SMITHSONIAN CONTRIBUTIONS TO ANTHROPOLOGY

VOLUME 11

A Comparison of Formative Cultures in the Americas

DIFFUSION OR THE PSYCHIC UNITY OF MAN

James A. Ford

SMITHSONIAN INSTITUTION PRESS

City of Washington

1969

A Publication of the

SMITHSONIAN INSTITUTION

United States National Museum

LIBRARY OF CONGRESS 69–60004

UNITED STATES GOVERNMENT PRINTING OFFICE, WASHINGTON, 1969

For sale by the Superintendent of Documents, U.S. Government Printing Office
Washington, D.C. 20402 - Price $7.75

Collaborators

Ripley P. Bullen, Florida State Museum, Gainesville, Florida

Michael D. Coe, Yale University, New Haven, Connecticut

Clifford Evans, Smithsonian Institution, Washington, D.C.

Gareth Lowe, New World Archaeological Foundation, Tuxtla Gutiérrez, Chiapas, Mexico

Richard S. MacNeish, Robert S. Peabody Foundation, Phillips Academy, Andover, Massachusetts

Ramiro Matos M., Universidad Nacional del Centro del Peru, Huancayo, Peru

Betty J. Meggers, Smithsonian Institution, Washington, D.C.

Gerardo Reichel-Dolmatoff, Universidad de Los Andes, Bogotá, Colombia

William Sears, Florida Atlantic University, Boca Raton, Florida

Paul Tolstoy, Queens College of the City of New York, New York

Preface

I have had an interest in the American Formative culture for some years and have searched for it with limited or no success in Colombia, Peru, Mexico, and the eastern United States. However, I stumbled into the present study entirely by accident. Meggers, Evans, and Estrada's *Early Formative Period of Coastal Ecuador* was published while Matthew Wallrath, Alfonso Medellín Z., and I were finishing the classification of several hundred thousand sherds from our excavations in Pre-Classic sites on the coast of Veracruz, Mexico. Wallrath was immediately impressed by the close resemblance of engraved wares from the Machalilla Phase to those we were working with from the site of Chalahuites. Upon careful reading of this well-illustrated tome, a number of unexplained resemblances between ceramics and other features of early North, Central, and South American cultures began to crystallize into patterns.

For six months after returning to the United States, I dutifully continued to work on the report of the Mexican excavations. The problem of Formative relationships, however, occupied more and more of my attention, and by the spring of 1966 the Veracruz paper had practically been shelved.

Correspondence with other archeologists working on the Formative led to plans to hold a week of discussion on this problem at the Florida State Museum in Gainesville. A grant toward the expenses of travel was made by the Wenner-Gren Foundation for Anthropological Research of New York, and the conference took place 17–22 October 1966. Participants were the collaborators listed on p. v, with the exception of Gerardo Reichel-Dolmatoff, who was unable to attend the session, but has actively collaborated in providing criticism and data. Those who came in the capacity of observers were James B. Griffin, University of Michigan; Otto Schöndube of the Museo de Arqueología, Mexico City; Takeshi Ueno, University of Tokyo; and Adelaide Bullen of the Florida State Museum. An agenda had been prepared in the form of preliminary versions of most of the charts included in this volume, and discussions of their shortcomings and implications were spirited and lengthy.

The archeologists listed as collaborators have given generously of their time, information, and opinions as this monograph developed. When each section was completed in tentative form, it was mimeographed and mailed to them for criticism and comment. In most instances I have incorporated the changes suggested, for each consultant has a unique knowledge of the prehistory of the regions where he has worked. Still, I cannot say that all collaborators are happy with the present form of this paper. A principal disquiet arises from the fact that I have glossed over details of chronological and areal information in some cases where these are well known. For example, Sears points to the fact that the east and west coasts of the northern part of the Florida Peninsula have distinct chronologies. So have southern and central Veracruz. Coastal Ecuador should be

represented by at least five regional columns, and to attempt to reflect the complex prehistory of Peru in two columns is absurd. Then too, some perfectly good chronologies
have been left off the charts. An example is the sequence in the Huasteca region of Mexico
developed by Ekholm (1944) and MacNeish (1947). This criticism is just; I admit to some
rather heavy-handed simplification.

It has become the admirable pattern in archeological reports to segregate carefully
and label the sections reporting factual data, comparisons, conclusions, and speculations.
This pattern cannot be followed here, for the obvious reason that the entire paper consists of comparisons, conclusions, and speculations. The comparisons are frequently
illustrated by selected specimens, but I wish it understood that these are merely samples.
The serious reader is advised to make extensive use of the field reports to which reference
is made, and to judge for himself the degrees of resemblance. I do not think that very
often I have left myself open to the criticism of having chosen unique or divergent specimens for comparison in an attempt to force conclusions.

Many of the comparisons would be more effective if we had knowledge of the relative
popularity of the various features in all areas. We do have this information for ceramics
in a number of chronologies, including the north coast of Peru (Virú), coastal Ecuador,
Soconusco, Tehuacán, and the Lower Mississippi Valley. Where available, this information has been used.

The collaborators also are not to be accused of agreeing with all the implications
and conclusions. MacNeish, for example, suggests that a long evolutionary development
of ceramics in northern South America waits to be discovered, of which the Puerto
Hormiga culture of Colombia may be a part. Alicia and Gerardo Reichel-Dolmatoff also
suspect that this may be true.

In addition to the collaborators to whom my debt is obvious, I wish to acknowledge
indebtedness to a number of others. First, to the Florida State Museum and its Director,
J. C. Dickinson, Jr., who has tolerated my rather single-minded preoccupation with this
problem. Also, I appreciate the generous forebearance of the National Science Foundation
and its Program Director for Anthropology, Richard Lieban. At the time of applying for
Grant GS–1002, I fully intended to produce reports on excavations in Veracruz, Marksville, and Poverty Point, Louisiana. Instead, the funds have been diverted into the
preparation of this paper.

For several years, Clarence Webb and I have been working on a report on additional
specimens from the Poverty Point site in the Lower Mississippi Valley. I am greatly
indebted to Webb both for his patience at the delay of the second Poverty Point paper,
and for permission to make advance use of some of the data.

Stephen Williams of Peabody Museum, Harvard, made available the papers of
Antonio J. Waring on the archeology of the Georgia coast in page proof, permitting me
to cite valuable data contained therein.

Robert Heizer of the University of California, Berkeley, has provided information
on his and Philip Drucker's recent work at La Venta.

To William G. Haag of Louisiana State University, I owe thanks for his interest
in the Formative problem, and for unpublished information on the Stallings Island
culture.

Bruce Trickey and Nicholas H. Holmes, Jr., have generously provided data on the
Bayou La Batre Phase of coastal Alabama.

Gregory Perino has loaned unpublished manuscripts reporting on his extensive work
on Illinois Hopewell.

Sherwood Gagliano, Raymond Baby, and Junius Bird provided valuable information
and answered a variety of questions.

Joan Booth, research assistant, typist, and language critic has worked conscientiously,
and most intelligently on the preparation of this paper. Timothy Anderson, Paul Frazier,
Kathy Notestein, and Bob Nininger have drawn the illustrations.

Anders Richter, Director, and Stephen Kraft, Managing Designer, of the Smithsonian Institution Press were most generous with advice on format, particularly in regard to the presentation of the large chronological charts for publication. Final editing and preparation of the manuscript for the U.S. Government Printing Office was by Joan Horn.

James A. Ford

Florida State Museum
Gainesville, Florida
February 1968

POSTSCRIPT

Typing was nearly completed on the final draft of this manuscript when James Ford was taken to the hospital, where he died a few days later on 25 February 1968. During the last ten months of his life, in spite of increasing weakness, he labored on what many of his collaborators believe to be one of the milestones of New World archeology. The fact that he succeeded in finishing it is a source of satisfaction to all of us, and a monument to the courage as well as the vision of a remarkable man.

It remains to us only to reiterate the appreciation expressed by Ford to the National Science Foundation, which has permitted continuation of his grant to cover remaining costs of preparation and the transportation of the manuscript and illustrations to Washington, and to J. C. Dickinson, who supervised the final clerical work and assured safe delivery of text and drawings to us.

Betty J. Meggers
Clifford Evans

Smithsonian Institution
Washington, D.C.
March 1968

Contents

Tables

Illustrations

FIGURES

CHARTS

A Comparison of Formative Cultures in the Americas

Diffusion or the Psychic Unity of Man

Introduction

DEVELOPMENT OF THE FORMATIVE CONCEPT

A half century ago, Herbert J. Spinden (1917) presented to the International Congress of Americanists held in Washington, a paper in which he postulated that the high civilizations from the Andes to Middle America were based on a common old cultural stratum. This stratum was supposed to have originated in Middle America, specifically in the region of the advanced Maya culture, and was thought to include maize agriculture, ceramics, crude handmade figurines, and ceremonial centers marked by pyramids that served as bases for temples. Spinden's theory seems to have been greeted with silence by his colleagues, and he himself neglected to elaborate on it in his later work. Ten years later the "Archaic" theory was criticized by Lothrop, and as Vaillant (1935a, p. 293) says, the ensuing discussion "changed the status of the 'archaic culture' from a conclusion to a problem." Indeed it could not be more, considering the amount of data and chronological information available.

At the time the Pueblo region of the United States Southwest was the bright spot in American archeology, where the researches of Morris, Nelson, Fewkes, and many others resulted in the first Pecos Conference and Kidder's "Outline" (1924). In the East, Holmes' (1903) regional review of ceramics was the handbook, and C. B. Moore was touring Southeastern rivers in the steamboat *Gopher* and publishing his field notes with magnificent illustrations.

In Mexico, handmade figurines had been found beneath the lava flow of the Pedregal, and stratigraphic excavations by Gamio had demonstrated a sequence of sub-Pedregal, Teotihuacán, and Aztec cultures. Uhle was making careful collections on the

coast of Peru and had found rocker stamped pottery in the shell heaps at Ancón.

After Vaillant worked out the sequence for the "Archaic" or "Pre-Classic" culture for the Valley of of Mexico in the 1920s, he and Lothrop attempted the correlation of early cultures in Middle America in terms of the "Q-complex", a group of specific traits that they also traced into the Mississippi Valley. They do not seem to have been very serious about this assay, and in any event were again frustrated by lack of chronological information. Most of the "Q-traits" cited in the eastern United States fall into quite recent time periods.

At the 23rd International Congress of Americanists held in 1928, Kroeber (1930) elaborated the thesis of a common archaic agricultural foundation, with identical food plants and similar techniques in weaving, metallurgy, and architecture.

The decades of the 1920s and 1930s saw the excavation of large sites in Middle America (Monte Albán, Teotihuacán, Uaxactún, and many others), which provided the Classic and Post-Classic cultural periods with a relative time scale, and thus made clearer the earlier age of the Pre-Classic or Formative.

Smaller scale but numerous excavations were conducted in the eastern United States and in Peru. As evidence accumulated, various archeologists undertook synthesis of parts of regions and then of regions as a whole. In the eastern United States, Cole and Deuel (1937) defined an Early Woodland basic cultural pattern and a later Mississippian pattern. This was a statement of the then popular Midwestern Taxonomic scheme, and this dichotomy still haunts the archeology of the area.

1

Five years later Ford and Willey (1941) offered an "outline" of Eastern archeology, which attempted to give chronology and direction of cultural diffusion. Dates were wrong and data on the early Burial Mound I and II stages sketchy, but the reader will note an essential agreement with the thesis of the present paper. Rigidity of viewpoint is not the exclusive prerogative of certain colleagues with whom the writer tends to disagree. Phillips (1940) also assessed Mesoamerican influences in the Southeast.

In the same year George Vaillant (1941) summarized the "Middle Cultures" of the Valley of Mexico in the opening chapters of *The Aztecs of Mexico*, and traced the chronology through succeeding phases up to the Conquest.

In 1941–1942 the Institute of Andean Research coordinated the work of representatives of various institutions, who were organized into ten field parties spaced from Chile to northern Mexico. The avowed purpose was to discover local chronologies and to find evidence of early inter-American cultural influences. The first objective was achieved with fair success, resulting in a number of important papers. Those that will be most useful here are Ekholm (1944) and Willey and Corbett (1954). Strong (1943) summarized the accomplishments of the projects and called attention to ceramic decorative techniques and motifs that were shared by the coastal Chavín of Peru, the Playa de los Muertos site in Honduras, and the Hopewellian Phase of the Mississippi Valley. These included zoned rocker stamping, wide-line incising, and zoned red painted designs.

About the same time, Tello (1943) described the discovery of the spectacular Chavín culture of Peru and pointed to its importance as the early pan-Peruvian Formative (to use current terms). Rebecca Carrión elaborated on the thesis in 1948.

In 1943, Drucker, Stirling, and others began to publish the results of excavations in the important Olmec sites on the Gulf coast of Mexico. The relative antiquity of this remarkable cultural phase, with its great ceremonial centers, monumental sculpture, distinctive art style, and lapidary industry in jade, began to be realized. Some authorities, notably Covarrubias (1946, p. 80), recognized Olmec as principally ancestral to both Mexican and Mayan civilizations, a point of view now generally accepted.

W. S. Webb and Snow in 1945 published an important summary of the Adena culture of the Ohio Valley. A second volume by Webb and Baby followed in 1957. Features of this eastern United States Formative Phase prompted Spaulding (1952) to propose that there had been a direct migration from Mesoamerica.

Willey (1945) outlined Peruvian archeology in terms of horizon styles. The earliest of these, Chavín, white-on-red, and negative horizons, are most pertinent to the present discussion.

As the result of excavation in the remarkable Maya site of Kaminaljuyú on the outskirts of Guatemala City, Kidder (Kidder, Jennings, and Shook, 1946) undertook extensive trait comparisons with other early Mesoamerican sites. His "General Discussion" summarized available knowledge of Maya and Mexican prehistory. A similar trait survey with illustrations was presented by Wauchope (1950) four years later, and this in turn was expanded by Sorenson (1955).

During this period, Griffin (1946) published an outline of the prehistory of the eastern United States which was filled with informative detail, but gave a flat picture of the culture periods. Facts were allowed to speak for themselves and intraregional hypotheses were avoided. The monumental *Archeology of the Eastern United States* (Griffin, ed., 1952) by Fay-Cooper Cole's students presents a similar picture.

The second cooperative project of the Institute of Andean Research concentrated the work of archeologists, ethnologists, and a geographer in the small Peruvian coastal Valley of Virú in 1946–1947. This produced knowledge of the Peruvian preceramic (Bird, 1948), and a detailed quantitative chronology for the ceramic phases (Ford, 1949; Strong and Evans, 1952; Collier, 1955). The Formative Chavín or Cupisnique Phase was firmly placed in relation to later cultures, and the work of Larco Hoyle was substantiated and elaborated.

An invitational conference held in New York in 1947, coordinated the results of the Virú project, and as comparative background, Armillas (1948) contributed an outline of Mesoamerican prehistory and discussed possible cross-ties with the Peruvian area, a theme also treated by Bennett, Strong, and Steward. Other comparisons were made by Jijón y Caamaño (1951b) in a paper presented at the 29th International Congress of Americanists in 1949.

In 1948, Bennett proposed the concept of a Peruvian co-tradition, and with Bird (Bennett and Bird, 1949) presented a more detailed prehistory of this region in the American Museum of Natural History handbook series. This was followed in 1951 by Willey's review of the Chavín problem, which was still considered to be uniquely Peruvian.

In 1953 Caso published a brief outline of Mesoamerican prehistory, and MacNeish (1954) in a section of his Panuco paper, followed the pattern set by Kidder and Wauchope of making extensive trait comparisons to other early Mesoamerican sites. This admirable practice was continued by M. D. Coe (1961) in his report on the Formative site at La Victoria, Guatemala.

In the decade of the 1930s, discoveries in brick-yard excavations in the northern suburbs of Mexico City had brought the rich cemetery of Tlatilco to the attention of archeologists. A remarkable quantity of Pre-Classic or Formative ceramics, figurines, and other artifacts have come from the commercial digging, as well as controlled excavations by the Mexican Instituto de Antropología. Porter's (1953) report on Tlatilco made the first comprehensive attempt to describe traits shared by the Mesoamerican Formative, the Chavín horizon of Peru, and the Hopewellian cultural manifestations of the eastern United States.

In a paper prepared in honor of the 75th anniversary of the Anthropological Society of Washington, Willey (1955) examined the question of the diffusion of traits between Mesoamerica and Peru. His list is in part the same as that treated by Porter: rocker stamping, negative painted pottery, tripod vessels, platform mounds, and metallurgy. The possibility of connection on the early lithic horizons was also considered. Willey concluded that contacts took place from preceramic times to the date of the Spanish Conquest.

Willey and McGimsey (1954) investigated shell middens on the Pacific coast of Panama in a planned search for early cultures. The Monagrillo Phase dates about 2000 B.C., clearly early Formative. The ceramic decorations feature scroll motifs made by incised lines ending in punctuations, a strange design for this early date.

In 1955, Gerardo and Alicia Reichel-Dolmatoff began publishing the results of their important excavations in shell middens on the north coast of Colombia. In rapid sequence over the next ten years, they developed a previously unsuspected ceramic chronology that runs from the earliest Formative at about 3000 B.C. up into the early centuries of the Christian Era. In their Momíl paper (1956), extensive trait comparisons are made to the Peruvian and Mesoamerican regions, and the cultural participation of Momíl (700–1 B.C.) in the movement of middle and late Formative influences is set forth.

The archeological career of Emilio Estrada of Ecuador only extended from 1952 to his unexpected death in 1961. This was a remarkably brief time for his notable accomplishments. Prior to 1955 the prehistory of the coast of Ecuador was little known, and most archeologists had the impression that, with the exception of some Mesoamerican-like traits in Esmeraldas Province, it was of minor importance. The team of Meggers, Evans, and Estrada have detailed in various publications a chronological sequence reaching back to 3000 B.C., which appears to be a principal key to the American Formative problem.

Estrada (1958, 1961; Estrada, Meggers, and Evans, 1962) was particularly interested in the relationships of the Ecuadorian Formative to early phases in Peru and Mesoamerica, and in the questions of possible connections with Asia. This latter aspect of the problem receives extensive consideration in Meggers, Evans, and Estrada (1965), where Valdivia ceramics are compared to pottery of the same age found on the island of Kyushu, Japan. Meggers (1966), and Meggers and Evans (1964) have continued this interest in specific trait resemblances in the New World Formative.

Over approximately these same years, Engel has conducted a program of research on the Peruvian coast, principally in the south. He (1963) has examined the preceramic cultural phases in admirable detail, and has investigated the Chavín horizon both on the north and central coasts and on the south coast, where it previously was unknown.

In 1958, Willey and Phillips published *Method and Theory in American Archaeology*, the major part of which was devoted to a historical-developmental interpretation of New World prehistory. A sequence of stages was used as an outline. "Formative" is defined as the earliest appearance of sedentary village life based on agriculture, and early cultural phases of North, Middle, and South America are described in terms of how well they conform to the definition; discussion of diffusion of traits was minimal.

About the same time, Ford, Phillips, and Haag (1955), and Ford and Webb (1956) described the Poverty Point culture (1200–400 B.C.) of the Lower Mississippi Valley. Although the authors were not aware of the fact at the time, this exposed an entirely new facet of the Formative problem in eastern North America.

Direct comparison of potsherds from Ecuador and Guatemala with the unique decorative technique of iridescent paint and other similarities almost as striking, led Michael D. Coe (1960) to publish an article on "Archeological Linkages with North and South America at La Victoria, Guatemala." In this he proposed that the traits had been exchanged by means of sea voyages about 1000 B.C. The thesis seems sound, for the materials are literally indistinguishable and are not found in intervening regions.

In Mexico, meanwhile, MacNeish began a twenty-year campaign in search of the origin of the domesticated plants that were the principal basis of New World agriculture. He skillfully blocked out the problem in a manner similar to a gold prospector searching for the mother lode. Botanical evidence suggested that maize had evolved from grasses native to the highlands. MacNeish's (1947, 1958) excavations in dry caves in Tamaulipas in northern Mexico, developed a cultural sequence with domesticated beans dating back to approximately 1000 B.C., maize to 3000 B.C., a variety of squash to 6000 B.C., and bottle gourds probably to 7000 B.C. Work in the Santa Marta Cave in Chiapas, southern Mexico (MacNeish and Peterson, 1962) demonstrated that maize had arrived with the earliest ceramics about 1500 B.C.

On the basis of this information, the semi-arid valley of Tehuacán in the state of Puebla, central Mexico, was selected as a probable region for maize domestication, and MacNeish (1961, 1962) mounted a three-year excavation program with an adequate field staff and the active cooperation of 30 specialists in various related disciplines. The results of the Tehuacán project, to be published in six volumes (Byers, ed., 1967–), will provide the most detailed chronology available in Mesoamerica from deep cave deposits stretching from 8000 B.C. up through the ceramic phases. Calendrical dating is based on 130 radiocarbon assays. The domestication and evolution of maize beginning about 5000 B.C. is clearly shown, and the first appearance of other important domesticates is also well dated. It is now clear that maize and other important food plants were cultivated in Mexico, and another group of plants in Peru, well before the beginning of the American Formative.

By 1960 a considerable body of information was available on New World prehistory, and there was general agreement that consolidation of knowledge could be effectively undertaken. This was accomplished in several symposia and volumes prepared principally as texts.

In 1962 a symposium on "Prehistoric Man in the New World" was held at Rice University in celebration of its semicentennial (Jennings and Norbeck, editors, 1964). Eighteen participants dealt with the various regions of the Americas, principally in terms of the history of cultural development.

Meggers and Evans (editors, 1963) organized a symposium entitled "Aboriginal Cultural Development in Latin America: An Interpretative Review," for the 35th International Congress of Americanists in Mexico City. Again, ten papers dealt with regional sequences as though they were nearly independent. Meggers (1963) contributed a summary that detailed the earliest occurrence of ten ceramic and five other traits in chronologies spaced from northern Mexico to Argentina. These included the stirrup spout, rocker stamping, zoned red paint, zoned hatching, excision, tripod bases, pedestal bases, white-on-red, and negative and polychrome paint. Later traits, the use of copper, elbow pipes, figurine molds, axe money, and shaft tombs were also discussed.

At this same 1962 Congress of Americanists, Prufer (1964) and Dragoo (1964) evaluated the evidence for deriving the Hopewell culture of the eastern United States, and the custom of mound burial, from Mesoamerica or from Asia. Neither author thought the available evidence very convincing.

In presenting the following discussion, I shall retrace some of the comparisons made by Strong, Porter, Willey, the Reichel-Dolmatoffs, Estrada, Evans, Meggers, and others. Also, new items will be added. That this can be done with somewhat more detail, and possibly clarity, is due to the fact that the proper type of information has now accumulated to the point where for the first time a substantial number of chronologies located in strategic geographical areas are available. The Literature Cited totals about 360 publications. A rough count was made according to publication date. Fifteen percent date before 1940, 52 percent date 1941–1960, and 33 percent date 1961–1968. This paper could not have been written in 1955; in 1975 it could be done much better.

DEFINITION OF FORMATIVE

Spinden called his postulated old agricultural-pottery base the "Archaic." Vaillant and others also applied this term to the early ceramic cultures of Mexico. Vaillant later proposed the term "Middle Cultures," leaving room for earlier phases to be discovered. Neither term, however, has been completely accepted and the Mexicans have preferred "Pre-Classic." Meanwhile, archeologists working in eastern North America have appropriated the name "Archaic" for the hunt-ing and gathering cultures that existed between the Paleo-Indian and the first appearance of ceramics, although the Archaic sometimes was considered to include early fiber-tempered pottery.

"Formative" has come into use to denote what in the Old World would be called early or initial Neolithic. Neolithic would be a perfectly good name, but Americanists have been very reluctant to commit themselves to any terminology that would seem to imply Old World relationships.

Willey and Phillips (1958, p. 144) have defined the Formative stage "by the presence of maize and/or manioc agriculture and by the successful socioeconomic integration of such an agriculture into well-established sedentary village life." This is a parallel to Childe's definition for the beginning of the Old World Neolithic as the point at which man became a food producer rather than a predator. Willey and Phillips were well aware of a certain ambiguity in this definition, yet they applied it to the classification of cultures with the consistency that any classificatory scheme imposes.

For present purposes there are two major defects in this definition. Both in the Mexican highlands and on the Peruvian coast, agriculture was practiced many centuries before such commonly accepted Formative traits as ceramics and polished stone tools came on the scene. The small settlements seem to have been sedentary, but perhaps were not "well-established sedentary village life." In other words, the population explosion had not started.

The second defect is that seemingly the earliest ceramics were not made by agricultural people at all. Initially they were manufactured by and spread by coastal groups who subsisted principally on shellfish. The marriage of agriculture and ceramics seems to have taken place halfway through the 3000-year long Formative in Andean South America, about 2000 B.C. in Mesoamerica, and probably not until 1000 to 500 B.C. in the southeastern United States, where, as in Ecuador, pottery had already been made for a millenium.

For these reasons it is preferable to define the Formative more loosely as the 3000 years (or less in some regions) during which the elements of ceramics, ground stone tools, handmade figurines, and manioc and maize agriculture were being diffused and welded into the socioeconomic life of the people living in the region extending from Peru to the eastern United States. At the start of this span of years, all these people had an Archaic economy and technology; at its end they possessed the essential elements for achieving civilization. That civilization did not develop in the Mississippi Valley is probably due to its relative isolation from the mutual cultural stimulation that took place in Nuclear America.

Inevitably the Formative concept has been subjected to the tripartite divisions that have become classic in archeology. People speak of "Early," "Middle," and "Late" Formative. Usually these are tied to specific culture areas as is M.D. Coe's (1961, pp. 133–144) "Proto-Formative," "Early Formative," "Late Formative," and "Proto-Classic" division for Mesoamerica. These divisions, however, will not fit the intercontinental picture.

As the writer has pointed out in regard to the establishment of pottery types or any other useful historical device, the classificatory units must be selected on the basis of a reasoned guess as to the actual sequence of events (Ford, 1962). That there is an empirical methodology for the selection of "traits," "types," or cultural phases that will reveal the historical facts when properly manipulated is a fallacy that at the moment is wasting thousands of dollars spent on computer time.

Obviously then, the division of the Formative will be a statement of the writer's guess as to what happened in these critical centuries. While this guess will be used as a partial framework in the following discussion, the evidence will be discussed in the conclusions.

An attempt will be made to break the tripartite formula and use only two terms: "Colonial Formative" and "Theocratic Formative." The Colonial Formative will be considered to extend from about 3000 B.C. to 1200 B.C., a period in which ceramics were being distributed over the Americas, apparently by the establishment of seaborne colonies. The beginning of the Theocratic Formative at 1200 B.C. is rather sharply defined by the first appearance of mound structures and other appurtenances of organized politico-religious control. Its ending, about 400 B.C. in nuclear areas, later in peripheries, is not so clear, but merges into a "Proto-Classic," apparently a period of reorganization and preparation for later cultural advance.

SELECTION OF EVIDENCE

If one were to attempt a complete listing of traits present during the Formative Period as defined here, its length would be overwhelming. In a study such as this, a selection obviously must be made. Many traits are of local or regional distribution, and consequently are irrelevant for interregional comparison. Even a list of more widely shared features is too long, and selection must be practiced. The traits utilized here in part reflect the author's special familiarity with particular complexes, and in part result from the way in which the problem was initially conceived.

As has been noted in the Preface, I stumbled onto the Colonial Formative when my attention was called to resemblances in decoration between Valdivia and Machalilla ceramics from coastal Ecuador and early pottery of Mexico and the southeastern United States. Verification of the correctness of this initial impression and interpretation of its significance required detailed analysis of vessel shape, decorative technique, and motif. As the case for diffusion became convincing to me, I was curious to see what associated features might also be shared. This led to examination of site form and composition, stone and pottery artifacts, manufacturing techniques, etc. Additional regions were added especially to the south (Peru) and northwest (Ohio, Illinois), and the prototypes of the large charts appended to this volume were designed to provide better understanding of chronological slopes in distribution. As traits were added, patternings in time and space began to emerge.

In compiling a list of traits for this purpose, it is difficult to know where to stop. I have come nowhere near to exhausting the possibilities. Ceramic features that have not been cited include toy vessels, large ollas with high outcurving necks, graters, interior decoration on bowls, pitcher-spout trays and bowls, duck or shoe-shaped pots, *candeleros*, boat-shaped vessels, castellated rims, and collanders, to say nothing of decorative elements such as line and panel burnishing, brushing, pinched decorations, the split circle motif, the U-motif perhaps representing an ear of corn, the meander, white slip, burnished black surfaces, gadrooning, and polychrome. Among other kinds of cultural elements are the construction of vaults made of stone or wood in mounds, the use of red pigment in burials, panpipes, potsherd disks, spindle whorls, stone cones, and small animal effigies. All of these traits moved on the Formative level. Others will certainly become evident with more careful analysis of art motifs and with review of physical anthropological evidence. Since archeologists have not agreed upon a quantitative criterion by which one may judge whether the evidence is sufficient, I have stopped at the point where I felt that my thesis was clearly established and further examples merely fortified it. Those who require more extensive proof are invited to pursue the analysis with some of the traits listed above.

A word should be said about the order of presentation of the traits, which may strike the reader as unsystematic or illogical. I fully agree, but since the traits differ widely in character, there is no obvious order of presentation in many cases. One consideration apparent from the beginning, however, was that if this material was to be published it would have to be presented visually in as compact a manner as possible. Principally, this involved inclusion of the data on the minimal number of chronological charts. Since the columns are standardized in width and the vertical chronological scale is uniform—both considerations important for comparing distributions—the traits had to fit into these space requirements. Obviously, therefore, traits of similar temporal and chronological position, which occupy the same positions on the charts, must be scattered over different charts and grouped with traits having different spatial and temporal distributions and with which they consequently may not be associated. This procedure made it possible to present all of the traits on 22 charts, but in some cases produced strange bed-fellows. While the arrangement in the text might have been changed, it seemed, likely that reference to the charts would be facilitated if the order remained the same for both.

SETTING THE STAGE FOR THE AMERICAN FORMATIVE

Unspecialized Mongoloid people, hunters of big game (elephants, large extinct bison, horses, and ground sloths), had crossed the Bering Strait land bridge at least by 12,000 B.C. By 9000 B.C. they had reached the southernmost point of South America. Their artifacts, principally known from projectile points, were of generalized Upper Paleolithic styles: stemmed and bifacially chipped.

Paleo-Indian cultures disappear at the time of the extinction of the Pleistocene megafauna, probably by 8000–7000 B.C., and the inhabitants of the two continents settled into what has been termed an "Archaic" way of life: the hunting of the smaller modern animals, fishing, the gathering of plant foods, and the collecting of sea products along the coasts. A large variety of projectile points marks the Early Archaic in North America. None shows the technical skill of the Paleo-Indian points.

About 3000 to 2500 B.C. what may be an old circumpolar complex of ground stone tools is added to the Archaic inventory of the northeastern United States and the St. Lawrence River Valley. These include slate points and semilunar knives, as well as adzes and curved-blade gouges. These and other forms are made of native copper in the Lake Superior region. The grooved stone ax may have appeared slightly earlier and is the principal ground stone tool to diffuse over most of the East. Bola stones are added to the list of weapons, and weights for the atlatl began to be made in the forms of "bannerstones" and "boatstones."

In the arid plateau country of the western United States and down the highlands of Mexico, a distinctive way of life developed in response to the environmental limitations. This Desert culture utilized the available small game, but a large proportion of subsistence depended on the collection of wild fruits and seeds. Stone mortars and flat grinding stones are a common tool of the Desert culture from an early date.

Desert culture people were interested in wild seed foods and now that the history of maize is known, it appears quite logical that maize should have been domesticated by people of this cultural pattern on the central Mexican plateau. The early spread of primitive and domesticated varieties to New Mexico, where they have been dated in Bat Cave between 3000 and 2000 B.C., is also understandable. The acceptance of this improved seed food involved little change in subsistence.

The Archaic pattern of life is less well known in South America. Lanning (1963a) has presented a preceramic sequence for coastal Peru in which pressure-flaked projectile points are replaced by crude percussion-flaked tools made from beach cobbles about 4000 B.C. The collection of wild seeds characterizes the latter part of the South American "Archaic," and milling stones are typical. These artifacts tend to disappear about 3000 B.C. with the appearance of cultivated plants and the establishment of permanent coastal villages. On the north Peruvian coast food came principally from the sea and was supplemented by the roots of wild plants. Shortly before 3000 B.C. domesticated squash, lima beans, and bottle gourds were cultivated. Cotton appeared around 3000 B.C., but maize was not added until about 1400 B.C., after the beginning of ceramics. The Peruvian Archaic also has yielded quantities of basketry, netting, and twined fabric. Fabric techniques and decorative designs show a high level of sophistication.

This then is a very brief summary of what is known of conditions in eastern North America, Middle America, and the Andean region of South America between 4000 and 3000 B.C., just prior to the appearance of the earliest ceramics. The entire region was populated, doubtless very thinly in less favorable localities, but small villages had formed on sea coasts where dependable food supplies were available. A hunting and gathering pattern of life had been established for thousands of years and the fact that the people began to select seeds and plant some of the formerly wild vegetables seems to have had little effect on their way of living. Probably there was a slight population increase.

Social organization undoubtedly was on the level of lineage bands. There is no evidence of organized community effort, no mounds, pyramids, or temple structures like those that later became so popular in these regions. So far not even evidence of organized community defense systems has been found. The thesis that peripheral groups of northern North America and southern South America have preserved numerous elements of the common American Archaic pattern has been developed in the researches of Nordenskiold, Cooper and others (summarized in Cooper, 1941). This seems to be a convincing reconstruction, but most are customs that leave no archeological record.

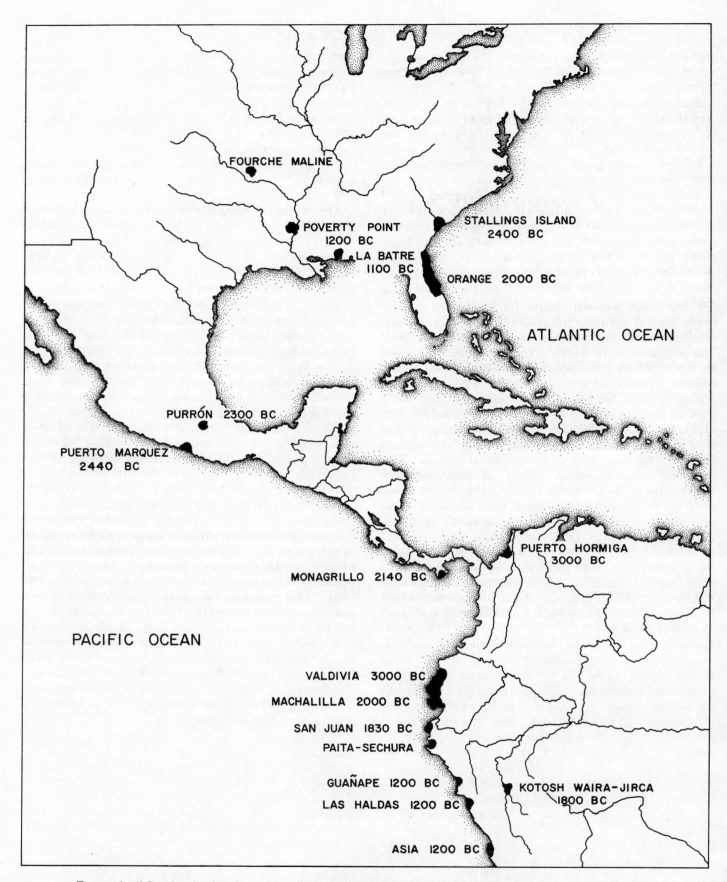

FIGURE 1.—Map showing locations of known Early Formative settlements in North, Central, and South America.

Chronology and Radiocarbon Dates

On the large fold-out charts (charts 1–22), fifteen chronological columns represent a range of history that supposedly lies between 3000 B.C. and A.D. 300. The geographical locations of these columns are shown on figure 1 and the inset maps on each chart. Each column equates with a more or less restricted geographical area, as will be explained, and has been selected for inclusion in a very arbitrary fashion. The first criterion is the quality of the information for the time span in which we are interested. The second criterion has been that of geographical spacing. The need to fairly represent events in approximately 7,000 miles of prehistory in a synoptic form has made it necessary to stand off from the data and view them as though through the wrong end of a telescope. Arbitrary lumpings have been made and *groserías* have been committed that set the teeth of area specialists on edge. I can only plead that the task would have been easier if manuscripts were still published on long scrolls as in early Medieval times, so there would be no limit to the chronological columns that we could align side by side.

Fortunately this problem of differentiating regional chronologies is comparatively simple in the early phases of the Formative, for the cultural traits being introduced were new, and apparently had few or no competing items to modify them. They retained, therefore, a basic similarity over distances much greater than was the case later when regional specialization began to develop, as it did in all parts of the Americas. The Chavín ceramics of 500 B.C. are practically pan-Peruvian; by A.D. 500 there is a bewildering number of distinct ceramic traditions in existence. At A.D. 100 the number of area chronologies would have to be multiplied several times 15 to picture the prehistory adequately, despite the leveling influences exerted by military conquests such as appear to be responsible for the wide spread of Mississippian, Teotihuacán, or Tiahuanaco cultures.

The 22 large, fold-out charts are all made from the same master drawing. Phase names are indicated and approximate temporal limits between phases are shown by dashed horizontal lines. Jagged lines mark limits of information. For example, in the Mobile Bay column a fiber-tempered phase is known, as is the Bayou La Batre, but the presumed continuity of occupation has not been established. The relatively wide bands of slanted lines indicate the time of the beginning of ceramics, where this has been determined.

I think it is safe to say that the relative dating of the phases is beyond question in all of these 15 columns, although the evidence varies in quality from one region to the other. It ranges from highly accurate quantitatively graphed ceramic sequences to superpositional evidence discovered more or less by accident as in Ohio. There may be some yet undiscovered phases that will have to be sandwiched in, and earlier phases will be identified, like the new Barra Phase in Chiapas. Then too the inevitable will occur. The next generation of graduate students, with or without real justification, will recut the segments of these continuums into what they hope will appear to be something new, and will give these bloody victims of a latter-day Solomon's judgment new names.

The datings of the phase limits are educated guesses made after considerable study of the opinions of the archeologists best qualified to make a guess in each region. For the most part, they follow these opinions very closely. These dating divisions were discussed at considerable length by the participants in the 1966 Formative Conference held at Gainesville, Florida, and a corrected version of the basic chart was submitted to each for review several weeks later. These

9

qualified opinions are of course based upon radiocarbon assays. While radiocarbon has introduced a degree of precision formerly unknown, and makes possible hemisphere-wide comparisons such as this will attempt to be, it does not have the precision of a tree-ring or calendrical date.

Some of the radiocarbon dates that are available for the phases in these fifteen chronologies are plotted on chart 1. The laboratory number has been placed at the indicated median date, and except where the 1-sigma range of probability was too short to extend beyond the number, it is shown by a black bar. Probably there is no need to remind the reader that there are two chances out of three that the actual date for the material under assay is within the range of the black bars. One chance remains that it is earlier or later.

The dates shown on chart 1 have been selected on two bases. First, they are dates for which the 1-sigma range runs into the temporal limits of the phase it is supposed to date. For example, date C–137 is 335 ± 210 B.C. and is supposed to date Ohio Hopewell. The date is earlier than the lower limits we have drawn for the Hopewell Phase, and its 1-sigma range lacks 25 years of arriving at our lower temporal limits for this phase. We have, therefore, excluded it from the chart and listed it in the tabulation as a "bad date." This date is by no means as "bad" as some others, but we have followed our rule in a strict and arbitrary fashion.

Some dates that agree perfectly with our temporal arrangement have been left off the chart simply because there is not room for them. For example, in the tabulation there are nine additional "good" dates for Ohio Hopewell, which are not shown on the chart because of lack of space.

Still other dates that have been left off the chart are really bad, and by no stretching of the laws of chance could be made to agree with our temporal placements. The chronology for Louisiana provides an unusual number of these. They do not agree with relative chronology in the area, and the temporal placement they indicate makes no sense when comparison is made to other neighboring chronologies; they also contradict other radiocarbon assays. All these categories—"good dates" listed on chart 1, "good dates" left off for lack of space, and "bad dates"—are tabulated on tables 1–13.

As is well known, there are several ways in which a date can go bad. The archeologist may make mistakes as to cultural or phase association of the charcoal or shell specimen, contamination may occur in the carbon deposited in the cells of the organism, in the ground, or in the handling of the specimens. It usually is impossible to make a guess as to what has gone wrong. Practically all of the dates being used here have been evaluated by the archeologists who are in the best position to pass judgment. Frequently this evaluation accompanies the sample description published in Radiocarbon, volumes 1–8. Other evaluations are given in relevant monographs, and still others have been published from time to time as separate papers: Wauchope, 1954; Libby, 1955; Radiocarbon Dates Association, Inc., 1958; Bullen, 1961; Griffin, 1964; Stoltman, 1966; Coe, Diehl, and Stuiver, 1967; etc. There would not be space here to review these evaluations. Instead we merely diagram and list the available dates in a wholesale fashion. It is hoped that this will give a rough idea of the amount and quality of the evidence for the chronological framework.

THE OHIO CHRONOLOGICAL COLUMN

This column includes a portion of New York State lying near the Great Lakes, to show the earliest cordmarked Woodland pottery that has been securely dated (Ritchie, 1962, 1965). It also takes in northern Kentucky to include early Adena (Webb and Snow 1945; Webb and Baby, 1957). In the centuries before and after the beginning of the present era, the principal attention is directed to the Classic Hopewell Phase of central Ohio (Mills, 1907, 1909, 1916, 1922; Moorehead, 1922; Shetrone, 1926; Magrath, 1945; Willoughby, 1922). Information from the Hopewell sites near Grand Rapids, Michigan, is also considered here (Quimby, 1941; Prahl, 1966).

Griffin (ed., 1952) has been used extensively, but the best recent summary of the archeology of the Midwest is Griffin, 1964. This the writer has tried to follow in both relative and calendrical chronology for both the Ohio and Illinois column.

Forty-seven radiocarbon assays are listed here that are applicable to the Ohio chronological column. Of these 38 or 81 percent agree with the phase dating shown on our charts (table 1, pp. 24–25).

The Late Archaic cultures of the Ohio region apparently were based on a hunting and gathering economy; there is no evidence that agriculture was practiced. The greatest concentrations of people were near river shoals where shellfish were available. Bannerstones (atlatl weights), adzes, and grooved stone axes are typical tools. Mound building was not practiced and the dead were placed in round pits in the refuse deposits. A curious phase of the Late Archaic is the "Old Copper Culture" that centers in Wisconsin. Tools manufactured from native free copper were widely traded.

A more complicated burial complex appears in this area about 1000 B.C. This includes cremation (popular in the later Adena Phase), red ochre scattered over the remains, and deposits of grave goods including tubular pipes, plummets, gorgets, birdstones, etc.

A thick, crude pottery with cord wrapped paddle impressions on both exterior and interior surfaces and straight sided amphoras with conoidal bases, were being manufactured in small quantities in the region from Minnesota to New England about 1000 B.C. Ritchie (1962) has described this as Vinette I ware, the name that is used here.

The Adena Phase begins about 800 B.C. The nature of the territory chosen for occupation suggests a dependence on agriculture, but there is no direct evidence. Ceramics are rare, and feature a plain ware that contrasts with the textured conoidal base Woodland pottery. The Adena people had brachycephalic skulls and practiced cranial deformation, a decided contrast to the more slender long-headed population of the Late Archaic. Some cultural items continue on from the Late Archaic, but new ones were added.

The Adena population and culture are quite clearly intruders into the Ohio-Kentucky region where they are found. Central America has been suggested as a possible origin. It appears more probable to the present writer, however, that, while the original population and basic elements for the phase (such as burial mound building) probably came from the Mississippi Valley from a culture related to the Poverty Point variety of early Formative, most of the development of Adena occurred in the Ohio-Kentucky region. From early to late in this phase, the burial mounds became larger. Although Adena was replaced by the Hopewell Phase in Ohio about 200 B.C., it continued to thrive in Kentucky.

The Hopewell Phase (200 B.C.–A.D. 300) is the earliest of the two cultural climaxes in eastern North America, and occurred in its most elaborate form in southern Ohio. It seems to have been a fusion of the local, already well-developed Adena traits, with ceramics and other features that came in from Illinois or the Mississippi Valley to the south. It is characterized by large geometrical earthworks, mound burial in elaborate log tombs, use of exotic stone such as obsidian, art forms made of copper, silver, and mica, copper helmets and breast plates, beautiful realistic carvings of animals and birds particularly on platform pipes, a core and blade industry, and ceramics decorated with line-bordered areas of rocker stamping depicting birds. Domestic pottery continued the cord-marked Woodland tradition.

Basic elements of the Hopewell culture extend over a large portion of the Mississippi Valley, from central Michigan to Louisiana and Florida, and from New York State west to the vicinity of Kansas City.

By A.D. 300 the Hopewellian traits have disappeared from the Ohio area, and the population reverted to a rather drab Woodland type of existence with a suddenness that suggests a relaxing of the social control that had produced the great earth monuments.

THE ILLINOIS CHRONOLOGICAL COLUMN

The alignment of the Illinois column is based upon Griffin's (1964) comparison of cultures and evaluation of radiocarbon dates. This column will be particularly difficult for the regional specialist to accept, for the somewhat different sequence in southern Illinois (Cole, et al., 1951; Fowler, 1959a, b; Griffin, 1941, 1952a, c, 1964; Maxwell, 1951; McKern, Titterington, and Griffin, 1945) is presented in the same frame as the chronology for the Illinois River Valley, where early phases of Hopewell are found (Cole and Deuel, 1937; Deuel, ed., 1952; McGregor, 1957; Bluhm, ed., 1960; Caldwell and Hall, 1964). The information from the Hopewell phase sites on Cedar River in Wisconsin (McKern, 1931) is also incorporated.

Of the 43 radiocarbon dates listed on chart 1, 35 or 81 percent agree with the temporal alignments used here (table 2, pp. 26–27).

The Illinois chronology is based on chance discoveries of superposition, and does not have a quantitative base. The contents and dating for the Early Woodland phases are not entirely clear. Some heavy crude cordmarked pottery similar to Vinette I of New York State has been found, and it is thought that this is associated with red ochre burials, but direct evidence is lacking. The earliest pottery in the southern part of the state consists of flat-base jars marked with plaited fabric impressions, the Baumer ware. Along the Illinois River the early Black Sands ware is decorated with straight line designs incised over cord malleated surfaces. This often has a rim decoration of nodes raised by punching from the interior.

A continuing but changing ceramic tradition in Illinois seems to lead directly to the Classic Hopewell Phase (300 B.C.–A.D. 300). The Central Basin Phase of early Hopewell is found in Illinois, but not in Ohio. Dentate and oval-shaped stamping are typical pottery decoration. Rims frequently have separate designs, and nodes are common. Late Hopewell in Illinois is similar to that in Ohio: log tomb burial in mounds, copper earspools, copper jacketed panpipes, effigy platform pipes, and pottery decorated with bird motifs formed by zoned rocker stamping are characteristic.

Illinois appears to be the center from which Hopewell diffused not only to Ohio, but also to Wisconsin, and southward down the Mississippi Valley. About A.D. 300 Illinois Hopewell disappeared, and Woodland culture replaced it.

THE GEORGIA COAST CHRONOLOGICAL COLUMN

The Georgia coast column rather specifically refers to the region around Savannah. The Stallings Island data are based on Moore (1897), Claflin (1931), Fairbanks (1942), Stoltman (1966), and Waring (in Williams, ed., 1968). Reference information for interior Georgia is Wauchope (1966), and for North Carolina, J. L. Coe (1964).

The radiocarbon dates for early periods on the Georgia coast have been evaluated by Bullen (1961), and the alignments in the column given here are those he has suggested both in print and verbally. Fifteen dates are available (table 3, p. 28). Of these, thirteen or 87 percent fall within the temporal limits assigned the several phases and are shown in chart 1.

The fiber-tempered pottery from the shell heaps near Savannah, Georgia, has long been a puzzle to archeologists, and the problem became more complex when radiocarbon showed that this was the earliest pottery in North America, dating back to more than 2000 B.C. Several writers have cited this as an example of the independent invention of ceramics (Bullen, 1960). Eight of the sites are doughnut-shaped shell rings, and excavation has shown that the oldest pottery is plain and is followed by drag-and-jab decorated ceramics. The balance of the culture content is typical of the Late Archaic sites of the Southeast: bannerstones, grooved axes, stemmed projectile points, etc.

Stallings Island seems to have been a long phase, ending about 500 B.C. It is succeeded by the Deptford Phase, which has not been thoroughly described, but is known from its ceramics. These are paddle marked, as is the early Woodland pottery to the northward, but the designs are large checks or check patterns in which the bands on the paddle are cut deeper in one direction than the other. Four feet appear on these vessels after 500 B.C. The inland location of Deptford sites suggests a degree of dependence on agriculture.

At about A.D. 100 the Deptford Phase is succeeded by the Swift Creek, in which the characteristic paddle stamped designs become curvilinear as well as rectangular and much more complex. Hopewellian traits are found in early Swift Creek burial mounds.

THE NORTH FLORIDA CHRONOLOGICAL COLUMN

This is another example of combining distinctive regional chronologies: the St. Johns area on the east coast at the base of the Florida Peninsula, where the early fiber-tempered Orange ceramic complex is followed by the rather colorless St. Johns phases (Wyman, 1875; Moore, 1894; Griffin and Smith, 1954; Goggin, 1952; Bullen, 1955, 1959; Bullen, A. and R., 1961), is lumped with the corresponding stretch of the Gulf coast, where the more spectacular Crystal River site is located and the Weeden Island complex existed several centuries after A.D. 1 (Moore, 1903, 1907; Greenman, 1938; Willey, 1949a; Sears, 1962; Bullen, 1953, 1966). Rouse (1951) and Ferguson (1951) have served as supplementary information for the Orange complex.

Time changes within the span of the early fiber-tempered ceramics on the St. Johns are rather well controlled by good vertical stratigraphy, and the radiocarbon dating discussed by Bullen (1961) is consistent. Bullen's dating has been followed for the early St. Johns phases, but the Transititional Phase he has proposed (1959) has been left out because similar transition is also found in other chronologies. To record them all would cut up our diagram to an excessive extent.

Fourteen radiocarbon runs are available for the north Florida chronology (table 4, p. 29). Of these, twelve (86 percent) conform to the phase dating used here.

The Orange complex of ceramics, most characteristic of the large shell mounds on the St. Johns River, also begins with a plain fiber-tempered ware, but it appears to start a century or so later than does the Stallings Island complex. Decorations, which start about 1600 B.C., are completely different from Stallings, as are the vessel shapes. By about 400 B.C. there has been a gradual change in the ceramics, and the untempered pottery of the Early St. Johns has become dominant. Some decorations continue from the Orange, but influence is also apparent from the Deptford pottery to the north and Tchefuncte from the west.

At A.D. 1 attention will turn from the St. Johns phases to the Gulf coast, where Crystal River and related sites were being built. Sears (1962) has been followed in dividing the data into Yent and Green Point Phases. The Yent Phase (A.D. 1–400) has typical Hopewell features, including cut animal jaws, copper jacketed panpipes, and bi-cymbal copper earspools. In addition to vessels with four feet, plain rocker and zoned rocker stamped decoration, and some unique vessel forms, there are several examples of negative painted pottery. The burials are in what Sears calls "continuous use" mounds, in contrast to the Green Point custom of making a central deposit of bones with a pottery deposit to the east and covering this with a small mound. The crude stele at Crystal River were also erected in the Yent Phase.

The Green Point Phase has less distinctive traits and some of the ceramics show relationship to the early Swift Creek Phase of Georgia and Troyville of the Lower Mississippi.

MOBILE BAY-FLORIDA NORTHWEST COAST CHRONOLOGICAL COLUMN

The geographical area represented by this chronological column is fairly restricted, being confined to the region of Mobile Bay on the Alabama coast, and adjacent Florida. Early description of cultural content is provided by Moore (1901, 1902), and the first chronological alignment was by Willey (1949a). More precise chronology, running from several centuries after the beginning of the Christian Era until almost the time of the arrival of the Europeans, has been worked out by Trickey (1958). Wimberly (1960) has described the ceramics of the Bayou La Batre and succeeding periods. Trickey and his associate Holmes have provided much additional unpublished data, including the new radiocarbon dates used on chart 1. Wimberly and Tourtelot (1941) have described the contents of the McQuorquodale Burial Mound, which has Hopewellian affiliations.

Sound vertical stratigraphy and seriation provide good control for the relative chronology. Continuity appears to exist in the data, except for a possible break between the early plain fiber-tempered pottery and the beginning of the Bayou La Batre.

Four radiocarbon dates are available for this column (table 5, p. 29). Of these, three or 75 percent agree with our phase dating. Assay M–824, 2150 ±250 B.C. is from preceramic levels at the stratified Bryant's Landing site. M–823, 1140±200 B.C. is from the Bayou La Batre cultural level. This has only one decorated pottery type, which features stamping with a large scallop shell.

The Santa Rosa Phase is dated from 100 B.C. to A.D. 400. This is the time of arrival of Classic Hopewell traits, including the construction of burial mounds, zoned rocker stamped ceramics, panpipes, platform pipes, copper earspools, etc. These traits were diffusing out of the Mississippi Valley Hopewellian centers. In western Florida and the Lower Mississippi Valley, the Santa Rosa-Marksville Phases are succeeded by the widespread Weeden Island-Troyville Phases about A.D. 400.

THE LOUISIANA CHRONOLOGICAL COLUMN

For the purpose of this study, the Louisiana or Lower Mississippi Valley chronological column will include information that extends geographically from the Gulf coast to about the latitude of Memphis, Tennessee. It is quite true that there is considerable regional variation in the prehistory over this wide expanse of territory, but most of it developed after the close of the Marksville-Hopewell Phases about A.D. 400. In the earlier centuries in which we are interested here, there was considerable cultural homogeneity.

The Lower Mississippi comparisons will be based on Ford (1936, 1951, 1952, 1963); Ford and Quimby (1945); Ford and Webb (1956); Ford, Phillips, and Haag (1955); Ford and Willey (1940); Phillips, Ford, and Griffin (1951); Gagliano and Saucier (1963); and McIntire (1958). In addition, data from extensive new private collections from the Poverty Point site will be used.

From the beginning of the Tchefuncte Phase (400 B.C.) to the period of aboriginal contact with the European settlers, there is a detailed quantitative ceramic chronology based on both stratigraphy and seriation. The priority of the Poverty Point Phase is well demonstrated by vertical stratigraphy at the Jaketown site (Ford, Phillips, and Haag, 1955), but there is as yet little time control within this long phase.

The radiocarbon dates for the Lower Mississippi Valley are more inconsistent and contradictory than for any other of the chronologies under consideration here. Of a total of 46 dates that supposedly apply to the phases shown on chart 1, only 23 (50 percent) fall within the time ranges assigned (table 6, pp. 30–32). Why this should be true is difficult to determine. Some of the charcoal specimens that were supposed to date the Tchefuncte Phase were selected from museum storage some ten years after excavation, so that contamination may have occurred. Other specimens, particularly those submitted to the Humble Oil Company Laboratory from the delta of the Mississippi River, are not from excavated sites. Their association with ceramics and thus their cultural significance was determined by surface collections, and there may be errors in these identifications.

Ford and Webb (1956) were inclined to accept a date of about 800–600 B.C. for the Poverty Point Phase, despite the fact that the radiocarbon results range from about 1200 to 400 B.C. Gagliano and Saucier (1963) have obtained dates ranging between 1800 and 1500 B.C. for what appear to be preceramic Poverty Point culture sites near Lake Pontchartrain. For this reason it now seems more logical to accept the dates from the Jaketown and Poverty Point sites at their face value.

The Poverty Point site is a complex geometrical earthwork, which if the dating is correct (1200–400 B.C.) stands out as a startling contrast to other sites and cultures in the eastern United States at that time. The site and culture bear precisely the same relation to their rather primitive neighbors as do the Olmec ceremonial centers of southern Veracruz and the coastal and highland Chavín sites of Peru.

The Poverty Point ceramic complex will be described in the following pages. There is a small proportion of fiber-tempered pottery, but most is clay-tempered and soft. Four feet, crude unzoned rocker stamping, and nodes around the rim are characteristic. It seems to be another Formative ceramic complex younger than, but comparable to Stallings, Orange, and Bayou La Batre.

The Tchefuncte Phase (400–100 B.C.) has simple burial mounds. Some sites are located in the interior, where agriculture may have been practiced, but others are coastal shell middens. The ceramic complex includes nearly all of the decorative techniques and motifs that were in the earlier Stallings, Orange, Bayou La Batre, and Poverty Point complexes.

The Marksville Phase (100 B.C.–A.D. 400) is the Lower Mississippi Valley version of Classic Hopewell. The features that characterize this horizon are so similar that it seems likely that the complex was developed in a fairly restricted geographical area and diffused from there. Marksville burials were in log tombs at the base of conical mounds built in two stages. Instances of two or more babies or children accompanying the bones of an adult are frequent enough to suggest child sacrifice. Some cremation was practiced.

THE VERACRUZ CHRONOLOGICAL COLUMN

An excellent relative chronology on the Mexican coast of the Gulf of Mexico has been left out of this comparison, both for lack of space and because on the Formative time level this region seems to be somewhat on the periphery of events This is the Tampico sequence in the Huasteca developed by Ekholm (1944), and added to by MacNeish (1954).

The Veracruz column on chart 1 represents the area from the vicinity of Zempoala in the central part of the state southward to the Coatzacoalcos River in the heart of the Olmec country. The northern part of the area includes the work of García-Payón (1966) at the sites of El Trapiche and Chalahuites, and recent unpublished excavations made by Ford, Medellín, and Wallrath at Chalahuites, Viejón, and Limoncito. For the southern portion there is available the work of the Smithsonian Institution group at La Venta (Drucker, 1947, 1952; Drucker, Heizer, and Squier, 1959); Cerro de las Mesas (Drucker, 1943b, 1955); and Tres Zapotes (Drucker, 1943a; Weiant, 1943). In addition, Michael Coe has provided unpublished data from excavations under way at the San Lorenzo site.

As with most of our columns, this one covers two closely related but distinctive ceramic provinces on the Formative level: the Zempoala region in the north, and the Olmec region in the south. In neither part of this region has an accurate relative chronology based on ceramics been established, but the general outlines of the sequence seem clear enough. Here the writer has followed the interpretation of M. D. Coe (1965) for the Olmec region, and his verbal advice during the 1966 Gainesville conference. This is already modified, however, by new radiocarbon dates.

The mounds built on this portion of the Gulf coast of Mexico from approximately 800 to 400 B.C. are not placed in any apparent order and have almost every shape except that of the rectangular flat-top pyramid. There are flat top L-shaped mounds, steep cones with pointed peaks, and elongated mounds with long ridge tops so narrow that they could not possibly have served as building foundations. The purpose for which these mounds were constructed is not clearly understood.

The phase names used in our Veracruz column are those that apply to the southern end of this region in the Classic Olmec country. As a result of the first year of work and new radiocarbon dates, M. D. Coe (1966) has defined a San Lorenzo Phase that dates 1200 to 900 B.C.

Michael Coe (1966, pp. 4–5) says

The bulk of San Lorenzo pottery is extraordinarily close to that of the Cuadros and Jocotal phases on the Pacific coast of Guatemala, where it has been radiocarbon dated to 1000–800 B.C. Shared here are brushed or striated tecomates, the dominant type at both Salinas La Blanca and San Lorenzo Tenochitlán; the use of interior finger punching or dimpling on the upper wall of these tecomates; tecomates slipped in a 7.5 R 4/4 red color; red-rimmed tecomates; plain rocker stamping (rare in San Lorenzo); abundant white-rimmed black ware; and deep bowls with exteriorly bolstered rims. These ceramic traits are also shared with the Chiapa I or Cotorra phase.

A more 'typically' Olmec pottery is also found in the San Lorenzo phase, a flat-bottomed bowl in black, grey, or white-rimmed ware with excised designs in the form of X's or stylized jaguar paws. This kind of pottery is well known at such Olmec influenced highland sites as Tlatilco or Las Bocas and has usually been thought to be Middle Formative. However, Gareth Lowe informs me that these excised designs occur with the type Pampas Black-and-white at the site of Altamira on the Pacific coast of Chiapas; this type belongs to the Cuadros phase there and at Salinas La Blanca in Guatemala. I now believe that the entire complex represented by Las Bocas (including the large hollow baby face figures), and present in the earlier graves at Tlatilco, belongs on an Early Formative horizon.

To return to the San Lorenzo phase, in the same deposits as these ceramics are many fragments of hollow and solid pottery figurines; the heads are in the purest Olmec style. It should be noted, however, that the style of eyes is very different from the usual La Venta or Conchas (Middle Formative) type, no punching being evident.

A notable feature of the La Venta Phase (1100–800 B.C.) is the formal arrangement of the mounds and ridges symmetrically about a center line that bears 8° west of north (Drucker, Heizer, and Squier, 1959, fig. 4). The Laguna de los Cerros site near Acayucán, Veracruz, has similar arrangement and orientation (Medellín, personal communication). These people were very good engineers.

The extremely rich content of Olmec culture is impossible to summarize in these pages. The ceramics are not too well known due to poor preservation at La Venta, but parallel the complex briefly described for El Trapiche. The characteristic representations of baby-faced dwarfs range in size from large stone heads seven feet in diameter to small jade figures with a typical bent-knee stance. Some clay figurines show individuals with similar features. Particularly impressive is a lapidary industry: the manufacture of beads and other small ornaments of jade. When it was first discovered, many Mesoamerican archeologists thought this sophisticated culture must date in the Classic Period. An early date, however, has now been demonstrated and most investigators agree that Olmec culture is the principal ancestor of later high cultural developments (M. D. Coe, 1963).

The naming of a Tres Zapotes and Cerro de las Mesas Phase is quite arbitrary. The two sites appear to overlap considerably in time. The "Tres Zapotes Phase" is principally what Coe has called "Tres Zapotes I," Weiant (1943) "Middle Tres Zapotes A," and Drucker (1943a, pp. 118–120) "Lower Tres Zapotes." M. D. Coe (1965, p. 694) places this in the Late Pre-Classic Period and says:

Strong continuities with the Middle Preclassic of the area are evident, but in general most resemblances lie with other Late Preclassic phases of Mesoamerica, such as Chicanel of the lowland Maya area, Chiapa IV and V at Chiapa de Corzo, and

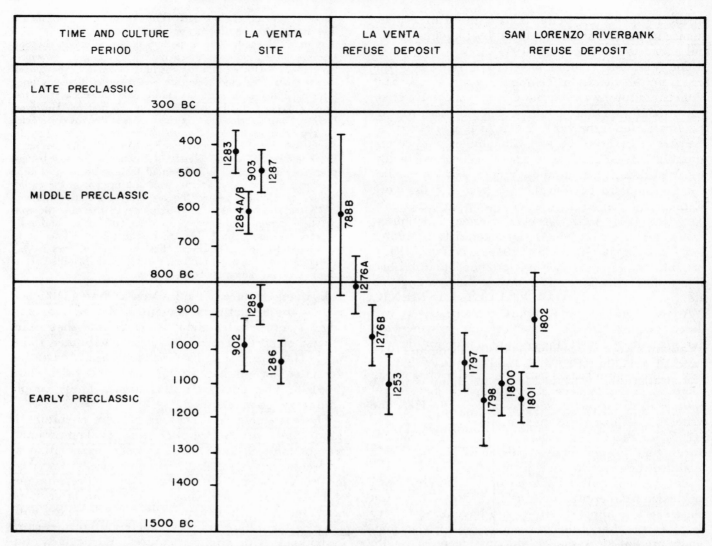

FIGURE 2.—Radiocarbon dates from the La Venta and San Lorenzo sites, Veracruz, Mexico (after Berger, Graham, and Heizer, 1967).

terminal Preclassic manifestations in the Valley of Mexico. Olmec and other Middle Preclassic phenomena are either absent or very weak, such as rocker-stamping, the double-line break, and the tecomate, although some Olmecoid clay figurines are still being manufactured. In the place of the Olmec art style is a new one, Izapan, which has a wide representation at this time in southern Mesoamerica.

The ceramic content is very succinctly described by Coe (1965). It clearly has developed out of the preceding La Venta Phase pottery, and tan, brown, black, and red slipped monochrome wares continue. Painted designs begin but no more than two colors are used. Some of the significant changes in form are the development of decorated labial flanges on bowls, and the appearance of pots with spouts, but without bridges. Figurines are handmade and continue to be principally nude females.

At the Tres Zapotes site, Mound G, a flat top earth pyramid faced with cut stone, seems to be of this phase. A stone stairway leads up the side. Olmec style large monuments are being replaced with Izapan style carvings.

The Cerro de las Mesas Phase is Proto-Classic. To quote M. D. Coe's summary (1965, p. 696):

. . . this is the famous Q-complex of Vaillant and Lothrop, with its pottery traits being swollen, mammiform supports, bridged spouts, spool-shaped pot stands, and lavish use of polychromed stucco. This complex is very well represented in the more luxurious tombs of the period in Mesoamerica (see the tombs of Chiapa VI—the Horcones phase—at Chiapa de Corzo, Lowe 1962), but is hardly to be found in the refuse deposits of more humble persons.

The elaborate burials in a circular mound at Cerro de las Mesas are described by Stirling (1941) and Drucker (1943b). It is worth noting that this is approximately the time level of the Hopewell Phase in the Mississippi Valley, Miraflores in Guatemala, and San Agustín in highland Colombia.

Temporal alignment of the Olmec region periods is based on the dates for the San Lorenzo site (Coe, Diehl, and Stuiver, 1967), which indicate a time range of approximately 1200–800 B.C., and the ten-year old set of Michigan dates publised by Drucker, Heizer, and Squier (1959) for La Venta, which suggest a range for the major occupation from 800–400 B.C. After charts were completed, Berger, Graham, and Heizer (1967) published re-assays of some of the same samples used in the earlier runs and some additional results from the University of California, Los Angeles Laboratory. These indicate that the La Venta site was in principal use between 1100 and 800 B.C., coeval with San Lorenzo.

The current information is summarized by Berger, Graham, and Heizer (1967) in a chronology graph reproduced here as figure 2. As the situation has been thoroughly discussed by these authors, the writer shall not review it in any detail.

As a consequence, it appears that the San Lorenzo-La Venta sequence shown in the Veracruz column of the twenty-two charts, is incorrect. The information, however, was received after the charts were completed and to change them was not practical. Considerable doubt also attaches to the exact dating of the succeeding phases in this column.

THE VALLEY OF MEXICO CHRONOLOGICAL COLUMN

Vaillant's work at Zacatenco (1930), Ticomán (1931), and El Arbolillo (1935) has been the classic example for stratigraphic work in Mexico for many years, but still presents a somewhat unclear picture of the Pre-Classic that has been difficult to interpret. The discovery and excavation of the extraordinary Tlatilco Cemetery has added to the complexity (Porter, 1953; Piña Chán, 1958; Lorenzo, 1965). In recent years Tolstoy has been reexcavating in an effort to clarify this portion of the chronology. In the most recent analysis, Tolstoy and Guenette (1965) reanalyze Piña Chán's data, and conclude that three phases may be recognized in the prehistory of the Valley between 1000 and 400 B.C. Oldest to latest these are Iglesia, Totolica, and Atoto. Iglesia and Totolica are thought to be roughly coeval with El Arbolillo II and are preceded by El Arbolillo I.

Tolstoy and Guenette conclude that the ceramics and other material from the Tlatilco Cemetery are either specialized burial furniture or are the product of an intrusive group of people, and that the site dates within the Atoto Phase and was of very short duration between 500 and 400 B.C. This view seems justified by the majority of the radiocarbon dates available. The Valley of Mexico chronology is now in a process of refinement and the phase names presented on chart 1 are already out of date. Of the 21 dates, 16 (71 percent) fall within the time range assigned (table 7, p. 33).

The time at which ceramics first appear in the Valley of Mexico is not known. Vaillant's El Arbolillo I Period has sophisticated monochrome pottery. Most common is a reddish brown "bay" ware (78 to 96 percent), which is made of "heavy coarsely kneaded clay, with a sandy temper that includes many crystalline particles" (Vaillant, 1935, p. 219). Tecomates or neckless jars, and ollas with necks seem to be common forms. Russet ware, black ware, and a very small percentage of white ware are accompanying features. Painted wares include white-on-red and red-on-yellow.

Vaillant's ceramic descriptions are difficult to use for comparative purposes, but apparently his early phase conforms fairly well to early ceramics in other parts of Mesoamerica.

The Tlatilco ceramic assemblage described by Porter (1953) and Piña Chán (1958) is clearly a specialized ceremonial complex, as Tolstoy and Guenette have concluded, but it is of very special interest because the exotic items show relations to Olmec of the Gulf coast and Chavín of Peru.

The earliest mound in the Valley of Mexico seems to be a small flat top pyramid at Tlapacoya, built in stages. It contained a tomb. This was followed a few centuries later at Cuicuilco by the 22-meter high truncated circular mound built of earth and faced with stone. Several centuries before the beginning of the Christian Era, the typical, highland ceremonial complex of temple pyramids arranged around courts became crystallized and culminated in the great structures at Teotihuacán.

THE TEHUACÁN CHRONOLOGICAL COLUMN

More than 130 radiocarbon assays have been made to date the various phases of the excellent 10,000-year long sequence established by MacNeish and his co-workers in the Valley of Tehuacán in the state of Puebla, Mexico. Probably the dating of this sequence is more accurate than any other in the Americas. The Tehuacán dates have not yet been published, but even if they were, it would be impossible to present them in the small space available here. For the Tehuacán column, the phase temporal limits shown by MacNeish (1964) have been followed. This placement was reviewed by MacNeish at the 1966 Gainesville meeting.

The primary contribution of the Tehuacán project has been the information on the domestication and evolution of the many New World food crops. It has been shown that maize, domesticated about 4000 B.C., evolved from a wild form that had a cob less than an inch in length. Chili pepper, avocados, gourds, amaranth, tepary beans, yellow zapote, and probably black and white zapote were all domesticated in the Coxcatlán Phase (5200–3400 B.C.).

The first ceramics appear in the Purrón Phase (2300–1500 B.C.). This is a crumbly, very crude ware with forms imitating the earlier stone vessels. Twenty years ago, archeologists would probably have interpreted this as another instance of the independent invention of ceramics, but MacNeish offers the possibility of earlier (as yet unfound) pottery in some other region.

In the succeeding Ajalpan Phase (1500–900 B.C.), the ceramics conform to a pattern that is widespread over Mesoamerica: well-made polished monochrome wares with occasional examples of red slip, reddish brown, black, tan, and rarely white. Usual forms are tecomates, flat-base pans, and jars. Decoration is rare and consists of rocker stamping, brushing, and incising. Female pottery figurines began to be made.

The Santa Maria Phase dates from 900 to 200 B.C. The settlement pattern consists of small hamlets of wattle and daub dwellings clustered about larger towns provided with ceremonial centers in the form of rectangular flat top pyramids with temples on them. The pottery is now white or gray in color. The flat-base pan is the dominant form and the balance are ollas, water bottles, and composite silhouette bowls. Bowls are incised on the interior of the bottom; there is some plain rocker stamping on the rim, and the techniques of engraving and negative painting occur. Farming is now the subsistence base, and woven cotton cloth is found.

Systematic irrigation was practiced by the time of the Palo Blanco Phase (200 B.C.–A.D. 700). Tomatoes, peanuts, lima beans, guavas, and turkeys were added to the list of domesticated items. Religious centers become more elaborate and have a larger population, which probably consisted of specialists and technicians. Pyramids, ball courts, and plazas are typical of the Mexican "Classic Period." Earlier pottery types begin to disappear and new forms arrive, including tripod bowls, bottles with spouts, and vertical-sided jars with slab legs.

THE CHIAPAS CHRONOLOGICAL COLUMN

The cultural content of the Chiapas column is based entirely on the work of the New World Archaeological Foundation under the direction of Lowe. An excellent quantitative ceramic chronology provides good control for the phases, which are assigned both numbers and names. We are here interested in phases Chiapa I through Chiapa VIII. Most of the information comes from papers in the Foundation series by Dixon (1959), Sanders (1961), MacNeish and Peterson (1962), Peterson (1963), Agrinier (1964), and Lowe (1962). In addition, Lowe has provided new data.

The phase calendrical limits shown here are based upon the estimates given by Peterson (1963, pl. 13) as modified by Lowe at the 1966 Gainesville meeting.

Ten radiocarbon dates are available for the Chiapas sequence (table 8, p. 34). Of these, eight (80 percent) conform to the phase dating used here.

The earliest ceramics in the Chiapa de Corzo sequence are white ware flat-base pans with low vertical or slightly outflaring side walls, a few of which have red paint, white monochrome jars with low necks, and large, unslipped neckless jars or tecomates. Sixty-six percent of the latter have decoration about the mouth: brushing; pinching; simple incised designs; a band of red slip; and smooth rocker stamping. The lips of these jars have the typical "comma-shape" thickening.

A concise resume of the Chiapas ceramic sequence

is given by Warren (1961) and quoted in part by Peterson (1963, pp. 121–123). In brief, it follows the pattern already familiar in the Tehuacán and Veracruz coastal regions. About 500 B.C. rather hard-fired white, brownish, and reddish orange mottled ceramics appear. There is a black slipped ware, and negative painting is introduced. Volcanic ash tempering replaces the sand of the earlier phases. New forms include the cuspidor bowls, chamferred cylindrical vessels, whistling jars, composite silhouette bowls, and incense burners with handles on the interior. Solid cylindrical and flat stamps with handles appear; figurines become abundant.

Labial and medial flange bowls are an innovation in Chiapa v (200–100 B.C.). White rim black ware was first made at this time, and Warren suggests that it developed from earlier examples at La Venta. Painted two-color wares have a variety of curvilinear decorations.

Chiapa vi (100–1 B.C.) has the features that mark the beginning of the Mesoamerican Proto-Classic.

The wide variety of vessel shapes and decoration includes features retained from earlier times as well as new ones. New items are Usulután ware, mammiform bowls with tetrapod supports and effigy decorations, stucco-decorated vessels, vessels with carved designs, conical tripod feet, jars with bridge spouts, effigy necks, and Monte Albán i gray ware. There is an increase in popularity of the white rim black ware bowls.

In his brief summary of the Chiapas sequence, Lowe (1959a) places the earliest use of platform mounds as bases for structures at 500 B.C., and notes that this is also the first occurrence of burials with offerings. He equates this period with the early Mamón Phase of the Petén in Guatemala. The complexity of ceremonial center sites and pyramidal structures increased rapidly, and the use of cut limestone for facing the pyramids was well developed at the Chiapa de Corzo site by the beginning of the present era.

THE SOCONUSCO, GUATEMALA CHRONOLOGICAL COLUMN

The cultural content of the area chronology for the northern part of the Pacific coast of Guatemala is based on M. D. Coe (1961) and Coe and Flannery (1967), as modified by verbal information at the 1966 Gainesville conference and later by correspondence with M. D. Coe, Lowe, and Susanna Ekholm (1966). The calendrical limits used in this paper are those suggested by Coe and Lowe. Seven radiocarbon assays are available for dating the Conchas and Cuadros Phases. All seven fall within the proper limits in this temporal framework (table 9, p. 34).

The early Barra Phase has recently been discovered by Lowe and his staff. This ceramic consists principally of flat-base pans and tecomate jars; the latter have brushed and incised decoration and comma-shaped lips. There is also a white slipped ware.

The most important site in this sequence is La Victoria, near the town of Ocós on the coast of Guatemala, reported by M. D. Coe (1961). It has ten low rounded mounds scattered about with no apparent arrangement, which contain superimposed floors and quantities of refuse. Stratigraphy was clear and showed four phases running from about 1400 B.C. to A.D. 200. Ceramics of the early Ocós Phase include the flat-base pan, and the neckless jar or tecomate. There were also smaller globular pots, which had long tripod legs. Decoration includes some unusual items: fabric marking, which is frequently zoned, and iridescent painting, which may or may not be zoned by incised lines. Rocker stamping was principally done with the edge of a scallop shell. Specular red slip is diagnostic.

While this paper was in preparation, Coe and Flannery (1967) interposed a Cuadros (1100–850 B.C.) and a Jocotal (850–800 B.C.) Phase between the sequence of Ocós-Conchas i. Cuadros has the typical large tecomates, some of which have rows of bosses bordering the mouth area raised by punching from the interior. A hard white ceramic and bowls with tripod feet also occur.

A polished black ware extends through Ocós and the following Conchas Phases. Excised decorations and engraved lines are filled with red pigment in the Conchas Phase. The large neckless jars are an unburnished red, and there is a white-to-buff ware. Fine wares begin. Composite silhouette bowls appear and the highly polished black ones have grooved side walls. Everted lips with incised decoration on the lip flange become prominent in the Conchas ii Phase. Figurines, which were nude females in the Ocós Phase, sometimes wear wrap-around skirts in Conchas. In the latter phase there are also napkin-ring earspools.

Coe set up a Crucero and Marcos Phase on the basis of material from the upper levels of the site.

The phase definitions are not clear, however, due to the scarcity of material and the fact that it is mixed with artifacts from the Conchas levels. The comparative section of the volume (M. D. Coe, 1961, pp. 120–136) is a thorough review of the Formative of Mesoamerica.

Near identity between iridescent-painted bowls, fingernail punctating, rocker stamp decoration, napkin-ring earspools, black polished composite silhouette bowls with grooved side walls, cuspidor-shaped bowls, line-burnished decoration, negative painting, red and white slip decoration, and grater bowls, prompted M. D. Coe (1961) to postulate that there had been direct contact by sea between the coast of Guatemala and of Ecuador in Ocós-Conchas and Chorrera-Tejar Phases (900–300 B.C.). This evidence seems to be unusually clear. The items compared are on the proper time level, they are complex, nothing similar is found in the intervening regions, and the traits are new in the areas to which they seem to have diffused.

THE NORTH COAST OF COLOMBIA CHRONOLOGICAL COLUMN

This column has been allowed to cover a rather long portion of the Caribbean coast of Colombia from the vicinity of Barranquilla at the mouth of the Magdalena River westward to the Isthmus of Panama. Here, Gerardo Reichel-Dolmatoff has reported on the excavation of the important sites of Barlovento (1955) and Puerto Hormiga (1961, 1965), and with his wife, Alicia, the site of Momíl (1956). Angulo Valdés (1962a, b) has described the site of Malambo. In some instances information will be included in this column from the burial mound of Cupica, which the Reichel-Dolmatoffs (1962) excavated on the north Pacific coast of Colombia.

The relative chronology for the north coast of Colombia has not been presented as a quantitative sequential continuum, but there seems to be little doubt about the temporal sequence of the various cultural phases. The outline presented by Angulo Valdés (1963) has been followed. In making the calendrical estimates for the several phases, however, the dating given in Meggers and Evans (1963, fig. 8) has been used rather than the estimates indicated in the text. This alignment seems to agree better with the apparent cultural connections of the Colombian phases to other regions.

Nine of the dates available for the north coast of Colombia column agree with the phase dating used here and seven do not (table 10, p. 35). Five of the seven come from the Malambo site, and if taken at face value would indicate that this phase dates about 1000 years later than it has been placed. Obviously either dates or relative placement are in error. Of the remaining two dates, that from the second level of the Cupica Mound seems to be too late and one date from Puerto Hormiga is too early for the round figure of 3000 B.C., which has been selected as the beginning date for the Puerto Hormiga Phase. Its 1-sigma range, however, lacks only 20 years of touching this date and it is excluded only by the strict rule being applied here. Obviously it is perfectly valid.

In the course of their work, the Reichel-Dolmatoffs have been very much aware of the problem of relating their newly discovered cultural phases not only to the little information that was available on Colombian prehistory before they began work, but also to known cultures in Peru, Ecuador, and Mesoamerica. The discussion in their Momíl paper (G. and A. Reichel-Dolmatoff, 1956, pp. 269–303) is the first consideration of the intercontinental diffusion of a long list of traits, many of which will be discussed later in this paper. The Puerto Hormiga paper (Reichel-Dolmatoff, 1965, pp. 45–53) also has a most informative review of the Early Formative in North and South America.

The following brief condensation of the north coast of Colombia sequence is taken in part from Angulo Valdés (1963) and in part from the several papers of the Reichel-Dolmatoffs. The Puerto Hormiga site is a ring-shaped shell midden located on the coast between the Magdalena and Sinú Rivers. Approximately half of the crude ceramics are tempered with vegetable fibers and are undecorated. The other half are heavily sand tempered and sometimes decorated with drag-and-jab incisions, zoned dentate rocker stamping, shell edge stamping, and parallel lines ending in punctations. Fairly elaborate animal heads are modeled on the ends of boat-shaped vessels. Most of the shapes seem to be hemispherical bowls with short borders slightly inclined toward the interior. They are either round or oval.

In the Barlovento Phase the people also seem to have subsisted, during part of the year at least, on shellfish. The pottery is globular, of a tecomate-like shape, and has decoration about the mouth consisting of scrolls formed by broad incised lines with punctated background. Red pigment was rubbed in the lines after firing.

Angulo Valdés (1963, fig. 8) places a San Jacinto Phase between Barlovento and Malambo; this we have not done for the sake of simplifying the chart. Apparently a very short phase, it sees the continuation of the incised curvilinear decorations, and the introduction of spouted vessels and zoomorphic lugs. In the Malambo Phase the modeled and incised zoomorphic adornos reach the peak of elaboration. The ceramics and other features indicate strong relations with the Barrancoid cultures of Venezuela and the Orinoco River delta. Abundance of griddle fragments suggests dependence on the cultivation of manioc.

Subsistence in the Momíl I and II Phases also seems to have been based on manioc. At this time there appear suggestions of contacts with Mesoamerica and the Andean region to the south. Red and black-on-white curvilinear painted designs appear for the first time. There is also a variety of zoned engraved designs, into which red pigment has been rubbed, and

zoned dentate stamped designs. Tubular pipes, roller and dentate stamps, small figurines, and a core and blade flint industry are also found.

The San Agustín Phase, located six hundred miles to the southward near the headwaters of the Magdalena River, yielded pottery very similar to that of Momíl I and II (Duque Gomez, 1964, pp. 462–466). Dates for San Agustín range between 555 B.C. and A.D. 1200. The Classic Period, in which Duque thinks the numerous monuments and the burial mounds with central stone vault tombs were constructed, apparently dates from approximately A.D. 500–800.

Angulo Valdés (1963, fig. 8) has placed Cupica Phases I and II between A.D. 1 and 500. This is a small mound built in stages, with burials interred from each stage, located in the Bay of Cupica on the north Pacific coast of Colombia. The mound was excavated and reported by Gerardo and Alicia Reichel-Dolmatoff (1962).

THE COASTAL ECUADOR CHRONOLOGICAL COLUMN

The excellent quantitative chronological column that exists for coastal Ecuador has been developed in the last twelve years and is principally the work of three investigators: Estrada (1957, 1958, 1961, 1962); Estrada, Meggers, and Evans (1962, 1964); Estrada and Meggers (1961); Evans and Meggers (1957); Evans, Meggers, and Estrada (1959); Meggers (1964); Meggers and Evans (1962, 1964); and Meggers, Evans, and Estrada (1965). An excellent summary written for the layman is Meggers (1966).

The calendrical subdivisions shown in the Ecuadorian column are taken from Meggers, Evans, and Estrada (1965, pp. 147–156, fig. 94). Thirty-eight radiocarbon assays are available and 32 (86 percent) of these fall within the limits of the phase they are supposed to date (table 11, pp. 36–37). For the remaining six dates, the 1-sigma range does not touch the temporal limits that have been set for the corresponding phase. It is difficult to maintain this strict rule for one date lacks only 35 years of being "good."

Although the authors divide Valdivia into four substages, there are only minor changes in the ceramic assemblage. It begins at 3000 B.C. with simple bowl and pot shapes, a hard well-fired polished ware that has an extraordinary variety of decoration. This includes techniques of broad-line incising, engraving with red pigment rubbed in the lines, excising, shell stamping, pebble polishing, red slipping, modeling, combing, and finger grooving. Somewhat later are

rocker stamping, zoned punctating, applique fillets, brushing, and carving. The Machalilla Phase, which begins at 2000 B.C., introduces new vessel shapes that include the composite silhouette bowl, and both straight neck and stirrup-spout bottles. Decorations are engraved, filled with red pigment, made with a multiple point tool, and for the first time, red paint on the natural vessel surface.

At approximately 1500 B.C. Estrada and Evans (1963, pp. 80–81) conclude that the pattern of life on the Ecuadorian coast was changed by invasion of cultural traits, if not people, from Mesoamerica. The Valdivia culture disappeared and traits such as napkin-ring pottery earspools, small obsidian blades struck from prepared cores, iridescent painting, zoned red and black painting, annular ring bases on vessels, and the cuspidor-shaped bowl apparently arrived from Mesoamerica to form the Chorrera Phase. The most important introduction appears to have been maize agriculture, a probability deduced from the fact that villages began to be established back from the coasts in terrain suitable for planting. As maize is known to have been domesticated in highland Mexico and has been identified in Peru as early as 1400 B.C., this seems a reasonable conclusion.

The Regional Developmental Period begins at 500 B.C., when seven specialized and distinctive cultures emerge on the Ecuadorian coast. White-on-red and negative decorated pottery are horizon markers. The

Bahía Phase seems to have developed the widest geographical contacts, for it includes such exotic Mesoamerican features as stone-faced platforms, figurine styles, pottery masks, and pottery stamps. There is also evidence for contact with the southern Peruvian coast.

About 200 B.C. there is additional evidence suggesting transpacific contact (Estrada and Meggers, 1961). The Regional Developmental Period ends about A.D. 500 and the succeeding and more complex Ecuadorian prehistory is not of interest here.

THE CENTRAL HIGHLAND PERU CHRONOLOGICAL COLUMN

The prehistory of the Peruvian highlands is best known in the north central part of the country, and the greatest amount of information comes from the excavations of W. C. Bennett (1944a), more extensively Tello (1943) at Chavín de Huántar, and the recent work of the University of Tokyo archeologists at Kotosh. It is the work at Kotosh that has given us the longest and oldest sequence and all of the available radiocarbon dates (Izumi and Sono, 1963). Recent summaries will be found in Kidder, Lumbreras, and Smith (1963), and in Kidder (1964).

Thirteen radiocarbon assays are available from the Kotosh sequence (table 12, p. 38). Most have been made by the University of Tokyo laboratory, and the information is in the form of mimeographed lists supplied through the courtesy of Professor Seiichi Izumi. Nine of these dates, or 69 percent fall within the calendrical limits assigned the phases and four do not.

The Archaic cultures of the Peruvian highlands are by no means as well known as those on the coast. Masonry construction of platforms, stairways, and buildings with wall niches precedes the appearance of pottery in the Kotosh Mito Phase (ca. 2000 B.C.). Ceramics are first found at 1800 B.C. and are by no means primitive. The neckless jar is a popular form, bowls and bridge-spout bottles occur, and decoration consists of burnishing, wide-line incising, and shallow incising. Evidence of maize agriculture is certain by 1200 B.C., the beginning of the Kotosh Kotosh Phase.

Clay spindle whorls, jet mirrors, polished stone knives, and clay figurines are also found. Post-fired painting of pottery is common. The Classic Chavín Phase dates between 800 and 250 B.C. For this phase evidence from Chavín de Huántar (Tello, 1960) supplements that from Kotosh. Very complex buildings were constructed of cut stones, and stone was extensively carved, both in relief and the round. The feline with prominently displayed fangs appears.

Izumi and Sono (1963, pp. 156–157) treat the Kotosh Sajara-patac and San Blas Phases (200–1 B.C.) together and their example is followed here: manos and metates; T-shaped stone axes; star-shaped and spherical polished stone club heads; and personal ornaments of mica and turquoise appear. Kotosh Well Polished, which has dominated the Chavín Period, lessens in frequency and its characteristic flat-base, stirrup-spout bottles disappear. Chocolate brown, zoned unpainted, and polished red slipped pottery are diagnostic. Bowls and neckless jars are usual shapes. A white-on-red decorated ware may be related to the white-on-red horizon style of the coast (Willey, 1948, p. 10).

Metal work begins in the Kotosh Higueras Phase at A.D. 1. On pottery, negative painting, applique fillets representing human faces, and zoomorphic adornos are frequent. Izumi and Sono (1963, p. 11) suggest that this period equates with the negative painted ceramic horizon of the coast.

THE NORTH AND CENTRAL COAST OF PERU CHRONOLOGICAL COLUMN

The high degree of similarity throughout coastal Peru in the centuries before the beginning of the present era makes it feasable to present the dates available from the north coast as far north as Chicama Valley and the central coast southward to Ancón on one chronological column. Discussion of late preceramic times will range as far south as Engel's (1963) work

in the Valley of Asia. Bird (1948) has provided much of the information on the preceramic culture of the Chicama and Virú Valleys in the north. Most of the content of the coastal Chavín or Cupisinque Phase of this same region is the work of Larco Hoyle (1941, 1945b), who also has reported on grave goods of the Salinar-Puerto Moorín Phase (1944). The reports of the Virú Valley project in 1946 and 1947 by W. C. Bennett (1950), Collier (1955), Ford (1949), Strong and Evans (1952), and Willey (1953) have been used. Tello (1943) and Carríon Cachot (1948) deal with the Chavín Phase sites of Moxeke, Sechín, and Pallka in Casma. Uhle (1913) and Willey and Corbett (1954) have described work in the Ancón and Supe shell heaps. Excavations at Las Haldas are by Ishida, et al. (1960). Engel (1956) has reported on work at Curayacu.

Radiocarbon dates for the Virú Valley sequence are discussed by Collier (1955, pp. 24–26). In general, the radiocarbon dating for the Peruvian coast is almost as contradictory as that for the Lower Mississippi Valley, but there are fewer assays involved. Out of 23 available, ten (43 percent) agree with the calendrical limits for the phases used here, and thirteen (57 percent) do not (table 13, pp. 39–40).

As in Mesoamerica, agriculture was practiced by the people living along the Peruvian coast a number of centuries before ceramics appeared. While the sea continued to provide a major part of the food supply, bottle gourds, a species of squash, lima beans, pepper, jack beans, and probably achira seem to have been cultivated. Cotton makes its appearance about 3000 B.C. and seems to be crossed with an Asiatic variety with 13 chromosomes (Kidder, Lumbreras, and Smith, 1963, p. 92). Stonework was very crude, principally the manufacture of large rough flakes knocked off beach cobbles. Maize has been dated back to 1200 B.C. and it is now clear that this was an importation from highland Mesoamerica, where its evolution has been demonstrated.

For the dating of the earliest ceramics on the Peruvian coast, I have followed Matos (1962, and personal communication), who places the early pottery at Ancón at 1700 B.C., a few centuries after the earliest ceramics at Kotosh in the highlands. The resemblances are close. This interpretation views the period of initial plain ceramics in Virú Valley and Las Haldas (dated at 1200 B.C.) as a result of stimulus diffusion.

The increasing importance of agriculture as a way of life, undoubtedly due to the arrival of maize, is shown by the fact that principal sites began to be located away from the beach, back up the alluvial valleys, where there is arable land capable of being irrigated.

Stone masonry buildings had already been in use in preceramic times, but the first appearance of religious architecture is about 800 B.C. By the beginning of the Classic coastal Chavín, Guañape-Cupisnique Phase (800–400 B.C.), modest adobe flat-top pyramids are being constructed in north coast valleys, but in Casma Valley the large and complex pyramids are comparable to the highland Chavín site. The temple structures at Moxeke and Sechín are decorated with large sculptures in clay, and stele-like stones have human figures engraved on them in Chavín style.

Coastal Chavín ceramics have been well described and illustrated by Larco Hoyle (1941). Highly polished flat-base, stirrup-spout bottles are a typical form. Decorative techniques include wide-line incising, rocker stamping, brushing, and red painted areas zoned by incised lines. Already, there is a difference between domestic and religious ceramics, which becomes more pronounced in later phases.

Regional specialization of ceramics begins at the end of the Chavinoid Phase, about 400 B.C. Larco Hoyle (1944) describes the north coast phase in Chicama as Salinar: it was named "Puerto Moorín" in Virú Valley. Vessel forms continue from the preceding Chavinoid Phase, as does zoned red decoration. White-on-red painted decorations and bottles with spouts and flat bridges mark this horizon. The population of the flat valley floors where crops may be irrigated was increasing rapidly.

Izumi and Terada (1966) have recently published descriptions of three early phases investigated on the Río Tumbes, just south of the Ecuador-Peru frontier. Although the writer shall not present a chronological column for that region, the material is of great interest for comparative purposes.

The earliest phase, marked by San Juan Coarse Incised ware (op. cit., pl. 25a), features broad-line incising with simple motifs, including the paneling of horizontal lines suggestive of Valdivia Incised. Red slip was also present. A radiocarbon date of 1830 ± 130 B.C. (sample BC42, op. cit., p. 71) seems to be about right.

The Pechiche Phase has two dates: 370 ± 130 B.C.; and 850 ± 120 B.C. (op cit., p. 71). This phase saw the introduction of white-on-red painting, negative painting, painting after firing, engraving, and pedestal bases for bowls.

The Garbanzal Phase shows many features shared with the Regional Developmental phases of Ecuador. On the basis of these resemblances, it should date between 500 B.C. and A.D. 500, but the four dates obtained from the top level of the Pechiche site in Garbanzal context, cluster about A.D. 1000–1100. The probable reasons for these apparent errors are discussed by the authors (op. cit., pp. 71, 73).

TABLE 1.—*Radiocarbon dates used for establishing the Ohio chronological column. Dates rejected as not in agreement with the chronology are cited, as well as those from which examples were selected for inclusion on chart 1. (RC designates the journal, Radiocarbon.)*

	PERIOD	LAB. NO.	REFERENCE	SITE	CULTURE	DATE
Dates Shown on Chart 1	Ohio Hopewell-Late Adena	owu–62	RC, 1964, vol. 6, p. 346	McGraw Site	Ohio Hopewell	A.D. 435 ±166
		c–136	Libby, 1955, p. 94	Hopewell Md. Group	Ohio Hopewell	1 B.C. ±200
		m–928	RC, 1961, vol. 3, p. 111	Hopewell Md. Group	Ohio Hopewell	A.D. 120 ±200
		c–139	Libby, 1955, p. 95	Hopewell Md. Group	Ohio Hopewell	94 B.C. ±250
		c–214	Libby, 1955, p. 94	Cowan Creek Md.	Late Adena	A.D. 441 ±250
		m–650	RC Dates Assoc. Inc., 1958	Rocky Fork Lake	Ohio Hopewell	A.D. 60 ±200
		owu–51	RC, 1964, vol. 6, p. 345	Mound City	Ohio Hopewell	A.D. 178 ±53
		m–974	RC, 1961, vol. 3, pp. 116–117	Cresap Md.	Late Adena	70 B.C. ±150
	Ohio Early Adena	m–929	RC, 1961, vol. 3, p. 111	Clough Md.	Early Adena	170 B.C. ±200
		c–759	Libby, 1955, p. 99	MS27	Early Adena	700 B.C. ±170
		c–942	Libby, 1955, p. 104	Toepfner Md.	Early Adena	830 B.C. ±410
		c–760	Libby, 1955, p. 99	MS27	Early Adena	219 B.C. ±175
		c–923	Libby, 1955, p. 104	Toepfner Md.	Early Adena	427 B.C. ±150
		m–19	RC Dates Assoc., Inc., 1958	Drake Md.	Early Adena	250 B.C. ±250
	Vinette I	c–192	Ritchie, 1962, p. 584	Oberlander No. 2	Vinette I	998 B.C. ±170
		y–981	Ritchie, 1962, p. 584	Hunter	Vinette I	852 B.C. ±68
		m–586	Ritchie, 1962, p. 584	Orient	Vinette I	1043 B.C. ±300
	Archaic	m–561	RC Dates Assoc. Inc., 1958	Bland Cave	Archaic	1080 B.C. ±250
Valid Dates Omitted from Chart for Lack of Space	Ohio Hopewell-Late Adena	c–874	Libby, 1955, p. 100	Florence Md.	Late Adena	A.D. 525 ±250
		m–194	RC Dates Assoc. Inc., 1958	Pt. Peninsula	Ohio Hopewell	230 B.C. ±300
		m–908	RC Dates Assoc. Inc., 1958	Gaines Md.	Late Adena	25 B.C. ±200
		m–570	RC Dates Assoc. Inc., 1958	Wagner Merk Md.	Late Adena	A.D. 90 ±200
		ucla–679a	RC, 1965, vol. 7, p. 341	McGraw	Ohio Hopewell	A.D. 140 ±80
		ucla–679b	RC, 1965, vol. 7, p. 341	McGraw	Ohio Hopewell	A.D. 190 ±80
		ucla–688	RC, 1965, vol. 7, p. 338	McGraw	Ohio Hopewell	A.D. 280 ±80
		m–1075	RC, 1962, vol. 4, p. 189	Gaines Md.	Late Adena	A.D. 390 ±200
		m–909	RC, 1961, vol. 3, p. 113	Gaines Md.	Late Adena	120 B.C. ±200

TABLE 1.—*Radiocarbon dates used for establishing the Ohio chronological column. Dates rejected as not in agreement with the chronology are cited, as well as those from which examples were selected for inclusion on chart 1.*—Continued

	PERIOD	LAB. NO.	REFERENCE	SITE	CULTURE	DATE
Valid Dates Omitted from Chart for Lack of Space	Ohio Early Adena	M–517	RC Dates Assoc. Inc., 1958	Toepfner Md.	Early Adena	350 B.C. ±200
		M–518	RC Dates Assoc. Inc., 1958	Toepfner Md.	Early Adena	330 B.C. ±200
		M–519	RC Dates Assoc. Inc., 1958	Toepfner Md.	Early Adena	250 B.C. ±200
		M–520	RC Dates Assoc. Inc., 1958	Toepfner Md.	Early Adena	400 B.C. ±200
		M–521	RC Dates Assoc. Inc., 1958	Toepfner Md.	Early Adena	460 B.C. ±200
		M–975	RC, 1961, vol. 3, p. 116	Cresap Md.	Early Adena	240 B.C. ±200
		M–976	RC, 1961, vol. 3, p. 116	Cresap Md.	Early Adena	290 B.C. ±150
	Vinette I	M–640	RC, 1959, vol. 1, p. 183	Morrow	Vinette I	570 B.C. ±250
		W–543	Ritchie, 1962, p. 584	Orient	Vinette I	763 B.C. ±220
		Y–1171	RC, 1963, vol. 5, pp. 331–332	Morrow	Vinette I	630 B.C. ±100
Dates not in Agreement with Phase Dating on Chart 1	Ohio Hopewell–Late Adena	C–126	Libby, 1955, p. 94	Drake Md.	Late Adena	A.D. 782 ±150 (too late)
		UCLA–685	RC, 1965, vol. 7, p. 338	McGraw	Ohio Hopewell	230 B.C. ±80 (too early)
		UCLA–679C	RC, 1965, vol. 7, p. 341	McGraw	Ohio Hopewell	A.D. 440 ±80 (too late)
		M–1432	RC, 1965, vol. 7, p. 130	Green Point	Middle Woodland	530 B.C. ±120 (too early)
		OWU–61	RC, 1964, vol. 6, p. 346	McGraw	Ohio Hopewell	A.D. 481 ±65 (too late)
		C–137	Libby, 1955, pp. 94–95	Hopewell Md. Group	Ohio Hopewell	335 B.C. ±210 (too early)
	Vinette I	C–794	RC Dates Assoc. Inc., 1958	Hunter	Vinette I	2450 B.C. ±260 (too early)
		Y–582	RC, 1959, vol. 1, p. 160	Lagoon Pond	Vinette I	A.D. 920 ±70 (too late)
	Archaic	Y–583	RC, 1959, vol. 1, p. 161	Lagoon Pond	Preceramic	A.D. 520 ±60 (too late)

TABLE 2.—*Radiocarbon dates used for establishing the Illinois chronological column. Dates rejected as not in agreement with the chronology are cited, as well as those from which examples were selected for inclusion on chart 1. (RC designates the journal, Radiocarbon.)*

	PERIOD	LAB NO.	REFERENCE	SITE	CULTURE	DATE
Dates Shown on Chart 1	Illinois Hopewell	A–80A	RC, 1959, vol. 1, p. 60	Dickison	Illinois Hopewell	A.D. 50 ±350
		A–80B	RC, 1959, vol. 1, p. 60	Dickison	Illinois Hopewell	130 B.C. ±200
		M–560	RC Dates Assoc. Inc., 1958	Rutherford Md.	Illinois Hopewell	A.D. 425 ±200
		M–453	RC, 1959, vol. 1, p. 179	Liverpool Md.	Illinois Hopewell	A.D. 480 ±200
		M–20	RC Dates Assoc. Inc., 1958	Havana	Illinois Hopewell	250 B.C. ±250
		M–378	RC Dates Assoc. Inc., 1958	Steuben	Illinois Hopewell	A.D. 290 ±250
		M–579	RC, 1959, vol. 1, p. 177	Kuhne	Illinois Hopewell	260 B.C. ±250
		M–378	RC, 1961, vol. 3, pp. 111–112	Steuben	Illinois Hopewell	A.D. 300 ±350
		M–758	RC, 1961, vol. 3, p. 112	McDougal Hartman Md.	Illinois Hopewell	320 B.C. ±200
		M–183	RC Dates Assoc. Inc., 1958	Pool	Illinois Hopewell	A.D. 210 ±250
		C–152	Libby, 1955, p. 95	Havana	Illinois Hopewell	386 B.C. ±250
		M–164	RC Dates Assoc. Inc., 1958	Knight	Illinois Hopewell	A.D. 250 ±300
Valid Dates Omitted from Chart 1 for Lack of Space	Illinois Hopewell	M–15	RC Dates Assoc. Inc., 1958	Pool	Illinois Hopewell	550 B.C. ±300
		M–439	RC, 1961, vol. 3, pp. 111–112	Steuben	Illinois Hopewell	160 B.C. ±200
		M–443	RC Dates Assoc. Inc., 1958	Bedford	Illinois Hopewell	A.D. 20 ±250
		M–444	RC Dates Assoc. Inc., 1958	Bedford	Illinois Hopewell	A.D. 10 ±250
		M–445	RC Dates Assoc. Inc., 1958	Bedford	Illinois Hopewell	A.D. 230 ±250
		M–446	RC, 1959, vol. 1, p. 180	Bedford Md.	Illinois Hopewell	A.D. 400 ±250
		M–545	RC, 1961, vol. 3, p. 112	Steuben	Illinois Hopewell	A.D. 50 ±200
		M–548	RC, 1961, vol. 3, p. 112	Steuben	Illinois Hopewell	60 B.C. ±200
		M–558	RC Dates Assoc. Inc., 1958	Wilson Md.	Illinois Hopewell	1 B.C. ±200
		M–559	RC, 1959, vol. 1, p. 176	Wilson Md.	Illinois Hopewell	50 B.C. ±200
		M–578	RC, 1959, vol. 1, p. 177	Kuhne	Illinois Hopewell	A.D. 280 ±200
		M–580	RC, 1959, vol. 1, p. 177	Kuhne	Illinois Hopewell	A.D. 160 ±300

TABLE 2. — *Radiocarbon dates used for establishing the Illinois chronological column. Dates rejected as not in agreement with the chronology are cited, as well as those from which examples were selected for inclusion on chart 1—Continued.*

	PERIOD	LAB NO.	REFERENCE	SITE	CULTURE	DATE
Valid Dates Omitted from Chart 1 for Lack of Space	Illinois Hopewell	M–759	RC, 1961, vol. 3, p. 112	Renchville Md.	Illinois Hopewell	40 B.C. ±200
		M–760	RC, 1961, vol. 3, p. 112	Caterpillar Md.	Illinois Hopewell	60 B.C. ±150
		M–1038	RC, 1962, vol. 4, pp. 186–187	Kamp Md.	Illinois Hopewell	A.D. 190 ±200
		M–1039	RC, 1961, vol. 4, p. 187	Kamp Md.	Illinois Hopewell	A.D. 10 ±150
		M–1040	RC, 1962, vol. 4, p. 187	Kamp Md.	Illinois Hopewell	30 B.C. ±150
		M–1041	RC, 1962, vol. 4, p. 187	Kamp Md.	Illinois Hopewell	A.D. 140 ±150
		M–1154	RC, 1963, vol. 5, p. 231	Snyders	Illinois Hopewell	A.D. 60 ±75
		M–1155	RC, 1963 vol. 5, p. 231	Snyders	Illinois Hopewell	A.D. 230 ±75
		M–1161	R, 1963, vol. 5, p. 233	Klunk Md.	Illinois Hopewell	A.D. 175 ±75
		M–1487	RC, 1965, vol. 7, p. 131	Snyders	Illinois Hopewell	A.D. 100 ±120
Dates not in Agreement with Phase Dating on Chart 1	Illinois Hopewell	M–256	RC Dates Assoc. Inc., 1958	Weaver	Illinois Hopewell	350 B.C. ±250 (too early)
		L–431c	RC, 1959, vol. 1, p. 21	Twenhafel	Illinois Hopewell	A.D. 510 ±100 (too late)
		M–440	RC, 1961, vol. 3, p. 112	Steuben	Illinois Hopewell	A.D. 625 ±200 (too late)
		M–441	RC, 1961, vol. 3, p. 112	Steuben	Illinois Hopewell	A.D. 675 ±200 (too late)
		M–489	RC Dates Assoc. Inc., 1958	Irving	Illinois Hopewell	A.D. 770 ±250 (too late)
		M–714	RC, 1962, vol. 4, p. 187	Snyders	Illinois Hopewell	A.D. 640 ±150 (too late)
		M–1160	RC, 1963, vol. 5, p. 233	Klunk Md.	Illinois Hopewell	920 B.C. ±75 (too early)
		M–1355	RC, 1964, vol. 6, p. 6	Klunk Md.	Illinois Hopewell	A.D. 600 ±110 (too late)

TABLE 3.—*Radiocarbon dates used for establishing the Georgia coast chronological column. Dates rejected as not in agreement with the chronology are cited, as well as those utilized on chart 1. (RC designates the journal, Radiocarbon.)*

	PERIOD	LAB NO.	REFERENCE	SITE	CULTURE	DATE
Dates Shown on Chart 1	Deptford	c–933	RC Dates Assoc. Inc., 1958	Booger Bottom	Deptford	154 b.c. ±140
	Stallings Island-Plain Fiber	m–39	RC Dates Assoc. Inc., 1958	Sapelo Is.	Plain Fiber	1750 b.c. ±250
		gxo–345	Stoltman, 1966, p. 872	Rabbit Mount	Plain Fiber	2515 b.c. ±95
		m–236	RC Dates Assoc. Inc. 1958	Dulany	Plain Fiber	1820 b.c. ±200
		o–1047	Bullen, 1961, p. 104	Bilbo	Plain Fiber	2175 b.c. ±115
		m–1278	RC, 1965, vol. 7, p. 134	Stallings Is.	Plain Fiber	1780 b.c. ±150
		m–267	RC Dates Assoc. Inc., 1958	Refuge	Stallings Is.	970 b.c. ±200
		gxo–343	Stoltman, 1966, p. 872	Rabbit Mount	Plain Fiber	2500 b.c. ±135
		m–1112	RC, 1963, vol. 5, pp. 239–240	Bilbo	Plain Fiber	1780 b.c. ±125
		m–1111	RC, 1963, vol. 5, pp. 239–240	Bilbo	Plain Fiber	1870 b.c. ±125
		m–1109	RC, 1963, vol. 5, p. 239	Bilbo	Plain Fiber	1750 b.c. ±125
	Archaic	m–1279	RC, 1965, vol. 7, p. 134	Stallings Is.	Preceramic	2750 b.c. ±150
		m–1277	RC, 1965, vol. 7, p. 134	Stallings Is.	Preceramic	2500 b.c. ±150
Dates not in Agreement with Phase Dating on chart 1	Stallings Island-Plain Fiber	o–1046	Bullen, 1961, p. 104	Bilbo	Plain Fiber	3550 b.c. ±115 (too early)

TABLE 4.—*Radiocarbon dates used for establishing the north Florida chronological column. Dates rejected as not in agreement with the chronology are cited, as well as those utilized on chart 1.* (RC designates the journal, *Radiocarbon.*)

	PERIOD	LAB NO.	REFERENCE	SITE	CULTURE	DATE
Dates Shown on Chart 1	Yent	I–1366	Personal comm. Ripley Bullen	Crystal River	Yent	A.D. 80 ±130
		I–1367	Personal comm. Ripley Bullen	Crystal River	Yent	A.D. 200 ±130
		I–1916	Personal comm. Ripley Bullen	Crystal River	Yent	30 B.C. ±100
		I–1464	Personal comm. Ripley Bullen	Crystal River	Yent	A.D. 350 ±210
		I–1464	Personal comm. Ripley Bullen	Crystal River	Yent	A.D. 530 ±125
	Orange	M–215	RC Dates Assoc. Inc., 1958	Cotten	Late Dec. Fiber	1070 B.C. ±200
		M–394	RC Dates Assoc. Inc., 1958	J–5, Zone 9, Chattahoochee R.	Transitional	1200 B.C. ±250
	Tick Island	G–596	Bullen, 1961, p. 104	Palmer	Early Dec. Fiber	1400 B.C. ±120
		G–598	Bullen, 1961, p. 104	Palmer	Early Dec. Fiber	1625 B.C. ±120
		G–597	Bullen, 1961, p. 104	Palmer	Early Dec. Fiber	1275 B.C. ±120
		M–1014	RC, 1962, vol. 4, p. 192	Summer Haven	Tick Island	1380 B.C. ±200
	Archaic	G–600	Bullen, 1961, p. 104	Palmer	Preceramic	2150 B.C. ±125
Dates not in Agreement with Phase Dating on Chart 1	Tick Island	G–599	Bullen, 1961, p. 104	Palmer	Early Dec. Fiber	2100 B.C. ±125 (too early)
	Archaic	M–264	RC Dates Assoc. Inc., 1958	Bluffton	Preceramic	750 B.C. ±500 (too late)

TABLE 5.—*Radiocarbon dates used for establishing the Mobile Bay-Florida northwest coast chronological column. Dates rejected as not in agreement with the chronology are cited, as well as those utilized on chart 1.* (RC designates the journal, *Radiocarbon.*)

	PERIOD	LAB NO.	REFERENCE	SITE	CULTURE	DATE
Dates Shown on Chart 1	Santa Rosa	M–822	Personal comm. Bruce Trickey	Bryant's Landing	Hopewell	90 B.C. ±150
	Bayou La Batre	M–823	Personal comm. Bruce Trickey	Bryant's Landing	Bayou La Batre	1140 B.C. ±200
	Archaic	M–824	Personal comm. Bruce Trickey	Bryant's Landing	Preceramic	2150 B.C. ±250
Dates not in Agreement with Phase Dating on Chart 1	Deptford	Gx–155	RC, 1965, vol. 7, pp. 48–49	Alligator Lake	Deptford	625 B.C. ±80 (too early)

TABLE 6.—*Radiocarbon dates used for establishing the Louisiana chronological column. Dates rejected as not in agreement with the chronology are cited, as well as those utilized on chart 1. (RC designates the journal, Radiocarbon.)*

	PERIOD	LAB NO.	REFERENCE	SITE	CULTURE	DATE
Dates Shown on Chart 1	Troyville	o–24	Greengo, 1964, p. 104	Thornton	Troyville	A.D. 540 ±100
		o–25	Greengo, 1964, p. 104	Thornton	Troyville	A.D. 530 ±100
		o–148	Greengo, 1964, p. 104	Mabin	Troyville	A.D. 650 ±100
		o–143	Greengo, 1964, p. 104	Manny	Troyville	A.D. 690 ±100
	Marksville	M–1196	RC, 1963, vol. 5, p. 240	Helena Crossing	Marksville	A.D. 210 ±75
		M–1197	RC, 1963, vol. 5, p. 240	Helena Crossing	Marksville	150 B.C. ±75
		M–1199	RC, 1963, vol. 5, p. 241	Helena Crossing	Marksville	A.D. 20 ±75
		M–1198	RC, 1963, vol. 5, p. 241	Helena Crossing	Marksville	A.D. 325 ±75
		o–49	RC Dates Assoc. Inc., 1958	Magnolia Md.	Marksville	A.D. 120 ±100
	Tche-functe	M–243	RC Dates Assoc. Inc., 1958	Big Oak Is.	Tchefuncte	270 B.C. ±200
		o–30	Ford and Webb, 1956, p. 121	Tchefuncte	Tchefuncte	250 B.C. ±110
	Poverty Point	L–195	Ford and Webb, 1956, p. 121	Poverty Point	Poverty Point	910 B.C. ±100
		L–114	Ford and Webb, 1956, p. 121	Jaketown	Poverty Point	400 B.C. ±80
		o–66	Ford and Webb, 1956, p. 122	Poverty Point	Poverty Point	1200 B.C. ±120
		L–272	RC Dates Assoc. Inc., 1958	Poverty Point	Poverty Point	710 B.C. ±80
		M–216	Ford and Webb, 1956, p. 121	Jaketown	Poverty Point	880 B.C. ±300
		M–403	RC Dates Assoc. Inc., 1958	Poverty Point	Poverty Point	900 B.C. ±250
		Schatzman	Ford and Webb, 1956, p. 122	Poverty Point	Poverty Point	389 B.C. ±200
		Schatzman	Ford and Webb, 1956, p. 122	Poverty Point	Poverty Point	735 B.C. ±210
		o–41	Ford and Webb, 1956, p. 121	Jaketown	Poverty Point	610 B.C. ±110
		G–578	Haag, pers. comm. (unpublished Humble Oil)	Linsley Site, 16 Or–40	Poverty Point	1900 B.C. ±130
		G–579	Haag, pers. comm. (unpublished Humble Oil)	Linsley Site, 16 Or–40	Poverty Point	1600 B.C. ±120
		G–580	Haag, pers. comm. (unpublished Humble Oil)	Linsley Site, 16 Or–40	Poverty Point	1750 B.C. ±120

TABLE 6.—*Radiocarbon dates used for establishing the Louisiana chronological column. Dates rejected as not in agreement with the chronology are cited, as well as those utilized on chart 1. (RC designates the journal, Radiocarbon.)*—Continued

	PERIOD	LAB NO.	REFERENCE	SITE	CULTURE	DATE
Dates not in Agreement with Phase Dating on Chart 1	Troyville	M–383	Ford and Webb, 1956, p. 120	Manny	Troyville	470 B.C. ±300 (too early)
		O–7	McIntire, 1958, p. 107	Perdue Ridge	Troyville	800 B.C. ±110 (too early)
		O–26	Greengo, 1964, p. 104	Thornton	Troyville	A.D. 770 ±100 (runs off chart)
		O–71	McIntire, 1958, p. 107	River Aux Chenes	Troyville	A.D. 20 ±110 (too early)
		O–77	McIntire, 1958, p. 107	River Aux Chenes	Troyville	A.D. 1090 ±100 (too late)
		O–104	McIntire, 1958, p. 107	Miller	Troyville	A.D. 960 ±100 (too late)
	Marksville	C–143	RC Dates Assoc. Inc., 1958	Crooks	Marksville	A.D. 792 ±250 (too late)
		C–154	Ford and Webb, 1956, p. 120	Bynum	Marksville	A.D. 674 ±150 (too late)
		O–80	Ford and Webb, 1956, p. 120	Magnolia Md.	Marksville	A.D. 1050 ±100 (too late)
		O–90	McIntire, 1958, p. 107	Metairie Ridge	Marksville	370 B.C. ±110 (too early)
		O–102	McIntire, 1958, p. 107	Metairie Ridge	Marksville	A.D. 510 ±100 (too late)
		O–107	McIntire, 1958, p. 107	Loutre Ridge	Marksville	250 B.C. ±110 (too early)
		O–123	McIntire, 1958, p. 107	Magnolia Md.	Marksville	A.D. 900 ±100 (too late)

TABLE 6.—*Radiocarbon dates used for establishing the Louisiana chronological column. Dates rejected as not in agreement with the chronology are cited, as well as those utilized on chart 1.* (RC designates the journal, *Radiocarbon.*)—Continued

	PERIOD	LAB NO.	REFERENCE	SITE	CULTURE	DATE
Dates not in Agreement with Phase Dating on Chart 1	Tchefuncte	c–150	RC Dates Assoc. Inc., 1958	Tchefuncte	Tchefuncte	A.D. 1317 ±150 (too late)
		c–151	RC Dates Assoc. Inc., 1958	Tchefuncte	Tchefuncte	A.D. 717 ±250 (too late)
		m–218	RC Dates Assoc. Inc., 1958	Little Woods	Tchefuncte	A.D. 380 ±250 (too late)
		o–12A	McIntire, 1958, p. 107		Tchefuncte	825 B.C. ±110 (too early)
		o–28	Ford and Webb, 1956, p. 121	Liberty Bayou	Tchefuncte	A.D. 50 ±110 (too late)
		o–42	Ford and Webb, 1956, p. 121	Tchefuncte	Tchefuncte	A.D. 1150 ±100 (too late)
		o–76	Ford and Webb, 1956, p. 121	ST–12	Tchefuncte	A.D. 520 ±100 (too late)
		o–101	McIntire, 1958, p. 107		Tchefuncte	1850 B.C. ±120 (too early)
		UCLA–687	RC, 1965, vol. 7, p. 339	Or–7	Tchefuncte	750 B.C. ±90 (too early)
	Poverty Point	o–46	Ford and Webb, 1956, p. 121	Jaketown	Poverty Point	200 B.C. ±110 (too late)

TABLE 7.—*Radiocarbon dates used for establishing the Valley of Mexico chronological column. Dates rejected as not in agreement are cited, as well as those utilized on chart 1.* (RC designates the journal, *Radiocarbon.*)

	PERIOD	LAB NO.	REFERENCE	SITE	CULTURE	DATE
Dates Shown on Chart 1	Teotihuacán I–III	y–644	RC, Supp., 1960, vol. 2, p. 57	Oztoyahualco	Teotihuacán I	A.D. 20 ±80
		st–162	RC Dates Assoc. Inc., 1958	Teotihuacán	Teotihuacán II	A.D. 230 ±65
		UCLA–609	RC, 1965, vol. 7, p. 344	Calle de los Muertos	Teotihuacán I	A.D. 150 ±80
		y–437	RC Supp., 1959, vol. 1, pp. 161–162	Tlalpam	Teotihuacán I	A.D. 25 ±60
		UCLA–610	RC, 1965, vol. 7, p. 344	Plaza de la Luna	Teotihuacán II	A.D. 200 ±80
		M–1283	RC, 1963, vol. 5, p. 249	Pyramid of the Sun	Teotihuacán I	A.D. 80 ±75
		M–1118	RC, 1964, vol. 6, pp. 13–14	Oztoyahualco	Teotihuacán I	A.D. 145 ±120
		M–663	RC Dates Assoc. Inc., 1958	Pena Rock Quarry	Teotihuacán I	90 B.C. ±200
		UCLA–611	RC, 1965, vol. 7, p. 344	Plaza de la Luna	Teotihuacán III	A.D. 250 ±80
	El Arbolillo I–II, Atoto, and Ticomán I	M–662	RC Dates Assoc. Inc., 1958	Zacatenco	Tlatilco	500 B.C. ±250
		y–1629	Tolstoy and Guenette, 1965, p. 91	Tlatilco	Tlatilco	810 B.C. ±160
		y–1626	Tolstoy and Guenette, 1965, p. 91	Tlatilco	Tlatilco	410 B.C. ±120
		M–661	RC Dates Assoc. Inc., 1958	Tlatilco	Tlatilco	990 B.C. ±250
		M–660	RC Dates Assoc. Inc., 1958	Tlatilco	Tlatilco	575 B.C. ±250
		y–1627	Tolstoy and Guenette, 1965, p. 91	Tlatilco	Tlatilco	710 B.C. ±50
		y–1628	Tolstoy and Guenette, 1965, p. 91	Tlatilco	Tlatilco	480 B.C. ±60
Dates not in Agreement with Phase Dating on Chart 1	Teotihuacán I–III	c–203	Libby, 1955, pp. 128–129	Pyramid of the Sun	Teotihuacán	484 B.C. ±500 (too early)
		c–422	Libby, 1955, p. 129	Atetelco	Teotihuacán II	294 B.C. ±180 (too early)
		c–423	Libby, 1955, pp. 129–130	Sun Temple	Teotihuacán	1474 B.C. ±230 (too early)
	El Arbolillo I–II	c–190	Libby, 1955, p. 129	Tlatilco	Tlatilco	4440 B.C. ±300 (too early)
		c–199	Libby, 1955, p. 128	Tlatilco	Tlatilco	1457 B.C. ±250 (too early)

TABLE 8.—*Radiocarbon dates used for establishing the Chiapas chronological column. Dates rejected as not in agreement with the chronology are cited, as well as those utilized on chart 1.* (RC designates the journal, *Radiocarbon.*)

	PERIOD	LAB NO.	REFERENCE	SITE	CULTURE	DATE
Dates Shown on Chart 1	Chiapa VII	GrN-1589	RC, 1964, vol. 6, p. 364	Chiapa de Corzo	Proto-Classic	A.D. 30 ±45
		M-977	RC, 1961, vol. 3, p. 120	Santa Marta Cave	Classic	A.D. 80 ±200
	Chiapa III	GrN-1524	RC, 1964, vol. 6, p. 364	Chiapa de Corzo	Chiapa II and III	560 B.C. ±45
	Chiapa I and II	GrN-1512	RC, 1964, vol. 6, p. 363	Chiapa de Corzo	Chiapa I, II	1060 B.C. ±50
		L-427	RC Supp., 1959, vol.1 p. 22	Chiapa de Corzo	Chiapa I, II	780 B.C. ±150
		GrN-774	RC, 1964, vol. 6, p. 363	Chiapa de Corzo	Chiapa I	1060 B.C. ±150
		M-978	RC, 1961, vol. 3, p. 120	Santa Marta Cave	Chiapa I	1330 B.C. ±200
		GrN-1172	Dixon, 1959, p. 41	Chiapa de Corzo	Chiapa I, II	935 B.C. ±60
Dates not in Agreement with Phase Dating on Chart 1	Chiapa I and II	GrN-1056	RC, 1964, vol. 6, p. 363	Chiapa de Corzo	Chiapa I	420 B.C. ±60 (too late)
		GrN-1525	RC, 1964, vol. 6, p. 364	Chiapa de Corzo	Chiapa I, II	220 B.C. ±50 (too late)

TABLE 9.—*Radiocarbon dates used for establishing the Soconusco, Guatemala chronological column.* (RC designates the journal, *Radiocarbon.*)

	PERIOD	LAB NO.	REFERENCE	SITE	CULTURE	DATE
Dates Shown on Chart 1	Conchas	W-836	RC, 1960, vol. 2, p. 181	La Victoria	Conchas II	200 B.C. ±240
		W-837	RC, 1960, vol. 2, p. 181	La Victoria	Conchas II	130 B.C. ±240
	Cuadros	Y-1151	RC, 1963, vol. 5, p. 333	Salinas La Blanca	Cuadros	765 B.C. ±105
		Y-1166	RC, 1963, vol. 5, p. 333	Salinas La Blanca	Cuadros	814 B.C. ±90
		Y-1154	RC, 1963, vol. 5, p. 333	Salinas La Blanca	Cuadros	928 B.C. ±105
		Y-1150	RC, 1963, vol. 5, p. 333	Salinas La Blanca	Cuadros	978 B.C. ±105
		Y-1167	RC, 1963, vol. 5, p. 333	Rio Naranjo	Cuadros	790 B.C. ±70

TABLE 10.—*Radiocarbon dates used for establishing the north coast of Colombia chronological column. Dates rejected as not in agreement with the chronology are cited, as well as those utilized on chart 1.* (RC designates the journal, *Radiocarbon*.)

	PERIOD	LAB NO.	REFERENCE	SITE	CULTURE	DATE
Dates Shown on Chart 1	Malambo	m–1176	RC, 1963, vol. 5, pp. 248–249	Malambo	Malambo	1120 B.C. ±100
	Barlovento	y–1318	Reichel-Dolmatoff, 1965, p. 53	Barlovento	Barlovento	1560 B.C. ±100
		y–1317	Reichel-Dolmatoff, 1965, p. 53	Canapote	Barlovento	1940 B.C. ±100
		w–743	RC, 1960, vol. 2, p. 180	Barlovento	Barlovento	1190 B.C. ±120
		w–739	RC, 1960, vol. 2, p. 180	Barlovento	Barlovento	1520 B.C. ±120
		w–741	RC, 1960, vol. 2, p. 180	Barlovento	Barlovento	1030 B.C. ±120
	Puerto Hormiga	i–1123	Reichel-Dolmatoff, 1965, p. 53	Puerto Hormiga	Puerto Hormiga	2552 B.C. ±250
		i–445	Reichel-Dolmatoff, 1965, p. 53	Puerto Hormiga	Puerto Hormiga	2925 B.C. ±170
		si–152	Reichel-Dolmatoff, 1965, p. 53	Puerto Hormiga	Puerto Hormiga	3020 B.C. ±70
		si–151	Reichel-Dolmatoff, 1965, p. 53	Puerto Hormiga	Puerto Hormiga	2870 B.C. ±100
Dates not in Agreement with Phase Dating on Chart 1	Cupica	m–1313	RC, 1964, vol. 6, p. 17	Cupica	Cupica II	A.D. 1215 ±100 (too late)
	Malambo	m–117	RC, 1963, vol. 5, p. 248	Malambo	Malambo	A.D. 650 ±75 (too late)
		m–1175	RC, 1963, vol. 5, p. 248	Malambo	Malambo	A.D. 60 ±100 (too late)
		m–1177	RC, 1963, vol. 5, p. 249	Malambo	Malambo	A.D. 1600 ±75 (too late)
		m–1178	RC, 1963, vol. 5, p. 249	Malambo	Malambo	A.D. 565 ±75 (too late)
	Puerto Hormiga	si–153	Reichel-Dolmatoff, 1965, p. 53	Puerto Hormiga	Puerto Hormiga	3090 B.C. ±70 (too early, 20 years)

TABLE 11.—*Radiocarbon dates used for establishing the coastal Ecuador chronological column. Dates rejected as not in agreement with the chronology are cited, as well as those utilized on chart 1.*

	PERIOD	LAB NO.	REFERENCE	SITE	CULTURE	DATE
Dates Shown on Chart 1	Regional Developmental	M–734	Meggers, Evans, Estrada, 1965, p. 153	Tarqui	Bahía	220 B.C. ±200
		SI–49	Meggers, Evans, Estrada, 1965, p. 153	Esteros	Bahía	350 B.C. ±65
		M–1315	Meggers, Evans, Estrada, 1965, p. 153	Esteros	Bahía	100 B.C. ±120
		SI–55	Meggers, Evans, Estrada, 1965, p. 153	Esteros	Bahía	480 B.C. ±60
		M–1316	Meggers, Evans, Estrada, 1965, p. 153	Esteros	Bahía	170 B.C. ±120
		SI–52	Meggers, Evans, Estrada, 1965, p. 153	Esteros	Bahía	400 B.C. ±65
		M–1319	Meggers, Evans, Estrada, 1965, p. 153	Esteros	Bahía	160 B.C. ±120
		W–834	Meggers, Evans, Estrada, 1965, p. 153	Esteros	Bahía	250 B.C. ±240
		W–833	Meggers, Evans, Estrada, 1965, p. 153	Esteros	Bahía	200 B.C. ±240
	Chorrera	SI–35	Meggers, Evans, Estrada, 1965, p. 153	Pepa de Huso	Late Chorrera	575 B.C. ±105
		SI–43	Meggers, Evans, Estrada, 1965, p. 153	Pepa de Huso	Late Chorrera	590 B.C. ±125
		1307	Meggers, Evans, Estrada, 1965, p. 153	Véliz	Late Chorrera	850 B.C. ±115
		SI–107	Meggers, Evans, Estrada, 1965, p. 149	La Cabuya	Machalilla-Chorrera	1370 B.C. ±170
	Valdivia	M–1317	Meggers, Evans, Estrada, 1965, p. 149	Valdivia	Valdivia A	2530 B.C. ±140
		SI–83	Meggers, Evans, Estrada, 1965, p. 149	Valdivia	Valdivia A	2580 B.C. ±55
		SI–84R	Meggers, Evans, Estrada, 1965, p. 149	Valdivia	Valdivia A	2590 B.C. ±150
		W–631	Meggers, Evans, Estrada, 1965, p. 149	Valdivia	Valdivia A	2500 B.C. ±200
		SI–22	Meggers, Evans, Estrada, 1965, p. 149	Valdivia	Valdivia A	2500 B.C. ±90
		M–1322	Meggers, Evans, Estrada, 1965, p. 149	Valdivia	Valdivia A	2670 B.C. ±140
		SI–84	Meggers, Evans, Estrada, 1965, p. 149	Valdivia	Valdivia A	2440 B.C. ±60
		W–630	Meggers, Evans, Estrada, 1965, p. 149	Valdivia	Valdivia B	2100 B.C. ±200

TABLE 11.—*Radiocarbon dates used for establishing the coastal Ecuador chronological column. Dates rejected as not in agreement with the Chronology are cited, as well as those utilized on chart 1.*—Continued

	PERIOD	LAB NO.	REFERENCE	SITE	CULTURE	DATE
Dates shown on Chart 1	Valdivia	sɪ–82	Meggers, Evans, Estrada, 1965, p. 149	Valdivia	Valdivia ʙ	2170 ʙ.c. ±65
		ᴍ–1318	Meggers, Evans, Estrada, 1965, p. 149	Valdivia	Valdivia ʙ	2220 ʙ.c. ±140
		sɪ–80	Meggers, Evans, Estrada, 1965, p. 149	Valdivia	Valdivia ʙ	2190 ʙ.c. ±60
		ᴍ–1321	Meggers, Evans, Estrada, 1965, p. 149	Valdivia	Valdivia ʙ	2150 ʙ.c. ±140
		sɪ–81	Meggers, Evans, Estrada, 1965, p. 149	Valdivia	Valdivia ʙ	2320 ʙ.c. ±60
		sɪ–85	Meggers, Evans, Estrada, 1965, p. 149	Valdivia	Valdivia ʙ	2220 ʙ.c. ±65
		sɪ–18	Meggers, Evans, Estrada, 1965, p. 149	Valdivia	Valdivia ʙ	2280 ʙ.c. ±100
		sɪ–16	Meggers, Evans, Estrada, 1965, p. 149	Valdivia	Valdivia ʙ	2270 ʙ.c. ±100
		w–632	Meggers, Evans, Estrada, 1965, p. 149	Valdivia	Valdivia ʙ	2240 ʙ.c. ±200
		sɪ–69	Meggers, Evans, Estrada, 1965, p. 149	Buena Vista	Valdivia c	1500 ʙ.c. ±50
		sɪ–78	Meggers, Evans, Estrada, 1965, p. 149	Valdivia	Valdivia c	2020 ʙ.c. ±65
Dates not in Agreement with Phase Dating on Chart 1	Machalilla	sɪ–108	Meggers, Evans, Estrada, 1965, p. 149	La Cabuya	Machalilla c	1030 ʙ.c. ±160 (too late)
		sɪ–67	Meggers, Evans, Estrada, 1965, p. 149	La Cabuya	Machalilla c	880 ʙ.c. ±45 (too late)
	Valdivia	ᴍ–1320	Meggers, Evans, Estrada, 1965, p. 149	Valdivia	Valdivia ᴀ	3200 ʙ.c. ±150 (50 years too early)
		sɪ–112	RC, 1965, vol. 7, p. 250	Valdivia	Valdivia ᴀ	1400 ʙ.c. ±200 (too late)
		sɪ–20	RC, 1964, vol. 6, p. 186	Valdivia	Valdivia ᴀ, ʙ	855 ʙ.c. ±105 (too late)
		sɪ–71	Meggers, Evans, Estrada, 1965, p. 149	Buena Vista	Valdivia c	2090 ʙ.c. ±55 (35 years too early)

TABLE 12.—*Radiocarbon dates used for establishing the central highland Peru chronological column. Dates rejected as not in agreement with the chronology are cited, as well as those utilized on chart 1.*

	PERIOD	LAB NO.	REFERENCE	SITE	CULTURE	DATE
Dates Shown on Chart 1	Kotosh Higueiras	N–62	Unpublished list provided by Izumi	Kotosh	Kotosh Higueras	A.D. 70 ±200
	Kotosh Chavín	N–65–2	Unpublished list provided by Izumi	Kotosh	Kotosh Chavín	870 B.C. ±120
	Kotosh Kotosh	N–66–a	Unpublished list provided by Izumi	Kotosh	Kotosh Kotosh	920 B.C. ±230
		N–67–2	Unpublished list provided by Izumi	Kotosh	Kotosh Kotosh	890 B.C. ±170
		Gak–261	Unpublished list provided by Izumi	Kotosh	Kotosh Kotosh	1120 B.C. ±110
	Kotosh Waira–jirca	N–69–2	Unpublished list provided by Izumi	Kotosh	Kotosh Waira–jirca	1150 B.C. ±130
		Gak–262	Unpublished list provided by Izumi	Kotosh	Kotosh Waira–jirca	1850 B.C. ±110
		Gak–765	Unpublished list provided by Izumi	Kotosh	Kotosh Waira–jirca	1830 B.C. ±90
	Kotosh Mito	Gak–766b	Unpublished list provided by Izumi	Kotosh	Kotosh Mito	1950 B.C. ±100
Dates not in Agreement with Phase Dating on Chart 1	Kotosh Sajara–patac	N–63–2	Unpublished list provided by Izumi	Kotosh	Kotosh Sajara–patac	A.D. 260 ±140 (too late)
	Kotosh Chavín	Gak–263	Unpublished list provided by Izumi	Kotosh	Kotosh Chavín	1200 B.C. ±150 (too early)
	Kotosh Mito	Gak–766a	Unpublished list provided by Izumi	Kotosh	Kotosh Mito	1670 B.C. ±100 (too late)
		Gak–764	Unpublished list provided by Izumi	Kotosh	Kotosh Mito	90 B.C. ±100 (too late)

TABLE 13.—*Radiocarbon dates used for establishing the north and central coast of Peru chronological column. Dates rejected as not in agreement with the chronology are cited, as well as those utilized on chart 1.*

	PERIOD	LAB NO.	REFERENCE	SITE	CULTURE	DATE
Dates Shown on Chart 1	Haldas–Curayacu	Gak–106	RC, 1962, vol. 4, p. 91	Las Haldas	Haldas-Curayacu	730 B.C. ±150
	Ancón	L–122c	RC Dates Assoc. Inc., 1958	Huaca Negra	Upper Early Guañape	1350 B.C. ±200
	Asia-Huaca Prieta	L–116A	RC Dates Assoc. Inc., 1958	Huaca Prieta	Asia-Huaca Prieta	1830 B.C. ±100
		c–315	Libby, 1955, p. 132	Huaca Prieta	Asia-Huaca Prieta	1622 B.C. ±220
		c–313	Libby, 1955, p. 132	Huaca Prieta	Asia-Huaca Prieta	2307 B.C. ±250
		c–316	Libby, 1955, p. 132	Huaca Prieta	Asia-Huaca Prieta	2430 B.C. ±270
		c–318b	Libby, 1955, p. 132	Huaca Prieta	Asia-Huaca Prieta	1600 B.C. ±600
		c–362	Libby, 1955, p. 132	Huaca Prieta	Asia-Huaca Prieta	2094 B.C. ±300
		c–598	Libby, 1955, p. 133	Huaca Prieta	Asia-Huaca Prieta	2348 B.C. ±230
		L–116B	RC Dates Assoc. Inc., 1958	Huaca Prieta	Asia-Huaca Prieta	1910 B.C. ±100
Dates not in Agreement with Phase Dating on Chart 1	Puerto Moorín	L–404A	RC Dates Assoc. Inc., 1958	Chanquillo	Puerto Moorín	350 B.C. ±80 (too early)
	Middle Guañape-Cupisnique	L–122A	RC Dates Assoc. Inc., 1958	Huaca Negra	Middle Guañape	1200 B.C. ±90 (too early)
		L–122B	RC Dates Assoc. Inc., 1958	Huaca Negra	Middle Guañape	3800 B.C. ±180 (too early)
	Haldas–Curayacu	Gak–107	RC, 1962, vol. 4, p. 91	Las Haldas	No cultural identification	1630 B.C. ±130

TABLE 13.—*Radiocarbon dates used for establishing the north and central coast of Peru chronological column. Dates rejected as not in agreement with the chronology are cited, as well as those utilized on chart 1*—Continued

	PERIOD	LAB NO.	REFERENCE	SITE	CULTURE	DATE
Dates not in Agreement with Phase Dating on Chart 1	Ancón	L–122D	RC Dates Assoc. Inc., 1958	Huaca Negra	Upper Early Guañape	2550 B.C. ±200 (too early)
		L–122F	RC Dates Assoc. Inc., 1958	Huaca Negra	Lower Early Guañape	2050 B.C. ±150 (too early)
		L–122G	RC Dates Assoc. Inc., 1958	Huaca Negra	Lower Early Guañape	3550 B.C. ±200 (too early)
		L–384A	RC, 1961, vol. 3, p. 71	Ancón	Ancón	A.D. 560 ±160 (too late)
	Asia-Huaca Prieta	C–75	Libby, 1955, p. 133	Huaca Prieta	Asia-Huaca Prieta	715 B.C. ±200 (too late)
		C–318A	Libby, 1955, p. 132	Huaca Prieta	Asia-Huaca Prieta	39 B.C. ±196 (too late)
		C–321	Libby, 1955, p. 132	Huaca Prieta	Asia-Huaca Prieta	1016 B.C. ±300 (too late)
		C–322	Libby, 1955, p. 133	Huaca Prieta	Asia-Huaca Prieta	1360 B.C. ±200 (too late)
		C–323	Libby, 1955, p. 133	Huaca Prieta	Asia-Huaca Prieta	682 B.C. ±300 (too late)

Geographical and Chronological Distribution of Selected Traits

SETTLEMENT PATTERN: VILLAGE PLAN AND CEREMONIAL CONSTRUCTIONS

CHART 2

Prior to 3000 B.C. the population of the Americas was sparse and probably for the most part the hunters and collectors wandered seasonally over a limited range of territory to take advantage of several natural food sources, as did the recent hunters of Canada and acorn collectors of California. MacNeish (1964) found that even the developing maize agriculturalists of the Mexican highlands occupied cave shelters only seasonally in their food quest. It seems safe to picture these people as organized into small kinship bands, many of which probably had a home village with permanent houses, which were not, however, permanently occupied.

Exceptions to this pattern occurred where the environment provided stable, readily available sources of food. At many favorable points along the sea coasts of all the Americas, there are large accumulations of seashells mixed with camp refuse that predate the appearance of ceramics. Such shell middens are also found near river shoals, as along the Tennessee River, where mussels formed the staple of diet.

Even where Archaic people concentrated in substantial numbers, there is little or no evidence of village plan, and there are no monuments that would reflect community organization of political or religious motivation. The shell heaps show that dwellings were strung out along water fronts, apparently arranged more for ready access to the food supply than for defense. Hostilities must have been fairly frequent during this time, but perhaps social control was so undeveloped that it could not be used for the effective planning of either offense or defense. The volunteer raiding parties of the historic peoples of northern North America or of eastern and southern South America were probably the pattern of the time. Islands in rivers and other naturally defensible localities were occupied, but compact deposits of refuse in areas that could have been readily defended by stockades are not a usual pattern.

Compact, almost circular, sea coast villages are a feature of the preceramic occupation of the Peruvian coast. Engel (1958, pp. 19–26) describes a number of localities, often on the shores of old filled-in bays, where compact deposits of refuse cap small rocky natural elevations or sand dunes. Huaca Prieta de Brujo excavated by Bird (1948) had retaining walls made of beach pebbles, and the sides of this 12-meter high refuse pile were so steep that they must have constituted an effective defense feature. Partially washed away by the sea, the remains of this big midden measure 125 by 50 meters. The similar but slightly smaller "Tell" of Pulpar is located a few kilometers up the beach, also in Chicama Valley. As is fairly common in preceramic times on the Peruvian coast, the houses were small subterranean structures of stone.

While these compact settlements were occupied before ceramics and maize agriculture appeared about 1200 B.C., they have not been dated before 2500 B.C. and so are coeval with the Valdivia and Machalilla occupations of the Ecuadorian coast, where a competent ceramic was being manufactured by coastal dwelling fishermen.

Although the Valdivia and Machalilla sites typically have a refuse deposit less than 2 meters deep, they also were usually placed on the crests of low hills along the beach, or the old shores of filled-in

41

bays. According to Meggers, Evans, and Estrada (1965, p. 15), "The deposit typically consisted of powdery soil containing large amounts of shell, sherd and other kinds of natural and cultural refuse. No evidence was found of walls, floors, or other kinds of structures, and no significant natural stratigraphy could be identified at any of the sites." Burials were occasionally found. An impressive feature of these middens is that they are quite compact and are roughly circular in form, a hundred meters or less in diameter. These villages could have been defended by stockades; whether they actually were is not known. The Punta Arenas site, occupied about 1500 B.C., is located on a small natural 50 by 80 meter rise in salt marsh on the north shore of the Gulf of Guayaquil, and was almost surrounded by the sea when it was occupied (chart 2–19). The midden deposit, slightly less than 50 centimeters deep, was around the edge of this low elevation, and the central part of the almost level area was free from refuse. This suggests that the dwellings were arranged around an open court.

The Puerto Hormiga site on the north coast of Colombia is located on a slight elevation alongside a marsh, which seems to be a filled-in arm of the Caribbean. Radiocarbon dates range from 3090 B.C. to 2552 B.C. Reichel-Dolmatoff (1965, pp. 7–8, fig. 1a–b) describes the midden as a ring 77 meters in diameter north to south, 85 meters east to west (chart 2–17). Shell and soil have been deposited to a depth of about 1.20 meters. Width of the ring varies from 16–25 meters. On the east side, there is a low place in the accumulation suggesting a gap in the circle of dwellings. The center of the ring was free of refuse.

The Barlovento site located on the coast near Cartagena, Colombia, has yielded radiocarbon dates from 1560–1030 B.C. (Reichel-Dolmatoff, 1955, pp. 247–272). It also is located beside a swamp that seems formerly to have been a waterway giving access to the beach a few hundred meters distant. Reichel-Dolmatoff (op. cit., p. 251) describes the site as follows: "The circle formed by the accumulations of these shells consists of six elevations, almost symmetrical, and more or less equidistant, in the forms of mounds connected with one another at their bases [chart 2–16]. The average elevation over the level area in the center of this circle is about 3 meters. . . . The total area covered by the shell heaps is about 100 × 100 meters; the level central court measures 15 × 20 meters."

The Monagrillo site on Parita Peninsula, Pacific coast of Panama, dating about 2000 B.C., has been described by Willey and McGimsey (1954). The shell midden occupies a low peninsula about 150 meters long and 80 meters wide, which now projects into tidal flats, formerly Parita Bay. The shell midden

forms two parallel ridges that run lengthwise on the low natural elevation. The shallow "trough" between the ridges proved to be deeper on excavation than it appeared on the surface. This suggestion of houses arranged about a central court is by no means as clear as in the sites described above.

Waring (in Williams, 1968, pp. 253–254) summarizes the fiber-tempered sites of coastal Georgia and adjacent South Carolina in the following words:

> (a) scattered occupations along marsh edges and bluffs
> (b) marsh middens
> (c) shell rings
>
> The scattered occupations are frequently quite extensive and suggest a looser, more open communal plan than do the great shell concentrations of Alabama and Tennessee.
>
> The marsh middens are shell deposits, some irregularly circular in shape, situated out in the marsh near the head waters of creek systems . . . [elsewhere described as 75 to 150 feet in diameter and 4 to 7 feet deep].
>
> Of the shell rings, eight have survived. These are circular enclosures of shell from fifty to three hundred feet in diameter, the walls of the enclosure being from two to nine feet in height [chart 2–3]. The area enclosed was apparently kept scrupulously clean. The walls themselves in cross-section show extensive evidence of fires and primary midden deposits. The great shell ring on Sapelo [Island] was one of three and was the center of extensive low midden deposits running two to three hundred yards in each direction.

Moore (1897, pp. 71–73) describes the Sapelo shell ring as follows:

> . . . a diameter, including the walls, of something over 300 feet. The walls have an average height of from 5 to 7 feet, and a thickness of about 50 feet at the base. They are flattened on the top where at present they have an average width of from 10 to 15 feet. They are covered with forest trees and are composed exclusively of shells, mainly those of oyster, with the usual midden refuse intermingled, such as fragments of bone, bits of earthenware, and the like. . . .

Waring and Larson report on their reexcavation of this ring in some detail (in Williams, 1968, pp. 263–278). The two shell specimens from this excavation gave an average date of 1750 ±250 B.C. (op. cit., p. 329).

It is tempting to suggest that the use of camp circles by North American Plains people, and the circular villages of the Amazon Basin may be retentions of an Early Formative or possible Archaic village plan.

Thus far, no hint of the practice of artificial mound construction has come from sites of the Early Formative dating before 1200 B.C. The circular and ring-shaped villages described above resulted from the careless, unplanned discarding of shells and other refuse around dwellings.

At various times after 1200 B.C., the Indians in the three Americas began to waste untold millions of man hours in the erection of tremendous monuments of earth, adobe brick, and stone that served no practical purpose. This is not unique, as attested by the pyramids of Egypt or the Medieval cathedrals located in small European towns. The spread of efficient maize agriculture, with the resultant population increase and increase of "leisure" time, are the factors that made this possible. It is also obvious that the strict social and political controls necessary to accomplish such great constructions have a religious base, complete with specialist priest-rulers. The striking art styles that accompanied early mound building also indicate marked craft specialization, including architects, engineers, sculptors, and artists.

Where cultural elements originated to spark this first burst of monument building is not yet known. Cultural isolationists may see it as a consequence of the improved food supply. Those inclined to cultural continuity can point to some striking Old World parallels.

There is a clear evolutionary sequence in settlement patterns in relation to the temple mound centers of the eastern United States, Mesoamerica, and the Andean region. Upon first appearance, the pyramids and their superimposed buildings tend to be used solely as religious centers. The populations they served lived scattered in small villages through the surrounding territory; the inhabitants of the centers were relatively few, probably functionaries and servants of the religious. Various centuries later a trend toward urbanization of these centers developed, and they became in some instances large cities. Chan-Chan, Pachacamac, and Arpulé in Peru, and Teotihuacán, Monte Albán, and Tenochtitlán in Mexico are examples.

According to present information, the earliest large scale ceremonial mound building was in the Olmec region on the Gulf coast of Mexico. At the San Lorenzo site, located on a small isolated plateau above a branch of the Coatzacoalcos River, Coe, Diehl, and Stuiver (1967) have obtained five radiocarbon dates that range between 1200 and 800 B.C. Stirling (1955, p. 9) describes the structures as follows: "The principal mound is conical in shape, although it may originally have been a pyramid. It is about 25 feet [7.5 m.] in height and stands at the south end of a rectangular plaza which is enclosed by earthen embankments. . . . A few other small mounds are erected near this central plaza, but they are without apparent regularity of orientation." In addition, there are nine small reservoirs or borrow pits, hexagonal in shape.

The original set of radiocarbon dates published by Drucker, Heizer, and Squier (1959, pp. 264–267) for La Venta has been supplemented by some reruns and additional dates by Berger, Graham, and Heizer (1967). These suggest that the site was occupied between 1100 and 800 B.C., essentially coeval with the San Lorenzo site.

La Venta, located on an island in a swamp near the coast, was much larger than San Lorenzo, but follows and elaborates its basic plan. The principal feature was first thought to be a flat-top pyramid (Drucker, Heizer, and Squier, 1959, pp. 6–15), but recent reexamination of the cleared structure proves it to be a large earth cone about 32 m. high with a very small flattened summit. Most unusual is the fact that the sides show 10 pronounced lobes or flutes extending from the summit to the base, a sort of "cupcake shape," quite unlike any other known mound structure (Heizer and Drucker, 1968).

The arrangement of structures at La Venta is complex and formal (chart 2–8). The excavators observed that the auxiliary features were symmetrically placed on either side of a center line that runs through the middle of this pyramid northward, bearing 8 degrees west of true north. Aligned with the outer edges of the pyramid are two linear mounds that extend parallel for 100 m. to the north. Between them is a low mound; beyond the linear mounds are two low platform mounds with enclosures formed by rows of columnar basalt. Outside of these, extending further north, are symmetrically arranged bracket-shaped ridges, also capped with basalt columns. Beyond, about 164 m. from the toe of the big fluted cone and directly on the center line, is a low mound that contained a basalt tomb provided with rich offerings to accompany the burials. An elaborate complex of mask-like pavements and offerings was placed on, or symmetrically to, either side of this line at various points. A variety of brilliantly colored earth was used in construction. Stone paving block and basalt columns were brought in from considerable distance, and unfired adobe bricks were also employed in construction.

Shortly after this time, mound building was widely practiced along the Gulf coast of Mexico. On the coast north of Veracruz, in the Valley of the Actopan River where García Payón (1966) has reported on excavations at El Trapiche and Chalahuites, there are dozens of impressive earth structures. Group plans are not discernible, probably due to the 4 to 6 meter sheet of alluvium that has buried their bases. The mounds range up to 15 meters high and are conical, cones resting on platforms, elongated mounds with steep sides and narrow-ridged tops; almost every form except the flat-top pyramids arranged about rectangular plazas that are usually thought of as the typical Mesoamerican plan. While some of these coastal mounds could and did serve as platforms for buildings, others are too steep and narrow at the summit. None have been carefully excavated and their use is unknown. The arrangement of rectangular pyramids about courts seems to begin about A.D. 300–500, when the early phases of such sites as Tajín were built.

There is no evidence for pyramid building having been associated with the Valley of Mexico Pre-Classic sites of Tlatilco, Ticomán, El Arbolillo, or Zacatenco. Armillas (1964, pp. 304ff) suggests that the isolated ceremonial center mounds, such as Cuicuilco and Tlapacoya, furnished the model on which true cities with large populations developed. Most notable of the cities in the valley is Teotihuacán. Millon, Drewitt, and Bennyhoff (1965, p. 34) offer evidence that the tremendous Temple of the Sun (chart 2–9) was built between A.D. 100 and 200. Apparently Teotihuacán had assumed its urban character by these dates, and thus may be the oldest true city in the Americas. The residence areas are apartment houselike buildings arranged in carefully laid out rectangular blocks, with city streets running at right angles. Streets and courts were paved with stone and cement, and underground drains were provided for water.

The Monte Albán site in Oaxaca is located on a steep hilltop, and apparently during its early phase (ca. 800–1 B.C.) was primarily a ceremonial center with temple pyramids. During Phase II (200 B.C.–A.D. 100), the process of urbanization began, but the population concentration never equaled that of Teotihuacán. Street arrangement was less precise due to the unevenness of the terrain.

In Tehuacán Valley the use of modest rectangular temple bases in groups of two or three, arranged about courts, began in the Santa Maria Phase (800–200 B.C.), more than a thousand years after the introduction of ceramics. During the Palo Blanco Phase (200 B.C.–A.D. 700), MacNeish (1964, p. 537) says: "They lived in wattle-and-daub villages or hamlets either oriented toward or adjacent to large hilltop ceremonial centers having elaborate stone pyramids, plazas, ball courts, and other structures. Some of these ruins covered whole mountain tops and in terms of population might be considered cities, albeit sacred cities."

In Chiapas, the first low field-stone platforms were constructed as building foundations between 1000 and 500 B.C. (Lowe, 1959b, pp. 11–21). Arrangement is not clear, and it is uncertain whether these were religious structures or not. By 600 B.C., however, the pyramids constructed at the site of Chiapa de Corzo form a well-developed ceremonial nucleus.

By the Horcones Phase (Chiapa VI, ca. A.D. 1) the low pyramids had cut-stone facings, and contained large tombs with adobe brick walls and timbered roofs (chart 2–12; Lowe, 1959a). The elaborate tombs show that the idea of erecting mounds for temple substructures had been combined with the simple conical earth mound erected over a central vault as at La Venta. Pyramids sometimes continued to have tombs, as at Kaminaljuyú and Palenque. A true urban phase, with cities comparable to Teotihuacán or Chan-Chan, does not seem to have developed in Chiapas.

There is no evidence of pyramid construction during the Ocós Phase on the Pacific coast of Guatemala (M. D. Coe, 1961). Low clay platforms for houses began in the Jocotal Phase (850–800 B.C.), and one site had a single rectangular pyramid 4 meters high (chart 2–15). Coe and Flannery (1967, pp. 89–90) state:

By Crucero times a significant population decrease had taken place in the Ocós area and most settlements had moved inland to the piedmont. The late Formative in the Guatemalan highlands and along the foot hills of the Pacific coast (the so-called 'Boca Coast') of both Guatemala and Chiapas, was a time of substantial pyramid building and monumental sculpture. Kaminaljuyú in the Miraflores Phase, Monte Alto, El Baúl and Izapa are some of the most impressive ceremonial sites of this period, and made important contributions to the development of Maya civilization.

In Lower Middle America, south of the Maya area, mound building never became popular. Baudez (1963, p. 47) says that in Costa Rica large burial mounds dating between 300 B.C. and A.D. 300 have been reported at Puerto Nuevo.

Ceremonial centers with temples built on platform mounds seem never to have developed to any great extent in Colombia. The Cupica Mound on the northern Pacific coast, reported by Alicia and Gerardo Reichel-Dolmatoff (1962), was a low 1.5 meter high domed structure built in four levels. Burials were made in pits cut down from each level, and apparently the locality was occupied for several centuries. Although no evidence of structures was found, the amount of refuse scattered through the soil and the method of building suggest the house mounds of Mesoamerica.

The earliest artificial mounds on the Ecuadorian coast appear to be associated with the Bahia Phase of the Regional Developmental Period (500 B.C.–A.D. 500). Estrada (1962, p. 72, fig. 116) describes and illustrates a group of low rectangular or irregularly shaped earth platforms at Esteros, which have since been destroyed. Jijón y Caamaño (1951b, figs. 23–24) provides plans for two rectangular platform mounds formerly existing in nearby Manta. Unlike the Esteros group, the latter had a stone facing and a stairway at one end. A clear example of mound arrangement around a plaza is provided by La Tolita, on the extreme north coast of Ecuador. Here, some 40 mounds ranging from 1–75 m. high and from 6 to 41 m. in diameter surround a broad plaza. Unfortunately, the dating of these constructions has not been ascertained.

In the late period, mound building became widespread on the coast. During the Milagro Phase (A.D.

700–1500) large mounds were erected for burial and as platforms for ceremonial structures. Neither stone facings nor stairways or ramps occur. In the highlands, however, extremely large earthworks were constructed, which characteristically included approach ramps (Jijón y Caamaño, 1951a, pp. 346–349). Unfortunately, dating is once again undetermined.

Construction with stone began quite early in both coastal and highland Peru; however, the imposing early constructions at the site of Kotosh are not true pyramids, but rather platforms with stone retaining walls, built against the sides of steep hills. Although some of the buildings placed on these platforms may have been ceremonial, the majority were clearly dwellings. House platform construction, necessitated by the terrain, remained a common Andean feature throughout aboriginal history.

The earliest true pyramid construction in the highlands may be represented by such complex buildings as Chavín de Huántar. If this sophisticated structure of cut stone was completely erected in the Chavín Phase (800–200 B.C.), it certainly represents the earliest example of advanced architecture in the Americas. In the contemporary Olmec culture of Mexico, mounds were being constructed of earth and infrequently had cobblestone facings. Tello (1960) makes it clear that the refuse on the site indicates occupation until the time of the Recuay Phase (ca. A.D. 1).

Comparable large Chavín Phase buildings constructed on adobe and stone-faced pyramids are found on the north coast of Peru (Carrión Cachot, 1948). Examples are Moxeke (chart 2–22), Sechín, and Pallka in Casma Valley. These remarkable constructions are varied in plan and details, and are even more sophisticated than later Peruvian pyramids. Emphasis is placed on details of ornamentation, such as niches and sculptured figures, and on the superimposed buildings rather than sheer mass of the supporting pyramid. In these respects and in the imaginative variation of plan, the Chavín Phase constructions resemble early Maya pyramids. The later Mochica (A.D. 1–600) pyramids of the north coast, by their simplicity and sheer size, are reminiscent of the pyramids of Teotihuacán.

The Chavín or Cupisnique Phase pyramids examined by the writer and Willey (1953) in Virú Valley on the north coast of Peru are much more modest than those just described (chart 2–21). These were flat-top square mounds, 1–3 meters high, with earth fill and conical adobe and fieldstone facings. No stairways are evident and details of the buildings once placed on top are not clear. They were built in groups of one to three in defensible, elevated localities, and sometimes were surrounded by stone walls strategically placed for defense.

The large Las Haldas site, located on the dry coast south of Casma Valley, has yielded a radiocarbon date of 1842 B.C. ± 100 from plant refuse that included gourds, cotton, and beans, but no maize or pottery. Here, Engel (1963, p. 11) found seven modest platforms inside a compound.

Many of the early Cupisnique Phase mounds in Chicama and Virú, typically built of conical adobes on valley floors distant from the rocky hillsides, have been covered with later mantles of construction dating into Mochica times. Mochica Phase (A.D. 1–600) pyramids constructed of rectangular adobes in Chicama Valley rose to over 30 meters. The Temple of the Sun in Moche Valley is the largest structure of this period.

Although these pyramids have terraced sides and usually stairways, as in Mesoamerica, the arrangement about a plaza did not develop to any marked extent on the Mochica time level. The big pyramids stood alone, although large walled rectangular courts were attached to some (chart 2–20).

After about A.D. 1000, when the coastal Tiahuanaco or Wari cultural phase blanketed the Peruvian coast, the construction of apartment dwellings within large, rectangular high walled quadrangles became the prevalent pattern. Many have a central court running the length of the quadrangle, with an adobe pyramid at either end. The ceremonial center had become incorporated into the dwelling unit. The large Chimú Phase sites of Chan-Chan in Moche, Apuríe in Lambayaque, and many other late sites consist of numerous dwelling compounds planned on this pattern.

While compact, nearly circular shell middens are fairly common in the Late Archaic and early ceramic phases in the eastern United States, simple ring-type dwelling areas are not known aside from the Stallings Island examples. However, the same principle of town planning is employed in the elaborate and unique Poverty Point site, located on an old channel of the Mississippi River over 200 miles from the Gulf of Mexico (Ford and Webb, 1956). Radiocarbon dates range from 1200–400 B.C., and while direct evidence is lacking, it seems likely that the economy of this large town was based on maize agriculture. Particular artifact resemblances to the Olmec Phase of the Gulf coast of Mexico will be cited, and a maize-based economy for that highly developed culture is clear.

The dwelling areas at the Poverty Point site consist of six concentric ridges, built of alternating layers of normally deposited refuse and intentionally added soil. They formed a circular town, 1.2 km. in diameter on the exterior (chart 2–7). The central court is about 800 meters in diameter. The ridges were originally interrupted for about 30 m. at eight points, so that eight level "aisles" gave access to the center. Between the gaps, the arc of the ridges was slightly flattened, forming a figure intermediate between circle and octagon.

On the west side of the town, there is a large earth mound, apparently a bird effigy, 23 m. high and headed west. About one mile to the north is a second bird-like mound, apparently unfinished, 18 m. high and headed north. Air photographs show that the engineering layout was perfectly symmetrical. The large western mound is about 8 degrees south of due west; the northern mound the same angle west of true north. While the basic plans are entirely different, the precise engineering and 8 degree west of north orientation are features of the Olmec sites of La Venta (Drucker, Heizer, and Squier, 1959, pp. 13–15, figs. 3–5), and Laguna de los Cerros (Alfonso Medellín Z., personal communication).

Although about 15 other sites of the Poverty Point Phase are now known, only one, the Teoc Creek site, has a suggestion of a circular village plan. Still, it seems probable that this and the less complex Stallings Island ring villages provided the pattern for the geometrical earthworks built during the later Adena and Hopewell Phases (900 B.C.–A.D. 200).

"Sacred circles," characteristic earthworks of the Adena Phase in the upper Ohio River Valley (chart 2–2), were so named by Squier and Davis (1848) because they could find no evidence for their practical use. Webb and Snow (1945, pp. 29–33), in their review of this feature, are almost equally at a loss. The earth embankments are narrow, vary from barely discernible rises to 2–3 meters high and from 16 m. to 100 m. in diameter. The average for 76 circles was 64 m. A borrow ditch is usually inside the ridge, impractical for a defensive work as Squier and Davis pointed out over a century ago; refuse is almost never associated with these earthworks in sufficient quantities to indicate their use as dwelling areas. On the east side, there is frequently a gap or gateway in the construction. Conical burial mounds were erected inside the circles or nearby.

Similar constructions of unknown use, but of more sophisticated geometric design, are common features of the Hopewell Phase in the Ohio Valley. The enclosures are circles, squares, or octagons, which are sometimes connected into complex figures (chart 2–1). The walls, which sometimes have ditches inside, range up to 5 m. in present height, and often have symmetrically located gaps or gates at corners and other points. Parallel ridges form "roadways" that lead from one group to another. As in the Adena Phase, conical burial mounds are usually associated. These geometric earthworks are most common in the

Ohio Valley from 100 B.C. to A.D. 200 and are also found at this time in Louisiana (chart 2–6). A series of mound groups featuring "roadways" and semicircles is located near Lake Okeechobee in southern Florida (chart 2–4).

In contrast to the circular villages and towns of an earlier date, these ceremonial centers have little associated dwelling refuse. Geometrical earthworks disappear from the eastern United States after the close of the Hopewellian Phase about A.D. 200–300.

Hilltop fortifications with earth or stone walls began to be built in eastern North America during the Adena Phase, and were occasionally constructed by later people. These are clearly defensive works, not to be confused with the class of geometrical earthworks.

Summary

Despite considerable variation in detail, there is a general consistency in the changing pattern of settlement plan and ceremonial centers in the Americas. During the Colonial Formative, ceremonial centers did not exist, and settlements were typically circular villages, sometimes with central courts. Religious construction started suddenly about 1200 B.C. and seems to be earliest in the Olmec area. There was wide variation in mound form and plans for both structures or groups were unformalized. The spread of mound building apparently was accompanied by maize agriculture. In North America, the earliest constructions were conical mounds erected to cover tombs; later geometrical earthworks probably grew out of the earlier circular villages. These were religious centers, not true towns.

The flat-top rectangular pyramid spread through Mesoamerica and into Peru on the Chavín time level, also as an isolated religious center. True urban concentrations around these centers apparently began in Mexico about A.D. 200 and flourished in the Peruvian area after the Wari Phase (A.D. 1000). A Middle American pyramid-temple pattern entered the Mississippi Valley about A.D. 400 and became popular after A.D. 900. By 1300, true urban centers surrounding the temple mounds had developed in that region also.

Comparisons

Takeshi Ueno and Kazuo Terada of the University of Tokyo have informed me that a number of Middle and Late Jomon sites are shell rings, or more commonly horseshoe-shaped with the opening toward the beach. For example, the Early Jomon site of Minamibori in central Japan is a crude C-shaped semicircle of pit houses about 50 meters in diameter, occupying the top of a small plateau.

The northern half of the Kasori site in the same region has a shell ring about 130 meters in diameter capping a roughly circular hill beside an old beach line. The shells were for the most part scattered outside the circle of pit houses. This portion of the site is dated as Middle Jomon. Immediately to the south lies a C-shaped ring of shell of Late Jomon date. This also crowns a knoll and is about 150 meters in diameter.

The Horinouchi shell midden is similarly situated around an elevated plateau near the beach. It is horseshoe-shaped, and dates early in Late Jomon.

Relative dating would not argue against the importation of this circular village concept from Japan. Also the isolated occurrence of Eskimolike pit houses on the north Peruvian coast is brought to mind. The similar Basket Maker III pit houses in northern New Mexico might be explained by diffusion from the Arctic (Roberts, 1929). If the Peruvian examples are not independent invention, they are probably related to the Jomon houses.

TOOLS

Core and Blade Industry

CHART 3

The making of parallel-sided flint blades, prismatic in section, evidently diffused into the Americas at 10,000 to 8000 B.C. This is a tool-making technique of the late phases of the Old World Paleolithic, and in a miniature form was particularly characteristic of the Mesolithic. It is an element of the British Mountain complex of the western Arctic (MacNeish, 1959). Long flint blades have been found from the Clovis type site in levels that yield bones of mammoth (Green, 1963). Blades are also dated about 8000 B.C. in the Tehuacán sequence of central Mexico. In highland Ecuador they appear to be part of the El Inga complex described by Bell (1960), and are found at an early date in the preceramic sequence at Ancón on the central Peruvian coast (Lanning, 1967, p. 41). Burins are an occasional accompanying tool.

This blade tradition is somewhat poorly defined, due to the apparent lack of cores. It is by no means as clear as is the microlithic blade tradition with tongue-shaped cores that entered the American Arctic about 4000 B.C. This latter did not spread southward and seems to have no connection with the history to be described below.

Evidently blades were a part of the initial spread of bifacially chipped projectile points on the Clovis time level (10,000–8,000 B.C.), but they rapidly disappeared in North America and are completely missing from the long Archaic sequences. In South America, bifacial chipping also completely disappears from the northern part of the Pacific coast in preceramic times.

Continuity in this tradition seems to exist only in highland Mexico. In the Tehuacán sequence, MacNeish (1961) found flint, prismatic blades dating continuously back to 8000 B.C. in the Ajuereado Phase. These were detached from cores on which the striking platform formed an angle of less than 90° with the working face (chart 3–23). True cylindrical fluted cores and the use of obsidian rather than flint, which were characteristic of the Aztec industry that lasted until Spanish contact, date after 2000 B.C. (chart 3–21).

The practice of drawing blades of obsidian from prepared cores does not begin in the Chiapas sequence until Chiapa II (1000 B.C.; chart 3–25). A similar initial date prevails for the Soconusco sequence, where the first blades are found in Conchas I (800–600 B.C.; chart 3–26). They are completely missing in the earlier Ocós Phase.

On the north coast of Colombia, the Reichel-Dolmatoffs (1956, pp. 235–238) found an abundant flint working industry confined to the Momíl I Phase (700–400 B.C.; chart 3, 29–31). This included cores with an angle of less than 90° between the striking platform and the face, from which blades were detached. It also included the detached blades and used blades, which had been worn down to the shape of "perforators." These latter will be described from the Poverty Point complex of the Mississippi Valley. That this industry is confined to Momíl I, which shows a number of other Mesoamerican traits, is quite striking. The technique does not continue in the Colombian sequence.

The blade technique was reintroduced on the coast of Ecuador after 1500 B.C. (chart 3–33). Meggers (1966, p. 56) says:

Small obsidian blades and flakes abound in Chorrera Phase refuse, another sharp contrast with the Early Formative situation. Although obsidian was the preferred material for stone implements in the highlands during preceramic times, it was not employed by people of the Valdivia and Machalilla Phases. Since both the material and the technique of chipping have deep roots in Mesoamerica, their appearance constitutes additional evidence of Mesoamerican contact. As often happened, the Ecuadorians outstripped their teachers, and many of the thin obsidian blades are straight, sharp-edged and as transparent as window glass.

So far as available evidence indicates, this core and blade industry did not rediffuse south of Ecuador on the Formative time level.

In the Valley of Mexico, Vaillant (1935, pp. 239–244) describes obsidian knives from Zacatenco and El Arbolillo. The knives are long blades pressed off a conical core. Flint fragments are quite rare. Most of the obsidian is streaked white-gray or golden green; black obsidian comprised only 10 percent of the Ticomán specimens. Only 21 examples of long thin obsidian blades are described by Lorenzo (chart 3–19; 1965, pp. 33–34) from Tlatilco. Apparently cores were not found; but judging from the illustrated blade, they were of the cyclindrical variety. This industry lasts until Aztec times.

It is probable that both in the Valley of Mexico sequence and in Veracruz, this technique extends back into preceramic times and connects up with the Paleo-Indian phase as at Tehuacán. Data are lacking, however, and for this reason the bars on chart 3 have not been extended back beyond the limits of chronological knowledge. Cores and blades are found in the earliest levels of excavations at El Trapiche and Chalahuites on the Veracruz coast (chart 3, 16–17). In these lower levels, in the excavations of Medellín, Wallrath, and the writer, there was a small portion of flint blades, but the majority were made of black obsidian. Higher up in the strata cuts, black was replaced by a translucent smoky gray obsidian (chart 3–15). Drucker (1952, p. 145) notes that black and gray obsidian were quite common in the La Venta excavations. No fragments with greenish tints were found. None of the blades were complete; all showed signs of extensive use. As in the highlands, this technique continues through succeeding periods.

Flint cores, blades, and worn-out blades (called "perforators") are the most abundant artifacts of the Poverty Point culture of the Lower Mississippi Valley (chart 3, 10–12; Ford and Webb, 1956). From the type site, 23,183 specimens of the industry have been collected and studied. Of these, 409 are cores, consisting of flint pebbles with a striking platform that forms an angle of about 50° with the face from which blades were detached. More common than unused blades are those with the edges extensively worn until they have the form called "perforators." In the Lower Mississippi this industry is confined to the 1200 to 400 B.C. period. In the Upper Mississippi Valley and the Ohio area, it is a marker of the Hopewellian Phase and dates from about 200 B.C.–A.D. 300 (chart 3,

1–4). At this time flake knives are found in Hopewell burial sites from western New York State to the eastern border of Kansas, and from the Great Lakes to the Florida Gulf coast (chart 3–7). Detailed references are too numerous to be listed here (Griffin, ed., 1952). Most of the cores in the Upper Mississippi Valley Hopewell have an acute angle between striking platform and the face from which blades were detached (chart 3–6). However, in Ohio Hopewell sites particularly, there are cores of cylindrical form (chart 3–2). These are principally of obsidian. Obsidian blades are also common. The core and blade industry disappears from the eastern United States at the end of the Hopewellian Phase, about A.D. 300.

Summary

The late Paleolithic-Mesolithic technique of striking long parallel-sided blades from prepared cores apparently was introduced into both North and South America on a Paleo-Indian time level, but was quickly abandoned everywhere except in highland Mexico. Here it continued until Formative times and had a secondary diffusion into northern South America. It continued into later phases on the Ecuadorian coast. The secondary diffusion into North America passed through the Lower Mississippi Valley between 1200 and 400 B.C. to become an element of the Hopewell culture, and as such, spread to a large part of the eastern United States between 200 B.C. and A.D. 300. It disappeared from the eastern United States after the decline of Hopewell.

Reamers

CHART 3

Beginning at the middle of Period A of the Valdivia Phase and extending into the Machalilla Phase on coastal Ecuador, Meggers, Evans, and Estrada (1965, p. 29, figs. 14, 69, pl. 20) found a number of reamers made of fine-grain sandstone and coquina (chart 3–34). These are described as about 5 cm. long, with a crudely shaped circular or oval handle with flattened sides. The working end is always circular in section, tapered toward the tip, and shows the effects of rotary use.

One use of these tools is clearly apparent at Valdivia. They were obviously used to manufacture the C-shaped shell fishhooks characteristic of early Pacific coast occupations from Chile to central California. Various stages in fishhook manufacture are shown by the authors (op. cit., fig. 19). A shell disk about 3 cm. in diameter was first roughed out and a small hole drilled in the center. This hole was then enlarged by rotary use of the reamers. The outer edge was smoothed off in a somewhat less accurate curve until the fishhooks assumed their final form.

At Tlatilco, Lorenzo (1965, pp. 34–35, fig. 40) found among the offerings of various burials eight reamers made of sandstone, basalt, obsidian, and flint (chart 3–18). The evidence of rotary motion indicated their use for the enlarging of small drilled holes.

Nine reamers have been found at the Poverty Point site in the Lower Mississippi Valley (chart 3–9). These are all made of sandstone, have roughly shaped handles enlarged at one end, and a tapered point showing rotary wear at the other. As no bone or shell is preserved at this locality due to the acid soil, whether or not fishhooks were manufactured must remain in doubt; however, the utility of these tools for enlarging drilled holes in stone objects is obvious.

The distribution of stone reamers is rather spotty, but it may be significant that they appear to be confined to the early part of the Formative. So far as is known, this apparently useful tool was not employed after 500 B.C.

Axes and Celts

CHART 4

In the Americas, three general classes of ground stone tools were provided with handles and used for woodworking. Earliest in North America seems to be the adze group, tools that have the blade hafted at right angles to the handle. These are both chipped and ground, and include the curved blade gouges that are an element of the Late Archaic in the New England and Great Lakes areas. Adzes are a characteristic of the Old Copper culture of Wisconsin, where they were made of both copper and stone, and date back to perhaps 3000 B.C. The ground stone adze has a respectable antiquity in Arctic sequences and along the Northwest coast. De Laguna (1947, pp. 154–162) has argued convincingly that this is a circumpolar culture element. Although the adze reached the Gulf coast of North America in the Poverty Point Phase, it does not seem to have diffused very strongly to the south.

The second group of woodworking tools is represented by full grooved and three-quarter grooved axes. The third group contains the ungrooved celts. In South America there is a special form, the ⊤-shaped axe. Perforated axes are quite late in the Andean region and will not be considered here.

Grooved Stone Axes

Crudely chipped stone axes are a fairly common element of the Late Archaic in the eastern United States (chart 4–19). These have a constriction about the middle for the attachment of a handle; this is some-

times polished, possibly representing a stage toward the development of the full ground axes. In North Carolina, J. L. Coe (1964, p. 113, fig. 110) places these in the Guilford complex, which is assigned a date of about 4000 B.C. Byers (1959, p. 239) in discussing the Atlantic coast of North America states that "Early horizons of this postulated coastal Archaic are characterized by choppers; grooved axes which in the earliest forms are chipped but not polished; . . ." In the Midwest they apparently last until the Fourche Maline Phase (Griffin, ed., 1952, fig. 131k).

Fully grooved ground stone axes are recognized as a persistent element of the Late Archaic in eastern North America, but the precise date of their appearance has not been determined to the satisfaction of all of the investigators. At the Modoc Rock Shelter in southern Illinois, Fowler (1959a, p. 36) found a polished stone axe in a context that suggests an age of about 5000 B.C. (chart 4–13). Griffin (1964, p. 231) indicates that grooved axes were in the New England area by 2300 B.C. They were well established on the coast of Georgia by the time of the introduction of ceramics at about 2400 B.C., and are an element of the preceramic of the Late Archaic Indian Knoll culture of Kentucky. Griffin (1952b, p. 356) suggests that at the end of the Archaic three-quarter grooved axes have begun to replace the fully grooved. This question is reviewed by Wauchope (1966, pp. 176–179), who illustrates a number of examples.

Ground stone axes lasted in the eastern United States until the centuries immediately preceding the beginning of the present era, when they were replaced by the celt. While celts predominated in the Poverty Point Phase of Louisiana (110 examples), grooved stone axes were also in use, as is shown by the finding of four specimens (chart 4–30).

These axes do not seem to be an element of the earlier Desert culture of the southwestern United States, but at about the time they disappear in the East, three-quarter grooved axes appear in the Pioneer stage of Hohokam, and run through the sequence (Gladwin, et al., 1937, fig. 44). This same type of axe is also an element of the Anasazi culture. In this region the celt form was never used.

There is no evidence in the Arctic regions to indicate that this element was introduced from Asia by way of the Bering Strait. The typical Arctic woodworking tool is the adze.

In the Valley of Mexico, two completely grooved stone axes were found in the Tlatilco Cemetery excavations (chart 4–37; Lorenzo, 1965, p. 25, fig. 16). They should date somewhere between 1200 and 400 B.C. Celts, however, were much more numerous in these deposits. There was a single example of an adze.

M. D. Coe (1961, p. 107, fig. 42c) describes a fragment of a grooved axe from the Conchas II deposits (600–300 B.C.) at La Victoria, Guatemala (chart 4–42). In his discussion, he cites A. V. Kidder's (1943) survey of grooved axes from Mexico to Nicaragua. The three-quarter grooved axe of the southwestern United States pattern is quite common in northern Mexico. Most of those found, however, from Mexico City southward are fully grooved like the earlier eastern North American Archaic form. Apparently the only temporally defined examples are those from Tlatilco and La Victoria.

The history of grooved ground stone axes in South America is not entirely clear. They are lacking in the early phases along the Pacific coast, which seems to be the diffusion route of many of the Formative traits we are tracing. Gonzalez (1963, pp. 110–111) suggests that they may have spread down the eastern edge of the Andes into northwestern Argentina where, along with pipes, they occur in the Early Ceramic Period (500 B.C.–A.D. 800).

That these items arrived in highland Bolivia, where the T-shaped axe was already established at a fairly early time, is evinced by their occurrence in Classic Tiahuanaco (W. C. Bennett, 1946, pp. 115–116), which dates in the first centuries of this era.

Tello (1960, pp. 306–308, figs. 137–138) found five or more fully grooved axes at Chavín de Huántar. Their precise date is dubious, however, for they were in water-deposited fill at the east and west ends of Building A, mixed with sherds of Chavín and Recuay styles. Tello thinks they were swept down from the building platform. If they are associated with Recuay ceramics, they date near the beginning of the present era.

Finds of grooved axes in lowland Bolivia by W. C. Bennett (1936, pp. 373, 385) seem to be in Incaic contexts, and a similar late date is obtained for grooved stone axes found near Huamachuco, northern highlands of Peru (McCown, 1945, p. 303, pl. 160).

Estrada (1958, fig. 54, 4–5) illustrates three-quarter grooved axes as elements of the Milagro Phase (A.D. 500–1500) in the Guayas Basin of Ecuador (chart 4, 47–48).

T-shaped Stone Axes

Stone axes with projecting ears to assist in lashing to the handle are an Andean trait that apparently never diffused north of Panama. Earliest examples of this form come from the Valdivia Phase deposits in coastal Ecuador (chart 4–54; Meggers, Evans, and Estrada, 1965, pp. 28–29, fig. 18, pl. 19q–r). They were made of gray-black diorite, pecked and polished.

Engel (1958, pp. 35, 37) in a survey of preceramic sites on the coast of Peru says that hatchets and axes with handles are lacking. Crude hand axes were found by Bird (1948) at Huaca Prieta in Chicama and also occur on the south coast. Brown (1926) describes earred stone axes in an apparent preceramic context from near the Ecuadorian border. As fragments of stone bowls accompanied them, however, this may be of a later preceramic date, possibly after 3000 B.C.

The T-shaped stone axe has not been reported from the Chorrera Phase, but Estrada (1962, fig. 98) illustrates a large possibly ceremonial axe of this shape from the Bahía Phase (500 B.C.–A.D. 500), on the north coast (chart 4–49).

At Kotosh in highland Peru, Izumi and Sono (1963, p. 147, pls. 104–105a–b) say "this lithic tool is almost absent before the Sajara-patac Period" (chart 4–58).

The T-shaped axes illustrated by Tello (1960, pp. 306–308, figs. 138b, 139a–c) from Chavín have the same dubious provenience as has been described for the grooved axes; they came from water-deposited fill with Chavín and Recuay ceramics. The Recuay date would correlate better with the dating of these tools at Kotosh.

W. C. Bennett (1946, p. 114) found a T-shaped axe in the early levels of his stratigraphic excavations at Tiahuanaco in Bolivia (ca. A.D. 1). T-shaped and grooved axes continue on through the Classic Tiahuanaco, and the T-shaped axe, made of bronze as well as stone, became a characteristic tool of the Inca. Strangely enough this tool is entirely missing from early phases on the Peruvian coast.

Lathrap (1958, p. 385) found T-shaped axes in all phases of the Yarinacocha sequence on the Ucayali River at the eastern foot of the Andes. The date of the earliest phase, Early Tutishcainyo, is uncertain.

The history of the T-shaped axe in Colombia is not clear. Duque (1964, p. 395, fig. 27–80) illustrates examples along with celt-shaped axes from tombs in San Agustín. He states that axes in general pertain to the late period, Mesitas Superior, which is given an approximate date of after A.D. 800 or 900. T-shaped stone axes appear in tomb collections from Nariño, where they accompany negative painted pottery (W. C. Bennett, 1944b, p. 53). These axes also occur in collections from tombs in the Quimbaya region of the Lower Cauca (op. cit., p. 76). They probably date somewhere between A.D. 500 and 1000.

Rectangular and Petaloid Celts

Celts, or ungrooved polished stone axes, are not found in the preceramic levels in either North or South America. These tools can usefully be divided into two classes, one of which tends to be rectangular in outline with almost parallel sides, slightly curved bit, and squared-off poll. The other, usually called a petaloid celt, has a rounded blade, generally a fat oval cross-section, and a tapered poll.

The rectangular celt, like the grooved and T-shaped stone axe, is usually made of fine-grain gray or black diorite or other tough metamorphic stone. The earliest examples come from the Valdivia Phase of Ecuador (chart 4–55; Meggers, Evans, and Estrada, 1965, pp. 28–29, pl. 19o–p). These are small blades, much smaller than are usual for this category, and it is possible that they were hafted in antler or bone socket pieces.

Estrada (1958, fig. 54) illustrates larger rectangular axes chipped and incompletely polished, that run through the Late Formative and the Regional Developmental Periods (chart 4, 52–53). These are thin rectangles in section, and some of the blades are asymmetrically sharpened suggesting that they may have been hafted as adzes. Estrada (1962, fig. 97) also illustrates rectangular hatchets with carved human features (chart 4–51) from the Bahía culture (500 B.C.–A.D. 500) in Manabí on the north coast of Ecuador. These are reminiscent of the anthropomorphic celts of the Olmec sites on the Gulf coast of Mexico.

One similar celt, rectangular in section, polished, and with a sharp edge, came from the Chavín Period deposits at Kotosh (chart 4–59; Izumi and Sono, 1963, pls. 106c–2, 166–12). Celts in general are extremely rare at Kotosh, and this example conforms more closely to the Chorrera style of Ecuador than it does to the rectangular celts with thick oval cross-section. Polished stone celts are conspicuously absent on coastal Peru.

The earliest celts in the north coast of Colombia sequence are in the Momíl I and II Phases (700–1 B.C.; chart 4, 45–46). These are of rectangular form with slightly curved blade and squared-off head. In cross-section, they are oval and fairly thick. This is the typical cross-section of Mesoamerican celts, in contrast to the thin rectangular section of the hatchets from Ecuador and Peru (Reichel-Dolmatoff, G. and A., 1956, pls. 26–11, 27, 8–9). Similar celts with squared polls come from the middle and late phase tombs of San Agustín, after A.D. 500 (chart 4–44; Duque, 1964, p. 395, drawing 27, 75–78). A single celt of petaloid form (chart 4–43) is illustrated in Duque (op. cit., fig. 74). A single rectangular celt came from Phase III in the Cupica Burial Mound (Reichel-Dolmatoff, G. and A., 1962, pl. 17–1). This accompanied Burial No. 5 and dates after A.D. 600.

W. C. Bennett (1944b, p. 76) describes polished celts as occurring in the collections of the Quimbaya

area. The shape of these tools is uncertain, for no illustrations are given. Trapezoidal celts, but with a rectangular section, are listed from most of the late sites that the Reichel-Dolmatoffs (1955, p. 241) examined in the Santa Marta region.

Ground celts were not found in the Monagrillo Phase of Panama. Willey and McGimsey (1954, p. 85, figs. 20a–b, 50m–o, r) illustrate very crude, generally rectangular examples made of fine-grained gray and black colored stone, which come from the Alvina and later phases. This seems to date approximately coeval with the Sitio Conte Phase after A.D. 500 (Ladd, 1964, pp. 201–202, pl. 18a–f).

On the Pacific coast of Guatemala, polished celts are lacking from the Ocós Phase, but do occur in Conchas I and II (chart 4–41; M. D. Coe, 1961, pp. 106–107, fig. 60q). These are made of greenish black stone, are oval in cross-section and are quite small, measuring about 3 cm. across the blade. As the polls are missing, it is uncertain as to whether they should be classified as rectangular or petaloid.

MacNeish and Peterson (1962, p. 28, pl. 5Ba) found a very small celt made of a hard volcanic stone in level 1 from the Santa Marta Rock Shelter. This zone has a radiocarbon date of about A.D. 90. Miniature celts, as well as the bit fragment of a medium-sized greenstone celt, were found by Sanders in the Chiapilla Phase (Chiapa IV–V, 450–100 B.C.; chart 4–40; Sanders, 1961, p. 43, pl. 11B r–u).

Although functional celts have not been reported before 800 B.C. in the Chiapas sequence, Lowe has given the information verbally that poorly smoothed celts are found in caches in Chiapa II (800–550 B.C.). The placing of celts in caches is a feature of Olmec sites of the Mexican Gulf coast, as will be discussed later.

MacNeish provides the information that the small cutting tools that run from the beginning of the Ajalpan Phase (1500 B.C.) to the end of Santa Maria (200 B.C.) are adzes. Celts with square polls run from 800 B.C. to about 1 B.C. (chart 4–39). Petaloid celts with tapered polls date from 200 B.C. to A.D. 500 (chart 4–38).

Lorenzo (1965, pp. 24–26, figs. 15–18) describes a single adze with curved cutting edge from the excavations at Tlatilco. This is reminiscent of the gouges of the North American Archaic. The most popular type of axe is a celt made of fine-grained stone with a thick oval cross-section. The polls seem to be squared off, which places these tools in the rectangular celt category.

Vaillant (1930, pl. 45) illustrates three rectangular celts from the middle levels of Zacatenco (chart 4, 35–36). One is made of jade, one of jade or serpentine, and the third of diabase. Ticomán celts are shown in

Vaillant's plate (1931, pl. 88). Similar specimens came from El Arbolillo (Vaillant, 1935, p. 244, table 18).

Celts are particularly characteristic of the Olmec sites on the Gulf coast of Mexico. Coe has informed me verbally that petaloid celts occur in the San Lorenzo Phase (1200–800 B.C.). This information comes from investigations still under way. Frequently at La Venta they are found in caches. Drucker (1952, pp. 164–166, pls. 55, 56a) points out that the beautifully polished examples made of jade are probably not workaday implements, but may have been regarded as articles of value. A considerable number are made of soft serpentine which, if the condition is not due to decomposition, could never have served as tools. Most of the Olmec celts have tapered polls, thick oval cross-sections, and curved blades giving a petaloid shape (chart 4, 31–32). A minority have the squared polls that place them in our rectangular class (chart 4–34). A pale bluish gray jade is the usual material. Celts made of soft serpentine tend to be larger and cruder than those of jade. "Several hundred" celts were found in the course of the first two seasons work at La Venta. Of these, four were decorated. Additional offerings of celts were found by Drucker, Heizer, and Squier in later excavations (1959, pp. 133ff, figs. 32–34). For example, Offering Number 1 had 20 large, roughly made "pseudo celts" of serpentine; Offering Number 2 had 51 neatly placed in layers. Wedel and Stirling found one offering with 253 celts. A cache of both celts and "pseudo celts" of serpentine were found beneath Monument 21 at San Lorenzo by M. D. Coe (personal communication).

The celts reported by Weiant (1943, p. 120, pl. 72, 1–14) from Tres Zapotes (chart 4–33) were made of fine-grained hard stone and conform to the rectangular category. Apparently only one jade axe is in the collection. This is perhaps nearer to the petaloid form than are the other axes. Celts were quite rare at Cerro de las Mesas (Drucker, 1955, pp. 58–60, pl. 48k). An unusual carved jade celt was, Drucker suggests, hafted like an adze.

From El Trapiche and Chalahuites, García Payón (1966, p. 171, pl. 81, 6–7) found several "chisels" made of hard stone. These are round in section and have narrow bits. As he says, there are no points of comparison with the celts from Tres Zapotes and La Venta. MacNeish found no celts in his excavations at Panuco. Ekholm (1944, p. 490, fig. 56a–p) describes both adzes, rectangular in section with asymmetrical blades, and small rectangular celts, oval in section. All come from Periods 5 and 6 (A.D. 900–1500). One adze was made of gray-green jade, while the remainder as well as the celts were "of fine-grain stones."

The adzes of the Poverty Point Phase in the Lower Mississippi Valley were of chipped stone with little or no evidence of grinding on the blade (Ford and Webb, 1956, p. 89, figs. 29f–g, 31 a–c). The 69 items mistakenly described as "ground stone adzes" (op. cit., pp. 89–91) are in reality what Drucker called "pseudo celts" at La Venta: crudely smoothed and made of soft green stone that could have had no utility for cutting wood. In one instance a cache of six of these objects was found at the Callion site in Arkansas. This is reminiscent of their common occurrence in caches at La Venta. To date, 129 of these crude green stone celts have been found at Poverty Point. This compares with 45 complete rectanguloid celts, 76 fragments, and two very handsome petaloid celts, one of serpentine, the other of hard gray stone. Both of these latter are thick oval in cross-section, and have slightly rounded symmetrical blades (chart 4–27).

Chipped stone celts continue into the Marksville Phase (Ford and Willey, 1940, p. 105, fig. 47o–r). Ground stone celts with oval cross-section, made of gray-green diorite and other igneous rock, were also found (chart 4–26, 4–28). One of these approaches the petaloid form (op. cit., fig. 49a). Celts are not common in the Troyville Phase, for the blade of only one occurred in the extensive excavation at Greenhouse, and none came from Greengo's (1964) excavations in the Yazoo Basin.

Willey (1949a, pp. 393, 449, pl. 42h–i) in his summary of the northwest coast of Florida, illustrates celts of oval section and pointed polls (chart 4, 23–24) from the Santa Rosa and Weeden Island Phases (100 B.C.–A.D. 700). A celt with more rounded poll (chart 4–25; op. cit., pl. 42j) is illustrated for the Fort Walton Phase (ca. A.D. 1200), and this form also occurs in Weeden Island. Goggin (1952, pp. 115–116) notes that celt-like cutting tools were made of the heavy lip of the pink conch, *Strombus gigas*. Stone celts made of hard local limestones and igneous and other imported rock, occur in the St. Johns I and II Periods (chart 4, 21–22). Most fall into the rectangular class (op. cit., pl. 6e–g), but "an occasional one is similar in form to the petaloid celt of the West Indies (pl. 6H)."

The Hopewellian Mandeville site located in the lower Chattahoochee River Basin yielded pointed poll greenstone celts, oval in section, which conform to what we are here calling petaloid (chart 4–20; Kellar, Kelly, and McMichael, 1962, fig. 3L–M). Wauchope (1966, pp. 180–185, figs. 114, 251a–m) describes two classes of polished celts in north Georgia. Those with oval section and squared or tapered polls first occur in "Late Archaic or Early Woodland context." The second class is thin, flat, and rectangular in section.

In a summary of Archaic traits, Fowler (1959a, table 10) places chipped stone adzes as beginning by at least 6000 B.C., ground stone adzes at about 4000 B.C., and celts at 2000 B.C., based on their occurrence in the Kentucky Archaic shell middens. The latter date is probably a thousand years too early, since these items first appear consistently over the Midwest with the earliest Hopewell and Adena cultural manifestations.

Polished stone celts are first recorded in the Baumer Phase of Early Woodland about 1000 B.C. (Fowler, 1961, p. 17, fig. 4), where they are rectangular in shape (chart 4–10). The celt with pointed poll, thick and oval in section (chart 4–8), occurs in the fully developed Hopewell beginning about 300 B.C. (McGregor, 1961, fig. 6), but the rectangular form continues. Copper celts are an element of Illinois as well as Ohio Hopewellian. These are thin, rectangular in section, and the blades were evidently sharpened by hammering, which produced a characteristic splaying (Mills, 1907, figs. 28–30). This feature was sometimes copied in the outline of the stone celts.

Webb and Snow (1945, p. 88) mention "celts of granite, and other igneous rock" as a common Adena trait. The Adena type was short and rectangular. The stone celts from the Ohio Hopewell sites are usually fairly long, thick oval in cross-section with tapered polls and rounded bits (chart 4, 2–3; Shetrone, 1926, figs. 41–44; Mills, 1907, fig. 62). Celts with squared polls were also made, but tend to have elongated proportions, rather than the short rectangular form. They were made of granite and other igneous stone. Apparently hornblende and other greenstones are not common. Both pointed poll and square poll celts of oval cross-section last on into the Mississippian phases in the eastern United States (A.D. 900–1700). They are occasionally made of greenstone. Monolithic stone axes, in which both blade and handle are carved, are an element of the Southeastern Cult dating about A.D. 1400. Small chipped axe blades with sharp round cutting edges appear in the Lower Mississippi Valley at this same time.

Summary

Full-grooved stone axes appear in the late phase of the North American Archaic, shortly before 4000 or 5000 B.C., and their origin is not clear. These are joined about 1000 B.C. by three-quarter grooved axes, a form that enters southwestern United States chronologies a millenium later. The occurrence of full-grooved stone axes in Mesoamerica is securely dated in only two instances about 1200–500 B.C.

This form may have spread down the eastern side of the Andes into highland Peru and northwestern Argentina about A.D. 500.

T-shaped stone axes apparently began about 2500 B.C. in Ecuador, but there is a gap in information of 1500 years before they become a fairly common element in the highland Peruvian cultures. In stone and bronze forms, they are characteristic tools of the Inca. Diffusion seems to be northward into Colombia, where they date after A.D. 500.

It is possible that the earlier celt-like tools of South America, beginning in the Valdivia culture and spreading briefly into Peru in the Chavín Phase, were hafted as adzes.

The origin of the stone celt with eliptical cross-section is obscure. We are distinguishing here between rectangular and petaloid outlines. Both first appear at 1200 B.C. in the Olmec area of Veracruz, where jade petaloid celts are particularly abundant. They are found rather sparingly in other Mesoamerican chronologies. The diffusion seems to be southward, as they arrive on the north coast of Colombia about 800 B.C. in rectangular form, and in petaloid form about A.D. 500.

Both rectangular and petaloid celts occur in the Poverty Point Phase in the Lower Mississippi Valley between 1200 and 400 B.C. They apparently begin on the northwest coast of Florida after 500 B.C., and in the Mobile Bay area there is a suggestion that the petaloid form may be older than the rectangular. This same date (500 B.C.) seems to hold for coastal and North Georgia. In the Illinois and Ohio areas, the rectangular form of celt seems to be the earlier, beginning about 900 B.C., and was joined by the petaloid form at the start of Classic Hopewell (ca. 300–200 B.C.).

It is perhaps significant that many of the celts in North America on the Hopewell horizon are made of a greenish serpentine hornblende, the available material most similar in appearance to the jade so commonly employed on the Mexican Gulf coast a few hundred years earlier. Caches of what Drucker calls "pseudo celts," so abundant at La Venta (1200–400 B.C.), are reported for Chiapas II (800–550 B.C.), and for Poverty Point (1200–400 B.C.). He (1952) has suggested that La Venta celts were probably objects of value. This may be the origin of the copper axe money found in the Milagro Phase of the coast of Ecuador and in western Mexico. Functional copper axes were also in use in the Andes at this time. Celts with curved human faces reminiscent of those found at La Venta, occur in the Regional Developmental Period (500 B.C.–A.D. 500) on coastal Ecuador.

Grinding Stones for Preparing Food

CHART 5

Among peoples who partially subsisted on wild seeds, some method of grinding was a necessity. From the dinosaurs up through the birds, nature provided a gizzard, and stones were ingested to grind the food, but unfortunately evolution did not give man this convenient device.

It is useful to differentiate between milling stones, which are irregularly shaped, flat slabs of rock on which a natural cobble handstone was used with a rotary motion; mortars, which tend to be deeper stone containers and on which a pestle was used with a pounding motion; and metates, flat slabs of stone on which a mano was used with a back and forth motion.

In eastern North America, milling stones are absent in Paleo-Indian sites and first occur in the Early Archaic. In the Stanfield-Worley Rock Shelter of northern Alabama, they are lacking in Dalton complex levels, which have dates of 7690 ± 450 B.C. and 6970 ± 400 B.C. (DeJarnette, et al., 1962, p. 85). In the upper levels of this locality, both grinding stones with small dimple-like depressions (called "nutting stones"), and bell-shaped pestles occur. While milling stones were not found, this lack is probably the luck of excavation. The initial date for the appearance of these items at this site is not known.

For comparison with his work at Modoc Rock Shelter in southern Illinois, Fowler (1959a, table 10) has analyzed the occurrence of grinding stones in early sites in southern Illinois, western Kentucky, and eastern Missouri. Radiocarbon dates indicate that "simple grinding stones" (milling stones), "pitted grinding stones" (deeper milling stones), nut stones, pebble hand stones, and bell-shaped pestles all appear between 8000 and 6000 B.C.

In the Piedmont region of North Carolina, J. L. Coe (1964, p. 115) found the earliest nut stones and large flat slabs on which "the grinding stone or mano was used with a circular motion" in his Halifax complex, which has a radiocarbon date of 3484 ± 350 B.C. (M–523).

The milling stones of the Eastern Archaic were presumably used for the grinding of wild seeds and nuts. Positive evidence of maize agriculture dates from about the beginning of the present era, but indirect evidence in the form of large sites in terrain suitable for agriculture, suggests that this practice was introduced into the East by 1200 B.C. The discovery of a Mesoamerican Formative type metate fragment and loaf-shaped mano at the Poverty Point site, reinforces this suggestion. The fragment was rectangular with rounded corners, 35 cm. long, 6 cm. thick, and dished on one side (chart 5–20). A similar metate, oval in

shape, 10 cm. thick, and 40 cm. long, is described by Wimberly and Tourtelot (1941, p. 14) from the McQuorquodale Mound (chart 5–14; Hopewell, ca. A.D. 1). This had been used on both faces, and in addition to the major concavity, there was a small nut-stonelike dimple at one end on each face.

If these are introduced examples of the Mesoamerican back and forth mano-metate method of grinding, they had no permanent influence on the customs of later agriculturalists in eastern North America, for milling stones continued to be typical artifacts on village sites until the end of the aboriginal period. The bell-shaped pestle, however, disappears from this tradition before 1000 B.C.

In historic times, the wooden mortar and pestle were in common use. Just when this practice began is not known. Sears reports the finding of a wooden pestle at the Fort Center site in south Florida. This has Hopewellian affiliations and should date A.D. 100.

Jennings (1964) has summarized the Archaic Desert culture in the southwestern United States. Flat milling stones and pebble handstones are characteristic of the small-seed harvesting culture, and at Gypsum Cave have been dated back to 8500 B.C. They are also characteristic of the Sulphur Spring stage of the Cochise culture dating about 5000 B.C., where they were found associated with remains of the American horse, dire wolf, and mammoth.

Jennings (op. cit., pp. 161–162) says that in the Great Basin after A.D. 1, the flat milling stone gave way to the mortar and pestle. He thinks that the use of mortars among many groups marked a greater emphasis on larger seeds, acorns, and pine nuts and reduced dependence on grass seed.

Mortars, rather deep and crude versions of the stone bowls made during the Snaketown sequence, run from Pioneer (A.D. 1) to recent periods. Basin-type metates with an eliptical basin in which a short handstone was used with a rotary motion, gradually decrease in frequency and end at the beginning of the Classic Period (A.D. 1100). The manos were short and loaf-shaped. Trough metates with elongated manos used with a back and forth motion, appear in the Pioneer stage and run through the Classic (A.D. 1–1300). These metates are obviously of the Mesoamerican Formative type. None have the feet that developed between 1000 and 1 B.C. in that region.

On the California coast, Heizer (1964, pp. 126ff) describes flat slab metates and bowl mortars in the Early Horizon of the Sacramento Valley (ca. 4000–2000 B.C.). The Middle Horizon (2000 B.C.–A.D. 300) has slab metates, but deep wooden mortars with stone pestles are the most common seed grinding tool. Large stone mortars, both bowl and slab forms with a basketry hopper attached, are characteristic of the Late Horizon after A.D. 300.

The preceramic cultures of Mesoamerica are best known from MacNeish's excavations in Tamaulipas, Chiapas, and particularly Tehuacán. The Tehuacán sequence gives the clearest picture of seed grinding techniques. MacNeish (1961, fig. 15) indicates that milling stones run from approximately 6000–3000 B.C. The bell-shaped pestle was in use between 6000 and 4000 B.C. (chart 5–28). The flat metate replaced the milling stone about 4000 B.C. and lasted until approximately 1000 B.C. (chart 5–27), when it was replaced by the metate with legs (chart 5–26). It is worth noting that the adoption of the metate on which grinding was done by back and forth motion, is correlated with an increased dependence on maize agriculture. Also beginning slightly before 6000 B.C. in the Tehuacán sequence are deep globular stone vessels, which may have been used as mortars in this early phase, but by 3000 B.C. before the appearance of ceramics, these had clearly developed into well-made, thin-walled containers. The early deep stone mortars resemble those of the California coast of the same time range.

Trough metates came from the excavations by Medellín, Wallrath, and Ford at Chalahuites and Limoncito on the coast of Veracruz. García Payón (1966, p. 171, fig. 80) also found some very crude examples from Chalahuites and El Trapiche. He illustrates a long cylindrical mano (chart 5–22). From Tres Zapotes, Weiant (1943, p. 118, pls. 66–5, 67–2, 68–13) found three metates with tripod feet. These had long manos, which extended over the edge (chart 5–21); they came from the upper levels of the site.

In reference to his "Middle Cultures" in the Valley of Mexico, Vaillant (1931, pl. 46) says that "The metates, manos, and grinding stones do not show any very visible change from one period to another. The Early Period deposits do not yield nearly so many fragments as the Middle or Late Period debris, but this may not be significant in the development of material culture, for the Early Period strata showed more evidence of discarded rubbish than of occupation. The support of metates is tripod. . . ."

The metates Lorenzo (1965, pp. 35–40) describes from Tlatilco were the trough type with both ends closed (chart 5–25). Outline was rectangular or oval and specimens showed varying degrees of use. There were flat-based metates as well as those having two legs to give them the inclination desirable for grinding. Manos, classified in some detail, range from oval to square in section and are the short form consistent with the trough-type metate. In regard to mortars at Tlatilco, Lorenzo (op. cit., p. 38) says, "It appears

that the inventiveness of the people of Tlatilco rose to a great height." Examples are circular, oval, or rectangular in shape, and some have three or four feet. The pestles are conical or bell-shaped. These items are not shown on chart 5, but it is clear that they are related to the late Mesoamerican mortars and pestles rather than to the crude tools of the Archaic. In Teotihuacán times, metates still retained the feature of legs, but generally were used with long cylindrical manos that extended over the edges of metates, so that they wore flat surfaces rather than the troughs characteristic of the Formative.

In the Santa Marta Rock Shelter, MacNeish and Peterson (1962, p. 28, pl. 5Ac) found river pebble mullers that had been used with a circular motion (chart 5–31). The milling stones were crude irregular slabs. The authors note: "Mullers or metates made in the same manner and probably used for the same purpose are common in northern Mexico in preceramic complexes in the period from 8000 to 4000 years ago." There were also two nut stones from the lower levels, which date between 6770 B.C. and the beginning of ceramics at about 1500 B.C. (chart 5–32).

Dixon (1959, fig. 53e–g) found trough-shaped metates in Pit 50 at Chiapa de Corzo (Chiapa I, 1400–800 B.C.). These are crudely shaped, but are clearly metates rather than milling stones (chart 5–30). Exactly when trough metates acquired feet or were replaced by flat metates in the Chiapas sequence is not clear. Agrinier (1964) mentions metate fragments in discussing the burials, but gives no details.

Crude milling stones or metates, rectangular and circular in outline, were found by M. D. Coe (1961, p. 102) in the Ocós Phase deposits at La Victoria on the coast of Guatemala (chart 5–36). He notes that these are similar to examples found by MacNeish in Tamaulipas. Small bell-shaped pestles were an associated artifact (chart 5–35; op. cit., p. 102, fig. 51p). Trough-shaped metates and short manos begin in Cuadros (Coe and Flannery, 1967, p. 63, pl. 21k, l), and last into the Conchas Phase (chart 5–34; M. D. Coe, 1961, p. 106, fig. 43).

Just when metates with legs were introduced into Guatemala is not clear, but trough metates, both oval somewhat crude ones and rectangular very well-made forms with three legs, come from the Esperanzo Phase (A.D. 400) at the site of Kaminaljuyú (chart 5–33; Kidder, Jennings, and Shook, 1946, pp. 140–141). The manos are short. Two large mortars were also found.

At the Puerto Hormiga site on the north coast of Colombia, Reichel-Dolmatoff (1965, pp. 38–39, pl. 7) found four examples of milling stones, which were flat slabs 15–20 cm. in diameter and 3–4 cm. thick with an oval depression on one face (chart 5–40).

He says, "It is evident that the movement of the handstones utilized for grinding was circular." Forty-one oval stones were found that showed use as hammers, but which may also have been used for grinding.

Like Puerto Hormiga, the Barlovento site was a village of coastal dwelling people who subsisted on seafood. Milling stones were not found. Instead, there were 17 examples of oval cobbles, flattened on two faces. Many of them not only had a depression in each of the flat faces but also similar depressions worked into the edges. Although these resemble nut stones of the North American Archaic, the symmetrical arrangement of the depressions is unusual (chart 5–39).

In the Momíl II Phase, Gerardo and Alicia Reichel-Dolmatoff (1956, p. 229, pl. 26–1) describe and illustrate typical Mesoamerican Formative metates; 20 examples were found. They are large sheets of rock, roughly oval or rectangular in shape, approximately 20 by 20 cm. (chart 5, 37–38). There were 59 manos showing extensive signs of use. These are oval or rectangular, 15–18 cm. long, 5 cm. in diameter, and taper to the ends. This is the time (500–1 B.C.) that numerous ceramic resemblances to Mesoamerica first appear on the north coast of Colombia. The fact that flat plates, which may be manioc griddles (op. cit., fig. 15), disappear when metates come into the Momíl sequence, suggests that the cultivation of maize replaced manioc at the beginning of Momíl II. The metate and mano do not seem to persist into the later periods. In Colombia, in fact, grinding stones are extremely rare.

The economy of the Valdivia sites on coastal Ecuador was oriented toward the sea, and maize agriculture did not arrive on the north coast of Peru until about 1500 B.C. For this reason, it is somewhat unexpected to find what appear to be Mesoamerican-type metate and mano fragments running through the Valdivia Phase. Meggers, Evans, and Estrada (1965, p. 27, fig. 11, pl. 16d–f) say that the metates are ovoid or rectangular in outline with round corners (chart 5–41). They have been used on one face, so that they have the trough form. The corresponding manos are flattened ovals in section and are well worn on one face. In the Machalilla Phase, there were no metates, but an oval handstone was found that had been pecked into shape. The wear implies that this mano was rubbed across a large grinding slab (op. cit., p. 112).

Estrada (1958, p. 107) indicates that metates with feet come from the Chorrera Phase. This seems, however, to be based on an example found by Dorsey from the island of La Plata, and the dating is uncertain. Two metate fragments are listed by Estrada, Meggers, and Evans (1964, p. 497) from the Jambelí Phase of the Regional Developmental Period (500

B.C.–A.D. 500). These have concave working surfaces. Meggers (1966, p. 104) also lists trough-shaped metates for the Tolita Phase of this same period. They evidently lasted into the Manteño Phase of the Integration Period (A.D. 500–1500). Estrada (1957, p. 144) describes Manteño manos as extending beyond the edges of the metates, having protuberances on the ends. He makes a comparison to Ekholm's Huasteca sequence, Periods II–VI. Grinding stones and manos are also found in the Puruhá Phase in the central highlands.

Izumi and Sono (1963, table 11, p. 148, pl. 177) found 12 manos and metates in the two upper levels of Mound KT at Kotosh in highland Peru. These are first in the Sajara-patac-San Blas Periods (200–1 B.C.). Some of the so-called metates illustrated (op. cit., pl. 177–3, 6) have circular depressions, and the grinding was probably done with a rotary motion. Others, however, are clearly of the Mesoamerican trough type, and consistently have closed ends (chart 5–42). The authors state (op. cit., p. 125) that most examples are more than 30 cm. in diameter; the largest measures one meter in diameter and weighs 441 pounds. Shape is circular, elliptical, or rectangular. Rough globular, oval, or cylindrical manos were found, and some of them in place on the metates. Also illustrated from Kotosh are a few stones with small pits, superficially similar to the nut stones of the North American Archaic (op. cit., pls. 175, 12–13; 176, 1–2). Their use is uncertain and since they are not listed in chronological tabulations, this feature is not shown on chart 5.

Stone containers that Tello (1960, pp. 300–304) terms ceremonial mortars are a feature of Chavín culture both in the highlands and on the coast. These range from vertical-sided flat-bottom bowls to elaborately carved birds and pumas with the bowls excavated in their backs. Exterior surfaces are engraved. That these were actually used for grinding food seems doubtful. Their small size and excellent finish argue against rough household use. The presence of maize is demonstrated at Kotosh by a drawing on a bottle from the earlier Kotosh Kotosh Phase (ca. 1000 B.C.), and it seems strange that the arrival of the Mesoamerican-type metate was delayed for six to eight centuries.

Manos and metates do not seem to last into later times in the Peruvian highlands. The making of breads is not a common Andean custom as it is in Mesoamerica, and the Peruvian Indians often consume their corn in the form of chicha.

Engel (1958, p. 38) says that metates appear in the preceramic levels of Culebras and Otuma, but are very slightly developed. The examples he illustrates from the Valley of Asia (1963, figs. 174–175) have oval depressions and look more like milling stones than true metates (chart 5–43). The handstones (op. cit., fig. 169) used with them are oval beach cobbles that suggest a circular grinding motion.

Willey and Corbett (1954, pl. 10m) illustrate a "stone metate" from the Aspero midden in Supe. Its details cannot be determined from the illustration, and the object is not described. A sandstone grinding slab came from the Huaca Negra site in Virú (Strong and Evans, 1952, p. 22). This had two faces, but again the method of grinding is not clear. Both were in a coastal Chavín context. Grinding stones do not occur in the later phases of the Peruvian coast.

Summary

Milling stones are quite characteristic of the Archaic of North America, coming into use after the end of the Paleo-Indian occupation (ca. 8000–6000 B.C.). They are accompanied by nut stones (use unknown), and in the Late Archaic by small bell-shaped pestles. Milling stones continue in the eastern United States until historic times, and the wooden pestle and mortar began to be employed by the beginning of this era, if not before.

Deep stone mortars appear on the North American Pacific coast about 4000 B.C. Milling stones and occasionally nut stones are found in the Late Archaic in the Andean region, but disappear after the beginning of pottery-making.

But for one anomaly, the history of the mano and metate would seem to be quite clear. The trough metate with a short mano begins in the highland Mexican area about 4000 B.C., and is associated with developing maize agriculture. Between 1000 and 500 B.C. the metate is provided with legs, and later the basin changes from the trough with either open or closed ends to the flat form used with a mano that projects beyond the sides. This latter remains in use in Middle America today. The early trough metate intrudes weakly into the Mississippi Valley between 1200 and 400 B.C. Diffusion to South America is somewhat stronger, and it appears on the north coast of Colombia and in the central highlands of Peru shortly after 400 B.C. The anomaly in the distribution is the unexpected presence of trough metates on the coast of Ecuador at 2000 B.C. Here, this tool continued in use until contact times. In Peru, it went out of use shortly after A.D. 500.

SMALL ORNAMENTS AND ARTIFACTS

The Lapidary Industry: Beads

CHART 6

While beads made of shell are a characteristic trait for the Late Archaic of the eastern United States, the manufacture of beads of hard stone is rare. Where they are found, there is reason to suspect a late date and possible Theocratic Formative influence. At the Carlson Annis shell mound in Kentucky, W. S. Webb (1950, pp. 300, 304) lists 9,646 shell beads, 1 copper bead, and 62 stone beads. These latter are made of soft stones: limestone, slate, and sandstone, and a substantial number are fossilized crinoid stems, a natural bead form that only needs drilling.

This lack of emphasis on small stone ornaments seems to be paralleled in the Desert culture of western North America, which extended from Oregon to southern highland Mexico in Late Archaic times. The use of olivella and haliotis shell for ornaments is characteristic, but in his survey, Jennings (1964) makes no mention of stone beads except in the Congdon II Phase of Oregon, where they are associated with

other probably Formative traits (nephrite celts, figurines, tubular pipes, cremated burials).

MacNeish's (1958; with Peterson, 1962) work in preceramic deposits in Tamaulipas and Chiapas, Mexico, and his unpublished excavations in Tehuacán Valley, seem to support the picture of a virtual absence of small beads and other ornaments carved of hard stone in the Archaic Period.

The preceramic cultures are poorly known or unknown for lower Middle America and the northern part of the Andean region. It is doubtless significant, however, that beads made of hard stone are missing from the early ceramic phases. For example, Willey and McGimsey (1954) do not report them from either the Monagrillo or Alvina Phases in Panama. They also are lacking from all of the early ceramic phases on the north coast of Colombia.

On the Ecuadorian coast stone beads are not found before the beginning of the Regional Developmental Period at 500 B.C.

Engel (1958, p. 39) does not list stone beads in his survey of preceramic sites on the Peruvian coast, but did find crude beads of lapis lazuli, steatite, and jadite in Unit 1 in Asia (Engel, 1963, pp. 54–55, fig. 122). As Chavinoid elements such as jet mirrors were also found, these beads may reflect this influence. A radiocarbon date of 1225±25 B.C. for this excavation confirms this impression.

Beginning about 1200 B.C. what may very well be termed a lapidary industry appears in the American Formative. In addition to the beads made of hard and rare stone that will be the central theme of this discussion, a variety of small pendants, realistic carvings of birds, and other items were manufactured.

Evidence of this industry is most abundant and perhaps earliest in the Olmec sites on the Gulf coast of Mexico. Here, emphasis was not only on monumental stone carving, but also on the manufacture of beads, pendants, earspools, and small masks of mottled green and white, yellowish green, and pale bluish green jade, serpentine, hematite, rock crystal (quartz), amethyst, and obsidian. Drucker (1952, pp. 166–168) says that the two basic forms of beads at La Venta were subspherical (chart 6, 13–14) and cylindrical (chart 6, 18–19). In addition he illustrated thin disk beads (chart 6–15). These three classes will be used here for descriptive purposes. Barrel-shaped beads will be included in the rubric subspherical.

Bead perforations are usually biconical. No instances were found of cylindrical drilling, which would indicate the use of a hollow drill. Although a few of the spherical beads are gadrooned, plain cylindrical beads from 3–6 cm. long are most common. Some have been modified by forming raised nodes on them suggesting sections of bamboo stem. Others have grooves around them at intervals as though the intention was to cut them into a number of pieces. These however, were ornamental. Two beads were carved in the form of duck heads.

Large tubular beads were occasionally associated with earspool flares at La Venta (Drucker, 1952, p. 168). A similar association at Kaminaljuyú (Kidder, et al., 1946, p. 113) suggests that these were used for ear pendants.

The excavations by Drucker, Heizer, and Squier (1959) added substantially to examples of the Olmec lapidary industry, but discovered no new bead forms. Beads were manufactured by sawing into form, probably with sandstone saws (op.cit., pl. 44a), and then drilled from either end.

From Tres Zapotes, Weiant (1943, p. 120, pl. 75) illustrates roughly spherical jade beads and small pendants. They are said to be moderately abundant, especially at the Ranchito site.

Beads are fairly prominent in the Cerro de las Mesas offerings (Drucker, 1955, pp. 60–67, pls. 51–54); 303 were found. The poor grade of jade, usual at La Venta, was less commonly used. Other types of

stone included calcite, serpentine, and a blue and white material that looked like turquoise. There was one alabaster bead. Many of the beads were irregular, unshaped pebbles; others approached the spherical form (chart 6, 11–12), and some of these were gadrooned; in one case the grooves were spiral. Tubular (chart 6–16) and "barrel-shaped" examples graded into one another. Several of the tubular beads are decorated. One has a face made by sawed lines and drill pits (chart 6–17). Three have spiral grooves, while five have encircling grooves cut at one or both ends.

Drucker notes that although the Cerro de las Mesas lapidary industry seems to have a definite Maya flavor, there are no specimens that can be recognized as trade pieces. In view of the comparative lack of the manufacture of beads, earspool flares, pendants, and other small objects in jade in the Chiapas sequences in southern Mexico, it might be suggested that the early Maya industry as illustrated by Kidder, et al. (1946, figs. 143–153), is probably derived directly from the Olmec area. The Olmec lapidary industry also provides a very probable source for the later beads, earspools, and other ornaments so common at the later highland sites of central Mexico. The flat disk form of bead seems to be confined to the La Venta site, and this shape is also missing in the early Maya site of Kaminaljuyú.

Considering the large number of burials uncovered in the Tlatilco Cemetery in the Valley of Mexico, beads of stone or shell are remarkably scarce. Lorenzo (1965, pp. 47–53, figs. 60–89) describes 100 small irregular-shaped disk beads, which came from a collar about the neck of one burial (chart 6, 21–22). These have flat faces, angular roughly shaped edges, biconical perforations, and are made of an unidentified green stone. They resemble the greenish slate beads from Poverty Point. The terminology used here is different from Lorenzo's: The single globular bead (op. cit., fig. 61) is a disk bead in my terminology, while his cylindrical bead (op. cit., fig. 62) conforms to my class of globular. Only three globular beads, all made of green jadite, were found at Tlatilco. The discovery of an oval bead (op. cit., fig. 63), two imitation teeth, and a bird bead will be discussed later.

Beads are equally scarce in Vaillant's Valley of Mexico sites. At El Arbolillo he found one of the crude flat discoidal beads and another spherical bead from the burial of a baby of late El Arbolillo I date (Vaillant, 1935, p. 244, fig. 25, 8–9). A "jaguar-tooth pendant" was purchased at the site. From Zacatenco he obtained one large bead or pendant made of soapstone (Vaillant, 1931, pl. 41–5). At Ticomán there were a few pottery beads and only two of stone, apparently spherical in form. One was of jade, the only jade ornament at the site. Vaillant (1935, p. 245) notes that in addition to jade ornaments, turquoise, pyrites, and "lucky stones" of quartz, opal, etc. were fairly frequent. The fact that cylindrical beads have not been described for this horizon may be a matter of chance. Most references are simply to "beads."

Beads are not very abundant in the Pre-Classic Chiapas sequence. Sanders (1961, p. 43) lists a large tubular bead crudely carved from limestone, apparently from Phases IV and V (Chiapilla). Lowe (1962, pl. 6b') illustrates a small jade bead of uncertain shape that dates in Phase VII. Although he does not deal with stone work, Peterson (1963, p. 114) reports that pottery beads, while scarce at Mirador, were found in levels IV and V. Both spherical and tubular shapes are present. Navarette (1959, p. 5) found a few cylindrical jade beads in the tomb from the San Agustín site which seem to date Late Pre-Classic (Chiapa IV–V). Agrinier (1964) lists the archeological burials from Chiapa de Corzo. While the number of burials for each phase varies considerably, a review of the occurrence of hard stone beads shows that most are of jade, and the greatest number occur in the Francesca Phase (Chiapa IV, 450–250 B.C.). While the shapes of most beads are not indicated, a necklace formed of 153 tubular jade beads (chart 6, 24–25), a bracelet made of 126 smaller tubular jade beads for the left arm, and 32 small circular beads for the right arm were found with Burial 115. This also had 50 tiny "circular" (disk) jade beads (chart 6–23) and 40 small olivella shells were in the pelvic region (op. cit., pp. 24–25).

M. D. Coe (1961, p. 108) and Coe and Flannery (1967) have analyzed 27,500 sherds from the La Victoria site, and 66,220 from Salinas La Blanca, covering the time from 1400 B.C.–A.D. 200 on the coast of Guatemala. In these refuse deposits they found only two beads; one a small, biconically drilled green jade globular bead (chart 6–26), the other a cylindrical pottery bead. The jade bead came from Conchas II levels. This is the more remarkable because these sites are very near the early Maya region of highland Guatemala, where a few centuries later beads and other work in jade are abundant.

Stone beads are not found in the sites of the Formative sequence on the north coast of Colombia. Gerardo and Alicia Reichel-Dolmatoff (1956, pp. 230–233), however, list small pendants, buttons, and other ornaments made of green slate, steatite, fossilized wood, green diorite, and other stone materials in the Momíl phases (700–1 B.C.). Apparently, the use of stone for the manufactured ornaments first becomes popular at this time on the north coast of South America. In addition, there are a number of ornaments and small objects of unknown use made of shell and bone (op.

cit., pp. 244–253). Stone beads are also lacking in San Agustín, Cupica, and other Colombian sites dating before A.D. 500. They do, however, become fairly abundant in the Quimbaya Phase of the Lower Cauca Valley (W. C. Bennett, 1944b, p. 76).

Small ornaments do not appear in the Ecuadorian sequence before the beginning of the Regional Developmental Period at 500 B.C. Shell pendants, disk beads, and small bird and human figures were found in the Jambelí culture (Estrada, Meggers, Evans, 1964, pp. 491–502). In this same phase are beads made of basalt, shale, serpentine, and chlorite schist (op. cit., fig. 13). These are both disk and globular shaped (chart 6, 27–28).

Beads and pendants of ceramics, bone, and stone came from all levels at the Kotosh site. There were 26 ceramic beads, 7 made of bone, and 19 tubular beads of stone (Izumi and Sono, 1963, p. 126, tables 11–13). The illustration of stone beads (op. cit., pl. 110b, 1–21) shows globular (chart 6, 29–30), tubular (chart 6–32), and disk forms (chart 6–31). The type of stone is not specified. In addition to beads, there are a number of thin stone pendants of rectangular, triangular, and circular shapes as well as small bead-like objects carved in the form of birds' heads. While in accordance with the distribution listed in Izumi and Sono's (1963) table 11, the bars representing the several stone bead types (chart 6) start at about 1500 B.C.; the earlier phases are represented by one example only, and it is by no means certain that the manufacture of stone beads extends back this far in the Peruvian highlands.

Beads made of bird wing bone, both disk and tubular, fish vertebrae, shell, and stone, described by Engel (1963, pp. 52–54, figs. 118–123), are fairly common in the preceramic site excavated in the Valley of Asia on the south coast of Peru. Stone beads were discoidal, tubular, trapezoidal, oval, and subrectangular. Materials are lapis lazuli, reddish brown steatite, green serpentine, and crude jadite. This excavation has a terminal radiocarbon date of 1200 B.C. Engel (1958, p. 30) notes that polishing is confined to jewelry, particularly beads of semiprecious stone. He suggests that they probably had been traded from the highlands. His statement that biconical drilling of hard stone appears at the end of the preceramic seems to date these items.

In their excavations at Ancón and Supe, Willey and Corbett (1954) found bird bone beads, but none made of stone.

Carving of small objects of hard stone is a feature of the Cupisnique Phase on the north coast of Peru. Larco Hoyle (1941, fig. 149; 1946, p. 153) illustrates a plate of the more unusual bead forms. These are made of colored quartz, turquoise, porphyry, lapis lazuli, slate, and anthracite, and are in a variety of shapes: globular (chart 6, 33–34), with incised circle and dot decoration or gadrooned, disk (chart 6, 35–36), human feet, small bird figures, human figures, human teeth, and ladles. There are also small buttons provided with two holes drilled at an angle from the back side so that they intersect. In addition, there are small cups and boxes carved of hard stone, both elaborately decorated (Carrión Cachot, 1948, pl. 24).

This highly developed lapidary industry on the Peruvian coast is the more striking because it did not continue through the phases immediately following Chavín.

Beads from the Poverty Point sites in the Lower Mississippi are made predominantly of red jasper, but also of crystal quartz, fluorite, brown jasper, and a few of obsidian. Softer stone such as red and green slate was also used. Shapes range from long tubular (chart 6, 9–10), barrel-shaped (chart 6–6), and globular, to thin disks (chart 6–7). There are also hour-glass forms and tubular beads decorated by low spiral or zig-zag ridges (chart 6–8). In addition, some tubular beads have been carved into what seems to be a bird form. Small jasper bird figures resembling seated owls, with a perforation through the back of the neck, are a characteristic item. There are also small bird heads very similar to the jade items that Drucker called bangles, found at La Venta (Drucker, 1952). The Poverty Point lapidary industry includes a number of additional ornamental items that are not properly beads, and which will be discussed in a following section (Ford, Phillips, and Haag, 1955, p. 126; Ford and Webb, 1956, pp. 101–103, figs. 37–38).

Considerable new information on the Poverty Point lapidary industry is being prepared for publication by Webb and Ford (ms). Included is a remarkable find of what seems to be a bead-maker's kit. This consists of pieces of red and green slate, which were in the process of being cut into long bars by sawing from both sides. Bars of this material are in various stages of being polished into cylindrical shape, and one bead blank 8 cm. long was partially drilled from both ends. As in all of the Poverty Point stone work, a solid drill is employed leaving a tapering hole.

Stone beads are not a feature of the succeeding Tchefuncte Phase, and are very rare in the Marksville Phase sites that have been excavated in the Lower Mississippi Valley (Ford and Willey, 1940, pp. 124–125). Copper (chart 6–5) and shell beads are present in all of these phases. Stone beads do not again become popular in the Lower Mississippi until after A.D. 1200.

While a few shell beads are found along the Gulf coast of Florida, and copper beads and other ornaments are found in the Santa Rosa Phase in the first centuries of this era, beads made of stone are very uncommon. Goggin (1952, p. 120) describes a few

for the St. Johns area, but they are not placed in time. A single jasper bead is reported by Ferguson (1951, p. 44) from a context that might be early St. Johns.

Since both Claflin (1931) and Williams (ed., 1968) have now adequately reported on the Stallings Phase, it is safe to say that stone beads are not a prominent element of this complex. In his survey of northern Georgia, Wauchope (1966, pp. 205–207) lists only two stone beads. Shell, bone, and pottery beads were found in the Georgia sites in the Mississippian Phase.

Along the lower Tennessee River in northern Alabama, beads are most characteristic of the burials found in shell mounds such as the Perry site (Webb and DeJarnette, 1942, pp. 58–69). Thirty occurrences of shell beads are listed and 16 stone beads. Most of the latter were long tubular or globular beads made of jasper. Precise dates of these occurrences are uncertain.

On the Hopewellian horizon in the eastern United States, there seems to be a tendency to make jewelry items such as earspools and finger rings of copper. This is reflected in the manufacture of beads (chart 6, 1–2). In general there are two types of copper beads found on this horizon. One is small and spherical, a drilled nugget, and the other is long and cylindrical, usually made by rolling a copper sheet.

Rolled sheet copper beads were found by Wimberly and Tourtelot (1941, p. 8) in the Hopewellian McQuorquodale site in southern Alabama (chart 6–4).

Although copper earspools, panpipes, and embossed plates came from the Crystal River site in Florida, beads were not found. They are, however, an element of the Hopewellian complex at the Mandeville site on the lower Chattahoochee River in Georgia (chart 6–3; Kellar, Kelly, and McMichael, 1962, fig. 3d).

In Illinois, beads are usually of shell in the Late Archaic and Early Woodland phases. Crinoid stems were also used (Fowler, 1961, fig. 4). Tubular and globular copper beads begin in Early Woodland, but become typical of the "Middle Woodland" or Classic Hopewell Phase (McGregor, 1959, fig. 5). At the Caterpillar Mound, Bluhm and Beeson (1960, fig. 5) found tubular copper beads on a string wound about the end of a wooden staff (chart 6–2). Usually, however, they are found at the neck, wrist, or ankles. Bone, shell (particularly conch columella), silver, and pearl beads are also characteristic of Illinois Hopewell.

While stone beads are not mentioned in the extensive tabulations of Adena Phase elements (Webb and Snow, 1945; Webb and Baby, 1957), there are numerous listings of pearl, shell, and copper beads.

The people of the Hopewell Phase of Ohio placed great emphasis on personal adornment, and beads were rather common. Many of these were made of the seashell marginella and the columella or Gulf coast conchs. Both tubular and globular copper beads were common (chart 6–1). Pearls were popular, and imitation pearls were made of clay and coated with powdered mica. Bird bones were also extensively used. Stone beads, however, are notable for their relative absence. It seems unnecessary to give a long list of references to demonstrate this point. The various types of beads so abundant in Ohio Hopewell mounds are adequately illustrated from the Hopewell group by Shetrone (1926, figs. 75–79).

Summary

Tubular, disk, and spherical beads were made principally of jade in the Olmec area beginning at 1200 B.C. They appear in the Formative levels of other Mesoamerican chronologies, although they are less abundant and other stones than jade are frequently used. Beads of hard stone are also a characteristic of the Chavín culture of Peru. Drilling with a solid drill is consistently found, except for one string found by Coe at the San Lorenzo site in the Olmec area. Similar beads made of hard stone, usually jasper, are abundant at Poverty Point in the Lower Mississippi Valley, and are occasionally found in the Late Archaic phases of the eastern United States. The Hopewell culture features beads, both tubular and globular, made of copper, shell, pearls, and more rarely of silver and meteoric iron. While shell and some stone beads continue in use, copper beads are quite rare in the eastern United States after A.D. 300.

The Lapidary Industry: Small Ornaments

FIGURES 3–5

In the Hopewell, Poverty Point, Olmec, Kotosh, and Cupisnique Phases, a number of small ornaments besides beads were manufactured of hard stone, and these show varying degrees of resemblances from one region to another. A careful comparison of the lapidary industries of these three regions would be highly desirable. Unfortunately the material from the Chavín-Cupisnique complex, principally in the collections of the Museo Rafael Larco Herrera of Lima, has not been completely published, and existing publications are not very clearly illustrated. In this section, therefore, the principal comparisons will be made of the Olmec and Poverty Point industries.

Bird motifs are fairly common among the small stone carvings at La Venta. Drucker, Heizer, and Squier (1959, p. 148, pl. 27a) illustrate and describe a greenish gray opaque jade plaque that represents a long-necked water bird (fig. 3g). Drucker (1952, pp. 169–170, fig. 48) also illustrates a fluted obsidian core upon which is engraved a very realistic representation of an eagle or other raptorial bird.

Small seated owls similar to the jasper examples from Poverty Point were not found at La Venta; however, the technique of suspending a figurine by means of a biconical hole drilled through the back of the neck, is present on some of the famous jade human figurines (Drucker, Heizer, and Squier, 1959, pl. 26). Weiant (1943, p. 120, pl. 74–3) illustrates "A nicely carved small parrott, of a hard yellow stone, perforated at the back of the neck, . . . said to have been found about a half mile north of Tres Zapotes" (fig. 3f).

In the earlier excavations of La Venta, a large number of small carved pieces of jade were found, each with two or more perforations, ranging in length from 1–2 cm., and only about 2 mm. thick (fig. 3i; Drucker, 1952, p. 171, pl. 58). One face is polished, and the small perforations are conical or biconical. Drucker postulated that they were intended to be sewn to clothing. In the excavation of Drucker, Heizer, and Squier (1959, p. 166, pl. 37), 13 additional "spangles" were found in Offering No. 5. The authors remark that "Some of them more obviously represent birdheads than do those of the 1943 season. One which is particularly noteworthy is quite clearly intended to represent the head of a duck and has two small bits of crystal set into the perforations." The resemblance of these jade spangles to the 114 red jasper spangles from Poverty Point is striking. Tubular beads in the form of birdheads are also found at La Venta (fig. 3j; Drucker, 1952, p. 168, pl. 57 A p–q). A brief discussion of realistic and "bird-monster" motifs in Olmec art is given by Drucker (op. cit., pp. 194–195).

Small stone carvings are not particularly abundant in the Tlatilco Cemetery. Lorenzo (1965, pp. 48–49) illustrates a small limestone bird figure carved in the round (fig. 3h), 3.5 cm. long. This has a hole drilled through the breast for suspension.

The Poverty Point complex in the Lower Mississippi, and particularly the Poverty Point site, is famous for the dozens of small jasper bird effigies that have been found (fig. 3a–b). These range from 1.0–2.5 cm. in height, are carved in the round from hard jasper, and are realistic representations of small fat-bellied owls. A biconically drilled hole through the back of the neck provides suspension. In other cases the bird figures are drilled lengthwise, so that in reality they are tubular beads. This drilling is also biconical. A third group of Poverty Point bird representations consists of thin birdheads also made of

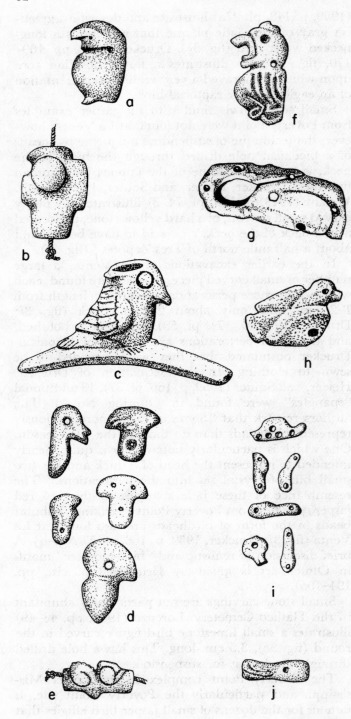

Poverty Point – Hopewell Olmec - Tlatilco

FIGURE 3.—Comparison of bird representations in the Poverty Point-Hopewell and Olmec-Tlatilco lapidary industries. *a–c, f–h,* Bird effigies. *d, i,* Thin spangles with bird features. *e, j,* Tubular beads. (*a,* after Ford and Webb, 1956, fig. 38i. *b, d–e,* after Webb and Ford, ms. *c,* after Mills, 1916, fig. 47. *f,* after Weiant, 1943, pl. 74–3. *g,* after Drucker, Heizer, and Squier, 1959, pl. 27a. *h,* after Lorenzo, 1965, fig. 68. *i–j,* after Drucker 1952: *i,* pl. 58; *j,* pl. 57a–p.)

jasper. These range from quite realistic representations to T- and L-shaped objects, which would not be suspected of representing birds (fig. 3*d*) if the transitional forms were not present. A fourth type of carved tubular bead at Poverty Point, also biconically drilled and made of jasper, is not so clearly a representation of a bird. In fact, it is not so certain what is represented.

At the Crystal River site of Florida, Moore (1903, p. 399, fig. 46) found a rock crystal pendant, which he suggests was carved to represent a bird. The abundance of pendants and beads from Crystal River (A.D. 1–600) probably justifies citing this complex as having a lapidary industry.

Willey (1949a, p. 547), in reference to this time horizon for the Gulf coast of Florida says, "In general, articles like stone beads, bar amulets, stone gorgets, stone pipes, and rock-crystal ornaments were more usual in Santa Rosa-Swift Creek than in Weeden Island."

In the Classic Hopewell complex of Ohio, birds were realistically carved as the bowls for platform pipes (fig. 3*c*). A substantial number of these pipes have been found and the representation is so excellent that the species can usually be identified. They range from ducks to small perching birds.

Although there is considerable work in small pieces of stone, particularly green slate, in the Momíl Phases on the north coast of Colombia, there are no representations of birds in this material. An interest in birds as well as animals, however, is shown by pottery rim adornos (Reichel-Dolmatoff, G. and A., 1956, fig. 13).

On the coast of Ecuador, small stone carving is rare before the beginning of the Regional Developmental Period at 500 B.C. Small representations of birds and human figurines are in the Jambelí culture carved in shell (Estrada, Meggers, and Evans, 1964, figs. 8–9).

Work in stone is somewhat more common in the Kotosh Phase of highland Peru. Among the objects illustrated by Izumi and Sono (1963, pl. 110B–22, -27) are what appear to be small birdheads, which are suspended by holes through the eyes.

The use of animal claws and teeth as pendants is a fairly common trait in many cultures. Representation of these items in bone and shell is also widely spread in time and space in the Americas. Imitations carved in jade, quartz, jasper, and other hard stones seem to have a more limited distribution, and are a peculiarity of certain Formative horizons in the Americas.

Representations of animal canines, jaguar canines according to Drucker (fig. 4*k*; Drucker, 1952, p. 162, pl. 57), occur at La Venta in pairs associated with earspools found accompanying burials, and apparently were pendants attached to these ornaments. All of these representations are made of jade, and in several cases are hollowed on the back so that the canines are translucent. In addition to the sets found in the early excavations, Drucker, Heizer, and Squier (1959, pl. 39) illustrate another set of jewelry, which also included canine representations. A single stone canine tooth came from Tres Zapotes (Weiant, 1943, pl. 76–13).

Lorenzo (fig. 4*j*; 1965, p. 48, fig. 64) records two stone canine teeth from Tlatilco. One is made of a green stone, the other of an unidentified stone. The perforation on one tooth is biconical, on the other single-conical. Vaillant (fig. 4*l*; 1931, pl. 40; 1941, pl. 16) also illustrates a jade canine tooth ornament from Zacatenco.

Five representations of either canine teeth or perhaps animal claws, have been collected from the Poverty Point site (fig. 4a–d). One of these is green slate, another quartz crystal, and the remainder are red jasper. Three of these are somewhat more comma-shaped than are the realistic jade canine teeth of the Olmec culture, and in this respect more nearly resemble ceramic decorative motifs found on ceramics and carved in copper and mica in the Classic Hopewell of the Upper Mississippi Valley.

The people of the Hopewell culture of Ohio were very much interested in animal teeth. They imported the canines of grizzly bears from the Rocky Mountains, and alligator teeth from the Lower Mississippi. Bear teeth are very commonly drilled and set with pearls. Imitation bear teeth of stone were found in the Hopewell Mound Group (Moorehead, 1922, fig. 35), and were represented in mica (Shetrone, 1926, fig. 139). Drilled dog, bear, and wolf canines, sometimes also set with pearls, are characteristic of the Classic Hopewell Phase of Illinois (Walker, 1952, pl. 8; Neumann and Fowler, 1952, pl. 77).

As an interesting sidelight, Drucker (1952, p. 162, fig. 46a, pl. 52) illustrates a typical set of Olmec jewelry consisting of jade beads, a human dwarf figurine, and pulley-shaped earspools. In this instance the pendants represent animal jaws (fig. 4*m*), perhaps deer jaws with teeth and incisors indicated. These resemble two objects of bituminous shale from a Marksville Phase (100 B.C.–A.D. 400) burial mound (fig. 4*e*), which Ford and Willey (1940, fig. 51f) illustrate and describe as probably grasshopper effigies. It now seems clear that these items are shown upside down, and that the lines thought to represent division in the thorax of the insect really mark the molar teeth. The canines are broken off. These also are imitation animal jaws.

Apparently the Formative people of the South American Andean region were little interested in canine teeth as ornaments, either taken from the animal or imitation. This seems a little strange in view of the common representation of the cat demon with his

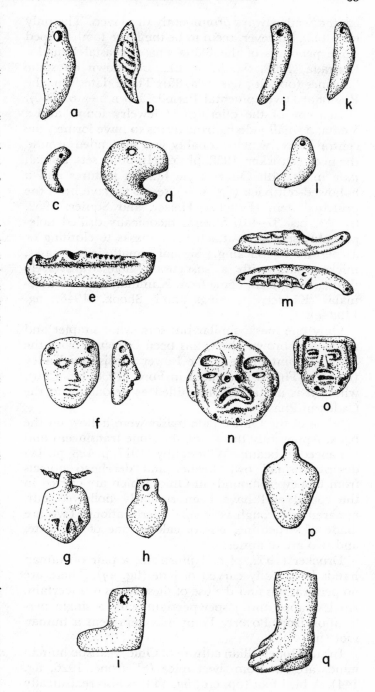

Poverty Point – Hopewell   Olmec – Tlatilco

FIGURE 4.—Comparison of small biomorphic ornaments in the Poverty Point-Hopewell and Olmec-Tlatilco lapidary industries. *a–d, j–l,* Animal canines or claws. *e, m,* Animal jaws. *f, n–o,* Human masks. *g–h, p,* Hearts or leaves. *i,* Foot. *q,* Hand. (*a,* after Moorehead, 1922, fig. 35. *b,* after Deuel, ed., 1952, pl. 77h. *c–d, g–i,* after Webb and Ford, ms. *e,* after Ford and Willey, 1940, fig. 51f. *f,* after Ford, 1936, fig. 15m. *j,* after Lorenzo, 1965, fig. 64. *k, m, p–q,* after Drucker, 1952: *k,* pl. 57a; *m,* pl. 57c; *p,* pl. 57A–r; *q,* pl. 54b. *l,* after Vaillant, 1931, pl. 40. *n,* after Drucker, Heizer, and Squier, 1959, fig. 43d. *o,* after Drucker, 1955, pl. 34b)

canine teeth always prominently displayed. The only examples, however, seem to be the large tooth-shaped stone pendants of the Bahía Phase, coastal Ecuador (Estrada, 1962, fig. 97 a, c), also shown on some figurines (op. cit., figs. 50a, 85). These date from the Regional Developmental Period (500 B.C.–A.D. 500).

In some of the offerings of jewelry found at La Venta, a small jade figurine seems to have formed the central piece, which probably was suspended around the neck (Drucker, 1952, pl. 52). In other sets, a small jade mask with Olmec style human features and a hollowed-out back (fig. 4n–o), seems to have been the principal item (Drucker, Heizer, and Squier, 1959, fig. 43, pls. 37–40). Several biconically drilled holes probably served to attach these masks to clothing or a perishable backing. Similar small jade masks, thicker, and with a suspension hole transversely through the head, come from Kaminaljuyú in Guatemala (Kidder, Jennings, and Shook, 1946, fig. 149d–e).

Only one mask, similar but somewhat simpler and made of a brown chert, has been collected from the Poverty Point Phase of the Lower Mississippi Valley (fig. 4f). This is illustrated in Ford (1936, fig. 15m), where it is mistakenly identified as belonging to the Caddoan Phase.

Some of the Olmec jade masks were hollow on the back. Apparently this made the stone translucent and enhanced its beauty. Willoughby (1917, p. 498, pl. 11) describes small owl, beetle, and deerhead objects from Hopewell mounds in Ohio, which are carved in the round and have been similarly hollowed out, apparently through very small perforations. Two are made of serpentine, one of calcite, one of red slate, and two are of antler.

Drucker (1952, pl. 54) illustrates a pair of human hands beautifully carved of jade (fig. 4q). There are no perforations and the use of these items is uncertain. An L-shaped thin jasper pendant with a single perforation from Poverty Point may represent a human foot (fig. 4i).

In the Hopewellian culture of Ohio, realistic human hands are cut from sheet mica (Shetrone, 1926, fig. 144). A bird foot (op. cit., fig. 143) is also realistically represented in this material. Designs cut from thin sheet copper appear to be bear paws (op. cit., fig. 152–7), and Moorehead (1922, fig. 38) shows a human thumb carved of cannel coal. Representations of spare parts are not common in the Formative of South America. Larco (1941, fig. 149), however, illustrates a stone bead that seems to be a crude animal or human foot from the Cupisnique Phase of coastal Peru.

From the tomb at La Venta, Drucker (1952, p. 169, pl. 57A–r) shows a small flat piece of pale blue-green jade, which he says represents either a heart or a leaf

(fig. 4p). He does not specify whether or not this object has a perforation in the stem from which it might have been suspended. Similar objects come from Poverty Point. One made of a gray stone has the stem perforated in the plane of the flattened body (fig. 4g). Nine others of jasper have drilled holes in the stem at right angles to the plane of flattening (fig. 4h). Thin circular, rectangular, and triangular pendants with a single drilled hole are also found at Poverty Point.

Similar pendants are described by the Reichel-Dolmatoffs from Momíl (1956, pp. 230–233), where they are usually made of green slate, a dark green stone, or steatite. Similar thin perforated tablets are illustrated by Izumi and Sono (1963, pl. 169). All of these items have conical or biconical drilled holes.

The typical Olmec technique of attachment for jade ornaments was to drill small holes close together at angles so that they met in the interior of the object. This is quite common on the edge of figurines and small jade masks. In Offering No. 2 at La Venta, Drucker, Heizer, and Squier, (1959, p. 149, pl. 28) found five small rock crystal objects slightly over 1 cm. in length which had pairs of "blind-drilled" holes at the ends and one side (fig. 5f). Although not identical these are very reminiscent of the fourteen small jasper buttons from Poverty Point (fig. 5a–b). They are circular or oval in outline and average about 1.0–1.5 cm. in diameter. The flat side has two blind-drilled holes; the other side is either strongly curved or rounds up to a definite ridge. Some specimens have the holes centered and in others they are placed near one edge. While most of the buttons are red jasper, a few are galena.

While stone buttons are not common in the Upper Mississippi Valley, buttons made of stone, clay, and wood, and coated with a thin plating of copper, silver, or meteoric iron, were "numerous" in the Hopewell Mound of Ohio (Shetrone, 1926, p. 170, fig. 98; Moorehead, 1922, pp. 120–121, fig. 16). These were flat on one face and domed on the other, similar to the jasper buttons from Poverty Point. The attaching string passed through holes in the flat face. It is probable that these objects were ornaments rather than true buttons. In any case it seems significant that after the decline of the Hopewell Phase, about A.D. 200, buttons of this shape were no longer made in the eastern United States.

The buttons that the Reichel-Dolmatoffs describe from Momíl (1956, pp. 248, 251, figs. 14–15, 17, 20), were of shell and bone, and were made more like shirt buttons, being thin circular disks with a depression in one face in which two small holes were drilled.

Among the quartz and turquoise beads from the Cupisnique Phase of coastal Peru, there is one object that appears to be a small stone button with two connecting drill holes made from one face.

From the columnar basalt tomb excavated at La Venta, Drucker (1952, p. 163, pl. 53a–b) illustrates half of a clam shell beautifully carved from light grayish blue jade (fig. 5g). A very small representation of a clam shell was found in Offering No. 7 excavated in 1955. This was about 1.5 cm. long made of "a very clear emerald-green jade" (Drucker, Heizer, and Squier, 1959, p. 174, pl. 40). Two additional clam shells made of jade came from the offering at Cerro de las Mesas (Drucker, 1955, pp. 49–50, pls. 40a–a', 46e). In discussing these finds, Drucker (op. cit., p. 66) suggests that they are earlier Olmec specimens kept as heirlooms.

C. H. Webb and the writer, in the process of preparing a second paper on specimens from the Poverty Point site in Louisiana, had been puzzled by two small pieces of red jasper about 1 cm. in diameter, thin, flat on one face, slightly rounded on the other, with one edge broken (fig. 5d). Each had a pair of drilled holes. The recent discovery of an unbroken specimen from Poverty Point solved the problem (fig. 5c). These are jasper representations of open shells. Their shapes are more similar to symmetrical seashells than to the mussels found in local rivers.

Drucker (1952, p. 163) describes, but does not illustrate, what seem to be two turtle effigies from La Venta: "At either end of a string of beads found in 1943 were two small rectangular pendants of jade with rounded corners, flat on one side, and a very low ridge down the axis on the other. A faint channel marking off the border on the ridged side increases the appearance of a turtle carapace. One of these objects has a sizable biconical perforation at the center of one end. The other is said to be perforated also . . . ."

A fragment of a very realistic turtle carapace from the Poverty Point site is made of polished brown limonite (fig. 5e). Complete, this object would have been about 6 cm. in diameter, flat on the bottom, and domed on the other side to about the proportions of the living animal. Incised lines mark off the plates of the shell in a realistic fashion. The edge of the broken part shows half of a conical drilled hole that passed through the carapace near one end.

Summary

Between 1000 and 1 B.C., an interest in the making of small ornaments of rare hard stone is manifested from Peru to the Mississippi Valley. Manufacture was by sawing and perforating with a solid drill. While the use of jade was confined to Mesoamerica, particularly the Olmec region, the softer green stone often employed in other regions may reflect a peculiar value for this material. A lapidary industry continues in the Maya area and Mexico. In Peru and the Mississippi Valley it disappears at the end of the Formative, but was revived at a later date in both regions.

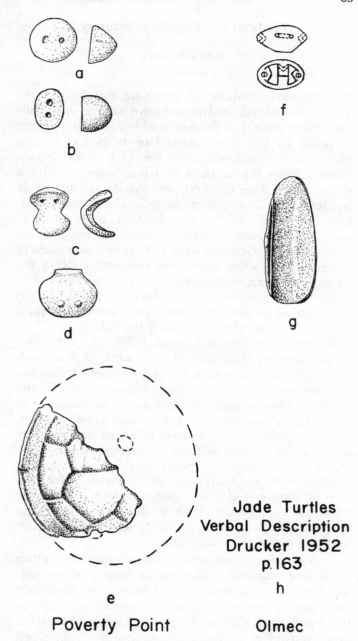

Jade Turtles
Verbal Description
Drucker 1952
p. 163

Poverty Point   Olmec

FIGURE 5.—Comparison of items of the Poverty Point and Olmec lapidary industries. a–b, f, Buttons. c–d, g, Clam shell effigies. e, h, Turtle effigies. (a–e, after C. H. Webb, 1968. f, after Drucker, Heizer, and Squier, 1959, fig. 37. g–h, after Drucker, 1952: g, pl. 53a; h, p. 163)

Tools of the Lapidary Industry

Sandstone Saws
CHART 7

The primary methods of roughing out hard stone among the American Indians were sawing and drilling. Pieces were then finished and brought to a degree of polish by use of abrasive. The method of sawing particularly characteristic of the Old World Mesolithic utilized the burin, a flint tool provided with a single tooth. This diffused into the American Arctic by 4000 B.C. It seems to have intruded southward into the middle of the continent at an early date, and has survived to recent times as the Eskimo splitting knife. Grooves were cut on opposite sides of material, and when they were sufficiently deep, the connecting area was broken away. Saws were employed in a similar manner. Emmon (1923, p. 43) describes bone and flint slab saws used with sand and water as an abrasive among the Eskimo.

Kidder, Jennings, and Shook (1946, pp. 118–124), in an extensive discussion of jade work at Kaminaljuyú, show that sawing is a very prominent technique and was employed in the same manner as used by the Eskimo. They suggest an additional technique, the use of string saws for which an abrasive was applied.

It is probable that a variety of edged artifacts was used for the cutting of softer materials. An ordinary looking flint projectile point was included in the bead-maker's kit found at the Poverty Point site. The accompanying slate materials show the sawing technique very clearly. Lack of abrasion on the edges of the projectile point is probably due to the relative hardness of the chert and slate.

It is apparent that saws made of wood and other perishable material leave no archeological record; however, saws of thin natural lamina of sandstone have been preserved. These are found from Peru to the Mississippi Valley in the same centuries as the first flourishing of the lapidary industry described above, and it is probable that they were an important tool in the production of beads and other jewelry. It also seems significant that they disappeared from most chronologies at about the beginning of the present era, when the lapidary industry also declined.

Twenty years ago De Laguna (1947, pp. 167–168) reviewed the distribution of saws in the Kachemak Bay III cultural phase of southern Alaska, possibly in the Dorset culture of the central Arctic, on the coast of California, and in Hohokam Vahki to Sacaton Phases. At Pecos they came from Pueblo III–IV. Based on the report of early saws in Manchuria, eastern Mongolia, and Japan, she considered the possibility that all of the American examples had diffused by way of the Bering Strait. De Laguna's discussion ends, however, with a very penetrating comment: "It may be that there were two centers of invention and diffusion; one in northern Asia, affecting Mongolia, Manchuria, Korea (?), and Japan, and which was probably the source from which the Aleut, Pacific Eskimo, Tena, and Salish types were derived; the other, perhaps as far south as Middle America (?), from which were derived the Hohokam, Pueblo, and southern California examples."

Giddings' (1964, p. 174, pl. 61, 1–2) discovery of sandstone saws in the Norton culture near the Bering Strait (date about 500 B.C.), lends additional weight to the possibility that this trait did come into North America by this route.

The earliest examples of sandstone saws elsewhere in the Americas are from Periods B and C of the Valdivia Phase of coastal Ecuador (chart 7–9; Meggers, Evans, and Estrada, 1965, pp. 29–32, fig. 15). They are also a feature of the Machalilla culture, 2000–1500 B.C. (op. cit., p. 112, fig. 70).

If these thin lamina of fine-grain sandstone with one beveled edge, dating about 2200 to 1500 B.C. on the coast of Ecuador, are an additional trait brought from southern Japan with the ceramic complex, then it appears that De Laguna's second thesis might be correct, and the diffusion was from the south as well as the west. The apparent gap in the occurrence of sandstone saws in the Ecuadorian Chorerra Phase may be due to the absence of complete reporting on the 1500–500 B.C. interval. One is described in the Jambelí culture beginning about 500 B.C. (chart 7–8; Estrada, Meggers, and Evans, 1964, pl. 6d).

Sandstone saws are not reported for the Kotosh or Chavín sites of highland Peru. Earliest on the Peruvian coast seem to be the saws found by Strong and Evans (1952, pp. 41, 44, fig. 7F) in the Huaca Negra site in Virú Valley. They disappear after the close of the Chavín-Cupisnique Phase.

On the north coast of Colombia, sandstone saws occur in Momíl I and II (chart 7–7). The Reichel-Dolmatoffs (1956, pp. 226–227, pl. 27, 5–6) found 36 examples in their excavation: lamina of gray sandstone 10 to 12 cm. long, about half as wide, and thickness up to 2 cm. The straight bifacial sawing edge was along only one side of each instrument. Apparently these tools do not continue in use in later phases. It will be recalled that while the lapidary industry of Momíl is certainly modest as compared to Cupisnique or Olmec, it marks the first appearance of the manufacture of small stone ornaments in the region.

While sandstone saws seem to be absent from the Soconusco sequence, M. D. Coe (1961, pp. 101, 105), and Coe and Flannery (1967, pp. 64–65) describe and illustrate "sherd abraders," which they suggest may have been used for sawing. These range from the Ocós to Crucero Phases. As the edges of some of these objects are curved rather than straight, and judging from the photographs do not have the characteristic bifacial tapering of the edge, they have not been cited as examples of the class of tools under consideration. In any event, a lapidary industry does not seem to have existed during these phases.

While sandstone saws have not been encountered in any of the sites reported by the New World Archaeological Foundation in Chiapas, Lowe has informed me that a set came from the site of San Isidro, and dates in the Chiapa IV Phase (450–300 B.C.).

There is a similar lack of published information for the Tehuacán chronology, but MacNeish has provided the information that these tools begin in the Ajalpan Phase shortly before 1000 B.C. and run into the Palo Blanco Phase. No illustrations are available.

Lorenzo (1965, p. 34, fig. 38) illustrates and describes 16 examples of sawlike tools from Tlatilco (chart 7–6). Materials were of "fine-grained stone," and sedimentary sandy slate. These clearly fall into our class of sandstone saws. Vaillant apparently did not find these tools.

A detailed discussion of the techniques for manufacturing small ornaments of jade and other hard stone is given by Drucker (1952, p. 172). That this is so closely comparable to Kidder, Jennings, and Shook's description of techniques at Kaminaljuyú, is another indication of a close relationship between the Olmec and Maya cultures. Many of the Olmec carvings exhibit cuts that could have been made with these tools, and at La Venta sandstone saws were discovered in the refuse (chart 7–5; op. cit., pl. 44a–b). Potsherd saws are also found (op. cit., pl. 42e–f, h), recalling the items in the Soconusco sequence.

Saws are a characteristic artifact of the Poverty Point Phase (chart 7, 3–4). A total of 111 have been collected from the type site. These tools last through the succeeding Tchefuncte Period (chart 7–2; Ford and Quimby, 1945, pp. 41, 43, fig. 11b–c, f), but after 100 B.C. disappear from the Lower Mississippi sequence. (The statement in the reference to the effect that they are found in later phases is incorrect.) Numerous stone fragments in the Poverty Point Phase, and bone, shell, and antler artifacts in Tchefuncte, clearly demonstrate the use of these tools. Saw cuts were made on opposite sides, and as they approached the center of the material, the remaining septum was broken.

Webb and Snow (1945, p. 90) describe stone saws from the Adena Phase (chart 7–1): sandstone or limestone slabs about 7 mm. thick. The working edge is straight, beveled from both sides, but is most unusual in that it is notched very regularly with 14–22 notches in each 5 cm. Saws do not last into the Hopewell Phase, and have not been reported from later cultures of the Midwest. The writer has no new information to add to De Laguna's citation of the occurrence of these tools in the Southwest beginning in the Vahki Phase (3100 B.C.) in Hohokam, and Pueblo III in Anasazi (A.D. 1000). It is quite possible that these items did come from the south as she suggests. The occurrences are a number of centuries too late to account for the earliest saws in the Lower Mississippi Valley.

Drilling Techniques
CHART 7

While chipped stone drills of a variety of handle shapes are quite common in the Archaic complexes, particularly in North America, it seems that they were principally used for perforating bone and other soft materials. Hard stone was drilled by two principal types of points. It is uncertain whether the bow or pump drill was in use, and the simple twirling of the drill stem between the hands lasted in Mesoamerica until contact times for ceremonial fire-making.

The two most common types of drill points are the solid drill and hollow drill. Solid drills, probably wood with a sand abrasive, produced a characteristic tapering hole. Hollow drills were probably sections of bamboo or tubular bones, such as those from bird wings. Also used with an abrasive, these produced drill holes with parallel sides and a projection of the stock material in the center of the hole. These two types of drill points seem to have different histories in the Americas.

Hollow drilling is particularly characteristic of the bannerstones (atlatl weights) that first appear in the late phase of the eastern United States Archaic about 5000 B.C. Joffre Coe (1964, pp. 54, 80–81, fig. 70) indicates that polished and drilled bannerstones were in use during the Stanley Phase in the Carolina Piedmont. Only one specimen, however, was finished and drilled with the cylindrical hole typical of the hollow drill. Coe estimates a date of the Stanley occupation as about 5000 B.C. At the Modoc Rock Shelter in Illinois, Fowler, and Winters (1956, table 1) found a hollow-drilled winged bannerstone in Zone 2. This has radiocarbon dates of 3675 B.C. and 6219 B.C. Fowler (1959b, p. 262) estimates that this bannerstone and the accompanying full-grooved polished axe, date about 5000 B.C. Although Griffin (1964) cites these figures, he seems to favor a more conservative dating for the Late Archaic, perhaps 3500–1000 B.C. From New England through the Midwest, bannerstones with characteristic tubular drilling are a common feature of Late Archaic preceramic sites.

Bannerstones occur in the Late Archaic on the Green River of northern Kentucky, but both this artifact and the method of drilling, seem to disappear with the appearance of the Adena Phase, when boatstones apparently replace bannerstones as atlatl weights. The small attachment holes drilled in these later forms are tapering.

It must be admitted that many of the published descriptions of artifacts do not specify the type of drilling, and judgment here is based on illustrations. From these it seems that the conical drill was the dominant form of tool through the Adena and Hopewell Phases (800 B.C.–A.D. 300) in the Ohio area.

In Illinois bannerstones began at 5000 B.C. and persist into the Late Archaic, where they disappear shortly after 1000 B.C. With the early Baumer ceramics of southern Illinois, thin gorgets become a prominent stone artifact (Cole, et al., 1951, fig. 65), as they are in the Kentucky Adena. These consistently have tapered drill holes made from one side. Solid drilling is prominent in the Illinois Hopewellian Phase and lasts on into the later Mississippian cultures.

A similar initial date for bannerstones is indicated for the south Atlantic coast. They are a common feature of the Late Archaic of north Georgia (Wauchope, 1966, p. 185, figs. 118, 252b). Waring found one in his excavation at Sapelo Island (in Williams, ed., 1968, fig. 93e). They persist into the time of the fiber-tempered Stallings Island complex, and Claflin (1931, pls. 45–46) gives an excellent illustration of a bannerstone broken during the drilling process. This shows the small central projection of stone left by the hollow part of the tubular drill.

Flat gorgets, apparently with tapered drill holes, were an accompanying artifact (Claflin, 1931, pl. 54h–j). This seems to be the beginning of the solid drilling technique which persists through the early ceramic phases of Georgia prehistory (Wauchope, 1966, pp. 185–187, fig. 119).

Bannerstones are listed by Goggin (1952, p. 43) as an element of the preceramic Mt. Taylor horizon. The type of drilling is not specified, but the hollow drill can be safely inferred.

Ground stone artifacts are very rare in Orange Phase shell middens along the St. Johns River in Florida, but a winged bannerstone fragment of a banded slate was reported by Bullen (1955, p. 11, fig. 3e) from the Bluffton site. This fragment does not include the central perforation, and again the method of drilling must be inferred. A similar inference is necessary for the flat gorgets that Moore (1903, pp. 399, 413) found at the Crystal River site. These probably had holes drilled with a solid drill.

Two tubular drilled bannerstones come from the lower level of the Mandeville site in southern Georgia (Kellar, Kelly, and McMichael, 1962, p. 344, fig. 3 o–p). This Hopewellian date is somewhat late for this artifact, suggesting peripheral survival, or that these bannerstones may be heirlooms.

Two "drilled atlatl weights" were found in levels 6 and 8 of Zone A at the Stanfield-Worley Rock Shelter in northern Alabama (DeJarnette et al., 1962, table 19). These atlatl weights are fairly common on a Late Archaic time horizon in the shell middens of northern Alabama along the Tennessee River, where they accompany tubular pipes, two-hole slate gorgets perforated with a solid drill, and steatite vessels (Webb and DeJarnette, 1942, pp. 69–80, pl. 94). Precise dates are not available. Neither bannerstones nor hollow drilling have been reported from the Bayou La Batre Phase of the Mobile Bay region, but the bar has been allowed to end shortly after 1000 B.C. on the presumption that this absence reflects the small amount of work that has been done. Wimberly (1960, fig. 68) illustrates a flat red slate gorget with a biconically drilled hole from the type-site. From the nearby McQuorquodale Mound, a Hopewellian Phase burial site, Wimberly and Tourtelot (1941, p. 13, fig. 10a–c) illustrate three additional gorgets with biconical solid drilling.

The Late Archaic of the Lower Mississippi Valley has not been worked out, and in general bannerstones or other artifacts showing hollow drilling are rare. Twenty-three bannerstones and fragments have been collected from the Poverty Point site, and where technique can be determined, these show evidence of hollow drilling. In addition, two beads have cylindrical perforations implying the same type of tool; however, the great majority of the 698 hard stone beads, 300 gorgets, and dozens of other pendants, buttons, etc., that have come from the site, show the use of the solid drill. Drilled artifacts are less abundant from Marksville sites, but this same technique was employed (Ford and Willey, 1940, fig. 50; Ford, 1963, fig. 14).

In discussing manufacture techniques employed in making jade jewelry at the Olmec site of La Venta, Drucker (1952, p. 172) says:

> Drilling was another frequently used process. No identifiable drills have been found, but it seems clear they were small and of some hard material, and were not like the hollow tubular drills that seem to have been so characteristic of highland Guatemala and Oaxacan jade carving. It seems likely that drilling was used to lay out features on the figurine blanks. One or more holes were drilled at the eyes, for each nostril, to mark the corners of the mouth, and in one instance along the line separating the arms from the body of the figurine.

When Drucker wrote this, the age of the Olmec culture was uncertain. It is now clear that Olmec jade is earlier than the jade ornaments from Monte Albán in Oaxaca and the early Maya sites of highland Guatemala. Corroboration of the relative lateness of tubular drilling in Gulf coastal Mexico is offered by the cache of jade ornaments from Cerro de las Mesas. Objects of Olmec style exhibit solid drilling (Drucker, 1955, pls. 27–54). Some items of Cerro de Las Mesas date, however, show the use of the tubular drill for making the eyes (op. cit., fig. 31c, g), and for lengthwise drilling (op. cit., fig. 37a–b). M.D. Coe (personal communication) reports examples of tubular drilling of magnetite beads from San Lorenzo.

The lapidary industry from the Tlatilco Cemetery in the Valley of Mexico is very modest in comparison to Olmec. Lorenzo (1965, pp. 47–51, figs. 60–75) carefully specified that biconical perforations are found in the three types of beads, in a jade banner-stone-like object, in imitation animal teeth, a quartz ornament, and hematite plates. Apparently the tubular drill was not known. In discussing craftmanship in general, Vaillant (1941, p. 143) says, "The Middle American people also developed tubular drills of bone and reed, which rotated by a bow and aided by an abrasive, could hollow out vases or bore out places that were otherwise inaccessible to the clumsy tools of the time." This statement obviously applies to the Post-Formative.

Both solid and cylindrical drilling occur in the Tehuacán sequence in highland Mexico, but there seems to be no lapidary industry in this sequence, and precise information as to the dating of these two drilling techniques is not yet available. It will, doubtless, be provided in MacNeish's forthcoming publications.

Lowe (personal communication) has stated that the solid drill was in use from Chiapa I to the end of the sequence. A considerable amount of hollow drilling appears in the Chiapa VI Phase (100 B.C.), and continues on into the end of the sequence.

Mason (1960, p. 29, pl. 12b) reports drill cores of white stone, probably marble, as "The most characteristic stone artifact . . ." from Mound 12, Chiapa de Corzo. He thinks they are by-products of the manufacture of earspool flares. Hicks and Rozaire (1960, pp. 17–18, pl. 2g) report 13 cylinders of white marble about 13 mm. in diameter from their excavations in Mound 13. These came from the Istmo Phase (Chiapa VII, A.D. 1–200).

The Soconusco sequence is remarkably lacking in work in hard stone. M. D. Coe (1961, figs. 51, 59) illustrates a few examples of drilling but these are potsherd disks, which could have been perforated with an ordinary stone point. This cannot be considered evidence of a true drill. Coe (op. cit., p. 108) describes a single jade bead from the Conchas Phase, which was biconically perforated; also, canine teeth of carnivores with the same type of drilling. This limited evidence is insufficient to indicate methods of drilling in the Soconusco column.

Kidder, Jennings, and Shook (1946, pp. 111–124) discuss the methods of manufacturing beads and other small ornaments of jade at Kaminaljuyú. Both solid and hollow drilling were employed. For roughing out, objects were both sawed and drilled. They suggest that the cores produced by hollow drilling were utilized in the manufacture of beads. In other instances two holes were drilled and the material between them was then cut by string sawing. Solid drills were apparently employed for small perforations in beads and pendants, while hollow drills were commonly used for making the large holes in earspool flares and the bowl-like cuts in the backs of carvings to render them translucent. Figurine eyes and other features (op. cit., fig. 48) were also indicated by hollow drill marks. The Kaminaljuyú sequence begins at about the Christian era.

While drilled shell beads and pendants are recorded for Puerto Hormiga on the north coast of Colombia (Reichel-Dolmatoff, 1965, fig. 4, 1–2), and a drilled potsherd came from the Barlovento Phase (Reichel-Dolmatoff, 1955, pl. 5–4), the first examples of drilling of stone are in the Momíl Phase. Gerardo and Alicia Reichel-Dolmatoff (1956, p. 230) describe four disk-shaped ornaments of green slate, which were perforated with a tubular instrument. Pendants, usually of this same material but also of other stone, show tapered holes. Biconical holes are also found in ornaments made from the wall of the conch shell (op. cit., p. 262). Information on later ornamental stone work in Colombia is very scarce. It seems, however, that both solid and hollow drilling continue. Gerardo and Alicia Reichel-Dolmatoff (1951, pl. 31–3) show an example of hollow drilling from the Magdalena region. Solid drilling occurs on the *Placas Sonajeras* of the Santa Marta region, and also in the perforation of beads (Reichel-Dolmatoff, G. and A., 1955, p. 211, pl. 3).

While a few perforated shell objects are reported from the early Formative phases of coastal Ecuador, there are no examples of drilled stone. The earliest occur in the Regional Developmental Period (500 B.C.), and are quite rare. From the Jambelí culture, Estrada, Meggers, and Evans (1964, pp. 501–502, fig. 13) illustrate basalt, shale, serpentine, and chlorite schist beads, which are stated to be biconically perforated. A drilled stone axe from the Milagro culture has a tapered hole (Estrada, 1958, fig. 54–1). The stone work from the Cerro Narrío Phase in highland Ecuador is illustrated by Collier and Murra (1943, pl. 47). Several of these objects show both sawing technique and solid drilling.

Judging by the illustrations in Izumi and Sono (1963, pls. 169–175), the solid drill was extensively employed in the Kotosh sequence for the manufacture of stone beads, pendants, and even for club heads, which had quite large central holes. All of these perforations taper from one or both sides, and a number of the objects are unfinished. Similar drilling is found in the stone work shown by Tello (1960, figs. 126, 134, 136) from Chavín, where drilled pits were extensively used in stone carvings to represent eyes, a trait shared with Olmec culture.

In the report on the late site of Huamachuco, McCown (1945, pp. 303–306) goes into admirable detail as to drilling methods. Apparently by this time hollow drills were in use for the making of large holes, such as in stone club heads, and solid drills were used for the perforation of beads. The precise date for the introduction of tubular drilling into highland Peru is not clear. Circular ornaments on the skirt of a statue found by W. C. Bennett (1946, pl. 36) at Tiahuanaco, and circles on Pucara style sculpture (op. cit., pl. 38), look as though they might have been made with a large hollow drill.

All of the drilling illustrated by Engel (1963, figs. 122, 165) from the preceramic of the Valley of Asia was done with the solid drill. In his survey of a number of preceramic sites along the Peruvian coast, Engel (1958, p. 46) states that the beads of this horizon show biconical holes.

The method of drilling used in manufacturing the beads and pendants of the Cupisnique-Chavín industry in Chicama Valley, is not entirely clear from Larco's (1941, fig. 149) illustration. It is probable that all were biconically drilled. The few stone ornaments found by Strong and Evans (1952, figs. 7–8) from this phase show this technique. The same is true for the scanty material from the succeeding Puerto Moorín and Gallinazo Phases (op. cit., figs. 15, 26). Apparently even the large holes of the carved stone mace heads have been drilled from either end in the characteristic manner of solid drilling (op. cit., p. 56; Collier, 1955, pp. 84–85, fig. 42). Turquoise beads from a Mochica Phase burial were also biconically drilled (op. cit., p. 166).

Worked stone artifacts of any kind are amazingly rare in the Post-Chavín phases on the north coast of Peru. Beads and elaborate massive earspools are found in Mochica graves, but aside from these items, the later Peruvians made little use of ornamental stone work.

Summary

Apparently the major tools employed in the lapidary industry that seem to have spread from the Olmec area of Mesoamerica into the Mississippi Valley and the Andean region between 1000 and 1 B.C., had different histories. Sandstone saws are first found in Ecuador about 2300 B.C., possibly an import from Asia, and after 1000 B.C. diffuse both into the Peruvian highlands and northward through Mesoamerica to the Mississippi Valley. Between 500 and 1 B.C., they fall into disuse in all regions.

It seems clear that drilling with a solid tool, perhaps a piece of hardwood with a sand abrasive, was the preferred method during the initial spread of the lapidary industry. It is quite possible that the technique of solid drilling extends further back in time than we have indicated for several of the columns, but if so it was not used for hard stone.

Drilling with a tubular instrument has been dated to 5000 B.C. in North America, where it is characteristic of the perforated bannerstones, but was temporarily replaced in popularity after 1000 B.C. by conical drilling, characteristic of the lapidary industry. Through Mesoamerica, cylindrical drilling does not begin until about the start of the present era (with the exception of Tehuacán). It is fairly common after 500 B.C. on the north coast of Colombia, but does not reach the Peruvian highlands until quite late in the Pre-Columbian sequence.

Earspools and Earplugs

CHART 8

Ear ornaments seem to be completely lacking in the preceramic Archaic of both North and South America, and in the Colonial Formative pottery-making cultures that date before 1500 B.C. The possible exception is two pairs of wood earplugs painted red, which Engel (1963, table 14, fig. 127) found in the fourth level of his excavations in Asia on the south coast of Peru.

Just where the use of ear ornaments originated in the Americas is not entirely clear, but they are certainly most abundant at an early date in the Olmec area on the Gulf coast of Mexico. The early forms are far from primitive experiments. Drucker (1952, pp. 160–161, fig. 43, pls. 52, 56) describes and illustrates beautifully made earspool flares and additional specimens were found in the later excavations of Drucker, Heizer, and Squier (chart 8–13; 1959, pls. 37–40). These are usually carved of jade, are quite thin, and have a cylindrical body on one side of which the material expands into a disk. In some cases the body and disk are made in two parts. A second disk or knob would have been necessary to hold the flares in the ear lobes, and it is thought that this was probably made of perishable materials. When found with burials, earspools usually were accompanied by pendants, long tubular bead-like cylinders, carved jaguar canines of jade, or similar items.

From the burials at Kaminaljuyú, Kidder, Jennings, and Shook (1946, pp. 106–111, figs. 43, 45) describe the early Maya jade earspools, frequently made up of four or more parts, and these later and more complex ornaments aid greatly in understanding the probable ways in which Olmec flares were assembled.

Although earspools are mentioned very casually in Drucker's (1943a, p. 88) discussion of clay ornaments from Tres Zapotes, almost every figurine from this site is shown with earspools. It is not possible, however, to determine whether these are of the flare or pulley type.

In the Cerro de las Mesas offering (Drucker, 1955, pp. 51–58, pls. 41–57), there were 36 large earspool flares and 10 small ones, as well as large jade disks with central perforations, which probably formed a backing for the ear ornaments. From the poorly finished specimens, Drucker was able to deduce the methods of manufacture: sawing, drilling, and polishing.

While napkin-ring or pulley-type earspools apparently were not found at La Venta, they do occur in the later Chalahuites site on the central coast of Veracruz. Medellín, Wallrath, and the writer found that fairly thick small, pulley-shaped spools crudely made of clay (chart 8–12) were succeeded by thin highly polished pulley-shaped spools of black ware (chart 8–11). One specimen from the later levels was made of obsidian; none were of jade.

Vaillant (1935, p. 237, fig. 25, 11–14) found long tubular earspools with turned-up ends (chart 8–16), apparently a variation of the napkin-ring type, in his El Arbolillo i and ii Phases (1200–600 B.C.). In Late El Arbolillo i he found a pair of flare-type earspools accompanying the burial of a baby (chart 8–18; op. cit., p. 244, fig. 25–7). A fragment of a similar earspool came from late deposits at Zacatenco.

At Ticomán, Vaillant (1931, p. 399, pl. 82) observed a sequence in earspool forms. Solid plain disks of pottery with a groove around the periphery came from early Ticomán (chart 8–17), while decorated disks (chart 8–14) and true napkin-ring or pulley-shaped forms (chart 8–15) were found in the middle periods. These types persisted through late Ticomán, where earspool disks with cut-out designs also were made.

It is certainly remarkable that no earspools have been found with the dozens of richly furnished burials excavated in the Tlatilco Cemetery. Lorenzo (1965, p. 49, fig. 73) describes and illustrates a single fragment of a thin, tubular earspool; however, they are commonly shown on the figurines (Porter, 1953, pl. 5; Piña Chán, 1958, vol. 2, figs. 15–16, 20, 29).

In the Huasteca sequence, short cylinders with slightly flared ends (in other words a variety of napkin-ring earspool) seem to range in time from about 500 B.C. to A.D. 800 (Periods I–IV; Ekholm, 1944, pp. 467–469, fig. 47). Long clay tubes without flared ends date Panuco II (ca. A.D. 1). Tubular earspools with tongue-like flanges on one end, also made of clay, are a characteristic of Period V (ca. A.D. 1000). These, of course, are a Post-Classic type. The plain, solid disk-type spool with a groove around the periphery, similar to those found by Vaillant at Ticomán, date in the Huasteca from Periods II–VI (A.D. 1–1500). Apparently the typical Olmec jade flares are missing from the north coast of Mexico.

Ear ornaments of any kind are absent from the Poverty Point and Tchefuncte Phases in the Lower Mississippi Valley. The first examples are found in burial mounds of the Marksville Period (chart 8–9). They are made of copper and are the typical earspool of the Hopewellian culture throughout the eastern United States. In the Crooks site in Louisiana, Ford and Willey (1940, p. 123, fig. 55b-d) state:

> The five spools found with burials are badly corroded. In shape they are similar: single concavo-convex discs about 4 cm. in diameter, and about 3 mm. thick (fig. 55c-d). A small hole had been pierced through the center of each. In four instances small masses of wood or shell were found adhering to the interior sides of the spools. It seems likely that these were the remains of small buttons which were fastened to the copper cones by strings through the central holes, thus keeping the flattened cones against the lobe of the ear.

This suggests that the "copper flares" were assembled in a manner quite similar to the jade earspool flares of the La Venta site. The Hopewellian artisans, however, were quick to take advantage of the malleability of copper, and most of the earspools consist of two copper flares connected by tubular copper rivets, or by inserting the ends of tubes formed on the flares into one another. Hopewellian copper earspools frequently had string wound around the central axis, possibly to protect the ear lobe from the metal. In some instances, they are not beside the skulls of the burials but are held in the hands (Ford, 1963, p. 17, fig. 11). This led Sears (personal communication) to suggest that these artifacts are not earspools but yo-yos, a toy that seems to have originated in the Philippines. The writer hesitates to take a stand on this interesting suggestion.

On the Lower Mississippi, copper earspools are replaced at the beginning of the Troyville Period by small solid clay plugs with a slight depression around the periphery (chart 8–10), which, except for the fact that they are thicker, suggest the clay disk spools of Ticomán and Huasteca Periods II-VI (Ford, 1951, p. 108, fig. 42a-c). Large pulley-shaped earspools sometimes plated with copper, are found in the later Mississippian phases, as are elaborate solid spools.

Along the Gulf coast of Florida, earspools first appear in the Santa Rosa Phase (100 B.C.–A.D. 400). They are usually bicymbal in shape, and are made of copper, sometimes plated with hammered silver or meteoric iron. A single cymbal-shaped spool or "flare" came from the McQuorquodale Burial Mound in southern Alabama (chart 8–8; Wimberly and Tourtelot, 1941, p. 8, fig. 10d). These items disappear about A.D. 400, at the beginning of the Weeden Island Phase.

Both cymbal and bicymbal copper earspools are a feature of the Yent Phase of the Gulf coast of north Florida, but do not continue into the Green Point (Sears, 1962, p. 13). These items are also reported from the lower levels of the Mandeville site in south Georgia (chart 8–6; Kellar, Kelly, and McMichael, 1962, fig. 3b). As in other sites reported by Moore, they are in a typical Hopewellian context that includes copper-jacketed panpipes, flake knives, figurines, platform pipes, and cut sheets of mica.

In the Florida State Museum collections, there is a fragment of a pulley-shaped earspool made of clay, 8 cm. in diameter, which came from the St. Johns I level of the Bluffton site (chart 8–7). A unique specimen for the Southeast, it resembles rare earspools from Illinois and Ohio.

Earspools do not arrive in the Georgia area until the Mississippian Period (A.D. 1000) when they have large disk forms, are made of wood or stone, and are plated with copper. Shell pins with a knob on one end, made from conch columella, are also a typical ear ornament of the Mississippian culture throughout the Southeast (Wauchope, 1966, pp. 196–198, figs. 135–137).

Copper earspools are a persistent feature of the fully developed Hopewell Phase of Illinois (McGregor, 1959, fig. 5). They are usually bicymbal (chart 8–5), sometimes have silver or meteoric iron plating, and string is frequently wound around the connecting axis. Again, at the Rutherford Mound (Fowler, 1957, p. 24, pl. 9), these objects were found in the hands of a skeleton rather than at the ears (chart 8–3). From the same site came a cache of nine beautifully made, thin, pulley-shaped earspools of cannel coal, sandstone, and pottery (chart 8–4). These range from about 7–18 cm. in diameter. One ring had pairs of delicate holes drilled at four points, spaced about its circumference. The rings were neatly stacked. While the small ones may well have been ear ornaments, Fowler is of the opinion that the larger examples are too big to have served this purpose (op. cit., pp. 31–33, table 3, pl. 14). Nevertheless, they have distinct grooves around the periphery.

Webb and Snow (1945) do not list either copper or stone earspools as a trait of the Adena Phase of Kentucky and Ohio. The achondroplastic dwarf depicted on the famous Adena pipe is clearly wearing a pair of large pulley-shaped earspools, but this may date late in the phase, coeval with Ohio Hopewell.

Copper earspools are an outstanding characteristic of the Classic Hopewell Phase of Ohio (100 B.C.–A.D. 300), and hundreds have been found. Willoughby (1917, pp. 493–495, pl. 5) discusses and illustrates the different ways in which the earspool halves were fastened together. In some instances, the hollow spaces were filled with clay, and both silver and meteoric iron were used as plating. Again, string is sometimes wound around the axis.

The high degree of resemblance in earspools over the entire Hopewell territory, from Michigan to Florida, and from western New York State to the eastern border of Kansas, argues that most were probably manufactured in a restricted locality and diffused by trade. The Lake Superior region was the source of the copper, and the Ohio region was probably the center of this industry between 100 B.C. and A.D. 300. It is perhaps unfortunate for Sear's yo-yo theory that realistic Hopewell figurines, such as those from the Turner group of Ohio, or the "Knight" figurines from Illinois, are shown wearing earspools of the copper bicymbal types.

A less popular type of earspool is a pulley-shaped ornament of stone. Pairs made of light red pipestone and black shale, 4–5 cm. in diameter, were found in the Tremper Mound (chart 8–1; Mills, 1916, pp. 375–376, figs. 106, 108–109).

Earspools disappear from the Ohio Valley at the end of the Hopewell Phase, and ear ornaments were not used again until the time of the Mississippian culture, when shell earpins were the most popular form.

The pulley-type earspool is found in the Estrella to Sacaton Phases of Hohokam in southern Arizona (Gladwin, et al., 1937, p. 128, pl. 18d). These ornaments are also worn by the figurines of this culture.

Returning to southern Mexico, the figurines from Chiapa Periods IV–V (450–250 B.C.) almost all wear earspools, but few of the actual artifacts have been recovered. Dixon (1959, fig. 51) found a stone figurine head with shapeless appendages that might be earspools, but there are no certain indications of these ornaments from the early pits 50 and 38 at Chiapa de Corzo. Agrinier (1964), in his study of burials at Chiapa de Corzo, lists six pairs of earspools ranging in date from Chiapa IV–VII (450 B.C.–A.D. 200), but does not illustrate them. At San Agustín, Navarette (1959, p. 5, fig. 10a) illustrates two translucent jade ear flares (chart 8–20), 3 cm. in diameter, which date 450–1 B.C.

Sanders (1961, p. 43, pl. 11Bp–q) found fragments of two long tubular pulley-shaped spools (chart 8–19) dating in Period V at the Santa Cruz site. One was made of dull gray stone, the other of white alabaster. Peterson (chart 8–21; 1963, p. 112, fig. 168) states that "A fair number of clay earplugs were found at Mirador, several in test pits. It is not known when the use of earplugs began, although figurines of Mirador III and later periods usually wear them. The earliest examples found at Mirador to date were located in Mirador IV levels. These clay earplugs generally have a tubular body with a wide flare on the front end, and are, on the average, quite small."

In the Soconusco on the Pacific coast of Guatemala, earspools are absent in the Ocós Phase, but are fairly abundant in Conchas I and II (M.D. Coe, 1961, pp. 103–104, tables 10–14, figs. 42d, 60a–b). They are of pottery, thin, polished, and vary in color from black to orange (chart 8–23). Diameters range from 2.6–7.0 cm. A few are decorated by incised lines filled with red or white pigment. In this same time range (800–300 B.C.), there are a lesser number of disk earspools (chart 8–22), 1–5 cm. in diameter, and 1–3 cm. in thickness. These are flat to slightly concave around the border, and are less well made than the napkin-ring type. Coe postulates that they might have been used to stretch the ear lobes.

The earliest earspools in the north coast of Colombia sequence are those represented in the ears of figurines of Momíl Phases I and II (700–1 B.C.; Reichel-Dolmatoff, G. and A., 1956, pl. 22). These clearly show a type of earspool with a marked depression in the center (chart 8–24). The Reichel-Dolmatoffs have hesitated to identify any objects as actual earspools; still, in the same deposit, they found 320 examples of small hollow cones of shell, 3–4 cm. in diameter at the base (chart 8–25; op. cit., pl. 31, 3–4). Some have holes through the peak of the cone. It is possible that these shell cones may be earspool flares used with an attached retaining disk, as were the jade flares of Mesoamerica.

No earspools have been found in either the Valdivia or Machalilla (3000–1500 B.C.) sites on the coast of Ecuador, nor are they shown on figurines. This negative evidence is weakened somewhat by the fact that most are females with long hair falling to their shoulders and hiding the ears.

The earliest earspools in the Ecuadorian sequence occur in the Chorrera Phase. They are thin, highly polished pottery cylinders 3–5 cm. in diameter, which are flared somewhat more strongly at one end than at the other (chart 8–27). These are identical to the pottery earspools of the Conchas Phases of the

coast of Guatemala (Evans and Meggers, 1957, p. 240, fig. 4), and are one of the several items that led M. D. Coe (1960) to postulate direct connection between the two regions. Figurines of the Mate type of the Chorrera culture also are shown with earspools (Estrada, 1962, figs. 72–73). These also wear helmet-like turbans reminiscent of the coeval figurines of Mesoamerica.

Earspools were in common use on the coast of Ecuador in some of the Regional Developmental phases. Again, this usually is shown in the figurines. They are illustrated, for example, from the Jambelí culture (Estrada, Meggers, and Evans, 1964, figs. 17b, 18a) and Manabí and Esmeraldas (chart 8–26; Estrada, 1957, fig. 86). A conical type made of pottery and shaped like a golf tee is especially characteristic of the Bahía culture (op. cit., fig. 35). During this phase, earspools tend to become large disks, and to have decorated faces, paralleling the evolution of these ornaments in Mesoamerica after A.D. 1. Estrada (1958, pp. 104–105) indicates that the clay earspool of the type "Chorrera-Zacatenco" extends into the Bahía Phase of the Regional Developmental.

From Kotosh in the Peruvian highlands, Izumi and Sono (1963, pp. 128–129) describe three "pulley-shaped" objects made of pottery, about 3.5 cm. in diameter, with a groove around the edge (chart 8, 28–30). While two are ring-shaped, one has four spokes in it like a wheel (op. cit., pls. 98a, 1–2; 155, 4–5). Three earspools of stone from the same upper levels (op. cit., pls. 110b, 29–31; 169, 20–21) are ring-shaped with grooves around the edges. One is black while another is red, and both are well polished. These come from the late San Blas and Higueras Phases. Although the authors seem uncertain as to the use of these objects, they are clearly earspools of the fully developed pulley type, such as are found near the beginning of the present era in Ecuador, Mesoamerica, and the Hopewell region.

Typical Chavín style stone carvings from the sites of San Pablo and Kuntur Wasi show stylized heads with prominently displayed fangs and wearing earspools (Carríon Cachot, 1948, figs. 16–17).

Larco (1941, fig. 55) illustrates a human effigy wearing earspools from coastal Peru. In one article (1945a, p. 17), Larco shows a pair of ear ornaments probably made of bone, with a monkey-like figure carved in low relief on the disk-shaped face of each (chart 8–31). Exactly how these were held in the ears is not clear from the illustration. Other ear ornaments from Cupisnique tombs are mosaic ornamental plaques of shell and turquoise (op. cit., p. 18).

Although earspools seem to have been in use by 500 B.C. on the north Peruvian coast, the precise form is not clear from the available publications.

Apparently they are not the simple napkin-ring or flare types common in the Formative to the northward, but rather are disk-shaped with decorated faces, more similar to the Early Classic spools of Mesoamerica. In later Peruvian phases earspools become quite elaborate, and the gold ornaments with inlay of turquoise and shell made during Mochica times are true works of art.

Summary

The delicate jade flares of the Olmec region may be the earliest form of earspools in the Americas. The source of this influence is unknown, and it first appears about 1000 B.C. Apparently, the custom of making these ornaments spread to the eastern United States on the Hopewell horizon about 200–100 B.C., and as native copper had been worked for a number of centuries before, earspools were manufactured from this material. The typical Hopewell earspool consists of two flares permanently joined together.

While the Olmec flare could not be held in the ear lobe without a backing, it seems to have developed into a delicate napkin-ring type of spool, usually made of pottery, several centuries before 500 B.C. These spools are turned outward sufficiently on the inner periphery to hold them in the ear lobe and they characteristically flare outward more strongly on the outer edge giving them a tapering profile. This type of earspool, which occurs in the Valley of Mexico between 1000 and 500 B.C., spread to the coast of Guatemala between 800 and 300 B.C., and apparently was carried by sea to the people of the Chorrera Phase on the coast of Ecuador.

True pulley-shaped spools, pottery or stone rings 3 cm. or more in diameter with a definite groove about the periphery, seem to date from a few centuries before the beginning of the present era in the Hopewell phases of Ohio and Illinois, in the Ticomán Phases in the Valley of Mexico, in the Regional Developmental Period of Ecuador, and the San Blas and Higueras Phases of the Peruvian highlands. The form of early earspools on coastal Peru is not clear. After A.D. 500, very elaborate metal and stone earspools with disk faces carved or set with mosaics were being manufactured in Mesoamerica and the Andean area. Spools of this type were also made in the Mississippi Valley after A.D. 900.

Less well-made solid earplugs, usually of clay, were used on the coast of Guatemala about 500 B.C., in the Valley of Mexico about the same date, and in the Lower Mississippi Valley about A.D. 500.

Mirrors

CHART 9

The first mirrors appear in American prehistory about 1000 B.C. The region where they seem to be most highly developed and probably the earliest, is that of the Olmec culture on the Gulf coast of Mexico. The seven mirrors found at the La Venta site are the subject of a special study by Gullberg (pp. 280–283, in Drucker, Heizer, and Squier, 1959). These are disk-shaped thin plates of magnetite, hematite, or ilmenite, 4–12 cm. in diameter, and less than 1 cm. thick. One face has been ground and polished in a concave form. Focal length ranges from approximately 6–57 cm. (chart 9–14). Gullberg says, "The polish of the specimen is excellent and probably represents the limit of perfection that the material will allow." Although there are minor irregularities of the curvature, he judges that the mirrors could be used for reflecting the sun to start a fire, or to reflect a picture in a camera obscura. The radius of the curvature becomes progressively greater toward the edges of the convexity similar to modern parabolic reflectors. Drucker, Heizer, and Squier (op. cit., pp. 181–183) discuss the method in which these mirrors were worn. A seated female figure shown in Drucker (1952, pl. 46–1) has an actual mirror on her chest, apparently suspended around her neck. Monument No. 23 (Drucker, Heizer, and Squier, 1959, fig. 58) appears to be wearing a mirror in a similar manner.

From the Valley of Mexico, Tolstoy provides the data that the small pyrite mirrors have come from his excavations at El Arbolillo. These are thin disks with flat faces. No examples of mirrors seem to have been found in the Tlatilco Cemetery.

Lowe (personal communication) says that pyrite mosaic mirrors occur in the Chiapas sequence beginning in Period IV about 450 B.C. Lowe also provides the unpublished information that the earliest mirrors known in the Soconusco area are of the mosaic pyrite type, and date in the Izapa Phase.

Gerardo and Alicia Reichel-Dolmatoff (1956, p. 297) describes plates of conch shell from the Momíl deposits, which are highly polished, and which they suggest were used as mirrors.

Meggers and Evans state (personal communication) that mirrors made of obsidian are an element of the Jama-Coaque Phase in Manabí on the north coast of Ecuador which belongs in the Regional Developmental Period. Although no illustrations are available, these appear to be mirrors of the Formative pattern, and the appropriate symbol has been placed in the Ecuadorian column. Later, in the Integration Period, pyrite mirrors had silver frames.

Five jet mirrors were unearthed in a fragmentary state at Kotosh in the Peruvian highlands. All of these came from Kotosh Kotosh levels (1200–800 B.C.), and examples are illustrated by Izumi and Sono (1963, p. 126, pl. 106b, 10–11, d–4). One mirror was circular, about 8 cm. in diameter (chart 9–21): the other squared with rounded corners, about the same size. They seem to be quite thin.

In the Valley of Asia, Engel (1963, p. 83, figs. 195–196, 201) found a baked clay rectangular tablet and a small rectangular slate plaque with polished mirrors fastened in them (chart 9–25), as though set in frames. The frames were decorated with glued-on disk beads made of shell and greenstone. Engle points to the fact that while Unit 1 is nominally preceramic, the tablet holding one mirror is of fired clay. The end date for this deposit is about 1200 B.C., and in several traits in addition to the mirrors, it shows Chavín influence.

Willey and Corbett (1954, pp. 66, 68, pl. 90) found a complete jet mirror and two fragments in their excavations at Ancón. The complete mirror was rectangular with rounded corners, 7.7 cm. long, 5.5 cm. wide, and 1.4 cm. thick. One surface is flat and highly polished, the other rough and round. Larco Hoyle (1941, p. 99) describes the jet mirrors of the coastal Chavín or Cupisnique sites in Chicama Valley. These are both rectangular and rounded, and some have a projection on the back that serves as a handle. The faces are highly polished and some of them are convex (Larco Hoyle, 1945a, p. 10). In Virú Valley, Strong and Evans (1952, p. 43, fig. 7h–k) found three jet mirror fragments at the Huaca Negra site. Two are rectangular and one is circular. Two have projecting handles carved on the back (chart 9–24).

No study has been made of the concave mirrors of the Chavín Phase to compare to Gullberg's analysis of Olmec mirrors. The fact, however, that concave mirrors were made in these two contemporary cultural phases is quite impressive. Mirrors do not continue in use in the Peruvian sequences after the close of the Chavín Phase about 400 B.C.

Among the exotic materials that were widely traded during the Hopewell Phase (ca. 100 B.C.–A.D. 200) in the eastern United States was sheet mica. The probable sources are in the Appalachian Mountains. In Hopewell sites of Ohio, particularly the Hopewell and Turner, this material is found cut into a variety of ornamental shapes (Willoughby, 1917, pp. 496–497, pl. 9). Generally, however, in the Hopewellian "provinces," mica is found in the form of sheets the size of the hand or larger, with or without cut edges.

While uncovering a burial in a Hopewell mound near Helena, Arkansas, that had such a sheet of mica about 11 cm. in diameter over one shoulder, the writer was impressed with the probability that these plates functioned as mirrors (chart 9–12). As soon as the earth was brushed off, a reflection of the excavator's ugly face could be plainly seen (Ford, 1963, p. 27, fig. 21d). These mica sheets are fragile and may have been provided with wood backs.

One of the burials in the McQuorquodale Burial Mound near Mobile Bay had a triangular-shaped mica plate in the region of the pelvis (chart 9–11; Wimberly and Tourtelot, 1941, p. 5, fig. 9).

From the Hopewellian Mandeville site in south Georgia, Kellar, Kelly, and McMichael (1962, pp. 344, 346, fig. 3h) say that from the early levels a large quantity of mica was found, some with cut edges. Mica sheets also came from the Crystal River site at the base of the Florida Peninsula (chart 9–10; Moore, 1907, p. 419).

McGregor (1959, fig. 5) illustrates mica sheets as typical artifacts of the Hopewellian Phase in Illinois. For example, in the Wilson Burial Mound, a sheet with cut edges was found at the head of what seemed to be the most important, or at least the most richly provided individual in Mound 5 (chart 9–9). This sheet measured 16×28 cm. (Neumann and Fowler, 1952, p. 188, pl. 59b).

In some instances mica was placed in the Hopewell mounds of Ohio in great quantities. Moorehead (1922, pp. 91–92) describes a deposit, apparently associated with a log tomb which he estimates as comprising 3000 sheets of mica. "They filled two barrels when packed for shipment to Chicago." Some sheets were 50 cm. in diameter, and 15 cm. thick. In reference to mica in the Ohio Hopewell mounds, Willoughby (1917, p. 496) says, "The crystals or plates are often of large size, and are frequently found with skeletons or as sacrificial deposits in the mounds."

While mica is occasionally found in burial deposits dating after the close of the Hopewellian Phase (A.D. 300–400), it is rare and not in large sheets. There is no indication that mica mirrors continue in use.

On the Classic time level and probably lasting well after A.D. 1000, a type of circular stone plaque, 7 to 25 cm. in diameter with thin sheets of pyrite glued on one face as a mosaic, is distributed from Panama to Pueblo Bonito in New Mexico. Kidder, Jennings, and Shook (1946, pp. 126–133, figs. 52–53, pls. 155–156) found a number of these items, beginning with the Esperanza Phase (A.D. 500) at Kaminaljuyú. They express doubt that these objects were actually reflecting mirrors due to the difficulty of setting the pieces of the mosaic in precisely the same plane; however, these must have been very brilliant ornaments. When found, the pyrite had usually oxidized into a yellow ochre, and only occasionally were the pyrite laminae preserved.

Thin circular stone disks of sandstone, slate, and fine grain gneiss occur in a Mississippian context (after A.D. 1000) through the central part of the Southeast. Webb and DeJarnette (1942, pp. 287–291, table 36, figs. 92–94) describe the distribution of these items:

> Nearly all are notched on the edges, and a few are elaborately engraved. Some are concave on one face as if used as palettes for grinding paint. Many have been found with lead or iron oxides smeared on them. Most of them have been found in graves. A few are drilled with a single hole for suspension. Many are decorated with one or more concentric incised circles. Such circles usually occur on the 'reverse' side, that is, opposite to the engraving, if any, or opposite the notches, where the notches are not duplicated on both sides.

It seems clear, to the writer at least, that these "paint palettes" are really backings that had mosaics of either galena or pyrite fastened on one face. These materials oxidize to white and yellow pigment respectively. The circles inscribed on the undecorated faces are the limits of the area of mosaic precisely as in the Mesoamerican examples. That some show slight concavity suggests that the tradition of concave reflectors persisted for a number of centuries.

Although Kidder, Jennings, and Shook may be quite correct that these composite reflectors would not be useful for arranging one's hair or face paint, it is probable that the primary function of aboriginal mirrors was to reflect sunlight. It also seems likely that the mosaic type developed from the one-piece Formative type mirror, perhaps in Mesoamerica, and had a secondary distribution which carried it to northern New Mexico and to eastern Tennessee.

Summary

One-piece mirrors of the Formative type have an erratic distribution through the Formative cultures between 1000 and 1 B.C. In the two areas where they were most popular, Olmec and coastal Chavín, they are occasionally convex. Mirrors in eastern North America are on the Hopewell horizon (100 B.C.–A.D. 300), and were made of mica. Between A.D. 500–1500 composite mirrors, mosaics with reflecting material glued to stone disk backing, diffused through Central America and the United States Southwest and East.

Comparisons

Mirrors are a common element of the Chou Dynasty of China, and were being traded into Japan in the first century A.D. (J. E. Kidder, 1957, p. 129.)

Finger Rings

CHART 9

Every small boy who has preempted the family television to watch cowboy and Indian classics is well aware that while the American aborigines were fond of personal adornment, finger rings are not usually considered a proper item of costume. As a matter of fact, they seem to be limited to the Formative horizon except in the Maya region. The source of the custom of making and wearing finger rings is not known, nor is it clear just where they first appear in the Americas. In this respect rings parallel the earspools previously discussed. Apparently they never became as popular as the ear ornaments, for relatively few have been found.

Probably the earliest example in Mesoamerica is a rather crude porous brown pottery specimen found by Vaillant (1930, pl. 41, bottom row, 4) in the early levels at Zacatenco (chart 9–16). Another ring made of stalactite came from the middle Zacatenco deposits (chart 9–15; op. cit., pl. 40–1).

In the Veracruz area, Weiant (1943, pp. 117–118, pl. 65) reports pottery finger rings from the Tres Zapotes site. One had a monkey's head modeled on it (chart 9–13), and two others were simple clay circlets. Drucker (1943b, p. 69) describes small "double rings" of brown or black ware, which have the plane of their loops placed at right angles to one another. It is uncertain as to whether these were finger ornaments or not.

Both shell and stone finger rings are found in the Hohokam culture of Arizona. Some of the shell rings are elaborately carved. Gladwin, et al. (1937, pp. 128, 144–145, fig. 57, pl. 18b) placed both varieties of rings in the Santa Cruz and Sacaton Phases. This should date from about A.D. 700–1000, considerably later than the occurrences in Middle and South America.

Webb and Snow (1945, pp. 26, 99) list 15 finger rings from seven different Adena burial mounds in the Kentucky-Ohio area. These are made of thin copper wire, which forms 1–3 spiral loops. This reflects the tendency in this region to make jewelry of copper rather than other materials. Fowler (1957, p. 24, pl. 9c) describes a skeleton that held copper earspools in each hand in the Rutherford Mound in Illinois. In each hand also were fragments of what appear to be finger rings cut from shell (chart 9–7).

In Chiapas, Mexico, Sanders (1961, p. 43, pl. 11Bx) illustrates a small ring made of shell, which he tentatively identified as an earplug flare (chart 9–17). The possibility that it might be a finger ring seems equally good. This dates in the Chiapilla Phase (Chiapa IV–V, 450–100 B.C.).

At the La Victoria site, coastal Guatemala, in the Conchas Phase deposits, M. D. Coe (1961, p. 98, fig. 42a) found a pottery ring (chart 9–19)

... of a size which would fit comfortably on the thumb but would be too big for the other fingers. On one part of the exterior is a strange face which is masked on the lower part below the nose. A more typically Conchas face with RE features is clearly of Tlatilco type, both in the type D eye treatment and in the masking (see Porter, 1953, pl. 5f). Faces with masks over the lower part also appear in Tres Zapotes (Weiant, 1943, pl. 25, 1–6) in a Formative context. Pottery rings of the same kind are known from Tres Zapotes (Weiant, 1943, pl. 65) and from the Las Charcas (Raul Moreno Collection) and Sacatepequez (Mata Amado Coll.) phases in the Valley of Guatemala area. It would seem to be late Conchas 2 in date at La Victoria.

Finger rings of bone are listed by Engel (1958, p. 39) as being an element of the preceramic culture in the Valley of Asia, coastal Peru. He says they continue into the Paracas Phase, where they are double so that they fasten the fingers together. Larco Hoyle (1941, figs. 171–172) illustrates carved bone rings found on the fingers of Cupisnique Phase burials (chart 9–22). These have Chavín style motifs. It seems probable that the rings found by Engel do not predate the Cupisnique Phase, for several other typical traits such as mirrors also come from the Asia preceramic deposits.

Summary

Finger rings are found sporadically from the Ohio Valley to coastal Peru, and were confined to the Chavín, Olmec, Adena-Hopewellian time level (1000–1 B.C.). They are made of bone in coastal Peru, of pottery in Mesoamerica, while in the Ohio region, like other ornaments such as earspools and beads, they were manufactured of copper.

Combs

CHART 9

De Laguna (1947, pp. 222–224) has given a thorough discussion of the distribution of the one-piece comb, usually made of bone or similar material, and the composite comb in which the teeth are fastened to the back. She points out that the one-piece comb has a wide occurrence in northern Asia, and goes back in time to Ertebølle culture in northern Europe and the Chou Bronze Age in China. The historic distribution in North America extends southward to the Iroquois, and in New York State it is first known from the Laurentian Archaic culture (3000–1000 B.C.).

The composite comb is an element of the Jomon culture in Japan. Birket-Smith (1937) has studied its distribution and finds that it is common in South America on the ethnological level. In North America it is distributed from the Aleutians down into the Northwest Plateau to such groups as the Nez Perce. It is also found among the Angmassalik Eskimo of east Greenland. De Laguna suggests that possibly the composite comb is the more ancient type and its distribution has been interrupted by the more recent introduction of the solid comb. As composite combs are frequently made of wood they are difficult to trace archeologically, and too much emphasis cannot be placed on their absence. On the north coast of Peru composite combs go back at least to the beginning of ceramics between 1500 and 1000 B.C., and as they have not been found between Peru and the Northwest Plateau region in North America, it is possible that this trait entered the New World both by way of the Bering Strait and directly across the Pacific to South America, as ceramics seem to have done.

The one-piece combs of the New York area tend to follow the Eskimo pattern in that they are elongated rectangles with decorated handles, and the teeth are formed on the end, not the side of the rectangle. This pattern continues into the time of the Iroquois culture, when the handles were frequently carved to represent deer or other animals.

On the relatively late prehistoric level, combs have been found in Fort Ancient sites on the Ohio River and at the Rose Mound in the Lower Mississippi Valley (Griffin, ed., 1952, fig. 123s).

In the Ohio area the oldest combs occur in the Adena Phase (chart 9, 3–4). Webb and Snow (1945, pp. 25, 96–97) list nine specimens from four different sites. These combs were commonly made of heavy bone in two parts, which seem to have been bound together side by side. The authors suggest that these may either have been for personal grooming, or for carding wool for spinning. Moorehead (1922, fig. 12b) illustrates a "carved object" of tortoise shell found with a burial in the Hopewell Mound Group (chart 9–2). This has a number of teeth projecting on one side and appears to be a rather elaborate type of comb. A comb closely resembling the one illustrated here from the Point Peninsula Phase of New York State, comes from a Hopewell Phase mound in Virginia (Griffin, ed., 1952, fig. 22n).

Perino (letter of November 9, 1966) reports from his unpublished work on Hopewell sites in Illinois: "Bone combs probably occur with Illinois Hopewell as one was recently found at Snyders which looks much like the Fort Ancient combs. We found a set of bone pins in Klunk Mound 6 that may have been bone scarifiers or the teeth of a comb having had a wooden handle" (chart 9–8).

Bone combs are rare in Mesoamerica. Sanders (1961, pl. 11B-y) illustrates a crude example from a Chiapa III (550–450 B.C.) context (chart 9–18).

Combs extend from Engel's (1963, table 14, p. 87) preceramic deposits in the Omas Valley through the Chavín Phase on coastal Peru. Carrión Cachot (1948, pl. 24) illustrates an elongated bone comb with teeth in the end from Ancón. A similar type from Cupisnique deposits is shown by Larco Hoyle (1945a, fig. 19). Willey and Corbett (1954, p. 70) describe wooden teeth from composite combs from the Lighthouse site (chart 9–23). Similar composite combs were found by Larco with Cupisnique burials in Chicama Valley.

In the Peruvian highlands, an elongated bone comb is illustrated by Izumi and Sono (1963, pl. 162–8) from Sajara-patac-San Blas levels in the

Kotosh site (chart 9–20). As we have noted above, Birket-Smith (1937) describes numerous examples of combs from South American ethnological records; and Meggers and Evans inform me that shell combs are found in the Guangala Phase in Ecuador (500 B.C.–A.D. 500).

Summary

The relative absence of both one-piece and composite combs in lower North America, Mesoamerica, and northern South America, may indicate that this trait was brought into the New World through the Bering Strait before 2000 B.C., and was introduced onto the coast of Peru a few centuries before 1000 B.C. The time of earliest popularity seems to be in the Hopewell Phase in North America and the Chavín-Cupisnique of the Andean region.

DISTINCTIVE ARTIFACTS

Figurines

Chart 10

Figurines have been extensively used for determining cultural relations and chronological sequence. This is particularly true in Mesoamerica where they are abundant, and archeologists have tended to follow Vaillant's example of setting up detailed classifications. While very useful for correlating closely related phases, an attempt to use these classifications in a general survey of the Americas would lead to considerable confusion. On chart 10 I have not attempted to impose any sort of classificatory arrangement, and merely placed arbitrarily selected examples in approximate time position in each of the columns. It will be noticed that interest flagged in Middle and South America after A.D. 1, when the custom of making figurines in molds became common.

In the Valdivia Phase of Ecuador, both stone and pottery figurines occur (chart 10, 79–86; Meggers, Evans, and Estrada, 1965, pp. 95–96). Stone figurines are divided into three types which form a sequence through Phases A and B (3000–2000 B.C.) from thin, flat natural slabs with a few lines engraved on them to represent arms or legs (op. cit., fig. 50, pls. 117a–q, 187h–j), through slabs notched at the lower ends to represent legs, to those that have crude but recognizable human faces and arms. The earliest simple form has parallels in Japan, as the authors point out (op. cit., pl. 187).

The pottery figurines are associated with Valdivia Periods B–D (chart 10, 79–84; op. cit., pp. 96–107, figs. 64–65). In contrast to the stone figurines, there is a decrease in realistic representation through the four types described. Beginning at 2000 B.C. the nude females have elaborate hair arrangements, sometimes hanging down to the waist, and well-modeled torsos. Between 2000 and 1500 B.C. the heads become conventionalized, torsos are stylized, and legs are reduced to short stubs. After 1500 the features are even less clearly depicted.

Estrada (1962, fig. 7) gives a chronological diagram of the sequence of figurines in Ecuador. This shows that solid and hollow figurines with helmet-like headgear (chart 10, 73–74; op. cit., fig. 71) first appear in the Late Formative (Chorrera), shortly before 500 B.C. Variation multiplies between 500 and 1 B.C. and includes male figures seated with crossed legs, wearing beards, and peaked caps (chart 10–70). Some of the female figures wear ankle length skirts; others are nude. Mold-made figurines appear in the first centuries of the present era, and the variety of types continues, both hollow and solid. Animal figurines become part of the complex also, and human features are engraved on stone celts (chart 10–72).

Figurines are relatively rare in the Peruvian sequences. At Kotosh, Izumi and Sono (1963, pp. 125–126, pl. 111a) found four of stone, which resemble the stone figurines of Valdivia. Also, principally in the Kotosh Kotosh Phase (1200–800 B.C.), they found 111 fragments of human figurines, and one fragment of an animal (chart 10, 88–89). Both standing and seated figures occur and examples are hollow as well as solid. Some are crudely modeled seated females with poorly represented arms and legs, but judging from illustrations, the typology is not very clear. Wide incisions, sometimes ending in pits as in the Mesoamerican Olmec, were used to represent the mouth, and decorative incisions are common on face and body, some filled with white, red, or yellow post-fired paint. Tello (1960, fig. 134) illustrates a crude stone figurine from Chavín de Huántar (chart 10–87). This again has drilled pits at the ends of lines that represent the eyebrows. He mentions its resemblance to the figurines of Ancón and Paracas, where they are associated with Chavín style pottery. An early figurine from the north coast, dating about 1200 B.C., was found by Bird (1962, fig. 52c) in the Huaca Prieta site; it is made of pottery, seated, knees raised, hands on knees, and wearing a pointed cap (chart 10–93).

In Colombia, adornos modeled in the form of animals and occasionally human heads, begin in Puerto Hormiga and are particularly prominent in the Malambo Phase (1000–700 B.C.). Angulo Valdés (1963, pl. 7a) illustrates a human head that might have come from a figurine (chart 10–69). The first certain occurrence of figurines (chart 10–68) is in Momíl I (800–400 B.C.): they are solid, and are made of a cream colored clay without slip (Reichel-Dolmatoff, G. and A., 1956, p. 294, pls. 22–23). The heads have curious lateral projections, which in some examples clearly represent pulley-shaped earspools (chart 10–67). Eyes are the slashed coffee-bean type, and noses are prominent. Figures are usually seated, legs spread apart, arms akimbo, and hands resting on knees. Heights vary from 4–8 cm. Fragments of larger hollow figurines with red slip are in Momíl II (400–1 B.C.). They also have coffee-bean eyes and seem to represent nude females, as did the preceding Momíl I type.

Considering the fact that the people of the San Agustín Phase cut so many large human representations from hard stone, figurines are remarkably rare. While the early phase, Mesitas Inferior, clearly is coeval with Momíl, it does not have the Momíl figurine types. Duque (1964, drawings 12–2, –3, –9) illustrates three clay figurine fragments and shows small crude stone figures (op. cit., drawing 30) which are so large that they can be considered miniature statues.

Figurines do not seem to be an element in the Monagrillo-Sarigua Phases of Panama, which apparently date from 2000 to possibly as late as 1000 B.C. They are also lacking in the Cupica sequence, just south of Panama on the Pacific coast of Colombia. This begins in the first centuries of the present era.

Small solid hand-made female figurines were not too common in the Ocós Phase (1400–1200 B.C.) on the Pacific coast of Guatemala; only 41 were found. The heads were fairly well formed, faces were sometimes caricatures, and the eyes were slits with very small punctations to represent the pupils (chart 10, 65–66). Figures were nude and in one case, apparently pregnant (M. D. Coe, 1961, p. 92, fig. 39). For some unknown reason figurines are absent from the Soconusco sequence during the Cuadros and Jocotal Phases. Conchas Phase figures (op. cit., pp. 93–98, figs. 54–58) are more abundant and show more variation (chart 10, 62–64). Most are solid, but a few are hollow. The faces tend to be plump, mouths are represented by a wide incision so that they appear open, and the pupils of the eyes are made with large punctations. Many seem to wear caps or headgear, and one has a cap with a pointed peak. The bodies, which could not be associated with heads, are again nude females; breasts are modeled, and the navel is indicated by a large punctation. In some instances, hands and feet are crudely modeled; in others, arms and legs taper to a point. There are also small bird and animal heads that probably come from effigies.

Larco (1941, fig. 153) shows a seated stone figure, which he tentatively identified as Cupisnique. From the coastal site of Las Haldas, Ishida (1960, figs. 60–61) illustrates fragments of a solid standing figurine that should date about 1200 B.C. (chart 10–92). Hands are folded on the chest as seems to be common on early South American figurines, but sex and state of dishabille are not apparent. From Ancón, Carrión Cachot (1948, pl. 25, 23–24) illustrates two standing figurines that seem to be hollow. One is a nude female (chart 10–90), the other of undetermined sex (chart 10–91). She mentions the similarity to figurines of Paracas. On the north coast molded figurines began to be made in the Mochica Phase after A.D. 500 (Strong and Evans, 1952, pp. 181–184, fig. 32). These are both hollow and solid and represent males and females, usually nude (Bennett, 1939, figs. 5a–b, d–e, 8g). The Post-Chavín figurines of Peru are comparatively rare, frequently are hollow, and measure from 15–30 cm. high. This larger size is characteristic for hollow figurines wherever they are found in the Americas.

Crude female figurines with coffee-bean eyes are an element of the Candelaria of northwestern Argentina (Alcina Franch, 1965, fig. 558). This probably has a late date judging from Inca resemblances in the associated pottery.

From the early Pit 38 at Chiapa de Corzo, Dixon (1959, p. 38, fig. 51) describes eight clay figurine fragments; arms, legs, and the head of a stone figurine (chart 10–61). This latter has a round blank face, apparently wears a cap, and has globular projections at either side that represent earplugs. Other pottery fragments were found in the earlier Pit 50 at Chiapa de Corzo (op. cit., p. 18, fig. 53a–b); these include two heads, flattened on the back, one of which has definite Olmec characteristics (chart 10–60). Apparently figurines were not very common in the Chiapas sequence between 1400 and 550 B.C.

At Santa Cruz, Sanders (1961, p. 44) recovered only six examples of Pre-Classic figurines, including two heads. One is grotesque (chart 10–56); the other wears a headdress, and has plump facial features and punctated eyes similar to the Conchas examples from Guatemala (chart 10–55).

Peterson (1963, pp. 78–110, figs. 114–165) gives a very comprehensive discussion of the figurine sequence from the Mirador site, which extends from Mirador IV (450 B.C.) to Post-Classic times. Figurines from Phases IV–VI are predominantly nude females, and are shown both standing and seated, in some cases with legs crossed in the "lotus position." Breasts are prominantly molded, and hands and feet poorly finished. Heads are flattened at the back, eyes indicated by slashes and punctations, and the figures frequently wear necklaces and earspools. Elaborate turban-like caps are usual. One figurine is holding an infant.

The Early Classic Santa Cruz Phase examples (Chiapa VIII–IX; A.D. 200–600) wore turban headdresses, and one had a beard. A large hollow head shows the nicely modeled face of an old man, and there are figurine representations of a dog, frog, and a monkey.

The complete figurine sequence from the excavations of Tehuacán Valley is not yet available. MacNeish (1961, fig. 15) has given a schematic presentation of figurine head types. Figurines appear in Late Ajalpan (chart 10, 51–54), and are solid, nude females as well as larger hollow figures (chart 10–53). Helmet-like headgear is characteristic and some of the heads are the Olmec baby-face type. Figurines continue on into later phases, but full details are not yet available.

Figurines are a prominent feature of the Valley of Mexico Formative, and Vaillant's typology has been followed rather closely by all who have worked in the area. Tolstoy (1958b, p. 87, graph 7) has seriated Vaillant's pottery samples, and has obtained a very clear-cut picture of the parallel figurine type sequence. Nearly all of the figurines are nude females wearing elaborate turban headdresses and earspools (chart 10–45). A few are seated, but most are standing. There is an extensive use of applique strips to form eyes, mouth, and ornaments. About 500 B.C. there is

a tendency for the legs in some of the types to become unnaturally swollen below the hips, a form that recalls the bulbous legs on tripod vessels that developed shortly after this time. There is also a tendency for bodies to be represented by flattened slabs of clay rather than shown in the round.

At Gualupita, George and Suzanna Vaillant (1934, pp. 50–53, figs. 14–15) found the large sometimes hollow realistic Olmec style figurines accompanying burials. They were somewhat at a loss to place these in the Valley of Mexico sequence, a difficulty still facing present-day investigators. Porter (1953, pp. 42–43, pls. 4–5) illustrates typical figurines from Tlatilco, most of which are found with burials, an unusual use for these objects in Mesoamerica. Other examples are given by Piña Chán (1958, vol. 2, pls. 13–23). These include typical male Olmec figures (chart 10–44), women holding babies, and female figurines of Type D, the realistic, graceful style that Vaillant places early in the sequence (Vaillant, 1930, pp. 115–119). The Pre-Classic hand-modeled figurines are succeeded by molded figurines, which are particularly characteristic and numerous at Teotihuacán.

From La Venta, Tres Zapotes, and Cerro de las Mesas, Drucker (1952, pp. 132–141, pls. 23–41; 1943a, pp. 76–90, pls. 26–27; 1943b, pp. 63–66, fig. 155, pls. 27–43, 49–52; Weiant, 1943, pp. 84–111, pls. 1–45) established a figurine classification modeled after Vaillant's, which to this reader at least, makes little contribution to problems of chronology. There is a basic similarity to the Valley of Mexico Pre-Classic in that most are nude females, standing, with poorly modeled arms and feet, and usually wearing turbans, somewhat simpler in arrangement than those in the highlands. The baby-face, droopy mouth Olmec figures wearing helmets are somewhat more common, as are males with beards and a curious peaked cap (chart 10–31). The old man or "Lirios" type is particularly common from Tres Zapotes (Drucker, 1943a, pls. 55–61). Headdresses in many cases resemble helmets, and the pupils of the eyes and the corners of the mouths are usually indicated by large punctations (chart 10, 33–34). Hollow figurines occur at Tres Zapotes (chart 10–32) and Cerro de las Mesas.

The jade figurines at La Venta are usually found in caches or in burials. All represent baby-faced males, who are either seated with legs crossed or standing with the bent knees of the achondroplastic dwarf.

Large hollow baby-faced figurines, solid Olmec baby faces, and ball players decorated with asphalt were found by M. D. Coe at San Lorenzo (chart 10, 38–39). Punched eyes are absent; these seem to be a local marker for the 800–500 B.C. time horizon, being also characteristic of Conchas I in Guatemala.

García Payón (1966, pp. 125–167) gives a thorough discussion of the figurines found at El Trapiche and Chalahuites on the central coast of Veracruz. Although his classification is simpler and occurrences are tabulated by levels, the chronology seems to be little clearer than that in the Olmec area, and approximately the same types are illustrated. Animal figurines are found in small numbers in both these complexes. In marked contrast to these simple Pre-Classic figurines are the large, hollow, complex figures illustrated by Medellín Zenil (1960) from the Proto-Classic sites of central Veracruz.

MacNeish (1954, pp. 586–589) analyzed the figures from his and Ekholm's (1944) excavations in the Huasteca for chronological differences, and developed 18 sequential types (MacNeish, 1954, fig. 20). The Olmec-like "pseudo baby face" type, falls in the Aguilar Phase dating about 800 B.C. The related negroid type runs from about 800–1 B.C. In general MacNeish's and Ekholm's figurines are quite comparable to those of the Olmec area and the Valley of Mexico, and it is probable that a similar sequence prevailed in both regions.

Over 500 figurines were found in the excavation of the Snaketown site of southern Arizona (Gladwin, et al., 1937, p. 233, pl. 195–207). These rather simple handmade nude females are obviously crude imitations of the Mesoamerican Formative examples. Many are armless, have exaggerated hips, and the legs end in points rather than modeled feet; others are seated. Figurines run through the Hohokam sequence and the changes in form have been worked out by Haury (op. cit., fig. 114).

Even cruder female figurines are rare in the Basket Maker III sites of the San Juan River region in northern New Mexico. Obviously an introduced trait, figurines did not become a feature of the succeeding Anasazi. After A.D. 500 clay figurines are found in Oregon in the Wakemup II Phase (Butler, 1959).

The earliest figurines in the eastern United States are from the Poverty Point Phase in the Lower Mississippi Valley (1200–400 B.C.; chart 10, 24–27). While 13 are discussed by Ford and Webb (1956, pp. 49–50, fig. 16), additional collections now make a total of 91 fragments available for study. There is no difficulty about the classification of Poverty Point figurines, for they all conform to one type. They represent nude females, sometimes pregnant, seated, with arms and legs shown by rounded projections. The hips are wide, but other sexual features are poorly represented. Most of the heads are broken off and few have been found. Heads attached to torsos are poorly modeled, and features are represented by simple slashes. On some there appears to be a belt around the waist. A red jasper figurine from the Jaketown site has facial features represented by incising (chart 10–23), but the body is a simple rectangular slab. A similar but cruder sandstone slab figurine comes from the succeeding Marksville Phase (chart 10–20), as does a standing figure made of quartz (chart 10–22). There is also a fragment of the head of a hollow figurine (chart 10–21). Rare clay figurines were made in the Lower Mississippi until about A.D. 600 (chart 10, 16–19; Ford, 1951, fig. 44).

Figurines are a fairly rare trait in fully developed Hopewell sites (100 B.C.–A.D. 200) in Illinois and Ohio. The remarkable figurines from Knight Mound, Illinois, described by McKern, Titterington, and Griffin (1945), are well modeled and represent both standing males and females, and females seated in a peculiar position with the legs bent to the side (chart 10, 5–8). The men wear breechcloths and the women, wrap-around skirts. Similar but cruder figures from other Illinois sites represent standing figures with the knees slightly flexed, a position very reminiscent of the standing jade figures from the Olmec site at La Venta (chart 10, 10–11).

Realistic figurines are illustrated by Willoughby from the Turner group of earthworks in Ohio (chart 10, 1–4; Willoughby, 1922, pp. 71–74, pls. 20–21). Male figures wear breechcloths, earspools, and a sort of headdress with knobs on it. They are shown standing, or seated, either cross-legged or with knees drawn up to the chest. One figure is kneeling, seated on his feet. A complete female figure wears a wrap-around skirt and has the hair arranged in a bun on the back of the head. These figures, as well as the "Knight" figurines from Illinois, were painted.

From the Mandeville site in Georgia, dating in Hopewell times, there is another realistic female dressed in a wrap-around skirt, and the upper torso and head of a figure wearing an elaborate turban (chart 10, 14–15; McMichael, 1964, pl. 8a, j–k).

In the Weeden Island burial mounds (A.D. 400–600), along the northwest coast of Florida, Moore (1902) found a series of hollow, standing male or female figures, 9–24 cm. high (chart 10, 12–13). These sometimes wear cap-like headdresses and have openings in the backs of their head so that they could serve as containers. These are several centuries later than the small solid Hopewell figurines, and their plump proportions are reminiscent of the Late Formative hollow figurines of Mesoamerica and Ecuador. Hunchback hollow human figure vessels, frequently kneeling and sometimes with spine showing as though they represent preserved bodies, occur in the eastern United States on the late Mississippian time level in Tennessee and Missouri. Small solid human and animal adornos attached to vessel rims have a similar date; however, true figurines are extremely rare after A.D. 500.

Summary

In general terms, there is a certain consistency in the Formative figurine sequences. Stone figurines, while rare, tend to be early. More attention is given to faces than to other parts of the body. The earliest clay figurines are nude females, sometimes obviously pregnant. Arms and legs either taper to points or in some cases are missing. Later in each sequence, both sexes are represented, and the figures wear clothing: wrap-around skirts for the females, and breechcloths for the males. Except in the Olmec region, large hollow figures also tend to be a late element.

There are some inter-areal comparisons of interest. Hair arrangement is emphasized in the Early Formative of South America, while helmets and caps are more popular in Mesoamerica. The Valdivia female figurines have the parting of the hair indicated by a wide groove. This trait is also present in Olmec figurines which do not wear head covering. Coe has suggested that this is an attribute of the were-jaguar. It could be explained, however, as a possible heritage from the earlier representations. This same parting of the hair is found on Poverty Point figurines from the Mississippi Valley. Many examples of two-headed females come from Valdivia and Tlatilco. This may be representation of a rare biological phenomenon, but perhaps it is significant in that so far as is known, it is confined to the Early Formative in both regions.

While the earliest figurines in both South America and North America are small and solid, and the larger hollow figurines appear at a later date, the two classes are found together at the beginning of the Veracruz and Tehuacán sequences in Mesoamerica.

Male figurines with beards and wearing peaked caps date about A.D. 1 on coastal Ecuador and Veracruz. Occasional representations of beards are found earlier on the large Olmec stone heads at La Venta, and later in the Mochica Phase of north coast Peru. Olmec figurines, usually made of jade on the Gulf coast of Mexico, represent achondroplastic dwarfs standing with the knees flexed. This flexed-knee stance is found on the famous Adena stone pipe (chart 10–9), and nearly all of the pottery figurines that have come from the Illinois and Ohio Hopewell sites.

The relative abundance of figurines can be measured only subjectively. Fairly common in Ecuador, hand-made figurines are rare in the early phases of Peruvian Formative, and absent thereafter. They are rather common through the Mesoamerican Formative, and become abundant when the molding technique began to be used in the early centuries of this era. In the Mississippi Valley and the eastern United States, hand-made figurines are practically confined to the Poverty Point-Hopewellian time level, where they are fairly infrequent, and disappear after A.D. 500. As in Peru, this looks like an introduced trait that lost its popularity after a few centuries. Mold-made figurines were never made in North America.

Comparison

Nude female figurines, which later acquire clothing, are a feature of Middle and Late Jomon in Japan. There is also a tendency toward exaggeration of the hips and thighs as is seen in Late Formative Mesoamerican examples (J. E. Kidder, 1957, pp. 41–47, figs. 40–43). A detailed chronological comparison should prove most interesting.

Tubular and Platform Pipes

CHART 11

In 1948 Porter published *Pipas Precortesianas*, a definitive study of available information on the history of smoking pipes in the Americas. The principal defect of this study was that, in the absence of the radio-carbon dates, she accepted the too late calendrical guesses of Ford and Willey (1941) for eastern North America. The basic thesis seems to be correct. Pipes developed from tubular to platform, to elbow and block forms in the eastern United States. The change from a one-piece "self pipe" to those having inserted wood stems is an important marker for early and late forms. Then about A.D. 900 platform pipes, which had survived and acquired characteristic forms on the Texas periphery, spread rapidly to Mexico and to South America as far as the Argentine and Chile.

Spaulding (1946) has suggested that the tubular pipe, the earliest form preserved to archeology, developed from the bone tubes used by shamans of northern Siberia and the Dorset culture of the American Arctic for extracting evil spirits in curing ceremonies. This seems a probable theory since it would account for the ceremonial and curing aspects of pipe smoking among the historic Indian groups.

What may be the earliest examples of tubular and elbow pipes of stone are found in the Congdon II Phase of Oregon, which Butler (1959) thinks begins somewhere between 1500 and 1000 B.C.

Meighan (1959) has discussed the distribution of pipes in coastal California. Long tubular steatite pipes first appear in the Late Horizon, which runs from A.D. 300 to the beginning of the Historic Period. In the

Southwest, stone tubular pipes first occur about A.D. 300 in the Basket Maker of the Four Corners region and in the Pine Lawn Phase of southwest New Mexico (Reed, 1964). In the eastern United States, Griffin (1964, pp. 234–235) says that tubular stone pipes date from the Glacial Kame sites of the Late Archaic shortly before 1000 B.C. Ritchie (1965, p. 178) states that cigar-shaped and the specialized blocked-end types appear in New York State at about 1000 B.C., the time of the earliest ceramics. Tubular pipes, sometimes in effigy form, are an element of the Adena culture (chart 11–3) of the central part of the Ohio River (800–100 B.C.). Simple tubular pipes of stone and pottery are found on this same time level in Illinois (chart 11–6), and reach the Gulf coast in Poverty Point (1200–400 B.C.; chart 11, 12–13) and St. Johns I times (400–1 B.C.; chart 11–8). In the eastern United States, the tubular is succeeded by the platform pipe on the Hopewellian time level (chart 11–2, 5, 7, 9–10) at approximately 100 B.C.–A.D. 300. Just how the development from tubular to platform shape occurred is not clear. There are no transitional forms.

There seem to be no pipes from Formative sites in Middle America. The nearest pipes in South America occur on north coastal Colombia. In the Momíl I levels, Gerardo and Alicia Reichel-Dolmatoff (1956, p. 219, pl. 19, 7–11) found 80 fragmentary cylinders that tapered to one end and had a very small perforation running through them (chart 11–33). All were broken at the other end, so that the authors were uncertain whether they were spouts for vessels or the mouth ends of tubular pipes. As no evidence was found for attachment to vessels, it seems probable that these are pipes from which the thin-walled tobacco chamber has been broken.

Tubular pipes are found in the Lake Valencia region of Venezuela in the Cabrera Phase, dating about 500 B.C. (Sanoja, 1963, p. 73).

Meggers (1966, p. 98) says that elbow pipes (chart 11–38) are a rare artifact in the Jama-Coaque Phase of the Regional Developmental of Ecuador (500 B.C.–A.D. 500). "The bowl is usually located in the body of a human or animal figure, but some pipes take the form of a human arm with the mouthpiece in the extended thumb."

Izumi and Sono (1963, p. 128, table 12, pls. 98b; 155, 1–3) found "fragmentary cylindrical clay objects" in "considerable quantity" (chart 11, 40–41). They say that "There are three kinds of shapes: some have a cylindrical shape with only one end open and the others are open at both ends; among the latter, there are some pieces having one end outflared like a trumpet (pl. 98a–14). The use of these objects is unknown." It seems quite clear that the cylindrical

objects with flared ends were tubular pipes. These date from Chavín times to the end of the Kotosh sequence (800 B.C.–A.D. 500).

Gonzalez (1963, p. 109) notes that pipes first appear in all complexes of his early ceramic period beginning between 500 and 1 B.C., and is of the opinion that along with grooved stone axes, pipes reached northwest Argentina from the north along the eastern slope of the Andes. He states that "From northwestern Argentina they crossed the cordillera into Chile and were incorporated into the Molle culture, an event that must have taken place during Molle I" (ca. A.D. 250).

As mentioned at the beginning of this section, Porter (1948) has given a picture of the later distribution of pipe forms, which seems to have occurred after A.D. 900 from east Texas, and to have involved the variations on the monitor or platform type of pipe.

Summary

The tubular "self pipe" without an inserted stem seems to be one of the elements that originated in North America and diffused directly to northern South America between 1000 and 1 B.C. Whether tobacco accompanied this original diffusion is not known. A later southward movement of platform pipe forms seems to have occurred about A.D. 1000. Unlike the earlier diffusion, this did involve Mesoamerica.

Flat and Cylindrical Stamps

CHART 11

The use of stamps for impressing designs, perhaps on the skin or on fabrics, seems to be earliest and most common in Mesoamerica, where it goes back to about 1200 B.C. These stamps are of two principal varieties: flat, either with or without projections on the back to serve as handles; and cylindrical, either solid or with a central perforation provided for an axle. The material is usually pottery, sometimes stone.

Porter (1953, pp. 41–42, pl. 13a–c) describes both these principal types from the Tlatilco site in the Valley of Mexico. Flat stemmed, perforated cylindrical, and solid cylindrical stamps were found. Designs were both negative and positive. The motifs included the hand, snake, scroll, and geometrical designs, and were quite bold. Several of the flat stamps were shaped like a human foot (chart 11, 21–22).

Drucker, Heizer, and Squier (1959, p. 258) list flat clay stamps as missing from La Venta and cylindrical stamps as rare. The two fragments found in strata excavation (Drucker, 1952, pp. 141–142) have heavy carving and deep design. Coe, who has recently reviewed Drucker's collection, informs me that in his opinion the bottle neck shown by Drucker (op. cit., fig. 40b) is a roller stamp (chart 11–19). If true, this not only adds a third stamp to the La Venta collection, but at the same time eliminates bottles with tall necks.

Both cylindrical (chart 11–16) and flat stamps were fairly common at Tres Zapotes. The flat stamps had square, elongated, rectangular, or circular faces (chart 11–18; Weiant, 1943, pp. 116–117, pls. 62–63). Drucker (1943b, pp. 67–68, figs. 200–208) says that stamps are relatively rare at Cerro de las Mesas, but both flat and cylindrical varieties (chart 11–15, –17) appear in collections of material purchased from the local people. Apparently García Payón (1966) did not find stamps in his excavations at Chalahuites and El Trapiche. The re-excavation of Chalahuites by Medellín, Wallrath, and Ford had similar results.

At Las Flores site in the Huasteca, Ekholm (1944, p. 472, fig. 48k-n) found five plain flat rectangular stamps. All date in Period V (A.D. 1000).

In the Chiapas sequence at Santa Cruz, Sanders (1961, pp. 43–44, pl. 11Aa–b, 11Bf–h) found two examples of cylindrical stamps (chart 11, 26-27). One of these came from the Burrero Period (Chiapa II, 800 B.C.), the other from Burrero-Chiapilla (ca. 400 B.C.). The carving on the cylinders is deep and wide, similar to that on the cylindrical stamps at Tlatilco. He also found three flat rectangular stamps (chart 11, 23–25), which date in the Chiapilla Period (ca. 450–250 B.C.). These have more delicate rectilinear designs.

M. D. Coe (1961, p. 105, fig. 59m), in the Soconusco of Guatemala, found fragments of large hollow cylindrical stamps in the Conchas II Phase (chart 11–29). They seem to last on into Crucero. Coe's comparative comments are worth quoting: "the distribution of roller stamps in time would lead one to believe that they are usually, if not always, confined to the Formative in Middle America. I strongly suspect that alleged occurrences of these objects in Classic contexts are due to redeposition." He points out that the bold deeply cut designs such as were found at Tlatilco, are confined to Chiapa II in the Chiapas region, which means they probably date between 1000 and 500 B.C. Other occurrences are cited at Kaminaljuyú and Copán. They are lacking at Zacaleu, which has no Formative levels. A single circular flat stamp with a spiral design (chart 11–28; op. cit., p. 109, fig. 61a) came from the Crucero-Marcos levels. Similar circular stamps are illustrated in the Valley of Mexico and Veracruz areas. Circular

flat stamps are also found at Zacaleu, and they seem to last up to Conquest times. Coe further states that long rectangular flat stamps persist into quite late times in the Guatemalan highlands.

At the Momíl site on the north coast of Colombia, Gerardo and Alicia Reichel-Dolmatoff (1956, p. 222) found a single flat circular stamp in Momíl I deposits (chart 11–30). This had a conical back, which served as a handle. Also from early Momíl deposits was a single cylindrical stamp, which had a crude zig-zag design and was not perforated (chart 11–32). In Momíl II, however, hollow cylindrical stamps are characteristic. These are made of a fine clay and have a variety of deeply incised designs, which were positive. That is, the printing surfaces express the design rather than making a colored background (chart 11–31).

Meggers (1966, pp. 75, 89, 98, 105, 115, 128) details the cylindrical and flat pottery stamps found in various phases of the Regional Developmental Period (500 B.C.–A.D. 500) on the coast of Ecuador (chart 11, 34–37), where they are a rather characteristic artifact. Patterns tend to be both bold and fine checkerboards, squares and zig-zags, as well as naturalistic curvilinear patterns of birds, monkeys, and floral designs. The flat stamps are provided with handles on the back, and are circular, long rectangular, or irregular in shape. Both flat and cylindrical stamps disappear from the Ecuadorian sequences after A.D. 500.

A single flat circular stamp was found by Izumi and Sono (1963, p. 130, pl. 154–12) at Kotosh in the Peruvian highlands (chart 11–39). This was small and crudely carved to produce a circle and dot design. It dates in the Kotosh Chavín Phase (800–400 B.C.).

With the earliest pottery in Huaca Prieta on the north coast of Peru, Bird (1948, p. 27) found both roller and flat stamps. Larco (1946, p. 153) states that stamps are a Cupisnique trait, but does not specify the type. Carrión Cachot (1948, pl. 24t) illustrates a flat stamp with handle from Ancón (chart 11–42), which bears S-figures.

Only one flat stamp is known from the Poverty Point complex of the Lower Mississippi Valley (chart 11–14). This is made of stone and has a flat round face on which is carved a cross and four circles. The upper part tapers to provide a handle.

Twelve engraved flat thin tablets have been found in the Adena sites in a quite restricted region of the central Ohio River Valley (chart 11–4). Webb and Baby (1957, pp. 83–101) describe these in some detail. Four show the head and beak of a raptorial bird, and four have formalized hand and foot forms. These are boldly engraved, and the use of the circle and dot is unusual for North America. The authors (op. cit., p.

96) note that two tablets have dark red stain on the face, and concluded that they were probably stamps used for decorating clothing or body.

Strangely enough, cylindrical stamps occur in the same region. They are usually made of stone, some perforated, some solid cylinders, and some spool-shaped as though intended for impressing designs on arms or legs. Holmes (1903, fig. 28) illustrates examples. Baby provides the information that those in the Ohio Historical Society collections and a large collection in the hands of a local collector are recorded as surface finds on Fort Ancient sites. (A.D. 1300–1600).

With the exception of circles and dots and small S-figures in Chavín, none of these Formative stamps were used to make impressions on pottery. A carved paddle probably made of wood was used in the southeastern United States for impressing pottery beginning about 500 B.C. and lasted up to the Historic Period. The model for this treatment is clearly the Woodland cord-wrapped and carved-face paddle. Paddle-impressed pottery is found quite late in the Peruvian coastal sequence, where it is associated with mold-made designs. This probably has no direct connection with the stamping tradition under discussion.

Summary

Both flat and cylindrical stamps appear in Meso-america about 1200 B.C. Their diffusion into South America seems to date about 800 B.C. Evidence of this influence into North America is much weaker: a single circular stamp from Poverty Point, and the flat tablets of the Adena Phase, which are not provided with handles on the back. The very late occurrence of roller stamps in the Fort Ancient Phase of the Ohio River Valley is one of those curious unexplained phenomena.

Bark Beaters

CHART 3

For the past several years, Tolstoy has been engaged in a study of the world-wide distribution on the several methods of manufacturing cloth by malleating the inner bark of certain trees such as the mulberry. A preliminary summary was published by the New York Academy of Sciences (Tolstoy, 1963).

Bark beaters in the American Formative conform to a single type, which also has an extensive diffusion through the Pacific Islands. A complete example was found by MacNeish in a dry cave deposit dating in the Palo Blanco Phase (200 B.C.–A.D. 900) in Tehuacán Valley (chart 3–20; MacNeish, 1961, figs. 13–1, 15). This had a rectangular stone head, with parallel ridges cut into both flat faces, and was strongly grooved around the periphery. A flexible withe handle was in place, bent around the peripheral grooves and tied securely where it crossed. Both ends extended about a foot and were tied together to form a handle. One piece of bark cloth was found in Santa Maria deposits.

García Payón (1966, p. 175, pl. 84–3) found one fragment of a bark beater in his excavation at El Trapiche. This was in Cut B, Level 12, well toward the bottom of the deposit in association with rocker stamped ceramics (op. cit., table 3).

Weiant (1943, p. 120, pl. 72, 15–17) in reporting on the excavation at Tres Zapotes says, "Several bark beaters were found, ranging in shape from rectangular to oval. These were grooved around the outer edge. The ridges on the beating surfaces are typically finely spaced on one side and widely spaced on the other. The excavated specimens were associated with upper Tres Zapotes ceramics" (chart 3–13). Similar stone bark beaters were encountered by Ekholm (1944, pp. 490, 493, fig. 56v-w) in his excavation in the Huasteca. These are described as grooved around the edges for hafting and with a scoring placed closer together on one face than on the other. Ekholm assigns these elements to his Period v and possibly the latter part of Period IV (ca. A.D. 1000).

In the past, it has usually been thought that bark beaters and bark cloth belong to the Classic and Post-Classic in Mesoamerica. As Vaillant (1941, p. 195) points out, many of the folding books, or *tonalamatl*, which survived the Spanish Conquest, are written on paper made from the bark of the *amate* or wild fig tree.

Bark cloth is not reported in the ethnological records of the eastern United States, and nothing resembling the typical Mesoamerican bark beater has been described in archeological reports. In a forthcoming paper on additional collections from the Poverty Point site, Webb and the writer (ms) will describe three oval stone objects about 7 cm. long, which have grooves around the edges and two faces that are slightly domed. These faces do not have the scoring lines usual on the Mesoamerican type of bark beater, and for that reason, Tolstoy has expressed some doubt that they actually were used for this purpose. Yet it is clear that these tools were hafted in the typical bark beater fashion. If they were not employed to malleate the cortex of bark, they must have been used for a similar purpose.

In the Plains area, a heavy grooved maul is used for crushing bones before they are boiled to render the grease. These are discussed by De Laguna (1947, pp. 164–166). Apparently they diffused southward from the Arctic. Gladwin, et al. (1937, p. 104, pl. 45) found seven grooved "hammerstones" in the Santa Cruz and Sacaton Phases at Snaketown. These are quite late and while some have markedly arched faces, others are nearly flat and could have served as bark beaters. They are much flatter than the grooved mauls, and it is possible that, like so many Snaketown traits, they diffused from Mesoamerica.

In the Chiapas sequence, four bark beaters of this type have been reported from a Chiapa VII context (A.D. 1–200). This information is provided by Lowe.

M. D. Coe (1961, fig. 41c) illustrates what may be a small fragment of a bark beater from Ocós Phase deposits (chart 3–27). A second artifact, more clearly a bark beater, of rectangular shape, grooved edges and scored flat faces, came from the surface of the Ocós site making dating uncertain (chart 3–28; op. cit., p. 110, fig. 42b).

On the coast of Ecuador, Estrada, Meggers, and Evans (1964, pp. 497, 539, pl. 6b–c) illustrate grooved face bark beaters from the Jambelí culture of the Regional Developmental Period (500 B.C.–A.D. 500). They say that the "two bark beater fragments are from sites that occupy an early and a later position, suggesting that this trait was present throughout the sequence." These beaters are somewhat anomalous in that the edges are squared and flat rather than grooved to provide for the handle. A similar example comes from the contemporary Bahía Phase (chart 3–32, op. cit., pl. 6a).

On the north Peruvian coast, Bird (1948, p. 25) found fragments of bark cloth in late preceramic context, but no beaters. This implies an age of slightly more than 1200 B.C. In recent times bark cloth was extensively made and used by tribes in the Amazon Basin, and it is possible that the specimens found by Bird were trade items from this source.

Summary

Although evidence is somewhat scattered, it appears that bark beaters, and by inference the manufacture of bark cloth, were introduced into the American Formative about 1000 B.C. In the selva regions east of the Andes, the custom of making bark cloth is still practiced today. This industry also lasted through the Classic and Post-Classic in Mexico, was used for book-making by the Aztecs, and today the Otomi Indians make bark cloth, which is purchased by art students at the National University of Mexico and painted with flowers and cock fight scenes.

The introduction of bark cloth manufacturing into North America in the Poverty Point Phase and late in the sequence at Snaketown is a possibility.

POTTERY AND STONE VESSELS AND APPENDAGES

Small Wide-mouth Pot

CHART 12

Small pots with globular bodies, in which the height is very nearly equal to the diameter, with wide mouth and short nearly vertical rims, are one of the two major shape groups in the Valdivia Phase of Ecuador between 3000 and 1500 B.C. (Meggers, Evans, and Estrada, 1965, fig. 54, 13–23). Variations on the bowl form are the second major group. The paste of the Valdivia pots varies from a rather sandy texture, Punta Arenas Plain (op. cit., pp. 43–44), and San Pablo Plain (op. cit., p. 45) to a paste that contains only a small amount of fine sand, Valdivia Plain (op. cit., pp. 72–74). In size these vessels range from about 10 cm. in diameter to 28 or 30 cm. Usually they tend to be small, between 14 and 24 cm.

From 3000 to 2000 B.C. more than 30 percent of the Valdivia pots have folded rims (chart 12, 49–52; op. cit., p. 90), and a number of these have either delicate notching formed by impressing an instrument in the lip at close intervals (op. cit., fig. 37–2), or the lip edges have been formed into a scalloped pie crust form by the fingers. It will be noted that these features of sandy paste and finely notched rims are early in the life cycle of this pot form in other regions where it will be described.

Later, from 2000 to 1500 B.C., the folded rims are replaced by rims that are not thickened, but have a definite channel on the interior (chart 12–48). This form is usually called a cambered rim. Meggers, Evans, and Estrada divide these curved rims into two classes: "angular cambered" and "curved cambered." Wide-mouth pots with cambered rims comprise about 20 percent of the Valdivia vessels at this time.

A substantial proportion of these pots are decorated, and the association of decorations with the several forms is given by Meggers, Evans, and Estrada (1965) in their table A. The earlier folded rim pots have decoration just below the rim fold and extending a short way down the vessel neck in the form of short vertical bands of combed lines, short vertical grooves made with the finger, narrow bands of fingernail punctations, scallop-shell stamp impressions that run horizontally and are arranged in panels, incised lines made with a pointed instrument similarly arranged in panels, and striated polishing. A notable decorative effect is named Valdivia Modeled (op. cit., pp. 66–67). This consists of a single row of nodes formed a short distance below the rim fold by pushing the vessel surface out from the interior with the fingertips. Finger impressions show plainly in the interior and the protuberances range from barely perceptible rises to pronounced bulges (op. cit., pl. 78). This treatment is confined to the early periods of Valdivia and does not continue into the late periods, where cambered rims are usual. On the pot shape, the two variations of the later cambered rim vessels also are frequently decorated. The decoration, however, is usually on the exterior of the rim, rather than below as with the folded rims. Applique fillets, fingernail punctating, broad-line incising, and nicked broad-line incising are usual decorations. Brushing, also found on both curving and angular cambered rims, is usually applied slanting on the rims, and on the body is carelessly crosshatched. A row of punctations at the lower edge of the decorated rims may be a replacement for the punched-out nodes (op. cit., fig. 35–1).

There is another change in vessel form in Valdivia pottery over this same range in time, but it occurs on bowl shapes, rather than the wide-mouth pot under discussion. This begins with four short, solid feet placed on plain or red-slipped simple bowls (chart 12–53). This feature had its maximum popularity between 3000 and 2000 B.C., and tends to be replaced between 2000 and 1500 B.C. by bases that have been pushed into a concave form. Both of these variations in base form disappear after 1500 B.C. (op. cit., p. 92). As will be pointed out later in other regions and at later times, these base forms are associated with the wide-mouth pot.

The wide-mouth pot form apparently is not found to the north in ceramics that date much before 1000 B.C. It is absent from the Puerto Hormiga and Barlovento complexes of northern Colombia, the Barra, Chiapa I, El Arbolillo, and San Lorenzo-La Venta of Mesoamerica, as well as the fiber-tempered Stallings Island and Orange complexes of the southern Atlantic coast of North America.

After the beginning of the Christian Era, this small wide-mouth pot is found on the Pacific coast of Colombia, but how the tradition was maintained after its apparent disappearance at the end of the

Valdivia Phase in Ecuador at 1500 B.C. is not clear. In the bay of Cupica, in the humid jungle of the north Pacific coast of Colombia, Gerardo and Alicia Reichel-Dolmatoff (1962) excavated a small mound that had been constructed in four levels. Burial pits had been dug from each level and the ceramics that accompanied these burials showed a clear sequence of forms. Radiocarbon dates are not available but Angulo Valdés (1962b, fig. 8) estimates that Phases I and II date between A.D. 1 and 500. Phase I has the small, wide-mouth pot form (chart 12–44; Reichel-Dolma-off, G. and A., 1961, pls. 3–1, –4, –5, –8; 4, 1–3, 5–6; 5–2, –5). Bodies are almost globular and the low rims that rise to the wide mouths have lightly notched lips, an added scalloped fillet, and are decorated with punctations. From the illustrations, it appears that two may have slightly cambered rims (op. cit., pls. 3–1; 4–6). On the shoulders of some of the vessels, there is a row of nodes formed by pushing out the vessel wall from the interior with the fingers. Decoration on the body consists of bands of straight lines, punctations, or curving bands of zoned hatching. Dentate stamping is zoned by incised lines in what looks like a bird motif (op. cit., pl. 5–3).

This small, wide-mouth pot form runs through the four phases of the Cupica Burial Mound (op. cit., pl. 14–2) and is also in the Murillo, Martincito, and Minguimalo Phases at the Minguimalo site on the San Juan River on the Pacific slope of the Andes. Two radiocarbon dates for the early and late phases of this stratified site are A.D. 832 and 1252, respectively, but Formative features are preserved to a remarkable extent. In the Murillo Phase some of the pots are decorated between lip and shoulder with incised concentric square and fret motifs (op. cit., fig. 4, pl. 2–1). The only painted designs are formed by narrow, red lines on the natural clay surface.

The most remarkable feature is the extensive use of nodes punched through from the interiors of the pots in the two latter phases of the Minguimalo site. These are made with a small, cylindrical instrument and the interior wall of the vessel is usually smoothed over so that the small protuberances that appear on the exterior wall have a hollow space behind them. More rarely the nodes are made inside the vessel lip. As is so often true with the similar nodes of the Alexander complex of the Tennessee River Valley, or in Early Illinois Hopewell of the eastern United States, the tops of the nodes are frequently knocked off with use of the vessels so that the hollow space is revealed. In Colombia several rows of nodes are arranged on the pot necks running parallel to the rim (op. cit., pp. 29–30, pls. 3–9). Crudely incised designs with rectangular motifs, or punctations and angular zoned hatching are accompanying decorative treatments. The small globular pot is described by Duque (1964, pp. 332–335) at the San Agustín site in the Central Cordillera of Colombia, and assigned to the phase Mesitas Medio. The time is probably near A.D. 1. Momíl-like decoration characterizes Duque's (op. cit., pl. 2) early phase, and nodes punched from the interior also occur.

The tradition of the small globular-bodied, wide-mouth pot continued in the highland Colombia, probably right up to the time of the Spanish Conquest. They are illustrated by Cubillos (1959, pl. 19a, c) from tombs in the adobe brick pyramid of Tulcán, on the outskirts of Popayán at the head of the Cauca River Valley. Also they are a part of the Río Bolo complex examined by Bennett and the writer further down the Cauca Valley (Ford, 1944, pl. IA–1). There are no radiocarbon dates for these occurrences, but it is doubtful if they predate the Spanish Conquest by more than a century or so.

Matthew and Marion Stirling (1964a) illustrate small, wide-mouth pots with globular bodies from a tomb in Coclé Province, Panama. One bears an excised design. Admittedly on the basis of little evidence, they consider that this ware is early. Vessels of similar proportions but considerably larger (15 to 30 inches in diameter) were found on Taboga and Taboguilla Islands, located a few miles from the Pacific entrance to the Panama Canal (Stirling, M. and M., 1964b). Brushing, simple crosshatched incising made with a multi-pointed tool, zoned crosshatching, tick marks on the edge of decorated areas, applique fillets, and stamping with the edge of a scallop shell look like Colonial Formative decorations. One vessel has shoulder bosses pushed out from the interior.

A row of nodes punched from the interior occasionally occurs in Mesoamerica on other vessel forms. Some of the large tecomates of the Barra Phase (1600–1400 B.C.) in the Soconusco have a single row bordering the rim, made with the finger. This feature continues on into the Cuadros and Jocotal Phases, where it is characteristic of Guamuchal Brushed (1200–800 B.C.; Coe and Flannery, 1967, pp. 28–30, decoration 11). From Tres Zapotes, Drucker (1943a, p. 59) describes similar nodes on ollas.

About 1000 B.C. the ceramics of the eastern United States were very limited as to decorations, shapes, and also geographical distribution. The cordmarked, pointed-base Woodland amphora was in use near the Great Lakes. The fiber-tempered, Stallings Island complex on the coast of Georgia has been described. The characteristic decoration is drag-and-jab punctating, which has been compared to Valdivia Drag-and-Jab Punctate. Only two shapes are known: simple bowls and simple bowls with inturned upper rim.

These forms have also been compared with those in Valdivia (see p. 109).

The Orange complex, also fiber tempered, was well established along the St. Johns River in Florida. The rather varied assemblage of incised decorations has been compared with the Machalilla complex of Ecuador, and it has been pointed out that the usual flat-base pan form is one that is early in the Mexican ceramic sequence.

The Bayou La Batre complex of the Mobile Bay area and the Poverty Point complex of the Lower Mississippi also were in existence at this time. The typical decorations have been described: characteristically scallop-shell rocker stamping for La Batre and crude rocker stamping for Poverty Point. A row of nodes below the rim area, formed by punching out the vessel wall from the interior, is found at Poverty Point (chart 12–30), but not at La Batre. Both complexes, however, share vessel shapes that contrast with the two early complexes to the east. These are a small vase with flat bottom and outslanting walls, and a small pot form (Wimberly, 1960, fig. 40). This latter has the size and proportions of the small, wide-mouth pot that is under discussion, but in a number of cases varies in the detail of base shape (chart 12, 23–33). Bases seem to be flattened and are provided with low crude rings, tetrapodal supports, or polypodal supports, this latter a sort of compromise between the ring base and feet. In most instances, bases appear to be absurdly small for the size of the vessels. It is possible that globular bodies are also present in these complexes, but as shape studies have thus far been dependent on sherds, this point remains obscure.

In the Lower Mississippi Valley, in the Illinois area, and probably in the intervening region as well, an apparent evolution of the wide-mouth pot form and of its associated decorations may be traced. The early phases have a tendency toward sand tempering of the paste, four feet, ring bases, or small, flat, heel bases. The rims are often thickened by folding, are bordered by a row of nodes punched from the interior, and lips are nicked or notched (chart 12, 10–12). The late phase is the Classic Hopewell pot with rounded shoulders and a small, flat base, which is either circular or square (chart 12, 7–8). Four feet are rare. The thickened rim was superseded by a thin cambered rim and the row of bosses by a row of large punctations (fig. 6 a–e). The scratchy, straight-line rim decoration is replaced by delicate incising that usually forms a crosshatched pattern. Rocker stamp and linear stamp decorations are associated with this form in its early phase; zoned rocker stamping forming bird motifs in the later one.

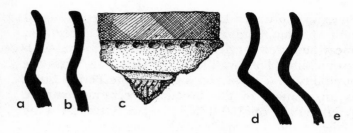

Mississippi Valley

Marksville — Hopewell Phase

ca. A.D. 100

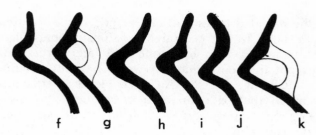

Peru. Tiahuanaco Phase

ca. A.D. 1000

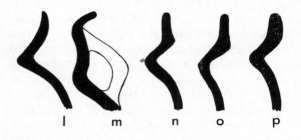

North Peru. Piura Phase

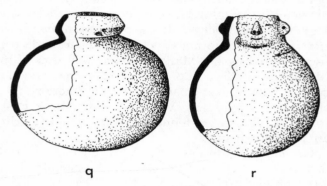

Coastal Peru. Gallinazo Phase

ca. A.D. — 100

Ecuador. Valdivia

Phase 2000 — 1200 B.C.

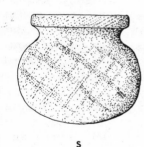

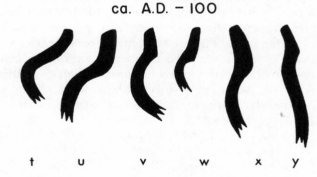

FIGURE 6.—Comparison of cambered rims in Marksville-Hopewell, Valdivia and the Peruvian Tiahuanaco, Piura and Gallinazo Phases. (*a*, after Ford, 1936, fig. 41 F. *b–c*, after Ford and Willey, 1940, fig. 41 *d–d'*. *d–e*, Louisiana State University collection. *f–k*, after Collier, 1955: *f–i*, fig. 50D; *j*, fig. 54F; *k*, fig. 56C. *l–p*, after Lanning, 1963b: *l*, fig. 14f; *m*, fig. 16f; *n*, fig. 20a; *o*, fig. 20e; *p*, fig. 20b. *q–r*, after Bennett, 1950: *q*, pl. 10D; *r*, fig. 10E. *s–y*, after Meggers, Evans, and Estrada, 1965: *s*, fig. 26–3; *t*, fig. 26–2; *u*, fig. 26–3; *v*, fig. 25–9; *w*, fig. 25–10; *x*, fig. 35–6; *y*, fig. 39–2, bottom)

It seems unlikely that this sequence of forms developed in the Mississippi Valley completely without outside influence, for the details of punched nodes and cambered rim form recapitulate the sequence of rim forms that terminated in the Valdivia Phase of Ecuador a thousand years earlier (fig. 6 *s–y*). How the transfer might have taken place remains a mystery. As noted above, no directly related forms have been found in Mesoamerica. They do occur in western Colombia, but the details of the sequence there are not entirely clear.

The small, wide-mouth pot does not disappear from the eastern United States with the decline of the Hopewellian cultural climax. An undecorated version appears to continue in the small, shell-tempered pot of the Early Mississippian Phase, and reverts to the rounded bases that characterized the Valdivia Phase pots. In the central Mississippi region, this is first tempered with limestone and later with shell. This pot frequently has two strap handles (Griffin, ed., 1952, fig. 151–4). An even clearer persistence occurs in the Caddoan area of southern Arkansas, where the pottery type "Cowhide Stamped" was made from about A.D. 1200 until the Historic Period (C. H. Webb, 1959, figs. 63a–g, 67k–1, 83g–h, 88i, 109). This features cambered rims, separate rim decoration, globular bodies, and body decoration consisting of zoned stamping.

The small wide-mouth pot also diffused down the Pacific coast of South America, but apparently at a somewhat slower rate. It retained the globular body of the Valdivia form, but in some instances the mouth diameter becomes relatively more restricted. Most impressive is the fact that it also retained the cambered rim. These rims do not develop the separate decoration featured by the Marksville-Hopewell rims of the Mississippi Valley, and instead of being smoothly curved, retain the angular ridge on the exterior that is characteristic of many Valdivia rims. Also the absurdly small handles found on a few Valdivia rims are fairly frequent.

Lanning (1963b, figs. 12i, 14, 15c, 16, 20) records this cambered rim and apparently the globular body form through his Sechura and Piura Phases on the far north coast of Peru (fig. 6 *l-p*). Influences of this form appear in Virú Valley in the Gallinazo Phase (ca. A.D. 1), where the cambered rim sometimes has human facial features modeled on it (fig. 6 *q-r*; Bennett, 1950, pl. 10B, D-E). The most popular occurrence of the small globular pot with cambered rim on the central part of the north Peruvian coast, however, coincides with the wave of reduced black ware, often with molded body decoration, which arrives about A.D. 1000 in the coastal Tiahuanaco Phase (fig. 6 *f-k*). Examples are illustrated by Collier (1955, figs. 50D, 53C, 54F, 56C-D), Strong and Evans (1952, figs. 39–1, 40–6, 44–5), and Ford (1949, fig. 6, 23–26). While the influence of this shape is quite marked on the north coast of Peru, it does not extend to other regions of the country. It is not associated with either rocker stamped decoration, or pushed out nodes or punctations forming a lower border to the rim. Neither do these vessels have feet. Evidently the northward and southward diffusions from coastal Ecuador were completely independent of each other.

It will have been noted that in the Americas, nodes punched out from the vessel interior are a rather consistent attribute of the early examples of wide-mouth pots. These nodes are found on a Woodland-like round and pointed base amphora at a date of about 3000 B.C. in north central Siberia, where in the Serovo

Phase of the upper Lena Valley they are associated with the amphora vessel form, fabric impression, linear and crescent dentate stamping, and drag-and-jab incising (Tolstoy, 1958a, p. 401). This raises the possibility that these nodes crossed the Bering Strait as an element of the Woodland ceramic pattern. Wright (1967, pp. 130–135) has recently evaluated the evidence and, in consideration of the long geographical gap and the relative lateness of the American examples, rather doubts that this diffusion occurred.

Summary

The small, wide-mouth pot with globular body is a prominent part of the Valdivia ceramic tradition when it is first known on the coast of Ecuador, at about 3000 B.C. In the course of 1500 years, folded rims with notched lips are replaced by cambered rims, and nodes punched out from the interior placed in a row at the bottom of the rim area are replaced with punctations. Straight-line rim decorations become prevalent.

These pots, with nodes punched from the inside around the shoulder, and with distinctive rim decoration and zoned stamped decoration on the body, are in northern Colombia and in southern Panama about the beginning of the Christian Era. Some centuries later they appear in highland Colombia decorated with several rows of nodes on the shoulders made with a pencil-size stick. Zoned crosshatching is one of the body decorations.

No precisely comparable vessel shape is known in Mesoamerica. However, this form appears about 1200 B.C. in the Lower Mississippi Valley, where it has lightly notched lips, folded rims, and the rim area is bordered by a row of nodes punched from the interior with a small stick. Rare body decoration is crude: unzoned rocker stamping, punctations, or scratchy straight-line incising. The body is slightly elongated toward the base, which is often provided with four small, solid feet. This form seems to have diffused up the Mississippi Valley to the Illinois area where it was strongly modified by the Woodland amphora shape. After 100 B.C. the Classic Hopewell pot is widely spread in the eastern United States. This is small, has globular body or flat base sometimes provided with four feet, and cambered rim decorated with fine straight-line motifs. Body decorations are frequently zoned, rocker stamped, bird motifs. This form persisted in the Caddoan region of Louisiana and Arkansas until historic times, and the small Mississippian pot with handles also may be related to this tradition.

In its southward diffusion, this form reached only to the central part of the north coast of Peru where it was associated with the black and molded ware of the Tiahuanaco Phase.

Paddle-stamped Woodland Amphora

CHART 12

By 1000 B.C. a contrasting variety of ceramic, to which Ritchie (1965, pp. 192–193) has given the name "Vinette I Ware," was being manufactured in New York State near the Great Lakes. This is described by Ritchie (1946, pp. 13–16) as "a moderately thick, coarse to medium grit-tempered, gray to black, or buff colored ware, derived from fairly large, unornamented, straight-sided, conoidal-based vessels, cord or fabric roughened over the entire surface, both outside and inside" (chart 12–5). Later he noted that the cordmarks ran in various directions on the exterior with a tendency toward the vertical; on the interior they were always horizontal. Lips were rounded and sometimes pointed, and coil-line breaks were common. Similar ware has been found westward to Minnesota and into New England (Griffin, 1964, pp. 235–236).

This "bag-shaped," conoidal-base vessel with surfaces textured from malleation with a cord- or textile-wrapped paddle, has no resemblances in either shape or surface finish to anything in the early Mesoamerican or South American Formative. It resembles very closely, however, the cordmarked ceramic that is found across northern Asia. This was first pointed out by McKern (1937), and the possibility of the diffusion of this Woodland ceramic across the Bering Strait has been more recently examined by Spaulding (1946) and Tolstoy (1953, 1958a). In his 1953 article, Tolstoy points out that textured-surfaced ceramics, including cordmarking, fabric marking, cord impressing, dentate stamping, shell stamping, plain and dentate rocker stamping, and combing are present in north central Siberia before 2000 B.C., and the distribution extends into Japan and the Kuriles. The conoidal-base amphora form is associated in the Lena River Basin, in Japan, and possibly in Kamchatka. These decorative techniques are also distributed westward into European Russia.

The possibility that this complex of textured-surface and dentate-stamped pottery of the Siberian Neolithic entered North America by way of the Bering Strait and gave rise to the highly similar early Woodland ceramics of the Great Lakes region, has interested archeologists for the last three decades. The obvious and apparently logical possibility that all New World ceramics originated from this diffusion has also been considered.

With the increased availability of radiocarbon dates, however, this theory has become much less attractive. One obstacle is the tremendous overland distance between the regions where the similar complexes are found in Siberia and the Great Lakes. Despite a reasonable amount of survey, only one geographically limited group of ceramics has been found between. This is on the Bering Sea and Arctic coasts of Alaska, where the earliest pottery has a flat-base jar form decorated with linear and check stamping applied with paddles (Griffin and Wilmeth, in Giddings, 1964, pp. 271–303). This pottery is not dated earlier than 500 B.C., too recent to be in the direct line of transmission.

Despite this conspicuous gap in our current knowledge, there still exists a possibility that at least the conoidal-base amphora form with paddle-malleated surfaces may have diffused across the Bering Strait from northern Siberia, and may have been made in very small quantities by the hunting tribes of the Canadian forests before 1000 B.C. This possibility is enhanced by two considerations: (1) No possible ancestral forms are known in the ceramics that date before 1000 B.C. anywhere south of the Great Lakes region. (2) Between 1000 B.C. and A.D. 500, this form and surface finish move slowly southward in North America, probably awakened and stimulated by the introduction of maize agriculture. They reached the Lower Mississippi Valley in a very weak form at the end of the Marksville Phase, about A.D. 400 (chart 12–26). The appearance on the coast of Georgia and in the Mobile Bay region seems to have been somewhat earlier, at the beginning of the Deptford Phase, about 500 B.C. (chart 12, 14–15, –21). At first the paddles were carved with check stamp patterns; cord-wrapped paddling followed very soon. Curvilinear pattern paddle stamping began shortly after A.D. 1 in the Swift Creek Phase.

The pointed-base amphora with cordmarked surface finish remained the dominant vessel form about the Great Lakes and in the Midwest until the native ceramic tradition ended in the seventeenth and eighteenth centuries of this era. There were, however, two intrusions of a basically plain ware and incised decorated tradition from the south which interrupted this continuity. The last was the spread of the Mississippian culture beginning at about A.D. 900. The earlier interruption began about 600 B.C. and lasted until the decline of the Hopewell culture, A.D. 300–400. This earlier intrusion, with which we are primarily concerned here, can be noted in the Baumer (Cole, et al., 1951, pp. 184ff), Black Sands (Cole and Deuel, 1937, pp. 199ff), Morton (ibid.), and Hopewellian Phases of Illinois and Wisconsin; and in the Adena and Hopewell Phases of Kentucky, Ohio, West Virginia, and Michigan. Ceramic traits that appear in the Upper Mississippi and Ohio

Valleys at this time include simple incised designs that tend to be confined to the rim area and may be placed over paddle-malleated surfaces as in Black Sands: linear stamping, rocker stamping, and, a few centuries before and after A.D. 1, the zoned rocker stamped designs of Classic Hopewell. Plain surfaces are prominent in early Adena pottery and the few incised designs are related to those of the earlier Orange Incised decorations of Florida (Griffin, in Webb and Snow, 1945, pp. 220–246). Folded rims, lightly nicked lips, and a row of nodes formed below the rim area by punching from the vessel interior with a small stick are particularly common in Illinois shortly after 500 B.C. Also a part of this general complex are small, flat bases, too small to appear practical, with a projecting heel. Sometimes these bases have four short feet.

M. D. Coe (1961, pp. 58–59, fig. 49) found cord- and fabric-marked pottery in the Ocós Phase of the Pacific coast of Guatemala. In the La Victoria paper, he seriously considered the possibility of influence from the North American Woodland tradition. At the present time, however, Coe (personal communication) considers this possibility as very unlikely because Ocós dates too early, the amphora vessel form is not found, and the impressions are much too delicate for direct comparison.

Griffin and Krieger (1947) describe cordmarked ceramics in the Valley of Mexico. These date in Aztec times, so that the possibility of late influence from the southeastern United States cannot be ruled out.

Tecomate or Neckless Jar

CHART 12

The large globular or egg-shaped neckless jar that is so prominent in the early ceramic complexes of Mesoamerica, where it is called a "tecomate," is entirely missing in the Valdivia and Machalilla Phases of Ecuador, the Puerto Hormiga Phase of northern Colombia, and the early fiber-tempered complexes of the southeastern United States. The earliest appearance of this form seems to be in high-land Mexico, where small rather crude stone vessels with incurving upper walls are in the Tehuacán sequence at 5000 B.C. (chart 12–41). After 2300 B.C. when ceramics first appear in the Purrón Phase, this form is made in pottery (chart 12–40), a rather soft crumbly ware, heavily tempered with grit, that twenty years ago might well have been interpreted as yet another example of the independent invention of ceramics. This tecomate shape was accompanied by flat-base pans, also apparently shaped in imitation of stone forms (MacNeish, 1964; M. D. Coe,

1963, p. 32). The fourth form of the early stone vessels in the Tehuacán sequence is the simple bowl.

Brush (1965) reports "sharply incurved neckless pots" as a shape of the early ceramics from Puerto Marquez on the Pacific coast of Mexico near Acapulco. The close resemblance of this "Pox pottery" to MacNeish's Purrón Phase ceramics was noted. A radiocarbon date from the preceramic levels of this site is 2940 ±130 B.C. Carbon from the lowest ceramic level dates 2440 ±140 B.C.

By 1500 B.C. the tecomate was the most popular form in the Tehuacán sequence. It had increased in size, was well made, and had rather thin walls and lips that were gracefully reinforced by adding clay on the interior to form what is called a "comma-shaped lip." A few had dentate rocker stamping about the rim at about 1200 B.C., and still fewer were painted with bands of specular red hematite encircling the mouth.

Similar tecomates formed 19 percent of the vessel shapes from Pit 50, Chiapa de Corzo (chart 12–42; Dixon, 1959, pp. 4–5, figs. 1, 52). This represents Chiapa I in the southern Mexico sequence, estimated to have a beginning date of 1400 B.C. Two-thirds of the vessels have decoration around the neck: fingernail punctations, brushing, incising, or rocker stamping. Twenty percent also have a band of red slip. Vessel walls are thin, and paste is brown to reddish brown in color, tempered with grains of white quartz. The tecomate form disappears at the end of Chiapa II, about 500 B.C.

MacNeish and Peterson (1962, pp. 30–33, table 9) also found the tecomate to be the earliest popular vessel form in the Santa Marta Rock Shelter in the state of Chiapas. Brushed surfaces are very common, and include crosshatched and curving pattern brushing. There is usually an exterior smoothed band encircling the vessel mouth, which occasionally was painted with specular red hematite or a thin white wash. Incising, grooving, and fingernail punctation are common in this rim area. One rim sherd has a row of nodes raised by punching from the interior with a small stick.

Tolstoy, who is now working on Formative in the Valley of Mexico, points out that large tecomates (at least 35 cm. in diameter) occur in Early and Middle Zacatenco (see Vaillant, 1930, p. 31, pls. 1n, 3z), El Arbolillo (see Vaillant, 1935, p. 221), and in the Tlatilco refuse (chart 12, 37–38; see Piña Chán, 1958, vol. 1, pp. 35–36, figs. 8f, g, r, 9c).

From his own excavations at El Arbolillo, Tolstoy states that tecomates form between 7 and 20 percent of the recognizable vessel forms in material corresponding to Vaillant's Bay and Dark Brown wares. They form minor percentages in the other monochrome wares. They are also in the Late Pre-Classic at Tlapacoya and Ticomán, where they constitute 11 to 14 percent of the Bay ware vessels. About one quarter of the vessel rims at El Arbolillo have the exterior reinforced collars of the variety illustrated by Vaillant (1935); others have rounded lips, but the "comma" shape is not usual. With this assurance, a drawing of a typical tecomate has been placed in the Valley of Mexico column (chart 12–37).

From the El Trapiche and Chalahuites sites near Zempoala on the central Veracruz coast, García Payón (1966) describes large, typical Formative tecomates in his "Café o Bayo" ware (chart 12–36; op. cit., p. 103, pl. 41), and red slipped over "Café o Bayo" (op. cit., p. 99, pl. 37). This form was also found with rocker stamped decoration bordering the mouth opening (op. cit., pp. 18–21, pl. 46). From re-excavations in the Chalahuites and Limoncito sites, Medellín, Wallrath, and the writer have recovered additional samples of this material and have determined that the typical Formative tecomate disappears at the beginning of the Remojadas Inferior Phase, or about 400 B.C. The majority of these neckless jars have the added thickness of the rim on the interior of the vessel mouth. On the central Veracruz coast, the sequence in surface finish and decoration parallels that in southern Mexico. The earlier examples have rough or brushed surfaces and rocker stamped decoration, while the later ones have fairly well-polished surfaces on which the polishing tracks show. The walls of these vessels appear to become thicker with time, and the paste is usually brown in color with white sand inclusions.

The recently discovered San Lorenzo Phase of southern Veracruz (1200–900 B.C.) has large striated or brushed tecomates, which frequently have a row of nodes about the mouth pushed out with the fingers from the interior (M.D. Coe, 1966). They are also sometimes decorated with a band of red slip around the mouth and occasionally with plain rocker stamping.

From La Venta, Drucker (1952, p. 117, fig. 39a) describes neckless jar forms that are strongly constricted toward the mouth:

> The rims continue the line of the walls on the exterior; on the inside they are usually heavily thickened, often twice the thickness of the wall in cross section. The maximum thickness is usually near the lip, tapering away in the distance of 3 to 5 cm. into the apparently fairly even wall width. Occasional rims are modified by flattening or beveling off the lip to produce a horizontal edge, but most of them round off to a blunt nearly symmetrical lip. Exterior surfaces are usually smoothed; interiors are rough from a short distance below the rim, work marks being very visible.

Rim diameters are described as ranging from 12 to 30 cm., with an average of about 22 cm. Incised

decorations of encircling lines are found, and handles are described and illustrated for this form. Handles are probably quite late, for they are also found at Tres Zapotes (Drucker, 1943a, fig. 27c) where the large tecomate form seems to be disappearing.

In the Soconusco on the Pacific coast of Guatemala, the tecomate form is found with earliest known ceramics, the Barra Phase, beginning at about 1600 B.C. (chart 12–43). By the time of the Ocós Phase (1400–1200 B.C.), M. D. Coe (1961, p. 48) notes that the neckless jar was a very popular form. The vessel walls were thin, the paste hard and compact, and in general technically superior to ceramics of the later phases. A variety of decoration was found on this vessel form and usually was zoned between wide incised lines that formed curving motifs. Roughening techniques included a variety of dentate stamping, cord-marking, fabric marking, punctating, and drag-and-jab punctating. Coe and Flannery (1967, fig. 8) diagram the changes in the decorated bands around the opening of these vessels through the Cuadros, Jocotal, and Conchas Phases. Brushing, punctating, fillet bands, and zoned red-and-white painting mark the later phases. The tecomate form disappears in the Conchas II Phase, about 500 B.C.

M. D. Coe (1961, p. 127) in the comparative section of his La Victoria paper, points out that Strong, Kidder, and Paul (1938, pl. 9) illustrate neckless jars from the Ulua River Valley in Honduras which closely resemble the forms found in Ocós and Chiapa I and II. Coe suggests that tecomates may be earlier than the painted pottery which the authors thought to be associated.

Neckless jars occur in the Monagrillo Phase of Panama, where Willey and McGimsey (1954, p. 61, fig. 9a–k) list them as Form 2. Judging from illustrations, the lips are not thickened in the typical "comma-shape" that characterizes this vessel in Mesoamerica and Peru. A small proportion have incised decoration (Monagrillo Incised) about the mouth opening, and some have red slip (Monagrillo Red). Willey and McGimsey (op. cit., p. 63) note that this form occurs in the thin, yellow ware with a better surface finish that tended to be clustered toward the base of their excavations and continues on into the thicker, coarser, Monagrillo Plain ware that formed the bulk of the pottery recovered.

Among the few and simple vessel forms of the Barlovento Phase on the north coast of Colombia, Reichel-Dolmatoff (1955, pp. 254–257, pls. 3–5) describes large and middle-sized vessels, approximately globular, subglobular, and semispherical, with rounded bases (chart 12–47). Although vessel walls are not very thick, averaging 8 mm., this ware was carelessly manufactured, roughly smoothed with a spatula or brush, and fired in an oxidizing atmosphere. Lips are rounded. A few have red slip daubed on in spots, but whether these are designs seems uncertain. Less than 4 percent of all sherds were decorated with a band of broad-line incised decoration that encircles the vessel mouth. Motifs are principally curvilinear, and punctations are employed to fill backgrounds. Small circles and dots are both impressed and drawn freehand.

Although this neckless jar form apparently cannot be traced through the succeeding Malambo Phase on the Caribbean coast, it does continue to be made in the central highlands of Colombia until a fairly late date (Ford, 1944, p. 21, fig. 3). As in the Peruvian sequence, the walls become thicker, the vessels larger, apparently less egg-shaped, and are globular. These jars sometimes were used as burial urns.

The large neckless jar seems to be entirely missing from the Ecuadorian sequence, not only from the Formative phases that date from 3000 to 1500 B.C., but from the later cultures as well. This is rather remarkable for this shape appears at the beginning of the Kotosh sequence in the Peruvian highlands (chart 12–55; Izumi and Sono, 1963, fig. 46) a few hundred kilometers southward. As Meggers and Evans have pointed out (1964, p. 6, fig. 1), the early tecomates of Kotosh more nearly resemble those of the Pre-Classic or Formative in Chiapas in southern Mexico than they do anything in the intervening region. Resemblances are found in the hard, sand tempered brown paste; the surface finishing which consists of scraping, then careless polishing so that the polished tracks of the tool are slightly separated and the scraped surface shows between them; the remarkable thinness of the walls considering the sizes of the vessels (25 to 60 cm. in diameter), and the characteristic thickened lips. Some of the decoration occasionally found around the mouths of these vessels in both regions consists of looped or arched incised lines, although somewhat more elaborate in the Andean region than in Mesoamerica (Meggers and Evans, 1964). In both regions there appears to be a tendency for these brushed, scraped, and decorated vessels to be early (ca. 1500–1000 B.C.), while the later vessels of this class (ca. 1000–500 B.C.) are unornamented and polished.

As in the earliest known ceramic complex of Mexico, the tecomate form in Peru is a substantial percentage of the vessel shapes. At Kotosh where this is the principal shape of Kotosh Polished Brown (Izumi and Sono, 1963, p. 122), the precise frequencies are not stated but, judging from illustrations, they are not low. Colors range from brownish black to reddish brown. A variety of wide-line incised and circle-and-dot decorations were placed in bands around the mouth, but in the Kotosh Chavín Phase decoration disappears. Vessel walls are thin in early examples, and lips were reinforced in characteristic comma-shaped fashion. These vessels measure up to 60 cm. in diameter. The egg-shaped body form of early periods becomes globular in the Sajara-patac Phase and incised decoration again appears.

On the coast at Ancón, Willey and Corbett (1954, p. 55) state that the "seed bowl" with comma lip is the most popular form. In Virú Valley, the earliest tecomates in the Guañape Phase are thin and do not have thickened lips (chart 12–57). By 500 B.C., large tecomates comprise between 30 and 40 percent of identifiable forms (chart 12–56; Ford, 1949, fig. 6; Strong and Evans, 1952, pp. 254ff, figs. 45–55). It is the dominant shape of Huacapongo Polished Plain and has thin side walls, comma lip, and scraped exterior walls with scraping marks partially obliterated by careless striated polishing. Paste color ranges from black to brown and abundant white quartz grains are used for tempering. Decoration is absent. Larco Hoyle (1941, fig. 135) illustrates a stone vessel of tecomate shape from the Cupisnique Phase of Chicama Valley.

The neckless jar remains a very popular form on the north Peruvian coast, where it runs through Chimú times. During the Mochica Phase, about A.D. 500, the paste of these vessels begins to be tempered with large grit and gravel rather than fine sand, is softer, and vessel walls are much thicker. Surfaces are no longer polished, vessels are larger, become globular rather than egg-shaped, and some have rims reinforced with exterior-applied flat strips that are occasionally decorated with simple incising. In Chimú times these vessels are sometimes found buried in the floors of houses, evidently to serve as cisterns or storage bins (Strong and Evans, 1952, pp. 271–272, fig. 42).

The large, neckless jar, so popular in the Formative phases to the south, is not a prominent form in the eastern United States, as a look at the illustrations of Griffin's (ed., 1952) study of the archeology of this region will show. As a matter of fact, it is known only from the Gulf coast and in a limited range of both time and geography. Earliest are four rim sherds in the Alexander collection from the Poverty Point site in Louisiana (chart 12–31). One of these is made of a much harder paste than the other pottery of the Poverty Point complex. It has the typical "comma-shaped" rim thickened on the inside; the mouth diameter is 15 cm. If the vessel was globular, it was about 40 cm. in diameter. The others are of typical crude paste. This collection also contains a fragment of a neckless jar made of fine grain sandstone (chart

12–33), nicely finished, and resembling the much earlier stone jars of MacNeish's Tehuacán sequence.

The notable appearance of the large, neckless jar form on the Gulf coast is after 500 B.C. The greatest number in the Florida State Museum collections date in St. Johns Ia Period (chart 12–18), in the northern one-third of the Florida Peninsula. The vessels are made of soft St. Johns temperless paste, but walls are rather thin (about 5 mm.) for vessel size. Mouth diameter ranges from 10 to 18 cm., while bodies vary from 30 to 45 cm. Bodies are globular and frequently covered with red slip, either in a broad band around the mouth or all over the vessel. One tecomate in the Florida State Museum collection has large bulges pushed out with fingers just below the band of mouth decoration, a practice more common in the Mesoamerican Formative. Lips are thin and infrequently have the "comma" profile so common to the south. Instead, there is often a thin broad exterior rim strap that is sometimes decorated with excised motifs. Some of the excised areas cut through red slip applied to the jar surface, others have red pigment rubbed into the excised areas. The technique of excising also has a pan-American distribution and will be discussed later (see pp. 131–133).

In his study of the Florida Gulf coast, Willey (1949a, pp. 496–498) describes a "flattened-globular bowl" and lists it as common. Moore's illustrations (1901, 1902, 1903) show a number of examples and the shape lasts through both early and late phases of the Weeden Island complexes, A.D. 400–800 (chart 12–20, –22). The vessels are frequently decorated on the shoulders with the typical scroll and meanders of the time. However, these later neckless jars appear to be smaller than is typical both for the St. Johns Ia Phase (400–1 B.C.) in the northern part of the Florida Peninsula, and for the Mesoamerican and South American Formative. In the Florida State Museum collections, however, there are four large, neckless jars with Weeden Island type decorations on the shoulder that have diameters between 40 and 45 cm. All come from a burial mound on the Gulf coast at the base of the Florida Peninsula. The large, neckless jar is unknown from other parts of the eastern United States, and in Florida decreases markedly in size after A.D. 500.

Summary

The large neckless jar, or tecomate, is not found in early Formative ceramics in northern South America. Like the flat-base pan it seems to have been copied from stone prototypes in the highlands of Mexico. With remarkably little change in shape, size, wall thinness, quartz tempering, reddish brown color, and scraping and careless polishing of exterior surface, it seems to have diffused to Peru shortly before 1500 B.C. Tecomates from early phases in Panama and Colombia are slightly different in details of construction. In both the Andean and Mesoamerican regions, there is a tendency for the early examples to bear decoration in a band around the mouth opening. This form substantially ends in Mesoamerica about A.D. 1, but continues in the Andean regions as a larger, thicker, and more globular jar.

Large tecomates are a minor element of the Poverty Point complex of the Lower Mississippi Valley, and diffused into a very limited area in Florida about 500 B.C. Here, they have the characteristic thinness of the vessel wall, but not the paste features and rarely the "comma-shaped" lip. The band of decoration about the mouth opening at first consists of excised designs and later of typical Weeden Island scroll motifs. After A.D. 600–700 the neckless jars on the Florida coast are of small size. Over this entire range, there is a tendency for either unthickened or comma-shaped lips to be early, and later for the rim to be reinforced with a broad exterior strap.

Flat-base Stone Bowl

CHART 13

The most ancient stone vessels that have been dated with some certainty in the Americas are in the highlands of central Mexico. In the Tehuacán sequence developed by MacNeish (1961, fig. 15), they date to 5000 B.C. (chart 13–25). These vessels have three forms: one is a deep, small-mouth jar, which seems to give rise to the large, neckless jar or tecomate so popular in early ceramic phases in Mesoamerica. The second is the round-base simple bowl. The third is a small, flat-base pan or bowl of stone that begins at 2500 B.C. and seems to be the model for the pottery pan-shaped vessels, also popular in this same region before and after 1000 B.C. As mentioned elsewhere, neither the neckless jar nor the flat-base pan are found in the early ceramics of northern South America.

In the early phases, the stone containers of the Tehuacán sequence are thick and somewhat crude, and there is some question as to whether they functioned as containers or actually were stone mortars to be used with the accompanying bell-shaped pestles. During the Coxcatlán Phase (5200–3400 B.C.), however, these items were better made, had thinner walls, were of hard, fine-grain stone, and almost certainly were containers (MacNeish, 1961, p. 26; 1964, pp. 533–535). The geographical range of these stone containers in preceramic times in Mesoamerica is somewhat uncertain, probably due to the limited number of excavations that have yielded material of this time level. They were not found in MacNeish and Peterson's (1962) excavations in the Santa Marta Rock Shelter in Chiapas, nor do they appear in MacNeish's cave work in Tamaulipas (MacNeish, 1947).

The distinction between well-made stone mortars and bowls manufactured to be used as containers is difficult in many instances. Lorenzo (1965, pp. 38–39) describes well-made circular, oval, and rectangular stone containers of about 25 cm. in diameter from excavations at the Tlatilco site as mortars. None seem to have the flat-base pan form that is found elsewhere in the Formative. A small bowl illustrated by Lorenzo (op. cit., fig. 48) is lenticular in form. Others are rectangular and have four feet.

Two fragments of well-made stone bowls with flat bases and outslanting low walls are described by García Payón (1966, pp. 175–176, pl. 85, 5–6) from the El Trapiche site of coastal Veracruz (900–400 B.C.). Both are of hard stone. The better polished example is 18.9 cm. in diameter and has a height of 4 cm. There is an incised line inside the lip. The other bowl, made of basalt, has a diameter of about 14 cm. García Payón calls attention to the similarity of these bowls to the flat-base pan ceramic that is found so abundantly in these same levels. The excavations by Medellín, Wallrath, and the writer in refuse deposits in the vicinity of García Payón's cuts, have yielded additional examples that conform very well to the description given above.

Fragments of stone bowls are reported by Weiant (1943, pp. 118–119, figs. 6, 12, pl. 66) from the Ranchito group of mounds at Tres Zapotes in Veracruz (chart 13–12). One is described as a "flowerpot" with flat base and outward flaring sides; another a flat-bottom bowl with a lug at either end; the third a flat oval dish. Stone bowls are also found in the San Lorenzo Phase (M. D. Coe, personal communication).

From Pit 50 at Chiapa de Corzo (Chiapa I), Dixon (1959, fig. 53f) illustrates a crudely pecked stone container that does not compare in finish or definite shape with the stone bowls described in the foregoing.

In the Soconusco sequence on the coast of Guatemala, M. D. Coe (1961, pp. 101–102, figs. 41a–b, 51q–r) illustrates well-made "stone bowls or mortars" from the Ocós Phase (chart 13–35). One is round, with a diameter of 18 cm. and 2 cm. thick. It is made of a fine-grain, gray-buff stone and while the interior is somewhat rough, the exterior is polished. The other is oblong in form and has low walls that curve up from a flat base. The width is 11.5 cm. and side walls are 4.6 cm. high. It too shows polishing. Bowls (or mortars) in the Conchas Phase are made of granite or tufa, and have bottoms somewhat thicker than in the Ocós Phase (op. cit., p. 106, figs. 42e–g, 61t). Diameters range from 18 to 32 cm.; heights about 6 cm. Most are polished on the interior.

At the Monagrillo site in Panama, Willey and McGimsey (1954, p. 74, fig. 12k) found a small bowl 5 cm. in diameter made of yellow siltstone. This fragment bore an incised decoration of curvilinear scrolls with the lines terminating in round dots and a triangular excised area, identical to the decoration of the accompanying ceramics.

Two fragments of well-made bowls of andesite with slightly flattened bases and curving sides are reported by Meggers, Evans, and Estrada (1965, p. 26, pl. 16a–b) from Valdivia Phase A and B on the coast of Ecuador (chart 13–44). The shape is that of a simple bowl, rather than the flat bowl with straight vertical or outslanting side walls that is the usual form in Mesoamerica and in the early ceramic levels of Peru.

Engel (1963, p. 50, fig. 145, and possibly figs. 174–175) describes and illustrates stone bowls from the preceramic constructions he excavated in the Valley of Asia on the south coast of Peru (chart 13–56). These also have the lenticular shape of the simple bowl. A radiocarbon date of 1225 ± 25 B.C. (op. cit., p. 12) for these deposits, indicates that these bowls were being made after ceramics were already established in the Peruvian highlands.

Small, well-made bowls with flat bases and vertical or outslanting sides, frequently with incised designs on the exterior of the walls, are a marker for the Chavín cultural phase both in the highlands and on the coast (chart 13–45, –49, –55). Strong and Evans (1952, p. 41) describe the undecorated fragment of a bowl made of granite-like stone that was 21 cm. in diameter at the lip. This came from Virú Valley and dates in the Guañape-Chavín Phase. Larco Hoyle (1941, figs. 129, 132–135) shows flat-base stone vessels in the form of pans, cylindrical jars, and globular jars from Cupisnique graves in Chicama.

Tello (1943, fig. 17) shows two stone vessels with flat bases and slightly outslanting walls. Both are decorated with incised designs, one of which clearly is a bird figure. One bowl comes from Nepeña Valley; the other from Santa. From the site of Chavín de Huántar, Tello (1960, pp. 300–304, figs. 126–133) describes and illustrates a series of "ceremonial mortars." These he divided into two categories: one in which hard stone is carved very realistically into bird and cat figures with the bowl in the back; and a second group comprised of flat-base pans with vertical or outslanting walls. These last are made of diorite, quartzite, andesite, and other hard stone, and often engraved with geometrical designs on the exterior walls (chart 13–54). One fragment has realistic figures of personages engraved on both exterior and interior. Additional mortars from both coastal and highland sites are illustrated by Carrión Cachot (1948, pl. 11). The simple bowl-shaped mortar that Lanning (1963a, fig. 3) found in the preceramic Piedras Gordas complex was certainly used for grinding.

In the excavations at Kotosh, Izumi and Sono (1963, p. 125, pls. 111c–4, 175–11, 11a–3, 171–16) found only three fragments of stone bowls. One of these is a footed vessel of marble, but the other two seem to be flat-base bowls with outslanting sides. They are well polished. One vessel is plain and the other has a crude human figure engraved on it.

Stone bowls, which were usually manufactured of steatite, and less frequently made of sandstone, are a common element of the Late Archaic Phase in the eastern United States. Bases are usually convex, but are also flat with the outslanting walls joining at a definite angle. Shape is circular, square, or oval, and diameter range from approximately 15 to 30 cm. Two lug handles a short distance below the rim are particularly common on the ends of the oval bowls. The frequency of occurrence of these vessels follows the axis of the Appalachian Mountains from New England to Georgia, apparently the result of the fact that steatite or "pot stone" outcrops occur in the formations of this old mountain system.

Without the benefit of much discussion, many American archeologists have assumed that the Indians of the eastern United States discovered this material and did the natural thing: they carved containers out of this fragile but fireproof "wood." Further, it has been suggested that the use of crushed steatite for tempering in the Middle Atlantic states may have been a step in the local evolution of pottery; a sort of sympathetic magic perhaps (J. L. Coe 1952; and in Griffin, 1952b, p. 305).

If this should happen not to be true, it becomes necessary to examine routes by which stone vessels might have entered eastern North America. Characteristic lamps and pots of steatite were made and used by the Eskimo and have a distribution from Greenland to the Bering Strait. This great geographical distribution, however, occurred after about A.D. 900, and apparently was a function of the spread of the Thule Phase of Eskimo culture. The source of practically all of the steatite in the Arctic seems to be in the territory of the Utkusagalik (pot place) just to the west of Hudson Bay. Steatite lamps and pots were also made by the earlier Dorset people in the central and eastern Arctic, possibly as early as 1000 B.C. Both Ritchie and Byers (Campbell, ed., 1962, pp. 98, 151) agree that differences in shape and the geographical gap make a connection between the Arctic and eastern United States traditions improbable.

If we broaden the definition to include hard stone,

the difficulty arises of distinguishing true vessels from stone mortars and lamps. Usually the mortars and lamps are relatively shallow. De Laguna (1947, pp. 221, 249–258) traces the temporal and geographical distribution of these items. The earliest occurrence of true stone vessels in the Bering Strait region seems to be in the Norton Phase, which Giddings (1964, p. 171, pl. 60, 3–6) dates a few centuries after 1000 B.C.

The use of stone to make containers of one type or another extends down the Pacific coast at least as far as Baja California. Stone mortars seem to be quite common in the California Middle Period, where they were in the process of replacing the earlier milling stones. Steatite vessels appear about the same time as ceramics on the southern California coast (2000 B.C.–A.D. 250), and apparently served similar functions. In the late prehistoric times in the vicinity of the Channel Islands, they were made in simple bowl, neckless jar, and even more complicated forms that may be copies of baskets. It seems very dubious that this California steatite industry could be directly related to that of the eastern United States.

Fragments of steatite vessels are said to be occasionally found in the so-called "Boreal Archaic" of New England at about 2000 B.C. (Griffin, 1964, p. 231). This early date may be questioned, for in the New York State sequence they mark the beginning of what Ritchie (1965, pp. 149ff) calls the "Transitional Stage" that seems to be securely dated at 1300 B.C. In North Carolina J. L. Coe (1964, p. 119) indicates that steatite vessel fragments first appear in the Savannah River occupation, for which he has a radiocarbon date of 2000 B.C. This date, however, must also be considered dubious, for the 62 steatite vessel fragments at the Gaston site actually were in ceramic-bearing levels. Coe (op. cit., pp. 112–113) concluded that they were brought upward from a lower stratum by aboriginal disturbance. Steatite vessels are not an element of the Savannah River complex as reported by Claflin (1931) and as analyzed by Fairbanks (1942). Both perforated and notched net sinkers made of steatite are found, but no containers.

Bullen (1959, pp. 43–53) presented evidence for the time placement of stone vessels in the eastern United States and concluded that the climax of manufacture centers in the centuries before and after 1200 B.C. Further, he suggests that in shape these vessels may be copies of the earlier ceramic forms rather than the reverse.

It undoubtedly is also significant that Gagliano and Saucier (1963) did not find stone vessel fragments at either of the two Poverty Point culture sites that they reported on near Lake Pontchartrain in Louisiana. Four radiocarbon dates from these sites ranged from 2490 to 1590 B.C. On the other hand steatite and sandstone vessel fragments are very common on the Poverty Point and Jaketown sites, which yielded radiocarbon dates from approximately 1200 to 400 B.C. (chart 13, 7–8; Ford and Webb, 1956, pp. 116ff). The fact that the incised lips on some of these stone vessels have the same motifs as do the lips of fiber tempered Orange Phase ceramics of the St. Johns River in Florida (chart 13–5), also appears to be significant. Bullen (1955) has demonstrated that on the St. Johns these lips are late in the phase, dating approximately 1000 B.C.

It is interesting to note that in spite of the distances between the Poverty Point site and any quarry source for steatite (or sandstone), this locality has probably yielded a greater quantity of stone vessel fragments than any other early site in the eastern United States. Webb removed 2,205 fragments from one large cache pit and collected 519 from the surface nearby. To date a total of 4,161 fragments of stone vessels has been collected and studied.

Many of the bowls are similar to the common form found up the Atlantic coast, in that they are roughly circular or oval in form with rounded bases. Some have lugs carved on the side walls just below the rim. In addition some of the fragments from Poverty Point indicate flat bases, a definite angle between base and side walls, and nearly straight walls that slope outward. This is an approach to the form usual in Mesoamerica (Ford and Webb, 1956, fig. 40). One fragment of a hard fine-grain stone and nicely finished on both surfaces, is a rim sherd of a neckless jar. Gouge marks made in the carving of the vessels are a usual feature of the Eastern steatite industry. A percentage of the fragments from Poverty Point, however, is well-smoothed on both surfaces. Although the manufacture and trade of steatite vessels seems to have substantially disappeared in the East by 500 B.C., there are a few instances of well-made vessels of hard stone in the Hopewell culture sites of Ohio. Also they occur rarely in the still later Mississippian sites, but there was no popular industry such as existed in the East at 1000 B.C.

It is very interesting that stone bowls run through the Hohokam sequence at Snaketown in southern Arizona (Gladwin, et al., 1937, p. 111, fig. 45, pls. 53–73). Early forms are a neckless jar with slightly constricted mouth, a simple bowl with rounded base, and flat-base bowls with straight slightly outslanting walls. A ring-base form is also present. Well made, but plain in the Pioneer Phase (A.D. 1–1000), they bear straight-line incised decoration in the Colonial and Sedentary Phases (after A.D. 1000), and complex effigy forms are also made. The authors of the Snaketown study are inclined to view this sequence as an indigenous development (op. cit., p. 115), but

as it repeats the Formative to Classic carved stone industry of central Mexico, it probably reflects the Mexican development.

Summary

While the lenticular or simple bowl-shaped stone vessels that are found early in the Ecuadorian and highland Peruvian sequences may really be mortars and owe their form to the convenience of adapting the shape of large boulders, it does appear that shortly before 1000 B.C. a flat-base stone bowl form with straight outslanting or nearly vertical walls diffused from Mesoamerica into Peru. Whether these were containers or were used to grind food or other materials does not obscure close resemblance in material and form.

The question of relationship of the stone bowls of the eastern United States to this same development is another matter. Material, as well as the characteristic shape, is different. The frequency of lugs in North America is another point of dissimilarity, although they have been described by Weiant (1943) from Veracruz. It is possible that the Late Archaic people of the East translated a common form of wooden container into a soft, easily carved stone. Yet the question remains of why this industry arose a few centuries before 1000 B.C., at the time stone bowls appear to have been diffusing to South America. Also why did the trait disappear a few centuries later, as many other introduced traits do?

If the appearance of this industry at this time is not coincidence, but diffusion from Mesoamerica, it is probable that stone bowls accompanied the Poverty Point group of ceramic traits. This inference is supported by chronology, abundance of the feature at the site, and the Mesoamerican-like forms of a few of the Poverty Point specimens.

Flat-base Pan

CHART 13

Large, pan-shaped pottery vessels with flat bases, walls that are relatively low in proportion to vessel diameter and rise from the vase at a sharp angle slanting slightly outward, are not known from the Ecuadorian sequence. They are, however, a very prominent form at the beginning of each of the older Mesoamerican chronologies, with the possible exception of the Valley of Mexico. In the Chiapa I Phase (1400–800 B.C.) in southern Mexico, for example, variations of this pan form comprise over 40 percent of all vessel shapes (Dixon, 1959, table 1, p. 7, fig. 1). In the Tehuacán sequence in the central highlands of Mexico, MacNeish (1964) has an excellent series of radiocarbon dates indicating that the Purrón Phase, in which the earliest ceramics are found, begins at approximately 2300 B.C. Here, crude, undecorated vessels have only four shapes: simple bowl, a small, wide-mouth olla, the tecomate, and the flat-base pan (chart 13–24).

In discussing the tecomate or neckless jar form above, it has been suggested that the shape in clay was copied from the earlier stone form, which goes back to approximately 5000 B.C. in the Tehuacán sequence. A similar origin is suggested for the flat-base pan, for there are also stone prototypes going back an equal length of time (MacNeish, 1961, fig. 15). Transfer of these two shapes from stone to ceramic in highland Mexico at 2300 B.C., would account for the absence of both shapes from the earlier cultural phases of northern South America. The latter include Valdivia (3000–1500 B.C.), Machalilla (2000–1500 B.C.), and Puerto Hormiga (3000–2000 B.C.).

The importance of the flat-base pan in the early portion of the Mesoamerican Formative culture history has not gone unnoticed by specialists in the area. Wauchope (1950, p. 230) unfortunately groups it with convex and concave-base composite silhouette bowls and so loses most of its value for comparison. MacNeish (1954, pp. 626–627) divides these vessels into two groups: "Flaring-sided, flat-bottom bowls," and "outsloping straight-sided flat-bottom bowls or dishes." The principal difference seems to be that the former group has slightly outcurved walls, and this distinction has not been maintained here. He traces the presence of this form from the Huasteca region to the Maya area, and shows it to be one of the earliest popular shapes. Its relative scarcity in the Valley of Mexico sequence is noted. There is some new information available since the date of MacNeish's paper, prominent among which is his new sequence in the Tehuacán Valley (in Byers, ed., 1967–).

A chronological graph of vessel shapes provided by MacNeish in advance of publication, shows the flat-base pan as being made in Tehuacán Valley from the earliest appearance of ceramics at 2300 B.C. to approximately A.D. 700. After the beginning of the Christian Era, however, these pans are small and often have feet. MacNeish also informs me that thickened and outflared decorated lips on this form begin about 900 B.C.

In the Ocós Phase (1400–1200 B.C.), M.D. Coe (1961, p. 48, figs. 18–20, 22p) refers to this as a flat-bottom dish, and describes and illustrates the shape for most of the pottery types present at that time (chart 13–36). It is found in brown unpolished ware, polished red, specular red, polished buff, and black ware. Most of these vessels are burnished on all surfaces

except undernearth the flat base. These pans are rather large, rim diameters varying from 20 to 35 cm. Beveled lips are common and some examples have simple crosshatched incised designs on the exterior of the walls, and panels of iridescent paint on the interior.

The flat-base pan form continues on through the Cuadros, Jocotal, and Conchas Phases (chart 13–34; Coe and Flannery, 1967, fig. 8). The "double-line break" design is found on the side walls between 1000 and 800 B.C., and in Conchas II (500–300 B.C.), everted lips with wide-line incised decoration and lip flanges occur. These are particularly characteristic of Conchas Orange.

Another feature at this time on the Pacific coast of Guatemala and the Veracruz coast of Mexico is the appearance of very low side walls, converting the bowl into a plate with upturned edge.

Flat-base pans apparently disappear in the Soconusco region at the beginning of the Crucero Phase (300 B.C.), their probable function as food serving dishes being taken over by composite silhouette bowls and bowls with flat bases but with low vertical side walls that round into the base (M. D. Coe, 1961, fig. 37b, f). The latter are here discussed as "simple bowls with flat bases." These same two forms also appear to replace the flat-base pan on the Gulf coast of Veracruz, apparently at about the same time.

"Vertical and flaring wall bowl" is the term used by Dixon (1959, pp. 4–5) in describing the Chiapa I (1400–800 B.C.) pottery from strata cuts at the site of Chiapa de Corzo (chart 13, 26–30). A substantial percentage of these pans were made of a white paste or are white slipped ware. Red slip was also employed. Lowe has indicated verbally that the form disappeared in Chiapa VI, as is shown on the chart. At this time (100–1 B.C.) the bowls from caches in Chiapa de Corzo Mound 17 are polished brown ware and either have flat bases with gently curving side walls, or composite silhouette shapes (Lowe, 1962, fig. 34). Evidently the sequence in popularity of the forms is very similar to that on the Pacific coast of Guatemala and the Gulf coast of Veracruz.

Peterson (1963, pp. 30–40) discusses the evolution of thickened lips, everted rims, and labial flanges in some detail. These rims are on flat-base pans, which are highly polished with a "waxy" feel from Periods III–V (550–100 B.C.). Often white or red-and-white bichrome in Period II (800–550 B.C.), Period III pans are monochrome and vary in color from midnight blue through shades of red and orange to light brown. Mottled surfaces are characteristic.

Lips have polished grooves numbering three to six all through the sequence, with a tendency toward the larger numbers in the older phases. Incising and engraved designs on these lips are confined to Phases III and IV (550–250 B.C.). These designs are often rather elaborate (op. cit., figs. 33–36). Edge scalloping and low relief modeling of frogs are rare and accompany the incised designs. Labial flanges attached just below the lip are common in Phases V–VI (250–1 B.C.), and frequently have an orange-colored vitreous slip.

The flat-base pan is an early dominant form in the Olmec region of southern Veracruz and Tabasco (chart 13–9, –11, –14, –16). The simple bowl is the only accompanying form that could have been used for food service in the San Lorenzo Phase (1200–900 B.C.). Typically this ware has a granular paste, in which white quartzite grain particles contrast with the dark brown color. Bases are flat and the low side walls form a sharp angle and slant slightly outward. Bottoms are frequently thinner than side walls, a peculiar feature for vessels with diameters ranging from 20–45 cm.

At La Venta, Drucker (1952, pp. 109–110) describes this pan as "Flat-bottomed dishes with flaring sides." He says that this was the most abundant vessel shape in the local wares: coarse white, coarse red, brown lacquer, and the "fine-paste" wares that occurred in orange, buff, gray, and black colors. Rim diameters range from 18 to 38 cm., walls are outslanted forming an angle of 110 to 130 degrees with the flat base, and vary from 4 to 7.5 cm. in height. No feet were found on this shape. Drucker says, "It is quite noticeable that many of the bases are thinner than the sides they support." This is a very consistent feature of these pans.

Polishing is described as covering both interior and exterior. That may be true for the La Venta site, but the pans from the El Trapiche and Chalahuites sites in the central coast of Veracruz are not polished beneath the base. Typically they are what has been described as streak-polished, brown in color with streaks of red that may have been produced by sprinkling the surface with coloring matter during the polishing process.

In both regions direct lips and side walls tapering from base to lip are most common. There are also a fair number of rims that increase in thickness toward the lip. The lips are flattened and are decorated (chart 13–13). This usually consists of fine engraved lines drawn parallel encircling the lip, or simple combinations of straight lines, crosshatching, etc. Red pigment was rubbed into the lines. Decoration is sometimes discontinuous, that is, lips will be crosshatched for 2 or 3 cm. and then have a plain area of equal length, followed by another short, decorated area. A few lips are everted and have polished wide shallow grooves. Occasionally the "double-line break"

motif is used on the lips: a pair of parallel incised lines that turn at intervals so that they run off the vessel lip.

At the Tres Zapotes site (400–1 B.C.) the flat-base pan form continues to be made of wares similar to those of La Venta, and flat, everted lips, sometimes scalloped and bearing decoration, become more abundant (Drucker, 1943a, pp. 48, 61,). Flanges below the lip are also present. Some of the bowls have three flat slab legs. The polychrome painting and bulbous legs with rattles in them that are found on some flat-base pan forms at Tres Zapotes almost certainly date at the beginning of the Classic Period and cannot be earlier than 100 B.C.

Vaillant's report on the ceramics of El Arbolillo does not make clear the frequency of the large, flat-base form. If it is present to any extent, it probably was included under the term "cajete" in the "Bay ware bowls" (Vaillant, 1935, pp. 219–222, table 17). He says (op. cit., p. 221), "Flare rim cajetes tend to mass more heavily in El Arbolillo I, but this numerical preponderance has no true diagnostic utility. . . . Flat-rim cajetes, which at Zacatenco showed a tendency to increase at the close of the Middle Period, are more consistent in their appearance during El Arbolillo II." These observations seem credible for they parallel tendencies in the flat-base pans of the Veracruz coast. The large pans are not mentioned in either Porter's (1953) or Piña Chán's (1958) description of the ceramics from the Tlatilco Cemetery site. Small bowls of this form however, are fairly common in the illustrations of both these papers (charts 13–19, –21.) The wares are described by Piña Chán as "Dark Coffee," "Black Polished," "Obscure Coffee," "White Polished," "Clear Coffee," and "Red Polished Interior." Apparently a number of the small pans bear wide-line incised, rocker stamped, and excised designs on the outer walls (Porter, 1953, figs. 7–10; pls. 6c, e–t, 11e, g–h; 12b, e; Piña Chán, 1958, vol. 1, figs. 33, 34c, h, 35n, p, r, z, a', c', 37d, m, n, 38f, 39x, 40w, 41d, k, 45y, 46d, j). As will be pointed out later, this small version of pan with side wall decoration is found early in the Peruvian sequences.

The flat-base pan appears to be missing from the Colombian and Ecuadorian chronologies. It occurs in both the highland and coastal sequences in Peru, although in both instances diameter is considerably smaller than usual in Mesoamerica. In the Kotosh column it runs from about 1200 B.C. (Kotosh Kotosh Phase) through the Chavín and Sajara-patac Phases, and ends with the San Blas Phase (A.D. 1; Izumi and Sono, 1963, fig. 46, pls. 40a, 43b, 47a–f). The bowls are 15 to 20 cm. in diameter and usually are classified by the authors as Kotosh Well Polished or Kotosh Grooved. Tello (1960, fig. 144i) also illustrates this form from Chavín de Huántar. In the Kotosh Kotosh Phase flanges project outward a short distance below the vessel lips (chart 13–47), and these are decorated with wide-line incised designs consisting of straight lines and punctations. Straight lines at alternate angles are a popular motif (Izumi and Sono, 1963, pls. 123, 1–6; 146, 28–45).

On the Peruvian coast these small versions of the flat-base pan are usually made of a dark reddish brown to gray ware with surface finish ranging from smoothed to polished (chart 13–53). On the coast, as in the highlands, these pans grade almost imperceptibly from perfectly flat bases to bases that are gently convex. Willey and Corbett (1954, p. 53) note that bases tend to be thinner than side walls and rims. Broad-line incised decoration and the zoning of punctated, rocker-stamped, hatched, or red painted areas are fairly common on this form (op. cit. pp. 37–56; Carrión Cachot, 1948, pl. 25, 1–16). If our alignment of the Ancón Phase is correct, this form seems to start at 1500 B.C. on the coast, somewhat earlier than in the highland sequence. In the Virú Valley column on the north coast, this flat-base pan is also small, but is rarely decorated. It is most common in the Guañape Phase (850–B.C.–A.D. 100) plain types (Strong and Evans, 1952, pp. 253–259). Flat-base pans disappear from the Peruvian sequences after A.D. 1.

While these small containers in the Peruvian sequence have a generalized resemblance to the large pans that are so common early in the Mesoamerican ceramic sequences, there are quite specific resemblances in size, color, surface finish, and decorations on the side walls with the small pans that Porter (1953) and Piña Chán (1958) have described for the Tlatilco ceramics in the Valley of Mexico.

Before A.D. 1 the flat-base pan form appears only in two quite limited geographical areas in the eastern United States. Between 1600 and 400 B.C., it is the dominant form in the Orange fiber-tempered ceramic complex that is found in the deep shell middens that, until recently, stood on the shores of the St. Johns River in northeastern Florida. The Formative relationships of the Orange complex as a whole have been discussed in the foregoing pages. Also the apparent relationship of this complex to the ceramics found in deep circular middens along the Fourche Maline River in eastern Oklahoma has been cited. It is here that the second early occurrence of this vessel is found. In both regions the impression of rather crudely twined textiles is occasionally found underneath the bases of these pans.

The third occurrence of this vessel form centers in the states of Tennessee and Kentucky, and is associated with the Tennessee Cumberland variety of Late Mississippian culture with a date of approximately A.D. 1400. These large shallow pans also have textile impressions on them and undoubtedly are correctly identified as having been made for the evaporation of salt (Holmes, 1903, pp. 27–31). There appears to be no evidence of continuity between the early and late occurrences of this form, and it is doubtful that they are related.

The flat-base pan vessels of the Orange Phase are similar to those of Mesoamerica in that they are large, the bases tend to be thinner than the side walls (Sears and Griffin, 1950), and all surfaces except the underside of the base have been smoothed and often polished. A high polish was impossible to achieve on the soft, fiber tempered ware of which Orange is made, but in some instances a surprisingly well-finished surface was produced. Some Orange specimens have loose red pigment applied to the base, as do some of the pans in the Trapiche Phase of Veracruz.

Bullen (1955) has demonstrated that thickened rims with flat lips decorated with straight-line incised motifs are a late feature of the Orange flat-base pans. This tendency toward decorated lips and labial flanges is shared by the other bowl forms that existed in the centuries just before 500 B.C. all the way to central Peru. These features will be the subject of a separate section (see pp. 136–138).

Composite Silhouette Bowl

CHART 13

Aside from the flat-base pan form, the history of which has just been traced, there seem to be three basic varieties of shallow bowls. Apparently most unspecialized, and therefore perhaps least useful for our purposes, is the simple shallow bowl with convex or slightly flattened base and side walls that round up to a direct, unornamented lip. The history of this shape is more complex than might be suspected, however, and it will be outlined later (see pp. 105–109).

The second bowl shape in degree of complexity, and apparently second from the point of view of age in the Americas, is a convex-base bowl with the upper rim turned sharply inward so that a definite angle is formed between base and rim. This form appears at the beginning of the Ecuadorian sequence (3000 B.C.), but is particularly popular in Valdivia Phases B–D (Meggers, Evans, and Estrada, 1965, fig. 54, 8–11).

The more complex "composite silhouette" bowls that will be discussed here have convex bases that are occasionally flattened or more rarely dimpled. The angle between base and side walls is quite definite, the side walls rise vertically or slant outward, and rims are usually curved outward or cambered.

These bowls first appear in the Ecuadorian sequence in the Machalilla Phase where they are rare (chart 13, 42–43; op. cit., fig. 90, 9–10). Here they are associated with the much more abundant inturned rim bowls mentioned above. These latter show a variety of upper wall profiles intermediate between the inturned and cambered side wall, suggesting that the composite silhouette bowl may have developed from the slightly earlier form. Shared features of polished surfaces, engraved decorations in which the lines are filled with red pigment, and red slip tend to reinforce this possibility. Still, after 1500 B.C. the histories of the two vessel shape traditions are distinct.

The rare composite silhouette vessels in the Machalilla Phase are tan to dark brown in color, mottled by uneven firing, are tempered with white quartz, and usually have surfaces ranging from striated polished to well polished. Some have red slip. Engraved decoration is usually on the exterior of the side walls. Motifs are straight-line, crossing bands of fine lines, or triangles filled with crosshatching (op. cit., pp. 117–119, type Ayangue Incised). A few have everted lips that are lightly scalloped.

Composite silhouette vessels continue as a minority form through the Chorrera and Regional Developmental Periods of the Ecuadorian sequence (chart 13–41). In the lower levels of the Pepa de Huso site (500–1 B.C.), they range from 12 to 38 cm. in rim diameter, have streaked polished surface finish, and have lip and occasionally shoulder flanges (Estrada, 1962, fig. 46).

Bowls with convex bases and cambered side walls are found in the Waira-jirca, Kotosh, and Chavín Phases of the Kotosh sequence (chart 13, 47–49; Izumi and Sono, 1963, fig. 44, F-58, F-59, F-62; pls. 130, 131, 1–10, 132, 1–5, 12; provenience is shown in table 8 on pages 137–138). Like the Peruvian version of the flat-base pan form discussed earlier, the proportions of these bowls tend to be different from the corresponding form in Mesoamerica in that they are smaller and have greater height in proportion to the diameter.

Surfaces are polished and some vessels have red slip, but the decorations on the side walls are rectilinear arrangements of wide lines, or grooves and dots. Red paint, white paint, or graphite are sometimes used in the lines. Human faces are also depicted on four raised bosses (op. cit., pls. 2–3, 45a–g, 46a–e, 47c–d). Tello (1960, fig. 160g–h) illustrates fragments of bowls of this shape from Chavín.

A few small bowls with convex bases and low side walls are illustrated from the Peruvian coastal site Supe by Willey and Corbett (1954, pl. 7d–e, g) and from Virú (Strong and Evans, 1952, fig. 37–6). These bowls, however, do not have the characteristic sharp angle between base and walls, and the side walls are not curved. This bowl form disappears from most of the Peruvian sequences by about the beginning of the present era. The size, proportions, rounded base, and slightly outcurved side walls are preserved in the delicate painted bowls of the Classic Nazca culture of the south coast. In these, the side walls and base join in a sharply curved shoulder rather than at the angle usual in the earlier bowls. A similar tendency seems to be operative in Mesoamerica, in that the beautifully painted bowls of Classic Maya also show a rounding of the shoulder angle (Longyear, 1952, fig. 115b, b′, e). The Classic composite silhouette bowl form was retained on the north coast, where today they are offered for sale on the market in Piura.

Gerardo and Alicia Reichel-Dolmatoff (1956, pp. 191–192, fig. 7J, O) state that their rim sherd Type J is diagnositic of the Momíl I Phase on the north coast of Colombia (chart 13, 37–40). We have placed the beginning of this phase at about 700 B.C. Type J rims are strongly outflaring or have labial flanges. They come from shallow composite silhouette bowls. The shoulder angles are sharp and show slight projection, though perhaps not enough to be called a basal ridge. Side walls are nearly vertical. The authors state that decoration is usually absent, but these bowls are well manufactured and polished.

While Gerardo and Alicia Reichel-Dolmatoff's stratigraphic tabulation (1956, p. 192) clearly shows that these Type J bowls with labial flanges reach their peak of popularity (about 6 percent) in the middle of the Momíl I time span, there is another type of carinated bowl that has its greatest frequency (16 percent) in the bottom level of the strata cut, suggesting that it is an ancestral form in declining popularity through Momíl I times. This is Type O, comprising bowls with convex bases, sharp shoulder angles, and almost vertical cambered side walls that taper in thickness from shoulder to direct lips. These bowls are red slipped and frequently decorated on the exterior walls with incised and dentate stamped designs.

Composite silhouette bowls with curved bases, nearly vertical cambered side walls and quite large basal flanges are limited to Momíl II times (250–1 B.C.). The edges of the flanges are frequently notched. In the Momíl ceramic sequence, from approximately 750–1 B.C., two trends are apparent: the composite silhouette bowl evolves from simple to complex hape in details of shoulder and lip embellishment, and polished red slipping and engraved decoration of the side walls are decreasing. In basic outline this parallels the history of the composite silhouette bowl in Mesoamerica, as will be pointed out later. The Reichel-

Dolmatoffs (1956, pp. 276–298) have presented considerable evidence to show the close relationship between the culture of the Momíl Phase and the latter half of the Formative of Mesoamerica, and the writer shall not attempt to reargue their case.

Whether the composite silhouette bowl arrived on the north coast of Colombia from Mesoamerica, or whether this particular item moved in the other direction is a problem unsolvable at present. It is clear, however, that it is the early form of this bowl in northern Colombia that shows the greatest degree of resemblance to the still earlier carinated bowls of the Machalilla Phase of coastal Ecuador.

The flat-base pan form dominates the food service dishes at the beginning of the ceramic sequence on the Guatemalan coast. The convex-base bowl with sharp shoulder angle and outcurving sides appears at the beginning of the Conchas I Phase at 800 B.C. on a white-to-buff ware that is new to the sequence, and as M. D. Coe suggests (1961, pp. 64–69, fig. 27j, 1) is possibly an import (chart 13–33). This form occurs also in Ocós Black ware (op. cit., fig. 30 b, d). These bowls are usually fairly small (average 14 cm. in diameter), are slipped and well polished, and a few are decorated with fluted horizontal lines inside the lip or on the outer wall, apparently made by impressing a rounded polishing tool deeper than usual.

In the Conchas II Phase (600–300 B.C.) the majority of the composite silhouette bowls have a streaky, brown-black surface polish (op. cit., pp. 69–70, Conchas Streaky Brown-black) that is produced by varying the pressure of the tool in the polishing process. This peculiar finish characterizes this time horizon through Chiapas and up the Gulf coast of Mexico as far as northern Veracruz. This form alternatively has a black finish (op. cit., p. 72, Ocós Black), and is sometimes made of an orange ware (op. cit., p. 79, Conchas Orange). These wares also have their parallels on the Mexican Gulf coast.

There are several changes in form details in the Conchas II Phase. These include a predominance of small, flat bases that usually are strongly concave or dimpled (chart 13, 31–32; op. cit., fig. 35i); lower walls that sometimes are straight between flattened base and shoulder angle; and pronounced basal ridges that are almost but not quite flanges. Upper walls also sometimes slant inward rather than have an outward flare. Everted lips that sometimes have engraved designs are another feature at this time (600–300 B.C.).

In Sanders' (1961) sequence at Santa Cruz in Chiapas, the flat-base pan dominates in the earliest Burrero Period (Chiapa II, 800–550 B.C.). This form continues on into the Chiapilla Period (Chiapa IV and V, 450–100 B.C.). Composite silhouette bowls

with sharp angles between the convex base and relatively low outcurving side walls also occur in the Burrero Gray and Burrero Cream wares (op. cit., figs. 17–18) that are most characteristic of the earlier period (800–450 B.C.). This ware seems to correspond to the Conchas White-to-buff, on which these forms first appeared in the Soconusco region (M. D. Coe, 1961, p. 66).

Chiapilla Polished Red of the Chiapilla Phase (450–100 B.C.) has this composite form with very low side walls (Sanders, 1961, fig. 20B). Occasionally there are basal flanges at the angle connecting base and side walls (chart 13–27).

The Santa Cruz site has a gap of approximately 500 years in its ceramic record, and the composite silhouette bowl appears again in the orange ware of the Santa Cruz Phase of the Early Classic (Chiapa VIII–IX, A.D. 200–350; op. cit., pp. 31–33).

The Mirador site, reported by Peterson (1963), covers most of the gap that exists in the information provided by Santa Cruz. The Mirador Phases, in addition to being named, bear the same roman numerals as does the Chiapas sequence, indicating the same spans of time.

Composite silhouette bowls with basal ridges, sometimes notched, and engraved decoration on side walls are particularly common in Mirador Periods IV–VI (450–1 B.C.). They occur in brown wares (op. cit., figs. 12d, g, n, p, q, u), bichrome ware (op. cit., figs. 17a–i), and in polished red engraved ware (op. cit., fig. 23), which Peterson terms "incised." Peterson (op. cit., pp. 41ff) describes a sequence of change in details of these bowls, which is illustrated in his figure 47.

MacNeish informs me that composite silhouette bowls with rounded bases and cambered vertical or outslanting sides first appear at the start of the Santa Maria Phase (900 B.C.) in the Tehuacán chronology (chart 13–22). They are usually made of a brown ware and are often polished. Everted lips bearing decoration appear on these bowls by 200 B.C., the close of the Santa Maria Phase, but data are not available as to the occurrence of basal ridges or feet.

Composite silhouette vessels are present through the range of time covered by Vaillant's excavations in Zacatenco and El Arbolillo, but the sequence in form details is not too clear. Bowls of this type are made of black and bay ware in the early phase at Zacatenco (chart 13–20; Vaillant, 1930, pls. 1b–c, f–m, p–d'). The thin, highly polished black ware is characteristically decorated on the side walls with wide polished "grooving" or flutes that run parallel to the rim. This form has engraved designs on the side walls in the Zacatenco Middle Period (op. cit., pls. 4–d, h, i, k–l, o–q) and usually is a polished black ware. One vessel of this shape has short, solid tripod feet. This same form is rarely painted with red-on-white designs. (op. cit., pl. 5, a–b), again with tripod feet. In the Late Zacatenco Period, composite silhouette bowls are common and have both solid and hollow tripod feet and painted designs (op. cit., pls. 8, a–d, g, n, 9c, h).

At Ticomán the composite silhouette vessel is very common, bears painted designs and often has tripod feet, either solid or hollow (chart 13–18). These are markers for the early part of the Classic Period.

Composite silhouette vessels, usually of simple shape, are a common form from the stratigraphic excavations of Piña Chán (1958) at Tlatilco and the nearby locality of Atoto. They occur in his types "Café rojiso o Bayo" (op. cit., fig. 8h–m, s–v); "Café obscuro" (op. cit., fig. 9g–o); "Café claro" (op. cit., fig. 9m–o); "Negro pulido" (op. cit., fig. 11 l–n); "Blanco pulido" (op. cit., fig. 12k–l); and "Blanco sobre rojo" (op. cit., fig. 13i–j).

This form is also common in the funerary ware that Piña Chán illustrates from the Tlatilco Cemetery. Elaborate modifications of basal ridge and lip do not seem to be present; no feet are found. The use of the Tlatilco Cemetery is estimated to have terminated about 400 B.C., and this is evidently before these features became fashionable in the Valley of Mexico.

In the Gulf coast Olmec region the simple bowls and flat-base pan forms also dominate the San Lorenzo Phase (1200–900 B.C.). This form lasts into the La Venta Phase, where it is joined by a much smaller proportion of what Drucker (1952, pp. 113–114, fig. 38f) terms "return side bowls with angular shoulders." The bowls are described as wide and shallow, ranging from 20 to 44 cm. in rim diameter. Bases are rounded, the shoulder angle is sharp, and side walls are strongly curved and often taper from junction of base to the lip. Rims are usually simple. Drucker says that this form occurs rarely, but is in all the wares found at La Venta, being slightly more common in the fine paste wares than in the coarse wares. He notes that this tendency is reversed at Tres Zapotes, where it is more common in coarse wares.

In the Tres Zapotes collection, Drucker (1943a, pp. 50–51) describes this shape (chart 13–10) as "composite silhouette dishes." The description is not very detailed but the illustrations show that the features of engraved decoration on the side walls, thickened flat and everted lips, and occasionally slight projection at the basal angle are present (op. cit., figs. 22, 23a–e, 32, 34d–e, 38n–p). These bowls are made of brown, black, and white-rim black ware.

A special variation of the composite silhouette form that is particularly characteristic of the Gulf coast as far north as central Veracruz is small, black ware bowls with flat bases, in which the portion of the bottom connecting base and side walls arches slightly upward instead of being straight or convex. This portion of the vessel is often thinner than either base or side walls. Surface is usually highly polished, and side walls often have a decoration of horizontal fluting (García Payón, 1966, pl. 8, 65–70). This distinctive form appears late in the strata cuts made at sites in the vicinity of Zempoala and probably dates 300–200 B.C.

Identical polished black ware bowls with fluted side walls and this peculiar composite silhouette are in the Conchas Phase of the Soconusco region and in the Chorrera Phase of Ecuador. This is one of the elements that M. D. Coe (1961, pp. 369–370, figs. 4k–1, 5i) cites as evidence for direct trade.

The ceramic chronology in the Huasteca on the northern Gulf coast of Mexico is based on the work of Ekholm (1944) and MacNeish (1954). The vessel forms in the oldest period, the Pavón, consist of ollas with small mouths, short flaring rims, and flat-base pans with short outward slanting walls (MacNeish, 1954, pp. 566–569, fig. 12, 7–12). Composite silhouette bowls appear to replace the flat-base pan in the Aguilar Phase (op. cit., p. 574). These are made of a white ware (Progresso White), a polished black ware (Ponce Black), and a polished red slipped ware (Aguilar Red). Decoration is rare on the black ware, and on the red ware usually consists of crosshatched areas, forming squares and triangles and parallel bands of lines that appear to have been drawn with a multipoint tool (op. cit., fig. 14).

In his comparative section MacNeish states (1954, p. 631) that "At Panuco this kind of vessel [composite silhouette bowl] first appears in the Ponce Period, reaches dominance in the Aguilar Period, then gradually diminishes through the Chila and El Prisco Periods." Following the chronological arrangements given in figure 4 of Meggers and Evans (ed., 1963), this means that the composite silhouette bowl starts about 1000 B.C., reaches a peak about 750 B.C., and disappears about A.D. 200–300.

First short and later long tripod feet begin to appear on these vessels in the Aguilar Period (750 B.C.). This seems to be several centuries earlier than in other parts of Mesoamerica. Incised and punctated designs in the bottoms of bowls (pseudo graters), which began in the flat-base pans that are in the earliest Huasteca Phase, also continue in some of the composite silhouette bowls, which usually have feet. Illustrations of these bowls from approximately 500 B.C. are given by Ekholm (1944). MacNeish also shows that two related features that have this same time range, i.e. begin in the Aguilar and reach a maximum popularity in the El Prisco Phase, are bowl lips with projecting scalloped flanges, and incised decoration (MacNeish, 1954, p. 635, fig. 36-1), and pronounced basal ridges on bowls (op. cit., pp. 635-636, fig. 37-7). A number of comparisons of these features cited by MacNeish are being neglected in this paper, simply because they do not occur in the vicinity of one of the selected chronologies. Most of his comparisons are with the Maya region.

The Davis site in Cherokee County, Texas, is reported by Newell and Krieger (1949). They (op. cit., pp. 224-232) very convincingly demonstrate the high degree of resemblance of the ceramics to Late Formative pottery in Mesoamerica. This includes composite silhouette or carinated bowls with scalloped lip flanges and engraved decorations on the side walls filled with red pigment (chart 13, 57-59). The black to dark brown color of the earliest pottery, as well as the high polish, are other Formative characteristics.

There has been considerable discussion as to the dating of the Davis site. Newell and Krieger (op. cit., pp. 219ff) made very careful comparisons to both the Mississippi Valley sequences and those of Mesoamerica, and concluded that Davis Phase I is coeval with Marksville, and could not have begun later than A.D. 500. In this they are supported by a radiocarbon date taken from charred corn cobs. The writer (Ford, 1951) opposed this view, pointing out that the traits coming through the Davis site do not appear in the nearby Mississippi and Red River Valleys until the beginning of the Plaquemine Phase, about A.D. 800-900. Many of the elements are in the Huasteca in Ekholm's Periods IV and V. This seems to be the most probable source for the movement into the Mississippi Valley.

Carinated bowls are particularly characteristic of the earlier Gibson and later Fulton Phases of Caddoan prehistory (Webb, 1959, fig. 19d-e, i), and lasted until the disappearance of ceramics early in the 18th century. They diffused eastward as far as central Georgia. The forms remained simple; the surfaces are always well polished, and are occasionally decorated on the side walls, but never acquire the feet or elaborate rims that characterize the composite silhouette bowls of the Classic Period in Mesoamerica.

Summary

Composite silhouette bowls first appear in Ecuador between 2000 and 1500 B.C., and the side walls have engraved decorations with red pigment rubbed into the lines, an association which is maintained through much of their diffusion.

Between 1200 and 300 B.C. this form is in highland Peru, but proportions are slightly different in that side walls are higher relative to diameter, the same tendency that was noted for the flat-base pan.

By 700 B.C. composite silhouette bowls are on the north coast of Colombia. They first appear in the Soconusco, Guatemala sequence at about 800 B.C. This date of approximately 1000-800 B.C. seems to be the time of the first appearance of unelaborated simple silhouette bowls in Chiapas, Tehuacán, Valley of Mexico, the Olmec region of Veracruz, and the Ekholm-MacNeish sequence in the Huasteca.

Everted lips, usually with decoration, and small basal ridges develop about 600-500 B.C. in these several regions, and by 400-300 B.C., basal flanges are common and well developed. While solid tripod feet are earlier in some areas, the typical bulbous and mammiform tripods of the Proto-Classic date after A.D. 1.

Composite silhouette bowls are in the Mississippi Valley after A.D. 900. Here they are polished and often have engraved decoration with red pigment rubbed in the lines.

Round-base Simple Bowl

CHART 14

Simple bowls with rounded or flattened bases might be considered as forms too "natural" to be capable of providing any archeological information. Primitive people certainly must have noticed that this form can be cut out of a large globular gourd, making an effective food serving dish as well as leaving a very useful container. To copy these vessels in clay when ceramics are first mastered would be only logical. Consequently, it is of interest to examine what is known of the history of simple bowls in the Americas, and attempt to determine whether their occurrence is a result of the logical operation of the mind of primitive man or of cultural diffusion.

In this study two variations of the simple bowl will be distinguished. One has a rounded or lenticular base and curves evenly up to the lip. It is relatively shallow in relation to diameter, which generally varies from about 10 to 30 cm. The second version differs from the first in that it has a relatively large flat bottom. Usually there is a distinct curvature between the base and the side walls. The chord of the curving side walls usually slants outward slightly; again these bowls are shallow relative to diameter. This attempted differentiation is not successful in many cases, for it is usually impossible to determine details of base form from rim sherds.

Both open and shallow simple bowls, as well as somewhat deeper bowls on which the upper walls curve inward slightly, comprise about 50 percent of the vessel forms and run through the Valdivia sequence in Ecuador (chart 14, 44–45; Meggers, Evans, and Estrada, 1965, fig. 54, 3–7). This shape bears a variety of decoration, including broad-line incising (op. cit., fig. 24, 1–2), brushing (op. cit. fig. 26–6), excising (op. cit., fig. 31–2), fine-line incising (op. cit., fig. 32, 1–3), fingernail punctation, pebble polishing (op. cit., fig. 40–3), polished plain (op. cit., fig. 42–4), and polished red slip (op. cit., fig. 44, 3–6).

The simple bowl form continued in use in coastal Ecuador through the Regional Developmental Period (500 B.C.–A.D. 500; chart 14, 39–43). In the Jambelí Phase of the Regional Developmental, simple bowls make up approximately half of the vessels. There is some variation in rim profile, and thickened lips seem to be prominent toward the end of the phase (chart 14–39).

Estrada (1962, table 3) places the occupation of the Pepa de Huso site in Manabí from 700 to 1 B.C. The stratigraphy seems clear in the four meters of refuse deposits and the sequence of rim forms is shown in his figure 46. A few examples of simple bowls are mixed in with the composite silhouette forms. All these bowls are marked by lip flanges with elaborate cutout and notched decoration (chart 14–41). The beginning of the use of lip flanges seems to be about 400 B.C.

Izumi and Terada (1966, p. 28, fig. 10) found simple bowls to be a popular form in the Pechiche Phase (850–370 B.C.) in the Tumbes region of north Peru. A few (op. cit., forms D4–5) have wedge-shaped thickened lips, flat on top. Everted lips (op. cit., form 6) are confined to the later Garbanzal Phase.

Shape studies in the Kotosh sequence of the Peruvian highlands unfortunately were made only on complete or restored vessels (Izumi and Sono, 1963, pp. 85–96). The shapes here classified as simple round-base bowls are numbered F–34, 47, 50, 51, 57. Their table 8 shows that these are almost confined to Kotosh Chavín and later phases. Judging by the chronological diagram (op. cit., fig. 46), these bowls are rare in the Chavín Phase and more common after 300 B.C. (chart 14, 51–54). They were commonly manufactured of Chocolate Brown (op. cit., pls. 40b–f, 41a) and Well Polished wares (op. cit., pl. 43a), and the side walls were decorated with wide-line rectilinear motifs. The concentric rectangle motif characteristic of Valdivia Broad-line Incised (Meggers, Evans, and Estrada, 1965, pl. 42a) is fairly

common. Another shared motif is horizontal parallel lines interrupted at intervals to form panels.

Simple bowls with a smooth curve between side walls and rounded base seem to be scarce or absent from the Ancón Phase on the Peruvian coast. Open bowls are numerous in Ancón Polished Black and Ancón Polished Red, but most seem to have an angle between side and base, and most of the bases are flat (Willey and Corbett, 1954, pp. 53–54). These bowls do appear at the beginning of the Guañape Phase (800 B.C.) in the Virú Valley sequence (chart 14, 57–59; Strong and Evans, 1952, pp. 253–256). They are rare or missing during the Gallinazo Phase, however, and only in the latter part of the coastal sequence do they seem to have become popular food serving dishes. At this time, many were made in molds.

Only one or two of the rim profiles that Reichel-Dolmatoff (1965, figs. 5–8) gives for the Puerto Hormiga (3000–2000 B.C.) pottery on the north coast of Colombia could have come from bowls. Practically all seem to be variations of the neckless jar.

The pottery of the Barlovento Phase (2000–1000 B.C.) also has a limited variety of forms. Again the neckless jar with broad-line incised decoration about the opening is dominant. Over 21,000 fragments were recovered and are described as one pottery type. In this type description Reichel-Dolmatoff (1955, p. 255) mentions semispherical vessels with rounded bases (chart 14–38). The latter become the most common form in the Malambo Phase (chart 14–37; Angulo Valdés, 1962 a, p. 80), where they have their greatest popularity toward the lower levels (estimated 1000 B.C.). The lips are rounded and sometimes incline slightly toward the vessel interior. This ware is usually streak polished and varies in color from gray to red; in the latter part of the phase, a red slip is applied.

The tendency toward deepening of the bowl form seems to continue in the Momíl Phase (800–1 B.C.). Gerardo and Alicia Reichel-Dolmatoff (1956, pp. 180) describe group B shapes as "semispherical vases with incised-dentated decoration." These are from 20 to 25 cm. in diameter and 10 to 15 cm. high. A second group of bowls is smaller but apparently of the same shape. This group H is described as "small semispherical containers with vertical side walls, or somewhat turned toward the interior, at times with a lip modified by thinning or thickening" (op. cit., p. 183). These too have the side walls decorated with incised decoration, somewhat different from that of the larger vessels.

These two groups are apparently those shown in the Reichel-Dolmatoffs' (op. cit., fig. 15) diagram of vessel shape evolution, second from the right at the top. After some hesitation, these vessels have been left off chart 14. They probably are derived from the simple bowl tradition, but have become so deep relative to diameter that they are approaching a beaker form. Simple bowls within the limits of the definition being applied here were manufactured at later dates on the north coast of Colombia, and as a matter of fact are found accompanying intrusive burials in the Momíl site (op. cit., pl. 33–6, –8).

Simple bowls also seem to be missing in the earlier phases of the Cupica Burial Mound on the Pacific coast of Colombia. Some rim sherds that may indicate this form are illustrated for Cupica Phase v, which seems to date about the fifth century of this era (Reichel-Dolmatoff, G. and A., 1961, fig. 11). This form also seems to be rare at San Agustín in the central Cordillera of Colombia. Duque Gomez (1964, pls. 24–87, –113, –114, 25–77, –102, –105) illustrates a few from the tombs, which should date from the early centuries of the Chirstian Era. Simple bowls are present in the ceramics of highland Colombia in late ceramic complexes (Ford, 1944, fig. 15f).

Simple silhouette bowls may be present in the Barra and Ocós Phases of the Soconusco region of the Guatemala coast, but M.D. Coe (1961) has not been able to present any positive evidence for the latter phase. Unless a fragment is large enough to show both rim and base, the lenticular form is difficult to determine. Rim sherds indicating the bowl shape are fairly common, but Coe is of the opinion that most bowls probably have flat bases. This form is found from the Cuadros to Conchas i Phases (1000–600 B.C.).

The early bowls in the Chiapas sequence are principally flat-base pans and simple bowls with side walls rounding to flat bases. The simple bowl with rounded base (chart 14, 25–26) seems to run from Chiapa ii times through vi (800 B.C.–A.D. 1). Sanders (1961, pp. 23–24, fig. 23) shows this form in polished black ware, which is decorated with engraved designs: simple motifs of hatched triangles, arrangements of straight lines, and zig-zags. In Chiapa v times simple bowls begin to have bichrome and polychrome painted decorations and one at least is illustrated with a short, solid conical foot that probably is a tripod (op. cit., fig. 44). In Santa Cruz Orange (Chiapa viii–ix, A.D. 200–600) there is a rare bowl with hollow tripod feet (op. cit., fig. 14b, pl. 6b).

According to the quantitative chronology MacNeish provided prior to the publication of his volume on Tehuacán ceramics (in Byers, ed., 1967–, vol. 3, fig. 7), the simple bowl with rounded bases appears about 1600 B.C. (chart 14, 19–21). It is shown for the gray wares that date about 400–200 B.C., which are probably early Monte Albán related. In the Palo Blanco Phase (100 B.C.) these simple bowls are made of El Riego Black and Orange ware and acquire low ring bases; about

A.D. 500 they have tripod feet. Flange lips bearing incised decoration date between 500 and 1 B.C.

It has been remarked before that it is difficult to obtain precise information from Vaillant's reports on his work in the Valley of Mexico. In referring to the simple silhouette in the bay, russet, and black wares (Vaillant, 1935, pp. 221–227) it is uncertain whether the bases are rounded or flat. Vaillant (op. cit., figs. 21–1, 22–8) does illustrate simple bowls in white ware from graves, which he dates late in El Arbolillo i. At Zacatenco the true simple bowl with convex base does not appear to occur until the Middle Period, corresponding to El Arbolillo ii (1000–600 B.C.), when it appears in incised decorated wares, red-on-white wares, and white wares (Vaillant, 1931, pls. 4c, n; 5 k–n; 6 i–j).

Piña Chán also is somewhat indefinite as to the precise forms of the bowls from his strata cuts in the early Tlatilco Phases that equate with El Arbolillo ii. When, however, he describes the vessels that accompanied the burials (the Atoto Phase), it is clear that simple bowls are a rather prominent feature. This shape is indicated on his table 1 (Piña Chán, 1958, vol. 1, p. 76; chart 14–17) as having a frequency of 34.19 percent. Although this figure probably does include some of the simple bowls with flat bases, which are here being treated separately, the illustrations given in his figure 33 and following, do show an impressive number of simple bowls with convex bases.

Simple bowls continue into the Ticomán Phase (400–100 B.C.) where they are decorated with red-on-yellow painted designs (chart 14–16). They are also made of a black-brown ware which apparently correlates with the chocolate brown ware that marks the end of the Formative in other parts of Mesoamerica. The former decreases in frequency through the Ticomán Phase (Vaillant, 1931, pp. 286–288, pl. 74). Composite silhouette bowls dominate this ware, with simple bowls in the minority. Many of the simple bowls have bird or animal heads modeled on the rim. Hollow conical, globular, mammiform, and effigy tripod feet begin to appear.

Simple bowls with rounded bases seem to be completely missing from García Payón's collections from El Trapiche and Chalahuites in Veracruz, as they are from the unreported excavations made by Medellín, Wallrath, and the writer. All the simple bowls have flat bases, where bases can be determined. Drucker (1952, fig. 38c) illustrates simple bowls from La Venta, but notes that "This classification is based on a series of rim sherds; the form is only conjectural" (op. cit., p. 111).

Drucker (1943a, fig. 13) and Weiant (1943, fig. 17b) illustrate a few bowls of simple lenticular profile from Tres Zapotes (chart 14, 12–13). Some have polychrome painted designs over a cream white slip. It is at this time (400–1 B.C.) that tripod supports and low annular bases begin to appear on these bowls, as well as other bowl forms (Drucker, 1943a, pl. 15c–e).

Not shown on chart 14 is the Huasteca chronology of Ekholm (1944) and MacNeish (1954). It appears fairly certain that the simple bowl of regular profile is not present here in the earlier phases. Whether the "hemispherical bowls" (MacNeish, 1954, p. 584, fig. 19, chart 5) that begin in the Ponce Phase have curving bases or not is a moot question. MacNeish lists them as "flat-bottomed" and they probably were. Tripod supports first appear in the Aguilar Phase and are common in the succeeding Chila Phase, which is Ekholm's Period I. They are long conical, short conical, short hollow conical, and animal effigy feet. Annular bases also occur.

The simple bowl form apparently is not found in the Poverty Point ceramic complex of Louisiana. It does occur in the Tchefuncte Phase (400–100 B.C.), where the bowls usually have red slip, but seem to be rare. Most of the bowls of simple form have either crude annular bases or four short feet. The simple bowl is somewhat more common in the Marksville Phase (100 B.C.–A.D. 400; chart 14, 10–11), where proportions range from moderately shallow to deep. Some bowls are decorated with zoned red slip or rocker stamping, and broad-line incising. The decoration covers the exterior including the base (Ford and Willey, 1940, figs. 22c, g, 23a, 29b, 39a, c, 40; Ford, 1963, figs. 31e, g–h, 34g–k). Some of the simple bowls from the Helena Crossing burial mound have beveled rims and red slip applied in vertical bands.

The simple bowl continues on through the Troyville Phase (A.D. 400–600), where it is often covered with red slip, or has red slip applied in line-bordered zones, or in areas not bounded by lines (chart 14, 8–9). The rims tend to be thickened and some bowls have four ears formed on the rims, a variety of labial flange (Ford, 1951, figs. 19–20, 22f, 23c, 24g–i, 25e–f, i, 31f). Cordmarked pottery, which arrives in the Lower Mississippi Valley at this time, also has this shape (op. cit., fig. 16b). The simple bowl form continued to be manufactured in the Southeast until historic times.

That the simple bowl of the proportions that are under consideration here was made during the Bayou La Batre Phase of the Mobile Bay area is not certain. The usual form is described as a "deep truncate-conoidal open bowl resting upon a small base platform" (Wimberly, 1960, p. 72). This platform is usually provided with either a crude annular base or four small feet. A hemispherical bowl with slightly constricted mouth is also described. These forms occur in the coeval Poverty Point Phase ceramics of the Lower Mississippi Valley. In both areas the vessels are proportionately deeper for diameter than are the simple bowls as defined here.

The earliest simple bowls that can be identified with certainty in the Southeast seem to be in the Santa Rosa Phase, 100 B.C.–A.D. 400 (chart 14–7; op. cit., p. 91). The round base bowls, somewhat deeper than are usual, have early stamped decoration (op. cit., figs. 58–59). Simple bowls continued in use in west Florida through the Weeden Island and succeeding phases, although not with the popularity that they had in the Mississippi Valley. Weeden Island bowls are relatively shallow and frequently have four ears on the rim, as do those of the Troyville Phase.

Simple bowls with convex bases do not seem to be an element of the Orange Phase (1300–400 B.C.) on the St. Johns River in north Florida. The only form made at this time was the flat-base pan. There are deep cups, possibly with rounded bases, which bear the Tick Island Incised decoration (1600–1300 B.C.), but although much smaller than is typical, these resemble the Mesoamerican (and north coast Colombian) neckless jar or tecomate more closely than the simple bowl.

Goggin (1952, p. 101) states that bowls are the most common form in St. Johns Plain ware, These are not, however, the shallow simple bowls that are under discussion in this section, and they are closer in shape to the Mesoamerican neckless jars.

Simple bowls with direct rims are also rare or missing from the Yent and Green Point Phases of the Crystal River site. There are two bowls of this form from the burial mound, both with heavy pronounced lip flanges (chart 14–6; Moore, 1903, figs. 25, 33). Bowls with horizontally projecting ears are characteristic of the Weeden Island Phase. Bowls from this and later periods with rounded bases tend to have vertical or inslanting upper walls (Willey, 1949a, fig. 69a, i).

Bowls seem to be the only form of container in the Stallings Island Phase near Savannah, Georgia, dated 1800–500 B.C. (chart 14–5). Rounded bases are a safe assumption, since no basal angles have been found. Claflin (1931, p. 14) estimates that these bowls have an average diameter of 16 inches and are 7 inches in depth. Rim diameters range from 8 to 20 inches. There are two varieties of rim treatment: One group of bowls has direct rims; on the other the upper few centimeters of vessel wall are turned sharply inward.

For the Deptford and following phases, the excellent summary of north Georgia archeology by Wauchope (1966) will be the source. The Deptford and early Swift Creek Phases apparently do not have the shallow simple bowl that is the subject of interest here (op. cit., figs. 6c, 9–11). Bowl-like forms are deeper and have conoidal bases. Perhaps between 500 B.C. and A.D. 300, this form is submerged by the Woodland paddle-stamped wares apparently moving down the Atlantic Seaboard. Lenticular simple bowls do appear in the Late Middle Woodland Phase in Napier Stamped (chart 14–4; op. cit., fig. 13d), which probably dates after A.D. 600. They are a fairly popular form in the Mississippian phases.

Shallow bowls of any form seem to be lacking in the Early Woodland paddle-impressed pottery of the Upper Mississippi Valley. The typical form is the deep amphora, but there are some examples of pointed base vessels of approximately equal height and diameter. Proportions are similar to the coeval steatite vessels.

Simple, shallow bowls first appear in the Illinois sequence on the fully developed Hopewell time level (ca. A.D. 1). They are not very common and some have the rim ledge that is called the "Brangenberg Rim" by midwestern archeologists (Deuel, 1952, pl. 35 s, v). Although relatively rare, this rim has a wide geographical distribution on the Hopewell time level. It has already been noted from the Crystal River site in Florida. It also occurred in the Helena Crossing burial mound in northeastern Arkansas (Ford, 1963) and at the Hopewell Mound Group in Ohio (chart 14–1; Shetrone, 1926, fig. 53).

Simple bowls continue in Illinois in the post-Hopewellian Late Woodland Phase (chart 14, 2–3; Maxwell, 1959, fig. 6). These are marked with a cord-wrapped paddle as are the accompanying and more abundant amphoras. The probable date is ca. A.D. 500. Bowl forms become common in the Mississippian phases and often have bird or animal heads and appendages attached to the rim, making them into effigy vessels reminiscent of the similar effigy bowls of the Mexican Proto-Classic.

Summary

It appears that in the Americas, at least, the shallow simple bowl with rounded base is not a "natural" form that people in all regions started making when they begin to manufacture ceramics. The form is oldest in the Valdivia Phase of Ecuador and diffused to highland and coastal Peru, where small flat-base pans were already established as food serving dishes, about 900 B.C. It has a time range of from 1900 to 700 B.C. on the north coast of Colombia, and disappears at least temporarily during the Momíl Phase.

Simple round-base bowls were present but not very popular in Mesoamerica, where they were in competition with flat-base pans and carinated bowls. After 500 B.C. they began to acquire low ring bases, tripod

feet, thickened lips, and lip ledges, which were often decorated. At about this same time most of these features appear in Ecuador.

The simple round-base bowl does not seem to be a form in the early paddle-marked Woodland pottery that probably entered North America across the Bering Strait. Its only early appearance in the East is in the fiber tempered Stallings ceramics, which were made in a very limited area on the coast of Georgia from approximately 2400 to 500 B.C. It does not continue into the later paddle stamped ceramic phases, except possibly in a form heavily influenced by the pointed-base amphora. Arguments have been presented to the effect that the Stallings pottery complex as a whole is a more-or-less direct importation from the Valdivia Phase of coastal Ecuador, where the simple bowl form was popular. If this is true it would explain the anomalous early appearance of this form in North America.

Shallow simple bowls with rounded base seem to have diffused over the eastern United States to a limited extent in the first centuries of the present era as an element of the Hopewell cultures. There is continuity in their manufacture along the Gulf coast, where Woodland ceramic influences were very attenuated. Thickened rims bearing decoration on the lip, and the development of four triangular ears are characteristic about A.D. 500. The form is fairly common in the Mississippian culture ceramics after A.D. 900, when effigy heads reminiscent of those found nine centuries earlier in the Valley of Mexico are rather common additions to the rims of simple bowls.

Simple Bowl With Flat Base

CHART 14

In the Valdivia Phase of the Formative on the Ecuadorian coast, there is a variation of the simple bowl in which the side walls curve in to a fairly large flat base. Like the curved-base simple bowl, these vessels were relatively shallow and were probably used for food service (chart 14, 48–50).

Although they run all through the Valdivia Phase (3000–1500 B.C.), apparently these flattened-base bowls are not numerous. They are found in Punta Arenas Plain (Meggers, Evans, and Estrada, 1965, pp. 43–45, fig. 22–6), a sandy paste ware, where they are undecorated and have plain lips. The form is also characteristic of Valdivia Broad-line Incised (op. cit., pp. 47–51, fig. 24, 1–4). In this type the rims are sometimes gracefully thickened on the interior, the side walls have wide-line incised decorations below the lip, and on some examples the rims are scalloped. This version of the simple bowl continues to be rare through the Chorrera and the Regional Developmental Periods (Meggers and Evans, personal communication).

Simple bowls with curving sides that either round into or have a definite angle between the side walls and the flat bottom also seem to be rare in the sequence at Kotosh, where they run through the Kotosh and Chavín Phases (900–200 B.C.; chart 14, 55–56). Like the flat-base pans that have been discussed in the foregoing, these bowls seem to be smaller in diameter than the Mesoamerican examples, and slightly deeper in proportion to diameter. Flat-base simple bowls bear the Kotosh Grooved decorations, which in technique and some motifs resemble Valdivia Broad-line Incised (Izumi and Sono, 1963, pls. 47a–d, 132, 7–11). With proportions somewhat more similar to the Mesoamerican examples, they are also found in Kotosh Well Polished (op. cit., pls. 43a, 128, 1–5). This same shape of bowl comes from the site of Chavín de Huántar (Tello, 1960, fig. 155j).

Simple bowls with flat bases seem to be earliest in Mesoamerica on the Pacific coast of Guatemala, where they are found in the Ocós Phase (1400–1200 B.C.; chart 14–36). They are made of Ocós Buff ware, which occasionally has notched rim fillets and stripes of iridescent paint on the interior, and of highly polished Ocós Black (M.D. Coe, 1961, figs. 21h–q, 22n, 29f).

The Ocós Black type, with the flat-base simple bowl as one of its forms, lasts into the Conchas Phase (chart 14–34; M.D. Coe, 1961, pp. 70–72, fig. 29f). The lips develop modest flanges and the double-line break motif is incised into the flat lip surface. There are also eccentric tabs projecting out from the rim flanges, possibly four arranged around the vessel lip. The proportions of the bowls appear to change, in that they become more shallow and the flat bases have greater diameter than in the Ocós Phase.

Simple bowls with flat bases and direct, flanged, and beveled decorated rims were also made through Conchas II Phase in Ocós Gray (op. cit., p. 73), Conchas Red-on-Buff (op. cit., p. 76), Conchas Fine White-to-Buff (op. cit., p. 80), and Conchas Fine Red-on-Cream (op. cit., p. 82). In the Crucero Phase (300 B.C.–A.D. 200) the simple bowls were usually of an orange colored ware that sometimes had red painted decoration (chart 14, 32–33; op. cit., pp. 84–86). On some of these bowls, the labial flanges have dropped a short distance down from the lip and they have eccentric ears or lobes. M.D. Coe (op. cit., p. 86) notes that "This is another good time marker for the late Formative, east of the Isthmus of Tehuantepec," and proceeds to cite similarities in Chiapa V Phase and other comparisons, which are unnecessary to repeat here.

The simple bowl with flat base and curved side walls with an angle between is much more common in Chiapas than is the convex-base simple bowl (chart 14, 27–31). As a food serving dish it is second in popularity to the flat-base pan. Dixon (1959) apparently did not find this form in the early deposits in Pits 38 and 50 at Chiapa de Corzo. Sanders, aside from one possible example in Burrero Gray ware (chart 14–31; 1961, p. 19, fig. 18), finds this form in the Chiapilla Brown type, which occurs in the Chiapilla Period of the Santa Cruz site (op. cit., p. 26, fig. 27). This is equivalent to Chiapa IV and V (450–100 B.C.). Sanders notes that the type is of special interest because it may be ancestral to the white-rim black ware of the Proto-Classic Period.

Flat-base simple bowls are also found in Chiapilla Polished Red (op. cit., fig. 21b). In Chiapilla Polished Black (op. cit., pp. 23–24, fig. 23) the side walls and lips are decorated with straight-line engraved designs that clearly belong to the Ayangue tradition. This is a diagnostic type of the Chiapilla Phase. The same bowl form is also found in Chiapilla Metallic (op. cit., pp. 26–27, fig. 28), which has its maximum frequency late in the Chiapilla Phase (ca. 100 B.C.). Among the minor types of this period, it occurs in burnished light brown (op. cit., p. 37, fig. 43) and with bichrome and polychrome painted designs (op. cit., p. 37, fig. 44).

In Peterson's (1963) sequence at the Mirador site, the white-rim black ware of Period V (250–100 B.C.) has the flat-base simple bowl form. It continues on into Period VI, where it is also made of polished brown-black ware (op. cit., p. 53, fig. 74), and sometimes has a vitreous slip (op. cit., p. 53, fig. 75). This form seems to disappear after Period VI (A.D. 200).

MacNeish indicates that the flat-base simple bowl is first found in the Tehuacán sequence after 1200 B.C. (chart 14, 22–24), where it is made of Coatepec Plain white wares. The double-line break rim decoration is fairly common in Canoas White after 900 B.C. It is also a form of the Quachilco Brown type that has a modest popularity maximum shortly before the beginning of the present era. Apparently this is the local equivalent of the Late Formative brown ware found in other Mesoamerican regions, but in the Tehuacán Valley it is in competition with the more abundant Monte Albán-related gray wares and so did not enjoy the popularity it achieved on the Gulf coast.

The flat-base simple bowl form continued until the end of the Tehuacán sequence. At various times it was manufactured of gray and orange ware, and was decorated with incising, striations, and both single color and polychrome painted designs.

Simple bowls with flat bases are illustrated by Piña Chán from his stratigraphic excavations at the site of

Atoto, near Tlatilco in the Valley of Mexico (chart 14–18). These are listed among the principal forms of "Café obscuro" (Piña Chán, 1958, vol. 1, fig. 37a). It seems to occur with less frequency in "Rojo pulido interior" (op. cit., fig. 40 o), "Rojo pulido estaca" (op. cit., fig. 42a), and "Café rojiso o Bayo" (op. cit., fig. 45r). This form seems to play a minor role in the Tlatilco ceramic complex; however, its fortunes in later phases are obscured. It is possible that Vaillant included it among the bowls from his stratigraphic excavations, but nowhere is it illustrated in his reports.

At the La Venta site in Veracruz, Drucker (1952, pp. 111–112, fig. 38d) seems to include most of the examples of the bowl form of interest here in the category, "Dishes with open-curved to incurved sides." Bases are described as varying from gently rounded to flat, thus the simple bowl with flat base is included. Rims are simple and direct, and no handles or feet were noted. A few appeared to have low annular bases. Low raised straps encircle the rims of some of the bowls and a few have flanges placed below the lip. One or more encircling lines, incised just below the lip, is the usual decoration. This form is listed as moderately abundant for Drucker's (op. cit., table 6) Coarse Buff, Brown, and White wares. It is "abundant" for Coarse Black, Fine Paste Buff Orange, and Fine Paste Gray Black. "Infrequent" is indicated for Brown Lacquer ware. The flat-base simple bowl and the curved-base simple bowl are almost certainly the principal forms of the black, brown, gray, and fine paste orange buff wares that have refired rims (op. cit., p. 92).

The Chalahuites and El Trapiche sites on the north coast of Veracruz reported by García Payón (1966), and our own unreported work in this same vicinity gives a somewhat clearer picture of the changes in bowl forms before and after 500 B.C. While the flat-base pan was being made from the beginning of this sequence, the simple bowl with large flat base becomes prominent toward the end of the time covered by these sites. It is made of a polished black ware (op. cit., pl. 4, 6–11), a white ware that sometimes has the double-line break motif incised below the rim and lip, and flanges and scallops that are decorated (op. cit., pl. 18, 2–8), black ware with refired white rims (op. cit., pl. 33–24, –27), red ware with refired rims (op. cit., pl. 33, 36–38), and polished brown ware.

These simple bowls with large flat bases continue into the Tres Zapotes Phase (chart 14–15), where they are made with thinner walls and have cream white slip (Drucker, 1943a, fig. 13a), or are of black ware (op. cit., fig. 34c), sometimes with refired white rims (op. cit., fig. 38e-k). Weiant (1943, figs. 17a–d, 32, 1–11, 47a–d) illustrates other specimens of this same form from this site. The flat and outflaring in-cised decorated lips and the scallops that characterize the several bowl forms in the centuries after 500 B.C., are well illustrated by Weiant (op. cit., figs. 39–42).

This same form of bowl continues into the Cerro de las Mesas Phase (A.D. 1–500), where it is commonly made in a brown or black ware (chart 14–14; Drucker, 1943b, figs. 12a–b, 13–21, pl. 15a). The double-line break incised decoration is found on white ware (op. cit., figs. 132–133). Polychrome painted designs are also associated with the form (op. cit., fig. 153).

In the Panuco sequence in the Huasteca, MacNeish (1954, p. 585, chart 5) shows the simple bowl, presumably with flat bottom, as starting in the early Ponce Phase at approximately 1000 B.C. and lasting through the Chila Phase. In his comparative section MacNeish (op. cit., p. 627) notes that this form of bowl is a good time marker for the Temple and Village Formative stages throughout much of Mesoamerica. Its absence in very early ceramics is also cited.

Simple bowls with flattened bases that approach the Mesoamerican form do not appear in the Mississippi Valley until the development of the Mississippian cultures after A.D. 1000. They seem to be a minor variation of the more abundant simple bowl form (Cole, et. al., 1951, fig. 10) and share with it features of incised decoration about the rim, outflaring rims, sometimes scalloped, and incised decoration on the out-turned lips.

Summary

While the simple bowl shape with both curved and flattened base was occasionally made of stone from the central coast of Peru to the eastern United States immediately before and after the times of the first appearance of ceramics in the several regions, there seems to be little reason to suspect that the later ceramic bowls were copies. Both forms are present in the Valdivia Phase of Ecuador, dating back to approximately 3000 B.C. In Peruvian chronological columns, however, and to the north, these shapes do not appear with the first pottery. The only exception to this statement seems to be in the Stallings Island Phase of coastal Georgia, where simple bowls are in early association with steatite bowls, some of which have identical forms.

From the coast of Ecuador to the latitude of the Valley of Mexico, both forms share the elaborating tendencies that mark the three centuries that precede the beginning of this era. These are tripod supports, annular bases, decorated lips, and lip flanges that are usually decorated and often have projecting ears. Refired oxidized rim areas are also characteristic of the Mesoamerican region between 1000 and 1 B.C.

Vessel Feet

CHART 15

Vessel feet, usually numbering four or three and of a variety of shapes, and annular bases, ranging from dimpled bottoms and low rings to tall pedestals, are a recurrent theme through a large part of New World ceramic history. There seems to be a degree of cohesion between these forms; in the regions and at the times where feet become large and elaborate, there also tends to be an accompanying emphasis on tall ornamental pedestal bases. These features have been used in both regional and interregional comparisons by a number of authors, including Wauchope (1950), Gerardo and Alicia Reichel-Dolmatoff (1956), MacNeish (1954), and Meggers and Evans (1963).

It appears to be valuable to make a distinction between vessels having four small feet, which seem to be earliest, and to have an origin in Ecuador, and the tripod vessels, usually bowls, that have a wide distribution in the Americas at a later date. As a matter of fact, the use of four and of three legs may well have different origins.

The oldest tetrapods are found in the Valdivia Phase of Ecuador, principally on the red slipped bowls that are classified as Valdivia Polished Red (chart 15–63; Meggers, Evans, and Estrada, 1965, pp. 76–80, figs. 43a, 44–5, pl. 103c). They are also on a few bowls of Valdivia Polished Plain (op. cit., fig. 42–2). These are not abundant and run from about the beginning of the sequence at 3000 B.C. to the first half of Valdivia B, approximately 2200 B.C. They are accompanied by dimpled bases, which will be discussed later.

The Valdivia tetrapods are short solid nubbin-like appendages placed so closely together on the bases of fairly large round-base bowls that they would not appear to have provided very stable supports. This method of placement is characteristic of tetrapods in other regions as will be noted.

Tetrapod supports do not occur in the Peruvian sequences. The four-legged vessels that were made are obviously animal effigies and can hardly be cited as examples of this tradition. They are also lacking from the early phases of Colombia that have been described by Reichel-Dolmatoff (1955, 1965) and Angulo Valdés (1962b). In the Momíl Phase, where tripod feet and low annular bases are common, what seem to be small toy vessels or toy benches with four feet were found in the early phase. Similar small objects in the later Momíl II had three feet (Reichel-Dolmatoff, G. and A., 1956, pp. 216–217, fig. 12–7). Except for the hollow swollen and mammiform examples of the Early Classic Period, tetrapod supports are also very rare in Mesoamerica. Although they seem to be missing from the collections of García Payón from El Trapiche and Chalahuites, a few examples of short nubbin tetrapods were found in the lower levels of the latter site, hardly abundant enough to justify putting them on the chart. Porter (1953, p. 41) reports two examples from Tlatilco and comments on their scarcity in highland Mesoamerica.

If there is a historical connection between the early use of tetrapods on the Ecuadorian coast between 3000 and 2200 B.C. and their reappearance in fair abundance at the start of the Poverty Point and Bayou la Batre Phases on the Gulf coast of the southeastern United States about 1000 B.C., both the geographical and temporal linkages are unknown at present. This situation recalls the fact that there are similar gaps in our information concerning the wide-mouth pot form, the use of a row of decorative nodes pushed out from the inside of the vessel just below the lip, and low ring bases. These features are associated when they are first found in the Lower Mississippi Valley. The decorative technique of rocker stamping that also accompanies these features, is somewhat more abundantly represented in early Mesoamerican ceramics.

Whatever their origin may be, the history of tetrapodal supports seems clear enough once they appear in eastern North America. Before 500 B.C. they are confined to the Poverty Point (chart 15–17) and Bayou la Batre (chart 15–12) Phases, and are entirely missing from the earlier fiber-tempered ceramics to the eastward on the Atlantic coast, the Orange and Stallings Island complexes. After 500 B.C. when the drag-and-jab decorative techniques of Stallings and the straight incised line motifs of Orange spread westward to form Tchefuncte, tetrapods diffuse eastward, where they are found in the St. Johns I Phase of Florida (chart 15, 9–10) and the Deptford Phase of eastern Georgia (chart 15–8). They are not abundant, are applied to the Woodland amphora form of vessel, particularly in Georgia in the Deptford Phase (Wauchope, 1966, figs. 6a–b, e, 7 o–q, 8u–w, 9z, nn), and disappear a century or so after the beginning of the present era.

Vessels with four feet are in the Illinois and Ohio regions (chart 15, 1–2) on the time level of the fully developed Hopewell culture, a few centuries before and after A.D. 1. They are found on the typical wide-mouth pot decorated with rouletted bird motifs, as well as the Woodland amphora which has paddle-stamped surfaces. They disappear about A.D. 300.

As was noted for the tetrapods of the Valdivia Phase of Ecuador, the feet of the four-footed vessels in the eastern United States are often placed more closely together than would seem to be functionally efficient. On the Hopewell time horizon they seem to be associated with and probably led to the practice of forming the vessel body into four rounded lobes that give a squared outline. In the Lower Mississippi it is clear that this is the origin of the rather common square flat bases that run through the Troyville and Coles Creek Phases until about A.D. 900 (Ford, 1951, figs. 13a, 16a, 17h, 21g, 23a, 25b, etc.).

Tripodal supports first appear on American ceramics sometime between 1500 and 1000 B.C. There is no indication as to how they may have evolved. Possibly they developed in some way from the earlier four-footed vessels, but as they are perhaps oldest in Mesoamerica, where tetrapods are rare, this may not be true.

Vessel supports, including feet, have been discussed in the regional and interregional comparisons already cited by Wauchope (1950), MacNeish (1954), Gerardo and Alicia Reichel-Dolmatoff (1956); a special survey of tripod supports in the Andean region was made by King (1948).

In the Ocós Phase of the Soconusco in Guatemala (1400–1300 B.C.), slightly bent long tripodal feet are found on small neckless ollas (chart 15–44) that sometimes have line-bordered bands of iridescent paint forming designs on the body and placed in bands around the mouth (M. D. Coe, 1961, p. 50, figs. 14–16). These seem to be the earliest examples of tripods in the Americas. These long tripod feet, bent at the point of attachment to the body, will be noted as an early form in other chronologies.

Tripods disappear from the Soconusco sequence until about 600 B.C., when they reappear in the Conchas II Phase on composite silhouette bowls made of Conchas White-to-buff ware (chart 15–43). These bowls have lines scored in the bottoms and functioned as graters (Coe and Flannery, 1967, fig. 8). Coe (1961, pp. 61, 67, fig. 26k) suggests that they are probably importations from another region. The legs are solid and are short tapering cones; more elaborate and hollow forms of legs are missing. For the Crucero Phase (300 B.C.–A.D. 200), Coe (op. cit., p. 84) states, "Resist decoration (i.e., Usulután) is absent, as are vessel supports."

There is a clear sequence in tripod support forms in the Chiapas region. Apparently they are entirely missing from Dixon's (1959) early pits at Chiapa de Corzo. Also they seem to be quite rare in the earlier deposits at the Santa Cruz site, which with a single gap runs from about 800–250 B.C. Sanders (1961, p. 42) only lists nine: small subglobular, large tubular and hollow, short nubbin (possibly tetrapod), and one mammiform.

From the cache and burial ware of the Horcones Phase (Period VI, A.D. 1–100) at Chiapa de Corzo,

Lowe (1962, fig. 8d) illustrates a single bowl with solid nubbin tripod feet (chart 15–40). The most characteristic vessel supports of this phase, however, are large mammiform feet, which have rattles in them and are placed four to the pot (chart 15–39). They are common on bowls, the pot form, flat-base beakers, and spouted vessels. Wauchope (1950, p. 233) states that this form "seem[s] to be diagnostic of the Proto-Classic ceramic complex . . . . They can be solid or hollow; they frequently (invariably?) occur on tetrapods."

In the Tehuacán sequence tripod vessels, usually bowls, first appear early in the Santa Maria Phase at about 800 B.C. (chart 15–35). They are short and usually solid. Slab leg feet and the bulbous hollow supports (chart 15–34) date in the succeeding Palo Blanco Phase, and while fairly abundant, never become so elaborate as in the lowland regions to the southward.

Porter (1953, pp. 40–41) states that the most characteristic tripod supports in the Tlatilco burial wares are long, solid, and tapering. In the illustrated examples they are attached to small globular neckless jars (chart 15–29), which gives them a close resemblance to the early tripod vessels of the Ocós Phase of coastal Guatemala. She also mentions a composite silhouette bowl with long hollow supports, open at the end. This has a parallel in the Chorrera Phase of Ecuador (chart 15–57; Estrada, 1958, p. 105). As MacNeish (1954, p. 635) has pointed out, short solid tripod feet seem to run through the early phases of Vaillant's El Arbolillo and Zacatenco excavations, but "in late Zacatenco and Ticomán times the type appears to be on the wane and is replaced by large hollow bulbous types" (chart 15–26). These become fairly elaborate, with pellets to form rattles, double hollow balls, and legs made in imitation of human or animal legs (Vaillant, 1931, pl. 75). Looped legs are also found.

Tripod feet apparently were not an element of the ceramic complex found at La Venta in southern coastal Veracruz, but a few of the short nubbin type are in the upper levels of Chalahuites, apparently beginning at about 600–500 B.C. (chart 15–22). A few of these feet were attached to simple bowl forms, which have rocker-stamped decoration in the interior, similar to the tripod grater bowls that are in the Conchas II Phase of the Soconusco, Guatemala.

After about 200 B.C. the usual varieties of Early Classic feet become fairly common. These include solid and hollow feet, the latter usually perforated and sometimes provided with rattles (chart 15, 18–19); and slab feet, both solid and hollow (Drucker, 1943b, figs. 73–81).

In the Huasteca sequence on the northern stretch of the Mexican Gulf coast, MacNeish (1954, pp. 585, 635, fig. 10) lists tripod feet on bowls beginning in the Aguilar Phase. This would be approximately 800 B.C. The early short and solid form is followed by long solid conical feet and feet that have been pierced. Short hollow feet with rattles make their appearance about the beginning of the present era, but never achieve the size and elaboration found in the southern part of Mesoamerica.

Tripod supports of relatively modest design continue to be made in the Huasteca in the succeeding centuries, and it was probably from this region that the tripods in the Mississippi Valley were derived.

Tripod supports in the Mississippi Valley are rare (Griffin lists 85 examples), and date in the later parts of the Mississippian and Caddoan Phases (chart 15, 3–5); probably all were made after A.D. 1300–1400. Geographically they are limited to the western part of the Southeast, the part closest to the presumed region of derivation in northeastern Mexico (Phillips, Ford, and Griffin, 1951, pp. 170–171, table 7, fig. 105). Both long and short solid feet, stem slab and bulbous hollow forms are found on globular bottles, which usually have long necks. Bowls with legs appear to be missing. A few bottles on the Mississippian time level have four feet. These are probably related to the bulbous Proto-Classic examples of Mesoamerica, for as Griffin states, there is no suggestion of connection with the use of tetrapods, on the Hopewellian horizon 1200 years earlier (op. cit., p. 170).

Tripod bowls, and more infrequently four-footed bowls, are a rare form in the ceramics of the Sacaton Phase, Sedentary Period of the Hohokam sequence at Snaketown in southern Arizona. All examples have solid feet and do not show the variation of forms found in the Mississippi Valley (Gladwin, et al., 1937, figs. 98, 108–109). McGregor (1941, p. 148, fig. 39) indicates that bowls with three feet begin in this sequence at A.D. 500.

From the Momíl midden on the north coast of Colombia, Gerardo and Alicia Reichel-Dolmatoff (1956, pp. 196–197, 276–277) present a clear sequence of vessel supports. Although they point out that these could belong to vessels having either three or four feet, no evidence of large four-footed vessels is presented and they were probably tripods. In Momíl I Phase (700–400 B.C.), the vessel supports were solid and were classed into four types. One of these types consists of tapering cylinders about 4 cm. long, which curve sharply inward just before they were attached to the globular body of the pot (chart 15–47, 49), "as though they were bent outward by the weight they supported" (op. cit., p. 196). In the details of both body form and the bent legs, these vessels resemble early tripods in the Ocós Phase of Guatemala and at Tlatilco. The second type is the short "nubbin" feet (chart 15–48), also common in early Formative of Mesoamerica. The Reichel-Dolmatoffs' third form is short feet attached to an almost flat griddle, or possibly a seat, while in the fourth group, short feet support cylindrical vessels with small basal flanges reminiscent of the later slab-foot cylindrical vessels of Teotihuacán style. In the Momíl examples, the feet are round.

Hollow tapering feet and hollow mammiform feet are found in the Momíl II Phase (400–1 B.C.; chart 15–46). Gerardo and Alicia Reichel-Dolmatoff (1956, pp. 286–288), in their very complete discussion of the distribution of mammiform feet, state that there is no evidence to indicate whether the vessels are tripods or have four feet as is usual in Mesoamerica.

From the famous San Agustín site at the headwaters of the Magdalena River, Duque (1964, pp. 141, 326–329, figs. 17, 79, 141) describes tripod vessels with globular bodies, and fairly long tapering legs that are bent to form a shoulder just below the point of attachment to the body. There is evidence that these are an element of his earliest Mesitas Inferior Phase, which dates approximately 500 B.C. to A.D. 100. They are a common form in the region, occurring also in Tierradentro. The resemblance to the globular body, bent leg tripod vessels of Momíl I, Ocós, and Tlatilco is remarkable.

Duque cites the fact that tripod vessels are found in the later cultural phases of Colombia, particularly in the Quimbaya region in the valley of the Cauca River. These, however, are different from the San Agustín specimens. For the later forms, a number of specific parallels can be drawn to the decorative tripod vessels of the Mesoamerican Classic.

Feet and annular bases are present in the Chorrera Phase of Ecuador (1500–500 B.C.). The feet may be tripods rather than tetrapods and are both the short nubbin type (chart 15–58), and more elongated tapering solid supports. Estrada (1958, p. 105, fig. 55) describes bowls with cylindrical hollow legs open at the ends (chart 15–57). These begin in late Chorrera (about 1000 B.C.), and continue in use into the Bahía Phase of the Regional Developmental (about 500 B.C.–A.D. 500). Estrada indicates that while this form of leg is fairly common in the late Ecuadorian Formative, it has been reported elsewhere only from the Tlatilco site in the Valley of Mexico on this time level.

Multiple solid supports, frequently tripods, but often with five or six feet, are characteristic of the Ecuadorian Regional Developmental Period (chart 15–55). Estrada's (1962) strata cuts at Pepa de Huso, Estero A, and Bahía J localities provide clear evidence for his earlier conclusions (1957, pp. 159–162) that tapering solid feet and the hollow cylindrical form precede the hollow mammiform and loop types of supports (chart 15, 53–54). These latter forms have very evident Mesoamerican resemblances and their appearance in Ecuador is around the beginning of the Christian Era. This is coeval with the beginning of these forms in northern Colombia and in Mesoamerica, where Wauchope (1950) notes that they are a time marker for the Proto-Classic.

With the exception of a few vessels that are clearly animal effigies, vessel supports are absent from the Peruvian highland sequence reported by Izumi and Sono (1963), and are also missing from the Chavín-related cultural manifestations of the northern and central coasts.

King (1948) has published a survey of the occurrence of tripod pottery in the Central Andean area, and despite the additional information accumulated in the twenty years that have elapsed, his principal conclusions still seem to be sound. King (op. cit., p. 107) states:

> Chronologically, tripods are earliest in the north highlands and on the central coast. Later Expansionist periods see a great increase in their distribution and frequency with the north coast and the south highlands yielding tripods of this date. In the central highlands tripod forms do not occur before the Inca Period and they are apparently absent in the north coast, central coast, and south highland region during the later Expansionist periods. With the advent of the Inca styles over the whole of the central Andean area we find that, except for the north highlands, the earlier forms of tripods disappear and are replaced by the Inca types, of which the brazier with cylindrical legs is most common.

King (1948, p. 103) notes that both vessel body forms and legs are quite varied in the central Andes, but it is worth mentioning that practically all have parallels in the Classic phases of Mesoamerica. Body shapes include "open bowls, convex-sided open bowls, straight-sided open bowls, hemispherical bowls, globular bowls, ollas, braziers, covered bowls, constricted mouth bowls, and animal forms. Likewise leg shapes are variable. These types are present in Peru and highland Bolivia: long-pointed conical, cylindrical, bulbous, short-stubby and lug legs, animal head."

King was certainly correct in his conclusion that the major part of the occurrence of these forms was in the "Expansionist" Period, the time of wide diffusion of the "Epigonal," coastal Tiahuanaco (or as it is now known, "Wari") ceramic styles. The beginning of this expansion is now placed in the centuries just before and after A.D. 1000 (Kidder, Lumbreras, and Smith, 1963, fig. 12). King (1948, p. 107) also seems to be correct in his postulation that at least some of the globular-bodied vessels with tripod supports were of

an earlier date. These recall the Ocós-Tlatilco examples.

Chronology for the Virú Valley on the north Peruvian coast was not available when King prepared his paper. Bennett (1944a, p. 101, fig. 32D–2) records the globular body form as an element of Recuay ceramics in the Callejón de Huaylas. In terms of the Virú sequence this characteristic Recuay pottery complex is coeval with the Gallinazo III Phase (Bennett, 1950, p. 117), which now is dated about A.D. 500. An illustration of the form has been placed in the highland Peruvian column on chart 15–65, but the more abundant occurrences of tripods on the A.D. 1000 level are too late to be shown here.

Summary

Vessels with small solid "nubbin" tetrapod supports were made in Ecuador between 3000 and 2200 B.C. Rare in Mesoamerica on early levels, they are in the Lower Mississippi Valley and the Mobile Bay region at about 1000 B.C. After 500 B.C. they diffuse eastward along the coast of the Gulf of Mexico and up the Mississippi Valley.

Early tripods, dating between 1500 and 1000 B.C. in coastal Guatemala, are globular-bodied vessels with long tapering feet that are bent near the point of attachment. Similar vessels come from Tlatilco. Apparently related forms are among the first tripods found on the north coast of Colombia (700 B.C.) and in the north highlands of Peru (A.D. 500). The arrival of tripods in the Mississippi Valley is still later (after A.D. 1200), and although bodies remain globular, they are provided with long bottle necks, and the feet are usually bulbous and hollow, or slab-shaped.

The use of feet on bowl forms seems to date to about 500 B.C. in Mesoamerica and to approximately the same time on the coasts of Colombia and Ecuador. Often these bowls are functioning graters, or are decorated in the interior. Both solid and hollow swollen feet, frequently "mammiform" in shape, and sometimes provided with pellets to make rattles, begin in Mesoamerica about the start of the present era. They may be slightly later in the Ecuadorian sequence. In most instances the latter vessels are multiple-footed rather than tripods.

Ring and Pedestal Bases

CHART 15

As has been remarked in the foregoing, the history of ring and pedestal bases roughly parallels that of vessel feet. They tend to appear in the same ceramic complexes and were often applied to the same vessel forms. Still, there is enough difference in the early history of these two varieties of vessel supports to warrant treating them separately.

If one insists on applying a strict definition, there are no annular base vessels in the Valdivia and Machalilla Phases of coastal Ecuador. However, on the polished red-slipped ceramic, where most of the tetrapodal supports are found, there are also examples of bowls with strongly dimpled bases (Meggers, Evans, and Estrada, 1965, p. 76, fig. 43b, pls. 98c, 116q). No additional clay has been added; the rounded bases of the vessels have been neatly pushed in to form dimples that range from 4 to 10 cm. in diameter and 2 to 10 mm. in depth.

The dimpled base will undoubtedly prove to be a useful linking trait. It appears on the Pacific coast of Guatemala in the Conchas and Crucero Phases (M.D. Coe, 1961, p. 83, fig. 35; Coe and Flannery, 1967, figs. 25d, 26d, 27, 29a-b, 31d, 32e, 33b-c), and is fairly common in Mesoamerican Classic ceramics. Earlier it is found in the Cerro de las Mesas Phase (Drucker, 1943b, fig. 12e'), at Tlatilco in the type "Café obscuro" (Piña Chán, 1958 vol. 1, fig. 36h), and in Pit 38 (700 B.C.) of Chiapa de Corzo (Dixon, 1959, p. 22, fig. 35). Dimpled bases also occur in the Mississippi Valley at the Belcher Mound in Belcher Engraved (Webb, 1959, p. 122), and in the late Mississippian Phase after A.D. 1200 (Ford, 1936, p. 151). The vessels with dimpled bases are usually bottles and shallow bowls. These seem to be associated with tripod and ring base pottery. However, this feature will not be traced in any detail here. The subject has been brought up to raise the question as to whether dimpled bases might possibly provide an ancestor for low ring bases. Instead of pushing the vessel base inward, the potter may have added a small rope of clay that performed the same function, i.e. made the vessel more stable on an irregular surface.

True low annular bases are first found in the coastal Ecuadorian sequence in the Chorrera Phase (1500–500 B.C.; chart 15, 61–62; Estrada, 1958, figs. 41–1, 55). Exact data of first appearance in this rather long phase and possible changes of form are unknown. Bowls seem to be the usual vessel form.

Tall pedestal bases become fairly common after 500 B.C. in the Regional Developmental Period (500 B.C.–A.D. 500; chart 15, 59–60). Occasionally these pedestals have open-work cutout designs as they do in Mesoamerica in the Classic Period. Pedestal bases increase in popularity in the last 10 centuries of Ecuadorian ceramic history. Low ring bases also occur in the Pechiche Phase of Tumbes near the Ecuadorian-Peruvian border. Izumi and Terada (1966, pls. 12, 28) date this phase between 850 and 370 B.C., coeval with Chavín.

Ring bases are not indicated for the various phases of the Kotosh sequence in highland Peru. In the Virú Valley coastal sequence, they first appear as low ring bases late in the Gallinazo Phase at about A.D. 400 (chart 15–64; Strong and Evans, 1952, pp. 265–266, fig. 40–5). They are also found in the Recuay Phase of about the same date in the Callejón de Huaylas. Low ring bases continue to be made on the north coast of Peru until the end of the ceramic sequence. Tall pedestal bases are in the Inca Phase, but are rare. In Peru these bases were used principally on bowls.

While tripod feet are found on pottery of the Ocós and Conchas Phases of the coast of Guatemala, ring and pedestal bases seem to be missing. Fragments that might be mistaken for such bases are identified by M. D. Coe (1961, figs. 26c, 29b) as parts of pottery stools. Incense burners had pedestal bases in the Crucero Phase (chart 15–45; Coe and Flannery, 1967, fig. 35).

Apparently ring base vessels are not found in the Chiapas sequence before the Horcones Phase (Chiapa VII). At this time (A.D. 1–100), dimpled or concave bases are rather common, but the ring bases are rare (chart 15, 41–42). Those illustrated by Lowe (1962, figs. 11b, 13b) are quite small, less than a centimeter in height. Tall pedestals are known at this same time but were used for incense burners. Accompanying ceramic features are the typical Proto-Classic items of swollen tetrapod vessel feet with rattles, and bridge-spout vessels. Ring bases continue into the Early Classic and Classic Periods in the Maya region, but never achieve the popularity, size, or elaborateness they acquired to the south.

In the Tehuacán sequence low ring bases first appear on bowls in the Palo Blanco Phase (chart 15, 37–38). This is a rather long period, which MacNeish thinks lasted from 200 B.C. to A.D. 700. The pottery types in which this is a fairly rare form, El Riego Black and El Riego Thin Orange, start being manufactured at the beginning of the phase, but the precise time of the introduction of ring bases is uncertain. By A.D. 500 the higher pedestal supports appear (chart 15–36).

Porter (1953, p. 41) states that at Tlatilco annular bases are "not uncommon and occur on many vessels with decorated rims and interiorly scored bottoms. Triangular-shaped openings are often present in the base supports." Piña Chán (1958, vol. 1, fig. 36y) illustrates a small cup with a base about as tall as the body of the cup.

Vaillant (1930, pl. 4a–b) shows a few annular base painted bowls from his Middle Period at Zacatenco (chart 15, 32–33). Tolstoy (1958b, p. 70) places this as equivalent with El Arbolillo II, here estimated to date a century or so before 500 B.C. High pedestal bases for bowls, with cutout areas in side walls, came from Vaillant's (1931 pl. 76k–n) excavations at Ticomán (chart 15, 30–31). Only three examples are illustrated in the report, in contrast to the much more numerous occurrence of both solid and hollow tripods.

In the strata excavations made at La Venta in southern Veracruz, Drucker (1952, p. 129) found annular supports in all levels, but gives no detail as to size and decoration (chart 15–25). The peculiar "potrests" that he also found in all levels are probably pottery stools similar to those from La Victoria. This type of support is not recorded from García Payón's excavations at Chalahuites and El Trapiche, but a very few quite low examples came from the upper levels of cuts made by Medellín, Wallrath, and the writer in the former site.

The low heavy annular bases that Drucker (1943a, p. 57; chart 15–24) found in the middle levels at Tres Zapotes may also be fragments of pottery stools. Annular bases for vessels, however, do occur rarely and tend to be tall and have cutout areas in the walls of the base (op. cit., fig. 41k–m, pl. 15e). Some of these vessels seem to be incense burners. These bases also seem to be rare from the Cerro de las Mesas deposits. Drucker (1943b, p. 60, fig. 12n′, u, w, w′) illustrates low ring bases on bowls and somewhat higher bases (chart 15–23) on tall slender vases. Dimpled bases occur at both sites.

In the Panuco sequence on the north Gulf coast of Mexico, podal supports are fairly common, but annular bases are not mentioned by either Ekholm (1944) or MacNeish (1954).

The ceramics of the Poverty Point and Tchefuncte Phases (1200–100 B.C.) of the Lower Mississippi Valley and the Bayou la Batre Phase (1100–100 B.C.) of the Mobile Bay area, beginning about this same date, include deep bowl-like forms with very crude ring bases (chart 15–11, –13, –14; Ford and Quimby, 1945, figs. 17d, 18b, c; Wimberly, 1960, figs. 38–40). These accompany the early examples of tetrapodal supports in the southeastern United States. They do not persist like the tetrapodal supports, however, and do not diffuse into the extreme Southeast or northward up the Mississippi Valley. A type of base in pre-Hopewell Upper Mississippi Valley pottery that may be related to the ring base is the small flat form with slightly projecting "heel" found in the Baumer and Crab Orchard Focuses of Illinois (Griffin, ed., 1952, figs. 96–23, 25, 98–1) and in the Adena ceramic complex.

As with podal supports, there seems to be a thousand-year gap in the eastern United States between these early examples of low ring bases and the reappearance of this feature on the late Mississippian horizon about A.D. 1300–1400 (Phillips, Ford, and Griffin, 1951, p. 158, fig. 101). At this time ring bases are found principally in the Mississippian Phase of Arkansas and Missouri (chart 15, 6–7), and tend to be fairly low. There are also tall pedestal bases with cutout designs similar to the Classic examples of Mesoamerica and South America.

Summary

Dimpled bases are earliest on the coast of Ecuador, followed by low ring bases, which apparently begin in the Chorrera Phase about 1500 B.C. These low ring bases diffused to Peru, where they were first made in the Gallinazo Phase about A.D. 400 and become common in the Expansionist Tiahuanaco ceramic tradition. In Mesoamerica, low ring bases seem to have first been made by about 800–600 B.C. on the Gulf coast and in the Valley of Mexico. They are in the Lower Mississippi Valley and adjacent Gulf coast at about this same time, but disappear after 500 B.C. and do not last into the Hopewellian Phase, in contrast to tetrapodal supports.

In northern South America and Mesoamerica, the tall annular bases, frequently with cutout designs, appear between 500 and 1 B.C. These do not diffuse into Peru until Inca times and arrive in the Mississippi Valley only one or two centuries after A.D. 1200.

Both tripod vessels and bowls with tall annular bases were being manufactured in north China toward the end of the Neolithic, about 2000 B.C.

Stirrup-Spout Bottle

CHART 16

Those who prefer a reasonable and rational interpretation of history, rather than a culturological one, might insist that the bottle form is another natural, inevitable, and practical shape that the American Indians easily could have imitated from nature. The bottle gourd was used on the coast of Peru as early as 3000 B.C. in the preceramic Huaca Prieta. It appears logical that this form was imitated in clay. If this did happen, however, it seemingly only happened once. The bottle form is earliest in the Machalilla Phase on coastal Ecuador, beginning at 2000 B.C. Some doubt may be thrown on even this example as an imitation of nature, for the straight-necked bottle is here accompanied by the stirrup-spout bottle, which certainly has no prototype in the natural vegetable kingdom.

Stirrup-spout bottles first appear in Machalilla Striated Polished Plain and Machalilla Embellished Shoulder (chart 16, 33–34; Meggers, Evans, and Estrada, 1965, pp. 137–139, figs. 78, 88, pl. 156). This is a well made sand tempered ceramic ranging from orange to dark grey in color, which has a characteristic surface finish formed by pebble polishing with the polishing tracks clearly apparent on most examples. Machalilla stirrup-spout vessels have globular or shouldered bodies, and the stirrup spout tends to be rather large at points of attachment to the body, narrowing as it approaches the orifice. The vertical portion of the neck is quite short. Stirrup spouts do not have a long duration in the Ecuadorian sequence, for they apparently disappear at the end of the Machalilla Phase at about 1500 B.C. (Estrada, 1958, fig. 55).

Stirrup-spout vessels are not found in the initial phase of the Peruvian highland sequence, but appear about 1100 B.C. in the Kotosh Kotosh Phase and run through the Kotosh Chavín to 300 B.C. (chart 16, 36–38). They occur in Kotosh Well Polished (Izumi and Sono, 1963, pp. 114–116, pls. 128, 6–8, 71a, 1–3) and Kotosh Grooved (op. cit., pp. 116–118, pl. 71a, 4–5). The ware is slightly tempered with sand, surfaces are well polished, and color ranges from dark brown to black. The bodies of the bottles are decorated with wide-line incising in Kotosh Grooved. The stirrup bridge tends to have a slightly greater diameter at the point where it is attached to the body of the bottle, and decreases slightly in diameter to the opening. The spout is longer than those of Machalilla bottles, but by no means so long and slender as became the case later in Mochica. This tendency toward characteristically massive spout form is better shown by the vessel from Chavín de Huántar illustrated by Tello (1960, pl. 48). This beautifully polished bottle has a flat bottom, which is also characteristic of coastal Chavín. A number of examples of the coastal Chavín or Cupisnique Phase stirrup spouts illustrated by Larco Hoyle (1945a, pp. 7–9, 11–14), vary from the massive spouts characteristic of the early period, to more delicate examples foreshadowing the slender spouts of the Mochica Phase on the Peruvian coast (chart 16, 41–43).

After 200 B.C. stirrup-spout bottles virtually disappear from highland Peru. They continue and even increase in popularity on the north coast, however, where they are characteristic of the Mochica Phase. Black ware stirrup-spout bottles were popular in Chimú times and are manufactured today in the vicinity of Piura, where they are offered for sale to tourists who pass on cruise ships.

Examples of stirrup-spout bottles are very rare between northern Peru and central Mexico. Bennett (1944b, p. 63) mentions four in the Quimbaya ceramics from northern Colombia and says that "none resemble the Peruvian style." Stirrup spouts also occur in the late Tairona culture of the Santa Marta region (op. cit., fig. 24e).

Stirrup-spout bottles have a very limited occurrence in Mexico, with the notable exception of the Tlatilco Cemetery, dating between 800 and 400 B.C. (chart 16, 10–11). Porter (1953, p. 40, fig. 12) was impressed with specific resemblances of the Tlatilco specimens to the coastal Chavín. She says, "This extraordinary shape is closely associated with Peru where it occurs in abundance. Stirrup spouts were unknown in Mexico on an early horizon until they were found in Tlatilco. In form, the Tlatilco specimens are almost identical with Peruvian examples from coastal Chavín sites (Covarrubias, 1950, pp. 155–156; Larco Hoyle, 1941, cover, and fig. 77a, d)."

Piña Chán (1958, vol. 1, figs. 43m, 44n; vol. 2, pl. 42) also illustrates examples. The rather specific resemblances to Cupisnique or coastal Chavín are indeed striking, including the black to brown polished surfaces. The Tlatilco examples emphasize the angular outlines for the body found in Cupisnique, rather than the globular bodies common in highland Chavín. It will be recalled that both globular and angular bodies occur in the earlier Machalilla Phase of Ecuador. In the Valley of Mexico, as in Chavín, the stirrups are massive and the spouts are short. Body decoration is formed by zoned red paint and broad incised lines in both regions.

In discussion of this form, Griffin (Phillips, Ford, and Griffin, 1951, table 8, pp. 171–172) lists eight other occurrences, which are concentrated principally in northwestern Mexico. He also cites examples from the eastern part of the Anasazi area in the southwestern United States, ranging in time from Basket Maker III until the 19th century. Griffin lists 28 examples of stirrup-spout bottles in the Mississippi Valley primarily in Missouri and Arkansas (chart 16, 1–2). These shell tempered vessels date in the late Mississippian, after A.D. 1200–1300, and in a crude fashion show the massive spouts and short necks attached to globular bodies characteristic of the Peruvian Formative. It is possible that this form survived to a very late date in northwestern Mexico, had a minor popularity in the Anasazi area, and passed into the Mississippi Valley by the Arkansas River trade route, which as Krieger (1946) points out, was in operation about A.D. 1200.

Summary

Stirrup-spout bottles have no prototype in nature. They are an element of the Machalilla Phase (beginning at 2000 B.C.) and their ultimate source is as mysterious as the derivation of the Machalilla complex as a whole. Their subsequent diffusion within the Americas seems clear enough: into Peruvian Kotosh and Chavín with characteristic large fat spouts, a long history in Peru up to modern times, and a rather long geographical jump to the Tlatilco Phase in the Valley of Mexico, where they seem to be unique in the Mesoamerican Formative. This was never a popular form in Mexico and apparently continued only in the western part of the country, from where they diffused into the Anasazi area of the southwestern United States. From here the form seems to move into the Mississippi Valley after A.D. 1200.

Straight-Necked Bottle

CHART 16

The bottle is missing from the Valdivia Phase of Ecuador, from Puerto Hormiga, and the early Formative manifestations in Panama and the eastern United States. It first appears in minor frequencies in the Machalilla Phase of Ecuador (2000–1500 B.C.; chart 16–35), where it is a shape of Machalilla Double-line Incised (Meggers, Evans, and Estrada, 1965, fig. 77–7) and more characteristically of Machalilla Striated Polished Plain (op. cit., fig. 88–11). In the latter type it is a companion of the stirrup-spout bottle discussed above. The form has a globular body and long slender neck, which flares slightly at the lip.

According to Estrada (1958, fig. 55) the simple bottle form disappears from the Ecuadorian sequence at the end of the Machalilla Phase (1500 B.C.). It is followed through the Chorrera Phase (1500–500 B.C.) by single-spout bottles with a strap handle attached to the neck and vessel shoulder. These are usually provided with a whistle and may be transitional forms in the development of the bridge-spout bottles to be discussed in the following section.

Simple-spout bottles do not occur in the earliest ceramic phase in the Peruvian highlands, the Kotosh Waira-jirca. Like stirrup-spout bottles, they begin at 1100 B.C. and run through Kotosh Kotosh and Kotosh Chavín to 400 B.C. (chart 16, 39–40). In these phases, bottles have both globular bodies (Izumi and Sono, 1963, pl. 44a) and bodies with flat bases (op. cit., pl. 129–9). The narrow necks tend to flare slightly at the lip, as did the Machalilla examples. The bodies are decorated with incised designs; one bears a rather realistic representation of an ear of corn (M. D. Coe, 1962). Similar bottles with characteristic Chavín-style incising are one of the principal forms illustrated by Tello (1960, fig. 144d, e, g, h, 166) from Chavín de Huántar.

Globular-bodied and flat-base bottles are also an element of the Cupisnique ceramics of the Peruvian coast. Larco Hoyle (1945a, pp. 10, 15) shows typical examples including a human head bottle (chart 16, 48–49), a form that becomes popular in the later Mochica Phase.

Simple bottles are not found in the early ceramic complexes that Duque describes from the site of San Agustín, Colombia, nor do they appear in the form sequence given by the Reichel-Dolmatoffs for the north coast of Colombia. Gerardo and Alicia Reichel-Dolmatoff (1956, p. 212, figs. 11–16) illustrate a very small "toy" bottle with quite short neck, apparently from late Momíl I deposits, but the form is rare.

Earliest bottles in northern Colombia appear to be in Cupica Phase IV (Reichel-Dolmatoff, G. and A., 1962, pl. 11), but they have very short necks, quite different from the long neck bottles under consideration. According to Angulo, this phase must date several centuries after A.D. 500. Although bridge-spout bottles and bottles with handles occur in Quimbaya ceramics of northern Colombia, and Peruvian-like double bottles continue into Chibcha ceramics, the simple bottle with a long spout is not a popular form.

Bottles are not found in the Ocós Phase of the Pacific coast of Guatemala. According to Coe and Flannery (1967, p. 23) they are completely missing from the Cuadros Phase, and their figure 8 shows a single form of the straight-necked bottle restricted to the Jocotal Phase about 850–800 B.C. (chart 16–24). The illustrated example is white slipped, has a band of red paint encircling the orifice, and rocker stamping on the short neck.

In the Chiapas sequence, true bottles do not make their appearance before the Horcones Phase (Chiapa VI, 100 B.C.–A.D. 1; chart 16–23; Lowe, 1962, fig. 10b, pl. 11b-2′). Apparently they are rare and are accompanied by variations on the bottle form very reminiscent of examples on the same time horizon on the Peruvian coast. These include double-bodied, joined bottles with bridges between human figures and spouts, whistling bottles, and spouted bottles, the latter being by far the most common form.

This simple bottle is completely missing from R.E. Smith's (1955) Uaxactún ceramic sequence, which extends from the Mamón through the Tepeu III Phases, from about 700 B.C. to A.D. 900.

In MacNeish's Tehuacán sequence (Byers, ed., 1967, vol. 3, fig. 7), the true bottle with small neck first appears about 1500 B.C. in Ajalpan Fine Red (chart 16–19). It continues in Ajalpan Coarse Red, Coatepec Buff, White, and White Rimmed Black (chart 16–18). Palo Blanco Phase bottles have outflaring lips (chart 16–17). Spouted bottles are a feature of the Proto-Classic, as in other Mesoamerican regions.

Bottles with globular bodies sometimes flattened on the bottom, and long necks that usually outflare at the lip, are characteristic of the pottery from the Tlatilco Cemetery (chart 16, 12–14). In color, these range from coffee and reddish brown to black. Surfaces are highly polished. Decoration consists of vertical gadrooning, designs made with wide round-bottom incised lines, red painting, rocker stamping in zones, spiral fluting, and excision with red pigment rubbed into the excised areas (Piña Chán, 1958, vol. 1, p. 76, figs. 15m, 34i-k, 35s-w, 37n-s, 39y-b', 43p-s, 44k-m, 45d', 46e-f, 49, table 1; vol. 2 pls. 24, 33, 34, 46; Porter, 1953, figs. 3, 9, pls. 6g-i, 7). The bottles at Tlatilco more nearly resemble those of the Cupisnique Phase of the Peruvian coast than anything in between. Here too there are examples of composite silhouette bodies (Piña Chán, 1958, vol. 1, fig. 43n, p), and there is a body with a human head on the bottle mouth (op. cit., fig. 44n) strongly reminiscent of an example illustrated by Larco Hoyle (1945a, p. 15).

Porter points out that polished bottles are common at the Playa de los Muertos site in Honduras (Strong, Kidder, and Paul, 1938), and are one of the numerous elements linking this site with Tlatilco (Porter, 1953, p. 65).

Simple long-necked bottles seem to disappear from the Valley of Mexico sequence at 400 B.C., and were not found by Vaillant at his excavations at Ticomán. This form also seems to be rare or absent from the succeeding ceramic complexes of highland Mexico.

In a personal communication, M. D. Coe provides the information that bottles, very similar to those shown in the Valley of Mexico column were found in the newly defined Olmec San Lorenzo Phase (1200–900 B.C.). He has recently reviewed Drucker's collection from La Venta in the United States National Museum and it contains no bottles. The supposed bottle neck illustrated by Drucker (1952, fig. 40b) is a perforated roller stamp.

Simple bottles seem to be missing on the northern part of the Gulf coast of Mexico. They were not found in the Zempoala region by either García Payón's or Medellín, Wallrath, and Ford's excavations in Formative sites. They are neither reported by Ekholm (1944) in his Huasteca sequence nor by MacNeish (1954) in his restudy of this sequence, in which earlier phases are described.

Before A.D. 900 the bottle form was entirely unknown in the eastern United States. At about this date it appears as a prominent element of the ceramics from the Davis site of the early Caddoan, or Gibson Phase, in east Texas (chart 16, 5–6; Newell and Krieger, 1949, figs. 31a, 33a, 45e). These bottles usually are made of dark brown to black ware, and have polished surfaces. Bodies are globular with flattened bases, and the long necks taper from the body to the lip. Body decoration is usually engraving, sometimes combined with excising, and red pigment was rubbed into the excised areas. There can be little doubt that these bottles are of Mesoamerican origin, for other elements of the Davis site ceramic complex point in the same direction: the engraving itself with red pigment rubbed in, "stepped" design motifs, and carinated and composite silhouette bowls. Bowls with interior engraved designs recall the functional graters or *molcajetes* Newell and Krieger (op. cit., pp. 224–232) point to parallels in various Mesoamerican sites.

While a number of features of this complex probably did come from the Huasteca, as was argued in the Greenhouse paper (Ford, 1951, pp. 124–129), it does not seem likely that this is the origin of the bottle form, for it apparently does not exist along the north Gulf coast of Mexico. The precise route of transmission is somewhat of a mystery at this time.

Bottles are a distinctive element of Mississippian cultural phases dating after A.D. 1200, and are undoubtedly derived from the earlier Caddoan examples. A study made by Phillips of 620 bottles is summarized by Griffin (in Phillips, Ford, and Griffin, 1951, pp. 158–159). Mississippian bottles incorporate some Mesoamerican features not found in the Davis site complex, such as small necks of even diameter flaring slightly at the lip, gadrooned bodies, and dimpled and annular bases. Some tall annular bases have decorated cutout designs. Red and white paint and negative painting are common decorations.

Bottles are known in the Southwest. McGregor (1941, p. 331, fig. 149) lists "vases with very tall slender necks and globular bodies . . . " as common in the Salado Branch dating between A.D. 1100 and 1450. This may be the route by which they entered the eastern United States.

Summary

Simple bottles with globular bodies and long necks are earliest on coastal Ecuador and characterize the Chavín-Cupisnique horizon of Peru. They are absent from early Colombian ceramic complexes. The earliest occurrence in Mesoamerica seems to be before 1000 B.C. At Tlatilco, they show features quite similar to those of the Peruvian coastal highlands. They are a minor form in the Jocotal Phase of coastal Guatemala, and in the San Lorenzo Phase of Veracruz, but seem to be entirely missing from the later periods of the Gulf coast of Mexico. Similar bottles are fairly common in the Mississippi Valley after A.D. 900, but the route of transmission from Mesoamerica is not clear at present.

Bridge-Spout Bottle

CHART 16

Although generally thought of as a Peruvian form, the earliest examples of bottles with spouts and bridges seem to be in the Chorrera Phase (1500–500 B.C.) on the coast of Ecuador (chart 16, 30–32). Estrada (1958, p. 101), says that whistling vessels,

> Abundant in the Chorrera culture, arrived in Peru in the Cupisnique Period, but the Ecuadorian forms of whistling bottles with straight spout and flattened handle arrived in Peru with the Salinar culture.
> In our work No. 3 [1957] page 59, we set forth our point of view about their Ecuadorian origin. They are found here throughout the distribution of the Chorrera culture, being completely diagnostic of it. They continue on in fewer numbers into the following Guangala culture. The construction of the whistle, figure 51, is the same in Peru as in Ecuador.

Not only does the bridge-spout whistling bottle appear to be earlier in Ecuador than in other regions in the Americas, there is in this region a suggestion that the form may have evolved from the simple bottle. During the Chorrera Phase (1500–500 B.C.) most of the bottles have centrally placed long spouts with the strap handle connecting spout and bottle shoulder. When modeled figures are placed on bottle shoulders after 500 B.C., the spout still occupies a central position and the figure is placed off to one side (chart 16, 28–29). This is in contrast to all the Peruvian bridge-spout bottles, including what seem to be earliest forms from the south coast (Wallace, 1962, fig. 3), where spout and figure are symmetrically placed.

It seems clear that the bridge-spout vessels entered Peru by way of the coast rather than the highlands, for they are missing in the latter region before A.D. 500. Whether they first appeared on the south coast and spread northward hinges (like negative painting) on the age of such complexes as the Cerillos Phase of Ica Valley described by Wallace (op. cit.). If the Chavinoid elements present there do indicate an age of 500–1 B.C., then these elements certainly came up from the south, and a sea route from coastal Ecuador to the south coast must be postulated. If, however, they moved southward down the Pacific coast with some time lag, the picture of the diffusion would be clearer. The Chorrera Phase bottles with large strap handles (Ecuador, 1500–500 B.C.) correspond to those of Salinar (Peru, A.D. 100–500; chart 16–47), while the figure and bridge-spout bottles of the Ecuadorian Regional Developmental (500 B.C.–A.D. 500) corre-

spond to the Gallinazo Phase (Peru, A.D. 500–800; chart 16, 44–46).

Bottles with long slender necks and attached handles apparently are not common in the Pechiche Phase (850–370 B.C.) in the Tumbes region of northern Peru, but they do occur, apparently without whistles, in this and the succeeding Garbanzal Phase (Izumi and Terada, 1966, p. 37, form B12, pl. 22b, 1–3, 5–7). This adds weight to a southward diffusion of this feature.

Bridge-spout vessels are certainly most numerous on the Peruvian south coast, where they last through the Paracas sequence up to Inca times. Along the entire coast they are particularly characteristic of the negative time horizon (ca. A.D. 500), and very commonly have modeled bird figures, are provided with whistles, and are decorated with negative paint. Bodies are round, rectangular, in the form of fruits, or may consist of double-connected globular receptacles, one of which bears the figure, and the other a spout, always connected by a bridge. With some changes in form these bridge-spout bottles run through all periods of the Peruvian coast up through the Inca conquest. Both single and double bridge-spout vessels are in the Recuay Phase of the Callejón de Huaylas. The appearance of bridge-spout vessels in the Peruvian highlands seems to be after the close of the Kotosh sequence, but before the beginning of Classic Tiahuanaco. The probable date is A.D. 500–600.

The Peruvian spout and bridge bottle seems to have arrived fairly late in highland Colombia. At San Agustín, Duque (1964, pp. 323–35, –42, –16, pl. 8–2, –4) shows examples of pedestal-base head vessels that come from tombs, which he dates in his Mesitas Media Phase (A.D. 500–800). He (op. cit., pp. 328–331) has discussed the distribution of this form in Colombia.

Gerardo and Alicia Reichel-Dolmatoff (1962, p. 3, pl. 8–2, –3) illustrate a globular bottle with two openings from the Cupica Burial Mound on the north Pacific coast (after A.D. 500). These openings, however, are not true spouts and they have no bridge. Probably there is no relationship to the Peruvian tradition. Bennett (1944b, fig. 13) shows both single and double-bridge-spout vessels (chart 16, 25–26). Birds decorated with red and white and negative painting come from the Quimbaya region of the lower Cauca Valley in Colombia. These pieces are clearly in the Peruvian tradition. A later Chibcha example (op. cit., fig. 20h) has joined bodies, each with a spout, and the spouts connected by a bridge.

The Peruvian type of spouted vessel has been sporadically found in Mesoamerica, approximately on the 500 B.C. time level. Porter (1953, p. 47) mentions both simple and bridge spout vessels and spouted whistling jars as being present at Tlatilco, but strangely enough neither she nor Piña Chán have provided illustrations. In regard to whistling jars, Porter (op. cit., p. 47) says:

> Whistling jars are worthy of mention. The Tlatilco ones are always animal effigy jars with the spout in the form of a tail. Tomb 33 of Monte Alban I, yielded a double-vesseled whistling jar with a bridge handle. One vessel represents an animal. Another such jar of the same period was found at Zimatlan. Other examples from Oaxaca are discussed by Kidder, Jennings, and Shook (1946, pp. 191–192).

She (op. cit., p. 77) makes further comparisons:

> Whistling jars are also a distinctly Peruvian feature although usually of slightly later date (Kidder, Jennings and Shook, 1946, p. 193). Larco Hoyle (1941, p. 35) reports one from Cupisnique, however, a double vessel connected by a flat bridge. Although not common, Pre-Classic examples of whistling jars in Meso-america include Tlatilco, Arenal Phase of Miraflores and Playa de los Muertos, Honduras. It seems unlikely that whistling vessels were invented independently in the two areas.

Lowe (1962, fig. 28, pl. 25a-1) illustrates a double-bodied vessel with bridge (chart 16–22), provided with a whistle surmounting the head of a figure on one side and a central opening as well as spout on the other. This dates in the Escalera Phase (Chiapa III, 550–450 B.C.).

Summary

Bottles with centrally placed spout and handle provided with a whistle are found in the Chorrera Phase on the coast of Ecuador (1500–500 B.C.). The early handle form appears in the Peruvian Puerto Moorín-Salinar Phase (A.D. 100–500) and the developed form with symmetrically arranged spouts was made after A.D. 500, the time of the negative painted decorative horizon. Although this form achieves a popularity peak on the south coast of Peru and may have been introduced there late in the Chavín Phase (after 500 B.C.), it seems more probable that it moved down from the north. The occurrence of bridge-spouts about 500 B.C. is mentioned for Mesoamerica, and one example is illustrated from Chiapas. This did not develop into a popular Mesoamerican form.

Teapot Vessel

CHART 16

Spouted vessels used by Wauchope (1950, p. 229, fig. 8) for comparative purposes in Mesoamerica are different in form from those of the Peruvian tradition: The former are never provided with whistles, are bottles or pots with a central opening and a short neck, and have spouts placed in a fashion very similar to those on a kettle or teapot. Wauchope points out that in his Village Formative Phase these spouts are generally free standing, while in the later Classic Phase, they have bridges tying them to the neck of the bottle.

Spouted vessels are missing from the La Victoria sequence described by M. D. Coe (1961) and from the continuation of this sequence given in Coe and Flannery (1967). They are also absent from the early part of the Chiapas sequence, first appearing in the Horcones Phase (Chiapa VI, A.D. 1–200), where they are fairly abundant and are always provided with bridges connecting spout and vessel neck (chart 16, 20–21).

MacNeish's diagram of the Tehuacán sequence shows teapot vessels (chart 16–16) in Quachilco Gray, which has a maximum frequency at about 300 B.C. The bridged spout variety begins at about this time and runs past A.D. 700 (chart 16–15).

Neither bridged nor unbridged spouts are present in Vaillant's series of Formative sites in the Valley of Mexico.

Earliest examples in southern Veracruz are in lower Tres Zapotes (chart 16–9; Drucker, 1943a, p. 51, fig. 24), where "Spouts are not uncommon. In only rare instances, and these are from Middle and Upper deposits, are spouts of the supported variety found in Polychrome ware. All the rest are stubby, unsupported, and slant outward from the vessel wall more than do the supported variety."

MacNeish (1954) discussed the significance of unbridged and bridged-spouted vessels, but did not find any in his excavations at the Pavón site in the Huasteca. Ekholm (1944, p. 394, figs. 24H, 25P, 25Q) illustrates two unbridged spouts and one bridge spout. One can be dated as Panuco V (approximately A.D. 1000).

Teapot vessels, often made into animal effigies so that the spout forms a tail as it frequently does in Mesoamerica, came into the Mississippi Valley shortly before the beginning of European contact (chart 16, 3–4). They are practically a marker of the early historic horizon. In fact, Quimby has suggested they may have been copied from European teapots. They are found principally along the lower Arkansas River. Red slip and red and white paint are the usual decoration. Griffin (Phillips, Ford, and Griffin, 1951, pp. 172–173, table 9, fig. 113) doubts that these vessels have any relationship to the earlier Mesoamerican forms. Although the transitional region is unknown, it seems likely that this is a peripheral retention of the earlier Mexican teapot with unsupported spouts.

Spouted vessels of the Mesoamerican variety both with and without bridges are found in the Peruvian

Andes on the late Tiahuanaco horizon, about A.D. 100–800 (Alcina Franch, 1965, figs. 515–12, 521–7, 20–21, 24).

Summary

Teapot-shaped vessels appear in Mesoamerica between 500 and 1 B.C. Early examples have free standing spouts, but after A.D. 1, there is usually a bridge tying the spout to the vessel neck.

J. E. Kidder (1957, figs. 22 1–n, 23, 44–56) illustrates similar teapot-shaped vessels from Tokai Province in Japan in the Jomon Horinouchi Phase.

POTTERY DECORATION

Red Slip and Zoned Red Slip

CHART 17

The use of red slip runs through the Valdivia Phase (3000–1500 B.C.; chart 17–42). It occurs as Valdivia Polished Red (Meggers, Evans, and Estrada, 1965, pp. 76–80), and on the decorated types, Valdivia Fine-line Incised, Valdivia Red Incised and Valdivia Red Zoned Punctate (op. cit., pp. 60, 81–82). According to the authors (op. cit., p. 76) "Exterior and rim interior of jars and both surfaces of open bowls are covered with a paper thin, rich, dark red slip." Surfaces are evenly polished. Most of the shapes are bowls, some with four feet. Valdivia Polished Red reaches a popularity maximum of about 40 percent toward the end of Period A. There is also a polished red slip type in the Machalilla complex, Machalilla Polished Red (op. cit., pp. 130–132). The zoning of red slip, or more properly red paint, on natural color vessel surfaces becomes prominent in this phase as Machalilla Red Banded. Red paint is combined with incised areas in Machalilla Incised and Red Zoned (op. cit., p. 134). Machalilla Red Incised has straight line engraved designs cutting through the red slip to reveal the color of the paste. These types are illustrated by Meggers, Evans, and Estrada (op. cit., pls. 145, 147–153).

The tradition of designs painted in red on the brown or tan natural color of the vessel will be mentioned in the following pages, but is not diagrammed on chart 17, nor is it considered the central theme of the red slipped tradition being traced.

Overall slip, zoned slip alternating with incising, and engraving cutting through red slip all continue through the Chorrera Phase and reach a maximum frequency in Tejar (chart 17–37; Evans and Meggers, 1957, p. 241). Polishing of the slip begins to decline in popularity in Chorrera and its place is taken by a thin red wash applied to unpolished surfaces, either all over the vessel or in patterns. This same sequence will also be noted in Mesoamerica.

Overall red slip never became a prominent type in the coastal Peruvian chronology of Virú Valley. Red paint zoned by incised lines begins about 500 B.C. and will be discussed later. This is followed by Puerto Moorín White-on-Red (Strong and Evans, 1952, pp. 295–301, figs. 55–56), a painted type belonging to a pan-Peruvian white-on-red horizon style (beginning about A.D. 100), which in turn is followed by extensive use of red and white paint in the Mochica style of the north coast. On the south coast in Ica, Wallace (1962) reports red slip between 500 and 200 B.C.

In the highland Kotosh sequence, polished red slip does not appear until the beginning of the Higueras Period, A.D. 1 (chart 17–44). Higueras Red (Izumi and Sono, 1963, pp. 106–107) apparently is an unslipped oxidized pottery; however, contemporary Kotosh Red Polished (op. cit., pp. 108–109, pl. 38) is a true red slipped ceramic. Broad-line incised decoration is common in the latter type. A peculiarity of Kotosh Zoned Unpainted is the fact that the vessels have an overall polished red slip except for a panel filled with incised decoration. This parallels Machalilla Incised and Red Zoned. Bowls are the usual form; a few vessels are jars.

The use of red slip in the Puerto Hormiga Phase on the north coast of Colombia is somewhat doubtful. In description of Puerto Hormiga Arenosa Esparcida, Reichel-Dolmatoff (1965, pp. 25–26) notes that at times small spots of red coloring can be seen (chart 17–36). That a fugitive red slip was in use is much clearer in the succeeding Barlovento Phase (chart 17–35). Reichel-Dolmatoff (1955, p. 258) says that the large globular hemispherical and oval vessels characteristic of this phase show that "Remains of red paint applied in a very irregular manner and forming spots are sometimes encountered on the upper parts of ollas and in the interior of wide mouth vessels. The color was applied in a very thin layer. . . . Frequently remains of paint or of the superficial wash can be seen only in the incisions, having eroded from the rest of the surface . . . ."

Angulo Valdés (1962b, p. 41) says that none of the sherds from the lower levels of the Malambo site are slipped, and that this feature is found in the middle and upper levels, where the vessel surfaces are well polished. He does not state the color of the slip, but it is possible that this is the point at which the earlier practice of applying a fugitive red wash changes to the application of a polished red slip. A true red slip, which occasionally was well polished, began to be applied in the Momíl Phases after about 500 B.C. (chart 17, 33–34; Reichel-Dolmatoff, G. and A., 1956, pp. 151–152). At the same time painted types appear: red-over-white, black-over-white, black-over-red, and polychrome. Red slipped vessels are semiglobular, composite silhouette, or shallow plates. Red slip is also common on the vessels from the Cupica Burial Mound (chart 17–32). Red slip and red and white paint continue in the Colombian ceramic tradition up to the time of European contact.

The Monagrillo Phase of Panama probably begins about 2000 B.C. Monagrillo Red (Willey and Mc-Gimsey, 1954, pp. 65–67) consists of deep jars, or bowls 20–30 cm. in diameter, which have red pigment covering the entire vessel or only the interior or exterior, or applied in a band around the rim, frequently on the inside as well as the outside. The type also includes simple red-on-buff designs on exterior walls. Motifs are horizontal bands, pendant triangles, semi-circles, or vertical painted bands.

M. D. Coe (1961, pp. 51–53, figs. 8, 10) found a substantial percentage of specular red slip in the lower levels of La Victoria site on coastal Guatemala (chart 17–29). This was placed on tecomates, simple silhouette bowls, and dishes. It was replaced by red slipped ware, which was both burnished and un-burnished. Coe and Flannery (1967, fig. 8) show the sequence of red slipped forms through the succeeding phases. Conchas Red Unburnished dominates between 700 and 300 B.C. (chart 17–27). This has large neckless jar vessel forms. At this same time, Red and White, Red-on-Cream, and Red on Unslipped wares were being manufactured.

From Pits 38 and 50 at the Chiapa de Corzo site, Dixon (1959) reports white monochrome, red and white bichrome, and occasional red slip applied about the rims of neckless jars or in the interior of bowls (chart 17–21). This slip seems to be well polished on bowls, but not on the neckless jars. Apparently at this time (Chiapa I, 1400–850 B.C.) there is no overall red slip in use in this region. In the Burrero Phase (Chiapa II, 850–500 B.C.) from Santa Cruz, Sanders (1961, pp. 17–18) describes Burrero Red, which has bands of red paint around the mouths of unpolished tecomates of varying color, bowls slipped usually in the interior and lightly polished, and composite silhouette vessels

that are usually painted inside the lip and sometimes also outside.

Chiapilla Polished Red (op. cit., pp. 20–23) has a more lustrous surface. This dates Chiapa IV–V (450–100 B.C.) and is found on both bowl and olla forms (chart 17–20). Bichrome and polychrome painting were also in use during this period. Occasional red paint is found at later dates in the Chiapas region, but overall red slipping seems to go out of favor after 100 B.C.

Ajalpan Fine Red, a polished red slip on bowls and bottle forms, begins about 1500 B.C. in the Tehuacán sequence (chart 17–19). Ajalpan Coarse Red, which consists of bands of red slip applied around the necks of large ollas, has a slightly later date, reaching a climax at about 900 B.C. (chart 17–18). About this same time red painting on the natural buff vessel surface reaches a modest maximum as Coatepec Red-on-Buff. These types are succeeded by Quichilco Red, which ranges from 400 B.C. to A.D. 200.

In his stratigraphic excavations at Tlatilco, Piña Chán (1958, vol. 1, table 1, p. 48, fig. 16d–i) found polished red slipped vessels in his middle levels (chart 17–17). Red slipped sherds formed less than 2 percent of the total. They were fragments of ollas with globular bodies and outcurving lips, and simple or composite silhouette bowls that usually have polished red interiors. Some had incised decoration on the exterior. Red-on-white, white-on-red, and red-on-buff painted designs start slightly earlier.

Porter (1953, p. 35, fig. 6) was impressed by the "Fair number" of the Tlatilco burial vessels decorated with red paint on natural surface, either as a band about the rim, or in areas accentuating details of vessel modeling.

At El Arbolillo, Vaillant does not consider red slip as a separate category, but describes most of the red painted types recognized by Piña Chán. At Zacatenco, Polished Red occurs in frequencies from about 1 to 5 percent (Vaillant, 1930, table 2). At Ticomán (Vaillant, 1931, pp. 284–286) burnished red ware is slightly more popular and is applied to bowls with tripod feet and annular bases (chart 17–16). In addition, in the middle and late periods there is an unpolished red that often tends toward a salmon shade.

Tolstoy's (1965, figs. 4–5) analysis of his excavations at Tlatilco and reanalysis of Vaillant's and Piña Chán's strata cuts suggest that polished red pottery is rare in the early half of the site occupation, but rises to about 8 percent frequency in the latter half. Red slip continues into the Teotihuacán horizons as San Martín Polished Red (Tolstoy, 1958b, pp. 29–30).

Overall red slip seems to be rare in the San Lorenzo Phase of Veracruz. According to M. D. Coe's pre-liminary mimeographed progress report, a few tecomates have overall slip, but a band of red slip about the mouth is more common (chart 17–12). Very close resemblance of these neckless jars to those of the Cuadros and Jocotal Phases of the Guatemalan coast is emphasized. Drucker (1952) lists a rare coarse red pottery for La Venta. This seems to be a red slip applied as rim bands or sometimes overall wash, on what he calls brown ware.

Red slipping over "Café o Bayo" ware is somewhat more common on this time level in García Payón's (1966, pp. 95–99) excavation at El Trapiche. Red slipping of shallow bowls is typical. Red slip also is very common on large ollas with outflaring lips (chart 17–10). Interiors of the lips are slipped and the olla shoulders have slip from the base of the neck to the maximum diameter. Viewed from directly above, the vessel looks as though it were covered with red slip, but this is not the case. Color varies from fairly bright dark red to an orange shade, and finish ranges from unpolished to polished.

At Tres Zapotes, Drucker (1943a, pp. 57–58) describes red slip ware very briefly as a subtype of brown ware. He mentions bowls with flat bases and flaring sides, a spouted vessel with unsupported spout, jars(?), and ollas, both neckless and with necks.

The red slipped ware from Cerro de las Mesas is also a minor subtype of the more common brown ware. The pigment is bright red, apparently contains mica, and is well polished. Drucker (1943b, p. 37) does not indicate vessel shapes beyond a statement to the effect that red slip was placed on brown ware vessel forms, and that bowls were not slipped under the base.

In the Huasteca, red slip first appears about 800 B.C. as Aguilar Red (MacNeish, 1954, p. 575). The slip is fairly bright red and is polished, except on some of the bases. Forms include recurved rim bowls with convex bottoms, sometimes with tripod feet.

Earliest red slip in the Mississippi Valley is Tchefuncte Red Filmed (chart 17–9). The slip is a fairly dark red and is applied only to bowls, covering both the interior and exterior surfaces. Frequency of occurrence of this type is less than 1 percent. In addition to the slipped sherds, there is some evidence that a fugitive red coloring matter had been applied to some of the vessels.

Red slip continues to have a low popularity through the Marksville Phase (Ford, 1963, fig. 34, table 1), but at this time is joined by red slip applied in areas and also zoned by incised lines. The three treatments, overall red slip and zoned and unzoned red paint, became more popular after A.D. 400 in the Troyville Phase (chart 17–8; Ford, 1951).

The earliest appearance of a substantial proportion of red slip in the southeastern United States is in the St. Johns area of Florida, where Goggin (1952, p. 102) describes Dunn's Creek Red (chart 17–3). This is found principally on large bowls, but also occurs on large neckless jars. This latter form sometimes has excised decoration about the neck (Oklawaha Incised), and a wide band of red slip serves as a background for the cutout designs. An accompanying type is St. Johns Red-on-Buff, which features simple geometric designs made with red paint on the buff or tan natural-colored surface of the vessel. Red slip continues into the Weeden Island time horizon, and is rather common in the eastern United States during the later Mississippian periods.

Summary

The feature of the application of a red slip or wash seems to have a fairly straightforward history in the Americas. It first appears on the coast of Ecuador at 3000 B.C. as a well-polished bright red coating. On the north coast of Colombia, there is a doubtful use of fugitive unpolished paint at this time. Polished painting does not start in the Colombian sequence until after 1000 B.C. Simple red slip did not diffuse to coastal Peru, but by 1500 B.C. red painting in zones bordered by incised lines was practiced. After A.D. 1 red slip was used as a ground color for white painted designs.

In most Mesoamerican sequences, the earliest red slip is polished as in Valdivia and later becomes unpolished. In the eastern United States, as in Colombia, the tradition begins as a fugitive paint, and polishing was not practiced until after A.D. 1.

The painting of red designs on natural vessel surfaces is a prominent device in the Machalilla Phase of Ecuador (2000–1500 B.C.). This tradition accompanies red slip from its earliest appearance in most of the Mesoamerican sequences and enters the eastern United States in the Marksville Phase (ca. A.D. 1). This variant has not been graphed.

Red Paint Zoned by Incised Lines

CHART 17

A distinctive variety of red painting has caught the attention of several writers who have made comparisons between the ceramics of North and South America (Strong, 1943; Porter, 1953; Willey, 1955b). These red-slipped areas are bordered by wide incised lines, which separate them from the natural surface of the vessel. Not only is there a close resemblance in the round-bottom incised lines and motifs to zoned rocker-stamped decoration, but the two are also closely associated in time range in the various areas.

The earliest zoned red paint is in the Machalilla Phase of Ecuador (2000–1500 B.C.; chart 17, 38–39). Meggers, Evans, and Estrada (1965, pp. 128–129, pl. 145) have called this Machalilla Incised and Red Zoned. A closely related type is Machalilla Punctate and Red Zoned (op. cit., p. 134, pl. 145). This decoration differs somewhat from red zoned designs that occur after 1000 B.C. in that it actually consists of areas filled alternately with incised lines and red paint. This same tendency can be noted in red zoned designs of the Chorrera Phase of Ecuador (chart 17–37; Estrada, 1958, fig. 43–6), and also is to be found in some of the early red zoned designs of coastal Peru (chart 17–47, –49).

Simple zoning of stamping by wide incised lines had already been practiced during the Puerto Hormiga Phase on the north coast of Colombia (Reichel-Dolmatoff, 1965, pl. 3–3, –4, –10). This could be the origin for the simplicity characteristic of the zoned red class after 1000 B.C.

Zoned red slip design appears on the coast of Peru in the Ancón Phase about 1500 B.C. By 1000 B.C. it has developed the motifs diagnostic of the Chavín Phase. Plume-like curving elements retain the natural color of the vessel surface while the background is painted red. Surfaces are beautifully polished. By 500 B.C. the designs have both curving and angular step motifs, which were forerunners of the geometric motifs of the Puerto Moorín or Salinar Phase (A.D. 100–600; chart 17–46). This technique of zoned red designs also occurs in the early phases of the Paracas culture on the south coast of Peru, but after approximately A.D. 600, it disappears from the Peruvian sequence.

Zoned red paint of the variety of interest here apparently is not found in the Kotosh sequence. Tello (1960, fig. 169) illustrates two examples of zoned black from the Temple of Chavín de Huántar (chart 17–43). Both red and black zoned ceramics from the same site are mentioned by Bennett (1944a, p. 87).

Earliest use of zoned red paint in the Colombian sequence is in the Malambo Phase (chart 17–31). This is somewhat atypical in that the red paint is applied to areas between modeled decoration. True zoning of various techniques becomes quite common in the Momíl Phase. This includes crosshatching, dentate stamping, and a minor proportion of zoned painting, which is confined to Momíl II (chart 17–30; Reichel-Dolmatoff, G. and A., 1956, pp. 198–199, pl. 15, 8–10). These few examples are not simple contrasting unpainted and painted areas, but rather stamp decorated areas contrasting with painted zones. Neither do the red slipped incised ceramics from the early stages at San Agustín (Duque, 1964, pp. 309–

310), nor those from Cupica (Reichel-Dolmatoff, G. and A., 1962) conform to the zoned type under consideration here. Both contrast areas of incised lines with red paint, in the tradition probably inherited from Machalilla.

In his comparative study of Pre-Classic ceramics in Mesoamerica, Wauchope (1950, p. 225) says, "Outline incising of painted areas seems to be clearly an Urban Formative and Proto-Classic manifestation, although an aberrant and possibly prototypical specimen appears in Early Zacatenco. This technique occurs in Cerro de las Mesas Lower I, Chukumuk I, Playa de los Muertos, Early Ticomán, Huasteca II, Chukumuk II, Late Ticomán, Balam, and Middle Tres Zapotes B."

Coe and Baudez (1961) have established a chronology in northwestern Costa Rica. The earliest period, dating in the first century of this era, features zoned red paint. Other ceramic decorations of this Zoned Bichrome Period are zoned dentate rocker stamping, engraving, incising, and wavy black painted lines produced by multiple brush technique. Vessel forms are usually jars with outflaring necks and "cuspidors." The red paint is bordered either by wide incised lines, or, apparently more frequently, by scratched or engraved lines. From the illustrations, it appears that lines were engraved after the paint was applied. A third engraved line is sometimes centered in the painted band and occasionally is zig-zag.

Ocós Specular Red (M. D. Coe, 1961, pp. 51–53) has well-burnished red slip made from hematite that has a high concentration of the crystalline form. On some neckless jars, painted and unpainted areas are separated by shallow grooves made before the slip was applied (chart 17–25). Other forms include thin wall neckless jars, dishes with beveled and gadrooned rims, flat-base pans, and bowls with simple silhouette, some of which have labial flanges. This design occurs in the same levels as zoned rocker stamping.

The Ocós type is succeeded by Conchas Red-on-Buff (chart 17, 22–23; op. cit., pp. 75–76). This again has very simple designs, and in some instances the red slipped areas are separated from unpainted areas by shallow incised lines. Forms are similar to those of the Ocós type. Coe and Flannery (1967, pp. 47–48) state that Conchas Red-on-Buff begins with the Jocotal Phase (850 B.C.), achieved its greatest variety and popularity in Conchas I, and disappeared rapidly at the end of Conchas II. This range is shown in their figure 8. Throughout this time, the type was accompanied by zoned red and white decorated pottery, and through Conchas II times by a red-over-cream design.

While polished red slip is fairly abundant in the Chiapas sequence, and red paint is applied to vessel rims, the practice of defining zones of red paint by incised lines does not seem to occur.

MacNeish provides the information that zoned red paint runs through the Ajalpan and Santa Maria Phases in the Tehuacán sequence, but illustrations are not available.

Red painted pottery zoned by wide incised lines is a fairly common feature at the Tlatilco site in the Valley of Mexico (chart 17, 13–15). Porter (1953, pp. 35–36, fig. 8, pl. 12D–E) says that the ceramic is characterized by a "warm brown color with red paint enclosed by a pre-slip and pre-polished groove." Piña Chán (1958, vol. 1, pp. 44–46, figs. 15, 46) includes these line bordered painted bands in his type "Rojo sobre Café." Motifs are simple geometric arrangements, sometimes with an extra incised line centered in the painted band. Despite the lack of complexity in design, Tlatilco Zoned Red shows more resemblance to the comparable decoration in the Peruvian Chavín Phase than it does to anything in between. Vaillant (1931, p. 275, pl. 70) describes these designs from Ticomán as Red-on-Yellow Incised.

Painted ware of any kind was extremely rare in the collections from La Venta; Drucker (1952, p. 104) says it constitutes only 25 out of 25,000 specimens. Of these most were red on brown and one is mentioned as having incising (chart 17–11). Red-on-brown sherds are somewhat more common from El Trapiche and Chalahuites. García Payón (1966, pp. 95–99) does not differentiate between line zoned and unzoned. Medellín, Wallrath, and Ford found a half dozen examples of line zoned sherds in the cut at Chalahuites. Red-on-brown painting seems to be equally rare at Tres Zapotes. White-on-red bichrome is mentioned by Drucker (1943a, p. 59), but zoning by incised lines apparently was not practiced. Red-on-brown ware continues at the Cerro de las Mesas site. Drucker (1943b, p. 38) describes three varieties. One of these has postfired engraved lines bordering the red painted area. This apparently is a late retention of zoned red paint, but will not be considered as in the mainstream of the diffusion we are trying to trace.

MacNeish (1954, p. 638, fig. 37–5), in the comparative section of his Panuco study, considers red paint outlined by incising as a linking trait in Mesoamerica. At the time he thought that it was on the Proto-Classic time horizon and pointed to occurrences in Early Zacatenco, Playa de los Muertos, and in Cerro de las Mesas. Several of his examples have engraved lines outlining the colored area. Typical zoned red, with the areas bordered by wide round-bottom incised lines, is found in the curious Tancól complex, most frequently on bowls. Ekholm (1944, p. 414, fig. 29a–e) considers this to be on his Period II level, which

dates the complex about A.D. 1. There is a striking resemblance to incised zoned red in the Lower Mississippi Valley as has been pointed out a number of times, but the resemblance to this decoration is closer in the Troyville Phase than it is in the Marksville.

Red paint zoned by wide round-bottom incised lines has been traced in the Lower Mississippi Valley and on the coast of the Gulf of Mexico by Ford (1951). It first appears as Marksville Red Filmed (chart 17–7; Ford and Willey, 1940, pp. 82–85, fig. 40). Designs are fairly complex, usually curvilinear, and the surface has a low polish. Frequencies of occurrence are very low. At the same time there are examples of red paint without bordering incised lines. This decoration is always found on bowls (Ford, 1963, fig. 34f, k). Red slip outlined by incised lines continued on into the Troyville Phase, where the type is named Woodville Red Filmed (chart 17–6; Ford, 1951, pp. 61–62). This also is found only on bowl forms and usually is on the interiors. In addition to the incised lines bordering the red painted area as was common at Tlatilco, there is frequently a third line centered in the painted band.

Zoned red slip is also characteristic of the coeval Santa Rosa and Weeden Island Phases on the northwest coast of Florida, where Willey (1949a, pp. 391–392, 422) describes Pierce Zoned Red and the later Weeden Island Zoned Red (chart 17, 4–5). Pierce Zoned Red is an element of the early phase at the Crystal River site on the Gulf coast at the base of the Florida Peninsula (chart 17–2).

Hopewell Zoned Red, with red painted areas bounded by wide incised lines, is a minor element of the Classic Hopewell of the Illinois River (chart 17–1; Griffin, 1952a, p. 118).

Summary

Although line zoned red paint was never a popular decoration in the Americas, its temporal and geographic distribution seems to be fairly simple. From a beginning of about 2000 B.C. on the coast of Ecuador, it is in coastal Peru by 1500 B.C. and after 1000 B.C. is a minor decoration of the Chavín complex, sharing the peculiar motifs that mark this art style. It continues on the Peruvian coast until about A.D. 500. In Ecuador and on the north coast of Colombia, where it seems to be established after 500 B.C., the idea of contrasting areas of incising and punctating or dentate stamping with red-painted areas seems to be inherited from the earlier Machalilla design arrangement.

Specular hematite and simple motifs mark this type on the coast of Guatemala after 1500 B.C. It seems to be absent in the Chiapas sequence, and plays a minor role at Tehuacán. As is the case with a number of other features, zoned red at Tlatilco after 1200

B.C. more nearly resembles Peruvian Chavín than anything in between.

After about 300 B.C. this decoration is rare in highland and Gulf coast Mexico, and scratched or engraved lines replace the earlier incised wide round-bottom grooves.

This design appears in the Mississippi Valley at 100 B.C. as a minor element in the Marksville Phase, and diffuses principally to the east along the Gulf coast of Mexico. With minor changes in detail, it lasts until about A.D. 600.

Unzoned and Zoned Rocker and Linear Stamping

CHART 18

The use of rocker stamping in bands or zones bordered by wide incised lines, contrasting with smooth bands, was among the first of the ceramic decorations to catch the attention of archeologists interested in inter-American diffusion. The occurrence of rocker stamping, usually unzoned, across northern Asia was also well known, and many (including the writer) have suspected that this may have been an element of the North American Woodland ceramic complex that had spread across Bering Strait.

For purposes of the following discussion, the numerous and fairly complex varieties of linear and rocker stamping will be divided into only two groups: decorations not arranged in line bordered zones and those that are. In the various local sequences there is considerable value in distinguishing between linear and rocker stamping, dentate vs. smooth rocker, and stamping with the edge of a scallop shell. These distinctions do not seem to be of equal importance when considering the intercontinental distribution, for in most regions these techniques group closely together in their temporal ranges.

In the early part of the Valdivia Phase on the coast of Ecuador (3000–2000 B.C.), Valdivia Shell Stamped (Meggers, Evans, and Estrada, 1965, p. 84, pl. 113a-k) comprises a very minor percentage of the Valdivia decorations (chart 18, 50–52). This is placed below the rim of vessels, which usually have folded rims, and the impressions of the edge of a scallop shell are arranged in panels with smooth areas between. Valdivia Rocker Stamped (op. cit., pp. 82–84, pls. 107–112) on bowls consists of one or two rows of rocked impressions that run parallel to the rim (chart 18, 45–49). Jar necks tend to be entirely covered (op. cit., pl. 112). On bowls, these rows are usually not continuous, but have gaps between them at intervals giving the impression of a variety of paneling. The tool used for Valdivia Rocker Stamped was smooth and was

impressed rather deeply as it was rocked back and forth.

Parenthetically it should be noted that the arrangement of decoration into panels with smooth areas between is a common feature of other Valdivia decorations (op. cit., figs. 34–4, 37, 1–2, pls. 74a, d-e, 75b, 80j, 83g, 101j, 109g, 110a). This arrangement is also rather common on the Middle Jomon designs from Japan, which the authors have used for comparison with Valdivia ceramics (op. cit., pls. 166d, 167g-i, 186b).

Both zoned and unzoned rocker stamping occur in the Chorrera Phase (chart 18, 42–44; Estrada, 1962, fig. 41a–c). Impressions are made with a smooth rocker in both cases, and the bounding lines of the zoned decorations are very narrow.

From the Puerto Hormiga site on the north coast of Colombia, pottery decorated with shell edge stamping zoned by wide incised lines seems to be equal in age (3000–2500 B.C.) to the stamping of Valdivia (chart 18, 38–40; Reichel-Dolmatoff, 1965, pp. 25–30, pl. 3). These impressions are not rocked; the shell was lifted to make each one. The line-bordered bands run parallel to the rim to form curvilinear motifs on the vessel body. This early example of zoned stamping is accompanied by drag-and-jab, and by depressions made with the finger that are accented by encircling lines. It will be recalled that a substantial proportion of the ceramics from Puerto Hormiga are fiber tempered and are undecorated.

Stamping of any sort seems to be absent in the Colombian sequence between 1900 and 700 B.C. In the Momíl Phase, however, it becomes rather popular and has several forms (chart 18, 35–37, 41). Unzoned dentate stamping, Momíl Cuneada (Reichel-Dolmatoff, G. and A., 1956, pp. 166–168, pl. 15, 1–4), is very scarce and occurs only in Momíl II. Momíl I is marked by Momíl Negra Dentada Fina (op. cit., p. 176, pl. 9, 1–5). These designs are formed by linear dentate stamping arranged in bands but without bordering incised lines (chart 18–37). Similar designs bordered by narrow incised lines (Momíl Dentada Zonificada, op. cit., pp. 174–175, pl. 9, 6–8) are confined to Momíl II (chart 18–35).

Zoned linear stamping comes from Phases I and II of the Cupica Burial Mound, located on the north Pacific coast of Colombia (chart 18, 33–34; Reichel-Dolmatoff, G. and A., 1961, pp. 293–294, pls. 3–5, 5–3). One of these sherds seems to have a motif representing a bird. The distribution and probable significance of dentate stamping in Colombia and to the north and south of it are discussed in the Reichel-Dolmatoffs' 1961 publication (pp. 289–290). Among the numerous similarities between the ceramics of San Agustín and Momíl, Duque (1964, p. 463) cites zoned dentate stamping. A sherd that he illustrates in his pl. 2i–47 probably could be lost among the Momíl ceramics.

In the Sarigua Phase of Panama (ca. 1000 B.C.), Willey and McGimsey (1954, p. 109, figs. 28–1, 29a–b, 48t–u) found shell stamping zoned between applique ridges. Some examples have a nested triangular motif and are on the side walls of composite silhouette bowls.

In the Kotosh sequence in highland Peru, rocker stamped designs are included along with several other techniques in Kotosh Well Polished (chart 18, 53–54; Izumi and Sono, 1963, pp. 114–116, pls. 68–69). According to the author's figure 46, Well Polished is confined to the Kotosh Chavín Phase (800–200 B.C.). The tool used for the rocker stamping was either plain or dentate. The dentations are very delicate and as the zig-zags were placed close together, it is difficult at times to determine the technique employed. The zoning lines are wide, round bottomed and, like the undecorated vessel surfaces, are well polished. Motifs are apparently expressed by the smooth areas leaving the background roughened by stamping. There are no complete vessels, but a number of sherds show the typical "feather" detail in which one bordering line curves sharply to meet the other (chart 18–53).

According to Matos (1962) zoned stamping begins on the central Peruvian coast in his period Ancón D, which dates after 900 B.C. This is the beginning of the Middle Guañape-Cupisnique Phase on the north coast of Peru (chart 18, 55–56). Examples of complete rocker stamped vessels, usually bottles, are illustrated by Larco Hoyle (1941, 1945a). These show the extraordinary diversity of motifs characteristic of Chavín-Cupisnique ceramic art. This same freedom of design will be noted for the motifs of Marksville pottery in the Lower Mississippi Valley.

Fine dentate rocker stamping zoned between wide incised lines to form curving motifs is an element of the Zoned Bichrome horizon (A.D. 1–100) defined by Coe and Baudez (1961) in northwest Costa Rica. Motifs are formed by curving elements, but cannot be determined from the small sherds. Like the zoned rocker stamping of the Playa de los Muertos site of the Ulua River Valley in Honduras (Strong, Kidder, and Paul, 1938), this zoned stamping more nearly resembles that of Cupisnique and Marksville than it does most of the early examples of rocker stamping in Mesoamerica.

Rocker stamping in the Ocós Phase on the Pacific coast of Guatemala runs from 1 to 7 percent in popularity. Shell edge stamping is the most common (chart 18–30, –32; M. D. Coe, 1961, p. 56, fig. 47a–y). This is accompanied by shell back stamping (op. cit., fig. 3k'), plain rocker (op, cit., fig. 48a), and

dentate rocker stamping (op. cit., fig. 48b). Application is sometimes in panels on the upper wall of tecomates with incising defining the panels. Although Coe and Flannery (1967, fig. 8) refer to this as zoning, it is not zoning in the sense the word is used here. One of the several varieties of stamping found at Ocós, however, has been zoned by incised lines so that the areas of stamping are separated by plain and polished areas of the vessel surface. Coe (1961, p. 57) states that the incised lines were usually drawn after the stamping had been applied. This is rather general in Mesoamerica and contrasts to the Peruvian and Mississippi Valley practice of drawing the boundaries first. Motifs are rather simple as compared with either Chavín or Marksville. Both zoned and unzoned rocker stamping run through the Cuadros Phase to about 850 B.C. and seem to disappear (chart 18–29, –31). An accompanying pottery type of Ocós, which seems to be unique in the Mesoamerican Formative, is line zoned cord or textile brushing (op. cit., pp. 58–59, fig. 49).

Rocker stamping is very rare in the Chiapas sequence, but occurs as unzoned smooth rocker placed around the rims of neckless jars (chart 18–28). Sanders (1961, p. 20, pl. 7A) found one example. Dixon (1959, pp. 17, 23, fig. 52) obtained a total of nine sherds in Pits 50 and 38 at Chiapa de Corzo.

Illustrations are not available for the stamped sherds found in the Tehuacán sequence. MacNeish provides the information that both zoned and unzoned rocker run from about 1100–900 B.C. and are followed by smooth rocker, which lasts until 500 B.C.

Rocker stamping is a minor decorative type at the Tlatilco site in the Valley of Mexico (chart 18, 26–27.). It is discussed and illustrated by Porter (1953, pp. 37–38, pls. 8A, 9H, 11F, G) and by Piña Chán (1958, vol. 1, figs. 35n, c', 36w, 37d–e, o). It occurs on three vessel forms: effigies, neckless jars or tecomates, and flat-base pans. The stamping tool is always smooth, and impressions were applied before the vessels were polished. Polished black and brown wares are most common. The rocker stamped areas are not zoned by incised lines to form complex motifs, as in Chavín or Marksville; rather, in most instances, the rows of stamping run parallel to the vessel lip and are interrupted at intervals so that they form panels. Limits of these smooth panels are marked by short vertical lines as in the early stamping of the Ocós Phase of Guatemala.

In his preliminary mimeographed report on the San Lorenzo Phase of Veracruz, M. D. Coe (1966) describes both plain and dentate rocker stamping, apparently unzoned. Almost certainly, some of this is rim decoration for the large neckless jars (chart 18, 24–25). Drucker (1952, p. 86, fig. 28a–c) describes plain rocker stamping from La Venta, which because of the curvature of the impressions, he thinks was made with the edge of a mussel shell. Stamping is rare but was found in all levels (op. cit., p. 129), mostly on coarse buff ware, less frequently on coarse brown ware.

García Payón (1966, pp. 109–113, pls. 43–44) found dentate rocker stamping both on the side walls and in the interior bases of flat-base pans. He also found at least one sherd with line zoned dentate stamping. A few additional examples were collected by Medellín, Wallrath, and Ford from Chalahuites (chart 18, 21–23). These include the typical Mesoamerican positioning of rocker stamping about the neck of the tecomate form. García Payón (op. cit., pp. 113–116) points out that rocker stamping is "excessively rare in Mesoamerica." He discusses its role there as a marker for Pre-Classic, and the significance of its occurrence both in eastern North America and in Peru. This decoration seems to disappear in Veracruz about 400 B.C.

The earliest rocker stamping in the Lower Mississippi Valley begins in the Poverty Point Period (1200–400 B.C.; chart 18, 19–20). It characteristically is made by a smooth tool or one with two points, and the rocker impressions run either parallel to the rim or vertically, covering the entire side wall of wide-mouth pots. Rows of punched out nodes delimit the rim and four small feet or crude ring bases are found on these vessels (Ford, Phillips, and Haag, 1955, fig. 22; Florida State Museum and Louisiana State University collections from Poverty Point site).

The use of unzoned rocker runs through the Tchefuncte Phase (chart 18–18; Ford and Quimby, 1945, pl. 2) with decreasing popularity into the Marksville (Ford, 1963, figs. 29, 30a). Paneling of decoration has not been noted in the earlier phases, but rare examples in the Marksville horizon (Ford and Willey, 1940, fig. 29c) suggest the practice common at Tlatilco (chart 18–17).

Zoned stamped decoration is very characteristic of Lower Mississippi Valley ceramics from about 300 B.C.–A.D. 600, running as high as 6 to 8 percent in popularity during the Marksville Phase (chart 18, 13–16), a ceramic complex which is 90 percent plain. Shell edge stamping zones by wide incised lines, Crooks Stamped, is the earliest of the zoned stamped types (op. cit., pp. 81–82, fig. 39). Typically, raptorial bird motifs are outlined by wide round-bottom incised lines and the background is filled with stamping. The design frequently covers the entire exterior of hemispherical bowls. This is succeeded by Marksville Stamped (op. cit., pp. 65, 74, figs. 28–34), in which the bird figures are outlined by the same type of incision while the background is filled with delicate dentate stamping, frequently so carefully applied that it has been mistaken for rouletting. Decoration covers the sides of wide-mouth pots from base to neck, and thin cambered rims typically have fine-line crosshatched designs and a row of hemiconical punctations as a lower border. Considerable variation in motif is usual, as is the case in the Chavín style of Peru.

After A.D. 400 zoned stamped material is classified as Troyville Stamped (chart 18–13; Ford, 1951, pp. 49–50, fig. 13). The crosshatched rims disappear, motifs become curvilinear, geometric, and repetitive, and the rocker stamping, which is now placed in the band that forms the motifs, again becomes smooth rather than dentate (Manny Stamped, Greengo, 1964, pp. 35–47, figs. 14–18; Troyville Stamped, pp. 47–50, figs. 19–20).

In the Mobile Bay area, rocker stamping begins in the Bayou la Batre Phase about 1100 B.C. (chart 18, 11–12). Wimberly (1960, pp. 64–70) has described the dominant decorations as both drag-and-jab impressions with a large scallop shell and rocker stamped impressions. He now agrees that there is only one type, in which the scallop shell was held with the inner face almost parallel to the vessel surface and the edge was rocked back and forth. These shell impressions cover the entire exterior surface of the crude cup-shape and wide-mouth pot vessel forms. Four or more feet and carelessly made low annular bases are common. There is no indication of paneling or zoning of the rocker stamping.

Unzoned stamping continues on into the Santa Rosa Phase (chart 18–10) as Santa Rosa Stamped (Willey, 1949a, pp. 376–378, fig. 24). Lips are delicately notched and four small feet are formed on some vessels. Zoned stamping occurs in this region between 100 B.C. and A.D. 400 (chart 18, 8–9). Alligator Bayou Stamped (op. .cit., pp. 372–374, fig. 22a–c) has more characteristics of the Louisiana Troyville Phase pottery than it does of the earlier Marksville. Although rocker stamping disappears from the Florida area after A.D. 500, the influence of these types persists into the Weeden Island Phase, as shown by the popularity of zoned decoration and bird motif.

Both zoned and unzoned smooth rocker stamped decoration, the latter on a small vessel with four feet, are in the Yent Phase at the Crystal River site at the base of the Florida Peninsula (chart 18–5).

Naples Dentate Stamped in Illinois (Griffin, 1952a, pp. 107–112, pls. 32–33) has a band of linear dentate stamping placed around the upper vessel wall, usually below a row of pushed out nodes. In some instances the stamp marks are oval rather than linear. These stamps are not rocked; the impressions are placed side by side. Vessel bodies are either cordmarked or smooth. Sometimes the stamping is arranged in panels very reminiscent of the paneling of the early stamping in the Valdivia Phase of Ecuador. This tradition survives in the Laurel Phase of Ontario and Saskatchewan (Wright, 1967).

Curvilinear zoned rocker stamping with typical Hopewell vessel shapes, with the characteristic cross-hatched rims, ranges in time from about 100 B.C.–A.D. 300 in Illinois (chart 18, 3–4). Vessels having these same characteristics were made over this same range of time at the Classic Hopewell sites in Ohio (chart 18, 1–2). Here they form a very minor percentage of the ceramics and are principally found accompanying burials. The domestic ware was the Woodland cordmarked bag-shaped vessel.

Summary

Wide-line zoned shell and dentate stamping are on the north coast of Colombia at about 3000 B.C., approximately the same time at which unzoned stamping begins on the coast of Ecuador. Both types are on the Ecuadorian coast between 1500 and 500 B.C., and the zoned variety of stamping becomes a prominent feature of the Chavín Phase of Peru between 800 and 1 B.C.

Although stamping of any kind is excessively rare in Mesoamerica, the unzoned variety is most prominent between 1400 and 600 B.C. Usually applied to the rims of tecomates and the side walls or interior bottoms of flat-base pans, it is frequently arranged in panels reminiscent of the common Valdivia practice.

In the spread of these decorations into the Mississippi Valley, unzoned stamping appears 500 to 800 years before the zoned variety. Paneling is most prominent in the Illinois area.

Marksville and Hopewell zoned stamped ceramics (200 B.C.–A.D. 300) have features more nearly resembling Cupisnique-Chavín of Peru than anything known in between. These include the use of wide lines incised before stamping, a tendency to roughen the background leaving the motif a smooth area, and the practice of forming feathers by making one incised line curve up to the other.

On the same time horizon (roughly 500 B.C.–A.D. 500), a divergent variety of zoned linear stamping is found on the north Pacific and the Caribbean coast of Colombia.

After A.D. 500 rocker stamping almost disappears from American ceramics. Rare zoned stamped vessels are found in the Maya area and in the lower valley of the Arkansas River.

Excised Decoration

CHART 19

Excised decoration is rare in the Valdivia Phase of coastal Ecuador, but runs from 3000–1500 B.C. (chart 19, 36–39). The design is usually applied to the rim exteriors of simple bowls or to the shoulders of bowls with strongly incurving rims. Triangles, I-, or T-shaped areas, and designs formed of broad lines with occasional spurs are common. Anthropomorphic faces were also made by this technique. Usually the excised areas were cut out after the vessel was polished with a pointed tool, which left scars in the bottoms of the excised areas. Enough sherds were found with red pigment in the excision to suggest that this was a common practice (Meggers, Evans, and Estrada, 1965, pp. 58–60, fig. 31, pls. 58–60).

In their comparisons Valdivia ceramics with Middle Jomon of southern Japan, Meggers, Evans, and Estrada (op. cit., pl. 177) illustrate very similar excised decorations from the Japanese sites. These also have red pigment rubbed into the cutout areas.

At least one excised sherd from the Puerto Hormiga site on the north coast of Colombia is illustrated by Reichel-Dolmatoff (1965, fig. 3–3, 5). The background of a circle and dot design appears to have been cut away.

While excising seems to disappear from the coastal Ecuadorian sequence about 1500 B.C., this same technique, but with a different set of motifs, is found in the Monagrillo Phase of Panama (ca. 2000 B.C.) as Monagrillo Incised (chart 19, 31–32). Willey and McGimsey (1954, pp. 63, 65, figs. 12a–c, 46, 47a–b 48a–g) describe and illustrate curvilinear, scroll-like motifs scratched into the vessel surface after the ware was sun dried. The incised lines terminate in gouged out punctations, and frequently triangular areas are excised where lines connect. There are also excised projections extending out from lines, which are widened at the ends. Because of its geographical proximity on the Parita Peninsula at Panama, Monagrillo designs have been placed in the Colombian column.

As Willey and McGimsey (op. cit., p. 131) point out, the spiral designs of Monagrillo with terminal pits are distinctive among early Formative motifs. They point to resemblance with types of the Arenal and Miraflores Phases of highland Guatemala, Los Barrancos on the lower Orinoco, and Weeden Island designs on the Gulf coast of Florida. This probably is a single decorative tradition, the history of which is yet obscure.

Excised designs run through Waira-jirca and Kotosh Kotosh Phases (1800–850 B.C.) in highland Peru (chart 19, 41–42). Izumi and Sono (1963) include this and other techniques in Kotosh Incised (op. cit., pp. 118–120, pl. 84), and Kotosh Grooved (op. cit., pl. 76a, 4, 14). The excision is usually geometrical and is always combined with incising, particularly motifs of broad incised lines forming hachured bands. These hatched zones usually have red pigment rubbed into them, while the excised areas were painted with yellow limonite and white calcium carbonate. These designs are on most common bowls and occasionally are on short neck jars.

The excising technique does not seem to last into the Chavín Phase and is not found later in the Peruvian sequence. It seems to be entirely missing from the Peruvian coast.

Excision, however, is widely distributed east of the Andes in the Amazon Basin. Rather complex excised designs are found in the Shakimu Phase of Lathrap's (1958) excavations on the Ucayali River in eastern Peru. This now has a radiocarbon date of 650 ± 100 B.C. (Y–1543), too recent to explain the presence of excision between 1800 and 800 B.C. at Kotosh. On the contrary, diffusion probably was eastward from the Andes.

On the coast of Guatemala excising appears on black ware vessels of the Conchas and Crucero Phases (ca. 800 B.C.–A.D. 200; chart 19, 25–27). Coe (1961, pp. 70–73, fig. 28) describes excised designs as an element of Ocós Black, noting that they appear toward the end of the time range of the type in the Conchas Phase. Coe and Flannery (1967, pp. 50–55, figs. 31–32) have redefined the later occurrence of Ocós Black into two types: Morena Black and Conchas Streaky Black Brown. Excising is confined to these black wares. Designs are simple excised areas, are painted with red pigment, and are usually placed on the side walls of composite silhouette bowls, which frequently have dimpled bases and flanged rims. Small excised areas also were combined with engraved lines as rim decoration. Unusual excised sherds from Salinas La Blanca, dating in the Cuadros and Jocotal Phases, are described and illustrated (op. cit., pp. 59–60, fig. 39).

A very minor amount of excising apparently occurs in Chiapas Phases I and II. There are no illustrated sherds, but Dixon (1959, p. 22), referring to the contents of Pit 38, says, "A design in relief made by carving occurs on an unclassified sherd. . . ." In the listing of traits rare in both Pits 50 and 38 (op. cit., p. 39), "carved decoration" is given as item 10.

So far as can be determined, the next examples are in the Horcones Phase, Chiapa VI (A.D. 100), where intricate designs are carved on brown ware and loose red pigment is rubbed into the incisions (Lowe, 1962, pl. 13m). Polished red ware is also carved with lattice

designs in this same phase (chart 19–22; op. cit., pl. 15u–v).

Ceramics with more sophisticated pictorial motifs and carved background first appear in the Uaxactún sequence in the Tzacol III Phase (ca. A.D. 500). R. E. Smith (1955, pp. 42–43) discussed the distribution of excising in Mesoamerica. He says it is largely confined to the Maya area and to the Valley of Mexico, and when found elsewhere may be considered the result of trade. These remarks apply to the early Classic time level. The related techniques of modeled carving and gouged and incised areas are also discussed by Smith (op. cit., pp. 43–45) as Early Classic time markers. In this study attention will be confined to the Formative examples.

MacNeish provides the information that excising was a very minor decorative technique during the Santa Maria Phase (900–200 B.C.) in the Tehuacán Valley in central Mexico. The appropriate symbol is placed on chart 19, but illustrations are not available.

At the Tlatilco site in the Valley of Mexico excising is a fairly common decorative technique and is found almost exclusively on black and dark coffee-colored polished wares (chart 19, 18–19; Piña Chán, 1958, vol. 1, figs. 35r–s, v–w, z, 37m–n, s, 48–49). Porter (1953, pp. 36–37, pl. 6) discussed this technique at Tlatilco and reviews its occurrence at early sites in Mesoamerica. Excising continues into the Classic as a variation of the type San Martín Incised (Tolstoy, 1958b, p. 22).

In the Olmec area of Veracruz, excision begins about 1300 B.C. in the San Lorenzo Phase (chart 19–15). Early examples are relatively simple geometrical motifs combined with engraved lines, usually on the side walls of flat-base pans and bowl forms of black or dark brown polished wares (Coe, 1966; García Payón, 1966, pp. 75–80, pls. 23–26). Although this design technique has very low frequency, it continues on through Tres Zapotes and Cerro de las Mesas. Weiant (1943, pp. 113–114, pl. 57) describes the curvilinear, often realistic designs, brought out by excising the background as "sculptured pottery." In Cerro de las Mesas, Drucker (1943b, p. 39, figs. 115–120) calls this "scraped" decoration and says that designs were made after drying and before firing the vessels, He notes the practice of rubbing pigment into the excised areas (chart 19–13). Red is the usual color; white pigment was used rarely.

The technique of excision is found in only one very restricted locality in the eastern United States at an early date. This is the base of the Florida Peninsula, where Goggin (1952) lists Oklawaha Incised as a type of the St. Johns IA early Phase (chart 19, 6–8), which we have dated between 400 and 1 B.C. (chart 1) The only published description of this type is by

Goggin (1948), in a mimeographed publication of very limited distribution. There are a number of examples, some complete, of Oklawaha Incised in the Florida State Museum collections. The ware has the typical soft, tan, untempered St. Johns paste. Vessel forms are limited to large globular neckless jars or tecomates, the form whose history is traced on chart 12. Both the tecomate forms and the excision technique are restricted to north Florida at this time. It seems very probable that they were brought in together. These jars sometimes have folded collars, are often red slipped, and have excised areas, which are triangular or "dog-bone" in shape, encircle the rim and are cut through the red slip where present. In other cases, red pigment apparently was rubbed into the areas of excision.

This unique appearance of excision in the eastern United States at this early date does not seem to have left any permanent influence on the ceramic traditions of the region, for the technique is completely missing elsewhere until about A.D. 900. At this date it appears at the George C. Davis site in east Texas as an element of a group of traits that came from Mexico into the Mississippi Valley to become a part of the Mississippian culture (chart 19, 9–10; Newell and Krieger, 1949). Holly Engraved (op. cit., pp. 81–90, figs. 29–32) is a polished black ware decorated with rectangular and curvilinear motifs that feature triangular areas of excision. Red pigment has been rubbed into the excised areas. Composite silhouette bowls and bottles are the usual form, and these also are Mesoamerican features that were moving into the Mississippi Valley by the same route.

Summary

The use of excised areas with red pigment rubbed in them begins at 3000 B.C. on the coast of Ecuador and lasts until 1500 B.C. Similar simple geometric designs occur in highland Peru between 1800 and 850 B.C. This same technique is in Panama about 2000 B.C., where it is usually employed in curvilinear designs with motifs that may be ancestral to another branch of the excising tradition.

Simple rectilinear excisions are a very minor element in the Mesoamerican Formative after 1000 B.C. The technique lasts on into Mesoamerican Classic, particularly in the Maya area, where quite elaborate, curvilinear, realistic designs are made by excising the background in contrast to simple Formative treatment, where the excision itself is used to express the decoration motif.

Between 400 B.C. and A.D. 200, excision was employed in the eastern United States only in a very limited area at the base of the Florida Peninsula. Here

it is associated with neckless jars, which have a similar limited temporal and geographical distribution. Excised designs intrude into the Mississippi Valley through east Texas after A.D. 900, to become a minor decorative technique on Mississippian ceramics.

Excision on the Formative level is marked by simple motifs, removal of the surface by repeatedly scratching with a pointed instrument, the practice of widening the ends of wide incised areas, and the use of small projections or spurs on excised lines. It shares with later Classic excising the feature of red ochre, or more rarely white pigment, rubbed into the cutout area.

Negative Painting

CHART 19

The decorating of pottery vessels by means of a negative or resist technique is a very specialized variety of painting which has a wide distribution in the Americas and lasts from about 800 B.C. well up into the Classic periods. The origin of this technique is obscure. Possibly it was transferred to ceramics from the textile batik process.

Earlier investigators thought that the areas of design not to be given the characteristic dark gray or black color were probably covered with a wax. The stain was then applied and the wax removed in the firing process. Robert Sonin of New York City, however, has recently conducted experiments that provide an alternative explanation. The vessels are first fired to the degree of hardness desired. Then a clay slip is painted in the areas that are to remain the ground color of the vessel. Next, an animal or vegetable substance is rubbed on the vessel. It does not seem to matter whether this substance is a grease or the juice of a plant. Any material that will carbonize may be used. The vessel is then subjected to low heat. This carbonizes the material on the unprotected areas, producing the characteristic black negative stain. Too much firing will burn out the carbon. The clay slip applied as a resist shrinks in firing, becomes flaky, and after the vessel cools may be rubbed off with ease. Some of Sonin's reproductions have fooled competent archeologists.

The region of greatest popularity of negative painting technique is northern South America and lower Middle America. The region of greatest age is not clear. It seems to appear on the scene about 500 B.C. from Ecuador to Veracruz. The earliest negative painting in the north coast of Colombia chronology is in Momíl I, and Momíl Negative A (chart 19–30; Reichel-Dolmatoff, G. and A., 1956, pp. 148–150, fig. 4, 1–4, 7–9). The dark color was applied in rectilinear motifs consisting of parallel lines. Execution is rather poor and the colors tend to be faint. Vessel shapes are composite silhouette bowls. Momíl Negative B (op. cit., pp. 165–166, fig. 4–6, –10, pl. 15–6) was made in Momíl II times (chart 19–29). It also was placed on composite silhouette bowls. The black color is brilliant in contrast to the earlier type and the painting is well executed and regular. Lines tend to be wide, and large triangular areas occur between the lines.

The technique of negative painting continues thereafter in limited quantity. In the earliest level at San Agustín, Mesitas Inferior, Duque (1964, pp. 301–302, drawing 11) described negative painting of bright black color over red slip (chart 19–28). Motifs are expressed both by the background color and by the black, and some are curvilinear in contrast to the earlier types from Momíl.

Negative painting becomes particularly popular in what might be called the Classic Colombian cultures, Quimbaya, in Antioquia, and in the southern part of the country in Nariño.

Estrada (1958, p. 73, fig. 38) listed the negative painting technique as an element of the late Chorrera Phase of Ecuador. Meggers and Evans inform me, however, that the technique probably does not appear before 500 B.C., and is now a trait used to recognize the beginning of the Regional Developmental Period (chart 19, 33–35). Types are described by Estrada (1957) as Guangala Negativo (op. cit., p. 46), Jama Negativo (op. cit., p. 99), and Coaque Negativo a Tres Colores (op. cit., p. 100). Other Ecuadorian types have negative painting applied over plain surface or red or yellowish red slip. Parallel lines and circular areas are characteristic. Estrada (1958, p. 101) briefly discussed the significance of negative painting in Ecuador, Mesoamerica, and Peru.

On the north Peruvian coast, negative painting occurs in the Pechiche Phase (850–370 B.C.) in Tumbes, immediately south of the Peruvian border. Izumi and Terada (1966, pp. 46–47, pl. 20a) found eleven sherds in various levels, some with negative paint on a white-slipped background.

In Peru negative painted pottery appears to form a pan-Peruvian style similar to the earlier white-on-red and Chavín horizon styles (Willey, 1945). A probable median date is A.D. 300.

The negative painting technique comes into the Higueras Phase in the Kotosh sequence after A.D. 1 (chart 19–40). Izumi and Sono (1963, p. 106) describe it as a decoration of the type Higueras Red. This is a red-slipped ware that was carelessly polished so that the polishing tracks show plainly. Negative painted vessels all seem to be large jars with small necks, usually with an animal effigy head on the shoulder and two horizontal loop handles. Motifs are principally crosshatching and bands of dark coloring with brown negative spots in them.

Negative painting is not found on the north coast of Peru until the Gallinazo Phase, about A.D. 500 (chart 19–43; Strong and Evans, 1952, pp. 301, 307, figs. 57–60). Motifs are usually wavy lines arranged in bands and circular areas. Vessel shapes are varied and include bridge spout jars, stirrup-spout jars, and large ollas, which sometimes have a modeled birdhead on the shoulder. These are similar to the Kotosh Higueras form but never have handles.

At about this same date (A.D. 500), three-color negative ware was manufactured in the Recuay region, along the central coast, and on the south coast of Peru. In the latter two areas, the decoration was frequently applied to the interior of open bowls.

Wallace (1962) has reported on an early ceramic complex in the Ica Valley on the south coast of Peru in which negative painted ceramics are associated with some Chavinoid decorative techniques. He estimates the date as 500–200 B.C. If correct, this would suggest that negative painting and probably accompanying traits of bridge spouts, napkin-ring earspools, and ring bases moved by sea to the Peruvian south coast and from there spread to other parts of the region. An alternative possibility is that the dates are too early and the associated Chavinoid traits lagged in time on this southern periphery of their distribution.

In the Soconusco sequence of Guatemala, a very minor percentage of negative painting is found on some Conchas White-to-Buff sherds (M. D. Coe, 1961, p. 82, fig. 53k). There is a possibility that this technique dates in Conchas I, but it is certainly present in Conchas II (600–300 B.C.). Parallel diagonal stripes are found on the white portions of red and white cuspidors, and the "cloudy Usulután" technique also occurred. Negative painting seems to be equally rare from the Crucero Phase (chart 19, 23–24). Coe and Flannery (1967, pp. 47–49) describe Usulután type painting on orange monochrome ceramics and also on the type Crucero Red-on-Orange (op. cit., figs. 25a–c, 26c). Although they note that the late Formative is very poorly known in the region, a Cerro del Tiestal complex is described (op. cit., pp. 91–92) that seems to be terminal Formative. The Usulután variety of negative decoration is an element of this complex.

Negative painting is quite rare in the Chiapa de Corzo sequence and is almost entirely of the Usulután variety. Peterson (1963, pp. 11–12) gives an excellent discussion. At Mirador he found "cloudy resist" pottery restricted almost entirely to Period III (550–450 B.C.; chart 19–21). The irregular splotches of black were applied to the interior and exterior of flat-base pans, shallow bowls, composite silhouette bowls, hemispherical bowls with restricted mouths, and cylindrical vessels. Peterson quotes Warren to the effect that this typical decoration runs through Periods III and IV at Chiapa de Corzo, where it is on brownish or reddish orange ware. Sanders (1961, p. 34) found only four sherds at Santa Cruz, all in the Santa Cruz Phase (A.D. 200–350; chart 19–20). With a considerable degree of uncertainty, the bar representing this technique runs from the beginning of Period III to the top of the Chiapas column.

The Usulután technique disappears at the beginning of the Classic Period at Uaxactún, but the negative technique with definite outlined motifs persists into Classic times (R. E. Smith, 1955, pp. 59–61).

MacNeish (personal communication) has indicated that a few negative painted trade sherds came into the Tehuacán sequence in the latter half of the Santa Maria Phase (approximately 500–200 B.C.). No samples are available for illustration.

Porter (1953, pp. 24–25) says that no negative painting was found on the burial vessels from the Tlatilco Cemetery, but a few sherds were recovered from the cemetery excavations. She points out that this technique is limited to the Ticomán complex of Vaillant (1931; chart 19–17). Piña Chán (1958, vol. 1, p. 111) places negative painting in the last of his three Tlatilco periods, but does not cite the evidence on which this is based.

Negative painting in the Valley of Mexico is the positive design type rather than the smudged Usulután variety to the south. It continues into Teotihuacán Phase I (chart 19–16) where it is fairly popular and decreases sharply in Phase II (Millon, Drewitt, and Bennyhoff, 1965, p. 32). Two- and three-color negative has developed by this time, and the technique was applied over a red or orange slip.

García Payón (1966, pp. 29–33) reports on negative painted sherds from the middle levels at the El Trapiche site, and gives an extensive discussion of this feature in early horizons in other parts of Mexico. As he points out, Drucker did not find the technique at La Venta. Excavations by Medellín, Wallrath, and Ford at Chalahuites support García Payón's initial date of approximately 600–500 B.C. The decoration usually consists of wide wavy lines placed on a red-slipped surface. The technique of negative painting extends up into the Remojadas Phases in central Veracruz. Drucker (1943a, p. 89; 1943b, p. 38) mentions negative painting at Tres Zapotes and Cerro de las Mesas (chart 19, 11–12). It was quite scarce and he considered it a probable trade item.

A small amount of negative painting appears in the eastern United States on the Classic Hopewell time level (100 B.C.–A.D. 300). Examples have been found in only two regions. One of these is at the Crystal River site on the Gulf coast at the base of the Florida Peninsula, where Sears (1962, fig. 3d-e) considers it to date in the earlier or Yent Phase (chart 19, 4–5). One vessel is a small wide-mouth pot with negative scrolls and round dots on the side walls. Another is a jar with restricted mouth that bears a negative design of angular parallel lines. Negative painted sherds decorated both inside and outside come from layers 3 and 4 of the Mandeville site in the lower Chattahoochee River Basin in southwest Georgia. Designs consist of broad and narrow bands of black, some of which have unpainted circular areas in them. Layer 3 has a radiocarbon data of A.D. 540±150 (Kellar, Kelly, and McMichael, 1962, p. 346).

The second area of occurrence is in central Illinois (chart 19–1). Thickened rims on simple bowls, the variety called "Brangenburg Rim", are in Classic Hopewell context at the Snyder's Site (Griffin, 1952c, pp. 118–119; Perino, personal communication). These rims have broad line, curving arch designs executed in negative technique on the widened lip.

After A.D. 300 the negative painting technique is entirely missing from the eastern United States sequences until the late Mississippian Phase beginning about A.D. 1200 (chart 19, 2–3). At this time it became fairly common on narrow spouted bottles and on the interior of shallow plates. It is found from southern Illinois and southern Indiana down into Arkansas and Tennessee. Decorative motifs are "sun symbols," crosses, and other designs characteristic of the so-called Southern Cult.

Summary

From Ecuador to Veracruz in Mexico, negative painting on ceramics suddenly appears about 500 B.C., at first made in very small quantities so that almost every investigator has considered it to be an imported trade item. Geometric designs of parallel lines, parallel wavy lines, circular negative dots, and triangular arrangements are usual. The Usulután "cloudy resist" designs of the Maya area seem to be a local development, otherwise there is a high degree of similarity throughout the geographical range of the technique.

Negative painting is first found in highland Peru about A.D. 1 and on the north coast after A.D. 500. A similar lag occurs in its initial introduction into North America.

Negative painting becomes popular through Ecuador, Colombia, and lower Central America on the uncertainly dated "Classic" horizon, perhaps A.D. 500–800. The use of additional color to form three- and four-color wares was common at this time. Its popularity through Mesoamerica probably has a similar date, and the second intrusion of the technique into the eastern United States after A.D. 1200 accompanied the group of Mesoamerican-like features that form the Southern Cult.

Thickened Decorated Lip, Outflaring Lip with Decoration, and Labial Flange

CHART 20

Thickened lips on bowls present in the Valdivia Phase of Ecuador occasionally have an inward bevel (chart 20, 49–50; Meggers, Evans, and Estrada, 1965, fig. 24–2). Some of these are decorated with simple, rectilinear wideline incised designs (op. cit., pl. 40a–1), encircling lines, interrupted lines, or crosshatching.

Decorated rims are also found in the Machalilla complex on carinated bowls with thickened or outflaring lips. These are engraved arrangements of straight lines or hatched triangles (chart 20, 46–48; op. cit., p. 118, shape 6; Estrada, 1958, p. 91, fig. 27, 1–3). Both forms are rare but appear to continue through the Chorrera Phase (chart 20–45, –51).

Labial flanges do not appear in the Ecuadorian sequence before the beginning of the Regional Developmental at 500 B.C. (chart 20–52). Flanges are rare; only a few modest ones are found in the Jambelí Phase (Estrada, Meggers, and Evans, 1964, figs. 23, 29). The greatest number and most elaborately decorated outflaring rims are found in the Bahía Phase (chart 20, 43–44; Estrada, 1962, figs. 45–48). Illustrations and charts show the frequency of these rims at the Pepa de Huso site. Meggers and Evans (1964) have given an extensive discussion of the distribution of outflaring decorated rims into the Barrancoid cultural level of Venezuela and out to the delta of the Orinoco.

Thickened flat lips are found on bowls of the Pechiche Phase (850–370 B.C.) of the Tumbes region of north Peru (Izumi and Terada, 1966, pp. 28–33, fig. 10–D4–5). Late in this phase, labial flanges are found below the rims of shallow, pedestal base compoteras (op. cit., p. 34, fig. 11, form P–7).

In the Kotosh sequence in highland Peru, there are no examples of thickened decorated lips or outflaring lips with or without decoration. However, in Kotosh Grooved (Izumi and Sono, 1963, pp. 116–118, pls. 44e–f, 133, 1–6) prominent flanges located on the vessel exterior below the lip are fairly common (chart 20, 53–55). These are usually decorated with broadline incised designs, frequently with paneled motifs reminiscent of Valdivia Broad-line Incised in Ecuador. These occur at the surprisingly early date of 1100–500

B.C., considerably earlier than basal flanges are found in Mesoamerica.

A possible source for these flanges in the Kotosh Phase is the Tutishcainyo Phase of eastern Peru (probable date 1000 B.C.). Carinated bowls with pronounced basal flanges were present. As Lathrap (1963) has suggested, there seem to be strong relationships to Venezuela along the eastern foot of the Andes.

A special and complex variety of rim decoration is found on the north coast of Colombia in the Malambo Phase (chart 20–41; Angulo Valdés, 1962b). Outflaring rim protuberances are decorated by modeled adornos and incising to represent geometrical and zoomorphic forms. As Angulo Valdés states, this complex is very closely related to the early phases of the Barrancoid ceramics of Venezuela and the mouth of the Orinoco River, which Rouse and Cruxent (1958) date between 1050 and 350 B.C.

Boat-shaped vessels with adornos at either end, from middle and lower levels of Malambo, are a characteristic Barrancoid form that later extends into the West Indies. Practically absent from other parts of the Americas, they are found in the early Puerto Hormiga Phase on the north coast of Colombia.

While Gerardo and Alicia Reichel-Dolmatoff (1956, pp. 189–194) show that approximately 14 percent of all vessel borders in Momíl I and II (700–1 B.C.) are decorated, the outflared lips bearing decorations, of particular interest here, are found principally in Momíl I (chart 20, 38–40; op. cit., fig. 7–J) on composite silhouette bowls. However, the decorations found on lips are not specified as to the period (op. cit., figs. 9, 12, 1–3). Shapes range from direct, sometimes slightly thickened lips (chart 20–37) to outflared. Decoration consists of punctations, parallel lines that encircle the vessel lip, and arrangements of straight incised lines or lines of dentate stamping. These form hatched zig-zag designs, or are placed in bands arranged at angles to one another, suggesting some of the Ayangue motifs.

Basal flanges are the only variety found in Momíl. They are fairly frequent, are on round-base bowls, and are limited to Momíl II (400–1 B.C.). The flanges are quite pronounced but only a few are decorated (chart 20–42; op. cit., pp. 182–183, fig. 6). Some have scalloped edges. Among other evidences of relations with coeval Mesoamerican cultures, the Reichel-Dolmatoffs (op. cit,. pp. 283–284) cite the occurrence of basal flanges in the two regions.

Both decorated lips and modest flanges are occasionally found in the ceramics of the Colombian highlands after A.D. 1, but apparently neither feature enjoys the popularity that prevailed for the thousand years before the beginning of the present era.

MacNeish (1954, pp. 635, 637, figs. 36–1, 37–7) in his survey of Formative traits in Mesoamerica points out that both decorated lips and basal flanges, which run from Aguilar to El Prisco times in the Panuco sequence of Mexico (approximately 1000–1 B.C.), are found from the Huasteca to the Playa de los Muertos site in Honduras. There is a suggestion by MacNeish that basal ridges may be later in popularity, as they are said to reach their maximum in the El Prisco Period (ca. 1 B.C.). Wauchope (1950) also uses the features of basal flanges and wide everted decorated lips in his comparative study. The latter he assigns to the Village and Urban Formative and the former to the Proto-Classic, thus indicating a tardiness in the appearance of flanges that is corroborated here.

In discussing "flat-base dishes with flaring sides," in his report on La Venta, coastal Veracruz, Drucker (1952, p. 109), says that the simple direct rim is most common; he continues: "The next most frequent rims, about 20 to 25 percent of the total rims of this type of vessel, widen rapidly toward the top, and are finished off in a flat bevel, ordinarily nearly horizontal. A rare type of rim is a wide everted one, either nearly flat, or sloping toward the outside. These rims occur in all wares but have a low frequency." Unfortunately he does not provide illustrations, a lack which is not repaired by Drucker, Heizer, and Squier (1959). Some illustrations for this period however, are given in García Payón's (1966, pl. 14) report on his excavations at El Trapiche. Others used here come from Medellín, Wallrath, and my unreported excavations from this same vicinity (chart 20, 12–14).

In the general Ranchito collection from Tres Zapotes, Weiant (1943, figs. 39–43) shows both thickened rims bearing engraved designs with red pigment rubbed in the lines, and outflaring lips, some scalloped, which have both engraved and wide incised line decorations (chart 20, 10–11). Drucker (1943b, figs. 91–99) also illustrated beveled and outflared lips from Cerro de las Mesas (chart 20, 8–9).

Porter (1953, p. 39) states that at Tlatilco, "Flattened incised rims are common on black-brown wares. The rim treatment varies from simple tabs spaced around the rim to continuous incised rims. These are decorated with short parallel lines incised in groups or a simple circumferential groove." (chart 20, 16–19).

This certainly suggests a close resemblance to the incised rims of the 1000 to 1 B.C. time range, but unfortunately, neither Porter nor Piña Chán show illustrations. Vaillant (1935b, table 17) indicates that thickened flared and flat lips run between 4 and 10 percent in the Bay ware *cajetes* from El Arbolillo.

He also fails to give adequate illustrations.

Data for the Tehuacán ceramic chronology have been taken from a pre-publication copy of the chronological graph prepared by MacNeish (in Byers, ed., 1967–, vol. 3, fig. 7). Outflaring rims, usually on flat-base pan forms, start with the beginning of the Santa Maria Phase (900 B.C.; chart 20, 20–21). They are on types Canoas Orange Brown, Rio Salado Gray, Quichilco Gray, and El Riego Gray. The use of flanges does not show on the diagram so the time range, if any, of this feature must remain in doubt.

In a personal communication, MacNeish has indicated that thickened flat lips with single straight-line decorations scratched on them, similar to those from Veracruz, date between 850 and 500 B.C. Accordingly, the appropriate symbol has been placed on chart 20, but without illustrations.

Decorated everted lips occasionally scalloped, with wide polished incised lines and engraved decoration including the double-line break motif occurred in Pits 38 and 50 at Chiapa de Corzo in southern Mexico. They are characteristic of white monochrome ware. Dixon (1959) dates these deposits from before 1000 B.C. to about 400 B.C. (chart 20, 24–28). Decorated everted and scalloped lips are also found in the Burrero Phase at Santa Cruz (Sanders, 1961, fig. 17), where they extend through the Chiapilla Phases to about 250 B.C. They occur on cream, polished red, and polished black wares. The well-polished variety of Chiapilla Polished Red has flanges placed on the exterior vessel wall below the lip. Apparently these are not decorated (chart 20–29).

Everted decorated lips bear even more elaborate designs in Peterson's (1963, figs. 33–36) Mirador III and IV (550–250 B.C.). Most of the straight line incised motifs are clearly in the Ayangue tradition. Scalloped lips are fairly common. In the Mirador sequence there is a decrease in width of the everted rims from early phase to the more narrow rims. Flattened thickened lips with straight line decoration similar to those from Veracruz are placed in Periods V–VI at Mirador (chart 20–23).

Peterson makes a distinction between labial and medial flanges, which are further down the vessel wall. This will not be attempted here. Medial flanges are found in Mirador IV–V; labial in V–VI. The two thus run from about 400–1 B.C. Some medial flanges are scalloped and some represent stylized frogs. Both frog and fish effigies (chart 20–22) are fairly common by the time of the Horcones Phase at about A.D. 1–100 (Lowe, 1962, fig. 17d, f).

Beveled rims, both with decorated and undecorated lips, are fairly common in the Ocós Phase of coastal Guatemala. Outflaring lips and labial ridges are present, but apparently not common (chart 20–34, –36).

Labial flanges seem to be missing from the Cuadros to Conchas II Phases. While two outflaring lips are illustrated by Coe and Flannery (1967, fig. 15d-e), for the Cuadros and Jocotal Phases, neither bear decoration. Everted rims become popular in Conchas I and II, particularly in Conchas Orange (chart 20, 30–33). Decoration consists of impressed polished and engraved lines. The double-line break is a common motif. Rim scallops are sometimes asymmetrical (chart 20–34). These rims last into the Crucero Phase, where some rims become quite narrow, although not enough so to be classed as thickened lips. Labial flanges become popular in the Crucero Phase (300 B.C.–A.D. 200; chart 20–35; Coe and Flannery, 1967, fig. 8). Apparently they were not decorated. In the later Maya ceramics, flanges are rather popular, particularly basal flanges on composite silhouette bowls.

Thickened, sometimes beveled, decorated vessel lips are a characteristic feature of the fiber-tempered Orange ceramic complex of the Atlantic coast of Florida (chart 20, 3–5). Bullen (1955) has demonstrated that these rims are late in the time range of Orange. We are here placing them from 800–500 B.C. Motifs of the Orange lip decorations show a remarkable resemblance to the type Ayangue Incised of the Machalilla Phase of Ecuador. This has been discussed in the foregoing pages.

Ten percent of the rim sherds of the steatite vessels that C. H. Webb (1944) found in a large cache at the Poverty Point site in Louisiana had decorated lips (chart 20–7; Ford and Webb, 1956, pp. 106–110, fig. 42). Again the principal motifs are arrangements of straight incised lines placed in bands that slant at alternate angles. There is a close resemblance to the late Orange Phase lips. Exact dating of these decorated lips in the Poverty Point Phase is unknown. (The ceramics of this phase do not have lip decoration.)

In later eastern United States ceramics, lip decorations are rare. They are most common in the Troyville Phase in the Lower Mississippi Valley, where incision is found on flattened lips and outflaring rims sometimes form four triangular ears spaced around the mouth of the vessel (chart 20–6; Ford, 1951, figs. 21g, j, m, 22e–f, 23i; 1936, figs. 35a, 37).

Bowls or plates with outflaring rims bearing painted and incised decoration, and bowls with flanges representing the fins of fish, quite similar to those made in Mesoamerica about A.D. 1, are elements of the Middle Mississippian Culture Phase dating after A.D. 1200 (chart 20, 1–2; Cole, 1951, fig. 9).

Summary

Decorated thickened outflaring rims are characteristic of bowl forms. They seem to be oldest in Ecuador, where they begin in the Valdivia Phase. Outflaring decorated rims begin at about 1000 B.C. in Colombia, 1300 B.C. in Guatemala, and between these dates in Chiapas, Tehuacán, and the Valley of Mexico. They start in Veracruz slightly later at 500 B.C., and come into the Mississippi Valley after A.D. 1200.

Thickened rims with flat lips date in the centuries before 500 B.C. in north Florida, Louisiana, Veracruz, and Tehuacán. They seem to be later in the Chiapas sequence.

Flanges date between 1500 and 1000 B.C. in Ocós, but seem to be more popular in South America where they appear between 1000 and 500 B.C. in the Peruvian highlands and later on the Ecuadorian coast. Most occurrences in Mexico date after 500 B.C. and are in the southern part of the country.

Broad-Line Incised Designs

CHART 21

Decorations composed of closely spaced broad incised lines are a recurrent theme through the American Formative. The incised lines tend to be 2 to 3 mm. wide and typically have rounded bottoms, U-shaped in section. It sometimes can be determined that they were made by cylindrical tools held at an angle to the vessel surface. These are the same broad incised lines that were used to bound rocker stamping and red paint, which are the accompanying zoned types in most regions.

This technique is earliest in the Valdivia Phase of Ecuador, where it has been given the name Valdivia Broad-line Incised (chart 21, 53–57; Meggers, Evans, and Estrada, 1965, pp. 47–51, pls. 30–42). It ranges from 3000 to 1500 B.C., gradually increasing in popularity to a maximum of about 6 percent. The incised lines made after the vessel surfaces were polished, are both U- and V-shaped in section. There are two prominent tendencies through this time range. First, more of the vessel surface tends to be covered by decoration, and second, curvilinear motifs increase in popularity at the expense of rectilinear. Motifs include 1–3 lines parallel to the vessel lips (op. cit., pls. 30–31), concentric rectangles (op. cit., pls. 32i, 42a), parallel lines with zig-zag or wavy lines between them (op. cit., pls. 34–35), one or two lines on the interior of vessel lip, usually two lines that form a curving or undulating fret (op. cit., pl. 40g-l), concentric rectangles or triangles covering the vessel bottom (op. cit., pls. 36–37), parallel straight lines interrupted at intervals by short vertical lines (op. cit., pl. 32a-d), and stylized faces (op. cit., pl. 41). Occasionally there are key-like figures (op. cit., pl. 42e). Vessel shapes are usually simple bowls, shouldered bowls with inslanted rims, and wide-mouth pots. On all these forms the decoration is applied principally to the shoulder. Broad-line incising is a recurrent element in Valdivia decoration. In Valdivia Nicked Broad-line Incised (op. cit., pl. 84) the lines are punctated, and in Valdivia Zoned Incised (op. cit., pl. 114), broad lines bound areas of crosshatching.

Meggers and Evans have informed me that wide-line incising runs through the Chorrera Phase, but illustrations have not been published. Rectilinear motifs with fairly narrow incising are present in the Bahía Phase of the Regional Developmental and are illustrated and described by Estrada (chart 21–47, 49; 1962, p. 38, fig. 54a-d).

Izumi and Terada (1966, p. 41) define broad-line incising as "a wide line with a U-shaped depression in section made with a blunt-pointed instrument." It dates early in the Pechiche Phase (850–370 B.C.) in the Tumbes region, north Peru. It is usually found on bowls, sometimes on the interior, and motifs are simple, often only lines encircling the rim.

Broad-line incising runs through the Kotosh sequence in central highland Peru. With predominantly rectilinear motifs, it is a decoration on most of the types described by Izumi and Sono (chart 21, 58–64; 1963). Motifs include rectilinear scrolls (op. cit., pls. 38a, 45a, 47a, 49d, 57a), concentric rectangles (op. cit., pl. 40c), short parallel horizontal lines interrupted by punctations or circle and dot (op. cit., pls. 40e, 41a, 53a, 1–5, 53b, 59, 62), and undulating frets (op. cit., pls. 57A–1, 58B–1). It will be noted that the motifs of this popular broad-line incising technique are shared with the broad-line incising of Valdivia. The circle and dot, so popular at Kotosh, is an accompanying Valdivia type (Meggers, Evans, and Estrada, 1965, pls. 62b, 104). At Kotosh, broad-line incising tends to be used in a band around the rims of bowls and other vessel forms, as was the case in the Valdivia type.

Most of the Kotosh motifs are rectilinear with the notable exception of the Kotosh Chavín Phase (800–200 B.C.), where the typical curvilinear lines on highly polished ceramics represent stylized catheads with prominent fangs and nonrepetitive scroll-like arrangements that very likely represent feathers (chart 21–60). These motifs are also found in the zoned rocker stamp type. Broad-line incising disappears from the Kotosh sequence at the end of the San Blas Phase (A.D. 1).

Broad-line incising, usually on polished surfaces with polished lines, is a prominent element of coastal Chavín or Cupisnique, and continues in very minor frequency into the Gallinazo Phase (chart 21, 66–68; Strong and Evans, 1952, pp. 325–326, fig. 65). The technique is well illustrated from Ancón by Willey and Corbett (1954) and from the north coast by Larco Hoyle (1941). At Ancón, the broad lines are used to bound rocker stamping, punctations, and red paint as well as serving as primary decoration. Matos Mendieta (1962) has been able to show that rectilinear arrangements, similar to those of Valdivia, and circle and dot motifs are earliest in the sequence (about 1000 B.C.). Typical Chavín curvilinear motifs occur between 800 B.C. and A.D. 100 (chart 21–67). A detail worth noting is that the ends of the "feather" design elements are formed by curving one line strongly so that it meets the other. This detail, already noted at Kotosh, is also found at Tlatilco in the Valley of Mexico and is prominent in the Marksville-Hopewell designs of the Mississippi Valley. Another feature shared by all three areas, is two characteristic kinds of arrangements. In one, the incisions outline bands, which could have been filled with either rocker stamping or red paint to form designs of those types. It is possible that a fugitive paint was applied to portions of these designs and has disappeared in the course of time. In the other class of motifs, the incised lines are placed closely together.

The placing of incised decoration in panels is another element shared by Chavín, Tlatilco, and Marksville (chart 21–68). Examples are illustrated by Larco Hoyle (1941, figs. 79, 89), and Izumi and Sono (1963, pls. 84b–13, 87a, 2–3, 87b, 2–3, 7, 138, 7, 9). This arrangement at the Tlatilco site is discussed and illustrated by Porter (1953, p. 36, fig. 7). Paneling is fairly rare in Mississippi Valley Hopewell (Squier and Davis, 1848, pl. 14).

Wide-line incising is used in the sand-tempered Puerto Hormiga ceramics of Colombia to outline stamped and punctated areas and to draw lines on modeled faces on the rims of vessels (chart 21, 45–46). Both surface finish and incising are crude.

Broad-line incising in curvilinear motifs is very characteristic of the succeeding Barlovento Phase (1900–1000 B.C.; chart 21, 41–44). It is used to outline smooth areas forming scroll-like motifs, and the background is punctated. There are also looped line motifs, in which punctations are frequently placed on the ridge between closely spaced lines.

Punctations at the ends of lines, which appear first in Puerto Hormiga, continue through Barlovento into the Malambo Phase (1000–700 B.C.). At this time there is also a considerable use of wide incised lines that sometimes end in punctations. These generally supplement the modeled adornos, but also have rectilinear scroll motifs reminiscent of Valdivia Broad-line Incised (chart 21–40).

The incising technique is fairly common in Momíl Phases I and II, but is usually used to bound areas of dentate stamping or punctations. The wide-line incised decoration of interest here is rare or absent. Gerardo and Alicia Reichel-Dolmatoff (1956, pp. 288–289) have briefly discussed this technique as a marker of early periods in northern South America.

Wide-line incising occurs in the early part of the Soconusco, Guatemala sequence, where it is used principally to bound areas of rocker stamping, textile impressions, or red paint. Very rarely it is used as a primary decoration (chart 21–35), and when it is, the motifs are simple parallel lines or crosshatching, rather than the rectilinear motifs of the early Formative of South America or the curvilinear patterns of the Chavín horizon. Another distinction is that wide lines were not incised while the paste was soft, but rather were impressed with a polishing tool when it was leather hard. M. D. Coe (1961, fig. 50a, c–f, i–j) terms this "indented line burnishing." This technique is also commonly used in coastal Veracruz. The majority of the line decorations in Ocós and Conchas were engraved and relate to the Ayangue tradition.

The Chiapas ceramic sequence presents a parallel situation to Soconusco. There is some wide-line incising scattered through the sequence, but for the most part motifs are in the Ayangue engraved tradition; Valdivia motifs are rare and scattered. They seem to be most common between 400 and 1 B.C. These rare examples are placed in the appropriate column on chart 21, 31–34. Interrupted lines on the vessel rim, an example which is shown on our chart 21–34, are identical to those found in Valdivia (Meggers, Evans, and Estrada, 1965, fig. 40a–b). Zig-zag lines and stepped motifs are other items shared by Valdivia and the Mesoamerican Formative.

Details of decoration are not available for the Tehuacán sequence, but probably parallel the typical Mesoamerican pattern.

Between 1200 and 1 B.C. wide-line incising is more prominent in the Valley of Mexico than in other parts of Mexico. Here too the lines are not truly incised, but are made by deeply impressing a polishing tool on a leather hard surface. The technique is extensively applied to zoned red painted areas, but also serves as primary decoration (chart 21, 25–28; Porter, 1953, fig. 5, pls. 9E, 10E, 11A–B, D–E; Piña Chán, 1958, vol. 1, figs. 8 o, 10i–l, o–p, 11n, q, 16f, k–m, 17a, j, 18k–l, q, numerous examples figure 33ff). Also, incising is used to express motifs related to those of Valdivia ceramics, as well as Machalilla. These include negative zig-zags with the background incised, checkerboard motifs, panel decoration, zig-zag lines placed between straight lines, and concentric

diamonds. The Machalilla-related motifs are bands of straight lines placed at angles, and extensive use of hatched triangles particularly when they are arranged in tiers (Piña Chán, 1958, vol. 1, fig. 47, 9–11).

Broad-line incised designs occur at the **La Venta** site (chart 21–22; Drucker, 1952, figs. 25, 34, pl. 20), and conform in general to the usual Mesoamerican pattern. There are some paneled arrangements (op. cit., pl. 20G), but the double-line break is more frequent. Incised designs are more common and distinctive at Tres Zapotes, where they are used on the outflaring lips (Weiant, 1943, figs. 39–43). In addition to both Valdivia and Machalilla-like motifs, there are some curvilinear designs reminiscent of Chavín (chart 21–20; op. cit., figs. 43f, 44c, 46a, 48e).

The most remarkable resemblances to broad-line incising of the Peruvian Formative-Marksville tradition are in the so-called Tancól complex that Ekholm (1944, pp. 412–417) found near Panuco in the Huasteca. While this complex has scattered resemblances through the late Formative of Mesoamerica, it stands apart in regard to the abundance of broad-line incising and zoned red slip. Ekholm dates Tancól as Huasteca II (ca. A.D. 1), and the presence of looped vessel supports and basal ridges on bowls seems to confirm the evidence of trade sherds found in the Pavón site levels. The majority of the incised Tancól sherds have spaced lines, and the motifs are drawn as though they were to outline zones of roughening. In at least three instances (Ekholm, 1944, fig. 28f, h, t) the outline bands end by one line curving strongly to meet the other, the characteristic "feather" of Chavín and Marksville. Most of the motifs are rectilinear, though a few curvilinear. Lip decorations are common and are usually short linear dashes interrupted by punctations. There is a resemblance to lips in the Ranchito collection of Tres Zapotes, but the motifs more nearly resemble the dash-and-dot rim decoration of late Kotosh and of Valdivia (Meggers, Evans, and Estrada, 1965, pls. 32a–c, 40a–b).

Broad-line incising with the characteristic round bottom lines has a popularity of about 7 percent in the Marksville Phase of the Lower Mississippi Valley (chart 21, 11–13; Ford, 1936, figs. 42n, p, s, 43g, j–k, n, 44k–m, o–s; Ford and Willey, 1940, figs. 35–37). Accompanying decorations are zoned rocker stamping and zoned red paint, and the small wide-mouth pots on which these designs occur often have delicately crosshatched rims. There is considerable variety in motif: concentric circles, concentric squares, diamonds, oval figures, and zig-zag bands of lines. Occasionally the lines are spaced as though to zone rocker stamping or red paint, and in these instances there is usually a stylized bird motif (chart 21–13).

Nearly always, this motif has the characteristic "feather" detail of band ending, which has been noted for the Tancól complex, rare in Tlatilco, but characteristic of Chavín. In Valdivia this incising is used primarily on vessel shoulders. In the Chavín Phase of Peru (800–300 B.C.), it characteristically covers the vessel wall down to the base, as it does in Tlatilco and Marksville. Incised line designs continue into the Troyville Phase, where the motifs tend to become repetitive scrolls and meanders. This type has been named Yokena Incised (Greengo, 1964, pp. 50–55). It incorporates the feature of punctations at the ends of lines first noted in the Monagrillo Phase of Panama. A rare rim decoration has the dash line and dot motif noted for Tancól in the Huasteca (chart 21–11). In a previous paper (Ford, 1952, pp. 350–354, figs. 12, 22), both the closely spaced and widely spaced varieties of incising have been traced eastward along the Gulf coast of Florida, and through time in the Lower Mississippi up to the beginning of European contact.

In the Mobile area, broad-line incising has a popularity of 3 percent and runs from 100 B.C. to A.D. 400 as the type Basin Bayou Incised (chart 21, 9–10; Willey, 1949a, pp. 375–376, fig. 22f–i).

In contrast to the accompanying zoned rocker stamped type, broad-line incising does not extend up the Mississippi Valley to the Hopewell areas of Illinois and Ohio.

Summary

Broad-line incising with rectilinear motifs began at 3000 B.C. on the coast of Ecuador and diffused to Peru at about 1800 B.C. in the highlands and 1000 B.C. on the coast. Tendencies toward complete coverage of side walls by decoration and curvilinear motifs become fully developed at 800–1 B.C. in the Chavín-Cupisnique Phase. A divergent and cruder use of incised lines occurred in the northern Colombian sequence. This technique is rare in Mesoamerica with the exception of the Tlatilco Cemetery, the Tres Zapotes Phase of Veracruz, and the Tancól complex in the Huasteca. Both Valdivia-like rectilinear motifs and curvilinear Chavín-like motifs are present.

In the Mississippi Valley and along the Florida Gulf coast, the technique begins at 100 B.C. and lasts until about A.D. 600. Both rectilinear Valdivia-like and curvilinear Chavín-like motifs were employed. The close spaced arrangements and the wider spaced zone-like motifs are characteristic.

Zoned-hatched Designs

CHART 21

Zoned crosshatching is a common decorative technique in the Formative of South America. This will be dealt with in a separate section. Here, attention will be centered on the practice of shading zoned areas by parallel incised lines. While crosshatching is found in Valdivia Phases A and B (3000–2000 B.C.), zoned hatching does not occur until the Machalilla culture (2000–1500 B.C.; chart 21–52). It is not very common and is one of the motifs included in Ayangue Incised (Meggers, Evans, and Estrada, 1965, pl. 132a–h). Usually pendant triangles are filled with slanting parallel lines. This is not zoned hatching in the same sense as in the Chorrera Phase, where the motifs are typically angular line bordered bands filled with slanting parallel lines, which form motifs (chart 21, 50–51). This latter arrangement continues into the Regional Developmental Period (500 B.C.–A.D. 500; chart 21–48).

Izumi and Sono have included zoned hatched decoration in their type Kotosh Incised (chart 21–62, –65; 1963, pp. 118–120, pls. 80b, 81, 83, 85a). Judging from the illustrations the design is rather popular. Broad-line incising is used to outline the zones and they are densely filled with fine-line hatching. Motifs are generally triangles, step design arranged in panels, squares, and concentric diamonds. There are a few curvilinear motifs, including scrolls and undulating bands. In some instances this design is combined with excised areas and the circle and dot. Usually red pigment is rubbed into the lines after firing; yellow and white are occasionally applied. Zoned hatching is confined to the Waira-jirca Phase (1800–1100 B.C.). Although it does not continue later in the Peruvian sequence, several of the characteristic motifs (such as a step design enclosed in rectangles) are found both in Early Tiahuanaco in Bolivia and occasionally in Cupisnique and Salinar on the coast.

In the Puerto Hormiga Phase on the north coast of Colombia, fine parallel lines, sometimes between incised lines, are used to roughen surfaces of modeled adornos placed on the vessel rim (Reichel-Dolmatoff, 1965, pl. 4). It is not certain that this is in the zoned hatching tradition under discussion, so these examples have been left off of the chart. Angular bands of zoned hatching occur in the Momíl Phase (700–1 B.C.), where they are accompanied by zoned punctations, cross-hatching, and dentate stamping (chart 21, 38–39; Reichel-Dolmatoff, G. and A., 1956, pl. 18, 5–13). Occasional examples are found in early Cupica (chart 21–36).

Zoned hatching has not been illustrated from the Soconusco region of coastal Guatemala.

In the Chiapas sequence a small amount of zoned hatching with curvilinear motifs is found in Periods IV–VI (450–1 B.C.; chart 21, 29–30). These are both incised and engraved on the side walls of flat-base pans and composite silhouette bowls. Line filled triangles are another hatched design element (Peterson, 1963, figs. 55, 56a).

MacNeish provides the information that there are examples of zoned hatching in the last centuries of the Santa Maria Phase of the Tehuacán sequence. Illustrations are not available, but his date of about 400 B.C. conforms very well to the occurrence of this technique in Chiapas.

Zoned hatching is fairly common in Tlatilco ceramics, but the motifs are all arrangements of line filled triangles and looped lines (chart 21, 23–24). Some of the triangles are placed in superimposed bands of decoration. These motifs are more reminiscent of the simple Machalilla arrangements than of the rectilinear and curvilinear scrolls that occur on the 500–1 B.C. horizon in Ecuador, Colombia, and Chiapas (Piña Chán, 1958, vol. 1, figs. 9j, 10i–1, p. 16f, k–1, 18j–1, 23f, other examples in figs. 33–39; Vaillant, 1935b, fig. 19c). This technique does not continue in the Valley of Mexico sequence.

Zoned hatching apparently does not start on the Gulf coast of Mexico in the Veracruz area until about 400 B.C. (chart 21–16, 18–19). It is expressed in two techniques: incising and very fine line engraving. The latter technique is most characteristic and has motifs of triangles, diamonds formed by hatching the background, crossed bands of hatching with one set interrupted where it crosses the other, and step bands formed by hatching the background. Red pigment is usually rubbed into the lines (Drucker, 1943a, pl. 20a, c; 1943b, figs. 82–114; Weiant, 1943, fig. 46e). Many of these motifs show remarkable resemblances to complicated Machalilla designs.

Similar fine engraved hatching appears in the El Prisco Black type from Ekholm's (1944, fig. 13k–1) sequence at Panuco, where it runs from his Periods I–III (500 B.C.–A.D. 500).

The zoned-hatched motif is present in a number of Orange fiber-tempered pottery collections from the St. Johns in Florida (chart 21, 5–6). There are some hints, however, that it begins fairly late in Orange, perhaps midway through the phase. Bullen (1955, p. 14) has shown that the Bluffton site appears to be earlier than South Indian Field and Cotton sites. There is a partial confirmation of this in a 1065 B.C. date for Cotton. Zoned-hatched designs are absent in the Bluffton collection, but common at the other two sites. They also extend on into the early phase of St. Johns I. In the foregoing comparisons between Orange and Machalilla decorations, the bands of hatching were the only prominent motif not found in the Ecuadorian phase. If in Florida this does date between 1000 and 300 B.C., a correlation with the Ecuadorian Chorrera Phase becomes possible, for identical patterns of hatched bands forming zig-zags were being made at that time.

Zoned hatching is not a ceramic design in the Stallings Island Phase on the coast of Georgia, but is found engraved on the bone pins that characterize this culture (chart 21–4; Williams, ed., 1968, fig. 63).

Bands of hatched lines forming angular motifs, as well as line-filled diamonds and triangles, are included in Lake Borgne Incised of the Tchefuncte Phase (chart 21, 14–15). The lines, however, are incised in a peculiar fashion, namely the drag-and-jab technique that at an earlier date was confined to the Stallings Island Phase of coastal Georgia (Ford and Quimby, 1945, pl. 4). Designs made by this same technique occur in the Tchula Phase of northern Mississippi, where the rims frequently have a row of small nodes punched from the vessel interior (Phillips, Ford, and Griffin, 1951, fig. 76b–c). On the sand-tempered Alexander complex pottery in the Tennessee Valley, the rectangular bands and their shading are incised. Nodes are also characteristic (Haag, 1939; Webb and DeJarnette 1942, pls. 100, 156).

Between about 600 and 200 B.C. rectilinear bands of zoned incising are found in Illinois, where they are characteristic of Baumer (chart 21, 1–3). Both incised lines and lines of punctation were employed to make the figures. Dentate stamping (J. W. Bennett, 1945, fig. 21b–e) was used to form similar designs. In early Hopewell (ca. 300 B.C.), the motifs become curvilinear and in most instances texturing is achieved by rocker stamping.

Zoned hatching substantially disappears from the Southeast at the time of Early Hopewell, with the exception of its use as background filler in scroll motifs of the Weeden Island and Troyville Phases on the Gulf coast. There is a limited revival, again sometimes with angular arrangements in Mississippian ceramics.

Summary

Zoned hatching is a specialized variation of the roughening of line bordered areas. It appears shortly after 2000 B.C. in Ecuador and highland Peru, with the more complex geometric motifs being found in Peru. By 800 B.C. rectilinear scroll motifs and occasional curvilinear designs were made in Ecuador and on the north coast of Colombia. Rectilinear and curvilinear versions of this design, both incised and engraved, are in the Chiapas, Tehuacán, and Veracruz, Mexican ceramic sequences at 500 B.C. The early occurrences at Tlatilco (1200–400 B.C.) have simple triangular motifs reminiscent of Machalilla. The earliest occurrence of rectilinear line-filled bands in the southeastern United States is in the Orange Phase of Florida at perhaps 800 B.C. These also characterize Tchefuncte in Louisiana, the Alexander complex in the lower Tennessee Valley, and the Baumer Phase of southern Illinois. The beginning date is about 500 B.C. In all of these areas there seems to be a tendency for rectilinear motifs to be early and for curvilinear designs to appear after 500 B.C.

Double-line Break Motif

FIGURE 7

The so-called double-line break motif, in which one or usually two incised or engraved lines run parallel to the vessel lip and then turn sharply and disappear off the edge of the lip, is a very common feature in Mesoamerican ceramics between 1000 and 1 B.C. (fig. 7a–d). Usually the point at which the lines turn and disappear is purely arbitrary. There are no features on the vessel rim correlated with this treatment.

A similar use of incised line is found in Valdivia Cut and Beveled Rim (fig. 7e–h; Meggers, Evans, and Estrada, 1965, p. 57, pls. 55, 56a–1), which runs through the Valdivia sequence in a very minor percentage. This decoration occurs on shallow bowls, usually with polished striated red slip and frequently with tetrapodal supports. The characteristic feature is that segments of the rim have been lowered slightly by carving, leaving rectangular elevations about 1–2 cm. long. The break in the incised lines rises up to these low projections.

In the Ocós Phase of Guatemala, a few examples of the line break motif end in shallow scallops on vessel rims (M. D. Coe, 1961, figs. 29a, c, 30 1). However, in later horizons while scalloped rims continue to be made, the breaks in this motif are not related to them. At Tres Zapotes, for example, while this motif continues as a lip decoration, it also tends to become a major side wall decoration (Weiant, 1943, figs. 12b, 13a). If the Mesoamerican double-line break motif did have this origin, the root of transmission from Ecuador is obscure, for no examples have been noted in the intervening area.

Human Face on Vessel Neck and Shoulder

CHART 22

Human faces, incised or modeled on vessel shoulders or necks, are to be distinguished from figurines which

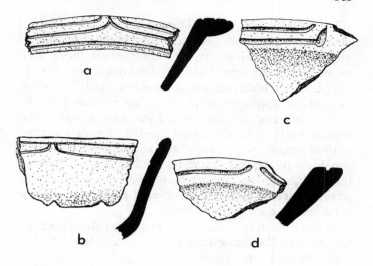

Mesoamerica. Double — line Break

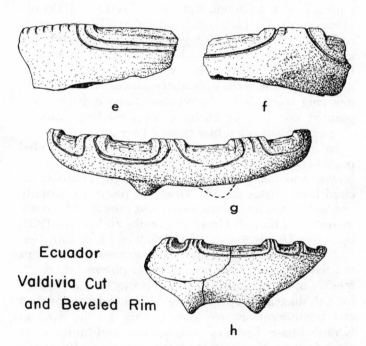

Ecuador

Valdivia Cut

and Beveled Rim

FIGURE 7.—Comparison of double-line break motif, Mesoamerica and Valdivia, Ecuador. (a–b, after Dixon, 1959: a, fig. 27c; b, fig. 28h. c–d, after M. D. Coe, 1961: c, fig. 29a; d, fig. 30k. e–h, after Meggers, Evans, and Estrada, 1965: e, pl. 56a; f, pl. 56f; g, pl. 55 1; h, pl. 55k)

never were attached to vessels, and from "adornos," which projected above the vessel rim. In the Valdivia Phase of Ecuador rectangular faces, incised with broad lines, are Motif 7 of Valdivia Broad-line Incised (Meggers, Evans, and Estrada, 1965, pp. 47–51, pl. 41). They usually are placed on the walls of bowls just below rounded lobes formed by the vessel rims (chart 22–45, –47, –49). These faces are also Motif 1 of Valdivia Excised (op. cit., pp. 58–60, pl. 58a–m) and are identical in style to the incised faces. Less numerous is the type Valdivia Embossed (op. cit., p. 57, pl. 57), which consists of faces rounded in outline, formed by applique strips smoothly welded into the vessel wall, and usually placed just below a rim lobe on the walls of bowls (chart 22–48). Small modeled animal heads were attached as adornos to vessel shoulders in the type Valdivia Nicked Rim or Nubbin (chart 22–46; op. cit., pp. 69–70, pl. 89). Crude straight incised lines are associated decoration. These occurrences date 2000–1500 B.C.

Similar human faces have not been described for the Machalilla Phase or for Chorrera. After 500 B.C. faces formed on round projecting lobes on vessel shoulders and modeled on vessel necks are fairly common in Ecuador (chart 22, 40–41).

In the Pechiche Phase (850–370 B.C.) of Tumbes, just south of the Ecuadorian-Peruvian border, apparently on the Chavín time level, Izumi and Terada (1966, p. 40, pls. 12, 24, 28) found that "The grotesque relief of the human face with a swollen eyelid and a vertically depicted eye is a distinctive feature of the Pechiche wares par excellence." These faces, modeled on the walls of beaker-like vessels, some with low ring bases, have Chavinoid characteristics, as is pointed out by the authors. Vertical loop handles give an overall resemblance to a beer mug.

In the Kotosh sequence of highland Peru, rounded protuberances are punched in the walls of carinated bowls, and facial features are made with broad incised lines (chart 22–53). Graphite paint was usually applied to the hair, eyes, nose, and mouth. These are included in Kotosh Grooved (Izumi and Sono, 1963, pp. 116–118, pls. 46c–h, 95a, 1–6, 95–1, 4, 6, 130, 1–4, 132–21). Anthropomorphic and zoomorphic designs are listed for the four later Kotosh phases (chart 22, 50–52; op. cit., table 10, p. 140), but in the chronological diagram (op. cit., fig. 46) heads on pushed out protuberances are shown only in the Kotosh Kotosh Phase. Faces of both animals and humans are abundant in Higueras Red (op. cit., pp. 106–107). The human faces here are quite different, being formed on vessel necks by means of applique pellets (chart 22–50). The eyes are "coffee bean-like" pellets with horizontal incisions. The mouths are similar, but longer, and the noses are modeled. Similar human faces are also found in Kotosh Red Polished (op. cit., pp. 108–110, pl. 94a) in the San Blas Phase. These faces are formed by incised lines and the nose is usually modeled. The eyes are circle and dot in most instances. Curiously enough, stylized faces do not seem to be a feature of Kotosh Well Polished, the type that marks the Chavín horizon.

Bird (1962, p. 158) illustrates two gourds found near the 2000 B.C. level at Huaca Prieta in Chicama Valley, which have faces carved in the rectangular style of the Valdivia incised faces (chart 22–60). This is several centuries before the introduction of ceramics on the coast.

Two incised human faces on vessel necks were found at Ancón by Willey and Corbett (chart 22, 58–59; 1954, figs. 2f, 8d). Again, this decorative feature seems to be missing through the coastal Chavín-Cupisnique. Human faces incised on vessel necks and applied as small rounded projections on vessel shoulders become very prominent in the Gallinazo Phase on the north coast (Strong and Evans, 1952, figs. 57–7, 58h, 63j–k, q–r, 64c, 67a–e). Similar small animal heads, some recognizable as owls (the *lechusa*), are also found at this time (A.D. 500–600; chart 22, 56–57). In post-Mochica times, human faces molded on vessel necks are quite common.

Faces formed by modeling and wide-line incising are an element of the Puerto Hormiga Phase on the north coast of Colombia (3000–1900 B.C.). These faces, both animal and human, project up above the rim, and were apparently placed at the ends of oval- or canoe-shaped vessels (chart 22, 38–39). The style is quite different from the rectangular incised faces of Valdivia, but in its simplicity does resemble the more rounded faces made by applique. It seems clear that this style in Puerto Hormiga (Reichel-Dolmatoff, 1965, pl. 4) provides an ancestor for the ceramic art of the Malambo Phase in Colombia and Barrancoid pottery of Venezuela. From 1900–1000 B.C. there seems to be a gap in this tradition, for similar faces are not found in the Barlovento Phase. Angulo Valdés (1962b) illustrates Malambo type faces in his plates 2–4 (chart 22–37). Many of these project above the rim and many are so conventionalized that it is impossible to determine whether animals or humans are represented. Some are obviously birds.

Animal heads as adornos seem to be fairly common in the Momíl Phase (chart 22, 35–36; Reichel-Dolmatoff, G. and A., 1956, fig. 13). Many look like dogs, others are clearly birds, and two or three appear to be human. One is a human skull. This type of ornamentation is absent both from Cupica and from the San Agustín ceramics. At a later date, however, stylized human faces, frequently with absurdly small arms placed on either side of the face, are common in northern Colombia (chart 22, 31–32).

Willey and McGimsey (1954, fig. 52j, 1) illustrate modeled adornos below the rims on La Mula complex vessels. This is later than Monagrillo, but the exact dating is uncertain. Projecting modeled adornos, human as well as animal faces, are fairly common in the Classic Period of Costa Rica and Guatemala.

Modeled heads and faces seem to be rare in the Soconusco sequence from the Ocós Phase. M. D. Coe (1961, fig. 40d–e, g–h) illustrates modeled animal heads, apparently of alligators and frogs, that project from the side walls of flat base pans (chart 22–30). In the orange pottery of the Conchas Phase, there is a stylized human face in low relief on the projecting flange of a bowl (op. cit., fig. 32d). A similar face is illustrated on red on buff pottery (chart 22–28; op. cit., fig. 33c). On the neck of a Conchas Red jar, Coe and Flannery (1967, pl. 271) illustrate a bat-like human face with Olmec style eyes (chart 22–29).

In the Chiapas sequence, human and animal effigy faces on the necks, rims, and bodies of vessels start at about 450 B.C. and run up into the Classic Period (chart 22, 25–27). These are principally modeled. Modeled faces from Mirador (Peterson, 1963, figs. 173–174) are mainly human. Modeled animal heads are abundant (op. cit., pp. 157–165), but most come from whistles and ocarinas. In the Horcones Phase (Chiapa VI, 100–1 B.C.), Lowe (1962, pl. 8, 2–4) describes human faces placed on the necks of spouted vessels, with bridge connecting spout and rim (chart 22–26). In Chiapa VIII (A.D. 200–400), Sanders (1961, fig. 34) illustrates very small button-like projections below the vessel rim, which have faces incised on them (chart 22–25).

Human faces and figures are fairly common in Mayan art. They are formed either by applique (Kidder, Jennings, and Shook, 1946, fig. 189), or are carved on walls of vessels by removing the background. At Uaxactún applique and modeling occur in all periods (R. E. Smith, 1955, p. 48). Animal head adornos on vessel rims are rare.

Complete data are not yet available on the Tehuacán ceramic sequence. MacNeish has verbally stated that early in the Santa Maria Phase (ca. 800 B.C.), there is at least one example of a human face carved on the side of a Canoas White vessel. No illustrations are available.

Small globular-bodied bottles, with enlarged necks that bear human faces and applique arms on the vessel shoulder, are at Tlatilco in black polished ware (chart 22–21; Piña Chán, 1958, vol. 1, fig. 35y), dark coffee ware (op. cit., fig. 37u), polished red (op. cit., fig. 41f), and red over coffee (op. cit., figs. 43 1, 44n). Also from the Tlatilco site are bowls with projecting flanges carved and incised to represent the heads and fins of fish and the heads and wings of birds. These are not exactly in the tradition being traced here, but they are closely paralleled by effigy bowls in the Mississippi Valley after A.D. 1200. Vaillant does not mention this feature from Ticomán, but Millon, Drewitt, and Bennyhoff (1965, fig. 95) illustrate an applique face

vessel which is probably from the Teotihuacán I Phase (chart 22–20). Another example of uncertain date (op. cit., fig. 110x) comes from the interior of the Pyramid of the Sun. Modeled and incised human faces and figures are common in later Valley of Mexico ceramics. In the Classic horizon at Monte Albán, representations of human figures and heads on vessel walls and necks become fairly common. The technique varies from painting to modeling and incising.

Both incising and low relief modeling are used to represent human faces on vessel necks from the La Venta site in the Olmec area (chart 22, 17–18). Drucker (1952, fig. 29) illustrates an Olmec style human or jaguar face with open mouth and prominent incisors (chart 22–18). A more clearly human face (op. cit., fig. 64) with the flaring nostrils and thick lip mouth of Olmec style comes from the lower levels of Tres Zapotes. Also from Tres Zapotes, Weiant (1943, pl. 56) illustrates a number of bulging vessel necks incised to represent human heads like those from the Valley of Mexico and Chiapas (chart 22–16). In coastal Veracruz a wide variety of human representations in ceramics extends on into Remojadas Inferior and the Classic horizons.

Representations of human faces on vessel walls and necks are not found at an early date in the eastern United States. The human head vessels of the Mississippian Phase (after A.D. 1200) are another problem.

Summary

The fairly rare but persistent trait of incising or modeling faces on vessel necks in low relief begins at 3000 B.C. in Ecuador and at approximately the same date in the Puerto Hormiga Phase of Colombia, where animal rather than human faces are emphasized. Modeled faces appear both in highland and coastal Peru at 1000 B.C. and after an apparent gap around 500 B.C. in the Chavín Phase, continue into later ceramic times. On the north coast they become molded in the Tiahuanaco Phase. This trait persists in the Regional Developmental of Ecuador. In Colombia faces on jar necks become quite popular after A.D. 600 in the northern part of the country. In the Soconusco of Guatemala modeled faces of the Ocós Phase are animals. Human faces, both incised and modeled with Olmec-like features are found between 800 and 400 B.C. In Chiapas, similar faces occur after 500 B.C. At least one example exists in the Tehuacán sequence, about 800 B.C. Jar necks incised to represent human heads are in the early phases (700–500 B.C.) of the Valley of Mexico. Human face representations begin about 900 B.C. in the Olmec ceramics of coastal Veracruz. Apparently this trait did not diffuse into the eastern United States.

Engraved Zoned Crosshatched Designs

CHART 22

Fine crosshatching, usually engraved after the vessel surface was dried, and bordered by engraved or incised lines, is a treatment closely related to the line zone hatching discussed in a previous section. It seems to have a somewhat divergent history. Zoned crosshatching is usually found on well-polished pottery and frequently red ochre has been rubbed into the lines, apparently after firing, for the pigment is loose and rubs off easily.

Valdivia Fine-line Incised (Meggers, Evans, and Estrada, 1965, p. 60, pls. 61–64, 183e-f) has a polished red surface (chart 22, 43–44). It has triangular motifs bounded and paralleled by straight engraved lines, and these triangles are frequently arranged in superimposed horizontal panels. Panels are also bordered by engraved lines. The triangles are arranged with points up and down, creating a smooth zig-zag band between them (chart 22–44). Engraved circle and dot elements were sometimes used between the triangles. This type begins at 3000 B.C. with a popularity of 2.5 percent and disappears at 1500 B.C. Some of the elements of this decoration are reported in the Machalilla type Ayangue Incised (op. cit., pp. 117, 119, pls. 131, 133–pv; chart 22–42), particularly in Motifs 1 and 4. Here again are found triangles with plain zig-zags between them and horizontal decorative bands, stacked one on another. Ayangue Incised lasts later than 1500 B.C. into the Chorrera Phase, where it becomes cruder and fine crosshatching disappears.

Zoned engraved crosshatching seems to be almost entirely absent from inland and coastal Peru. The rare exceptions are a few examples in coastal Chavín (chart 22, 54–55), Willey and Corbett (1954, p. 43, fig. 7e–l) established Ancón Zoned Hatched for the occurrences of this technique at the sites of Ancón and Supe on the central coast.

The earliest zoned crosshatching on the north coast of Colombia is in the Momíl Phase (chart 22, 33–34), where the Reichel-Dolmatoffs (1956, pp. 145–146, pl. 7–6, –7, –9) have assigned it the name "Momíl Negra Incisa." Almost a thousand sherds place the type in Momíl I Phase (ca. 500 B.C.). The designs are engraved on polished black ware; characteristic forms are globular-bodied vessels and composite silhouette bowls. Motifs consist of undulating plain bands encircling the vessels, with the background roughened with delicate crosshatched engraved lines. One or two lines are centered in the undulating bands. White pigment is commonly rubbed in the cuts.

The resemblance to the common Valdivia and Machalilla engraved zig-zag motif is close. That the undulating motifs of Momíl are curvilinear conforms to the trend away from the rectilinear designs during the Colonial Formative that can be noted in other decorative groups (the wide-line incised decorations, for example.)

Engraved designs do not appear in the Soconusco sequence from the Ocós through the Crucero Phases. In the Chiapas sequence, rectilinear crosshatched engraved designs are among the decorations in Chiapilla Polished Black (chart 22, 22–24; Sanders, 1961, pp. 23–24, figs. 22–23, pl. 6d, h). This dates predominantly Chiapa IV–V (450–100 B.C.). These designs continue on into Santa Cruz Black (op. cit., pp. 30–31, figs. 14j, 33), which reached its maximum in the Santa Cruz Phase (A.D. 200–600). Sanders recognizes that this is a continuing engraved black ware tradition in which a hard, well-fired, polished ware was replaced by a softer, cruder, smoother, but unpolished black ware. The latter frequently has white rims produced by refiring in an oxidized atmosphere. The earlier Chiapilla type has a variety of forms, mostly bowls with composite silhouettes; the later Santa Cruz features the flat-base pan. Zoned crosshatching is but one of the engraved decorations on these two pottery types. The full range of motifs, however, shows very striking resemblance to the engraved wares of the Machalilla Phase of Ecuador, rather than to the Momíl I Phase black ware described above. An excellent case can be made for the direct importation of Chiapilla Polished Black from the coast of Ecuador. The varied vessel forms also reflect forms present on the coast of Ecuador. Only in the later Santa Cruz Black does this black surface finish and decoration become consistently associated with the Mesoamerican flat-base pan. In Peterson's (1963) Mirador sequence, straight-line engraved designs, including delicate crosshatching, are found on polished brown and polished red ware (op. cit., figs. 12n, 23, 25) in Periods IV–VI (450–1 B.C.). They also last until Period VIII (op. cit., fig. 56a, d), but apparently are not as popular as at Santa Cruz.

Curvilinear motifs and zoned crosshatching bordered by wide incised lines occur in the Archaic and Early Classic (A.D. 300–800), and on orange ware at the Maya site of Copán (Longyear, 1952, fig. 56). This suggests that the bordering of crosshatched areas by broad lines may be later than the use of fine lines similar to those used for the crosshatching.

In his survey of Pre-Classic ceramics, Wauchope (1950, pp. 226–227, fig. 7) considers that this technique is typical of the Urban Formative and Proto-Classic. He cites examples from Middle Tres Zapotes, Chukumuk II, Salcaja, Chama I, and the Balam Phase at Zacualpa.

Zoned crosshatching occurs rarely in the Tlatilco ceramics in the Valley of Mexico (chart 22–19; Piña Chán, 1958, vol. 1, fig. 47–25; Porter, 1953, pl. 6a, h–i). While triangular motifs filled with simple hatching resemble the Ayangue group of motifs, these rare crosshatched examples tend to be curvilinear.

In the Olmec area on the Gulf coast of Mexico, very delicate zoned engraving first occurs in the Tres Zapotes Phase at about 500 B.C. (chart 22–14). Rectilinear arrangements, crosshatched triangles, lines centered in smooth bands, as well as a few curvilinear motifs are found. These decorations are characteristically on black ware, and red or white pigment has been rubbed into the lines. Weiant (1943, figs. 13b–c, 21d, 41e) illustrates both body and lip decoration. Drucker (1943a, figs. 22d, 30, 39–40, pl. 20) also illustrates examples of this technique on black and brown wares. Similar motifs from Cerro de las Mesas are given by Drucker (chart 22–13; 1943b, figs. 82–84, pl. 19e–f). In excavations in Chalahuites and Limoncito, Medellín, Wallrath, and Ford found zoned engraved designs in the upper levels, but they are quite rare; as a matter of fact, the total of decorated sherds in these levels is not more than 2 or 3 percent.

In the northern part of the state of Veracruz, zoned crosshatching with red pigment rubbed into the lines is an element of Ekholm's (1944, fig. 9t) Zaquil Black Incised. It starts in Panuco III (A.D. 150–500), but is relatively popular and dates mainly in Panuco IV, approximately A.D. 500–900.

Among the Colonial Formative ceramic complexes in the southeastern United States, zoned crosshatching is a minor element only in the fiber-tempered Orange pottery of Florida (chart 22–8; Moore, 1894, p. 619), where it is not engraved but incised with a pointed tool. However, it is fairly common on the bone pins that are a feature of the Stallings Island and Orange ceramic phases (chart 22–7, –9). Decorated pins with excellent Colonial Formative motifs are also found in "preceramic" but probably coeval sites along the Tennessee River and in Kentucky (for example, W. S. Webb, 1950, fig. 15). The pin shown on chart 22–7 has an angular key-like motif formed by a smooth band with background crosshatched. A line is centered in the smooth band, and the decoration is repeated in horizontal, superimposed panels.

Engraved human bone and other objects come from the Hopewell site in Ohio at a date of about 100 B.C.–A.D. 200 (chart 22, 1–3). In contrast to the earlier bone pins mentioned above, these motifs tend to be curvilinear. The earliest of these designs in the Mississippi Valley are the engraved plummets of the Poverty Point Phase (1200–400 B.C.; chart 2–12), of

magnetite and highly polished. At least a dozen have been found bearing delicate crosshatching bordered by heavier engraved lines.

Delicate incised (not engraved) zoned crosshatching is a fairly common feature of the Weeden Island Phase of the Gulf coast of Florida, and the coeval Troyville Phase of Louisiana (chart 22, 10–11). This features smooth bands forming undulations or scrolls, with a line frequently centered in the band and the background delicately crosshatched. Other variations have punctated, hatched, or painted background (Willey, 1949a, pl. 26c). These examples date about A.D. 500–800, and seem to provide the motifs for many of the later Caddoan designs.

While the fine-line engraving techniques of decoration on black and brown ware very similar to Mesoamerican Formative come into east Texas about A.D. 900, zoned crosshatched motifs are not an element of the Alto ceramic complex (Newell and Krieger, 1949). They are abundantly represented, however, in the later Fulton Phase of Caddoan ceramic art (chart 22, 4–6; Webb, 1959, fig. 108). Designs and techniques diffused eastward and persisted from about A.D. 1200–1500. Motifs on these Mississippian examples are usually curvilinear scrolls or meanders formed by plain bands, often with a line centered in them. The backgrounds are roughened by delicate crosshatching. Similar zoned decorations are found on shell gorgets. In many instances zoning lines are broad, and crosshatching is made by fine lines.

Summary

Zoned engraved crosshatching starts on the coast of Ecuador about 3000 B.C., and lasts there until about 1000 B.C. A century or so after 1000 B.C., curvilinear zoned crosshatching appears briefly in coastal Peru in the Chavín horizon, but is more abundant on black ware on the north coast of Colombia. There is a small representation of this technique in the Tlatilco site in the Valley of Mexico. Curvilinear designs seem to have little relation to the late Formative Mexican tradition. The zoned crosshatched engraving that appears in Chiapas at 500 B.C. is initially on polished black ware and is very similar to Machalilla-Chorrera examples. What seems to be a reflection from the Chiapas material extends along the Gulf coast of Mexico from 400 B.C.–A.D. 600 in small quantities.

The earliest engraved designs in the eastern United States are on the bone pins of the Stallings Island Phase, the plummets of Poverty Point, and human bone in the Hopewell site in Ohio. These appear to be early examples of the Ayangue influence. Engraved ceramic designs first come into east Texas about

A.D. 800–900, but the curvilinear crosshatched background motif in which we are interested first appears on the coast of Florida as incised decoration about A.D. 500. True engraved decoration with background crosshatched develops in the later Caddoan and Mississippian Phases (A.D. 1200–1700).

SUMMARY OF TRAIT DISTRIBUTIONS

The trait diffusions traced in the foregoing can be classified into four general categories based on place and time of first appearance in the Americas, and as to time and apparent method of their spread.

1. Groups of features, principally ceramics, transported by sea during establishment of small colonies during the Colonial Formative. With the exceptions noted, all ceramic features could have been derived from the Valdivia and Machalilla complexes.

a. Valdivia (3000–1500 B.C.), coastal Ecuador. Apparently derived from the Middle Jomon Phase of southwestern Japan.

b. Puerto Hormiga (3000–1900 B.C.), north coast of Colombia. Principally derived from Valdivia, coastal Ecuador. Trait of vegetable fiber tempering and boat-shaped vessels not accounted for.

c. Stallings Island (2400–500 B.C.), coast of Georgia, south Atlantic coast of the United States. Fiber tempering derived from Puerto Hormiga; vessel shapes and decorations from Valdivia.

d. Puerto Marquez (ca. 2400 B.C.), Pacific coast of Mexico, state of Guerrero. Published description not very detailed, but similar to Purrón.

e. Purrón (2300–1500 B.C.), central highland Mexico. Probably the result of an inland diffusion from an unknown coastal settlement. Shapes derived from local stone vessels.

f. Machalilla (2000–1500 B.C.), coastal Ecuador. Origin unknown.

g. Orange (2000–400 B.C.), St. Johns River region, Florida, south Atlantic coast of the United States. Early phases related to Puerto Hormiga and Barlovento, north coast of Colombia; vessel shapes, Purrón related. Majority of ceramic decorations resemble Machalilla, coast of Ecuador, Ayangue engraved tradition.

h. Monagrillo (ca. 2000 B.C.), Panama. In part related to Purrón, in part to Valdivia, but with an unexplained decoration motif.

i. Kotosh Waira-jirca (1800 B.C.), highland Peru. In part related to Valdivia, but not so directly as coastal localities. Part of ceramic complex unexplained.

j. Negritos (probably ca. 1500 B.C., no radiocarbon dates), north coast of Peru. Valdivia related.

k. Guañape (1200 B.C.), Virú Valley, Peru. Purrón vessel shapes; decorations, Valdivia related.

2. Traits that are earliest in the Valdivia and Machalilla Phases of coastal Ecuador, but which diffused subsequent to the Colonial Formative, principally between 1000 and 1 B.C.

a. Ring-shaped villages.
b. Sandstone saws.
c. Reamers for enlarging drilled holes.
d. Rectangular celts.
e. Clay figurines.
f. Small wide-mouth pots with cambered rims.
g. Composite silhouette bowls.
h. Simple bowls with rounded, convex bases.
i. Simple bowls with flat bases.
j. Bowls with four solid feet.
k. Low ring bases (begin in Ecuador, Chorrera Phase).
l. Bottles with small necks.
m. Stirrup-spout bottles.
n. Bridge-spout bottles.
o. Red slip and red painted areas.
p. Rocker stamping.
q. Excised designs with red pigment rubbed into cutout areas.
r. Thickened flat lips, decorated.
s. Wide-line incised decorations.
t. Double-line break.
u. Line zoned hatching.
v. Incised and modeled faces on vessel shoulders and necks.
w. Line zoned crosshatched decorations.

3. Traits that are earliest in North America (including Mexico) and diffused principally between 1000 and 1 B.C.

a. Nutting stones.
b. Milling stones.
c. Metate and mano.
d. Tubular drilling.
e. Tubular pipes.
f. Full and three-quarter grooved stone axes.

g. Tecomate or large neckless jar.

h. Pottery flat-base pan.

i. Stone flat-base pan.

j. Negative painted decoration.

4. Traits that first appear in the Theocratic Formative and diffuse between 1200 and 1 B.C.

a. Mound building and ceremonial centers.

b. Beads made of hard rare stone; disk, tubular, round, and barrel-shaped.

c. Lapidary industry. Small carvings made of hard rare stone.

d. Solid drill bit for hard stone (may go back earlier but diffused at this time) related to lapidary industry.

e. Earspools of stone and metal.

f. Mirrors made of jet or mica.

g. Finger rings: stone, pottery, shell, bone, or copper.

h. Combs.

i. Flat and cylindrical stamps.

j. Bark beaters.

k. Petaloid celts.

l. Tripod vessels, long as well as short legs.

m. Teapot-shaped bottles.

n. Flanges on bowl walls, often decorated.

Colonial Formative Diffusion in the Americas

In this chapter and the following one, the attempt will be made to evaluate the significance of the trait distributions selected for review by placing them in the context of the various cultural complexes to which they belong and comparing these complexes with one another.

According to the information available at present, the making of pottery during the Colonial Formative (3000–1500 B.C.) was confined to a few rather small geographical areas that were widely spaced over the Americas. Doubtless additional groups or colonies of sites will be found, but it seems improbable that they will be numerous, or that they will have a continuous geographic distribution.

With the exception of two localities (Tehuacán, Mexico and Kotosh, Peru), all of the known Colonial Formative sites are coastal shell middens, obvious remains that should not be difficult to locate and identify, if the archeologist knows what he is looking for. For more than ten years investigators have been aware of this, and parts of the coasts of Peru, Ecuador, and Colombia have been surveyed in a fairly thorough fashion. In contrast, the coasts of Central America and Mexico have received little attention aside from limited areas in Panama and Guatemala. The Gulf and south Atlantic coasts of North America are comparatively well known.

The Colonial Formative localities that are known at present are as follows:

ECUADOR

Valdivia Phase A–C (3000–1500 B.C.)
At least 30 localities, all shell middens, clustered principally along the coast of Guayas Province.

Machalilla Phase (2000–1500 B.C.)
Four localities, shell middens, three adjacent to Valdivia sites, one a few miles to the north.

COLOMBIA

Puerto Hormiga (3000–1900 B.C.)
One site, shell ring about 80 m. in diameter, 1.2 m. in height.

PANAMA

Monagrillo Phase (ca. 2000 B.C.)
Three sites, shell middens.

PERU

Negritos Phase (no date)
Coastal site.

Guañape Phase (ca. 1200 B.C.)
Coastal shell midden.

Kotosh Waira-jirca (ca. 1800 B.C.)
Inland site, stone terrace and building construction.

MEXICO

Puerto Marquez (ca. 2400 B.C.)
One site, shell midden.

Purrón (2300–1500 B.C.)
One site, cave deposit.

SOUTHEASTERN UNITED STATES

Stallings Island Phase (2400–500 B.C.)
Approximately 20 sites, shell middens, of which eight are shell rings.

Orange Phase (2000–400 B.C.)
Approximately 12 sites, large shell middens.

Bayou la Batre (1100 B.C.)
Two sites, shell middens.

Poverty Point (1200–400 B.C.)
Two coastal sites, shell middens, date about 1500 B.C. About 25 interior sites probably date 1200–400 B.C.

There are several conclusions to be drawn from a survey of Colonial Formative diffusion, and it seems practical to state them at the beginning rather than the end of this discussion.

1. The early spread of ceramics appears to have been by sea. The voyages were of considerable length and small colonies were established among local people. Meggers, Evans, and Estrada (1965) have postulated that early trans-Pacific contacts were probably the result of accident: a lost boatload of fishermen. In the Americas there is reason to think that colonizing voyages were not only intentional, but that they were repeated and that contact continued. Parallel sequences of traits supporting this view will be cited in the following pages.

2. In the colonized areas it may be expected that two things will happen to the ceramic tradition. First, isolation and lack of stimulation may result in a gradual decline in the quality of the product. The second effect is diametrically opposite. Local people at varying distances from these centers of the new technology may begin tentative attempts at pottery-making. If their initial efforts were as crude as the first Basket Maker pottery of the Four Corners region of the United States Southwest, undecorated pottery might have been made for some time before competence was achieved and the art began to approach the level of the pattern. Ultimately, the ceramic industry probably would become stabilized at a lower level than in the donor region.

3. Only a portion of the complete donor complex was transported to each colony. Why this should be so is not clear. Possibly there was family specialization, so that the cluster of traits taught local people depended on the composition of the boat passengers.

4. There are a few new vessel forms found in colony regions that do not occur in the parent complex. In highland Mexico it seems clear that two shapes that became quite important, namely the flat-base pan and the neckless jar or "tecomate," were copies of traditional shapes of stone vessels. Probably the oval or "boat-shaped" vessel, which first appears in Puerto Hormiga and later became popular in Venezuela and the West Indies, had a wooden prototype. This is a very practical shape for containers made from small tree trunks. In the history of American ceramics, it is remarkable how rare are such "new" vessel shapes. The transfer of decorations from gourds, textiles, or other perishable material is also a possibility, but appeal to this level of explanation rarely seems necessary.

ARCHEOLOGICAL COMPLEXES

The Valdivia and Machalilla Cultures of Coastal Ecuador

The discovery of the highly sophisticated Valdivia ceramic complex with an apparent initial date of about 3000 B.C. in shell middens on the coast of Ecuador, has been an unexpected surprise to American archeologists. In the Valdivia sites underlying preceramic levels have not been found. Neither do there appear to be any simple early developmental stages. This well-polished pottery with an unusually wide variety of incised, engraved, excised, punctated, applique, brushed, red-slipped, impressed, and rocker-stamped decorations appears suddenly, and nowhere in the Americas have possible antecedents been found.

Meggers, Evans, and Estrada (1965), the discoverers of Valdivia, have cited a number of ceramic similarities in the coeval Middle Jomon pottery of western Japan, particularly from the island of Kyushu. On this basis, a trans-Pacific voyage from Japan to Ecuador is postulated.

The features of Valdivia ceramics will not be summarized, nor will the similarities to Jomon be reviewed. The reader is advised to have Meggers, Evans, and Estrada's (1965) report conveniently at hand. In the following discussion, the Valdivia Phase will be accepted as having existed on the coast of Ecuador with a number of internal changes from 3000–1500 B.C.

An even more puzzling enigma is presented by the Machalilla ceramic complex which is found in separate villages scattered along the Ecuadorian coast among Valdivia sites, and which dates from 2000 to 1500 B.C. Any possible antecedents in the Americas or in Asia are unrecognized at present.

The problems of the origins of Valdivia and Machalilla are not directly germane to the theses presented here, which focus on events within the Americas. When an allusion is made to a similar feature in China or Japan, the writer is not presenting an argument, merely pointing out a parallel in need of further study.

The Puerto Hormiga Phase of North Coastal Colombia

Meggers, Evans, and Estrada (1965, p. 168) compare Puerto Hormiga ceramics to those of Valdivia and find a number of traits in common. Reichel-Dolmatoff (1965, pp. 50–51) concludes that the differences make relationship improbable. Since the final reports of both complexes were published in the same year, and were consequently not available to these authors, the evidence may be usefully reevaluated here.

Fiber and Sand Tempering

Forty to fifty percent of the Puerto Hormiga pottery is heavily tempered with vegetable fiber, has poor surface finish, and lacks decoration. Twenty to thirty percent has a smaller fiber content and shares decoration with the remaining pottery which is tempered with sand. The use of fiber tempering has not been observed in Valdivia ceramics, all of which contain fine or coarse sand.

Parenthetically it seems worthwhile to quote J. E. Kidder (1957, p. 7) in reference to the Jomon ceramics of Japan: "The pottery is always hand-made, often by the coiling process, and is at first baked in an open fire at a temperature between 400° and 500° c. The tempering material in the early periods is fiber, and later may be sand usually strongly micaceous in content. The sand varies from extremely coarse to fine; small quartz crystals are often clearly visible."

Vessel Shapes

Shapes of Puerto Hormiga vessels are limited. Most common are semiglobular bowls up to 30 cm. in diameter and 15 cm. deep, which have vertical or slightly incurved lips. Lips are simple and often thinner than vessel walls (fig. 8a). This form is very similar to a popular Valdivia bowl form (fig. 8g; Meggers, Evans, and Estrada, 1965, fig. 54, 3–5) that runs through the sequence. The oval- or boat-shaped vessels with modeled adornos on the ends that are a minor feature of Puerto Hormiga (fig. 8b), are not present in the Valdivia complex. It has already been suggested that this may be an imitation of a wooden form.

Scallop-shell Stamping

In comparing features, Reichel-Dolmatoff's discussion will be followed (1965, pp. 28–30). Additional data and illustrations are provided by Reichel-Dolmatoff (1961, pls. 1–2; 1965, fig. 3, pls. 3–5), and Meggers, Evans, and Estrada (1965, pl. 188). Scallop-shell stamping is zoned by broad incised lines in Puerto Hormiga (fig. 8c). These impressions are parallel,

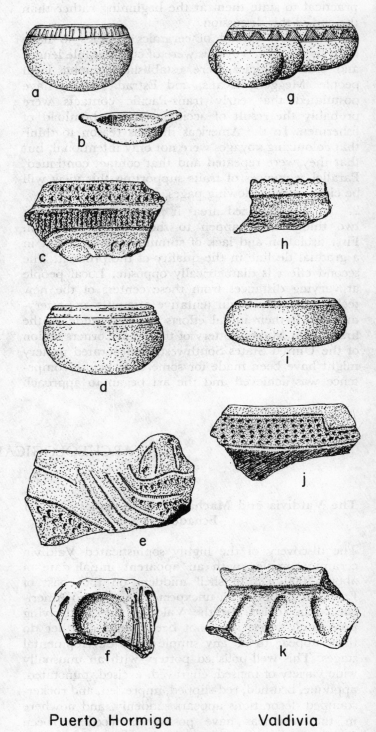

Puerto Hormiga   **Valdivia**

FIGURE 8.—Resemblances between vessel shapes and decorations of the Puerto Hormiga Phase, Colombia and the Valdivia Phase, Ecuador. a, g, Semi-globular bowls. b, Boat-shaped vessel. c, h, Shell-edge stamping. d, i, Horizontal incised lines. e, j, Zoned punctate. f, k, Finger grooving. (a–f, after Reichel-Dolmatoff, 1965: a, pl. 3–9; b, p. 27; c, pl. 3–10; d, p. 28; e, pl. 5–8; f, pl. 3–8. g–k, Meggers, Evans, and Estrada, 1965: g, fig. 32–3, 54; h, pl. 113b; i, fig. 24–3; j, pl. 105f; k, pl. 65a)

not rocked. Except for the curious and early fine-line incising, zoning is absent in Valdivia A-C decorations. The rare sand-tempered type Valdivia Shell Stamped (fig. 8h; op. cit., p. 84, pl. 113a–k) usually has the parallel scallop-shell impressions placed in panels like the arrangement of incised designs. This type dates 3000–2000 B.C.

Horizontal Incised Lines

Reichel-Dolmatoff (1925, p. 28) describes but does not illustrate the simple decoration of two or three parallel lines that encircle the rim just below the lip. Lines are broad, round-bottom, and irregular, 3 to 5 mm. wide. This decoration has a frequency of about 25 percent of decorated sherds. An illustration is furnished (fig. 8d) based on the description. Meggers, Evans, and Estrada (1965, pp. 47–51, pls. 30–31) list this design, usually on the rims of globular bowls with slightly incurving rims as Motif 1 of Valdivia Broad-line Incised (fig. 8i). One to three lines occur, but a single line is most frequent. Although the type increased from fractional percentage to about 6 percent from 3000-1500 B.C., this motif declines from an initial popularity of around 50 percent within the type during Periods A–B to a minority occurrence in Period C (Meggers, Evans and Estrada, 1965, Appendix table 7).

Punctated Decoration

Reichel-Dolmatoff (1965, pp. 28–29) describes three varieties of punctated decorations. One has punctations, which are usually comma-shaped and made with the instrument held at an angle, zoned by broad incised lines and sometimes used in conjunction with the modeled adornos (fig. 8e). Punctations, including a few comma-shaped examples, occur in minor frequency in Valdivia (Meggers, Evans, and Estrada, 1965, pp. 80–81, pls. 100–101), but usually are arranged in panels not bordered by incised lines. Valdivia Red Zoned Punctate (fig. 8j; op. cit., pp. 81–82, pl. 105) has very simple rectilinear or curving undulating broad lines bounding areas of punctation on the cambered rims of bowls.

Finger-made Dimples

Sixty-one Puerto Hormiga sherds have oval areas pushed into the vessel surface with the finger, which are generally surrounded by incised decoration and are sometimes filled with red pigment (fig. 8f). This seems to be a late feature at Puerto Hormiga. Areas punched out with the finger are more common in Valdivia ceramics (Meggers, Evans, and Estrada, 1965, pl. 78) than are pushed-in areas, but the latter do occur. In Valdivia Punctate (op. cit., pl. 100 d, r)

elongated areas are pushed in, apparently with the fingers (fig. 8k). Short grooves of this type are characteristic of Valdivia Finger Grooved (op. cit., pp. 61–62, pl. 65). No incised decoration accompanies this latter treatment; neither was red pigment applied. However, both decoration by punching in the vessel wall with the fingers, and the use of post-fired red pigment are shared by Puerto Hormiga and Valdivia.

Adornos

Rather sophisticated modeled and incised adornos, apparently heads of reptiles or rodents, are a feature of Puerto Hormiga ceramics (fig. 9a). This is clearly an ancestral form of the modeling in the Barrancoid ceramics of later date in Colombia (Malambo Phase, 1000–700 B.C.) and Venezuela. Incised lines ending in punctations, circle and dot, small elevated clay buttons with centered punctation, small excised areas, and brushing are all features of Puerto Hormiga modeling.

The Valdivia adornos also appear to represent animals but are much cruder and simpler (fig. 9d; Meggers, Evans, and Estrada, 1965, pp. 69–70, pl. 89). Modeling is careless, eyes and mouths are indicated by short slashes, and the vessel body is covered with crude parallel hatching or crosshatching.

Drag-and-Jab Incising

Drag-and-jab incising is a minor feature in Puerto Hormiga (Reichel-Dolmatoff, 1965, p. 29). A pointed tool was used and impressed at intervals to make teardrop-shaped impressions arranged around the rims of bowls (fig. 9b). The broad-line, double-point, drag-and-jab Valdivia decoration runs horizontally encircling the vessels and may be interrupted to form panels (fig. 9e).

Circle and Dot

Two sherds from Puerto Hormiga are decorated with small circle and dot designs placed between straight incised lines running parallel to the vessel lip (fig. 9c). At least one (Reichel-Dolmatoff, 1965, fig. 3–5) appears to have the background excised. These two decorations are identical to a treatment included in the Valdivia Red Incised type of Valdivia Periods A and B, 3000–2000 B.C. (fig. 9f; Meggers, Evans, and Estrada, 1965, p. 81, pl. 104). In Valdivia an interlocking fret design is often placed below the row of circle and dot; in Puerto Hormiga this is missing.

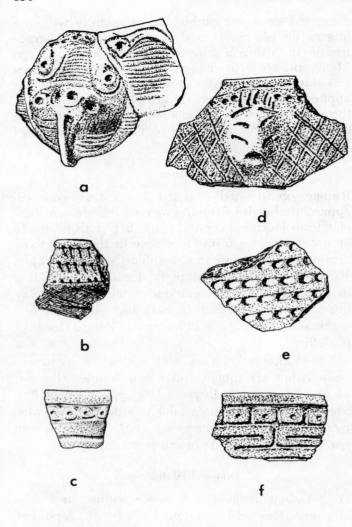

Puerto Hormiga   **Valdivia**

FIGURE 9.—Resemblances between pottery decorations of the Puerto Hormiga Phase, Colombia and the Valdivia Phase, Ecuador. *a, d,* Adornos. *b, e,* Drag and jab. *c, f,* Circle and dot. (*a–c,* after Reichel-Dolmatoff, 1965: *a,* pl. 4–5; *b,* pl. 3–7; *c,* fig. 3–5. *d–f,* after Meggers, Evans, and Estrada, 1965: *d,* pl. 89f; *e,* pl. 80i; *f,* pl. 104 b–c)

Summary

FEATURES PROMINENT in Puerto Hormiga ceramics and lacking in Valdivia.
1. Fiber tempering.
2. Boat-shaped vessels.
3. Use of dots at the ends of lines.
4. Zoning of shell stamping, parallel hachure, or punctations by broad-line incising.

FEATURES SHARED.
1. Sand-tempered pottery.
2. Common bowl shape with slightly incurving rim.

3. Prominent use of one to three incised lines drawn parallel to bowl rim.
4. Use of wide round-bottom incised lines.
5. Scallop-shell impressions placed parallel, not rocked (although motifs are different).
6. Red slip; often polished in Valdivia; more crudely finished in Puerto Hormiga.
7. Loose red pigment rubbed into decoration.
8. Depressions in vessel surface as decoration.
9. Adornos on vessel surface; elaborate in Puerto Hormiga, crude in Valdivia.
10. Drag-and-jab incising (limited use and narrower lines in Puerto Hormiga).
11. Circle and dot in horizontal panels with excised background; rare in Puerto Hormiga, but almost identical to Valdivia execution.

It is a curious fact that the features present at Puerto Hormiga but missing from Valdivia ceramics nearly all tend toward the Barrancoid complex of Venezuela, which was to have a profound effect on the later ceramic traditions of the Orinoco Basin, the Antilles, and the eastern flank of the Andes as far south as Peru.

Both Puerto Hormiga and Valdivia were in existence for about 1000 years following 3000 B.C. Both groups of people were coastal dwellers and subsisted primarily on sea products. Puerto Hormiga was a circular village; one Valdivia village appears to have a similar shape. Both complexes share the crude South American coastal chipped stone industry.

The reader is now faced with the classic dilemma of American archeology: either both complexes were independent inventions of ceramics, or one derived from the other. Those who choose the first conclusion should stop reading here and head for the roulette wheel and dice table. Obviously they have a superior faith in, and perhaps mastery of, the laws of probability and coincidence than does the writer.

The ground rules rather arbitrarily laid down at the beginning of this discussion favor the derivation of Puerto Hormiga ceramics from Valdivia. A major part of Puerto Hormiga ceramics can be derived from Valdivia, but the reverse is far from true. The new features in Puerto Hormiga tend toward the Barrancoid ceramics along the Caribbean coast; they are not reflected back down the Pacific coast.

The Monagrillo Phase of Panama

Willey and McGimsey (1954, p. 58) have characterized the Monagrillo ceramic complex of the Parita Peninsula, south coast Panama, as simpler and cruder than any other known for Middle America or the Andean region. Both the appearance of the pottery and a radiocarbon date of 2140 B.C. certainly justify considering this complex as Colonial Formative.

Moderately tempered with sand, including white quartz grains, the Monagrillo pottery was coiled, crudely finished by scraping, carelessly polished, and predominantly undecorated.

As crude as is Monagrillo Plain to begin with, it degenerates with time, a condition so notable that at the Zapotál site, Willey and McGimsey (op. cit., pp. 94–95) set up a separate late plain type, Zapotál Plain. This has larger temper particles, is less dense and compact, and the surfaces have holes and scars from loss of temper particles and some surface crackling. In the lower levels of the midden, there were concentrated 200 to 300 sherds of a thin yellow ware that had the best smoothed finish.

Bowl Shapes

Moderately deep to deep bowls, 10 to 15 cm. in diameter, are described as the most common form (fig. 10a; Willey and McGimsey, 1954, p. 61). Rims are vertical or incurving and are direct; lips are rounded, thickened, or flattened. Bases are rounded, and while sometimes slightly flattened, are never truly flat. Folded rims on these bowls (op. cit., rim 4, p. 61, fig. 9m–v) are late at Monagrillo. This deep bowl is also the dominant Puerto Hormiga form (fig. 10f), and is popular in the Valdivia ceramics, as was noted above.

Shallow bowls (op. cit., p. 61, fig. 10q–t) found at Monagrillo (fig. 10b) are not described from Puerto Hormiga, but are common at Valdivia (fig. 10g) where they run through the sequence (Meggers, Evans, and Estrada, 1965, fig. 54, 6–7).

Tecomate-shaped Jars

Willey and McGimsey (1954, p. 61, fig. 9a–k, form 2) state that "Other characteristic Monagrillo Plain forms are a subglobular bowl or jar with a markedly incurved rim and relatively small orifice. . . ." Sizes of these vessels are not indicated, but rim profile illustrations show a few examples of lips reinforced on the interior in the characteristic "comma-shaped lip," making it seem fairly certain that these are fragments of large neckless jars or "tecomates" (fig. 10c).

The history of the tecomate has been traced (see pp. 92–95). This form, absent from Valdivia-Machalilla and from Puerto Hormiga, began to be manufactured in substantial frequencies shortly before 2000 B.C. with the first appearance of ceramics in MacNeish's (1961) Tehuacán sequence in central highland Mexico (fig. 10h). It is also an important form in Brush's (1965) Puerto Marquez complex in Guerrero, Mexico.

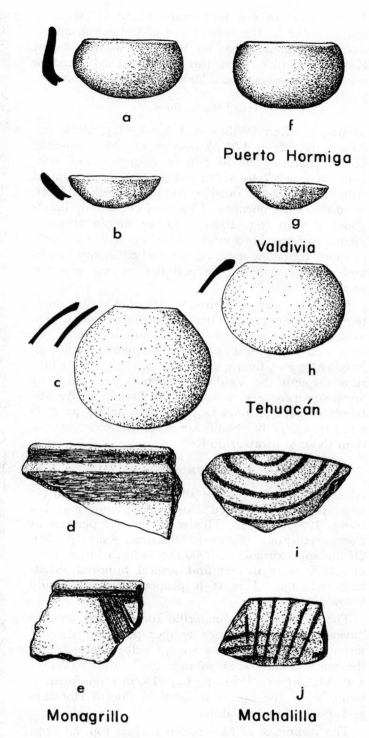

FIGURE 10.—Resemblances between vessel shapes and decorations of the Monagrillo Phase of Panama and the Puerto Hormiga Phase of Colombia, the early part of the Tehuacán sequence in Mexico, and the Valdivia and Machalilla Phases of Ecuador. a, f, Deep bowls. b, g, Shallow bowls. c, h, Tecomates. d–e, i–j, Red banding. (a–e, after Willey and McGimsey, 1954: a, fig. 8o; b, fig. 10t; c, fig. 9a, i; d, fig. 12g; e, fig. 12j. f, after Reichel-Dolmatoff, 1965, fig. 6. g, i–j, after Meggers, Evans, and Estrada, 1965: g, fig. 54, 6–7; i, pl. 150c; j, pl. 150g; h, after Byers, ed., 1967–, vol. 3, fig. 7)

By the start of the Barlovento Phase (1900 B.C.), it is popular on the north coast of Colombia, and it reached highland Peru by 1800 B.C. in the earliest Kotosh ceramics. That this form reached Panama from the northwest about 2000 B.C. appears probable.

Red Slip on Bowls

Monagrillo Red (Willey and McGimsey, 1954, pp. 65–67, fig. 12e–j, 47d–1) consists of "Medium-deep bowls, probably 20–30 cm. in diameter, and sub-globular bowls," to which red slip has been applied either to cover the outside, inside, or both surfaces, or to restricted portions of the surface, usually bands about the lip (fig. 10d–e). Other simple arrangements include horizontal bands encircling vessels, pendant triangles, semicircles attached to rim bands, and vertical panels. Incised line zoning was not practiced.

Red slip was sometimes applied to the sand-tempered pottery of Puerto Hormiga, but it was evidently of poor quality and motifs cannot be determined. Overall red slip, frequently well polished (Meggers, Evans, and Estrada, 1965, pp. 76–80), runs through the Valdivia sequence. Red bands or areas are rare and restricted to Period A. Arched bands of painted lines begin in Machalilla at 2000 B.C. (fig. 10i–j), but bands are somewhat more narrow than those of Monagrillo Red.

Engraved Decoration

About 18 percent of the sherds from the Valdivia deposits were decorated (Meggers, Evans, and Estrada, 1965, p. 42). This ratio ran 6.2 percent in Puerto Hormiga (Reichel-Dolmatoff, 1965, p. 28). Of the approximately 20,000 sherds from Monagrillo, about 70 were incised and several hundred sherds had red slip. This is a proportion substantially below 1 percent.

The 70 sherds of Monagrillo Incised ware tend to "average somewhat finer temper particles, the exterior surfaces are almost always well-smoothed, and the ware is somewhat thinner (6–7 mm.)" (Willey and McGimsey, 1954, p. 65). Decoration forms a band below the lip, as is usual in Puerto Hormiga and much of early Valdivia.

The technique of Monagrillo Incised (op. cit., pp. 63–65, figs. 12a–d, 46, 47a–c, 48a–d) is the scratching of lines into the hard dry vessel surface, probably before firing. I am using the term "engraving" for this treatment. Motifs are predominantly curvilinear scrolls, meanders, and keys (fig. 11a), but rectilinear elements are also present. Dot punctations at the ends of lines are common (fig. 11b), triangular areas are excised where lines meet, and some examples have red pigment rubbed into incisions.

The new discoveries of early ceramics since Willey and McGimsey (op. cit., pp. 128–132) wrote their comparative section on Monagrillo have provided no potential direct ancestor for Monagrillo Incised. Most of the essential elements however, existed in northern South America before 2000 B.C., with the possible exception of the curvilinear scroll motif with roughened background. Curvilinear motifs in general are late and rare in the Valdivia-Machalilla sequence. They are present in Puerto Hormiga, with shell stamping used to roughen line-zoned areas, but sherds are too small to determine the decorative patterns.

Engraved lines, the excision of triangular areas where lines meet, and red pigment rubbed into the depressed areas are present in Puerto Hormiga (fig. 11d) and frequent in Valdivia. Round punctations at the ends of lines were common in Puerto Hormiga, where the lines were broad incisions (Reichel-Dolmatoff, 1965, pls. 3, 8–9; 4; 5, 5–6, 8–9); they are less common in Valdivia, where excised lines often end in broad triangular-shaped excised areas (fig. 11e; Meggers, Evans, and Estrada, 1965, pls. 56n, 59h–k).

That scroll motifs were developing in the north Colombian coastal region at this time is further indicated by the frequency of this arrangement in the Barlovento Phase (1900–1500 B.C.), which features broad-line incising, scroll and undulating band motifs with background roughened by punctations or parallel lines, and red pigment in incisions. Neckless jars or tecomates are the dominant vessel form (Reichel-Dolmatoff, 1955, pls. 3–5).

Excised Rectilinear Designs

Monagrillo sherds with rectilinear undulating bands combined with excised areas (fig. 11c; Willey and McGimsey, 1954, figs. 12c, 48a) have parallels in Valdivia Excised (fig. 11f), which dates prior to 2000 B.C. (Meggers, Evans, and Estrada, 1965, pl. 59a).

Willey and McGimsey (1954, p. 131) cite resemblances between Monagrillo incised and the engraved black-brown ware of the Arévalo to Miraflores Phases (800 B.C.–A.D. 100) of highland Guatemala. It may be noted that the same elements are also found along the Gulf coast of North America in the Weeden Island Phase (A.D. 400–600). Possibly this reflects the northwestern diffusion of a decorative family featuring a curving scroll motif with the background hatched or punctated, and punctations at ends of lines. The eastern branch, which also features broad-line incising, adornos, etc., is represented by the Barrancoid ceramics of Colombia, Venezuela, and the Antilles.

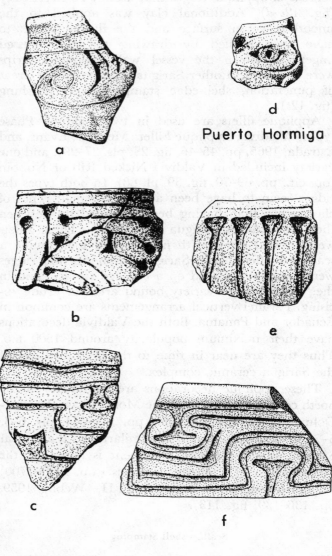

Monagrillo   **Valdivia**

FIGURE 11.—Resemblances between pottery decorations of the Monagrillo Phase of Panama, the Puerto Hormiga Phase of Colombia, and the Valdivia Phase of Ecuador. *a*, *d*, Curvilinear scrolls. *b*, *e*, Enlarged termination of incisions. *c*, *f*, Undulating bands combined with excision. (*a–c*, after Willey and McGimsey, 1954: *a*, fig. 46c; *b*, fig. 47a; *c*, fig. 12c. *d*, after Reichel-Dolmatoff, 1965, pl. 5–3. *e–f*, after Meggers, Evans, and Estrada, 1965: *e*, pl. 59 1; *f*, pl. 59a)

Summary

Since the elements of Monagrillo Phase ceramics were in existence in northwestern South America and Middle America (the tecomate form) at 2000 B.C., the most economical theory is to regard the complex

as having been composed of a selection from this background, brought to the south coast of Panama by early seafarers.

The Sarigua Phase of Panama

Willey and McGimsey (1954, pp. 105–110) have described a single site of the Sarigua Phase, a small shell midden located in a filled-in marsh in Parita Bay, Panama. The pottery is simple, and bears no resemblance to Monagrillo or any other known complex in lower Middle America or Colombia.

It seems clear that the Sarigua complex precedes the painted ware pottery assemblages in Panama, and Willey and McGimsey argue that it probably follows Monagrillo. As the latter has an approximate age of 2000 B.C., Sarigua probably dates around 1500 B.C. It seems appropriate then to search for comparative traits on this general time level.

Composite Silhouette Bowls

Fifty-four percent of the 275 sherds found are plain, tempered with quartz sand and quite thin (4–8 mm. with an average of 5 mm.). Surfaces are well smoothed and polished. The most common shape is a medium deep bowl with rounded base. Rims are outcurved and some show the marked shoulder angle of the composite silhouette bowl (fig. 12*a*), but whether this was the only bowl form or not, is uncertain. The history of composite silhouette bowls is shown on chart 13. They first appear in the Machalilla Phase (2000–1500 B.C.) on coastal Ecuador (fig. 12*f*; Meggers, Evans, and Estrada, 1965, fig. 90, 9–10).

Jars with Collars

The authors thought that some of the rims from Sarigua represented "globular jars with restricted orifices and short collars" (fig. 12*b*). Globular jars with wide mouths reached a popularity of 30–40 percent about 1400 B.C. toward the end of the Valdivia Phase and are also found in Machalilla (fig. 12*g*; Meggers, Evans, and Estrada, 1965, fig. 54–17).

Sarigua Plain shares the features of sandy paste, unusual thinness (4–8 mm. Sarigua; 3–6 mm. Punta Arenas), folded rims, and most vessel shapes with the Valdivia type Punta Arenas Plain. Range of firing color, dark gray to light tan, is also similar (op. cit., pp. 43–45). Punta Arenas Plain appears in the Valdivia sequence between 2000 and 1500 B.C., and became the dominant type with a maximum frequency of about 55 percent after 1500 B.C. (op. cit., fig. 52).

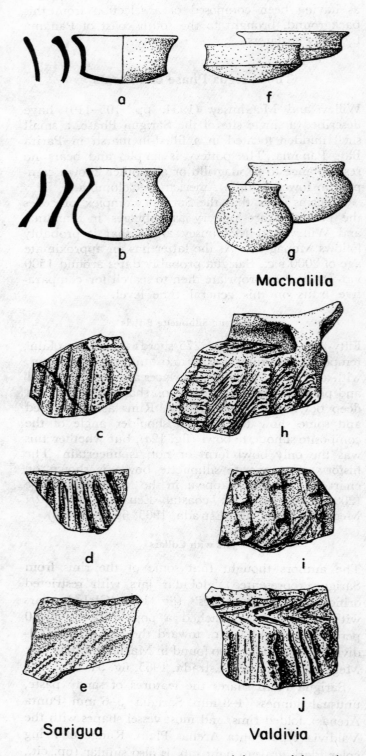

Machalilla

Sarigua   **Valdivia**

FIGURE 12.—Resemblances between vessel shapes and decorations of the Sarigua Phase of Panama and the Valdivia and Machalilla Phases of Ecuador. *a, f,* Composite silhouette bowls. *b, g,* Globular wide-mouth jars. *c–e, h–j,* Applique decoration. (*a–e,* after Willey and McGimsey, 1954: *a,* fig. 28 c, l, i; *b,* fig. 28 j–k; *c,* fig. 48n; *d,* fig. 48s; *e,* fig. 29b. *f–j,* after Meggers, Evans, and Estrada, 1965: *f,* fig. 90–9, 10; *g,* fig. 90–11, 13; *h,* pl. 88 l; *i,* pl. 27 l; *j,* pl. 88k)

Applique Decoration

The decoration named Sarigua Applique (Willey and McGimsey, 1954, p. 109, figs. 29d–e, 48n–o, s) consists of applique ridges that usually run vertically (fig. 12c–d). Additional clay was applied to the smoothed vessel surface and the fluting seems to have been formed by drawing the close-pressed finger tips down the vessel wall. Applique strips were also used in other Sarigua types to bound areas of punctation, shell-edge stamping, and brushing (fig. 12e).

Applique fillets are used in two Valdivia Phase types: Valdivia Applique Fillet (Meggers, Evans, and Estrada, 1965, pp. 45–46, fig. 23, pls. 27–29), and one variety included in Valdivia Nicked Rib or Nubbin (op. cit., pp. 69–70, fig. 39, pl. 88). In both types the ridges seem to have been applied as small ropes of clay rather than having been squeezed up between the fingers as in Sarigua (fig. 12h–j). These fillets were pressed down with fingers or a tool, giving a scalloped effect. Like Sarigua Applique, the ridges were sometimes placed on a brushed surface, and in the "Nicked Rib" variety bound areas of crude incising. Parallel vertical arrangements are common in Ecuador and Panama. Both the Valdivia decorations have their maximum popularity around 1500 B.C. Thus they are near in time to the presumed age of the Sarigua ceramic complex.

These applique decorations are continued on the north coast of Colombia in the Momíl Phase (Reichel-Dolmatoff, G. and A., 1956, pp. 141–144, pls. 6–3, 5–7; 10, 2–5, –8). A curious similarity to the typical Sarigua fingertip-raking treatment is found in the Fulton Phase of Caddoan ceramics (A.D. 1200–1700) of northwestern Louisiana (C. H. Webb, 1959, pp. 136–139, fig. 113).

Scallop-shell Stamping

Sarigua shell stamping comprised 9 percent of the complex. Somewhat carelessly applied impressions of the edge of a scallop shell are divided into rectilinear or curving zones by low applique ridges (figs. 12e, 13a). Shell stamping zoned by broad incised lines was introduced on the Caribbean coast of Colombia in the Puerto Hormiga Phase considerably earlier than the Sarigua examples, and bounding of incised areas dates about 1500 B.C. on the Coast of Ecuador as noted above. Both the applique ridge technique and stamping with the edge of scallop shell are in the Valdivia Phase (fig. 13d); however, they are not used in combination.

Zoned Punctating

Sarigua Punctate (Willey and McGimsey, 1954, p. 109, fig. 29a) has a popularity of less than 4 percent. In this type applique ridges bound dot, teardrop, and short slashes made with a pointed tool (fig. 13b). Once again the elements, but not the precise zoning arrangement, are available in the earlier Valdivia ceramics. Similar punctations zoned by incised lines occur in the Barlovento Phase of northern Colombia, where they date approximately 1900–1000 B.C. (fig. 13e; Reichel Dolmatoff, 1955, pls. 4–5).

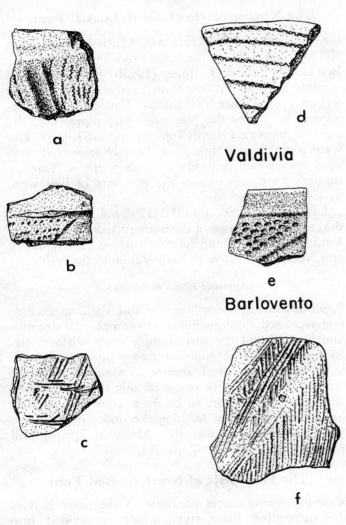

Valdivia

Barlovento

Sarigua   Valdivia

FIGURE 13.—Resemblances between pottery decorations of the Sarigua Phase of Panama, the Barlovento Phase of Colombia, and the Valdivia Phase of Ecuador. a, d, Scallop shell stamping. b, e, Zoned punctation. c, f, Brushing. (a–c, after Willey and McGimsey, 1954: a, fig. 48u; b, fig. 48q; c, fig. 48w. d, f, after Meggers, Evans, and Estrada, 1965: d, pl. 113k; f, pl. 45n. e, after Reichel-Dolmatoff, 1955, pl. 5–8)

Brushing

Sarigua Striated, with about 15 percent frequency, features combing or brushing of the vessel surface with a stiff brush (fig. 13c). Applique ridges do not seem to be associated. Similar brushing is one of the principal Valdivia Phase techniques about 1500 B.C. (fig. 13f; Meggers, Evans, and Estrada, 1965, pp. 51–52). As in the Sarigua type, this is applied at various angles to roughen the vessel surface.

Summary

Sarigua ceramics, quite distinct from the earlier Monagrillo complex of Panama, appear to have drawn upon a different set of features that were available in Ecuador at a date shortly after 1500 B.C.

The San Juan Phase of North Coastal Peru

In Tumbes, the northernmost of the Peruvian coastal river oases, actually on the south side of the Bay of Guayaquil, a team of archeologists from the University of Tokyo found a simple, and apparently early ceramic which was named San Juan Coarse Incised (Izumi and Terada, 1966, pp. 18–25, 69–70, pl. 25a). A charcoal sample from this level dated at 1830 ± 130 B.C. (op. cit., p. 71). The sherd sample was limited and as no rim sherds were found, the vessel shapes are not known. The ware is described as thin, tempered with fine sand, very friable, and ranging from red-brown to buff. Surfaces are smoothed, but not polished. Izumi and Terada consider that this San Juan material dates in the early Formative, and the fact that parallels to this simple assemblage occur in the nearby Valdivia complex suggests that they are correct.

Zoned Large Punctations

The carelessly drawn punctations bordered by broad incised lines (fig. 14a–b; Izumi and Terada, 1966, pl. 25a, 6–7, 9) are similar to the sherds that Meggers, Evans, and Estrada (1965, pp. 86–87, pl. 113p–r) have described as Technique 2 of Valdivia Zoned Incised (fig. 14e–f). Valdivia sherds are hard and have polished surfaces, in contrast to the soft and poorly smoothed San Juan material.

Horizontal Incised Lines

One San Juan sherd appears to have crudely incised horizontal lines that are broken so that they form panels (fig. 14c). If true, this can be equated with Valdivia Incised, Motif 3 (fig. 14g; Meggers, Evans, and Estrada, 1965, pp. 63–66, pl. 74a–f, 75b, k).

Applique Fillets

The two San Juan sherds with applique strips applied to the surface and impressed along the ridge top (fig. 14d) are comparable to what Meggers, Evans, and Estrada (1965, pp. 69–74, pl. 88) describe as a variant of Valdivia Nicked Rib or Nubbin (fig. 14h).

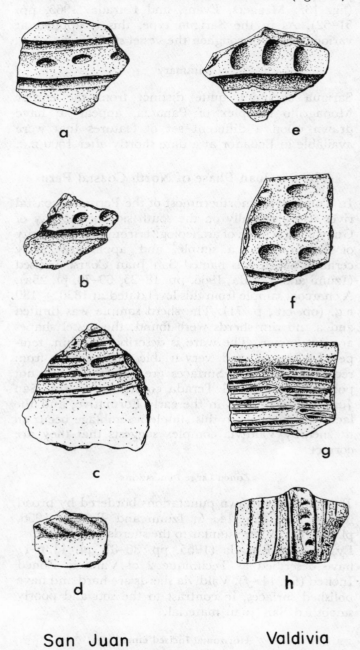

San Juan   Valdivia

FIGURE 14.—Resemblances between pottery decorations of the San Juan Phase of north coastal Peru and the Valdivia Phase of Ecuador. a–b, e–f, Zoned large punctations. c, g, Horizontal incised lines. d, h, Applique fillets. (a–d, after Izumi and Terada, 1966: a, pl. 25a–9; b, pl. 25a–7; c, pl. 25a–2; d, pl. 25a–10. e–h, after Meggers, Evans, and Estrada, 1965: e, pl. 113r; f, pl. 113q; g, pl. 75b; h, pl. 88g)

Like the early applique strip decorated vessels of the Guañape Phase further down the Peruvian coast, the San Juan examples are not associated with brushing or incising.

Summary

Izumi and Terada conclude that the radiocarbon date of ca. 1800 B.C. is correct for the San Juan complex, and that it belongs to the early Formative. The resemblances they have cited, and which are essentially repeated above, support their conclusion.

The Negritos Style of North Coastal Peru

On the coasts of the Piura and Chira Valleys, some 200 kilometers down the coast from Tumbes and the Ecuadorian border, Lanning (1963b) has presented a ceramic chronology based on presence and absence seriation of surface collections. Earliest in this sequence he places the Negritos style, represented by only 13 decorated sherds (op. cit., pp. 152–153). The ware is rather soft, thin, and heavily tempered with sand with some quite large white particles. Interior surfaces were wiped and the exteriors of half were smooth, half brushed.

Lanning (op. cit., pp. 198–199) points to the fact that the limited range of decorations resembles certain Valdivia motifs to the north, and less closely Early and Middle Guañape in Virú Valley to the south.

Applique Fillets and Nodes

Resemblances between Negritos and Valdivia include finger-pressed applique fillets, sometimes with straight-line incisions on the surrounding vessel surface (fig. 15 a, e). Punctated nodes or ridges pushed out with the fingers from vessel interior in a row around the base of the vessel neck occur on one sherd (fig. 15b). The only rim appears to be from a jar with a short neck. The method of forming the nodes is similar to Valdivia Modeled (fig. 15f; Meggers, Evans, and Estrada, 1965, pp. 66–67, pl. 78).

The Paita Style of North Coastal Peru

Valdivia resemblances continue in the early half of the succeeding Paita style, which is divided into Phases A–D (Lanning, 1963b, pp. 153–165). Jars with flaring or "concave" cambered necks are the prominent form. These latter are late in the Valdivia Phase. The applique ridge decoration now more nearly resembles the Guañape variety (fig. 17c), but also has parallels in Valdivia (fig. 17f). Rows and zones of small punctations, notched fillets, and rows of hollow protuberances are other typical Paita decorations.

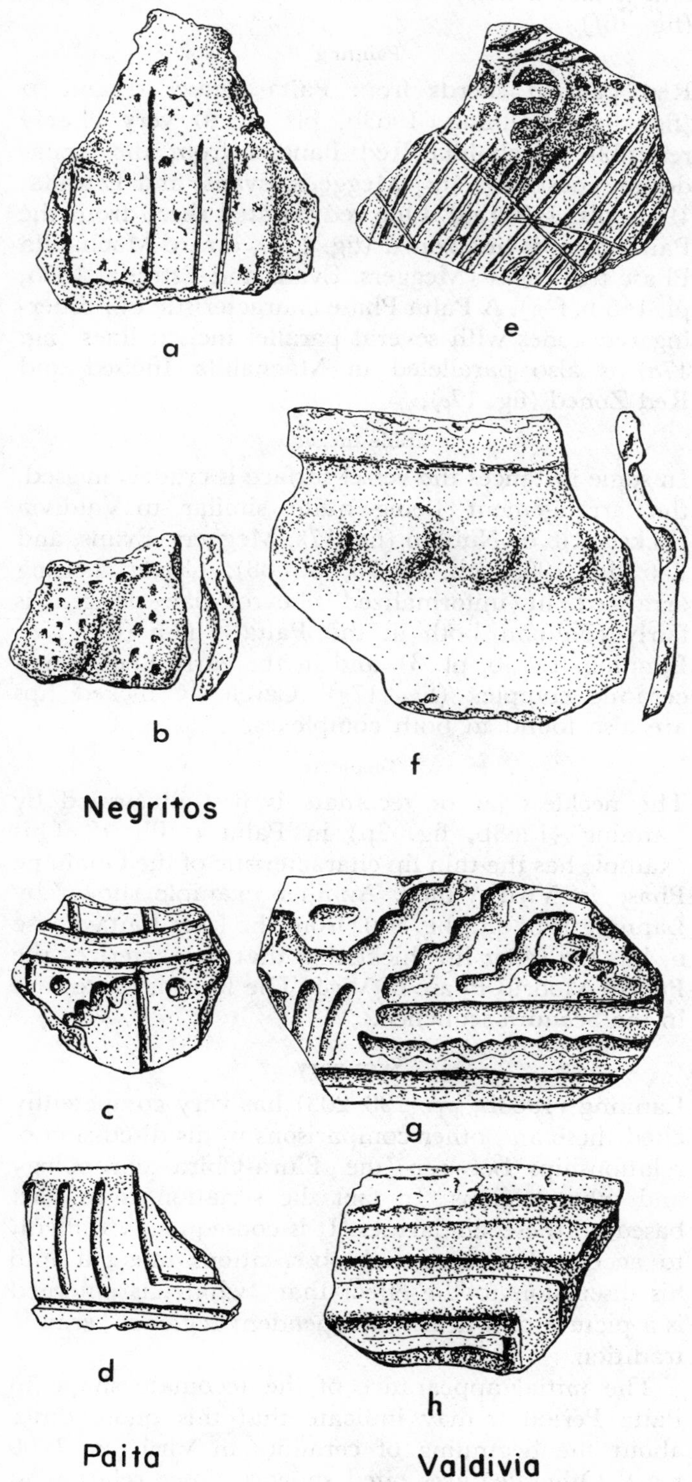

Wide-line Incising

Lanning (1963b, fig. 21a, k–m) illustrates examples of wide-line incising from the Paita B Phase (fig. 15c–d) that resemble Valdivia Broad-line Incised (fig. 15g–h; Meggers, Evans, and Estrada, 1965, pp. 47–51).

Cambered Rims

The channeled or cambered jar rims that are late in the Valdivia sequence (fig. 16 g–h; Meggers, Evans, and Estrada, 1965, fig. 54, 21–23) have counterparts in the Paita D Phase (fig. 16c; Lanning, 1963b, fig. 4b), and become popular later (op. cit., figs. 11b, 12i, 15d, 16d–g, 20). The distribution of this feature is discussed in more detail elsewhere (pp. 86–87).

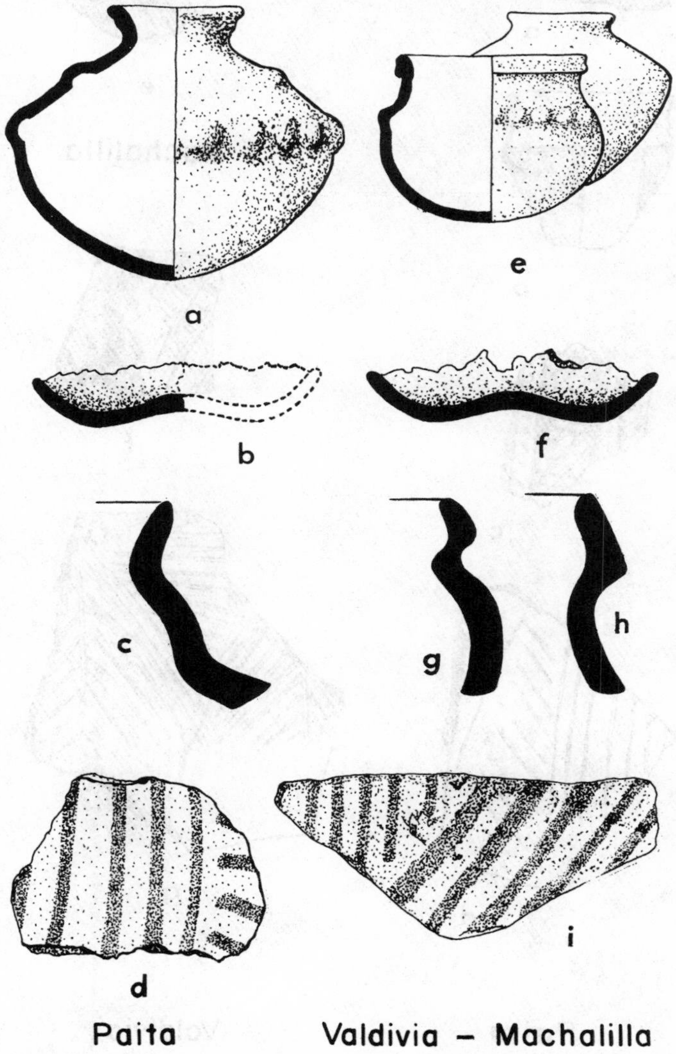

Negritos

Paita   **Valdivia**

FIGURE 15.—Resemblances between pottery decorations of the Negritos and Paita Phases of north coastal Peru and the Valdivia Phase of Ecuador. a–b, e–f, Applique fillets and nodes. c–d, g–h, Wide-line incising. (a–d, after Lanning, 1963b: a, pl. 1b; b, pl. 1c; c, fig. 2d; d, fig. 21a. e–h, after Meggers, Evans, and Estrada, 1965: e, pl. 89 l; f, pl. 78b; g, pl. 39j; h, pl. 38c)

Paita   **Valdivia – Machalilla**

FIGURE 16.—Resemblances between vessel shapes and painted decorations of the Paita Phase of north coastal Peru and the Valdivia-Machalilla Phases of Ecuador. a, e, Jars with angular shoulders. b, f, Indented base. c, g–h, Cambered rim. d, i, Red banding. (a–d, after Lanning, 1963b: a, fig. 3; b, fig. 21f; c, fig. 4b; d, pl. 4 l. e–i, after Meggers, Evans, and Estrada, 1965: e, figs. 36, 84–6; f, fig. 43b; g, fig. 26–5; h, fig. 35–6; i, pl. 150s)

Jars with Angular Shoulders and Indented Bases

Lanning's (1963b, figs. 3, 5a, 9, 21g–h) illustrations indicate that by Phase c the Paita jars have developed an angular shoulder at the point of maximum circumference (fig. 16a). This feature is not found in Valdivia jars, which have globular bodies, but does occur in some Machalilla jar forms (fig. 16e; Meggers, Evans, and Estrada, 1965, fig. 77, 6–7).

Also in Lanning's figure 21f is a profile of an indented vessel base (fig. 16b). This dates from Paita B

and is also a fairly common feature of Valdivia jars (fig. 16f).

Painting

Red painted sherds from Paita Phases c and d (fig. 16d; Lanning, 1963b, pls. 7, 9) very closely resemble Machalilla Red Banded from the Ecuadorian coast (fig. 16i; Meggers, Evans, and Estrada, 1965, pls. 149–153). One red painted sherd from the Paita series is line zoned (fig. 17b), a rare Machalilla Phase treatment (Meggers, Evans and Estrada, 1965, pl. 145 b, f–g). A Paita Phase characteristic of bordering red zones with several parallel incised lines (fig. 17a) is also paralleled in Machalilla Incised and Red Zoned (fig. 17e).

Crude Incision

In some instances the vessel surface is crudely incised, the arrangement being quite similar to Valdivia Nicked Rib or Nubbin (fig. 17f; Meggers, Evans, and Estrada, 1965, pp. 69–70, pl. 88). Crude incising arranged in unformalized chevron-like designs is fairly common both in the Paita Phase (fig. 17d; Lanning, 1963b, pl. 3), and in the early Ecuadorian ceramic complex (fig. 17g). Carelessly nicked lips are also found in both complexes.

Tecomate

The neckless jar or tecomate is first illustrated by Lanning (1963b, fig. 2p) in Paita c Phase. This example has the thin lip characteristic of the Guañape Phase in Virú Valley. Another example shown by Lanning (op. cit., fig. 6g), from the later Paita Phase d, has the inner lip thickening that characterizes the Puerto Moorín Phase of Virú. The form is quite rare in the Sechura sequence.

Summary

Lanning (1963b, pp. 198–203) has very competently cited these and other comparisons in his discussion of relationships between the Piura-Chira chronology and other regions. In fact the seriation is in part based on these similarities. It is consequently difficult to accept the occasional observations injected into his discussion to the effect that "what has emerged is a picture of a nearly independent regional ceramic tradition . . . ."

The initial appearance of the tecomate shape in Paita Period c may indicate that this phase dates about the beginning of ceramics in Virú (ca. 1200 B.C.). Other features cited show a closer relation to the Ecuadorian chronology than to the central part of the north coast of Peru.

The Kotosh Site, Central Peruvian Highlands

A date of 1950 B.C. for the preceramic Mito Phase, and 1150, 1830, and 1850 B.C. for the pottery of the

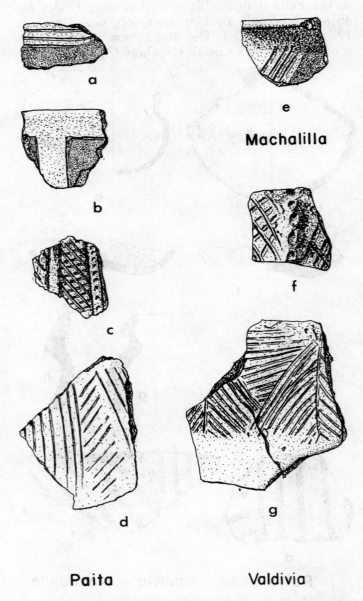

Machalilla

Paita   **Valdivia**

FIGURE 17.—Resemblances between pottery decorations of the Paita Phase of north coastal Peru and the Valdivia and Machalilla Phases of Ecuador. a, e, Multiple incised lines bordering red-slipped zones. b, Line zoned red slip. c, f, Incision between applique ribs. d, g, Incised chevron-like designs. (a–d, after Lanning, 1963b: a, pl. 2a; b, pl. 2e; c, pl. 2j; d, pl. 3i. e–g, after Meggers, Evans, and Estrada, 1965: e, pl. 145c; f, pl. 88f; g, pl. 76d)

Kotosh Waira-jirca delimit the beginning of ceramics with some precision and certainly place it during the Formative in the central Peruvian highlands. While broad-line incising and polishing of vessel surfaces suggest a generalized resemblance to the Ecuadorian Formative, there are many features that are new for the Americas. For example, 36 percent of the Waira-jirca decorations are fine parallel hatching zoned by broad incised lines to form usually rectilinear motifs (Izumi and Sono, 1963, table 10). Rectangles crossed by diagonal bands of hatching and stepped elements are also common. Undulating bands are a motif shared with Valdivia (fig. 18 *e*, *j*), but the zoned effect is more like the zoned shell stamping of Puerto Hormiga (op. cit., pl. 80b–85a).

Looped or Arched Lines

Twelve percent of Waira-jirca decorations are arrangements of arched or looped narrow or broad incised lines, usually around the mouths of large neckless jars or tecomates (figs. 18*a*, 20; Izumi and Sono, 1963, pls. 87–88). Similar looped or arched lines on this same jar form are a prominent decoration of the coeval Barlovento Phase of northern Colombia (Reichel-Dolmatoff, 1955, pls. 3–5).

Similar arched incised lines, usually drawn on a brushed ground, are found on early tecomate forms in Mesoamerica (Dixon, 1959, figs. 51 1–m, 54j; Chiapa I, 1400–800 B.C.). On the coast of Ecuador parallels occur in Machalilla (fig. 20*d*; Meggers, Evans, and Estrada, 1965, pls. 131c, g, m, o, 132e, 133v, 144t, x).

Vessel Shapes

The presence of the tecomate and the flat-base pan (in its smaller diameter Andean version) in the earliest Kotosh ceramics (fig. 18*a*–*b*), argues for the presence of Mesoamerican influence at this early date, 1800 B.C. (fig. 18*f*–*g*). These features are missing on the Pacific coast of South America at this time. Perhaps this is the beginning of a communication route that was to culminate in the Olmec-Chavín florescences. A form of maize probably accompanied these ceramic features. Its presence is proven by an illustration in the Kotosh Kotosh Phase, 1200–800 B.C. (fig. 18*d*).

Bottles with long slender necks and stirrup-spout bottles first appear in the Kotosh Kotosh Phase (fig. 18*c*–*d*). These have an initial date of 1100 B.C. and are comparable to the two bottle forms present earlier in Machalilla (fig. 18*h*–*i*).

Rectangular Spirals

An incised rectangular spiral motif is fairly popular in the Kotosh Kotosh Phase (fig. 19*a*; Izumi and Sono, 1963, pls. 40c, 45a, d, 47a, 57a, 2–5); a variant center-

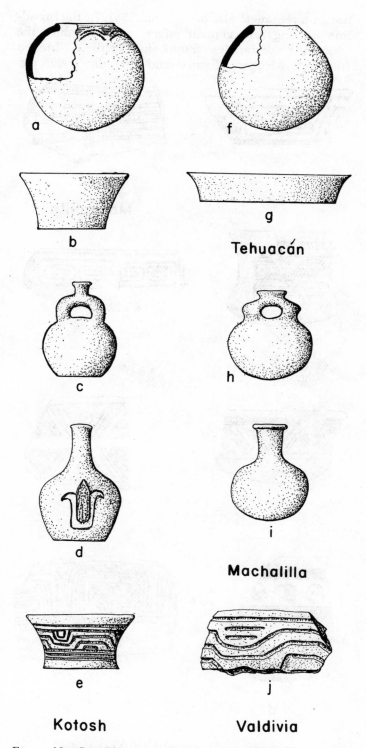

FIGURE 18.—Resemblances between vessel shapes and decorations from the Kotosh site, central highlands of Peru, the Valdivia and Machalilla Phases of Ecuador, and early Tehuacán, Mexico. *a*, *f*, Tecomate. *b*, *g*, Flat-base pan. *c*, *h*, Stirrup-spout jar. *d*, *i*, Simple bottle. *e*, *j*, Undulating incised bands. (*a*–*e*, after Izumi and Sono, 1963: *a*, fig. 46x; *b*, fig. 46ix; *c*, fig. 46vi; fig. 46vii; *e*, fig. 46ix. *f*–*g*, after Byers, ed., 1967–, vol. 3, fig. 7. *h*–*j*, after Meggers, Evans, and Estrada, 1965: *h*, fig. 88–12; *i*, fig. 88–11; *j*, pl. 38j)

ing on a rectangle also occurs (fig. 19b). In the broad-line incising and general effect, this resembles the concentric rectangles found in Valdivia Incised (fig. 19f; Meggers, Evans, and Estrada, 1965, pls.

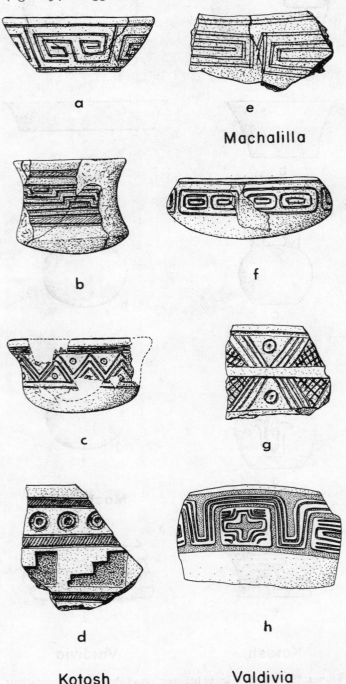

Machalilla

Kotosh   **Valdivia**

FIGURE 19.—Resemblances between pottery decorations from early phases of the Kotosh site, central highlands of Peru, and the Valdivia and Machalilla Phases of Ecuador. a, e, Rectangular spiral. b, f, Concentric rectangles. c–g, Ziz-zag motifs and circle and dot. d, h, Excision. (a–d, after Izumi and Sono, 1963: a, pl. 47a; b, pl. 49d; c, pl. 49a; d, pl. 84a–2. e–h, after Meggers, Evans, and Estrada, 1965: e, pl. 138 o; f, pl. 42a; g, pl. 62b; h, pl. 59b)

42a, 161e–h). In Valdivia, these sometimes appear to be conventionalized faces. However, in the detail of being a true spiral rather than a concentric arrangement, it is more comparable to motifs found in Machalilla (fig. 19e; op. cit., pl. 138o), which is also closer in time to the occurrence at Kotosh.

Zig-zag Motifs and Circle and Dot

The circle and dot is rare in Valdivia (fig. 19g), and common in Kotosh (fig. 19c–d, 20b–c), where it reaches a peak of popularity in the Sajara-patac-San Blas Phase. Zig-zags are common in Valdivia; fairly rare in Kotosh.

Excision

Although motifs differ, the technique of excision is found both in Valdivia Phases A and B, 3000–2000 B.C. (fig. 19h), and in Kotosh Waira-jirca, 1800–1100 B.C. (fig. 19d). Red pigment is rubbed into excised areas in each region. The stepped motif common in Kotosh is found in Valdivia Incised.

Interrupted Horizontal Lines

Two or more short horizontal incised lines, frequently ending in dots and interrupted to form panels, often with a circle and dot in the space between lines (fig. 20b–c), form 23 percent of the decorations of the Sajara-patac-San Blas Phase (200–1 B.C.) at Kotosh (Izumi and Sono, 1963, pls. 52b, 12–14, 17–25; 53a, 1–5, most of b; 59; 61a; 62). A similar but crude paneling of incision without the circle and dot is found in Valdivia Incised, and Valdivia Broad-line Incised (fig. 20e–f).

Summary

As pointed out by Meggers, Evans, and Estrada (1965, p. 174), Kotosh affiliations appear to be with the Puerto Hormiga, Barlovento, and Momíl Phases of northern Colombia, and an intermontane route is suggested. Relationships to the ceramics of Yarina-cocha have been cited both by Izumi and Sono (1963, p. 155), and Meggers, Evans, and Estrada (1965, pp. 176–177). Shared features include incised rims, boat-shaped vessels, and elaborate lateral flanges on bowls. Details of this possible route of diffusion are not yet entirely clear.

It is interesting that the circle and dot, dots ending lines, and the linked chains on the heads of bone pins (Izumi and Sono, 1963, pl. 102b, 3–4) are Asiatic Iron Age traits that crossed the Bering Strait into the Eskimo art of Alaska at about the same time as they appear in Kotosh (Collins, 1937, pp. 300–303; Larsen and Rainey, 1948, pp. 130–132). The S-element may also belong to this complex. Lanceolate ground stone knife blades are another Kotosh element (Izumi and Sono, 1963, pl. 167) that resembles Eskimo artifacts and probably have Asiatic origin. The history of the semilunar knife, panpipes, metallurgy, and a number of other Andean traits also needs investigation in the light of this possibility.

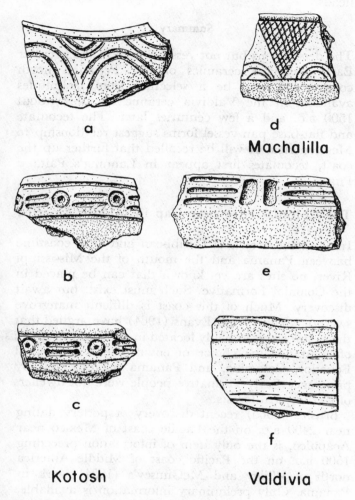

Machalilla

Kotosh

Valdivia

FIGURE 20.—Resemblances between pottery decorations from the Kotosh site, central highlands of Peru, and the Valdivia and Machalilla Phases of Ecuador. *a*, *d*, Arched lines. *b–c*, *e–f*, Interrupted horizontal lines. (*a–c*, after Izumi and Sono, 1963: *a*, pl. 88a–8; *b*, pl. 53a–2; *c*, pl. 53b–10. *d–f*, Meggers, Evans, and Estrada, 1965: *d*, pl. 131g; *e*, pl. 32a; *f*, pl. 74f)

The Guañape Phase of North Coastal Peru

The first ceramics in Virú Valley on the north coast of Peru appear about 1200 B.C. and stand somewhat apart from the earlier (ca. 1800 B.C.) initial ceramics at Ancón on the central coast and Kotosh in the highlands.

At this point only the unique features of the early Guañape complex will be considered. Its relationships have been discussed by Meggers, Evans, and

Estrada (1965, pp. 168–169). After 800 B.C. with the beginning of the coastal Chavín or Cupisnique Phase, the north coast was incorporated into the general picture of Peruvian ceramic development.

Approximately 90 percent of the earliest pottery in the Virú Valley sequence (Period M–N on the arbitrary scale; Ford, 1949, fig. 4) was plain, black to dark brown in color, with sparse white quartz tempering, scraped on the interior, low track polish on exterior, made usually into large, egg-shaped neckless jars. This is the Central American tecomate form lacking in the early phases of Ecuador, Colombia, and Piura-Chira Valleys. This pottery is thin, with an average thickness of 6 mm.

Applique Fillets

There are three decorative techniques. Guañape Finger-pressed Rib (Strong and Evans, 1952, pp. 277–279, fig. 45) has two variations: relatively large ropes of clay running horizontally and roughly pressed onto the vessel wall with the fingertips, and smaller ropes running vertically that are more flattened with the fingers. The resemblance to Valdivia Applique Fillet (Meggers, Evans, and Estrada, 1965, pp. 45–46, pls. 27–29) is very close, especially in regard to the latter Guañape type. The Valdivia decoration is occasionally applied in simple rectilinear patterns and placed on vessel rims, practices not found at Guañape. The Valdivia type begins about 1700 B.C., and after 1500 B.C. has a popularity of 2 to 3 percent; the Guañape type begins with a frequency of 4–5 percent at approximately 1200 B.C. and disappears about 800 B.C.

Guañape Incised Rib (Strong and Evans, 1952, pp. 279–282) is simply a version of the finger-pressed type, on which a tool rather than fingers was used to weld the clay strips to the vessel wall (fig. 21a–d). It also has both horizontal and vertical versions, but in the latter there are indications of simple geometrical patterns as described in the Valdivia type.

In the detail of tool rather than fingers used to impress the applique ridges, the Guañape type more nearly resembles Valdivia Nicked Rib or Nubbin (fig. 21f–h; Meggers, Evans, and Estrada, 1965, pp. 69–70). The latter, however, has crudely incised lines between the ridges, a feature lacking in Virú. The Valdivia type is rare, scattered from early to late phases, while the Virú types begin with a frequency of about 3 percent and end in the Chavín-Cupisnique Period.

Applique Nodes and Finger Punching

The third early Virú type, described as Guañape Modeled (Strong and Evans, 1952, pp. 282–283, fig.

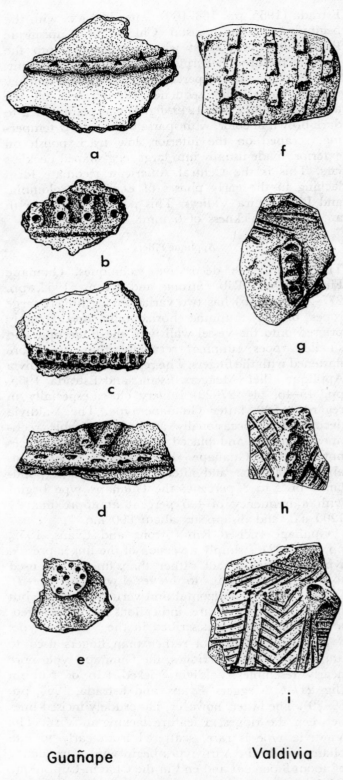

Guañape   **Valdivia**

FIGURE 21.—Resemblances between pottery decorations of the Guañape Phase, Virú Valley, Peru and the Valdivia Phase of Ecuador. *a–d, f–h,* Ornamented applique fillets. *e, i,* Applique nodes. (*a–e,* after Strong and Evans, 1952: *a,* fig. 45a; *b,* fig. 45c; *c,* fig. 46a; *d,* fig. 46g; *e,* fig. 47e. *f–i,* after Meggers, Evans, and Estrada, 1965: *f,* pl. 27a; *g,* pl. 88c; *h,* pl. 88f; *i,* pl. 89j)

47), consists of pushed-in areas as well as small applique nodes. The latter were simple round bosses decorated with punctations (fig. 21*e*), or in one instance with an animal face. These resemble the nubbins of Valdivia Nicked Rib or Nubbin (fig. 21*i*; op. cit., pl. 89), which sometimes represent animal heads.

Summary

The decorations but not vessel shapes in the peculiar Early Guañape ceramics on the Peruvian north coast could well be a selection from techniques available in the Valdivia ceramic complex about 1500 B.C. and a few centuries later. The tecomate and flat-base pan vessel forms suggest relationship to Mesoamerica. It will be recalled that further up the coast, tecomates first appear in Lanning's Paita c Phase.

The Colonial Formative Gap in Middle America

In the long stretch of Caribbean and Gulf coastline between Panama and the mouth of the Mississippi River, no sites are yet known that can be placed in the Colonial Formative. Such must exist, but await discovery. Much of this coast is difficult mangrove swamp. Meggers and Evans (1964) have argued that these sites were probably located in semi-arid stretches of coast, for the choice of environments in coastal Ecuador, Colombia, and Panama suggests that by preference Early Formative people were not dwellers of wet tropical forests.

Brush's (1965) recent discovery of pottery dating near 2400 B.C. on the Pacific coast of Mexico near Acapulco, is the only item of information preceding 1500 B.C. on the Pacific coast of Middle America north of Willey and McGimsey's (1954) work in Panama. Only preliminary information is available, but the close resemblance to the Purrón Phase ceramics of highland Tehuacán Valley suggests that this complex may be derived from the highlands, rather than the reverse. Probably the earliest pottery of coastal Mexico should show more resemblances to Puerto Hormiga, Machalilla, or Valdivia. If the diffusion of pottery manufacture was by sea, then the newly landed voyagers and the people to whom they taught the art would not be likely to change either shapes or designs drastically. True, their imitations might not be very competent, but they should be recognizably similar to the models.

The people of the interior, in highland Mexico, were already well-established cultivators of maize by 2000 B.C. Their need for ceramic storage and cooking vessels would seem to be somewhat greater than that of seafood eaters. These highland people, basically of the Archaic Desert culture, already had a container tradition in the form of vessels laborously cut from stone and probably also wood. The two principal forms were the flat-base pan with low outslanting walls, and the tecomate. The earliest highland pottery known was manufactured in these two shapes.

Most of the ceramics that Mesoamerican authors have called Early Formative date after 1500 B.C., and in terms of the divisions proposed here, pertain principally to the beginning of the Theocratic Formative. Most of the ceramic features can be traced to Valdivia and Machalilla.

The Stallings Island Complex of the Georgia Coast

Moore (1897) and particularly Claflin (1931) brought the fiber-tempered pottery found in shell heaps near the mouth of the Savannah River to the attention of archeologists. The ceramics of the Stallings Island, as well as the fiber-tempered Orange complex of the Atlantic coast of Florida, have been described by Sears and Griffin (1950). The surprisingly early radiocarbon date of around 2000 B.C. has been discussed by Bullen (1961). This date, about 1000 years before the appearance of either the paddle-stamped Woodland pottery of the Great Lakes region or any other known complex of North America, has led to the suggestion that the sequence from preceramic to plain to decorated pottery on the south Atlantic coast is a case of independent invention of the pottery art.

In a recent article (Ford, 1966), an attempt was made to relate both the Stallings Island complex and the Orange Phase of Florida to the early Formative of northwestern coasts of South America. These arguments will be repeated here, but not exactly in the same form, for there is now new information available.

Two new dates for the plain fiber-tempered ware have recently been published by Stoltman (1966). These came from Rabbit Mount, a small midden located in the Savannah River swamp, and date 2500±135 B.C., and 2515±95 B.C.

The Waring Papers provide considerable additional information on the Stallings Island complex. Of particular interest are reports on Waring's excavations at the Bilbo site (Williams, ed., 1968, pp. 152ff), a circular shell midden about 100 feet in diameter located in a marsh. Clear ceramic stratigraphy in the five feet of deposit near the center shows initial plain pottery, with linear punctated, punc-

tated, and incised decorations higher up in the midden (op. cit., fig. 70).

Waring (Williams, ed., op. cit., p. 191) is of the opinion that the Stallings Island site, described by Claflin (1931), persisted later than did Bilbo. All of the material from the lower level is fiber tempered, with sand tempering confined to the upper levels. Vessel shapes were round, deep bowls, and the bowls with sharply inturned rims that Claflin describes do not occur in the earlier Georgia middens (Williams, ed., 1968, fig. 72). In addition to the drag-and-jab decoration found in Stallings, Bilbo ceramics contain a number of designs made by incising lines horizontal to the rim and then spacing punctations in them. The Bilbo site is also remarkable for the number of bone pins with engraved heads (op. cit., figs. 63–64). The acceptable radiocarbon date from Bilbo is 2165 B.C. Another fiber-tempered ceramic site described by Waring is Dulaney (op. cit., p. 208). This yielded a date of 1810 B.C.

Another important locality is a shell ring on Sapelo Island (op. cit., pp. 263–278), which yielded a radiocarbon date of 1750 B.C. It was found that baked clay balls, probably used as cooking stones, decreased in frequency as plain fiber-tempered pottery increased, and that the decorated wares were again in the upper levels of the midden As at Bilbo, punctations made in lines previously drawn horizontally to the rim were a fairly common decoration. The three shell rings at Sapelo and five others along the coast near the mouth of the Savannah River are not positively identified by Waring as unintentionally accumulated midden deposits, but judging from his description of hearths and occupational levels, it seems probable that they were. They vary from 50 to 300 feet in diameter (op. cit., p. 253).

The early Stallings Island fiber-tempered complex is confined to a relatively restricted region near Savannah, extending along the coast and inland up the rivers. Waring (Williams, ed., 1968, p. 219) points to the fact that fiber-tempered pottery found further in the interior along the Tennessee River bears decoration that occurs in Georgia on a post-Stallings horizon, and so probably has a later date.

The Puerto Hormiga shell heap (3000–1900 B.C.) on the north coast of Colombia has a ring shape (Reichel-Dolmatoff, 1965) identical to the shell rings of the Georgia coast. The later site of Barlovento (1900–1000 B.C.) in the same region (Reichel-Dolmatoff, 1955), is an irregular arrangement that might be interpreted as a hollow square. The ten Valdivia shell middens of coastal Ecuador tend to be compact areas, rather than elongated shell ridges stretched along the shoreline is as the case with many later shell middens. One Valdivia site, Punta Arenas

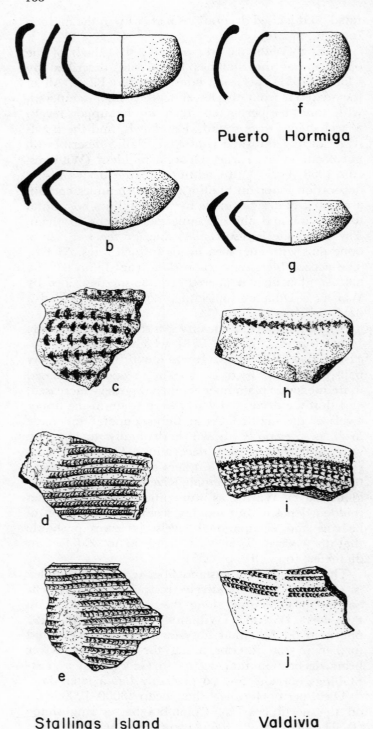

Puerto Hormiga

Stallings Island   Valdivia

FIGURE 22.—Resemblances between vessel shapes and decorations of the Stallings Island Phase, south Atlantic coast of North America, the Puerto Hormiga Phase of Colombia, and the Valdivia Phase of Ecuador. *a, f,* Deep rounded bowls. *b, g,* Shouldered bowls. *c, h,* Punctations in incisions. *d–e, i–j,* Drag and jab. (*a–b, d–e,* after Claflin, 1931: *a–b,* pp. 14–16; *d–e,* pl. 18. *c,* after Williams, ed., 1968, fig. 56c. *f,* after Reichel-Dolmatoff, 1965, p. 26. *g–j,* after Meggers, Evans, and Estrada, 1965: *g,* fig. 40–6; *h,* pl. 81i; *i,* pl. 79a; *j,* pl. 80j)

(Meggers, Evans, and Estrada, 1965, fig. 3), is roughly oval in shape, conforming to the hilltop on which it is placed, and the center is free of refuse. These could well have been towns defended by stockades with the dwellings arranged about round or rectangular plazas.

In the centuries before and after 2000 B.C there are few known ceramic complexes in the Americas to which the Stallings Island pottery may be compared. Approximately contemporary parallels to all of its features, however, may be found in two regions: the north coast of Colombia, and the Guayas coast of Ecuador. In paste characteristics, Stallings compares directly with Puerto Hormiga ceramics of Colombia (Reichel-Dolmatoff, 1961, 1965). In the Puerto Hormiga complex, about half the pottery is tempered with vegetal fibers, and the remainder has sand tempering in varying quantities. All Stallings pottery is fiber tempered, but sand has also been added to about half of the vessels. It is poorly fired, soft and thick, and surfaces are carelessly smoothed.

While village plan and the tempering of Stallings pottery resemble Puerto Hormiga (3000–1900 B.C.), shapes and decorations are almost identical to some of the features popular in the Ecuadorian Valdivia ceramics about 2000 B.C.

Simple and Shouldered Bowls

Stallings vessels are predominantly simple deep bowls, 15 to 30 cm. in diameter with upper walls vertical or slightly incurved (fig. 22*a*). A variation of this bowl, particularly prominent at the Stallings Island site, has the upper few centimeters of the wall turned sharply to slant inward (fig. 22*b*).

This deep bowl form is common to Monagrillo, Puerto Hormiga (fig. 22*f*), and Valdivia ceramics. However, the inturned rim version has very specific resemblances in details of rounded interior and sharp exterior angle with occasional ridge to a shape common in the Valdivia complex (fig. 22*g*; Meggers, Evans, and Estrada, 1965, figs. 25–7; 40–6; 46–3; 54, 8–9). This shape reaches a popularity of about 20 percent between 2000 and 1500 B.C., coeval with Stallings Island.

Punctations in Incised Lines

The earliest decoration on fiber-tempered pottery from the Bilbo and Sapelo localities on the Georgia coast consists of rows of punctations, incised lines in which punctations have later been made, and to a minor extent, drag-and-jab incision, this latter to become the dominant form in the Stallings Island Phase. The peculiar technique in which lines are first drawn and punctations later placed in them (fig. 22*c*), corresponds to Valdivia Nicked Broad-line

Incised (Meggers, Evans, and Estrada, 1965, p. 68, fig. 38, pls. 81–84). The incisions are broader in Valdivia, and a single line around the rim is usual (fig. 22*h*) rather than the multiple lines found at Bilbo.

Drag-and-Jab Incision

The type Stallings Island Punctated was made by a drag-and-jab technique. A tool about the size of a pencil, usually round but sometimes rectangular, was held at an angle and as the line plowed along the vessel surface, the tool was jabbed to form the characteristic punctated lines (fig. 22*d*). In some instances it can be determined that a double-pointed tool was employed. On most sherds the lines are closely spaced and run parallel to the rim. Lines frequently are not continuous, but form panels with smooth areas between (fig. 22*e*).

A technique of drag-and-jab with a pointed tool was employed by the Puerto Hormiga potters (Reichel-Dolmatoff, 1965, pls. 3–7, 5–2), but for more precise parallels such as size of tool, multiple point, lines parallel to rim, and arrangement in panels, we may refer to the Ecuadorian type, Valdivia Multiple Drag-and-Jab Punctate (fig. 22*i–j*; Meggers, Evans, and Estrada, 1965, pp. 67–68, pls. 79–80, 170e–h, 183h–i). Some Stallings motifs are zig-zags (fig. 23*a*), not found in the comparable punctated Valdivia type but common in the contemporary Valdivia Broad-line Incised (fig. 23*f*; op. cit., pls. 32–35). Valdivia Multiple Drag-and-Jab Punctate occurs in frequency of less than one percent between 2000 and 1500 B.C. and thus is coeval with the Stallings Island decoration.

Punctations in Rows and Panels

Accompanying but less popular decorations in the Stallings complex are simple punctations, crudely jabbed into the vessel surface with a sharpened tool similar to a pencil point. These are arranged in zig-zag patterns and also were placed in panels on the inturned rims of bowls (fig. 23*b–c*; Claflin, 1931, pl. 14). Similar decorations are lacking in Puerto Hormiga, but are illustrated as Technique 6 of Valdivia Punctate (fig. 23*g–h*; Meggers, Evans, and Estrada, 1965, pp. 80–81, pls. 100–101). Valdivia Punctate runs through the sequence in very small frequencies, and thus is coeval with the similar Stallings Island decoration.

Finger-pressed Dimples

In discussing Stallings Island ceramics, Waring writes: "Some large, roundish to ovoid dimple-like impressions were noted which had apparently been done with the finger tips" (Williams, ed., 1968, p.

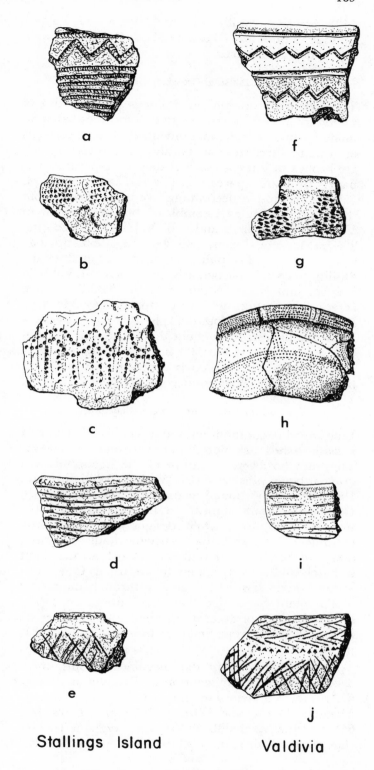

Stallings Island **Valdivia**

FIGURE 23.—Resemblances between pottery decorations of the Stallings Island Phase, south Atlantic coast of North America, and the Valdivia Phase of Ecuador. *a, f,* Zig-zag line. *b–c, g–h,* Punctations in rows and panels. *d, i,* Paneled incising. *e, j,* Crosshatched incising. (*a–e,* after Claflin, 1931: *a,* pl. 20; *b–c,* pl. 16; *d–e,* pl. 15. *f–j,* after Meggers, Evans, and Estrada, 1965: *f,* pl. 35f; *g,* pl. 101j; *h,* pl. 100r; *i,* pl. 74f; *j,* pl. 73k)

160); however, no illustrations are provided. Finger-tip indentations are a feature of both Puerto Hormiga and Valdivia ceramics.

Paneled Incising, Crosshatched Incising

The fourth decoration on Stallings pottery, also of minor frequency, is crude straight-line crosshatching made with a pointed instrument, and arrangements of straight lines running parallel to the rim, which are broken at intervals so that they are separated into panels by blank spaces (fig. 23d–e; Claflin, 1931, pl. 15). These simple decorations are also missing from the Puerto Hormiga assemblage, but are present in Valdivia as Motifs 2 and 3 of Valdivia Incised (fig. 23i–j; Meggers, Evans, and Estrada, 1965, pp. 63–68, pls. 73–75). The panel arrangement noted for the Stallings types is particularly prominent in Valdivia Incised, and is also common in the Middle Jomon ceramic decoration used for comparison by Meggers, Evans, and Estrada (op. cit., pls. 166–167) Valdivia Incised is present throughout the Ecuadorian Formative sequence, and at 1500 B.C. has a frequency of about 15 percent. It also is contemporary with the beginning of the Stallings decorative type.

Line-zoned Hatching and Crosshatching

Line-zoned decorations with alternate roughened and smooth bands are not found on Stallings pottery. They are however, a feature of the beautifully engraved bone pins such as Waring (Williams, ed., 1968, figs. 63–64) found at the Bilbo site (fig. 24a–d). Decorative motifs appear to be expressed by the smooth areas, and while designs are dominantly rectilinear, a minority have curving motifs. Zig-zags, diamond figures, and a checkerboard arrangement of hatch and smooth diamonds are usual. One rectilinear S-motif has a line running through the center of the plain band (fig. 24a), and there are superimposed panels of decoration. Similar but less ornate bone pins came from Stallings Island (Claflin, 1931, pl. 38).

In all details except the curvilinear motifs, these decorations are reminiscent of the Ecuadorian pottery designs of Valdivia Fine-line Incised (fig. 24 e, g; Meggers, Evans, and Estrada, 1965, p. 60, pls. 61–64), and the Machalilla Phase type, Ayangue Incised (fig. 24f,h; op. cit., pp. 117–119, fig. 73, pls. 131–134).

Summary

This completes the rather simple inventory of Stallings decorations. All, as well as the vessel forms, existed in the Valdivia complex between 2000 and 1500 B.C. Stallings pottery is much cruder than Valdivia,

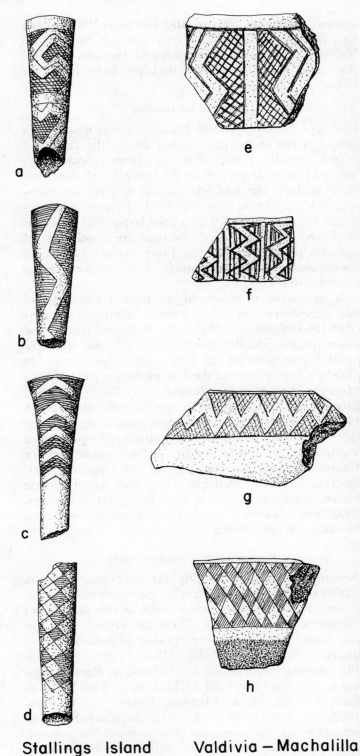

Stallings Island   Valdivia–Machalilla

FIGURE 24.—Resemblances between line-zoned hatching and crosshatching on engraved bone pins of the Stallings Island Phase, south Atlantic coast of North America, and pottery vessels of the Valdivia and Machalilla Phases of Ecuador. (a–d, after Williams, ed., 1968: a, fig. 63b; b, fig. 63h; c, fig. 63j; d, fig. 63n. e–h, after Meggers, Evans, and Estrada, 1965: e, pl. 64p; f, pl. 134j; g, pl. 63n; h, pl. 133k)

and in the feature of fiber tempering and occasional use of sand tempering resembles the coeval Puerto Hormiga ceramics of the Caribbean coast of Colombia. This leads to a postulation that somewhere in lower Middle America, there may be a few coastal middens that served as way-stations in the transfer of the ceramic technique from Ecuador to Georgia, and that the features from the Caribbean coast of Colombia were acquired at these stations.

The Orange Complex of Florida

It has also been known to southeastern archeologists for some time that a fiber-tempered pottery complex of an age almost equal to Stallings was associated with the large shell middens that formerly existed along the St. Johns and Indian Rivers on the Atlantic coast of Florida. This Orange complex was first described by Wyman in 1875 and later by Moore in 1893. Fortunately, other excavations were made in the 1930s, for now these heaps have been almost totally destroyed to provide road material. The lower levels of a number of these deposits are preceramic; pottery appears about 2000 B.C. (Bullen, 1961), and decoration begins at approximately 1600 B.C. The range of decoration is much wider and quite different from the Stallings Island sites 150 miles up the Atlantic coast, and there seems to be no evidence of trade.

One of the recent salvage excavations was in the Bluffton site (Bullen, 1955). A remaining fragment of the deposit was 16 to 18 feet deep. Ceramics were confined to the upper 4 to 7 feet, and decorated pottery was found only in the top 2 feet. Bullen (op. cit., p. 7) seems to have evidence of a trend toward thickening of the fiber-tempered ware. Plain pottery ranged from ⅛ to ½ inch in thickness, with an average of ¼ inch. Bullen states that "Orange Incised vessels were made of the same paste as plain fiber-tempered containers. Walls average a little thicker, about ⅜ of an inch."

Flat-base Pans

The principal vessel form of Orange pottery has a flat base, 20 to 40 cm. in diameter (fig. 25a; Sears and Griffin, 1950). The walls rise at almost a right angle, are relatively low (6–15 cm.) in comparison to vessel diameter, and are either vertical or more commonly slope outward slightly. Some vessels seem to be square rather than circular (fig. 25b), and occasional rim sherds have low rounded ears. Lips are rounded, thickened and flat, or beveled. These latter often have incised decorations.

While this fiber-tempered pottery is fairly thick (8–18 mm.), vessel bases are often thinner than walls. Some basal fragments have matting impression, and

on a number there is loose red pigment underneath the base. Much of this ware is remarkably well smoothed considering its fiber content. Incised decoration occurs on the walls, lips, and occasionally on the inner surface of walls and bottoms.

This pan shape, lacking in the early South American Formative, is characteristic of the first pottery known in Middle America (fig. 25f). Its history has been discussed on pp. 98–101 and chart 13. Size and proportions are similar, but the grit-tempered pans to the south are fairly well smoothed and polished on all surfaces except the base. In the features of un-polished bases, bases thinner than walls, and thickened flattened lips decorated with straight-line incision, they are similar to the Orange pans.

From our unreported excavations at the Chala-huites site, coastal Veracruz, Mexico, 10 percent of the pans had loose red ochre smeared under the base as do some Orange examples. However, fabric-impressed bases are not known from Mesoamerica.

Tick Island Incised

The early decorations in the Orange Phase were found on the top of plain pottery levels at the Palmer and Bluffton sites (Bullen, 1961, p. 104; 1955). The more elaborate motifs and decorated lips were lacking; only two motifs were found. One was the curvilinear Tick Island Incised, the other an unnamed arrangement of incised concentric diamonds.

Tick Island Incised has been illustrated and described by Holmes (1894, pp. 123–124), Sears and Griffin (1950), and Bullen (1955, fig. 2a-c). Tick Island stands apart from the later Orange motifs in that it features broad-line curvilinear scrolls arranged around the vessel necks, and the spaces between scrolls are crudely punctated. Small circles with a dot centered in them were often drawn in these fields of punctations (fig. 25d-e). A rarer design has rows of punctations alternating with incised lines (op. cit., fig. 2e). The circle and dot was also used in this variety.

Scroll motifs are not found in the early Ecuadorian Formative. They are, however, the prominent element of the Barlovento Phase on the north coast of Colombia (1900–1000 B.C.). Reichel-Dolmatoff (1955, pl. 4, 1–9) illustrates curvilinear scrolls made by broad incised lines forming decorative bands around the necks of globular tecomate shape vessels (fig. 25h-i). Punctations fill the spaces between scrolls, and circle and dot elements are arranged in these fields of punctations. Alternate rows of punctations and broad incised lines are another motif (op. cit., pl. 3-5, −10). The Barlovento pottery is tempered with small amounts of sand, possibly accidental amounts of

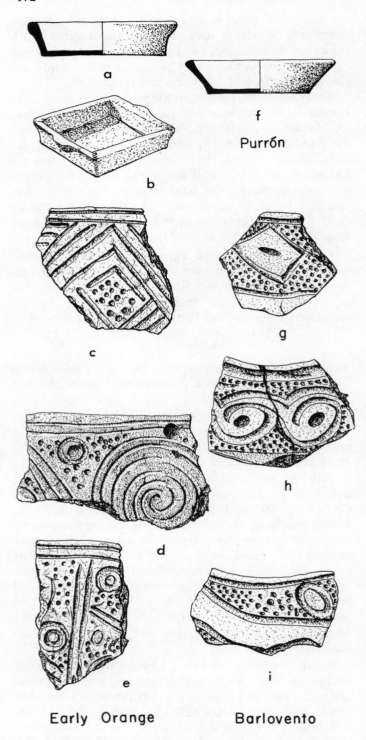

Purrón

Early Orange   Barlovento

FIGURE 25.—Resemblances between vessel shapes and decorations of the early part of the Orange Phase, south Atlantic coast of North America, the Purrón Phase of Tehuacán, Mexico, and the Barlovento Phase of Colombia. *a–b, f,* Flat-base pan. *c, g,* Broad-line diamond. *d–e, h–i,* Incised curvilinear scroll combined with fields of punctations containing circle and dot elements. (*a–b, d, f,* Florida State Museum collections. *c, e,* after Holmes, 1894: *c,* fig. 12, p. 124; *e,* fig. 9, p. 123. *g–i,* after Reichel-Dolmatoff, 1955: *g,* pl. 5–1; *h,* pl. 4–1; *i,* pl. 3–1)

ground shell, and possibly ground potsherds. Surfaces are carelessly finished.

Neither Tick Island Incised nor the concentric diamond motif is present in later Orange Phase sites such as South Indian Field (Ferguson, 1951), Cotton (Griffin and Smith, 1954), or Summer Haven (Bullen, 1961). The designs recur, however, on early pottery of the Adena Phase.

Broad-Line Diamonds

This precise concentric diamond arrangement (fig. 25*c*) has not been illustrated from northwestern South America where so many other comparisons are found; however, the constituent elements of this motif are present. Concentric rectangles and squares are present in Valdivia ceramics (fig. 25*g*; Meggers, Evans, and Estrada, 1965, pls. 42a, 161e-h), executed in broad-line incising. The diamond, although made by a single broad line and with punctated background is found in the Barlovento Phase of Colombia (Reichel-Dolmatoff, 1955, pl. 5–1). Holmes (1894, pp. 123–124, figs. 9–12) illustrates a couple of sherds from Clarence B. Moore's excavations at Tick Island that may be early Orange decorated; at least Tick Island Incised was found. These bear concentric diamond designs executed with wide, round-bottom lines, very similar to the Valdivia and Barlovento examples cited. One sherd has a small ear or spout formed on the lip. These ears, common at Bluffton (Bullen, 1955, fig. 1), seem to be another feature of early Orange. A variety of similar rim modifications are found in Valdivia ceramics.

Ayangue Tradition

Most of the Orange decorative motifs resemble those of the engraved pottery of the Machalilla Phase of Ecuador (2000–1500 B.C.). These decorations also last on into the Chorrera Phase (1500–500 B.C.). How late they persist is not known, for the latter phase has not been adequately reported. Resemblances are mostly confined to two types: Ayangue Incised, and Machalilla Double-line Incised. To distinguish this group, it shall be referred to as the Ayangue tradition. It has an extensive distribution in Mesoamerica after 1500 B.C.

Meggers, Evans, and Estrada (1965, fig. 89) show that Ayangue Incised increases in popularity through the Machalilla Phase, to reach a maximum frequency of about 6 percent at the end of this phase and the beginning of Chorrera. This maximum dates approximately 1600–1400 B.C. Considering the approximate nature of our guess dates, this is very close to the appearance of the decorations to be described below in the Orange ceramics of Florida.

The Machalilla designs were engraved with a pointed tool after the vessel surfaces had sometimes been red slipped and were fairly well polished. Orange surfaces were well smoothed, and designs were drawn with a pointed instrument while surfaces were soft enough for incisions. The narrow lines contrast with the earlier Tick Island and Stallings Island Incised. The Orange decorations are twice or more the scale of the corresponding designs in Machalilla; they look like crude cartoon imitations. (The drawings in our figures 26–30 are not to scale.)

Incised Herringbone Motifs

Crude herringbone motifs, in which lines are closely spaced, are arranged both horizontally and vertically on the walls of Orange pan-shaped bowls (fig. 26a–b). Both arrangements occur in Machalilla Double-line Incised (fig. 26f–g; Meggers, Evans, and Estrada, 1965, pp. 123–124), which differs from the Orange herringbone motifs in that the lines are engraved with a tool having two points. However, multi-pointed tools were used in the Florida decoration assemblage.

Crossed Bands of Incised Lines

Bands of lines drawn at 45 degrees to the rim so that they cross are common to both complexes. Two versions of this motif are found. In one the bands are simply drawn across one another (fig. 26c, h). In the other, one set of bands is broken as it crosses so that it appears to pass behind (fig. 26d–e, i–j). This latter is prominent in Mesoamerican ceramics about 800 B.C. In Orange it is not so well drawn. The bands stop at the point of crossing, but often do not continue. It is in some of the four- to six-line band decorations that multi-pointed tools were employed (fig. 26c). These recall the two-point engravers of Machalilla.

A related motif is that of bands of straight lines leaning at about 45 degrees alternately to right and left (fig. 27a–b, f–i). More common in Orange than Machalilla, these bands and other motifs are arranged in superimposed horizontal panels that are bounded by two incised lines and encircle the vessels (fig. 27a, h–i). In the Ecuadorian sequence, similar horizontal paneling is a very prominent feature of the earlier Valdivia Fine-line Incised (Meggers, Evans, and Estrada, 1965, p. 60, fig. 32, pls. 61–64).

A variation of this leaning band of lines motif has only a few lines (3–5) in each band bordered by a line of punctations. A fairly common body decoration in Machalilla, this variant is found principally on flattened vessel lips in Orange (fig. 27c, j). As flat lips seem to be late in the Orange Phase, this suggests a late date for the decoration. This is consistent with

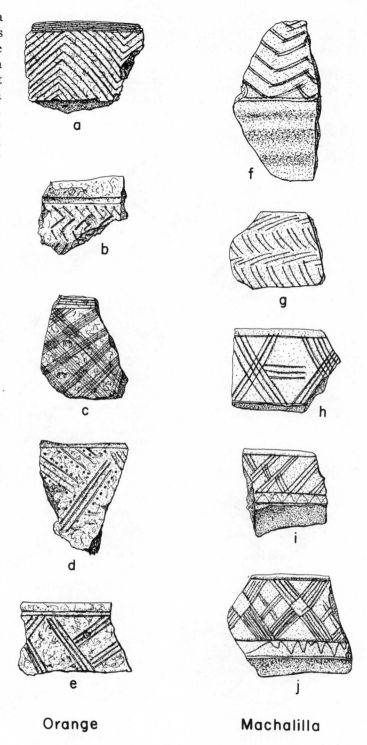

Orange   **Machalilla**

FIGURE 26.—Resemblances between pottery decorations of the Orange Phase, south Atlantic coast of North America, and the Machalilla Phase of coastal Ecuador. a–b, f–g, Incised herringbone motif. c, h, Crossed bands of incised lines. d–e, i–j, Crossed bands with one discontinuous element. (a–d, Florida State Museum collections. e, after Sears and Griffin, 1950, Fiber-tempered Type 8–3. f–j, after Meggers, Evans, and Estrada, 1965: f, pl. 137n; g, pl. 138b; h, pl. 133n; i, pl. 133c; j, pl. 133b)

its continuation into the succeeding St. Johns Phase. It also occurs in Tchefuncte and other later ceramics in the eastern United States.

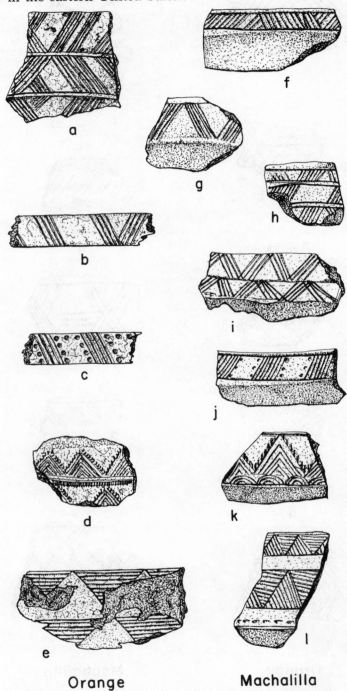

Orange   Machalilla

FIGURE 27.—Resemblances between incised decorations of the Orange Phase, south Atlantic coast of North America, and the Machalilla Phase of coastal Ecuador. *a–b, f–i*, Bands of alternatingly slanting lines. *c, j*, Slanting lines bordered by punctation. *d–e, k–l*, Line-filled triangles. (*a–d*, Florida State Museum collections. *e*, after Ferguson, 1951, pl. 2q. *f–l*, after Meggers, Evans, and Estrada, 1965: *f*, pl. 132k; *g*, pl. 132 1; *h*, pl. 132u; *i*, pl. 132i; *j*, pl. 132x; *k*, pl. 132e; *l*, pl. 132f)

Line-Filled Triangles

Line-filled triangles appear in both Orange and Machalilla. In some examples, the filling lines slant parallel to one leg of the triangle. Somewhat more unusual are nested chevrons (fig. 27*d–e, k–l*).

Dots or Tick Marks Bordering Motifs

The custom of occasionally bordering units of decoration with small tick marks was practiced in both regions. These marks had two variations: a row of punctations, or a row of short dashes attached to the decorative element like a fringe of tassels (fig. 27*c–d, j–k*).

Hatched Diamonds or Squares

Squares and diamonds filled with hatched lines are a feature of both Orange and Machalilla ceramics. Hatching in alternate squares placed at right angles, gives a "basket-work" effect. This is fairly common in Orange (fig. 28*a*), perhaps less so in Machalilla (fig. 28*e*), and is a persistent minor element in Middle Formative of Mesoamerica.

Hatched diamonds are large and crude in Orange (fig. 28*b*), delicate and engraved on polished surfaces in Machalilla (fig. 28*f*). In the latter, alternate diamonds are not hatched so that a checkerboard effect is achieved.

Zig-zag Bands with Hatched Backgrounds

Triangles arranged in a band with apex alternately up and down, and separated so that a smooth band between them forms a zig-zag, are fairly common both in Orange and Valdivia. Orange examples are usually hatched, Valdivia ones crosshatched (fig. 28*c, g*).

Crosshatched and Hatched Bands

Crosshatched line-bordered bands are used in Orange, Valdivia, and Machalilla Phases to form angular motifs. The Valdivia examples are hatched in two ways. Usually lines run at 45 degrees to the axis of the band. In the other arrangement the crosshatching lines run lengthwise and at right angles. The latter unusual treatment is the only arrangement that seems to be used in Machalilla and Orange (fig. 28*d, h–i*).

Late Orange Features

Three features found in the Orange ceramics cannot be compared to the Ecuadorian Machalilla Phase. These are the wide flattened lips bearing incised decoration (fig. 29*a–b, e*), vessel decoration consisting of angular hatched bands (fig. 29*c*), and similar bands formed by parallel lines (fig. 29*d*). These features appear to be late in Orange (Griffin and

Smith, 1954, p. 43), possibly too late to have been derived from the Ecuadorian phase. There are suggestions of relationships with Formative ceramics dating after 1000 B.C.

In geographical terms, the outflared decorated vessel lips find their closest comparisons in the lips of flat-base pans on the Gulf coast of Mexico (fig. 29 f–g) and in the highlands. MacNeish informs me that in Tehuacán these lips date between 850–550 B.C.

Zig-zag lines bordering bands of hatching are rather common in the late Orange Phase collections. These seem to be related to the rectilinear zoned hatching (pp. 141–142, chart 21). Through Mesoamerica this specialized version of the group of zoned hatched and crosshatched decorations, seems to date between 1000 and 500 B.C. In Ecuador it is found in the Chorrera Phase, and in highland Peru in Kotosh Waira-jirca.

Similar large triangular motifs with plain bands of vessel surface between wide bands of parallel hatching (fig. 29d) also lack exact parallels in Machalilla. They may, however, reflect the common use of parallel-line bands in that phase (fig 29i).

Rare Orange Decorations

There are several relatively rare features of Orange decoration that should be considered. One is a rectilinear undulating line motif, which Griffin and Smith (1954, fig. 3–6) illustrate from a widened vessel lip (fig. 29e). This is similar to a motif of Machalilla Double-line Incised (fig 29j; Meggers, Evans, and Estrada, 1965, pl. 137a), but is much more common in the broad-line incising of the earlier Valdivia types (op. cit., pls. 59a, 178b).

A piece of tortoise shell from the Cotton site has an engraved meander design based on interlocked T-figures (fig. 30a; Griffin and Smith, 1954, pl. 2–6). This rather complex design is very similar to engraved motifs found on Valdivia Red Incised (fig. 30b; Meggers, Evans, and Estrada, 1965, p. 81, pls. 102–103).

Discussion

This is very nearly a complete inventory of ceramic features of the fiber-tempered Orange ceramics of Florida. Comparable features have been cited from contemporary phases in northern Colombia and coastal Ecuador. I venture to suggest that the resemblances are close enough to indicate direct contact by ocean voyages, rather than diffusion. However, it is again necessary to postulate an undiscovered ceramic complex in a few coastal shell middens somewhere in lower Middle America, where the

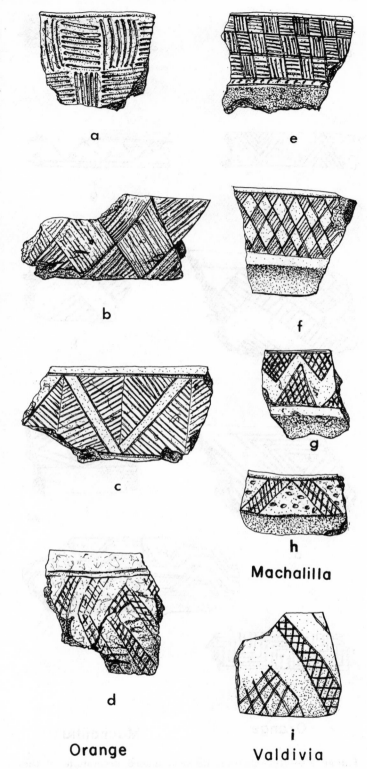

FIGURE 28.—Resemblances between incised decorations of the Orange Phase, south Atlantic coast of North America, and the Machalilla and Valdivia Phases of coastal Ecuador. a–b, e–f, Hatched diamonds or squares. c, g, Zig-zag bands with hatched backgrounds. d, h–i, Crosshatched bands. (a–d, Florida State Museum collections. e–i, after Meggers, Evans, and Estrada, 1965: e, pl. 134a; f, pl. 133k; g, pl. 131a; h, pl. 133p; i, pl. 64j)

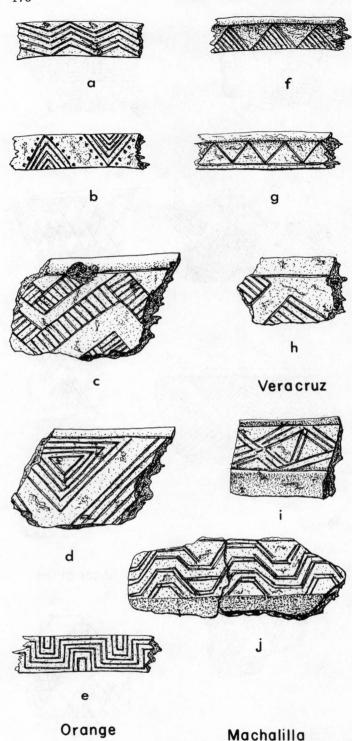

features of the flat-base pan (highland Mexico) could be combined with fiber tempering and the Tick Island motif (north coast of Colombia), and the numerous Machalilla decorative motifs. That the contact was not a one-way single trip is indicated by the parallel chronological position of later features such as decorated thickened rims and zoned hatched designs.

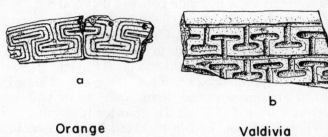

FIGURE 30.—Resemblances between interlocked T-figures in decorations of the Orange Phase, south Atlantic coast of North America, and the Valdivia Phase of coastal Ecuador. (*a*, after Griffin and Smith, 1954, pl. 2–6. *b*, after Meggers, Evans, and Estrada, 1965, pl. 178b)

The Fourche Maline Complex of Oklahoma

Along the Fourche Maline River in eastern Oklahoma, there is a small colony of sites marked by deep middens approximately circular in shape. While the pottery is grit tempered, features of vessel shape and decoration are remarkably similar to the Orange complex of Florida (Newkumet, 1940). Radiocarbon dates are not available. This strange Fourche Maline complex may well represent a direct migration from the St. Johns region of Florida, dating somewhere between 1000 and 500 B.C. It seems to have had no immediate influence upon the Poverty Point ceramics in the nearby Mississippi Valley, but what may well be decorative motifs diffused from Fourche Maline become prominent in the early phases of Illinois Hopewell after 500 B.C.

The Bayou La Batre Complex of the Mobile Bay Region

A third early ceramic complex is known from several shell middens located on streams that empty into Mobile Bay on the Gulf coast of the southeastern United States. The type site and the characteristic pottery have been described by Wimberly (1960). Since Wimberly's investigation, Bruce Trickey and Nicholas Holmes (personal communication) have excavated the Bryant's Landing shell midden and have obtained radiocarbon dates of 79 B.C for the Hopewell-related Santa Rosa level, 1129 B.C. for the

FIGURE 29.—Resemblances between incised decorations of the Orange Phase, south Atlantic coast of North America, Veracruz region of Mexico, and the Machalilla Phase of coastal Ecuador. *a–b, f–g,* Incised decoration on flattened lip. *c, h,* Angular hatched bands. *d, i,* Bands of parallel lines. *e, j,* Rectangular undulating line. (*a, c–d, f–h,* Florida State Museum collections. *b, e,* after Griffin and Smith, 1954: *b,* fig. 3–4a; *e,* fig. 3–6; *i–j,* after Meggers, Evans, and Estrada, 1965: *i,* pl. 134v; *j,* pl. 137a)

La Batre level, and 2139 B.C. for the lowest preceramic deposits. Fortunately, Trickey and Holmes' stratigraphy is somewhat clearer than that from the University of Alabama excavations, and permits a clearer definition of the La Batre complex.

There are a few plain fiber-tempered sherds in the Bayou La Batre level, but most of the pottery compares to Stallings Island and Orange ceramics only in the fact that all three are somewhat cruder in manufacture than later Southeastern pottery. The pottery is clearly manufactured by coiling, a point somewhat in doubt for the other two early complexes. It is tempered with moderate amounts of coarse sand and fine gravel, is harder than the other Southeastern Formative wares, and ranges from buff to dull orange in color. Forms range from deep vessels with outslanting walls, 18–30 cm. in rim diameter, to globular-bodied pots with incurved upper walls. Rims are direct; sometimes lips are slightly flattened or notched. Outward curved rims may be a late form. Bases are small for vessel size, are flat, and have four small wedge or mammiform-shaped feet, or crude annular rings. There are also what Wimberly terms "pseudo-annular bases," which are flat rather than concave on the exterior.

Flaring-side Cup

At approximately 1000 B.C. there is no known ceramic to the south with which the flaring-side cup form may be compared (fig. 31a–b). In the tapering sides and small base, it has a generalized resemblance to the Woodland amphora being made in the vicinity of the Great Lakes at this time, but cordmarking and other Woodland ceramic features do not reach the Gulf coast for almost a millenium.

Globular Pot

The globular pot with tetrapod or annular base is perhaps easier to identify (fig. 31c). Its history is detailed on pp. 112–115 and chart 12. Similar shapes seem to originate in Valdivia (fig. 31h) and were manufactured as late as 1 B.C. in the early Cupica Phase on the north Pacific coast of Colombia (Reichel-Dolmatoff, G. and A., 1962). Subglobular and globular pots, 25–30 cm. in diameter and about 20 cm. high, with wide mouths and out-turned lips, are the dominant Momíl 1 form (Reichel-Dolmatoff, G. and A., 1956, pp. 178–179). They are decorated with dentate stamp designs in straight-line motifs. Four feet on small globular-bodied vessels are a feature of Valdivia (fig. 31f) and of both Momíl Periods (700–1 B.C.) on the Caribbean coast of Colombia (fig. 31g; op. cit., p. 212, fig. 12–7). Detached short feet of uncertain number are also

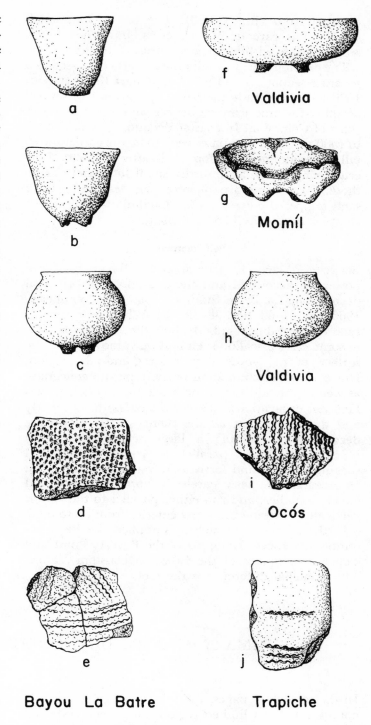

FIGURE 31.—Resemblances between vessel shapes and decorations of the Bayou La Batre Phase, Gulf coast of North America, and those of the Valdivia Phase of Ecuador, the Momíl Phase of Colombia, the Ocós Phase of Guatemala, and the Trapiche Phase, Gulf coast of Mexico. a, Flaring cup. b–c, f–g, Small tetrapod feet. h, Globular pot. d–e, i–j, Shell stamping. (a–e, after Wimberly, 1960: a–c, fig. 40; d, fig. 42a; e, fig. 39b. f, h, after Meggers, Evans, and Estrada, 1965: f, fig. 42–2; h, fig. 42–8. g, after G. and A. Reichel-Dolmatoff, 1956, fig. 12–7. i, after M. D. Coe, 1961, fig. 47k. j, after García Payón, 1966, pl. 45–15)

common (op. cit., p. 288). The use of four small solid feet is rare in Mesoamerica, but when found seems to date within a few centuries of 1000 B.C.

The distribution of annular bases is also discussed in a separate section (pp. 115–117 and chart 15). At about 1000 B.C. they made their first appearance in several of the Mesoamerican sequences and on the north coast of Colombia. In coastal Ecuador they date back to 1500 B.C. Low ring bases seem to be the earlier form; tall bases do not develop until after 500 B.C. Low crude ring bases, as absurdly small for vessel size as those of La Batre, are an infrequent feature on thick sand-tempered pottery of the Chalahuites-El Trapiche complex on the Gulf coast of Mexico.

Shell Stamping

Between 20 and 30 percent of the Bayou La Batre pottery is decorated and there is only one principal decoration, La Batre Stamped (fig. 31d; Wimberly, 1960, pp. 64–68, figs. 38–39, 42). When he wrote the type description, Wimberly had the impression that in some cases a scallop shell had been moved over the surface of the vessel with a drag-and-jab motion. However, a reexamination of the type site collection, as well as the additional materials from Trickey and Holmes' excavations, has convinced both Wimberly and the writer that all the sherds of the type were decorated by holding a large scallop shell with inner face almost parallel to vessel surface and rocking it back and forth as it was moved forward. Impressions are very carelessly applied, are placed closely together, and run either parallel to the rim or vertically, covering the vessel exterior from lip to base.

In the manner in which it is applied, La Batre resembles the rocker stamping of the Poverty Point and Tchefuncte Phases of the Lower Mississippi Valley. The principal difference is the tool.

Between 1 and 2 percent of the Bayou La Batre shell-stamped impressions are the more conventional shell edge type (Bayou La Batre Scallop Impressed; Wimberly, 1960, pp. 68–70, fig. 39a–b). These impressions are linear, not rocked, and one sherd shows attempts to line up the impressions into a simple design pattern (fig. 31e).

Summary

This simple Bayou La Batre complex, dating apparently at 1000 B.C., shares no features with either the Orange Phase ceramics of Florida or the Stallings material from coastal Georgia. Except for a few plain fiber-tempered sherds in the deposits, there is no evidence of contact. It does have features in common with the Poverty Point Phase ceramics of the Lower Mississippi Valley.

Impressions of a scallop shell, both linear and rocker, are a minor but persistent part of the unzoned rocker stamp tradition. Through Mesoamerica (fig. 31i–j) this tradition dates between 1000 and 500 B.C., the proper date to provide a source for Bayou La Batre Stamped. On the coast of Ecuador, it goes back to 3000 B.C. Here, however, stamping occurs in bands about the vessel rims rather than as overall surface roughening.

With the exception of the flaring-side small base cup, all of the features incorporated in the Bayou La Batre complex were in existence on the 1000 B.C. time horizon through much of Mesoamerica and in Colombia. However, these elements usually were incorporated in ceramic assemblages of much greater complexity and sophistication. It seems probable that Bayou La Batre represents a third introduction of selected pottery features onto the southeastern coast of North America.

SUMMARY AND SPECULATION ABOUT THE COLONIAL FORMATIVE

In the preceding pages, the features of early ceramic complexes of ten limited regions have been reviewed and compared. There is good reason to suspect that in each instance these complexes represent the first introduction of ceramics into their respective region.

The number of sites known for each region is small, ranging from one to about 30, and for the most part they are shell middens located on coasts or up rivers giving ready access to the sea.

Each group of sites appears to be geographically isolated. While this may be in some cases an illusion

due to lack of knowledge of intervening areas, in more thoroughly surveyed regions such as the coasts of the southeastern United States or northern Peru, the early geographical distribution is similar to that of the European colonies placed on the North American east coast prior to A.D. 1700.

In the earlier of these colonies, those which have yielded radiocarbon dates prior to about 2000 B.C., the complete ceramic inventory shows a marked resemblance to a selection of features of the Valdivia Phase of the coast of Ecuador. This is true of Puerto

Hormiga (3000 B.C.) on the north coast of Colombia, Stallings Island (2400 B.C.) on the Atlantic coast of the United States, Monagrillo (2100 B.C.) on the Pacific coast of Panama, and probably the San Juan Phase of the Tumbes, Peru region.

Two tendencies can be noted in the earliest pottery of most of these areas. First, in the Stallings Island, Monagrillo, and San Juan Phases, there is a tendency for at least a proportion of the ware toward the base of the deposits to be thinner, and to a degree better finished than that of immediately later date. This same tendency is displayed in later Formative complexes such as the Orange Phase of Florida, and the Negritos and Guañape of coastal Peru. It has also been noted by M.D. Coe (1961) at La Victoria on the Guatemalan coast, and by Kidder, Jennings, and Shook (1946) at Kaminaljuyú in the highlands.

In addition to being relatively thin, the earliest ceramics of the west coast of South America from Panama to the north coast of Peru, are similar in having a moderate amount of sand tempering in which there are large white particles, usually quartz (but thought by Lanning to be crushed limestone in Piura).

After an initial production of relatively thick pottery in Period A, the pottery of the Valdivia-Machalilla Phases is quite thin. If the several complexes described above were colonies transplanted more or less directly from the Ecuadorian coast, then the tendency toward thicker, and in some cases less well-finished pottery, may represent a temporary degeneration in ceramic technology.

In the Guañape Phase of Peru, the Purrón Phase of highland Mexico, and the Orange and Stallings Island Phases of the southeastern coast of the United States, there is an initial period of undecorated pottery. These are the instances where the transition from preceramic to ceramic deposits has been observed. Whether there are similar initial phases for the other colonies is unknown.

While the individuals who brought the techniques of pottery-making into a new region should have made competent pottery, it appears that their neighbors, who were learning, started in a modest fashion, satisfied to create a useful container without decoration. The pride of craftsmanship that motivates the application of decoration could have developed later. These two tendencies toward the production of a thicker and perhaps stronger ceramic, and the gradual adoption of the practice of decoration are not inconsistent.

If the ceramic assemblages described above do represent colonies of people who landed on coasts far from their homelands, there is evidence that most did not remain isolated, for the sequence of changes in features parallels those that took place in the nuclear region. These have been pointed out for the Orange Phase of Florida, the Monagrillo-Sarigua sequence of Panama, the Puerto Hormiga-Barlovento sequence of the north coast of Colombia, and the Negritos-Paita sequence of Piura in northern Peru.

The Theocratic Formative

What appears to have been the spread of the knowledge of ceramic manufacture to various parts of the Americas between 3000 and 1500 B.C. has been described. The mechanism seems to have been primarily sea voyages by coastal dwelling people, and the addition of this new technology apparently had little or no effect on the Archaic pattern of living in the areas to which it was introduced. While some diffusion away from the coasts can be seen, as in highland Mexico and Peru, there seems to have been no general eagerness to adopt and elaborate the new art.

The real initial impetus to the American Formative pattern of life occurred between 1500 and 1000 B.C. Apparently it was based primarily on the rapid and perhaps simultaneous diffusion of two important cultural patterns. The basic one was undoubtedly the spread of maize agriculture from its point of origin in highland Mexico. Without this efficient addition to the various plant foods collected and cultivated in a limited fashion in the several regions, the population increase that made the Formative cultural florescence would not have been possible.

It often happens in human history, however, that important practical advances are taken for granted and the real driving forces of a cultural revolution are intangible ideas, particularly religious concepts (Willey, 1962). This seems to have been the case in the Americas where the sudden appearance of a religio-political group of ideas began to produce the monumental mound structures, large stone carvings, a lapidary industry for personal adornment, and the distinctive art styles that are preserved for the admiration of the students of pre-Columbian art. The high points of this first wave of organized religion and political control were the Olmec culture of a very limited area of the Gulf coast of Mexico (1200–400

B.C.), the Chavín culture of Peru (800–400 B.C.), and the Poverty Point-Hopewell cultures of the Mississippi Valley (1200 B.C.–A.D. 200). These were true cultural revolutions; revolutions that apparently were not imposed by military force. Suddenly really tremendous amounts of labor were absorbed in the construction of religious edifices, and marked social stratification can be inferred from burial practices.

While the three major regions developed distinctive standardized versions of the basic mound building pattern and art styles, communication between them seems to have been accelerated. This is reflected in parallels in pottery and other artifacts.

Present evidence indicates that Olmec is the parent complex and that it was established fully developed on a very limited stretch of the Gulf coast of Mexico at 1200 B.C. Some suggestions exist that possibly earlier sites are on the Pacific coast of the state of Guerrero, Mexico, but this is as yet uncertain.

Again the key question of the American Formative: did this religio-political complex develop in situ, or is it an import? There are no suggestions of Olmec features in the earlier ceramic complexes of coastal Ecuador, which clearly do seem to be imports. Neither are there hints of developmental stages in known Mexican complexes that immediately predate 1200 B.C. The Tehuacán sequence of MacNeish and associates is very near to the Olmec areas and shows no hint or early developmental Olmec. As a matter of fact, if it were not for a few baby-faced figurines, the reviewer of the Tehuacán sequence would not suspect that this sophisticated complex fluorished between 1200 and 400 B.C. in the nearby lowlands. Unlike Chavín or Hopewell, Olmec remained a very geographically restricted phenomenon.

A few cultural traits and ceramic features have passed up and down the Americas in the millenium preceding the beginning of the present era, when these religio-political systems were in the process of becoming established and crystalized. Movements of sizable groups of people apparently occurred, and traits were also diffused from group to group. It seems necessary to infer migratory movements to account for the spread of the religio-political system, and particularly for brachycephaly and cranial deformation. The minor ceramic traits upon which the archeologist is so dependent, may have been diffusing from group to group. However, if so, they show remarkably little modification by the cultural filters through which they passed.

It has been possible to present the ceramic colonization of the Colonial Formative as neat packaged units. However, most of the items that diffused during the Theocratic Formative have a beginning in the Americas before 1200 B.C., and continue on after the estimated date of 500 B.C.–A.D. 300, the approximate end of the Theocratic Formative.

Ceramics of Poverty Point, Louisiana

The fourth early ceramic complex in the Southeast comes from the large planned geometrically arranged town, the Poverty Point site in the Lower Mississippi Valley. Although the initial date is 1200 B.C., approximately coeval with Bayou La Batre, the complex Poverty Point culture clearly relates to the Theocratic rather than the Colonial Formative. When excavations were made at the site (Ford and Webb, 1956, pp. 105–106), only 53 sherds were found. Thirty-two of these were plain fiber tempered, 17 thick, soft, coarse clay tempered, and three thinner and harder sherds from undoubted Poverty Point context but which were incorrectly identified as the later Coles Creek Plain. One of these latter came from a fire bed at the base of a 20-foot high conical mound that yielded radiocarbon dates clustering around 1000 B.C. (op. cit., pp. 121–122). A second sherd was a few inches above a fireplace in the dwelling area, which dated 910 ±100 B.C.

In the last 10 years, a local collector, Carl Alexander, in the course of accumulating over 21,000 additional specimens from the site, has collected 293 more sherds from the surface and excavated from the walls of gullies. About half of these sherds are decorated and thus we begin to accumulate information on the ceramic industry, which was certainly not popular among the inhabitants of this locality; a total of 363 ceramic sherds as compared to 4,161 steatite sherds and uncounted hundreds of thousands of clay balls made for pit baking.

While a minority of the Poverty Point sherds are thick and fiber tempered, the majority are tempered

with lumps of clay, are very soft and poorly fired, and range up to 1 cm. in thickness. Some are quite thin

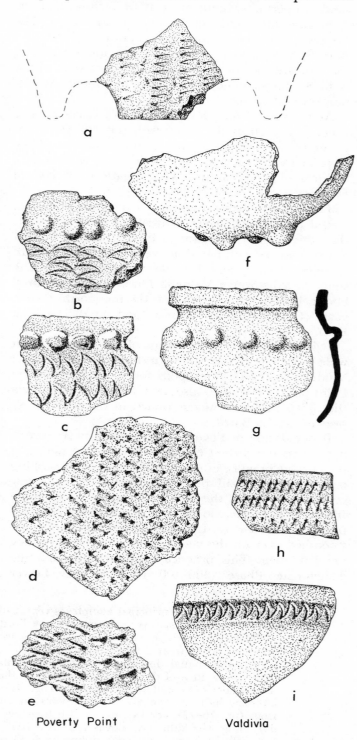

Poverty Point   Valdivia

FIGURE 32.—Resemblances between vessel features and decorations of the Poverty Point Phase, Lower Mississippi Valley and the Valdivia Phase of Ecuador. *a, f,* Tetrapod feet. *b–c, g,* Nodes pressed out from the interior. *d–e, h–i,* Smooth rocker stamping. (*a–e,* Florida State Museum collections. *f–i,* after Meggers, Evans, and Estrada, 1965: *f,* pl. 98a–b; *g,* pl. 78b; *h,* pl. 112g; *i,* pl. 108c)

and hard, indistinguishable from later clay-tempered wares. Also a proportion have varying amounts of sand tempering. Manufacture is by coiling, and the deep vase and wide-mouth pot form are usual. The Poverty Point and the contemporary Bayou La Batre ceramics that were being manufactured to the east are more similar to one another than either is to Stallings Island or Orange, but there are significant differences.

As the reader may have begun to suspect by this time, nearly all of the features of the Poverty Point ceramics, with the exception of the crudeness of the ware, may be directly compared to a selection of features of the Valdivia Phase pattern of coastal Ecuador.

The history of the wide-mouth pot form has been traced (pp. 86–90). Here, it is sufficient to point out that this earliest appearance in the eastern United States may be compared to vessel shapes 14–23 of Meggers, Evans, and Estrada (1965, fig. 54). The shape lasted through Valdivia Phase D, possibly until about 1000 B.C. It continued on the north Pacific coast of Colombia, in Panama, and on the coast of Peru.

It is not known whether some of the Poverty Point wide-mouth pots had globular bases like the usual Valdivia form. The tetrapods found on the Poverty Point pottery (fig. 32a) also have parallels in Valdivia (fig. 32f), as has been mentioned in discussing their presence in La Batre.

If our dating of Poverty Point ceramics is correct, it presents the earliest examples in North America of the curious practice of forming decoration by pushing out a row of small protuberances or nodes a few centimeters below the rim by pressing from inside the vessel with the end of an instrument the size of a pencil (fig. 32b–c, g). Usually the resultant holes are smoothed over on the vessel interior; sometimes they are left open. This practice continued through the Tchefuncte Phase (400–100 B.C.) in the Lower

Mississippi (Ford and Quimby, 1945), and occurs in the related Tchula Phase of northern Mississippi (Phillips, Ford, and Griffin, 1951, pl. 76; Ford, Phillips, Haag, 1955, pp. 62–75, figs. 20a–c, 21d, 22b). It is a common feature of the sand-tempered Alexander ceramic complex along the Tennessee River in northern Alabama (Heimlich, 1952), and is found on the fabric and cordmarked Baumer pottery of southern Illinois (Cole, et al., 1951, pp. 184–200). It also lasts into the early phase of Illinois Hopewell culture (ca. 300 B.C.). These bosses are found to the north in Minnesota and extend into southern Ontario and Manitoba (Wright, 1967).

From the mouth of the Mississippi to the latitude of the southern end of Lake Michigan, these nodes punched through to mark off a rim area are immediately followed by the Classic Hopewell vessel rim, which usually is cambered, delicately crosshatched, and has a lower border of large hemiconical punctations.

Twenty-seven of the sherds from Poverty Point have rocker-stamped decoration (fig. 32a–c), careless zig-zag stamped impressions that run parallel to the rim or vertically from below the rim area, if indicated, to the base. Basically similar to La Batre Stamped, Poverty Point employed a smooth or notched tool rather than the edge of a scallop shell (fig. 32a–e). These sherds may be classified as Tchefuncte Stamped. Smooth rocker stamping is found in the early Formative of Mesoamerica, but like the punched-out nodes discussed above, it is most often on the rims of large neckless jars. Probably some of the examples of Valdivia Rocker Stamped (Meggers, Evans, and Estrada, 1965, pp. 82–84, fig. 46, 4–5) where the impressions are found on the neck areas of small wide-mouth globular pots, provide the closest similarity (fig. 32h–i). On the Ecuadorian coast, this dates in Valdivia C (2000–1500 B.C.). The technique continues into the following Chorrera Phase, but this has not been well described.

The review of the principal complexes representing the Theocratic Formative in North, Middle, and South America was not completed by Ford. His working outline includes a chapter entitled "Olmec-Chavín-Hopewell," in which he apparently expected to compare these complexes in the manner that he treated representatives of the Colonial Formative. Since the review of the chronological and spatial distribution of the individual traits involved was completed, the reader can derive some idea of the scope and variety of the evidence by referring especially to the following discussions: core and blade industry (pp. 47–48), rectangular and petaloid celts (pp. 50–53), lapidary industry (pp. 57–70), earspools and earplugs (pp. 70–74), mirrors (pp. 74–76), finger rings (pp. 76–77), combs (pp. 77–78), figurines (pp. 78–82), flat and cylindrical stamps (pp. 83–85), composite silhouette bowls (pp. 101–105), unzoned and zoned rocker and linear stamping (pp. 128–131), and mound building (pp. 43–46). The "Summary of Trait Distributions" (pp. 148–149) calls attention to additional traits. The concluding chapter (pp. 188–193) summarizes Ford's views.

A Historical Reconstruction

In the foregoing pages the reader has been presented with the grubby details that are the building blocks for archeological reconstructions of history. If he has become seriously interested, it is hoped that many of the references have been consulted, for the more complete information they provide cannot possibly be presented here.

This section will attempt a historical reconstruction of the spread of Formative cultural elements through the Americas. The archeological approach is severely limited by the nature of the evidence with which it can work, and it is also clear that a number of pieces of the skeleton-like picture puzzle are still missing. Enough evidence is now available, however, to sketch in the major outlines. Where key data are lacking the writer will not hesitate to postulate its nature and probable location. Prediction of this sort is one of the most useful features of a historical model, and is essential to logical programs of field research.

Wauchope (1950), Willey (1955), Reichel-Dolmatoff (1957), Meggers, Evans, and Estrada (1965, pp. 157–178), and others have discussed portions of this history in considerable detail. They all have concluded that there was evidence for cultural connections for the geographical regions they have considered. While much of the same ground will be covered, the writer will not presume to repeat all of their arguments, but will attempt to present some new ones.

At about 3000 B.C. after a long sea voyage from the southwestern Japanese Islands, a group of fishermen landed on the coast of Ecuador. Meggers, Evans, and Estrada (1965), who have presented the evidence in support of this happening, so novel in terms of currently accepted theory about New World cultural development, have modestly suggested that perhaps this was a single boatload of fishermen, lost at sea in a storm, who were unwillingly brought to the shores of America by the North Pacific ocean current.

There is reason to suspect, however, that this might have been more in the nature of an exploring and colonizing expedition involving a number of individuals of both sexes and varied skills. Subsequent events in the Americas suggest that these people had a seafaring, exploring, and colonizing tradition, similar to that of the later Polynesians and Vikings. Solheim (1964, pp. 360, 376–384) has offered statistical evidence to show that one of three sources of the Malayan and Polynesian ceramic traditions was influenced from the Japanese Islands at an estimated date of 1000 to 500 B.C. The extensive spread of this "Sa-huynh-Kalany" tradition in the southwestern Pacific certainly implies a seafaring tradition. Most of the ceramic shapes, decorative elements, and design motifs are similar to those postulated to have spread to the Americas between 3000 and 1000 B.C.

The compact roughly circular villages that the immigrants established were clustered along a limited stretch of the coast of Ecuador, and evidence of the complex sophisticated ceramic tradition extends to the initial levels of the deeper middens that have been tested. Rather than a few castaway fishermen being cordially received by local people to whom they taught the art of ceramics, this suggests that competent artisans were in charge of this industry from the start. The ceramic arts do not degenerate, as occurred during some of the later movements inside the Americas, but after about 2300 B.C. pottery is actually better made than the contemporary wares on the Japanese Islands.

The remarkable variety of the Valdivia ceramics suggests that more than one or two individuals, or lineages, founded and maintained this tradition. The highly selective fashion in which certain elements of the complex were spread to other parts of the Americas, also argues that specialization in this craft had already developed. Furthermore, as varied as it is, the Valdivia ceramic complex does not represent the entire range of pottery manufactured at 3000 B.C. in southwestern Japan. As with the early English settlement at Jamestown in Virginia, the products manufactured corresponded to the experience and training of the craftsmen brought from the mother country.

Compact, almost circular villages or C-shaped arrangement of houses with the open side of the C facing the beach, are characteristic of the Middle Jomon of Japan (information from Takeshi Ueno and Kazuo Terada). While the clustering of houses close together for defense may be a practical feature without historical significance, the modest plan of arranging dwellings about an open court may have been a trait imported to the Americas at this time.

At about 3000 B.C. cotton appears in preceramic sites on the coast of Peru to the south. The botanical evidence suggests that this may be the result of a cross between a 13-chromosome Asiatic cotton and a lintless South American relative. Asiatic cotton seeds may well have been part of the baggage of the settlers on the Ecuadorian coast (Silow, 1953; Hutchinson, 1963).

The people living along the desert coast of Peru before 3000 B.C. collected wild food plants as well as produce of the sea. Just as in Mesoamerica at this time, selection of superior plants, and probably planting and cultivation, had developed to a limited extent so that a primitive sort of agriculture was already being practiced. The plants domesticated included bottle gourds, a species of squash, lima beans, peppers, jack beans, probably a variety of canna, and a number of other plants.

While the series of crania available to Munizaga (1965, p. 228) from Valdivia sites was limited in number, he concludes that it "represents a very homogeneous brachycranic type that probably corresponds to a family group." Still more impressive is the fact that these earliest round-headed people contrast markedly with the still earlier dolichocephalic peoples of both the North and South American preceramic or Archaic phases. Munizaga continues: "This new group may be to a large degree the source of the brachycrany observed in populations associated with the later potterymaking periods on the Peruvian coast." This would be quite an achievement for a single boatload of lost fishermen.

Meggers, Evans, and Estrada (1965) have presented an excellent ceramic chronology for the 1500-year span of the Valdivia ceramic complex, and this shows that the Middle Jomon-like features are not all present from the earliest known levels. Some are injected into the development at later times. Unless this is a consequence of sampling error, it raises the possibility that there may have been repeated contacts with the Japanese Islands.

The Valdivia ceramic complex, which appears suddenly about 3000 B.C. in a limited region on the coast of Ecuador, is by no means primitive. The unusually extensive range of decorations comprises a large part of the techniques (aside from painting) employed in the Americas in the succeeding centuries. These include applique fillets, wide-line incising, brushing, pattern brushing, engraving, excising with red pigment rubbed in lines, fingernail punctating, tool punctating, nodes pushed from the interior, applique nodes, drag-and-jab incising, track polishing, red slipping, scallop-shell stamping, and rocker stamping. A minor technique of cord impression was to have no effect on later design. The design motifs are also quite familiar to those who have worked with American ceramics. It is notable that they are almost entirely limited to rectilinear arrangements; lines parallel to vessel rim often broken to form panels, rectangles, undulating frets, interlocking T-shaped designs, zig-zags, stepped designs, slanting arrangements of parallel lines, triangles filled with crosshatching, and both incised and modeled human faces.

Vessel shapes of the Valdivia complex are less varied. They include simple and shouldered bowls, sometimes provided with four short feet, and globular-bodied wide-mouth pots. These latter initially have folded and later cambered rims; loop handles are occasionally provided. Nicked, scalloped, and castellated rims occur on both bowls and pots, as do dimpled bases; however, a number of vessel shapes later to become popular are missing.

Within a few years a group of people appears to have proceded up the Pacific coast of South America and established a colony on the Caribbean coast of present-day Colombia. At the Puerto Hormiga site, a small ring-shaped village was placed on an inlet a short distance from the sea. A limited selection of Valdivia ceramic features was introduced: sand tempering, the simple deep bowl form, scallop-shell stamping, horizontal incised lines, punctated designs, finger node dimples, modeled adornos, drag-and-jab incising, and circle and dot made by excising the background. The zoning of scallop-shell edge stamping by wide incised lines has not been found in the parent ceramics, but the elements are present. The use of vegetable fibers as tempering and the making of oval, boat-shaped vessels are new items. It has been suggested in the foregoing that perhaps the boat-shaped vessels were copies of wooden bowls carved from small tree trunks. That fiber tempering was practiced in Early Jomon in Japan may or may not be significant.

About 2400 B.C. a remarkably long voyage was made on the Atlantic coast of the Americas. The point of origin is not known, but it was probably within a few hundred miles of the Isthmus of Panama. It should be a small coastal circular village where a broader spectrum of Valdivia ceramic features was manufactured than at Puerto Hormiga, but which shared with this latter complex the practice of mixing vegetable fibers with the pottery clay. The route probably passed through the straits of Yucatán, around western Cuba, through the Florida straits, and northward to the mouth of the Savannah River. The Gulf Stream would certainly have assisted, and may have been the reason that a landing was not made on the nearer coasts of the Gulf of Mexico.

On offshore islands, islands in the Savannah River, and on old channels now changed to swamp, some 20 or more characteristic small circular compact settlements were founded, and shell middens began to accumulate. At least eight villages were ring-shaped. Which and how many localities were established by colonists, and which may have been occupied by local people in process of acculturation is not known. At any rate, undecorated pottery underlies decorated in some deposits. In others, notably the type site, decorated sherds are found in the bottom levels.

Except for the fiber tempering, in which it resembles Puerto Hormiga, the Stallings Island pottery shapes and decorations are remarkably similar to a small part of the Valdivia assemblage. The former include deep simple bowls and similar bowls with sharply inturned rims. Decorations are lines incised parallel to the rim with punctations spaced in them, horizontal wide drag-and-jab lines sometimes made with a double-pointed tool and arranged in panels, zig-zag lines, narrow incisions arranged horizontally in panels, careless crosshatching, and point punctations sometimes arranged in panels. In a few examples, rim decoration differs from that on the vessel body. More complex engraved decorations on the heads of the associated bone pins resemble Valdivia incised ceramic designs.

The stone artifacts in these early Savannah area sites are typical of the late phase of the Archaic culture that extended over the eastern United States at 2500 B.C. These include stemmed projectile points, "bannerstone" atlatl weights, and grooved stone axes. Apparently, there was close contact with the preexisting population.

The method of burial found by Claflin (1931)— skeletons flexed in small pits with very little grave goods—conforms to the usual Southeastern Archaic pattern. However, in so far as could be judged, the skeletons themselves do not. It is now well known that the Late Archaic and preceramic population was dolichocephalic. Claflin (op. cit., pp. 43–44) states that despite the fragmentary nature of the bones of some 80 burials uncovered, "it can be said in general that the Stallings Island people were brachycephalic and did not as a rule practice cranial deformation." Also somewhat remarkable for the time and place is an adult skull fragment showing circular trephination in the parietal region. The first stages of healing had occurred before the patient succumbed, according to Hooton (in Claflin, op. cit., p. 45).

No trephination has been found in the limited cranial material from the early Ecuadorian sites. To the south the first adequate sample of human crania of an early date has been reported by Engel (1963, pp. 10, 67–69) from late preceramic deposits in the Valley of Asia. The date is before 1200 B.C., but apparently well within the time limits of the ceramic phases. Fifty skulls were studied. They have tabular deformation, and two have been trephined, one of them twice.

It was also at this early date, about 2300 B.C., that the art of pottery-making arrived in the highlands of central Mexico, where MacNeish (1964) has reported simple, crude "crumbly" ceramics in the Purrón Phase (2300–1500 B.C.) in Tehuacán Valley. He (op. cit., p. 536) states: "The pottery, the earliest thus far found in Mesoamerica, has the same vessel forms as the stone bowls and ollas of the previous period. This pottery may not be the first modeled in Mexico, but only an imitation of still earlier pottery (yet unfound) in some other areas." This seems to be a very astute guess, and the source of such influence should be a coastal locality inhabited by seafaring people who had brought the techniques from the coasts of northwestern South America. Whether Brush's (1965) discovery of initial ceramics above nonceramic levels at Puerto Marquez near Acapulco, with a date of 2440 ±140 B.C., represents such a colony is uncertain; forms include the highland "tecomate" or neckless olla, suggesting influence from the highlands rather than the reverse.

Probably the spread of the knowledge of ceramic technology inland from a colony on one of the coasts of Mexico was a diffusion process, not the direct movement of groups of people such as is postulated for the coastal settlements. Already established in the highlands were populations who, some two millenia earlier, had begun to improve their lot as typical Desert pattern collectors of wild seeds by selecting and intentionally planting superior varieties. This experimentation with wild foods seems to have been widespread in the Late Archaic of the Americas. The domestication of principally root-type food plants in

Peru has been mentioned. Just when wild plant collectors become agriculturalists is a matter of the degree of dependence placed on cultivated plants. The people of the central Mexican highlands were not full-fledged agriculturalists in 2300 B.C., but in addition to canavalia, beans, and probably pumpkins, they had developed a primitive maize past the point where it had crossed with the wild grass, teocentli. By 1500 B.C. these and additional plants, among them cucurbits, amaranth, chili, avocado, zapote, and cotton, permitted major dependence on agriculture.

These highland Mesoamericans already had a tradition of containers in the form of stone vessels carved into three distinctive shapes. One was a globular jar without a neck, or as the modern Mexican name indicates, a gourd-like vessel or "tecomate." Another was a bowl or pan-like vessel with flat base and low slightly outslanting side walls. These may also have been carved in wood, in view of the fact that wooden flat-base pans are still in use in the Coatzacoalcos River region of southern Veracruz. Simple bowls were the third shape. When the diluted and filtered knowledge of ceramics reached the emerging highland agriculturalists, pottery began to be manufactured in these traditional forms. A fourth form was a small, crude, wide-mouth olla, possibly a poor imitation of the Valdivia olla. Decoration was not applied.

By 1500 B.C. or the beginning of the Ajalpan Phase in Tehuacán, ceramic technology had achieved a higher level of competence, agriculture had advanced, and certain unique Mesoamerican vessel forms had spread to Florida in North America and to central Peru. There is evidence that maize agriculture was a prominent factor in this diffusion, particularly to Peru. One supporting item is the fact that the typical Mexican mano and metate made a temporary intrusion into both Peru and the Mississippi Valley. These container forms and maize agriculture also became associated with the first wave of highly organized and demanding religion to sweep the Americas.

In 2100 B.C., the association of ceramics with full-fledged agriculture and the building of even modest ceremonial centers was centuries in the future. The Monagrillo village, established on a peninsula in what is now a filled-in arm of Parita Bay on the Pacific coast of Panama, was clearly the home of people dependent on the sea. Bowl forms, red slip, and decorations made by engraved lines, excising, and rectilinear motifs were Valdivia-related. However, the Mesoamerican neckless jar or tecomate was also present as a minor shape, suggesting that by 2100 B.C. it had begun to spread southward along the Pacific coast.

By 1800 B.C., neckless jars had become the principal form of the Barlovento Phase, which replaced Puerto Hormiga on the north coast of Colombia. These have bands of wide-line incised decorations in rectilinear and curvilinear motifs around the mouth. Barlovento is also a village that was arranged in a crude circle.

At this time (1800 B.C.), small settlements appeared along the Peruvian coast. The San Juan Phase of Tumbes has pottery decorations featuring horizontal incised lines broken so that they form panels, large punctations zoned by broad incised lines, and applique fillets, all Valdivia-derived decorations. At the mouths of the Piura and Chira rivers, further to the south, the poorly known Negritos Phase shows Valdivia ceramic resemblances.

During this long stretch of time from 3000 to 1200 B.C., many of the Archaic peoples of the north Peruvian coast continued their former way of life, showing little inclination to adopt the blessing of pottery available a few hundred miles to the north in Ecuador, as well as at rare settlements nearer at hand. They did acquire cotton, and two carved gourds found by Bird (1962) in Huaca Prieta preceramic levels have Valdivia rectangular face decorative motifs. Collection of seafood and the rather casual cultivation of cotton, bottle gourds, squash, achira (*Canna edulis*), and several varieties of beans, provided the subsistence.

At about 1800 B.C. ceramics reached the central highlands of Peru, where people were already living in masonry apartment house-like villages. The earliest pottery is by no means primitive, and while the wide-line incised decorations have rectilinear motifs reminiscent of Valdivia, they are not such exact copies as those found in coastal colonies. Also, the earliest Kotosh ceramics show resemblances to a quite different portion of the Valdivia complex than do the coastal colonies cited above. Here, it was the wide-line incised and zoned-hatched motifs that were adopted. The small wide-mouth pot and the open bowls may well be copies of Valdivia forms, but there are two additional shapes not found in the Ecuadorian sequence. One is the large globular tecomate with scraped and crudely polished surfaces and curving (looped and arched) wide-line decoration about the mouth. The second is the flat-base pan with slightly outflaring sides. This latter has the smaller diameter and relatively higher sides characteristic of the Andean version of this form.

Exactly how these two vessel shapes of Mesoamerican origin became part of the Kotosh complex is not clear. They occur in the earliest ceramic complexes on the central and north Peruvian coasts, but the full range of Valdivia-derived decoration represented at Kotosh is lacking. Also, for the most part, the radiocarbon dates are too late. Meggers, Evans, and Estrada (1965, p. 175) have suggested that possibly these influences entered Peru via the Andes. Some vessels have pitcher-like spouts, as at Tlatilco in Mexico, but this does not become a popular American feature. Similar spouts are common in Japan at this time.

At about 2000 B.C. a second group of people landed on the Guayas coast of Ecuador, bringing with them the Machalilla culture. These were also round-headed people, but they introduced a custom apparently unknown earlier in the Americas. This was the practice of deforming the skulls of babies by applying pressure to the back of the head and to the frontal region. This somewhat bizarre method of beautification in varied forms was to become the hallmark of the people having the highest developed civilizations in the Americas: the Inca, Maya, and Aztec. The custom spread into North America to the Pueblo peoples of the Southwest, and the Mississippian peoples of the East. In the Amazon Basin, some remote tribes still continue the practice.

The Machalilla villages were placed along the same stretch of coast already occupied by the Valdivia people. These newcomers also subsisted on products of the sea and left small circular to ovoid shell middens. A remarkable fact is that in spite of the close proximity of the two peoples, and apparently peaceful relations, their ceramic traditions maintained their complete individuality for some 500 years (2000–1500 B.C.).

Machalilla ceramics were on about the same level of competence as the Valdivia ones, and their distinctive shapes and decorations were to produce a marked effect on later traditions. Shapes included composite silhouette bowls, bottles with straight necks, and stirrup-spout bottles. Decorations were principally applied after the vessel surface was polished and hard. The engraved designs, referred to here as the "Ayangue tradition," featured hatched and cross-hatched triangles, squares, diamonds, and bands of parallel lines in simple but characteristic slanting arrangements. Simple angular motifs engraved with a double-pointed tool are also part of this tradition. The other principal decoration of the Machalilla Phase is red paint applied in simple designs on natural vessel surfaces, which were then polished causing the paint to smear.

The origin of the Machalilla people and their distinctive pottery is not known at present. Similar ceramics in early Mesoamerican complexes all date after 1500 B.C., at least 500 years too late to be ancestral. In the engraving technique, some decorative motifs, and some simple vessel forms, Machalilla has a basic similarity to Valdivia. Possibly it represents a second colonizing venture from some unknown point

on the coast of Asia. A seafaring tradition need not have been confined to the Japanese Islands.

At about 2000 B.C. or shortly thereafter, a second colonization by pottery-making people seems to have occurred on the south Atlantic coast of North America. Evidence is centered in a series of deep shell middens spaced along the shores of the St. Johns River, in what is now the state of Florida. Like the Stallings Island settlements 150 miles to the north, established some 400 years earlier, the crude pottery that was first deposited in these middens was tempered with plant fiber. A similar developmental sequence also prevails, in that plain pottery is the first to appear (in some middens at least), and this was followed, perhaps from 1800 to 1600 B.C., by decorated types.

These general parallels exhaust the similarities between the two complexes. After an initial period in which the only decoration resembles that of the Barlovento Phase of Colombia, the varied Orange decorations are clearly derived from the Ayangue tradition of Machalilla. The makers of the Orange ceramic did their best to achieve a polished surface finish comparable to the model, and succeeded remarkably well considering the nature of the fabric. The dominant vessel shape, however, is not one found in the early Ecuadorian Formative. It is instead the Mesoamerican flat-base pan, which here was sometimes made square instead of circular.

As with the Stallings Island immigrant group, it is necessary to postulate an undiscovered way-station, perhaps on the Caribbean coast of Central America, where the traits of fiber tempering, the Barlovento decorative motifs, and the characteristic vessel shape were acquired.

Orange and Stallings Island coexisted on the southern Atlantic coast only 150 miles apart for 1,500 years (2000–500 B.C.) and neither ceramic complex seems to have had the least effect on the other. This isolationism is directly comparable to that of the Valdivia and Machalilla ceramic complexes on the coast of Ecuador between 2000 and 1500 B.C. It is quite evident, however, that the Orange potters were not cut off from stylistic trends occurring to the south. After 1300 B.C., they began to provide their pan-shaped vessels with wide flat lips decorated with the straight-line motifs fashionable at this time in Mesoamerica and northern South America. They also adopted the angular zoned-hatch motifs that became popular there at about the same time.

If the original group of Machalilla people did follow the Valdivia group to the coast of Ecuador, this sequence of events appears to have been repeated several generations later in migrations to the south Atlantic coast of North America.

Between the initial settlement and about A.D. 500, there seems to have been only a limited diffusion of the two fiber-tempered ceramic traditions in the Southeast. The Stallings Island complex probably did not spread more than 100 miles from the Savannah River region. Orange is thinly dispersed over the northern half of the Florida Peninsula as far south as Indian River. There does, however, seem to have been a colony of people with Orange tradition ceramics established on the Fourche Maline River in what is now the eastern part of the state of Oklahoma.

A few centuries after 1500 B.C., the American cultures received a shock that was to change their character profoundly. This was the sudden introduction of a religio-political system demanding great public works. It is not known with certainty where this first appeared, but the Olmec region on the Gulf coast of Mexico seems to be the best guess. At least, it was here that a remarkable ceremonial complex, infinitely advanced over anything else in the Americas at that date, had developed by 1200 B.C. Appearance of organized religion marks the end of what is here called the Colonial Formative and the start of the Theocratic Formative Period.

As a result of recent excavations at the San Lorenzo site and new series of radiocarbon dates, Coe, Diehl, and Stuiver (1967) have concluded that the peak of Olmec art with its monumental stone carvings did not occur toward the end of the phase, but was already flourishing between 1200 and 800 B.C. New dates for the La Venta site support a similar time range.

We are in ignorance as to what sparked the Olmec civilization. Some have speculated that the cultivation of maize, spread down from the Mexican plateau, provided an adequate subsistence base, and the development of such a sophisticated culture was a normal and inevitable result. This seems unlikely for several reasons. First, the seasonally hot and humid jungles of the Coatzacoalcos River are a most unlikely environment. Most of the later civilizations reached their highest development in the more temperate mountain valleys. Secondly, pre-Olmec cultural phases are not known on the coast, but have been well studied by MacNeish and his associates in Tehuacán Valley (in Byers, ed., 1967–), a short distance inland. In this sequence there is no hint of earlier developmental stages that would lead to the unique features of Olmec.

The third argument against the independent, local development of Olmec is an example of circular reasoning. Instances of the spontaneous and independent invention of cultural items, such as ceramics, are becoming increasingly rare. It now seems that they exist only where archeologists have not yet discovered the steps that led up to the event. Experience thus argues against the probability of the spontaneous development of Olmec ceremonialism.

Exotic elements in the Olmec culture include the construction of complex ceremonial centers, involving rectangular, conical, and "linear" mound arrangements precisely engineered and accurately oriented. The principal mound at La Venta is 80 m. high and has the form of a fluted cone. It does not seem to be a temple base and its primary purpose is unknown. Colored earth was used in different stages of mound construction, and elaborate offerings were made. Huge basalt blocks weighing up to 20 tons were transported 80 miles, carved into full round baby-faced heads, and set up in the ceremonial plazas. When the San Lorenzo site was abandoned about 800 B.C., dozens of statues of a variety of forms were buried.

The La Venta site, larger than San Lorenzo, has a similar basic plan. Orientation of this and another Olmec site is 8 degrees west of true north. Pavements in the form of jaguar masks appear to have been intentionally buried and ceremonial caches of jade carvings, and particularly celts, were encountered arranged symmetrically on the center line of the site.

A mound at the north end of La Venta had been erected over a tomb made of columnar basalt. This early example of tomb building was to be followed in later centuries by wood, adobe, or stone tombs for important personages in the Maya area, in Colombia, and in the Mississippi Valley. Principal burials were covered by cinnabar, and the bones of juveniles suggest child sacrifice, also a practice of the Mississippi Valley Hopewell Phase.

It was the Olmec who provided the Maya with the long count cyclical calendar. It should be mentioned (if with a casually skeptical air), that the initial date for this device is 3113 B.C. (Morley, 1946, p. 284), rather close to the estimated date of the first appearance of ceramics in the Americas.

Small carvings in jade and other rare types of stone, baby-faced figurines, earspools, beads, representations of animal teeth and claws, and a variety of other ornaments are among the outstanding art objects produced in pre-Columbian America. This is also the time and place of the first appearance of two animal deities that continued to dominate the American pantheon for centuries. These were the jaguar or cat god, and a rapacious bird. Mirrors, finger rings, panpipes, flat and cylindrical stamps appear at this time. Olmec figurines of fired clay show that cranial deformation was extensively practiced. In addition to the baby-faced representation, there are men wearing neat Van Dyke beards. Bearded figurines are late in the phase.

While the traits cited are new, most of the Olmec ceramic complex is not. In addition to the Mesoamerican flat-base pan and tecomate shapes, it includes traits derived from both the Valdivia and Machalilla ceramic traditions. In vessel shapes, these are composite silhouette bowls, ring bases, bottles, and wide-mouth ollas. In decoration, they include broad-line incising, engraving with Ayangue tradition motifs, excision, rocker stamping, and differential polishing. Some vessels have white slip, while bowls of reddish brown or black ware have light colored oxidized rims; however, tripod pots with both long and short legs, highly polished black ware, and the complex negative technique of ceramic decoration are new.

Shortly after 1500 B.C., a unique pottery decoration appears briefly on the Pacific coast of Guatemala in the Ocós Phase. A cord or fabric textured surface was first produced. Broad incised lines were then drawn to outline zones. Finally, the texturing was erased within the line bordered zones with a polishing tool. This technique for making zoned decoration did not spread, so far as available evidence indicates. It is remarkably similar to what J. E. Kidder (1957, pp. 123, 149, fig. 26) calls zoned or erased cord impressed in the Horinouchi ceramic style of central Japan.

Most Mesoamerican specialists now agree that Olmec, with its vigorous art and emphasis on ceremonialism, was a principal ancestor for both Maya and highland Mexican civilization. Apparently, it also had a profound effect on cultures in both North and South America on the same time level (1200–500 B.C.). People in the Mississippi Valley and Peru received the blessings of maize agriculture during this period, but in turn paid the price of being saddled with ceremonial systems that must have absorbed just about all the spare time gained by the acquisition of a more efficient and reliable food source.

Some archeologists have been reluctant to accept indirect evidence for the practice of maize agriculture. Yet when people begin to establish sizable villages back from the coast in terrain eminently suited for cultivation, as they did in Ecuador after 1500 B.C., it seems logical to presume that this is the point at which they adopted the subsistence pattern known to have prevailed through the following centuries. The simultaneous appearance of other Mesoamerican traits, particularly metates and manos, strengthens the assumption that maize had been added to the list of cultivated plants native to the northern Andean region.

Finds of preserved cobs show that maize arrived on the north coast of Peru about 1400 B.C., to be followed two centuries later by the first ceramics, which in-corporated a very modest and limited selection of applique and other decorations from the Valdivia tradition. It is notable, however, that the two prominent vessel forms were Mesoamerican in origin: the flat-base pan and the tecomate.

As is shown by a realistic drawing of an ear of corn and the appearance of metates and manos, maize arrived at the highland site of Kotosh about 1000 B.C., 800 years after the beginning of pottery manufacture. This obviously was not the beginning of agriculture for this region, which has an impressive list of plant domesticates to its credit, including the potato.

It is a long way from the Olmec area of southern Mexico to the coast and highlands of Peru, where the remarkable Chavín culture phase flourished from 800 to about 200 B.C., but the evidence suggests that there was direct communication that had little or no immediate effect on the lives of the people between. While the respective dates (1200–500 B.C. and 800–200 B.C.) suggest that influences flowed from the Mexican center to Peru, the Chavín people were not passive imitators of Olmec, but developed vigorous modification of the basic patterns as the new features spread over northern Peru. The precise steps by which Chavín developed are not yet known, but it apparently crystallized rather rapidly.

The pyramids built in some of the coastal valleys for temple bases were modest affairs. In the valleys of Nepeña and Casma, however, the sites of Cerro Blanco, Moxeke, Sechín, and Pallka were large stepped pyramids decorated with nitches containing sculptured figures or with large stone slabs carved in bas-relief. Most remarkable is the pyramid temple of Chavín de Huántar, which has given its name to the culture. Located in the central highlands, this is a complex stepped pyramid faced with cut stone, provided with stairways, and decorated with carved stone heads that project from the walls. Buildings, courts with standing carved stele, and a complex of subsurface galleries are notable features of this structure. While the date of these buildings within the Chavín Phase is not known, the sculptural detail, as well as accompanying ceramics, identify them with this culture. The emphasis in Chavín constructions is on the pyramid rather than the arrangement of mound structures about courts as in Olmec. This differential emphasis continued in succeeding cultural phases in both regions.

The baby-faced individual is not present in Chavín sculpture, which features the jaguar with the canine teeth prominently displayed and birds usually identified as condors. These two animals have relatively minor roles in Olmec. The third animal, which later became prominent in Mesoamerican art, is common in Chavín, but rare in Olmec. This is the serpent.

Superior engineering skill is evident in the constructions in both regions. The San Lorenzo site (Olmec) and Chavín de Huántar are both precisely oriented with the cardinal directions.

Resemblances of the Chavín ceramic style to pottery of this time level in Mesoamerica, particularly at the Tlatilco Cemetery, have been cited by Porter (1953, pp. 74–79) and later writers. While some of the shared traits may derive from the common ceramic heritage, the simultaneous appearance of heavy curvilinear version of the wide-line incised tradition and the extensive modeling of vessel bodies into human, animal, and vegetable representations, suggest a reestablishment of communications.

In the preceding pages, several traits have been cited that seemed to have spread rapidly through the Americas on the 1000 to 1 B.C. time level, and then for the most part to have disappeared or changed form radically. Items that arrive with the Chavín horizon in Peru and are also found in Olmec include a lapidary industry represented in beads and small pendant ornaments made of hard, rare stone, sandstone saws for manufacturing these items, finger rings, mirrors ground and polished from one piece of black stone with both flat and concave faces, pulley-shaped earspools, mosaic work (jade plaques in Olmec, turquoise in Chavín), roller and flat stamps, and several ceramic features such as rocker stamping zoned by broad incised lines forming curvilinear realistic motifs, and red slip treated in a similar fashion.

Neither the Olmec nor the Chavín art style was formalized and repetitive, unlike those which developed later in both Mesoamerica and Peru. Both emphasized feline motifs. There was a wide range of variation, within stylistic limits; stone carving in the round tended to be realistic, if imaginative. The same was true for modeling in ceramics; there was little repetition. Heine-Geldern (1959a, b) has pointed out both stylistic and motif resemblances to the contemporary Middle and Late Chou Period art of China, and an Asiatic origin for this entire new religious complex is not to be ruled out.

The vigor of the Chavín culture is demonstrated by the short space of time in which it spread over a greater part of the Peruvian highlands and coast. Geographically it covered much more territory than the Olmec florescence in Mexico. The minor extent to which the ceramics and other features were modified indicates that it was accepted as a markedly new and superior block of cultural features; apparently nothing existed that offered successful competition. There is little evidence of military construction, suggesting that the adoption was voluntary. This is in marked contrast to the warfare that characterized the later pan-Peruvian cultural horizons: the Huari or Tiahuanaco, and the Inca.

Chavín is now recognized as the principal base for the later developments of civilization in Peru. The construction of ceremonial centers continued, the pyramids became larger, but not more tastefully ornamented. The engineering seems to have degenerated. By Tiahuanaco times the people on the coast apparently could measure the sides of their large quadrangles with fair accuracy, but the corners were never right angles, and precise orientation was neglected.

A physical anthropological study of Formative populations, as well as of the practice of cranial deformation, is badly needed. Munizaga (1965) shows that while fronto-occipital deformation initially spread down the Peruvian coast about 1400 B.C., it was followed by the more pronounced cuneiform or Chavín-Cavernas variety about 800–700 B.C. The Chavín variety of deformation resembles the few examples that Munizaga described from the Machalilla Phase. Stewart is cited to the effect that intentional deformation decreases in frequency in later periods on the Peruvian coast.

While skeletal material has not been preserved in the Olmec heartland, some of the figurines show pronounced fronto-occipital deformation (Drucker, 1952, pl. 29), and this same type of deformation is dominant in the Tlatilco Cemetery.

Duque (1964, p. 458) has shown that while the occupation of San Agustín in highland Colombia extended from about 500 B.C. to A.D. 1200, the majority of the remarkable sculptures and mounds with central tombs probably date A.D. 400–900. The comparison that he makes to the megalithic art of both Olmec and Chavín clearly demonstrates affiliations with these two prior traditions.

San Agustín was a ceremonial center but, as Duque (op. cit., pp. 418–421) has pointed out, it is a center or rather a fairly extensive region marked by tombs of the dead, which were buried both in subterranean vaults and in central stone vaults in conical mounds. San Agustín lacks the formal arrangement of Olmec or Chavín sites, and pyramids constructed as temple bases are also absent. However, the conical mounds with central vaults made of stone are reminiscent of Mound A–2 at the Olmec site of La Venta. Monolithic sarcophagi have been found at both sites.

The people of eastern North America began to be relieved of the boredom of spare time about 1200 B.C., when the Poverty Point site was settled in the Lower Mississippi Valley. Although a few coastal shell middens at the mouth of the river incorporated characteristic traits of this culture as early as 1500 B.C., it was only three centuries later that sites began to appear upriver, in terrain better suited for agriculture. A typical Mesoamerican metate and mano suggest that maize and perhaps other Mexican cultigens were added to what apparently was a preexisting primitive agricultural pattern.

The Poverty Point site was a large town, 1207 meters in diameter, built on six concentric ridges forming a slightly curved-sided octagon, perhaps reflecting the simple ring village form established in the Southeast in the earlier Stallings Island Phase (2400–500 B.C.). The tremendous amount of earth moved to form the 18.6 km. of dwelling ridge and to build the 23 m. and 18 m. high bird effigy mounds certainly indicates strict control of the community. The possibility exists that other symmetrically arranged effigies lay to the east and south sides of this town, in terrain now erased by river action.

The accurate engineering of Poverty Point, and the placement of the mounds 8 degrees to the left of true cardinal directions, are reminiscent of the Olmec sites, La Venta and Laguna de los Cerros, which were symmetrically built about center lines that also bear 8 degrees west of true north.

The single 6 meter high conical mound at Poverty Point is slightly apart from the formal arrangement and covers a fire bed that served for the cremation of human remains. A similar conical structure of this date excavated near Baton Rouge, Louisiana, gave clear evidence of a crematory fire on the floor of a rectangular building 9 meters square. Evidence for the practice of cremation is lacking at Olmec sites thus far investigated, and the purpose of the numerous conical mounds of Formative age along the Mexican Gulf coast is not known. As direct burial is relatively rare there, cremation remains a possibility.

A number of the artifacts used by the Poverty Point people are clearly inherited from the preceding Eastern Archaic. These include boatstone and bannerstone types of atlatl weights, bola weights, the so-called gorgets, a variety of projectile point shapes, and the grooved axe. At the same time, the complex has tools and ornaments new for the East, but which show relations to the Formative pattern to the south. Among these are celts, the "pseudo celt" crudely shaped of soft green colored stone, a prepared core and blade industry (which disappears at the end of the Hopewell Phase, A.D. 300), pottery female figurines, sandstone saws, and the use of solid drills for perforating hard stone. Monumental stone work is lacking, but the lapidary industry shows striking parallels to Olmec. Where the early Mexican people employed jade, the harder jasper was generally used at Poverty Point. The Poverty Point obsession with birds, as shown in mound construction, stone vessel decoration, and small jasper beads, was to continue through the later Hopewell Phase.

It was during this millenium preceding the beginning of the present era that several North American Archaic traits spread to South America. These include the grooved axe and the drilling of stone with a tubular, rather than solid bit. Tubular pipes apparently skipped Middle America and diffused directly to northern South America. From there they seem to have spread along with grooved axes east of the Andes to northwest Argentina. Probably the bola, so characteristic of Eastern Archaic, followed the same route. Missing in Mesoamerica, it disappears from eastern North America after A.D. 500.

The rare and crude ceramics of Poverty Point also show relationships to the Formative to the south, although not specifically to the Olmec area. Unzoned rocker stamping is rare but widespread in Mesoamerica at this time. The wide-mouth pot form, four feet, and the practice of punching a row of nodes below the rim with a small tool are somewhat more common in northwestern Colombia. The typical Mesoamerican nodes are on the tecomate jar and are made with the fingers. However, there are a few examples of tecomate-shaped jars with thin walls and the typical comma-shaped lip in the Poverty Point complex.

By 1000 B.C. the practice of mound burial had diffused to the western Great Lakes. Cremation was generally practiced, and when bones were deposited they often were liberally sprinkled with red ochre. This latter practice gave its name to the "Red Paint" culture of New England and the "Red Ochre" burials of Illinois. A similar use of red coloring matter is found in burials of the Olmec Phase of Mexico and the Cupisnique-Chavín of coastal Peru.

The practice of burial mound building (and possibly a rudimentary sort of maize agriculture) seems to have preceded Formative ceramics into the Upper Mississippi Valley. At first, this very well may have been diffusion from the Lower Mississippi, a modest reflection of Poverty Point mound building practices. Tubular pipes, gorgets, birdstones (probably atlatl hooks), and the use of galena cubes were other traits of the period.

Another element already in the area was stimulated to a greater or at least a more obvious expression by the arrival of the new cultural pattern. This was a pottery modeled and compacted by malleating the vessel walls with a paddle. Characteristically, this paddle was wrapped with cords or netting fabric, or had a design carved on it.

Paddled "bag-shaped" pottery seems to have circumpolar distribution. It is oldest in northern Europe, where it is the characteristic Ertebølle vessel of the Mesolithic. In the Lena Basin of nothern Siberia, it first appears in the Early Neolithic (Tolstoy, 1958a). By the Serovo Phase (3000 B.C.), this pottery still has conoidal bases, and is simple and fabric stamped, cordmarked, or dentate stamped, sometimes with a row of nodes punched from the inside. Adzes and gouges of nephrite, stone fish lures, lamellar perforators, compound fishhook shanks, and sandstone shaft straighteners are typical tools.

The remarkable resemblance of these northern Siberian cultural phases of about 5000–3000 B.C. to the American Woodland cultures of the Great Lakes region has caught the attention of several American archeologists (including the writer), and caused them to postulate Bering Strait as the probable route by which ceramics entered the Americas. Increased chronological information and adequate radiocarbon dating have required modification of this thesis, but have not negated it entirely. It now appears that at least two major ceramic traditions existed in Asia, and that before 3000 B.C. both had influenced the Japanese Islands (Fairservis, 1959, pp. 88–91). The paddle-stamped northern tradition has just been described. Cordmarking and punched-out nodes from this tradition entered into the Jomon complex of the northern Japanese Islands. The southern tradition consisted of coiled, predominantly plain, incised, punctated, and later painted wares in olla, bowl, and bottle forms. This latter was the principal source of the Valdivia and Machalilla ceramics which played the dominant role in early American ceramic history.

The knowledge of ceramic history in the Bering Strait region extends back only to about 600 B.C., when Norton Check-stamped pottery was being made. Still, it appears probable that elements of the paddle-molded bag-shaped Arctic pottery and some accompanying traits had passed that way several centuries earlier, for they were in the Great Lakes-New England region when southern influences began to arrive about 1000 B.C.

Once awakened and stimulated by the arrival of agriculture, the Woodland pottery tradition rapidly became popular and dominant in the region north of the Ohio River, and with only two temporary invasions of the southern plain ware were to remain dominant until the end of aboriginal pottery after A.D. 1700.

Webb and Snow (1945, pp. 310ff) bring out quite clearly the fact that the population of the Adena Phase of the central Ohio River Valley was brachycephalic with high skull vaults, and practiced occipital and fronto-occipital cranial deformation. At about 900 B.C. the sudden appearance of this practically pure population into eastern North America where (with the exception of the Stallings Island group) slender-bodied longheads had been the only type of man, led the authors to postulate a direct migration from Central America, a thesis that Spaulding (1952) supported. The writer considers this hypothesis to be sound, but suggests the Poverty Point Phase of the Lower Mississippi as a way-station. Unfortunately there is, as yet, no evidence as to a Poverty Point physical type.

Traits brought into the Ohio Valley by the Adena people, or which preceded them a century or so by diffusion, include large conical mounds built over cremations on the floors of buildings (rectangular in Poverty Point; sometimes rectangular, but usually circular in Adena), "sacred circles," the celt form of axe, sandstone saws, bird motifs, and very probably, maize agriculture. Other traits of probable Mesoamerican origin not yet found in Poverty Point include tablet-like stamps and finger rings.

Adena ceramics are another element of southern origin. They consist predominantly of crude, plain, flat-based pots, which sometimes have four small feet and small punched-out nodes about the rim. Rare incised decoration resembles a variety of the fiber-tempered Orange ware of Florida, as Griffin has noted. As might be expected, there is a minority of cord- and fabric-marked Woodland ware in these sites; whether it is early or late in the phase is not known.

About 500 B.C. the isolationism of the Stallings Island, Orange, and Poverty Point ceramic complexes was broken down, and the respective techniques began to spread to other parts of the Southeast. Rocker stamping and tetrapodal supports diffused into Florida, while elements of all three ceramic complexes combined in the Lower Mississippi to form the Tchefuncte complex (400–1 B.C.). This breakdown of barriers may have been effected by the arrival of productive maize agriculture, as occurred a thousand years earlier on the coast of Ecuador. The earliest direct evidence of maize in the East, however, dates only a century or so before the beginning of the present era in Ohio and Virginia.

The population of the Tchefuncte Phase was a mixture of the earlier longheaded Archaic peoples and the new broadheaded ones (Snow, in Ford and Quimby, 1945; Collins, 1941). Snow (Webb and Snow, 1945, pp. 310–343) found a similar mixture in the Classic Hopewell population of Ohio and approvingly quotes Collins to the effect that this is a blending of the Archaic longheaded populations with the broadheaded people who practiced deformation and entered the Southeast from Mexico. Evidently the endogamy that characterized the Adena population started breaking down about 500 B.C., when this formerly "pure" group started mixing with the local population.

By 400 B.C. the Poverty Point Phase had disappeared from the Lower Mississippi to be replaced by the unspectacular Tchefuncte, which blends the Poverty Point, Stallings Island, and Orange ceramic traditions. Our interest consequently moves to the Upper Mississippi where the Hopewell culture was developing. At the same time the Adena culture was becoming established in the Ohio Valley, the Central Basin version of Early Hopewell was appearing in Illinois. Ceramic features such as nodes punched from the interior, dentate stamping arranged in panels, and incising of the Orange-Tchefuncte tradition were being placed on Woodland-shaped vessels with cord and fabric-marked bodies. Presumably, there was also a mixture of native and intrusive populations.

About 200 B.C. the fully developed Hopewell culture replaced Adena in what is now the state of Ohio, and began the 300-year climax that was to influence the entire eastern United States. Mound groups were still isolated ceremonial centers, but extensive geometric earthworks were built. Important burials were placed in log tombs and provided with rich grave goods, which included items traded from distant places, like conch shells, obsidian, grizzly bear teeth, mica, and copper ornaments. The finding of children in tombs with a bundle of bones from an adult suggests human sacrifice.

The Hopewell tombs are reminiscent of the basalt-log tomb at La Venta, the log tombs at Kaminaljuyú, and the stone vaults in the mounds at San Agustín in Colombia. Earspools and finger rings made of copper are Mesoamerican traits introduced during the earlier Adena Phase. Mirrors of mica and panpipes jacketed with copper are confined to Hopewell. Panpipes are found on this time level on the Gulf coast of Mexico and coastal Ecuador, and later became popular in the Andean region, but despite their abundance in eastern North America from 100 B.C. to A.D. 300, they did not subsequently continue in use. Another Mesoamerican trait that vanished from North America after the close of the Hopewell Phase is the striking of blades from prepared cores, which was introduced at 1200 B.C. into Poverty Point.

Hopewell thus appears to be a several centuries delayed efflorescence of the Olmec-Chavín religio-political stimulus. While the latter cultures provided the foundations in their respective regions on which the later civilizations were constructed, Hopewell was submerged by the awakened Woodland cultures about A.D. 300, and the prehistory of most of the eastern United States entered a very dreary phase until the arrival of fresh Mesoamerican influences at A.D. 900, this time coming overland through Texas.

Willey and Phillips (1958) have outlined the later history of the Americas. In Mesoamerica and the Andean region of Peru and Bolivia, the Middle Formative cultural wave gave rise to vigorous developments in the early centuries of the present era. Regional specialization rapidly occurred, strong political control developed, and arts entered a Classic stage. By A.D. 800 to 1000 a warfare pattern had developed, cultural emphasis moved from religious to more secular interests, and small empires began to rise. These in turn were forcibly merged into larger units, a process that the Spanish terminated in the early 16th century when they destroyed the "barbaric" civilizations of the Aztec and Inca.

This then, is how a part of the available evidence on the history of the spread of Early Neolithic or Formative culture traits in the Americas appears to the writer. There doubtless are many errors of fact and interpretation, but the major outline seems fairly clear, although it is certain that a substantial number of American archeologists will not agree. Particularly will they be repelled by the fact that a considerable part of this interpretation reinforces the thesis that a substantial part of American high culture development is based on the trans-Pacific importation of knowledge, techniques, and undoubtedly people.

These gentlemen, who prefer the traditional concept that American civilization arose independently of Old World developments, or that Aztec and Inca civilizations had little common foundation, should be reminded that an alternative explanation was provided a century ago by Adolf Bastian, who believed that "the psychic unity of mankind constantly impelled societies to duplicate one another's ideas" (Lowie, 1937, p. 29). If this is ture, it appears that the Middle Jomon-Valdivia ceramic comparisons

and a number of the other examples cited in this paper support to a remarkable degree the "psychic unity" of mankind.

Archeologists have shown little interest in examining the philosophic bases of their studies. While utilizing the thesis that trait resemblances (in adjacent geographic regions) are evidence for contact, when faced with an unexplainable origin of a trait they have fallen back on independent invention theory.

The origin of American civilizations has a significant bearing on an important anthropological question that remains in debate after a century of development of the discipline. Did man create his culture out of innate capabilities responding to needs and desires, or is culture a superorganic phenomenon that has evolved according to its own laws, with man's role that of a more or less fortunate inheritor, depending on the time and place in which he chanced to live?

Literature Cited

AGRINIER, PIERRE
> 1964. The archaeological burials at Chiapa de Corzo and their furniture. Papers of the New World Archaeological Foundation, no. 16, publ. no. 12. Brigham Young University, Provo, Utah.

ALCINA FRANCH, JOSÉ
> 1965. Manual de arqueología americana. Aguilar, S.A. de ediciones. Madrid.

ANGULO VALDÉS, CARLOS
> 1962a. Evidencias de la serie Barrancoide en el norte de Colombia. Revista Colombiana de Antropología, vol. 11, pp. 73–88. Bogotá.
> 1962b. Evidence of the Barrancoid series in north Colombia. *In* The Caribbean: Contemporary Colombia, edited by A. Curtis Wilgus, pp. 35–46. University of Florida Press, Gainesville.
> 1963. Cultural development in Colombia. *In* Aboriginal cultural development in Latin America: An interpretative review, edited by Betty J. Meggers and Clifford Evans. Smithsonian Misc. Coll., vol. 146, no. 1, pp. 55–66. Washington, D.C.

ARMILLAS, PEDRO
> 1948. A sequence of cultural development in Mesoamerica. *In* A reappraisal of Peruvian archaeology, edited by Irving Rouse. Society for American Archaeology Memoir 4, pp. 105–111.
> 1964. Northern Mesoamerica. *In* Prehistoric man in the New World, edited by Jesse D. Jennings and Edward Norbeck, pp. 291–329. University of Chicago Press, Chicago.

BAKER, FRANK; GRIFFIN, JAMES B.; MORGAN, RICHARD G.; NEUMANN, GEORG K.; and TAYLOR, JAY L. B.
> 1941. Contributions to the archaeology of the Illinois River Valley. Transactions of the American Philosophical Society, vol. 32, part 1. Philadelphia.

BAUDEZ, CLAUDE F.
> 1963. Cultural development in lower Central America. *In* Aboriginal cultural development in Latin America: An interpretative review, edited by Betty J. Meggers and Clifford Evans. Smithsonian Misc. Coll., vol. 146, no. 1, pp. 45–54. Washington, D.C.

BELL, R. E.
> 1960. Evidence of a fluted point tradition in Ecuador. American Antiquity, vol. 26, pp. 102–106.

BENNETT, JOHN W.
> 1945. Archaeological explorations in Jo Daviess County, Illinois. University of Chicago Publications in Anthropology: Archeology Series. Chicago.

BENNETT, WENDELL C.
> 1936. Excavations in Bolivia. American Museum of Natural History, Anthropological Papers, vol. 35, pp. 329–507. New York.
> 1939. Archaeology of the north coast of Peru. American Museum of Natural History, Anthropological Papers, vol. 37, part 1. New York.

BENNETT, WENDELL C.—Continued

1944a. The north highlands of Peru: Excavations in the Callejón de Huaylas and at Chavín de Huántar. American Museum of Natural History, Anthropological Papers, vol. 39, part 1. New York.

1944b. Archaeological regions of Colombia: A ceramic survey. Yale University Publications in Anthropology, no. 30. New Haven.

1946. The archeology of the central Andes. *In* Handbook of South American Indians, edited by Julian H. Steward. Bureau of American Ethnology Bulletin, no. 143, vol. 2, pp. 61–147. Washington, D.C.

1948. The Peruvian co-tradition. Memoirs of the Society for American Archaeology, no. 4, pp. 1–7.

1950. The Gallinazo group: Virú Valley, Peru. Yale University Publications in Anthropology, no. 43. New Haven.

BENNETT, WENDELL C., and BIRD, JUNIUS B.

1949. Andean culture history. American Museum of Natural History, Handbook series, no. 15. New York.

BERGER, RAINER; GRAHAM, JOHN A; and HEIZER, ROBERT F.

1967. A reconsideration of the age of the La Venta site. *In* Studies in Olmec archaeology. Contributions of the University of California Archaeological Research Facility, no. 3, pp. 1–24. Berkeley.

BIRD, JUNIUS

1948. Preceramic cultures in Chicama and Virú. *In* A reappraisal of Peruvian archaeology, assembled by Wendell C. Bennett. Society for American Archaeology Memoir, no. 4, pp. 21–28.

1962. Art and life in old Peru: An exhibition. Curator, vol. 2, pp. 147–210. New York.

BIRKET-SMITH, KAJ

1937. The composite comb in North America. Ethnos, vol. 2, pp. 33–37. Stockholm.

BLUHM, ELAINE A., editor

1960. Indian mounds and villages in Illinois. Illinois Archaeological Survey Bulletin, no. 2. University of Illinois, Urbana.

BLUHM, ELAINE A., and BEESON, WILLIAM J.

1960. The excavation of three Hopewell mounds at the Caterpillar Tractor Company. *In* Indian Mounds and Villages in Illinois, edited by Elaine A. Bluhm. Illinois Archaeological Survey Bulletin, no. 2, pp. 1–24. University of Illinois, Urbana.

BROWN, CHARLES BARRINGTON

1926. On stone implements from northwest Peru. Man, vol. 26, no. 6, pp. 97–101, London.

BRUSH, CHARLES F.

1965. Pox pottery: Earliest identified Mexican ceramic. Science, vol. 149, pp. 194–195. Washington, D.C.

BULLEN, RIPLEY P.

1953. The famous Crystal River site. Florida Anthropologist, vol. 6, no. 1, pp. 9–37, Florida Anthropological Society.

1955. Stratigraphic tests at Bluffton, Volusia County, Florida. Florida Anthropologist, vol. 8, no. 1, pp. 1–16. Florida Anthropological Society.

1959. The transitional period of Florida. Newsletter, Southeastern Archaeological Conference, vol. 6, pp. 43–53. Chapel Hill.

1961. Radiocarbon dates for Southeastern fiber-tempered pottery. American Antiquity, vol. 27, pp. 104–106.

1963. The earliest pottery in Southeastern United States, 2000–1000 B.C. and its case as an independent invention. VIᵉ Congrès International des Sciences Anthropologiques et Ethnologiques, 1960, volume 2, no. 1, pp. 363–367. Paris.

1966. Stelae at the Crystal River site, Florida. American Antiquity, vol. 31, pp. 861–865.

BULLEN, ADELAIDE K., and RIPLEY P.

1961. The Summer Haven site, St. John's County, Florida. Florida Anthropologist, vol. 14, nos. 1–2, pp. 1–15. Florida Anthropological Society.

BUSHNELL, G. H. S.

1951. The archaeology of the Santa Elena peninsula in south-west Ecuador. Cambridge University Press.

BUTLER, ROBERT R.
1959. Lower Columbia Valley archaeology: A survey and appraisal of some major archaeological resources. Tebiwa: Journal, Idaho State University Museum, vol. 2, pp. 6–24. Pocatello.

BYERS, DOUGLAS S.
1959. The eastern Archaic: Some problems and hypotheses. American Antiquity, vol. 24, pp. 233–256.

BYERS, DOUGLAS S., editor
1967–. The prehistory of the Tehuacán Valley. Vol. 1, Environment and subsistence. Vol. 2, The non-ceramic artifacts. Vols. 3–6, in preparation. University of Texas Press, Austin.

CALDWELL, JOSEPH R., AND HALL, ROBERT L., editors
1964. Hopewellian studies. Illinois State Museum Scientific Papers, vol. 12. Springfield.

CAMPBELL, JOHN M., editor
1962. Prehistoric cultural relations between the Arctic and Temperate zones of North America. Arctic Institute of North America, Technical Paper, no. 11. Washington, D.C.

CARRIÓN CACHOT, REBECA
1948. La cultura Chavín: Dos nuevos colonias: Kuntur Wasi y Ancón. Revista del Museo Nacional de Antropología y Arqueología, vol. 2, no. 1, Primer semestre, pp. 99–172. Lima.

CASO, ALFONSO
1953. New World culture history: Middle America. In Anthropology Today, edited by A. L. Kroeber, et al., pp. 226–237. University of Chicago Press, Chicago.

CLAFLIN, WILLIAM H., JR.
1931. The Stallings Island mound, Columbia County, Georgia. Papers of the Peabody Museum of Archaeology and Ethnology, Harvard University, vol. 14, no. 1, pp. 1–47. Cambridge, Massachusetts.

COE, JOFFRE L.
1952. The cultural sequence of the Carolina Piedmont. In Archaeology of Eastern United States, edited by James B. Griffin. University of Chicago Press, Chicago.
1964. The Formative cultures of the Carolina Piedmont. Transactions of the American Philosophical Society, vol. 54, part 5. Philadelphia.

COE, MICHAEL D.
1960. Archaeological linkages with North and South America at La Victoria, Guatemala. American Anthropologist, vol. 62, pp. 363–393.
1961. La Victoria, an early site on the Pacific coast of Guatemala. Papers of the Peabody Museum of Archaeology and Ethnology, Harvard University, vol. 53. Cambridge, Mass.
1962. An Olmec design on an early Peruvian vessel. American Antiquity, vol. 27, pp. 579–580.
1963. Cultural development in southeastern Mesoamerica. In Aboriginal cultural development in Latin America: An interpretative review, edited by Betty J. Meggers and Clifford Evans. Smithsonian Misc. Coll., vol. 146, no. 1, pp. 27–44. Washington, D.C.
1965. Archaeological synthesis of southern Veracruz and Tabasco. In Handbook of Middle American Indians, vol. 3, part 2, pp. 679–715. University of Texas Press, Austin.
1966. Preliminary report on the first season's work at San Lorenzo Tenochtitlán, Veracruz (mimeographed).

COE, MICHAEL D., AND BAUDEZ, CLAUDE F.
1961. The zoned bichrome period in north western Costa Rica. American Antiquity, vol. 26, pp. 505–515.

COE, MICHAEL D.; DIEHL, RICHARD; AND STUIVER, MIZE
1967. Olmec civilization, Veracruz, Mexico: Dating of the San Lorenzo phase. Science, vol. 155, no. 3768, pp. 1399–1401. Washington, D.C.

COE, MICHAEL D., AND FLANNERY, KENT V.
1967. Early cultures and human ecology in south coastal Guatemala. Smithsonian Contributions to Anthropology, vol. 3. Washington, D.C.

COLE, FAY-COOPER; BELL, ROBERT; BENNETT, JOHN; CALDWELL, JOSEPH; EMERSON, NORMAN; MACNEISH, RICHARD; ORR, KENNETH; and WILLIS, ROGER.
    1951.   Kincaid: A prehistoric Illinois metropolis. University of Chicago Press, Chicago.

COLE, FAY-COOPER, and DEUEL, THORNE
    1937.   Rediscovering Illinois: Archaeological explorations in and around Fulton County. University of Chicago Publications in Anthropology: Archeology Series. Chicago.

COLLIER, DONALD
    1955.   Cultural chronology and changes as reflected in the ceramics of the Virú Valley, Peru. Fieldiana: Anthropology, vol. 43. Chicago Natural History Museum, Chicago.
    1962.   The central Andes. In Courses toward urban life: Archaeological considerations of some cultural alternatives, edited by Robert J. Braidwood and Gordon R. Willey. Viking Publications in Anthropology, no. 32, pp. 165–176. New York.

COLLIER, DONALD, and MURRA, JOHN V.
    1943.   Survey and excavations in southern Ecuador. Field Museum of Natural History, Anthropological Series vol. 35. Chicago.

COLLINS, HENRY B., JR.
    1937.   Archeology of St. Lawrence Island, Alaska. Smithsonian Misc. Coll., vol. 96, no. 1. Washington, D.C.
    1941.   Relationships of an early Indian cranial series from Louisiana. Journal of the Washington Academy of Sciences, vol. 31, no. 4, pp. 145–155. Washington, D.C.

COOPER, JOHN M.
    1941.   Temporal sequence and the marginal cultures. Catholic University of America, Anthropology Series, no. 10. Washington, D.C.

COVARRUBIAS, MIGUEL
    1946.   Mexico south: The isthmus of Tehuantepec. New York.
    1950.   Tlatilco: El arte y la cultura preclásica del valle de Mexico. Cuadernos Americanos, vol. 51, pp. 149–162.

CUBILLOS CHAPARRO, JULIO CÉSAR
    1959.   El Morro de Tulcan (pirámide prehispánica). In Arqueología de Popayán, Cauca-Colombia. Revista Colombiana de Anthropología, vol. 8, pp. 215–357. Bogotá.

CUMMINGS, BRYON
    1933.   Cuicuilco and the archaic cultures of Mexico. University of Arizona Social Science Bulletin, no. 4.

DEJARNETTE, DAVID L.; KURJACK, EDWARD B.; and CAMBRON, JAMES W.
    1962.   Standfield-Worley Bluff Shelter excavations. Journal of Alabama Archaeology, vol. 8, nos. 1 and 2. University of Alabama.

DE LAGUNA, FREDERICA
    1947.   The prehistory of northern North America as seen from the Yukon. Society for American Archaeology Memoir 3.

DEUEL, THORNE, editor
    1952.   Hopewellian communities in Illinois. Illinois State Museum Scientific Papers, vol. 5. Springfield.

DIXON, KEITH A.
    1959.   Ceramics from two preclassic periods at Chiapa de Corzo, Chiapas, Mexico. Papers of the New World Archaeological Foundation, number 5, publication no. 4. Brigham Young University, Provo, Utah.
    1964.   Culinary shoe-pots: The interamerican diffusion of a cooking technique. Actas y Memorias 1, XXXV Congreso Internacional de Americanistas, Mexico, 1962, pp. 579–586. Mexico, D.F.

DRAGOO, DON W.
    1964.   Relationship of the eastern North American burial cult manifestation to Central America and the Old World. Actas y Memorias 1, XXXV Congreso Internacional de Americanistas, Mexico, 1962, pp. 101–111. Mexico, D.F.

DRUCKER, PHILIP
    1943a. Ceramic sequences at Tres Zapotes, Veracruz, Mexico. Bureau of American Ethnology Bulletin, no. 140. Washington, D.C.
    1943b. Ceramic stratigraphy at Cerro de las Mesas, Veracruz, Mexico. Bureau of American Ethnology Bulletin, no. 141. Washington, D.C.

1947. Some implications of the ceramic complex at La Venta. Smithsonian Misc. Coll., vol. 107, no. 8. Washington, D.C.

1952. La Venta, Tabasco: A study of Olmec ceramics and art. Bureau of American Ethnology Bulletin, no. 153. Washington, D.C.

1955. The Cerro de las Mesas offering of jade and other materials. Bureau of American Ethnology Bulletin, no. 157, pp. 25–68. Washington, D.C.

DRUCKER, PHILLIP; HEIZER, ROBERT F.; and SQUIER, ROBERT J.
1959. Excavations at La Venta, Tabasco, 1955. Bureau of American Ethnology Bulletin, no. 170. Washington, D.C.

DUQUE GOMEZ, LUIS
1964. Exploraciones arqueológicas en San Agustín. Revista Colombiana de Antropología, Suplemento no. 1. Bogotá.

EKHOLM, GORDON F.
1944. Excavations at Tampico and Panuco in the Huasteca, Mexico. American Museum of Natural History, Anthropological Papers, vol. 38, part 5, pp. 321–506. New York.

EKHOLM, SUSANNA M.
1966. Mound 30a and the early middle Preclassic ceramic sequence at Izapa, Chiapas, Mexico. Unpublished Masters Thesis, Columbia University, New York.

EMMON, G. T.
1923. Jade in British Columbia and Alaska and its use by the natives. Indian Notes and Monographs, no. 35, Museum of the American Indian, Heye Foundation. New York.

ENGEL, FREDERIC
1956. Curayacu, a Chavinoid site. Archaeology, vol. 9, no. 2, pp. 98–105.

1958. Algunos datos con referencia a los sitios precerámicos de la costa Peruana. Arqueológicas No. 3., Instituto de Investigationes Antropológicas. Museo Nacional de Antropología y Arqueología. Lima.

1963. A preceramic settlement on the central coast of Peru: Asia, unit I. Transactions of the American Philosophical Society, new series, vol. 53, part 3. Philadelphia.

ENGLE, NANCY
1957. Prehistoric human figurines of the eastern United States and their significance. Unpublished Masters Thesis, University of Illinois, Urbana.

ESTRADA, EMILIO
1957. Prehistoria de Manabí. Publicación del Museo Víctor Emilio Estrada, no. 4. Guayaquil.

1958. Las culturas pre-clásicas, formativas o arcaicas del Ecuador. Publicación del Museo Víctor Emilio Estrada, no. 5. Guayaquil.

1961. Nuevos elementos en la cultura Valdivia: Sus posibles contactos transpacíficos. Publicación del Sub-Comité Ecuatoriano de Antropología, Instituto Pan Americano de Geografía e Historia. Guayaquil.

1962. Arqueología de Manabí central. Publicación del Museo Víctor Emilio Estrada, no. 7. Guayaquil.

ESTRADA, EMILIO, and EVANS, CLIFFORD
1963. Cultural development in Ecuador. In Aboriginal cultural development in Latin America: An interpretative review, edited by Betty J. Meggers and Clifford Evans. Smithsonian Misc. Coll., vol. 146, no. 1, pp. 77–88. Washington, D.C.

ESTRADA, EMILIO, and MEGGERS, BETTY J.
1961. A complex of traits of probable transpacific origin on the coast of Ecuador. American Anthropologist, vol. 63, pp. 913–939.

ESTRADA, EMILIO; MEGGERS, BETTY J.; and EVANS, CLIFFORD
1962. Possible transpacific contact on the coast of Ecuador. Science, no. 135, pp. 371–372. Washington, D.C.

1964. The Jambelí culture of south coastal Ecuador. Proceedings of the United States National Museum, vol. 115, no. 3492, pp. 483–558. Washington, D.C.

EVANS, CLIFFORD, and MEGGERS, BETTY J.
1957. Formative period cultures in the Guayas Basin, coastal Ecuador. American Antiquity, vol. 22, pp. 235–247.

EVANS, CLIFFORD; MEGGERS, BETTY J.; and ESTRADA, EMILIO
    1959.   Cultura Valdivia. Publicación del Museo Víctor Emilio Estrada, no. 6. Guayaquil.
FAIRBANKS, CHARLES H.
    1942.   The taxonomic position of Stalling's Island, Georgia. American Antiquity, vol. 7, pp. 223–231.
FAIRSERVIS, WALTER A., JR.
    1959.   The origins of Oriental civilization. The New American Library of World Literature, Inc. New York.
FERGUSON, VERA MASIUS
    1951.   Chronology at South Indian Field, Florida. Yale University Publications in Anthropology, no. 45. New Haven.
FORD, JAMES A.
    1936.   Analysis of Indian village site collections from Louisiana and Mississippi. Department of Conservation, Louisiana Geological Survey, Anthropological Study, no. 2. New Orleans.
    1944.   Excavations in the vicinity of Cali, Colombia. Yale University Publications in Anthropology no. 31. New Haven.
    1949.   Cultural dating of prehistoric sites in Virú Valley, Peru. *In* Surface survey of the Virú Valley, Peru. American Museum of Natural History, Anthropological Papers, vol. 43, part 1, pp. 31–89. New York.
    1951.   Greenhouse: A Troyville-Coles Creek period site in Avoyelles Parish, Louisiana. American Museum of Natural History, Anthropological Papers, vol. 44, part 1. New York.
    1952.   Measurements of some prehistoric design developments in the southeastern states. American Museum of Natural History, Anthropological Papers, vol. 44, part 3. New York.
    1962.   A quantitative method for deriving cultural chronology. Technical Manual I, Dept. of Social Affairs, Pan American Union. Washington, D.C.
    1963.   Hopewell culture burial mounds near Helena, Arkansas. American Museum of Natural History, Anthropological Papers, vol. 50, part 1. New York.
    1966.   Early Formative cultures in Georgia and Florida. American Antiquity, vol. 31, no. 6, pp. 781–799.
FORD, JAMES A.; PHILLIPS, PHILIP; and HAAG, WILLIAM G.
    1955.   The Jaketown site in west-central Mississippi. American Museum of Natural History, Anthropological Papers, vol. 45, part 1. New York.
FORD, JAMES A., and QUIMBY, GEORGE I., JR.
    1945.   The Tchefuncte culture: An early occupation of the Mississippi Valley. Society for American Archaeology Memoir no. 2.
FORD, JAMES A., and WEBB, CLARENCE H.
    1956.   Poverty Point, A late Archaic site in Louisiana. American Museum of Natural History, Anthropological Papers, vol. 46, part 1. New York.
FORD, JAMES A., and WILLEY, GORDON R.
    1940.   Crooks site: A Marksville period burial mound in La Salle Parish, Louisiana. Department of Conservation, Louisiana Geological Survey, Anthropological Study, no. 3. New Orleans.
    1941.   An interpretation of the prehistory of the eastern United States. American Anthropologist, vol. 43, no. 3, pp. 325–363.
FOWLER, MELVIN L.
    1952.   The Clear Lake site: Hopewellian occupation. *In* Hopewellian communities in Illinois, edited by Thorne Deuel. Illinois State Museum Scientific Papers, vol. 5, no. 4, pp. 131–173. Springfield.
    1957.   Rutherford mound, Hardin County, Illinois. Illinois State Museum Scientific Papers, vol. 7, no. 1. Springfield.
    1959a.   Summary report of Modoc Rock Shelter 1952, 1953, 1955, 1956. Illinois State Museum Report of Investigations, no. 8. Springfield.
    1959b.   Modoc Rock Shelter: An early Archaic site in southern Illinois. American Antiquity, vol. 24, pp. 257–270.
    1961.   The early Woodland period. Illinois Archaeology Survey Bulletin, no. 1, pp. 17–20. University of Illinois, Urbana.

FOWLER, MELVIN L., and WINTERS, HOWARD
  1956. Modoc Rock Shelter preliminary report. Illinois State Museum, Report of Investigations, no. 4. Springfield.
GAGLIANO, SHERWOOD M., and SAUCIER, ROGER T.
  1963. Poverty Point sites in southeastern Louisiana. American Antiquity, vol. 28, pp. 320–327.
GARCÍA PAYÓN, JOSÉ
  1950. Restos de una cultura prehistórica encontrados en la región de Zempoala, Veracruz. UNI-VER, Organo de la Universidad Veracruzana, Tomo 2, no. 15, pp. 90–130. Jalapa.
  1966. Prehistoria de Mesoamérica, Excavaciones en Trapiche y Chalahuites, Veracruz, Mexico, 1942, 1951, y 1959. Cuadernos de la Facultad de Filosofía, Letras y Ciencias, Universidad Veracruzana, vol. 31, Jalapa.
GIDDINGS, J. L.
  1964. The archeology of Cape Denbigh. Providence, Rhode Island.
GLADWIN, HAROLD S.
  1937. Independent invention versus diffusion. American Antiquity, vol. 3, no. 2, pp. 156–160.
GLADWIN, HAROLD S.; HAURY, EMIL; SAYLES, E. B.; and GLADWIN, NORA
  1937. Excavations at Snaketown: Material culture. Gila Pueblo Medallion Papers, no. 25. Globe, Arizona.
GOGGIN, JOHN M.
  1948. Some pottery types from central Florida. Gainesville Anthropological Association, Bull. 1 (mimeographed). Gainesville.
  1952. Space and time perspective in northern St. John's archaeology, Florida. Yale University Publications in Anthropology, no. 47. New Haven.
GOGGIN, JOHN M., and SOMMER, FRANK H., III
  1949. Excavations on Upper Matecumbe Key, Florida. Yale University Publications in Anthropology, no. 41. New Haven.
GONZALEZ, ALBERTO REX
  1963. Cultural development in northwestern Argentina. In Aboriginal cultural development in Latin America: An interpretative review, edited by Betty J. Meggers and Clifford Evans. Smithsonian Misc. Coll., vol. 146, no. 1, pp. 103–117. Washington, D.C.
GREEN, F. E.
  1963. The Clovis blades: An important addition to the Llano complex. American Antiquity, vol. 9, pp. 145–165.
GREENGO, ROBERT E.
  1964. Issaquena: An archaeological phase in the Yazoo Basin of the Lower Mississippi Valley. Society for American Archaeology Memoir, no. 18.
GREENMAN, EMERSON F.
  1938. Hopewellian traits in Florida. American Antiquity, vol. 3, pp. 327–332.
GRIFFIN, JAMES B.
  1941. Additional Hopewell material from Illinois. Indiana Historical Society, vol. 11, no. 3. Indianapolis.
  1943. The Fort Ancient aspect: Its cultural and chronological position in Mississippi Valley archaeology. Ann Arbor.
  1945. The significance of the fiber-tempered pottery of the St. John's. Journal of the Washington Academy of Sciences, vol. 35, no. 7, pp. 218–223. Washington, D.C.
  1946. Cultural change and continuity in eastern United States archaeology. In Man in Northeastern North America, edited by Fredrick Johnson. Papers of the Robert S. Peabody Foundation for Archaeology, vol. 33, pp. 37–95. Andover, Mass.
  1947. The Spruce Run earthworks: A forgotten Adena site in Delaware County. Archaeological and Historical Society Quarterly, vol. 56, pp. 188–200. Columbus.
  1952a. Some early and middle Woodland pottery types in Illinois. In Hopewellian communities in Illinois, edited by Thorne Deuel. Illinois State Museum Scientific Papers, vol. 5. Springfield.
  1952b. Culture periods in eastern United States archeology. In Archeology of eastern United States, edited by J. B. Griffin. University of Chicago Press, Chicago.
  1952c. A preview of the ceramic relationships of the Snyders Site, Calhoun County, Illinois. In The Snyders site, Calhoun County, Illinois. The Greater St. Louis Archaeological Society, St. Louis, Missouri.

GRIFFIN, JAMES B.—Continued
  1964.   The northeast Woodlands area. *In* Prehistoric man in the New World, edited by Jesse
            D. Jennings and Edward Norbeck, pp. 223–258, University of Chicago Press,
            Chicago.
GRIFFIN, JAMES B., editor
  1952.   Archeology of eastern United States. University of Chicago Press.
GRIFFIN, JAMES B., and KRIEGER, ALEX D.
  1947.   Notes on some ceramic techniques and intrusions in central Mexico. American An-
            tiquity, vol. 12, pp. 156–168.
GRIFFIN, JOHN W., and SMITH, HALE G.
  1954.   The Cotton site: An archaeological site of early ceramic times in Volusia County,
            Florida. Florida State University Studies in Anthropology. no. 16, pp. 27–60.
            Tallahassee
HAAG, WILLIAM
  1939.   Type description Alexander Incised. News Letter of the Southeastern Archaeological
            Conference, vol. 1, no. 1.
HEIMLICH, MARION DUNLEVY
  1952.   Guntersville Basin pottery. Geological Survey of Alabama, Museum Paper 32. Mont-
            gomery.
HEINE-GELDERN, ROBERT
  1959a. Chinese influences in Mexico and Central America: The Tajín style of Mexico and the
            marble vases from Honduras. Actas del 33rd Congreso Internacional de Ameri-
            canistas, Costa Rica, 1958, pp. 195–206. San José.
  1959b. Representation of the Asiatic tiger in the art of the Chavín culture: A proof of early
            contacts between China and Peru. Actas del 33rd Congreso Internacional de Ameri-
            canistas, Costa Rica, 1958, pp. 321–326. San José.
HEIZER, ROBERT F.
  1964.   The western coast of North America. *In* Prehistoric man in the New World, edited
            by Jesse D. Jennings and Edward Norbeck, pp. 117–148. University of Chicago
            Press, Chicago.
HEIZER, ROBERT F. and DRUCKER, PHILIP
  1968.   The La Venta fluted pyramid. Antiquity, vol. 42, no. 165, pp. 52–56 and pl. 12.
HICKS, FREDERICK, and ROZAIRE, CHARLES E.
  1960.   Mound 13, Chiapa de Corzo, Chiapas, Mexico. Papers of the New World Archaeo-
            logical Foundation, no. 10. Brigham Young University, Provo, Utah.
HOLMES, WILLIAM H.
  1894.   Earthenware of Florida: Collections of Clarence B. Moore. Journal of the Academy
            of Natural Sciences of Philadelphia. vol. 10, part 1, art. 2, pp. 105–128. Philadelphia.
  1903.   Aboriginal pottery of the eastern United States. Bureau of American Ethnology
            Annual Report, vol. 20, pp. 1–120. Washington, D.C.
HUTCHINSON, JOSEPH
  1963.   The history and relationships of the world's cotton. Annual report of the Smithsonian
            Institution 1962, pp. 497–515. Washington, D.C.
ISHIDA, EIICHIRO, et al.
  1960.   Andes, The Report of the University of Tokyo Scientific Expedition to the Andes in
            1958, no. 1. Tokyo.
IZUMI, SEIICHI, and SONO, TOSHIHIKO
  1963.   Andes 2: Excavations at Kotosh, Peru, 1960. University of Tokyo Scientific Expeditions
            to the Andes. Tokyo.
IZUMI, SEIICHI, and TERADA, KAZUO
  1966.   Andes 3: Excavations at Pechiche and Garbanzal, Tumbes Valley, Peru, 1960. Uni-
            versity of Tokyo Scientific Expeditions to the Andes. Tokyo.
JENNINGS, JESSE D.
  1964.   The desert west. *In* Prehistoric man in the New World, edited by Jesse D. Jennings
            and Edward Norbeck, pp. 149–174.
JENNINGS, JESSE D., and NORBECK, EDWARD, editors
  1964.   Prehistoric man in the New World. University of Chicago Press, Chicago.
JIJÓN Y CAAMAÑO, JACINTO
  1951a. Antropología prehispánica del Ecuador. Quito.

1951b. Las civilizaciones del sur de Centro América y el noroeste de Sud América. Papers of the 29th International Congress of Americanists, New York, 1949, pp. 165–172. New York.

KELLAR, J. H.; KELLY, A. R.; and McMICHAEL, E. V.
1962. The Mandeville site in southwest Georgia. American Antiquity, vol. 27, pp. 336–355.

KIDDER, A. V.
1924. An introduction to the study of Southwestern archaeology, with a preliminary account of the excavation at Pecos. Papers, Southwestern Expedition, Phillips Academy, no. 1. Yale University Press, New Haven.
1943. Grooved stone axes from Central America. Carnegie Institution of Washington, Notes on Middle American Archaeology and Ethnology, no. 29. Washington, D.C.

KIDDER, ALFRED V.; JENNINGS, JESSE D.; and SHOOK, EDWIN M.
1946. Excavations at Kaminaljuyú, Guatemala. Carnegie Institution of Washington, Publication no. 561. Washington, D.C.

KIDDER, ALFRED, II
1964. South American high cultures. In Prehistoric man in the New World, edited by Jesse D. Jennings and Edward Norbeck, pp. 451–486. University of Chicago Press, Chicago.

KIDDER, ALFRED, II; LUMBRERAS, LUIS G.; and SMITH, DAVID B.
1963. Cultural development in the central Andes—Peru and Bolivia. In Aboriginal cultural development in Latin America: An interpretative review, edited by Betty J. Meggers and Clifford Evans. Smithsonian Misc. Coll., vol. 146, no. 1, pp. 89–101. Washington, D.C.

KIDDER, J. EDWARD, JR.
1957. The Jomon pottery of Japan. Artibus Asiea, Supplementum 17, Institute of Fine Arts, New York.

KING, ARDEN R.
1948. Tripod pottery in the central Andean area. American Antiquity, vol. 14, pp. 103–116.

KRIEGER, ALEX D.
1946. Culture complexes and chronology in northern Texas, with extension of Puebloan datings to the Mississippi Valley. University of Texas, Publication no. 4640. Austin.

KROEBER, ALFRED L.
1930. Cultural relations between North and South America. Proceedings of the 23rd International Congress of Americanists, New York, 1928, pp. 5–22. New York.

LADD, JOHN
1964. Archeological investigations in the Parita and Santa María zones of Panama. Bureau of American Ethnology Bulletin, no. 193. Washington, D.C.

LANNING, EDWARD P.
1963a. A pre-agricultural occupation on the central coast of Peru. American Antiquity, vol. 28, pp. 360–371.
1963b. A ceramic sequence for the Puira and Chira coast, north Peru. University of California Publications in American Archaeology and Ethnology, vol. 46, no. 2, pp. 135–284. Berkeley.
1967. Peru before the Incas. Prentice Hall, Englewood Cliffs, New Jersey.

LARCO HOYLE, RAFAEL
1941. Los Cupisniques. Casa Editora "La Crónica" y "Variedades". Lima.
1944. Cultura Salinar. Síntesis monográfica. Buenos Aires.
1945a. Los Cupisniques. Sociedad Geográfica Americana. Buenos Aires.
1945b. La cultura Virú. Sociedad Geográfica Americana. Buenos Aires.
1946. A cultural sequence for the north coast of Peru. In Handbook of the South American Indians, edited by Julian H. Steward. Bureau of American Ethnology Bulletin, no. 143, vol. 2, pp. 149–175. Washington, D.C.
1948. Cronología arqueológica del norte del Peru. Hacienda Chiclín, Trujillo, Peru.

LARSEN, HELGE, and RAINEY, FROELICH G.
1948. Ipiutak and the Arctic whale hunting culture. American Museum of Natural History, Anthropological Papers, vol. 42. New York.

LATHRAP, DONALD W.
1958. The cultural sequence at Yarinacocha, eastern Peru. American Antiquity, vol. 23, pp. 379–388.

LATHRAP, DONALD W.—Continued
> 1963. Possible affiliations of the Machalilla complex of coastal Ecuador. American Antiquity, vol. 29, pp. 239–241.

LEWIS, THOMAS M. N., and LEWIS, MADELINE KNEBERG
> 1961. Eva: An Archaic site. University of Tennessee Study in Anthropology. Knoxville.

LIBBY, WILLARD F.
> 1955. Radiocarbon dating. University of Chicago Press, Chicago.

LONGYEAR, JOHN M., III
> 1952. Copan ceramics. A study of southeastern Maya pottery. Carnegie Institution of Washington, Publication 597. Washington, D.C.

LORENZO, JOSÉ L.
> 1965. Tlatilco III, los artefactos. Serie Investigaciones no. 7, Instituto Nacional de Antropología e Historia, Mexico, D.F.

LOWE, GARETH W.
> 1959a. The Chiapas project, 1955–1958. Papers of the New World Archaeological Foundation, no. 1, publication no. 3. Brigham Young University, Provo, Utah.
> 1959b. Archaeological explorations of the Upper Grijalva River, Chiapas, Mexico. Papers of the New World Archaeological Foundation no. 2, publication no. 3. Brigham Young University, Provo, Utah.
> 1962. Mound 5 and minor excavations, Chiapa de Corzo, Chiapas, Mexico. Papers of the New World Archaeological Foundation no. 12, publication no. 8. Birgham Young University, Provo, Utah.

LOWIE, ROBERT H.
> 1937. The history of ethnological theory. Farrar and Rinehart, Inc., New York.

MacNEISH, RICHARD S.
> 1947. A preliminary report on coastal Tamaulipas, Mexico. American Antiquity, vol. 13, pp. 1–15.
> 1954. An early archaeological site near Panuco, Veracruz. Transactions of the American Philosophical Society, vol. 44, part 5, pp. 539–641. Philadelphia.
> 1958. Preliminary archaeological investigations in the Sierra de Tamaulipas, Mexico. Transactions of the American Philosophical Society, vol. 48, part 6. Philadelphia.
> 1959. Men out of Asia, as seen from the northern Yukon. University of Alaska Anthropological Papers, vol. 7, no. 2.
> 1961. First annual report of the Tehuacán archaeological-botanical project. Project Reports, no. 1. Robert S. Peabody Foundation for Archaeology, Andover, Mass.
> 1962. Second annual report of the Tehuacán archaeological-botanical project. Project Reports, no. 2. Robert S. Peabody Foundation for Archaeology, Andover, Mass.
> 1964. Ancient Mesoamerican civilization. Science, vol. 143, pp. 531–537.

MacNEISH, RICHARD S., and PETERSON, FREDRICK A.
> 1962. The Santa Marta rock shelter, Ocozocoantla, Chiapas, Mexico. Papers of the New World Archaeological Foundation, no. 14, publication no. 10. Brigham Young University, Provo, Utah.

MAGRATH, WILLIS H.
> 1945. The North Benton mound: A Hopewell site in Ohio. American Antiquity, vol. 11, pp. 40–47.

MASON, J. ALDEN
> 1960. Mound 12, Chiapa de Corzo, Chiapas, Mexico. Papers of the New World Archaeological Foundation, no. 9. Brigham Young University, Provo, Utah.

MATOS MENDIETA, RAMIRO
> 1962. La cerámica temprana de Ancón y sus problemas. Tesis de grado en la Facultad de Letras, Universidad Nacional Mayor de San Marcos, Lima.

MAXWELL, MOREAU S.
> 1951. Woodland cultures of southern Illinois. Logan Museum Publications in Anthropology, Bull. 7. Beloit College, Beloit.
> 1959. The late Woodland period. In Illinois Archaeology. Illinois Archaeological Survey Bulletin, no. 1, pp. 27–32. University of Illinois, Urbana.

McCOWN, THEODORE D.
> 1945. Pre-Incaic Huamachuco: Survey and excavations in the region of Huamachuco and Cajabamba. University of California Publications in American Archaeology and Ethnology, vol. 39, no. 4, pp. 223–400. Berkeley.

McGregor, John C.
1941. Southwestern archaeology. John Wiley and Sons, New York.
1952. The Havana site. *In* Hopewellian communities in Illinois, edited by Thorne Deuel. Illinois State Museum Scientific Papers, vol. 5, no. 2, pp. 43–91. Springfield.
1957. Prehistoric village distribution in the Illinois River Valley. American Antiquity, vol. 22, pp. 272–279.
1959. The middle Woodland period. *In* Illinois archaeology, edited by Elaine A. Bluhm. Illinois Archaeological Survey Bulletin, no. 1, pp. 21–28. University of Illinois, Urbana.

McIntire, William G.
1958. Prehistoric Indian settlements of the changing Mississippi River delta. Louisiana State University Studies, Coastal Studies Series, no. 1. Baton Rouge.

McKern, W. C.
1931. A Wisconsin variant of the Hopewell culture. Bulletin of the Public Museum of the City of Milwaukee, vol. 10, no. 2, pp. 185–328. Milwaukee.
1937. An hypothesis for the Asiatic origin of the Woodland culture pattern. American Antiquity, vol. 3, pp. 138–143.

McKern, W. C.; Titterington, P. F.; and Griffin, James B.
1945. Painted pottery figurines from Illinois. American Antiquity, vol. 10, pp. 295–304.

McLurkan, Burney R.; Field, W. T.; and Woodall, Ned J.
1966. Excavations in Toledo Bend reservoir. Papers of the Texas Archaeological Salvage Project, no. 8. Austin.

McMichael, Edward V.
1964. Veracruz, the Crystal River complex, and the Hopewellian climax. Hopewellian Studies, Illinois State Museum Scientific Papers, vol. 12, pp. 123–132. Springfield.

Medellín Zenil, Alfonso
1960. Cerámicas del Totonacapán: Exploraciones arqueológicas en el centro de Veracruz. Universidad Veracruzana, Instituto de Antropología, Jalapa.

Meggers, Betty J.
1963. Cultural development in Latin America: An interpretative overview. *In* Aboriginal cultural development in Latin America: An interpretative review, edited by Betty J. Meggers and Clifford Evans. Smithsonian Misc. Coll. vol. 146, no. 1, pp. 131–145. Washington, D.C.
1964. North and South American cultural connections and convergences. *In* Prehistoric man in the New World, edited by Jesse D. Jennings and Edward Norbeck, pp. 511–526. University of Chicago Press, Chicago.
1966. Ecuador. Ancient Peoples and Places series, vol. 49. Praeger, New York.

Meggers, Betty J., and Evans, Clifford
1962. The Machalilla culture: An early Formative complex on the Ecuadorian coast. American Antiquity, vol. 28, pp. 186–192.
1964. Especulaciones sobre rutas tempranas de difusión de la cerámica entre Sur y Mesoamérica. Hombre y Cultura, Tomo 1, no. 3, pp. 1–15, Revista del Centro Investigaciones Antropológicas de la Universidad Nacional, Panama.

Meggers, Betty J., and Evans, Clifford, editors
1963. Aboriginal cultural development in Latin America: An interpretative review. Smithsonian Misc. Coll., vol. 146, no. 1. Washington, D.C.

Meggers, Betty J.; Evans, Clifford; and Estrada, Emilio
1965. Early Formative period of coastal Ecuador: The Valdivia and Machalilla phases. Smithsonian Contributions to Anthropology, vol. 1. Washington, D.C.

Meighan, Clement W.
1959. Californian cultures and the concept of an archaic stage. American Antiquity, vol. 24, pp. 289–305.

Millon, Rene; Drewitt, Bruce; and Bennyhoff, James A.
1965. The Pyramid of the Sun at Teotihuacán: 1959 investigations. Transactions of the American Philosophical Society, vol. 55, part 6. Philadelphia.

Mills, William C.
1902. Excavations of the Adena mound. Ohio Archaeological and Historical Society Quarterly, vol. 10, no. 4, pp. 452–479. Columbus.
1907. The explorations of the Edwin Harness mound. Ohio Archaeological and Historical Society Quarterly, vol. 16, pp. 113–193. Columbus.

MILLS, WILLIAM C.—Continued
> 1909.   Explorations of the Seip mound. Ohio Archaeological and Historical Society Quarterly, vol. 18, pp. 269–321. Columbus.
>
> 1916.   Exploration of the Tremper mound. Ohio Archaeological and Historical Society Quarterly, vol. 25, no. 3, pp. 263–398. Columbus.
>
> 1922.   Exploration of the Mound City group. Ohio Archaeological and Historical Society Quarterly, vol. 31, no. 4, pp. 423–584. Columbus.

MOORE, CLARENCE B.
> 1893.   Certain shell heaps of the St. John's River, Florida, hitherto unexplored. The American Naturalist, vol. 27, pp. 605–624. Philadelphia.
>
> 1894.   Certain shell heaps of the St. John's River, Florida, hitherto unexplored. American Naturalist, vol. 28, part 5, pp. 15–26. Philadelphia.
>
> 1897.   Certain aboriginal mounds of the Georgia coast. Journal of the Academy of Natural Sciences, vol. 10, part 1, pp. 4–138. Philadelphia.
>
> 1901.   Certain aboriginal remains of the northwest Florida coast, part I. Journal of the Academy of Natural Sciences, vol. 11, part 4, pp. 419–497. Philadelphia.
>
> 1902.   Certain aboriginal remains of the northwest Florida coast, part II. Journal of the Academy of Natural Sciences, vol. 12, part 2, pp. 125–335. Philadelphia.
>
> 1903.   Certain aboriginal mounds of the Florida central west-coast. Journal of the Academy of Natural Sciences of Philadelphia, vol. 12, pp. 361–438. Philadelphia.
>
> 1907.   Crystal River revisited. Journal of the Academy of Natural Sciences of Philadelphia, vol. 13, part 3, pp. 406–425. Philadelphia.
>
> 1908.   Certain mounds of Arkansas and of Mississippi. Journal of the Academy of Natural Sciences of Philadelphia, vol. 13, part 4, pp. 481–600. Philadelphia.
>
> 1912.   Some aboriginal sites on Red River. Journal of the Academy of Natural Sciences, vol. 14, no. 4, pp. 482–640. Philadelphia.
>
> 1918.   The northwestern Florida coast revisited. Journal of the Academy of Natural Sciences, Philadelphia, vol. 16, part 4, pp. 514–577.

MOOREHEAD, WARREN K.
> 1922.   The Hopewell mound group of Ohio. Field Museum of Natural History Publication 211, Anthropological Series, vol. 6, no. 5. Chicago.

MORLEY, SYLVANUS G.
> 1946.   The ancient Maya. Stanford University Press.

MUNIZAGA, JUAN R.
> 1965.   Skeletal remains from sites of Valdivia and Machalilla Phases. Smithsonian Contributions to Anthropology, vol. 1, appendix 2. Washington, D.C.

NAVARETTE, CARLOS
> 1959.   Explorations at San Agustin, Chiapas, Mexico. Papers of the New World Archaeological Foundation, no. 3, publication no. 3. Brigham Young University, Provo, Utah.

NEUMANN, GEORG K., and FOWLER, MELVIN L.
> 1952.   Hopewellian sites in the Lower Wabash Valley. *In* Hopewellian communities in Illinois, edited by Thorne Deuel. Scientific Papers, Illinois State Museum, vol. 5, pp. 175–248. Springfield.

NEWELL, PERRY H., and KRIEGER, ALEX D.
> 1949.   The George C. Davis site, Cherokee County, Texas. Society for American Archaeology Memoir 5.

NEWKUMET, PHIL J.
> 1940.   Preliminary report on excavation of the Williams mound, Leflore County, Oklahoma. Oklahoma State Archaeological Society, vol. 3, no. 2, pp. 1–9. Tulsa.

ORR, KENNETH G.
> 1952.   Survey of Caddoan area archaeology. *In* Archaeology of eastern United States, edited by James B. Griffin, pp. 239–255. University of Chicago Press, Chicago.

PARSONS, LEE A.
> 1963.   A doughnut-shaped vessel from Kaminaljuyú, with a distributional analysis of this unusual form. American Antiquity, vol. 28, pp. 386–389.

PETERSON, FREDRICK A.
> 1963.   Some ceramics from Mirador, Chiapas, Mexico. Papers of the New World Archaeological Foundation, no. 15, publication no. 11. Brigham Young University, Provo, Utah.

PHILLIPS, PHILIP
    1940.   Middle American influences on the archaeology of the southeastern United States.
            In The Maya and their neighbors, pp. 349–367. D. Appleton-Century, New
            York.

PHILLIPS, PHILIP; FORD, JAMES A.; and GRIFFIN, JAMES B.
    1951.   Archaeological survey on the lower Mississippi Alluvial Valley, 1940–1947. Papers
            of the Peabody Museum of American Archaeology and Ethnology, vol. 25, Harvard
            University.

PIÑA CHÁN, ROMÁN
    1958.   Tlatilco. Serie Investigaciones, vol. 1 and 2, Instituto Nacional de Antropología e
            Historia. Mexico, D.F.

PORTER, MURIEL NOÉ (see also Weaver, Muriel Porter)
    1948.   Pipas precortesianas. Acta Antropológica, vol. 3, no. 2. Mexico, D.F.
    1953.   Tlatilco and the preclassic cultures of the New World. Viking Fund Publications in
            Anthropology, no. 19. New York.

PRAHL, EARL J.
    1966.   The Muskegon River survey: 1965 and 1966. The Michigan Archaeologist, vol. 12,
            no. 4, pp. 183–210. Ann Arbor.

PRUFER, OLAF H.
    1964.   Hopewell versus Meso-America and Asia. Actas y Memorias I, XXXV Congreso
            Internacional de Americanistas, Mexico, 1962, pp. 113–120. Mexico, D.F.

QUIMBY, GEORGE I., JR.
    1941.   The Goodall focus: An analysis of ten Hopewellian components in Michigan and
            Indiana. Indiana Historical Society Prehistoric Research Series, vol. 9, no. 1.
            Indianapolis.

RADIOCARBON DATES ASSOCIATION, INC.
    1958.   Key-sort cards of radiocarbon dates. Quincy Mail Advertising Co. Braintree, Mass.

RADIOCARBON (formerly *Radiocarbon Supplement*)
    1959–1968.   Volumes 1–10. American Journal of Science, Yale University.

RADIOCARBON MEASUREMENTS
    1967.   Comprehensive Index, 1950–1965. American Journal of Science. Yale University,
            New Haven.

REED, ERIK K.
    1964.   The greater Southwest. *In* Prehistoric man in the New World, edited by Jesse D.
            Jennings and Edward Norbeck, pp. 175–191. University of Chicago Press, Chicago.

REICHEL-DOLMATOFF, GERARDO
    1955.   Excavaciones en los conchales de la costa de Barlovento. Revista Colombiana de
            Antropología, vol. 4, pp. 247–272. Bogotá.
    1957.   Momíl: A Formative sequence from the Sinú Valley, Colombia. American Antiquity,
            vol. 22, pp. 226–234.
    1961.   Puerto Hormiga: Un complejo prehistórico marginal de Colombia (nota preliminar).
            Revista Colombiana de Antropología, vol. 10, pp. 347–354. Bogotá.
    1965.   Excavaciones arqueológicas en Puerto Hormiga (Departmento de Bolivar). Antro-
            pología 2, Ediciones de la Universidad de los Andes. Bogotá.

REICHEL-DOLMATOFF, GERARDO and ALICIA
    1951.   Investigaciones arqueológicas en el Depto. del Magdalena, Colombia—1946–1950.
            Boletin de Arqueología, vol. 3, nos. 1–6. Bogotá.
    1955.   Investigaciones arqueológicas en la Sierra Nevada de Santa Marta, part 4. Revista
            Colombiana de Antropología, vol. 4, pp. 189–245. Bogotá.
    1956.   Momíl: Excavaciones en el Sinú. Revista Colombiana de Antropología, vol. 5, pp.
            109–333. Bogotá.
    1961.   Investigaciones arqueológicas en la costa Pacífica de Colombia ɪ: El sitio de Cupica.
            Revista Colombiana de Antropología, vol. 10. pp. 237–330. Bogotá.
    1962.   Investigaciones arqueológicas en la costa Pacífica de Colombia ɪɪ: Una sequencia
            cultural del bajo Río San Juan. Revista Colombiana de Antropología, vol. 11, pp.
            9–72. Bogotá.

RITCHIE, WILLIAM A.
    1946.   A stratified prehistoric site at Brewertown, New York. Research Records of the Roch-
            ester Museum of Arts and Sciences, no. 8. Rochester.

RITCHIE, WILLIAM A.—Continued
  1962.   The antiquity of pottery in the Northeast. American Antiquity, vol. 27, pp. 583–584.
  1965.   The archaeology of New York State. The Natural History Press, Garden City, New
          York.
ROUSE, IRVING
  1951.   A survey of Indian River archaeology, Florida. Yale University Publications in Anthro-
          pology, no. 44. New Haven.
ROUSE, IRVING, and CRUXENT, JOSÉ M.
  1958.   An archeological chronology of Venezuela. Social Science Monograph VI. Pan Ameri-
          can Union, Washington, D.C.
SANDERS, WILLIAM T.
  1961.   Ceramic stratigraphy at Santa Cruz, Chiapas, Mexico. Papers of the New World
          Archaeological Foundation, no. 13, publ. no. 9. Brigham Young University, Provo,
          Utah.
SANOJA, MARIO
  1963.   Cultural development in Venezuela. *In* Aboriginal cultural development in Latin
          America: An interpretative review, edited by Betty J. Meggers and Clifford Evans.
          Smithsonian Misc. Coll., vol. 146, no. 1, pp. 67–76. Washington, D.C.
SEARS, WILLIAM H.
  1962.   Hopewellian affiliations for certain sites on the Gulf coast of Florida. American Antiq-
          uity, vol. 28, pp. 5–18.
SEARS, WILLIAM H., and GRIFFIN, JAMES B.
  1950.   Fiber-tempered pottery of the Southeast. *In* Prehistoric pottery of the eastern United
          States, edited by James B. Griffin, University of Michigan. Ann Arbor.
SHETRONE, HENRY C.
  1926.   Explorations of the Hopewell group of prehistoric earthworks. Ohio State Arch-
          aeological and Historical Quarterly, vol. 35, no. 1, pp. 5–227. Columbus.
SILOW, R. A.
  1953.   The problems of trans-Pacific migration involved in the origin of the cultivated cottons
          of the New World. Proceedings of the Seventh Pacific Science Congress of the Pacific
          Science Association, vol. 5, pp. 112–118. Wellington, New Zealand.
SMITH, ROBERT E.
  1955.   Ceramic sequence at Uaxactún, Guatemala. Middle American Research Institute,
          Tulane University, vol. 1, publ. no. 20. New Orleans.
SOLHEIM, WILHELM G., II
  1964.   Pottery and the Malayo-Polynesians. Current Anthropology, vol. 5, no. 3, pp. 376–384.
SORENSON, JOHN L.
  1955.   A chronological ordering of the Mesoamerican Pre-Classic. Middle American Research
          Institute, Tulane University Publication, no. 18, pp. 41–70. New Orleans.
SPAULDING, ALBERT C.
  1946.   Northeastern archaeology and general trends in the northern forest zone. *In* Man in
          northeastern North America, edited by Frederick Johnson. Papers of the Robert
          S. Peabody Foundation for Archaeology, vol. 3, pp. 143–167. Andover, Mass.
  1952.   The origin of the Adena culture of the Ohio Valley. Southwestern Journal of Anthro-
          pology, vol. 8, no. 3, pp. 260–268.
SPINDEN, HERBERT
  1917.   The origin and distribution of agriculture in America. Proceedings of the 19th Inter-
          national Congress of Americanists, Washington, D.C. 1915, pp. 269–276. Wash-
          ington, D.C.
SQUIER, EPHRAIM G., and DAVIS, EDWIN H.
  1848.   Ancient monuments of the Mississippi Valley. Smithsonian Contributions to Knowl-
          edge, vol. 1. Washington, D.C.
STIRLING, MATTHEW W.
  1941.   Expedition unearths buried masterpieces of carved jade. National Geographic Maga-
          zine, vol. 80, no. 3, pp. 277–302.
  1955.   Stone monuments of the Río Chiquito, Veracruz, Mexico. Bureau of American Ethnol-
          ogy Bulletin, no. 157, pp. 1–68. Washington, D.C.
STIRLING, MATTHEW W. and MARION
  1964a. El Limón, an early tomb site in Coclé province, Panama. Bureau of American Ethnol-
          ogy Bulletin, no. 191, pp. 247–254. Washington, D.C.

1964b. Archeological notes on Almirante Bay, Bocas del Toro, Panama. Bureau of American Ethnology Bulletin, no. 191, pp. 255–284. Washington, D.C.

STOLTMAN, JAMES B.
1966. New radiocarbon dates for Southeastern fiber-tempered pottery. American Antiquity, vol. 31, no. 6, pp. 872–874.

STRONG, WILLIAM DUNCAN
1943. Cross sections of New World prehistory. Smithsonian Misc. Coll., vol. 104, no. 2, pp. 1–46. Washington, D.C.

STRONG, WILLIAM DUNCAN, and EVANS, CLIFFORD
1952. Cultural stratigraphy in the Virú Valley, northern Peru: The Formative and Florescent epochs. Columbia Studies in Archaeology and Ethnology, vol. 4. Columbia University Press, New York.

STRONG, WILLIAM DUNCAN; KIDDER, ALFRED, II; and PAUL, A. J. D.
1938. Preliminary report on the Smithsonian Institution-Harvard University archeological expedition to northwest Honduras, 1936. Smithsonian Misc. Coll., vol. 97, no. 1. Washington, D.C.

SUHM, DEE ANN, and KRIEGER, ALEX D.
1954. An introductory handbook of Texas archeology. Bulletin of the Texas Archeological Society, vol. 25. Austin, Texas.

TELLO, JULIO C.
1943. Discovery of the Chavín culture in Peru. American Antiquity, vol. 9, pp. 135–160.
1960. Chavín, cultura matriz de la civilización andina. Universidad Nacional Mayor de San Marcos, primera parte. Lima.

TOLSTOY, PAUL
1953. Some Amerasian pottery traits in north Asia prehistory. American Antiquity, vol. 19, pp. 25–39.
1958a. The archaeology of the Lena Basin and its New World relationships, part I. American Antiquity, vol. 23, no. 4, pp. 397–418.
1958b. Surface survey of the northern Valley of Mexico: The Classic and Post-Classic periods. Transactions of the American Philosophical Society, vol. 48, part 5. Philadelphia.
1963. Cultural parallels between southeast Asia and Mesoamerica in the manufacture of bark cloth. Transactions of the New York Academy of Science, Series II, vol. 25, pp. 646–662. New York.

TOLSTOY, PAUL, and GUENETTE, ANDRE
1965. Le placement de Tlatilco dans le cadre du Pré-Classique du Bassin de Mexico. Journal de la Société des Américanistes, tome 54–1, pp. 47–91. Paris.

TRICKEY, BRUCE E.
1958. A chronological framework for the Mobile Bay region. American Antiquity, vol. 23, pp. 388–396.

UHLE, MAX
1913. Die muschelhugel von Ancon, Peru. 18th International Congress of Americanists, London 1912, pp. 22–45. London.

VAILLANT, GEORGE C.
1930. Excavations at Zacatenco. Anthropological Papers vol. 32, part 1, pp. 1–197. American Museum of Natural History, New York.
1931. Excavations at Ticomán. Anthropological Papers vol. 32, part 2, pp. 199–451. American Museum of Natural History, New York.
1935a. Early cultures of the Valley of Mexico: Results of the stratigraphical project of the American Museum of Natural History in the Valley of Mexico, 1928–1933. Anthropological Papers, vol. 35, part 3, pp. 281–328. American Museum of Natural History, New York.
1935b. Excavations at El Arbolillo. Anthropological Papers, vol. 35, part 2, pp. 137–279. American Museum of Natural History, New York.
1941. Aztecs of Mexico. Doubleday-Doran and Co. New York.

VAILLANT, GEORGE C. and SUZANNA B.
1934. Excavations at Gualupita. Anthropological Papers, vol. 35, part 1, pp. 1–135. American Museum of Natural History. New York.

WALKER, WINSLOW M.
     1952.   The Dickinson mound group, Peoria County. *In* Hopewellian communities in Illinois,
                 edited by Thorne Deuel, Illinois State Museum Scientific Papers, vol. 5, pp. 13–41.
                 Springfield.
WALLACE, DWIGHT T.
     1962.   Cerillos, an early Paracas site in Ica, Peru. American Antiquity, vol. 27, pp. 303–314.
WARREN, BRUCE W.
     1961.   The archeological sequence at Chiapa de Corzo. *In* Los Mayas del sur y sus relaciones
                 con los Nahuas meridionales. Sociedad Mexicana de Antropología, VIII, Mesa
                 Redonda, pp. 75–83. Mexico, D.F.
WAUCHOPE, ROBERT
     1950.   A tentative sequence of Pre-Classic ceramics in Middle America. Tulane University,
                 Middle American Research Institute, publication 15, pp. 211–250. New Orleans.
     1954.   Implications of radiocarbon dates from Middle and South America. Tulane University,
                 Middle American Research Records, publ. 18, vol. 29, pp. 17–40. New Orleans.
     1966.   Archeological survey of northern Georgia with a test of cultural hypothesis. Society
                 for American Archaeology Memoir 21.
WEAVER, MURIEL PORTER (see also Porter, Muriel)
     1967.   Tlapacoya pottery in the museum collection. Indian Notes and Monographs, no. 56.
                 Museum of the American Indian, Heye Foundation, New York.
WEBB, CLARENCE H.
     1944.   Stone vessels from a northeast Louisiana site. American Antiquity, vol. 9, pp. 386–394.
     1959.   The Belcher mound, a stratified Caddoan site in Caddo Parish, Louisiana. Society
                 for American Archaeology Memoir 16.
     1968.   The extent and content of Poverty Point culture. American Antiquity, vol. 33, pp.
                 297–321.
WEBB, CLARENCE H., and FORD, JAMES A.
     MS.   Poverty Point culture and the American Formative.
WEBB, WILLIAM S.
     1940.   The Wright mounds: Site 6 and 7, Montgomery County, Kentucky. The University
                 of Kentucky Reports in Anthropology, vol. 5, no. 1. Lexington.
     1950.   The Carlson Annis mound: Site 5, Butler County, Kentucky. The University of
                 Kentucky Reports in Anthropology, vol. 7, no. 4. Lexington.
WEBB, WILLIAM S., and BABY, RAYMOND S.
     1957.   The Adena people, no. 2. Ohio State University Press, Columbus.
WEBB, WILLIAM S., and DEJARNETTE, DAVID L.
     1942.   An archeological survey of Pickwick Basin in the adjacent portions of the states of
                 Alabama, Mississippi, and Tennessee. Bureau of American Ethnology Bulletin, no.
                 129. Washington, D.C.
WEBB, WILLIAM S., and FAUKHOUSER, W. D.
     1931.   The Tolu site in Crittenden County, Kentucky. The University of Kentucky Reports
                 in Archaeology and Anthropology, vol. 1, no. 5. Lexington.
WEBB, WILLIAM S., and HAAG, WILLIAM G.
     1939.   The Chiggerville site: Site 1, Ohio County, Kentucky. Reports in Anthropology, vol.
                 4, no. 1. University of Kentucky, Lexington.
WEBB, WILLIAM S., and SNOW, CHARLES E.
     1945.   The Adena people. University of Kentucky Reports in Archaeology and Anthropology,
                 vol. 6. Lexington.
WEIANT, C.W.
     1943.   An introduction to the ceramics of Tres Zapotes, Veracruz, Mexico. Bureau of Amer-
                 ican Ethnology Bulletin, no. 139. Washington, D.C.
WICKE, CHARLES R.
     1965.   Pyramids and temple mounds: Mesoamerican ceremonial architecture in eastern
                 North America. American Antiquity, vol. 30, pp. 409–420.
WILLEY, GORDON R.
     1945.   Horizon styles and pottery traditions in Peruvian archaeology. American Antiquity,
                 vol. 11, pp. 49–56.
     1948.   Functional analysis of "horizon styles" in Peruvian archaeology. *In* A reappraisal of
                 Peruvian archaeology, Society for American Archaeology Memoir 4, pp. 8–15.

1949a. Archeology of the Florida Gulf coast. Smithsonian Misc. Coll., vol. 113. Washington, D.C.

1949b. The southeastern United States and South America: A comparative statement. *In* The Florida Indian and his neighbors, edited by John W. Griffin, pp. 101–106. Interamerican Center, Rollins College, Winter Park, Florida.

1949c. Excavations in southeast Florida. Yale University Publications in Anthropology, no. 42. New Haven.

1951. The Chavín problem: A review and critique. Southwestern Journal of Anthropology, vol. 7, no. 2, pp. 103–144.

1953. Prehistoric settlement patterns in the Virú Valley, Peru. Bureau of American Ethnology Bulletin, no. 155. Washington, D.C.

1955. The interrelated rise of the native cultures of Middle and South America. *In* New interpretations of aboriginal American culture history, Anthropological Society of Washington, 75th Anniversary volume, pp. 28–45. Washington, D.C.

1962. The early great styles and the rise of pre-Columbian civilizations. American Anthropologist, vol. 64, pp. 1–14.

1966. An introduction to American archaeology, volume 1: North and Middle America. Prentice-Hall Inc., Englewood Cliffs, New Jersey.

WILLEY, GORDON R., and CORBETT, JOHN M.

1954. Early Ancón and early Supe culture. Columbia Studies in Archaeology and Ethnology, vol. 3. Columbia University Press, New York.

WILLEY, GORDON R., and McGIMSEY, CHARLES R.

1954. The Monagrillo culture of Panama. Papers of the Peabody Museum of Archaeology and Ethnology, Harvard University, vol. 49, no. 2. Cambridge, Mass.

WILLEY, GORDON R., and PHILLIPS, PHILIP

1958. Method and theory in American archaeology. University of Chicago Press, Chicago.

WILLIAMS, STEPHEN, editor

1968. The Waring papers: The collected works of Antonio J. Waring, Jr. Papers of the Peabody Museum of Archaeology and Ethnology, Harvard University, vol 58. Cambridge, Mass.

WILLOUGHBY, CHARLES G.

1917. The art of the great earthwork builders of Ohio. Annual Report of the Smithsonian Institution, 1916, pp. 489–500.

1922. The Turner group of earthworks, Hamilton County, Ohio. Papers of the Peabody Museum of Archaeology and Ethnology, vol. 8, no. 3. Harvard University. Cambridge, Mass.

WIMBERLY, STEVE B.

1960. Indian pottery from Clarke County and Mobile County, southern Alabama. Alabama Museum of Natural History, Museum Paper 36. University, Alabama.

WIMBERLY, STEVE B., and TOURTELOT, HARRY A.

1941. The McQuorquodale mound: A manifestation of the Hopewellian phase in south Alabama. Geological Survey of Alabama, Museum Paper 19. University, Alabama.

WOOD, RAYMOND W.

1962. A stylistic and historical analysis of shoulder patterns on Plains Indian pottery. American Antiquity, vol. 28, pp. 25–40.

WRIGHT, J. V.

1967. The Laurel tradition and the Middle Woodland period. National Museum of Canada Bulletin, no. 217, Anthropological Series 79. Ottawa.

WYMAN, JEFFRIES

1875. Fresh-water shell mounds of the St. John's River, Florida. Memoirs of the Peabody Academy of Science, vol. 1, no. 4, pp. 1–94. Salem, Mass.

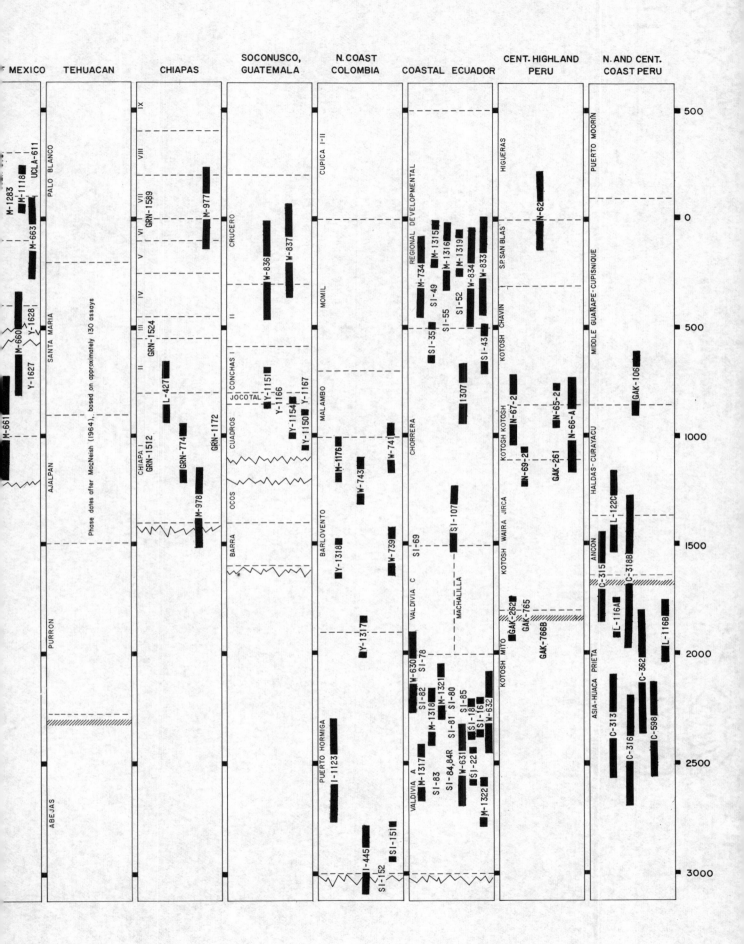

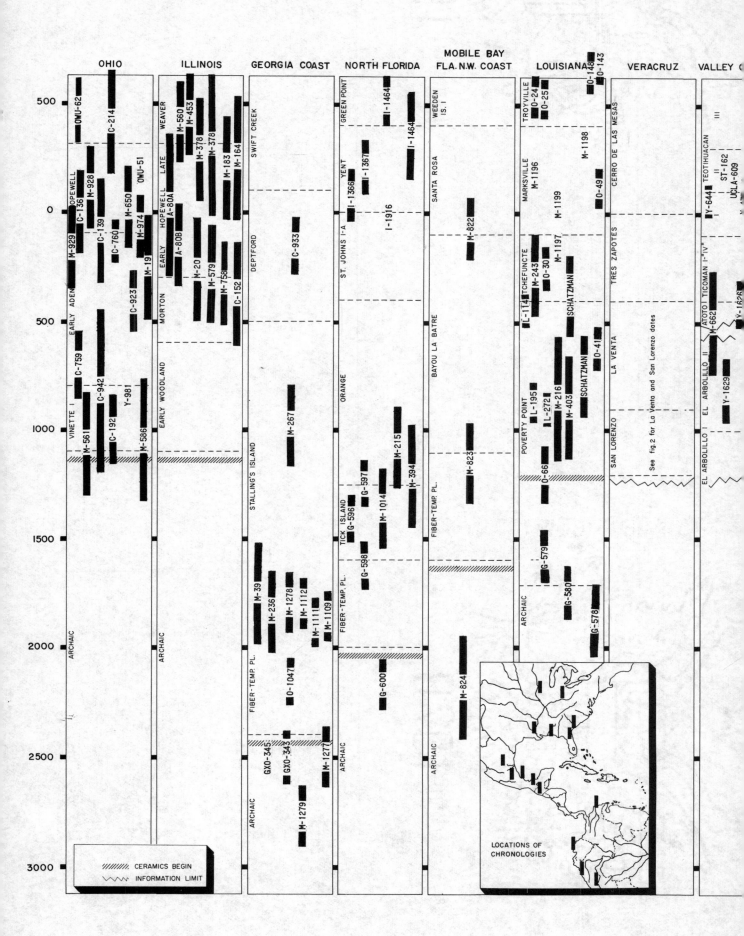

RADIOCARBON DATES USED FOR ESTABLISHING THE REGIONAL CHRONOLOGIES

CHART 1

Black bars represent the 1-sigma range for each date; where there is no black bar, the laboratory number occupies an area equal to or greater than the 1-sigma range. References for all dates are provided on tables 1–13.

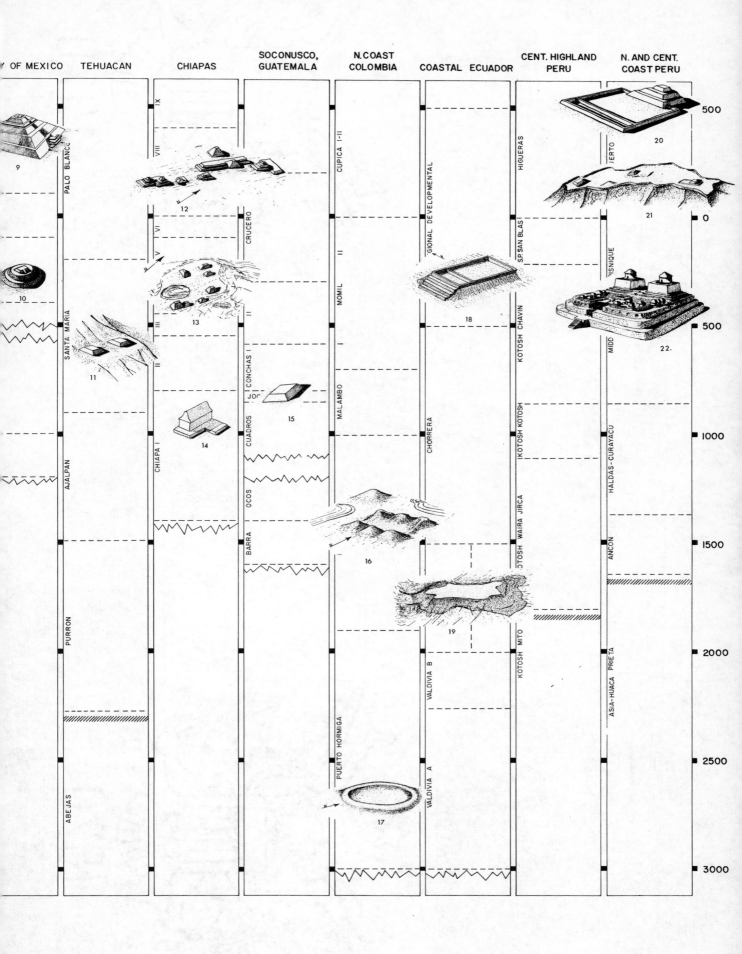

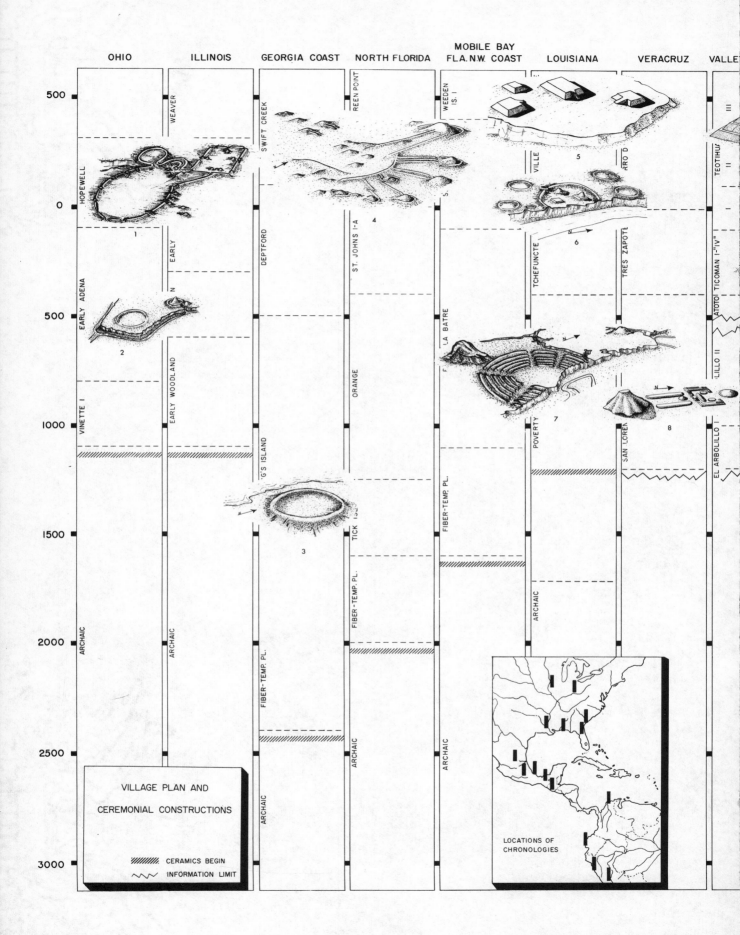

OHIO   ILLINOIS   GEORGIA COAST   NORTH FLORIDA   MOBILE BAY FLA. N.W. COAST   LOUISIANA   VERACRUZ   VALLE

500

0

500

1000

1500

2000

2500

3000

VILLAGE PLAN AND
CEREMONIAL CONSTRUCTIONS

▨▨▨ CERAMICS BEGIN
〜〜〜 INFORMATION LIMIT

LOCATIONS OF
CHRONOLOGIES

WEAVER

HOPEWELL

EARLY ADENA

VINETTE I

ARCHAIC

EARLY

EARLY WOODLAND

ARCHAIC

SWIFT CREEK

DEPTFORD

G'S ISLAND

FIBER-TEMP. PL.

ARCHAIC

REEN POINT

ST. JOHNS I-A

ORANGE

TICK ISS

FIBER-TEMP. PL.

ARCHAIC

WEEDEN IS. I

S.

FIBER-TEMP. PL.

FIBER-TEMP. PL.

ARCHAIC

VILLE

TCHEFUNCTE

POVERTY

ARCHAIC

RRO D

TRES ZAPOTE

SAN LOREN

TEOTIHU

ATOTI TICOMAN I-IV

LILLO II

EL ARBOLILLO I

1
2
3
4
5
6
7
8

SETTLEMENT PATTERN: VILLAGE PLAN AND CEREMONIAL CONSTRUCTIONS

CHART 2

1. Mills, 1907, fig. 1 (Harness Mound)
2. Griffin, 1947, pl. 1 (Spruce Run)
3. Williams, ed., 1968, fig. 89 (Sapelo Shell Ring)
4. Willey, 1949c, fig. 8 (Big Mound City)
5. Ford, 1951, figs. 1, 3, pls. 1–3 (Greenhouse Site)
6. Marksville Site (unpublished notes of W. Haag and J. A. Ford)
7. Ford and Webb, 1956, figs. 2, 6 (Poverty Point)
8. Drucker, Heizer, and Squier, 1959, figs. 3–5; Heizer and Drucker, 1968, pl. 12 (La Venta)
9. Millon, Drewitt, and Bennyhoff, 1965, fig. 3 (Teotihuacán)
10. Cummings, 1933, p. 52 (Cuicuilco)
11. MacNeish, 1962, pp. 38–39 (Santa Maria Phase)
12. Lowe, 1959a, fig. 5b (Chiapa de Corzo)
13. Lowe, 1959a, fig. 4b (Los Tres Cerritos)
14. Lowe, 1959b, fig. 34
15. Coe and Flannery, 1967, p. 89 (Jocotal Phase)
16. Reichel-Dolmatoff, 1955, p. 264 (Barlovento)
17. Reichel-Dolmatoff, 1965, fig. 1b (Puerto Hormiga)
18. Estrada, 1962, fig. 11
19. Meggers, Evans, and Estrada, 1965, fig. 3 (Punta Arenas)
20. Bennett, 1946, pl. 52 Top (Mochica Period, Chicama Valley)
21. Willey, 1953, fig. 18 (Puerto Moorín, Cerro Bitín Site)
22. Carrión Cachot, 1948, pl. 6 (Moxeke)

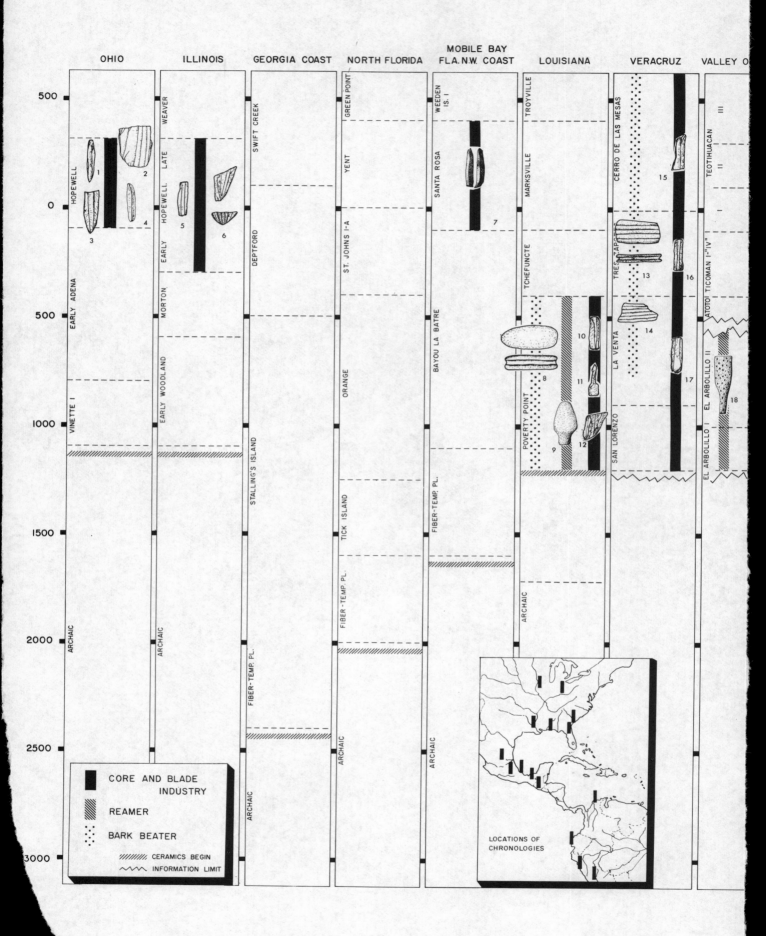

OHIO   ILLINOIS   GEORGIA COAST   NORTH FLORIDA   MOBILE BAY FLA.N.W. COAST   LOUISIANA   VERACRUZ   VALLEY O

500
0
500
1000
1500
2000
2500
3000

OHIO: HOPEWELL, EARLY ADENA, VINETTE I, EARLY ADENA, ARCHAIC

ILLINOIS: WEAVER, LATE HOPEWELL, EARLY HOPEWELL, MORTON, EARLY WOODLAND, ARCHAIC

GEORGIA COAST: SWIFT CREEK, DEPTFORD, STALLING'S ISLAND, FIBER-TEMP. PL., ARCHAIC

NORTH FLORIDA: GREEN POINT, YENT, ST. JOHNS I-A, ORANGE, TICK ISLAND, FIBER-TEMP. PL., ARCHAIC

MOBILE BAY FLA.N.W. COAST: WEEDEN IS. I, SANTA ROSA, BAYOU LA BATRE, FIBER-TEMP. PL., ARCHAIC

LOUISIANA: TROYVILLE, MARKSVILLE, TCHEFUNCTE, POVERTY POINT, ARCHAIC

VERACRUZ: CERRO DE LAS MESAS, TRES ZAPOTES, LA VENTA, SAN LORENZO

VALLEY O: TEOTIHUACAN III, II, I, ATOTOI TICOMAN I-"IV", EL ARBOLILLO II, EL ARBOLILLO I

CORE AND BLADE INDUSTRY
REAMER
BARK BEATER
CERAMICS BEGIN
INFORMATION LIMIT

LOCATIONS OF CHRONOLOGIES

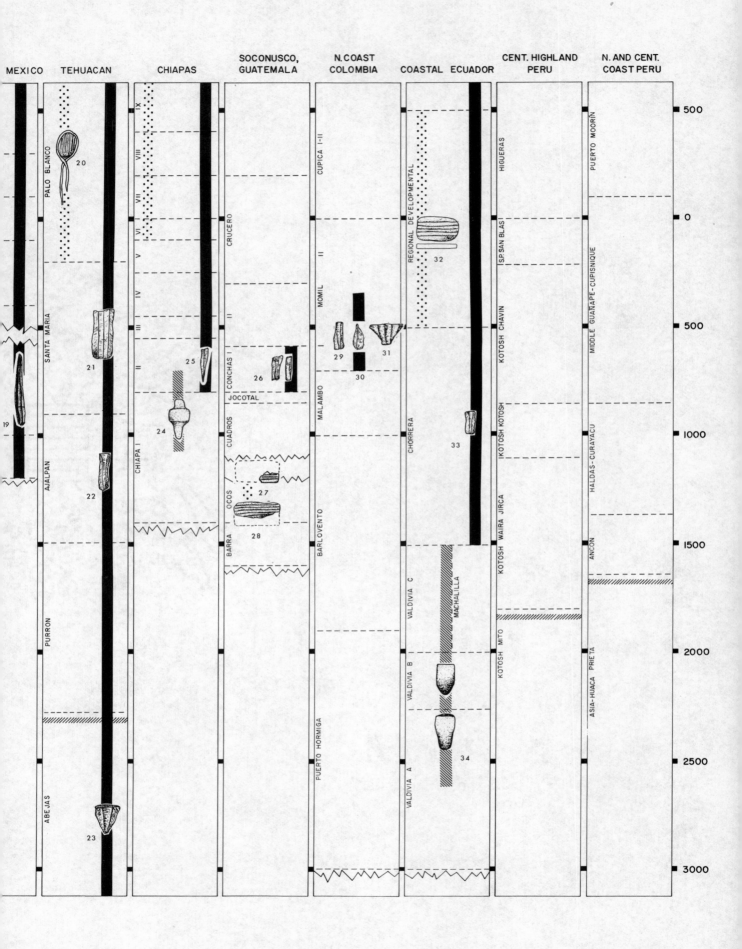

MEXICO	TEHUACAN	CHIAPAS	SOCONUSCO, GUATEMALA	N. COAST COLOMBIA	COASTAL ECUADOR	CENT. HIGHLAND PERU	N. AND CENT. COAST PERU

CORE AND BLADE INDUSTRY, BARK BEATERS, AND REAMERS

Chart 3

1. Mills, 1907, p. 179, fig. 63
2. Mills, 1907, p. 180, fig. 64
3. Shetrone, 1926, pp. 41–43, fig. 12
4. Mills, 1907, p. 179, fig. 163
5. McGregor, 1952, pl. 18c
6. Fowler, 1952, pl. 48d
7. Kellar, Kelly, and McMichael, 1962, fig. 3c
8. Poverty Point, unpublished notes
9. Poverty Point, unpublished notes
10. Ford and Webb, 1956, fig. 26o
11. Ford and Webb, 1956, fig. 26a′
12. Ford and Webb, 1956, pp. 77–79, fig. 26a–e
13. Weiant, 1943, p. 120, pl. 72–15
14. García Payón, 1966, pl. 84–3
15. Florida State Museum Collection
16. García Payón, 1966, pp. 171–175
17. García Payón, 1966, pp. 171–175
18. Lorenzo, 1965, fig. 40
19. Lorenzo, 1965, fig. 37
20. MacNeish, 1961, fig. 13–1
21. MacNeish, 1961, fig. 15
22. MacNeish, 1961, fig. 15
23. MacNeish, 1961, fig. 15
24. Dixon, 1959, p. 19, fig. 53c
25. Sanders, 1961, p. 43
26. M. D. Coe, 1961, pp. 107–108, fig. 60j–k
27. M. D. Coe, 1961, fig. 41c
28. M. D. Coe, 1961, fig. 42b
29. Reichel-Dolmatoff, Gerardo and Alicia, 1956, pl. 28–15.
30. Reichel-Dolmatoff, Gerardo and Alicia, 1956, pl. 28–12.
31. Reichel-Dolmatoff, Gerardo and Alicia, 1956, pp. 235–236.
32. Estrada, Meggers, and Evans, 1964, pl. 6a
33. Estrada, 1962, fig. 92i
34. Meggers, Evans, and Estrada, 1965, p. 29, fig. 14

4. Mills 1907, p. 179, fig. 183
10. Ford and Webb, 1956, fig. 26d
15. Florida State Museum Collection
16. Garcia Payon 1966, pp. 121-123
17. Garcia Payon, 1966, pp. 121-123
18. Lorenzo, 1965, fig. 40
19. Lorenzo, 1965, fig. 37

33. Estrada, 1964, fig. 92
34. Meggers, Evans, and Estrada, 1966, p. 79, fig. 34

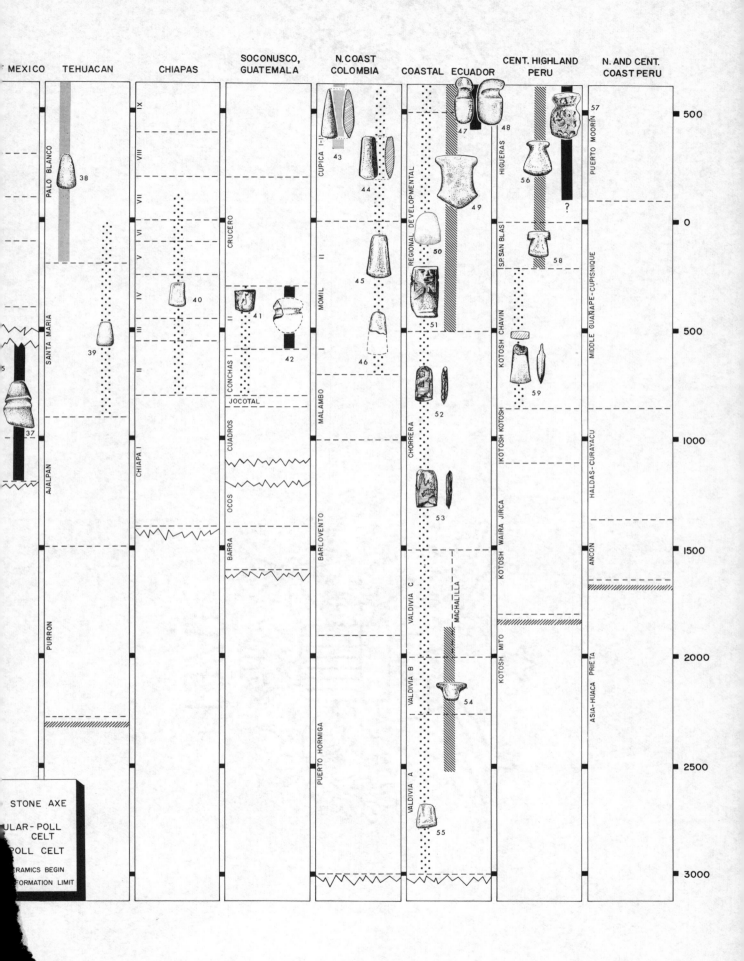

STONE AXE
ULAR-POLL
CELT
POLL CELT
ERAMICS BEGIN
FORMATION LIMIT

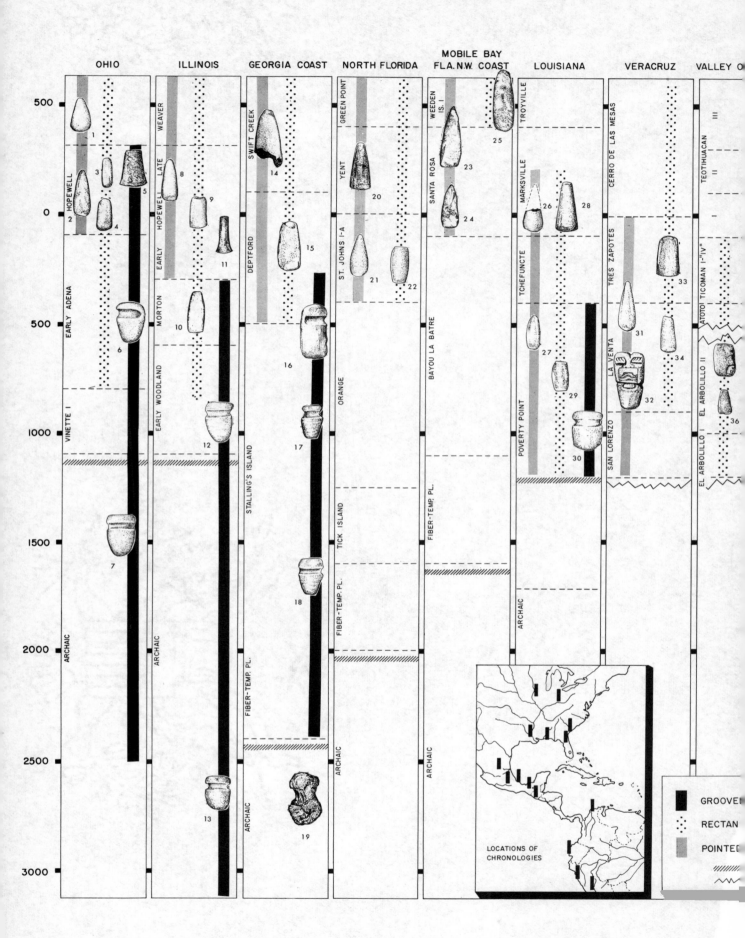

| OHIO | ILLINOIS | GEORGIA COAST | NORTH FLORIDA | MOBILE BAY FLA. N.W. COAST | LOUISIANA | VERACRUZ | VALLEY O |

LOCATIONS OF
CHRONOLOGIES

GROOVE
RECTAN
POINTED

AXES AND CELTS

CHART 4

1. Mills, 1907, fig. 62
2. Shetrone, 1926, fig. 41
3. Shetrone, 1926, fig. 41
4. Shetrone, 1926, fig. 41
5. Griffin, 1952b, fig. 32m
6. Shetrone, 1926, fig. 45
7. Griffin, 1952b, fig. 29m
8. McGregor, 1959, fig. 6
9. Fowler, 1952, pl. 49c
10. Fowler, 1961, fig. 4
11. McGregor, 1959, fig. 5
12. Griffin, 1952b, fig. 96–16
13. Fowler, 1959a, fig. 12m
14. Wauchope, 1966, fig. 251h
15. Wauchope, 1966, fig. 251e
16. Wauchope, 1966, fig. 108b
17. Claflin, 1931, pl. 48c
18. Claflin, 1931, pl. 48b
19. Griffin, 1952b, fig. 162H
20. Kellar, Kelly, and McMichael, 1962, fig. 3L
21. Goggin, 1952, pl. 6h
22. Goggin, 1952, pl. 6 o
23. Willey, 1949a, pl. 42i
24. Willey, 1949a, pl. 42h
25. Willey, 1949a, pl. 42j
26. Ford and Willey, 1940, fig. 49b
27. Ford and Webb, 1956, fig. 31e
28. Ford and Willey, 1940, fig. 49a
29. Ford and Webb, 1956, fig. 32a
30. Alexander Collection, Poverty Point Mound
31. Drucker, 1952, pl. 55
32. Drucker, 1952, pl. 56a
33. Weiant, 1943, pl. 72–1
34. Drucker, 1952, pl. 55
35. Vaillant, 1931, pl. 45
36. Vaillant, 1931, pl. 45
37. Lorenzo, 1965, fig. 16
38. MacNeish, 1961, fig. 11–24
39. MacNeish, personal communication
40. Sanders, 1961, pl. 11B-t
41. M. D. Coe, 1961, fig. 60q
42. M. D. Coe, 1961, fig. 42c
43. Duque, 1964, drawing 27–74
44. Duque, 1964, drawing 27–75
45. Reichel-Dolmatoff, Gerardo and Alicia, 1956, pl. 26–13
46. Reichel-Dolmatoff, Gerardo and Alicia, 1956, pl. 27–8
47. Estrada, 1958, fig. 54–5
48. Estrada, 1958, fig. 54–4
49. Estrada, 1962, fig. 98
50. Bushnell, 1951, fig. 27a
51. Estrada, 1962, fig. 97E
52. Estrada, 1958, fig. 54–8
53. Estrada, 1958, fig. 54–6
54. Meggers, Evans, and Estrada, 1965, pl. 19r
55. Meggers, Evans, and Estrada, 1965, pl. 19p
56. Izumi and Sono, 1963, pl. 106b–1
57. Tello, 1960, fig. 137, lower right
58. Izumi and Sono, 1963, pl. 104–1
59. Izumi and Sono, 1963, pls. 106c–2, 166–12

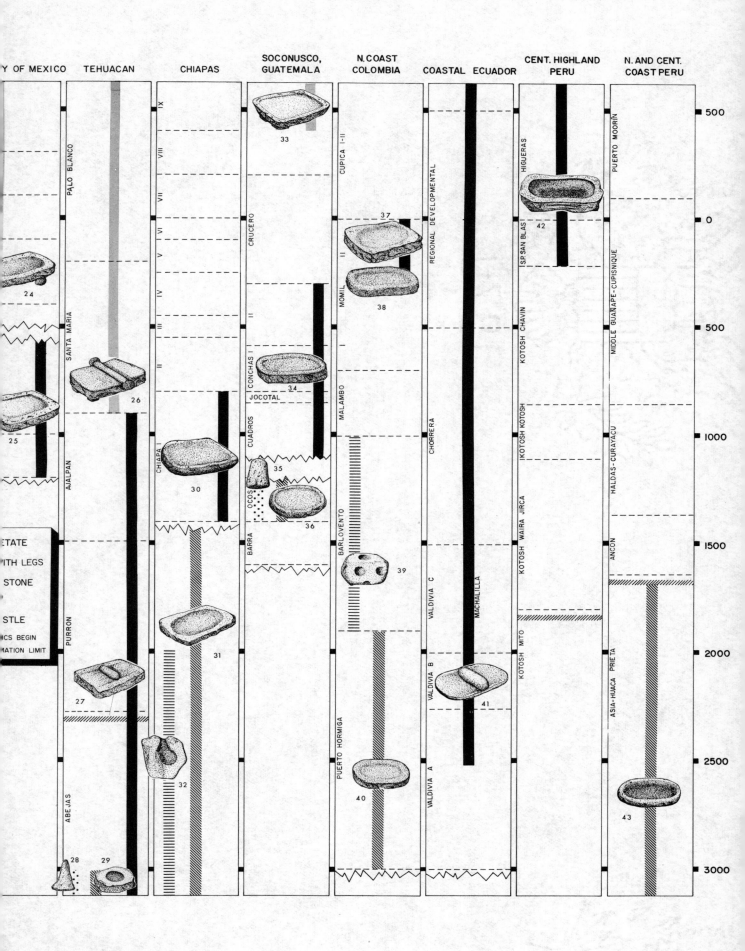

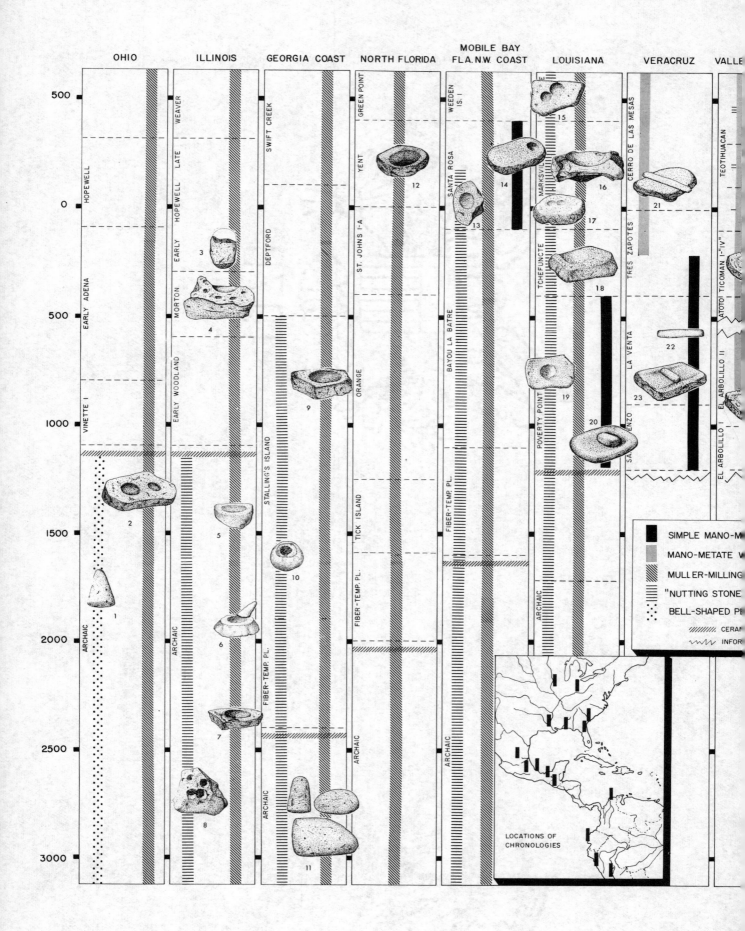

OHIO   ILLINOIS   GEORGIA COAST   NORTH FLORIDA   MOBILE BAY FLA. N.W. COAST   LOUISIANA   VERACRUZ   VALLE

SIMPLE MANO-M
MANO-METATE V
MULLER-MILLING
"NUTTING STONE
BELL-SHAPED Pl
CERA
INFOR

LOCATIONS OF CHRONOLOGIES

GRINDING STONES FOR PREPARING FOOD

CHART 5

1. Griffin, 1952b, fig. 29o
2. Webb and Haag, 1939, fig. 10
3. Griffin, 1952b, fig. 95–11
4. Griffin, 1952b, fig. 95–12
5. Cole, et al., 1951, fig. 67–43
6. Fowler, 1961, fig. 4
7. Fowler, 1959a, fig. 12k
8. Fowler, 1959a, fig. 12 1
9. Claflin, 1931, pl. 50
10. Claflin, 1931, pl. 51
11. Lewis and Lewis, 1961, pls. 31b, 32a, 32c
12. Florida State Museum Collection
13. Wimberly and Tourtelot, 1941, fig. 9
14. Wimberly and Tourtelot, 1941, p. 14
15. Ford, 1951, fig. 47j
16. Ford, 1951, fig. 48
17. Ford and Willey, 1940, fig. 49e
18. Ford and Quimby, 1945, fig. 11a
19. Ford and Webb, 1956, fig. 34a
20. Florida State Museum, Alexander Collection
21. Weiant, 1943, pl. 67–2
22. Garcia Payón, 1966, pl. 81–5

23. Florida State Museum Collection
24. Lorenzo, 1965, fig. 42
25. Lorenzo, 1965, fig. 41
26. MacNeish, 1961, fig. 15
27. MacNeish, 1961, fig. 15
28. MacNeish, 1961, fig. 15
29. MacNeish, 1961, fig. 15
30. Dixon, 1959, fig. 53e
31. MacNeish and Peterson, 1962, pl. 5Ac
32. MacNeish and Peterson, 1962, pl. 5Ae
33. Kidder, Jennings and Shook, 1946, fig. 58h
34. M.D. Coe, 1961, fig. 43d
35. M.D. Coe, 1961, fig. 51p
36. M.D. Coe, 1961, fig. 41g
37. Reichel-Dolmatoff, Gerardo and Alicia, 1956, p. 229
38. Reichel-Dolmatoff, Gerardo and Alicia, 1956, pl. 26–1
39. Reichel-Dolmatoff, Gerardo and Alicia, 1956, pl. 26–6
40. Reichel-Dolmatoff, 1965, pp. 38–39
41. Meggers, Evans, and Estrada, 1965, pl. 16 O–F
42. Izumi and Sono, 1963, pl. 112a
43. Engel, 1963, fig. 175

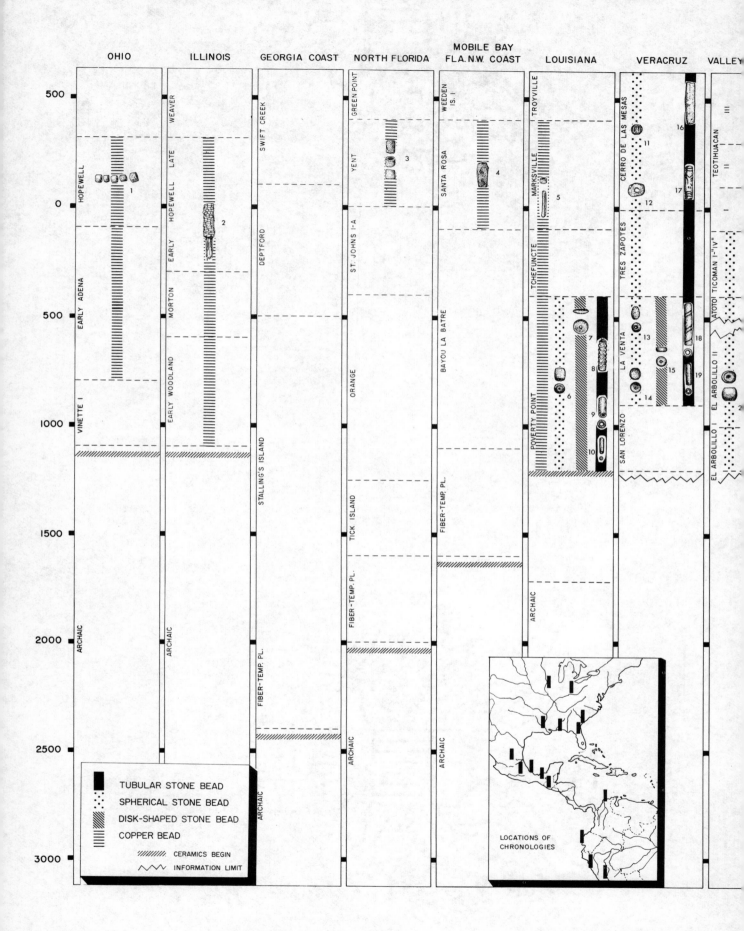

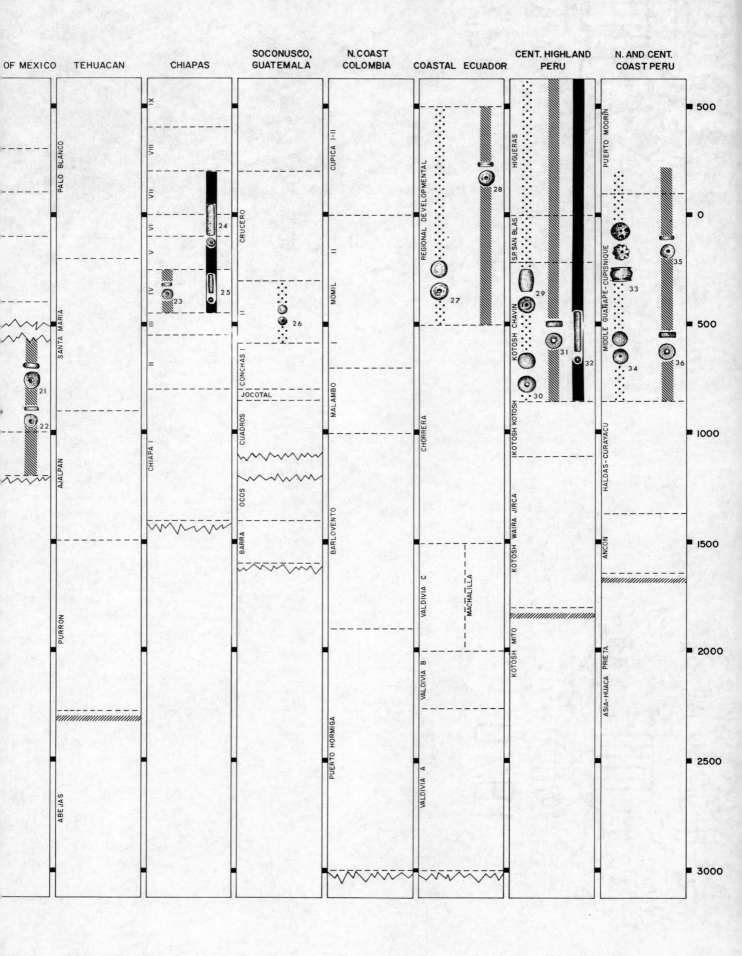

THE LAPIDARY INDUSTRY: BEADS

Chart 6

1. Shetrone, 1926, fig. 79
2. Bluhm and Beeson, 1960, fig. 5
3. Kellar, Kelly, and McMichael, 1962, fig. 3d
4. Wimberly and Tourtelot, 1941, fig. 10e
5. Ford and Willey, 1940, fig. 55e
6. Ford and Webb, 1956, fig. 37m
7. Ford and Webb, 1956, fig. 37e
8. Ford and Webb, 1956, fig. 37s
9. Ford and Webb, 1956, fig. 37g
10. Ford and Webb, 1956, fig. 37t
11. Drucker, 1955, pl. 51
12. Drucker, 1955, pl. 51
13. Drucker, Heizer, and Squier, 1959, pls. 28 and 52a
14. Drucker, Heizer, and Squier, 1959, pls. 28 and 52a
15. Drucker, Heizer, and Squier, 1959, pls. 28 and 52a
16. Drucker, 1955, pl. 53
17. Drucker, 1955, pl. 53
18. Drucker, Heizer, and Squier, 1959, pls. 28 and 52a
19. Drucker, Heizer, and Squier, 1959, pls. 28 and 52a
20. Lorenzo, 1965, fig. 62
21. Lorenzo, 1965, fig. 60
22. Lorenzo, 1965, fig. 60
23. Agrinier, 1964, p. 25
24. Agrinier, 1964, p. 25
25. Agrinier, 1964, p. 25
26. M. D. Coe, 1961, p. 108
27. Estrada, Meggers, and Evans, 1964, fig. 13
28. Estrada, Meggers, and Evans, 1964, figs. 7d, 13
29. Izumi and Sono, 1963, pl. 110b–5
30. Izumi and Sono, 1963, pl. 110b–1
31. Izumi and Sono, 1963, pl. 110b–3
32. Izumi and Sono, 1963, pl. 110b–19
33. Larco Hoyle, 1941, fig. 149
34. Strong and Evans, 1952, p. 40
35. Larco, 1941, fig. 149
36. Strong and Evans, 1952, p. 40

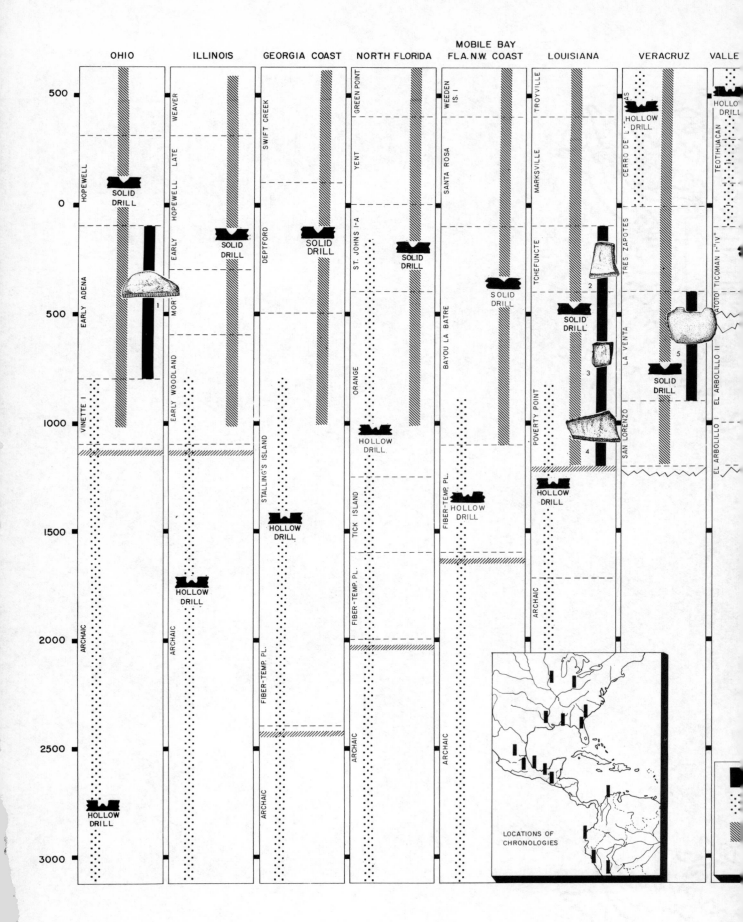

MOBILE BAY

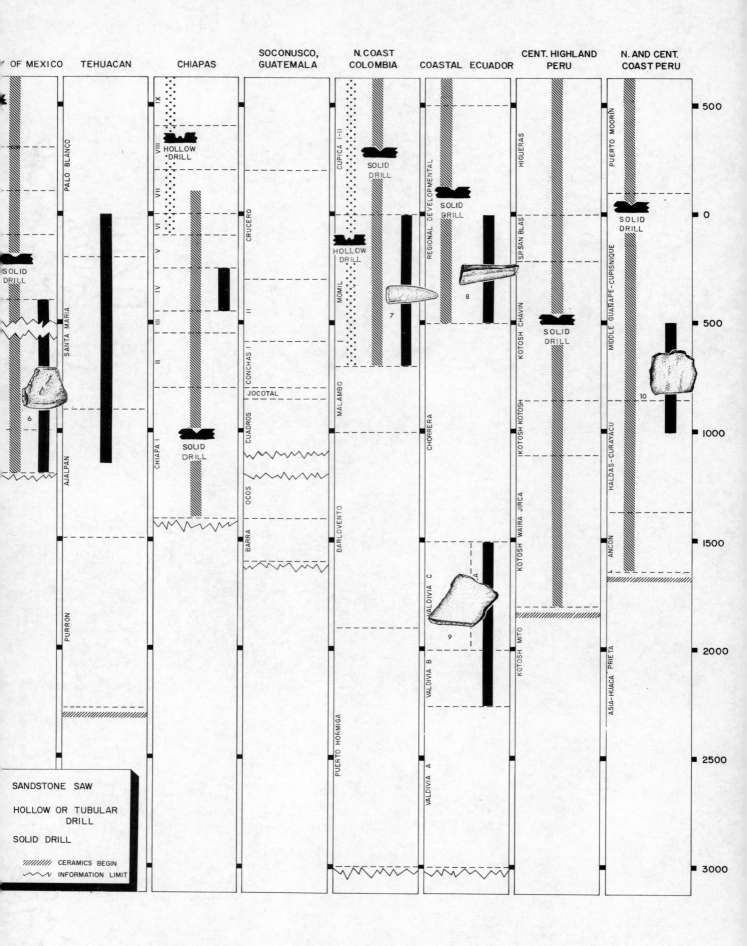

SANDSTONE SAWS, SOLID AND TUBULAR DRILLS

Chart 7

Illustrations of drilling techniques do not refer to individual specimens, but to tool types in general; for detailed information on sources, see pp. 67–69.

1. Webb and Snow, 1945, p. 90
2. Ford and Quimby, 1945, fig. 11f
3. Ford, Phillips, and Haag, 1955, fig. 47h
4. Ford and Webb, 1956, fig. 34h–i
5. Drucker, 1952, pl. 44a

6. Lorenzo, 1965, fig. 38
7. Reichel-Dolmatoff, Gerardo and Alicia, 1956, pl. 27–5
8. Estrada, Meggers, and Evans, 1964, pl. 6d
9. Meggers, Evans, and Estrada, 1965, fig. 15a
10. Strong and Evans, 1952, fig. 7f

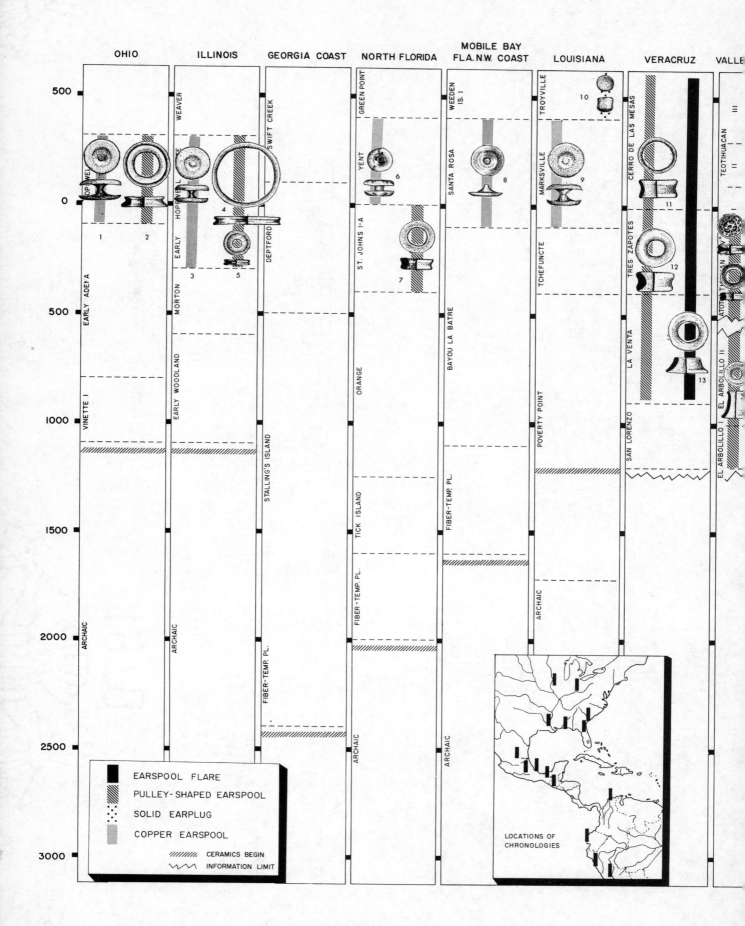

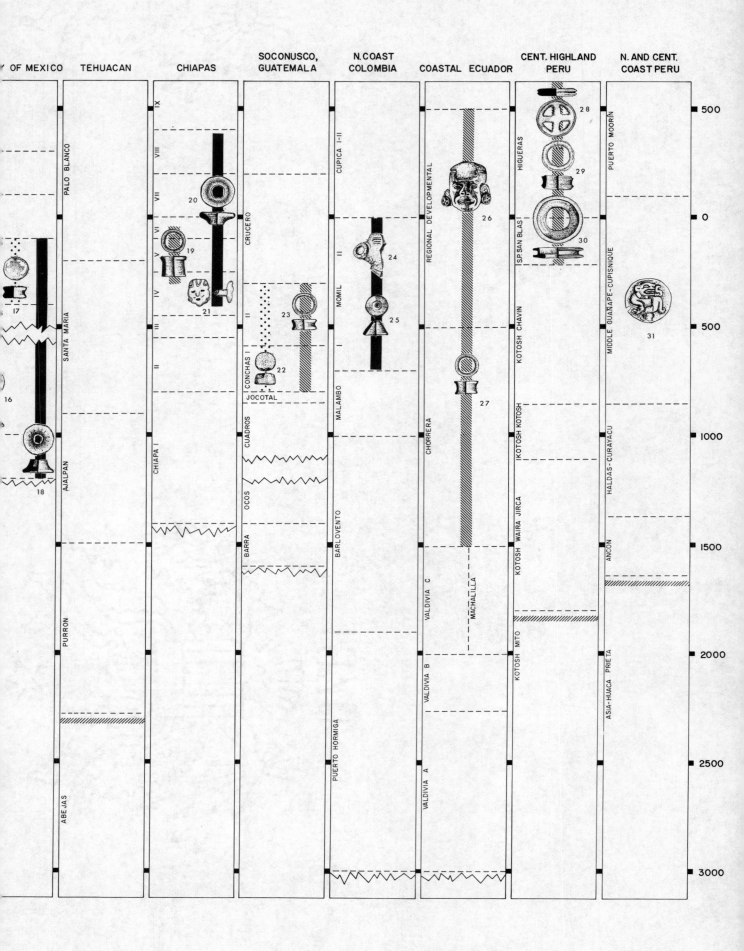

OF MEXICO   TEHUACAN   CHIAPAS   SOCONUSCO, GUATEMALA   N.COAST COLOMBIA   COASTAL ECUADOR   CENT. HIGHLAND PERU   N. AND CENT. COAST PERU

EARSPOOLS AND EARPLUGS

CHART 8

1. Mills, 1916, fig. 106
2. Shetrone, 1926, fig. 100
3. McGregor, 1959, fig. 5
4. Fowler, 1957, pl. 14–1
5. Fowler, 1957, pl. 14–8
6. Kellar, Kelly, and McMichael, 1962, fig. 3b
7. Florida State Museum Collection
8. Wimberly and Tourtelot, 1941, fig. 10d
9. Ford, 1963, fig. 11
10. Ford, 1951, fig. 42a
11. Florida State Museum Collection
12. Florida State Museum Collection
13. Drucker, Heizer, and Squier, 1959, pl. 39b
14. Vaillant, 1931, pl. 82
15. Vaillant, 1931, pl. 82
16. Vaillant, 1935, fig. 25

17. Vaillant, 1931, pl. 82
18. Vaillant, 1935, fig. 25–7
19. Sanders, 1961, pl. 11B–p
20. Navarette, 1959, fig. 10a
21. Peterson, 1963, fig. 168
22. M.D. Coe, 1961, fig. 60c
23. M.D. Coe, 1961, fig. 42d
24. Reichel-Dolmatoff, Gerardo and Alicia, 1956, pl. 22–4
25. Reichel-Dolmatoff, Gerardo and Alicia, 1956, pl. 31, 3–4
26. Estrada, 1957, fig. 86
27. Evans and Meggers, 1957, fig. 4
28. Izumi and Sono, 1963, pl. 155–4
29. Izumi and Sono, 1963, pl. 169–21
30. Izumi and Sono, 1963, pl. 155–5
31. Larco Hoyle, 1945a, p. 17

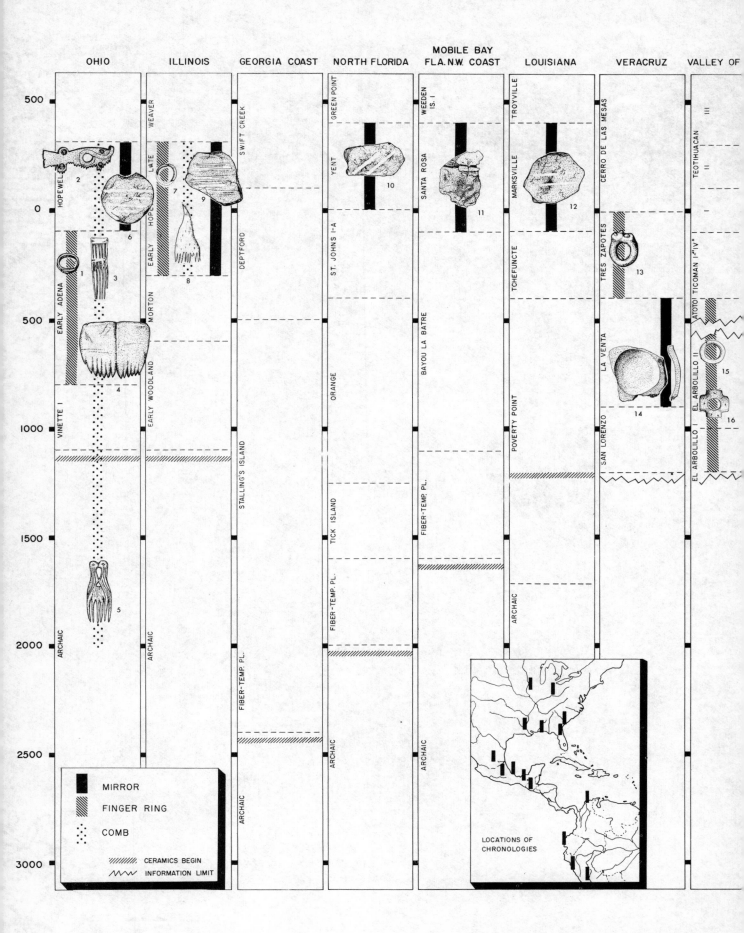

OHIO ILLINOIS GEORGIA COAST NORTH FLORIDA MOBILE BAY FLA. N.W. COAST LOUISIANA VERACRUZ VALLEY OF

MIRROR

FINGER RING

COMB

CERAMICS BEGIN

INFORMATION LIMIT

LOCATIONS OF CHRONOLOGIES

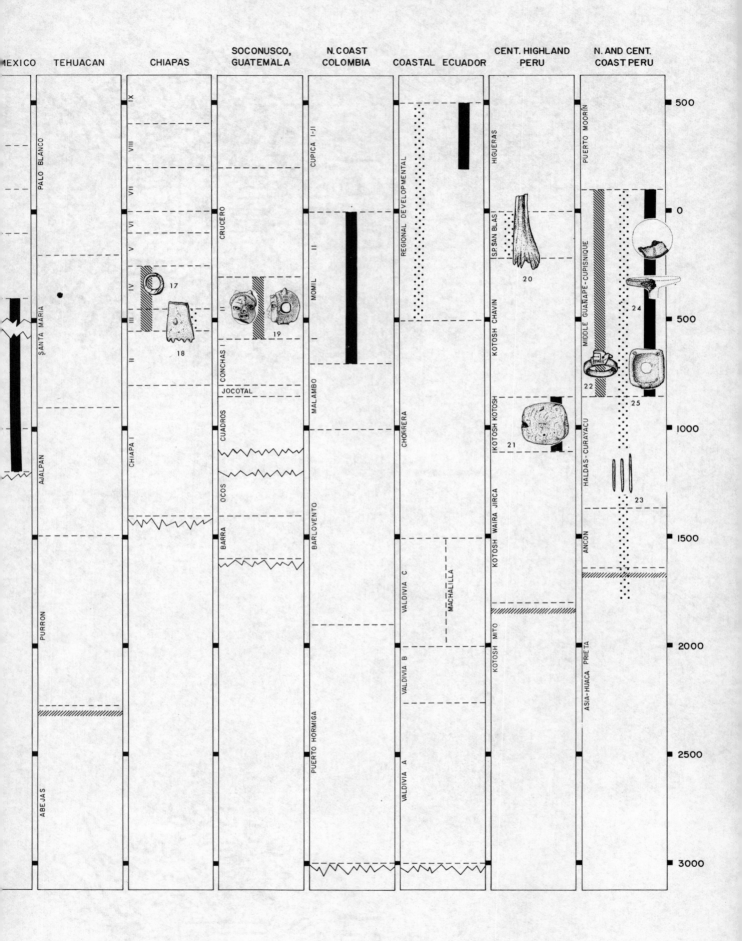

MEXICO | TEHUACAN | CHIAPAS | SOCONUSCO, GUATEMALA | N. COAST COLOMBIA | COASTAL ECUADOR | CENT. HIGHLAND PERU | N. AND CENT. COAST PERU

500

0

500

1000

1500

2000

2500

3000

COMBS, MIRRORS, AND FINGER RINGS

CHART 9

1. Mills, 1902, p. 458, fig. 5
2. Moorehead, 1922, fig. 12b
3. Griffin, 1952b, fig. 16–1
4. Mills, 1902, fig. 22
5. Ritchie, 1965, pl. 40
6. Mills, 1907, fig. 57
7. Fowler, 1957, pl. 9c
8. Perino, personal communication
9. Neumann and Fowler, 1952, pl. 59b
10. Moore, 1907, p. 419
11. Wimberly and Tourtelot, 1941, fig. 9
12. Ford, 1963, fig. 21d
13. Weiant, 1943, pl. 65
14. Drucker, Heizer, and Squier, 1959, fig. 49
15. Vaillant, 1930, pl. 40–1
16. Vaillant, 1930, pl. 41– bottom row, 4
17. Sanders, 1961, pl. 11B–x
18. Sanders, 1961, pl. 11B–y
19. M. D. Coe, 1961, fig. 42a
20. Izumi and Sono, 1963, pl. 162–8
21. Izumi and Sono, 1963, pl. 106b–11
22. Larco Hoyle, 1945a, p. 19
23. Willey and Corbett, 1954, p. 70
24. Strong and Evans, 1952, fig. 7j–k
25. Engel, 1963, fig. 196

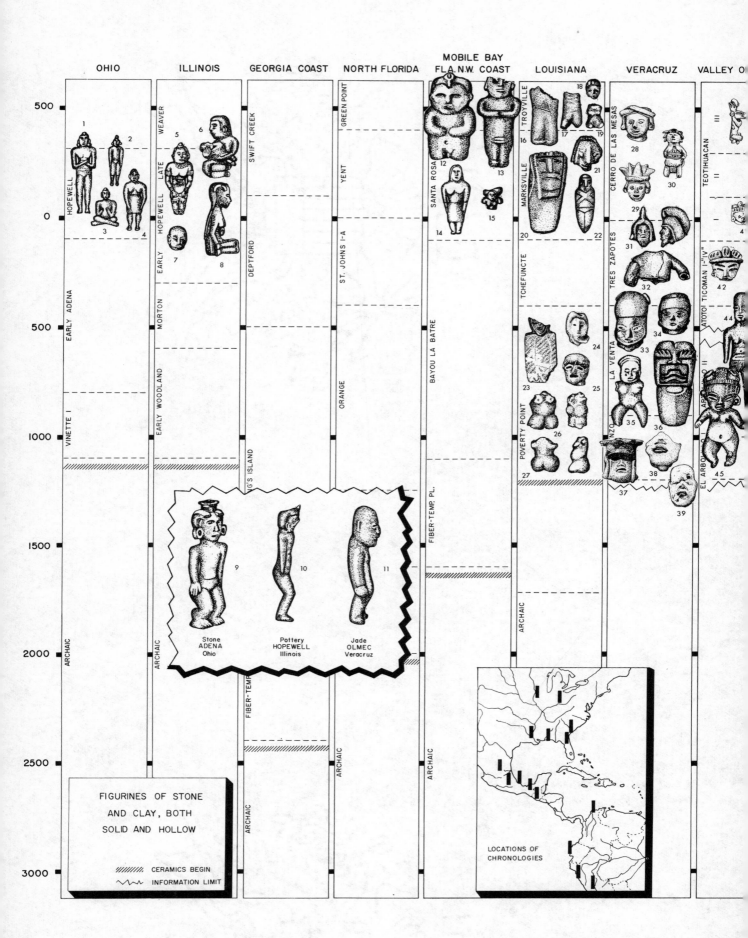

FIGURINES OF STONE
AND CLAY, BOTH
SOLID AND HOLLOW

////// CERAMICS BEGIN
〜〜 INFORMATION LIMIT

LOCATIONS OF
CHRONOLOGIES

Stone
ADENA
Ohio

Pottery
HOPEWELL
Illinois

Jade
OLMEC
Veracruz

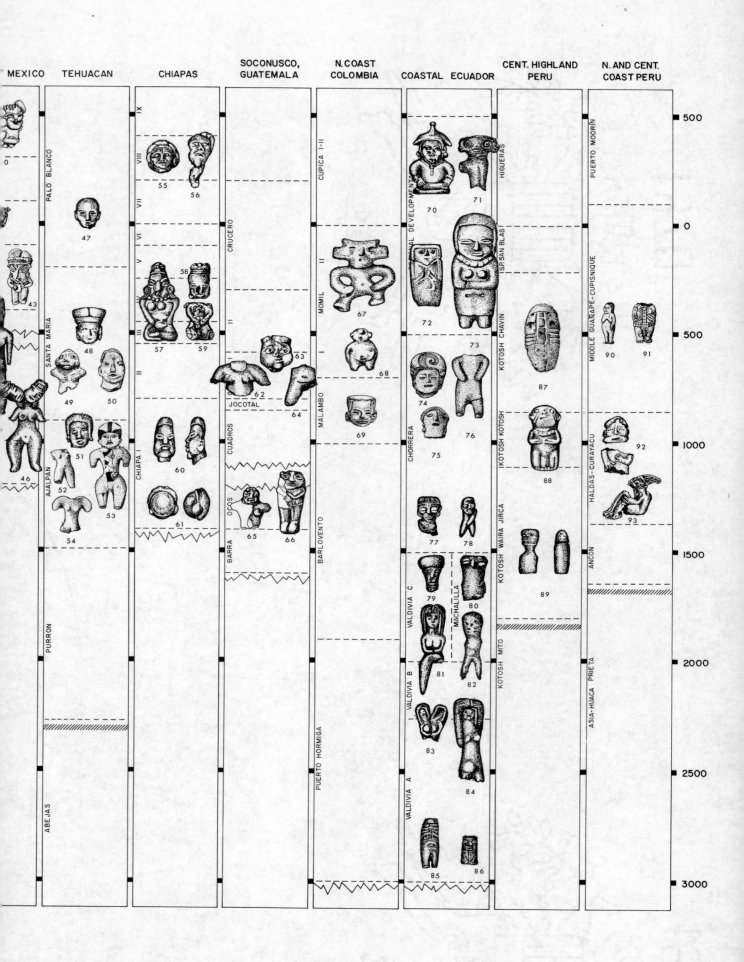

MEXICO   TEHUACAN   CHIAPAS   SOCONUSCO, GUATEMALA   N. COAST COLOMBIA   COASTAL ECUADOR   CENT. HIGHLAND PERU   N. AND CENT. COAST PERU

FIGURINES

Chart 10

1. Willoughby, 1922, pl. 21g
2. Willoughby, 1922, pl. 21a
3. Willoughby, 1922, pl. 21f
4. Willoughby, 1922, pl. 21b
5. McKern, Titterington, and Griffin, 1945, pl. 24
6. McKern, Titterington, and Griffin 1945, pl. 22
7. N. Engle, 1957
8. N. Engle, 1957
9. Webb and Baby, 1957, fig. 22
10. N. Engle, 1957
11. Drucker, 1952, pl. 49
12. Moore, 1902, fig. 32
13. Moore, 1902, fig. 22
14. McMichael, 1964, pl. 8A
15. McMichael, 1964, pl. 8J
16. Ford, 1951, fig. 44f
17. Ford, 1951, fig. 44i
18. Ford, 1951, fig. 44a
19. Ford, 1951, fig. 44c
20. Ford and Willey, 1940, fig. 51a
21. Ford and Willey, 1940, fig. 53b
22. McLurkan, Field, and Woodall, 1966, fig. 14j
23. McCormick Collection
24. Ford and Webb, 1956, fig. 16k
25. Poverty Point, unpublished notes
26. Ford and Webb, 1956, fig. 16d
27. Ford and Webb, 1956, fig. 16f
28. Drucker, 1943b, pl. 29
29. Drucker, 1943b, pl. 35
30. Drucker, 1943b, pl. 42a
31. Drucker, 1952, pl. 28L
32. García Payón, 1966, pl. 69–24
33. García Payón, 1966, pl. 62–1
34. García Payón, 1966, pl. 53–1
35. García Payón, 1966, pl. 60–2
36. Drucker, 1952, pl. 56
37. Photograph provided by Michael Coe
38. Photograph provided by Michael Coe
39. Photograph provided by Michael Coe
40. Millon, Drewitt, and Bennyhoff, 1965, fig. 106a
41. Millon, Drewitt, and Bennyhoff, 1965, fig. 101–1
42. Vaillant, 1931, pl. 55
43. Vaillant, 1931, pl. 64
44. Piña Chán, 1958, vol. 2, pl. 16
45. Piña Chán, 1958, vol. 2, pl. 20
46. Piña Chán, 1958, vol. 2, pl. 28
47. MacNeish, 1961, fig. 15
48. MacNeish, 1961, fig. 15
49. Willey, 1966, fig. 3–14g
50. Willey, 1966, fig. 3–14a
51. MacNeish, 1961, fig. 15
52. Willey, 1966, fig. 3–13k
53. Willey, 1966, fig. 3–15
54. Willey, 1966, fig. 3–13j
55. Sanders, 1961, pl. 10B–e
56. Sanders, 1961, pl. 10B–m
57. Peterson, 1963, fig. 114a
58. Peterson, 1963, fig. 119d
59. Peterson, 1963, fig. 119c
60. Dixon, 1959, fig. 53a
61. Dixon, 1959, fig. 51
62. M. D. Coe, 1961, fig. 57c
63. M. D. Coe, 1961, fig. 54b
64. M. D. Coe, 1961, fig. 57f
65. M. D. Coe, 1961, fig. 39j
66. M. D. Coe, 1961, fig. 40f
67. Reichel-Dolmatoff, Gerardo and Alicia, 1956, pl. 22–6
68. Reichel-Dolmatoff, Gerardo and Alicia, 1956, pl. 22–14
69. Angulo Valdés, 1962b, pl. 7a
70. Estrada, 1962, fig. 128a
71. Estrada, Meggers, and Evans, 1964, fig. 15a
72. Estrada, 1962, fig. 97E
73. Estrada, 1962, fig. 71
74. Photograph provided by Clifford Evans
75. Photograph provided by Clifford Evans
76. Photograph provided by Clifford Evans
77. Estrada, 1962, fig. 71
78. Estrada, 1962, fig. 71
79. Meggers, Evans, and Estrada, 1965, pl. 118q
80. Meggers, Evans, and Estrada, 1965, pl. 158a
81. Meggers, Evans, and Estrada, 1965, pl. 120a
82. Meggers, Evans, and Estrada, 1965, pl. 125a
83. Meggers, Evans, and Estrada, 1965, pl. 123cc
84. Meggers, Evans, and Estrada, 1965, pl. 123u
85. Meggers, Evans, and Estrada, 1965, pl. 118j
86. Meggers, Evans, and Estrada, 1965, pl. 118b
87. Tello, 1960, fig. 134
88. Izumi and Sono, 1963, pl. 100c
89. Izumi and Sono, 1963, pl. 111, 4–5
90. Carrión Cachot, 1948, pl. 25–23
91. Carrión Cachot, 1948, pl. 25–24
92. Ishida, 1960, nos. 60–61
93. Bird, 1962, fig. 52c

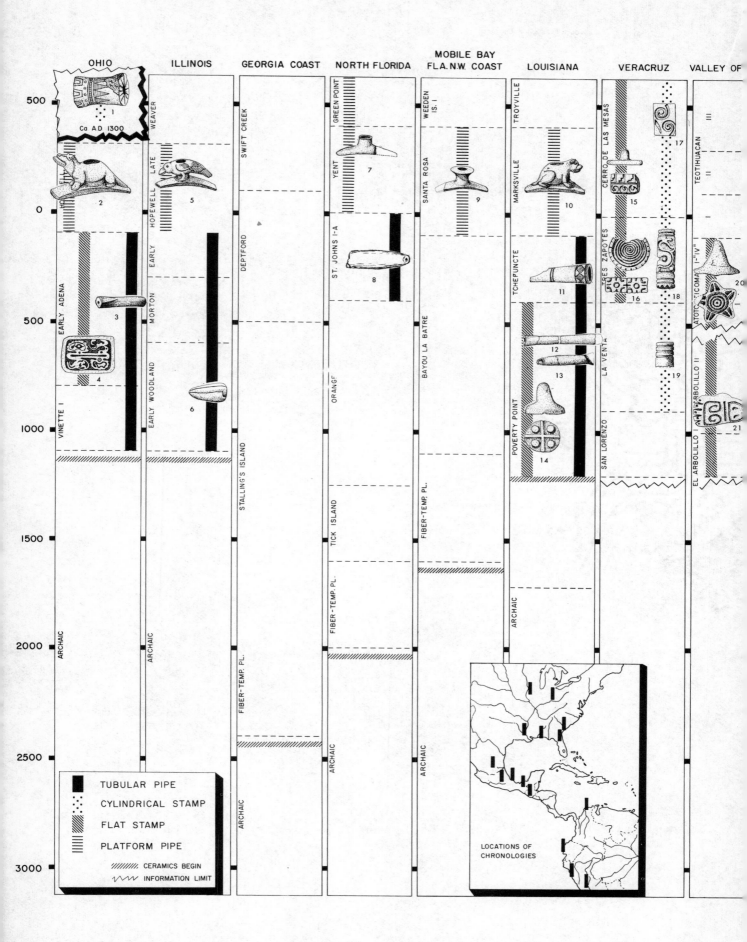

MOBILE BAY

OHIO   ILLINOIS   GEORGIA COAST   NORTH FLORIDA   FLA. N.W. COAST   LOUISIANA   VERACRUZ   VALLEY OF

500

Ca A.D. 1300

0

500

1000

1500

2000

2500

3000

TUBULAR PIPE

CYLINDRICAL STAMP

FLAT STAMP

PLATFORM PIPE

///// CERAMICS BEGIN

∿∿ INFORMATION LIMIT

LOCATIONS OF
CHRONOLOGIES

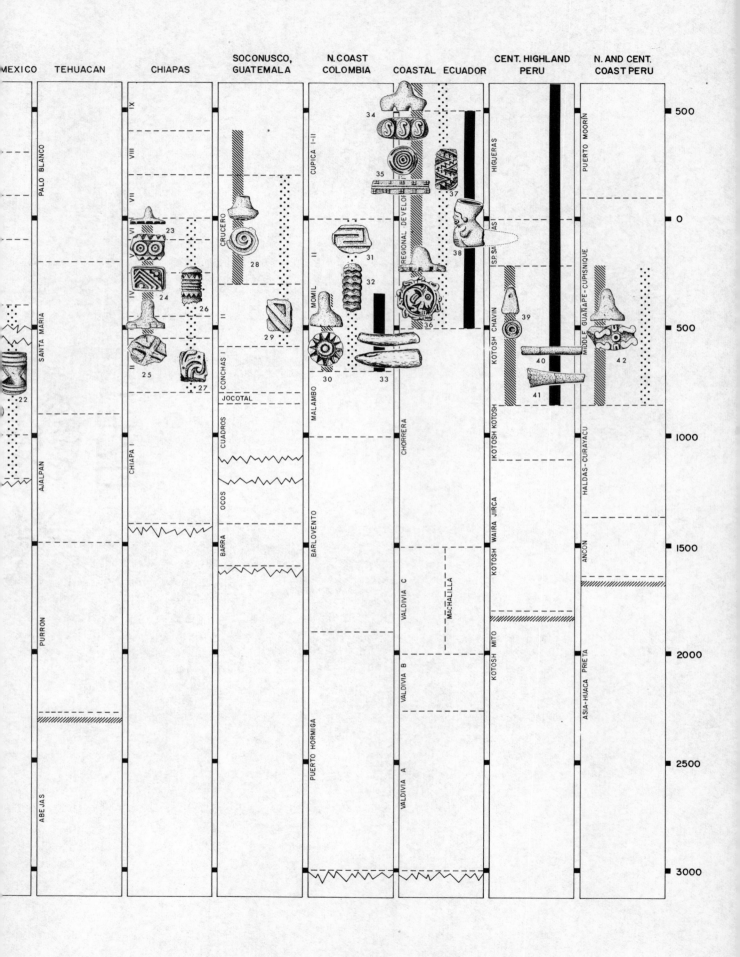

TUBULAR AND PLATFORM PIPES, FLAT AND CYLINDRICAL STAMPS

CHART 11

1. Holmes, 1903, fig. 28
2. Mills, 1916, fig. 10
3. Griffin, 1952b, fig. 31b
4. Webb and Baby, 1957, fig. 38
5. McGregor, 1959, fig. 5
6. Perino, personal communication
7. Sears, 1962, fig. 2m
8. Moore, 1894, fig. 112
9. Kellar, Kelly, and McMichael, 1962, fig. 3e
10. Ford and Willey, 1940, fig. 52a
11. Ford and Quimby, 1945, fig. 7k
12. Ford and Quimby, 1945, fig. 7a
13. Ford and Quimby, 1945, fig. 7c
14. Poverty Point, unpublished notes
15. Drucker, 1943b, figs. 203, 205
16. Weiant, 1943, pl. 62
17. Drucker, 1943b, fig. 202
18. Weiant, 1943, pl. 63
19. Drucker, 1952, fig. 40b
20. Vaillant, 1931, pl. 83e
21. Porter, 1953, pl. 13c
22. Porter, 1953, pl. 13b
23. Peterson, 1963, fig. 170

24. Sanders, 1961, pl. 11B–g
25. Peterson, 1963, fig. 170
26. Peterson, 1963, fig. 170
27. Sanders, 1961, pl. 11A–b
28. M.D. Coe, 1961, fig. 61a
29. M.D. Coe, 1961, fig. 59m
30. Reichel-Dolmatoff, Gerardo and Alicia, 1956, pl. 20–3
31. Reichel-Dolmatoff, Gerardo and Alicia, 1956, fig. 11–1
32. Reichel-Dolmatoff, Gerardo and Alicia, 1956, pl. 20–8
33. Reichel-Dolmatoff, Gerardo and Alicia, 1956, pl. 19, 10–11
34. Estrada, 1958, fig. 51–2
35. Estrada, 1962, fig. 93
36. Meggers, 1966, pl. 36
37. Meggers, 1966, pl. 36
38. Estrada, 1957, fig. 111
39. Izumi and Sono, 1963, pl. 154–12
40. Izumi and Sono, 1963, pl. 98b–13
41. Izumi and Sono, 1963, pl. 98b–14
42. Carrión Cachot, 1948, pl. 24–t

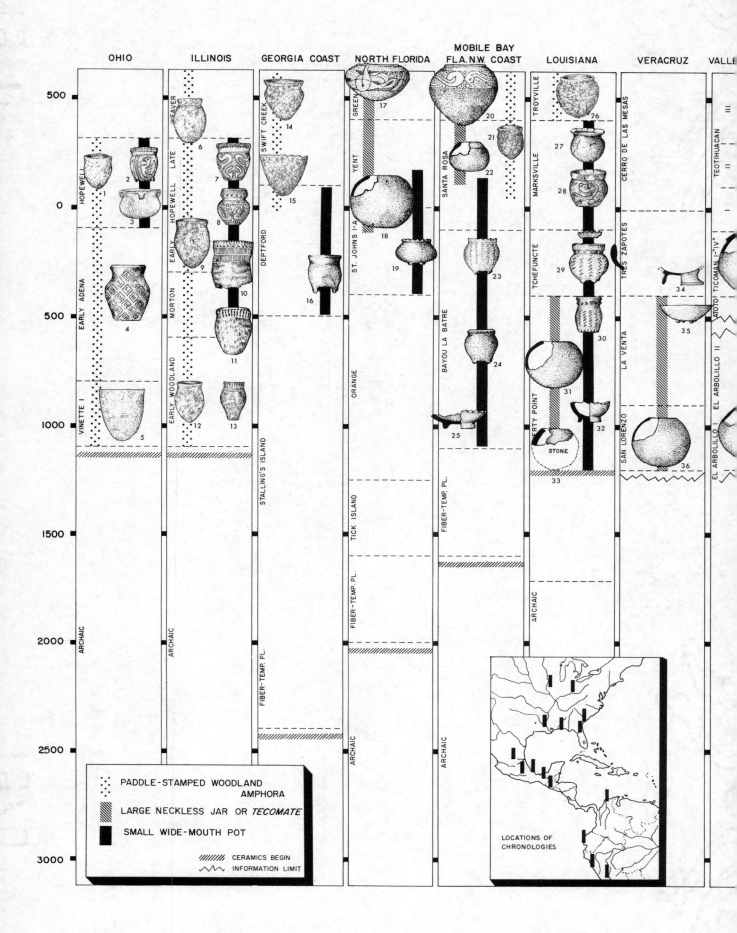

OHIO

ILLINOIS

GEORGIA COAST

NORTH FLORIDA

MOBILE BAY
FLA. N.W. COAST

LOUISIANA

VERACRUZ

VALLE

500

0

500

1000

1500

2000

2500

3000

HOPEWELL
EARLY ADENA
VINETTE I
ARCHAIC

WEAVER
LATE HOPEWELL
EARLY HOPEWELL
MORTON
EARLY WOODLAND
ARCHAIC

SWIFT CREEK
DEPTFORD
STALLING'S ISLAND
FIBER-TEMP. PL.
ARCHAIC

GREEN
YENT
ST. JOHNS I-A
ORANGE
TICK ISLAND
FIBER-TEMP. PL.
ARCHAIC

SANTA ROSA
BAYOU LA BATRE
FIBER-TEMP. PL.
ARCHAIC

TROYVILLE
MARKSVILLE
TCHEFUNCTE
RTY POINT
STONE
ARCHAIC

CERRO DE LAS MESAS
TRES ZAPOTES
LA VENTA
SAN LORENZO

TEOTIHUACAN
ATOTO TICOMAN I-"IV
EL ARBOLILLO II
EL ARBOLILLO I

PADDLE-STAMPED WOODLAND AMPHORA

LARGE NECKLESS JAR OR *TECOMATE*

SMALL WIDE-MOUTH POT

CERAMICS BEGIN
INFORMATION LIMIT

LOCATIONS OF CHRONOLOGIES

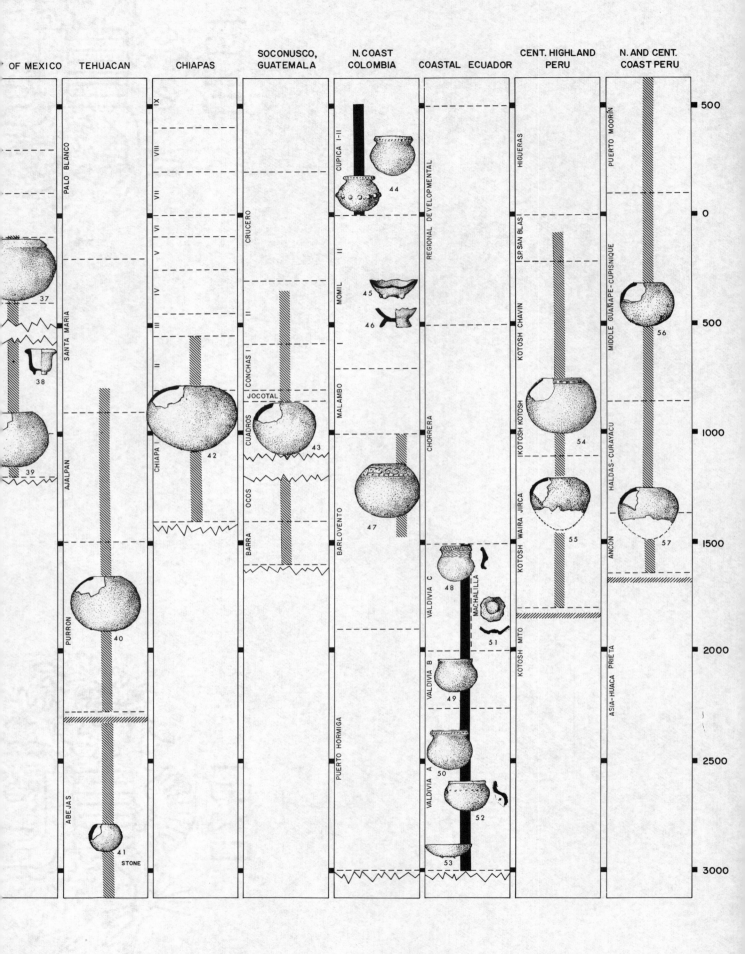

OF MEXICO TEHUACAN CHIAPAS SOCONUSCO, GUATEMALA N. COAST COLOMBIA COASTAL ECUADOR CENT. HIGHLAND PERU N. AND CENT. COAST PERU

PALO BLANCO
SANTA MARIA
AJALPAN
PURRON
ABEJAS

IX VIII VII VI V IV III II

CRUCERO
CONCHAS I JOCOTAL
CUADROS
OCOS
BARRA

CUPICA I-II
MOMIL II
MALAMBO
BARLOVENTO
PUERTO HORMIGA

REGIONAL DEVELOPMENTAL
CHORRERA
VALDIVIA C MACHALILLA
VALDIVIA B
VALDIVIA A

HIGUERAS
ISP. SAN BLAS
KOTOSH CHAVIN
IKOTOSH KOTOSH
KOTOSH WAIRA JIRCA
KOTOSH MITO

PUERTO MOORÍN
MIDDLE GUAÑAPE-CUPISNIQUE
HALDAS-CURAYACU
ANCON
ASIA-HUACA PRIETA

37
38
39
40
41 STONE

42
43

44
45
46
47

48
49
50
51
52
53

54
55

56
57

500
0
500
1000
1500
2000
2500
3000

TECOMATE, SMALL WIDE-MOUTH POT, AND PADDLE-STAMPED WOODLAND AMPHORA

CHART 12

1. Griffin, 1952b, fig. 40
2. Griffin, 1952b, fig. 32s
3. Willoughby, 1922, pl. 22 bottom
4. Webb and Snow, 1945, fig. 2
5. Ritchie, 1946, p. 13, pl. 8–5
6. Griffin, 1952b, fig. 37u
7. Perino, personal communication
8. McGregor, 1959, fig. 5
9. Griffin, 1952b, fig. 37n
10. Griffin, 1952a, pl. 32a
11. Cole and Deuel, 1937, pl. 1–7
12. Griffin, 1952b, fig. 37g
13. Fowler, 1959a, fig. 4
14. Wauchope, 1966, fig. 10f
15. Wauchope, 1966, fig. 6c
16. Wauchope, 1966, fig. 6b
17. Florida State Museum Collection
18. Florida State Museum Collection
19. Florida State Museum Collection
20. Florida State Museum Collection
21. Willey, 1949a, pp. 388–389
22. Willey, 1949a, fig. 42c
23. Wimberly, 1960, figs. 40–41
24. Wimberly, 1960, fig. 40
25. Wimberly, 1960, fig. 39d
26. Ford, 1951, fig. 16a
27. Ford and Willey, 1940, fig. 21
28. Ford and Willey, 1940, fig. 31c
29. Ford and Quimby, 1945, fig. 17b, pl. 2a

30. Poverty Point Site, Alexander Collection
31. Poverty Point Site, Alexander Collection
32. Ford and Quimby, 1945, fig. 18b–c
33. Poverty Point Site, Alexander Collection
34. Weiant, 1943, fig. 19d
35. Florida State Museum Collection
36. Florida State Museum Collection
37. Vaillant, 1930, pl. 1n; Tolstoy, personal communication
38. Porter, 1953, fig. 14
39. Vaillant, 1930, pl. 1n; Tolstoy, personal communication
40. MacNeish chart, personal communication
41. MacNeish, 1961, fig. 15
42. Dixon, 1959, fig. 1
43. M. D. Coe, 1961, fig. 29n
44. Reichel-Dolmatoff, Gerardo and Alicia, 1961, pls. 3–1, 4–1
45. Reichel-Dolmatoff, Gerardo and Alicia, 1956, fig. 12–7
46. Reichel-Dolmatoff, Gerardo and Alicia, 1956, fig. 10–1
47. Reichel-Dolmatoff, 1955, pls. 3–5
48. Meggers, Evans, and Estrada, 1965, fig. 35–6
49. Meggers, Evans, and Estrada, 1965, fig. 41–5
50. Meggers, Evans, and Estrada, 1965, fig. 41–2
51. Meggers, Evans, and Estrada, 1965, fig. 43b
52. Meggers, Evans, and Estrada, 1965, fig. 36–1
53. Meggers, Evans, and Estrada, 1965, fig. 42–2
54. Izumi and Sono, 1963, pl. 124–1
55. Izumi and Sono, 1963, pls. 50b, 139–8
56. Ford, 1949, fig. 9
57. Ishida, 1960, p. 195, fig. 6

CHART 12

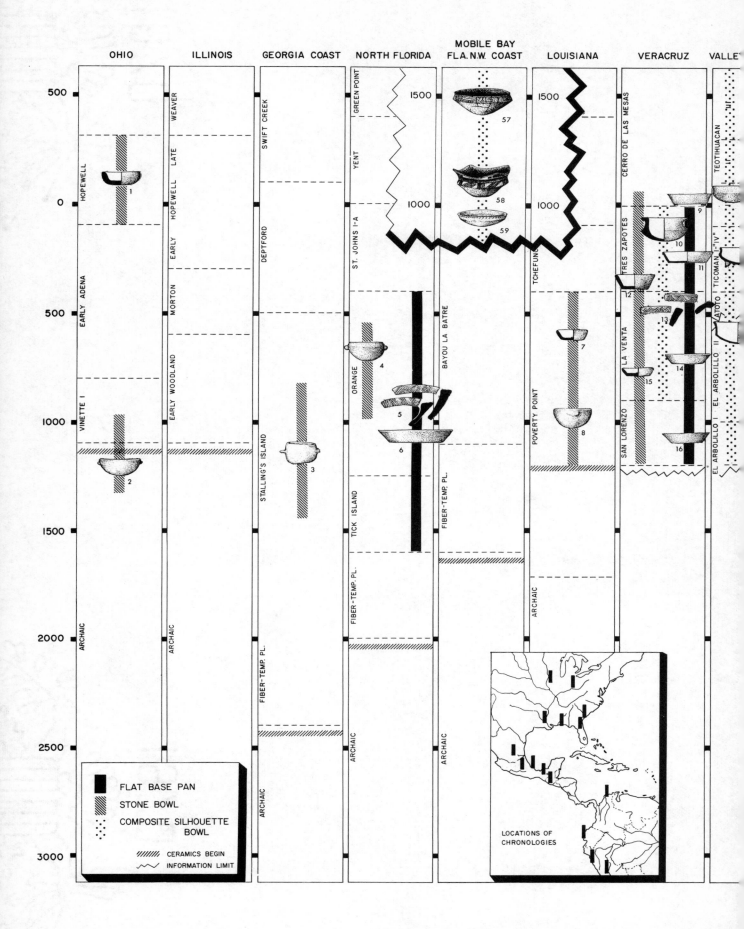

| OHIO | ILLINOIS | GEORGIA COAST | NORTH FLORIDA | MOBILE BAY FLA. N.W. COAST | LOUISIANA | VERACRUZ | VALLE |

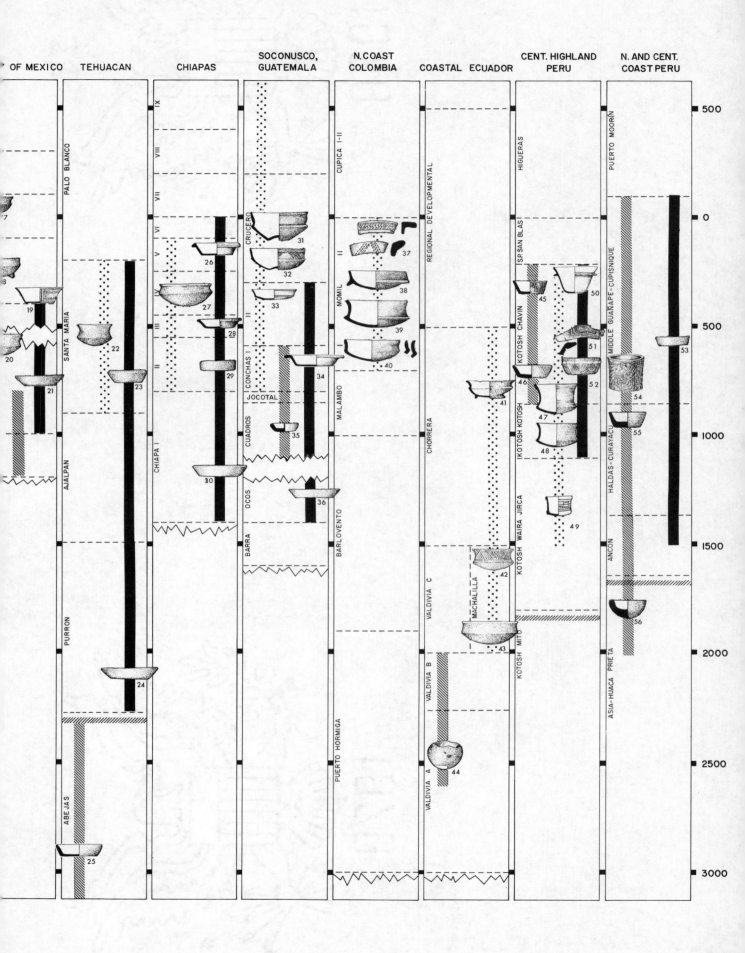

FLAT-BASE PAN, STONE BOWL, AND COMPOSITE SILHOUETTE BOWL

CHART 13

1. Shetrone, 1926, p. 129, figs. 56–57
2. Ritchie, 1965, pp. 158–161, pl. 52
3. Wauchope, 1966, fig. 131–B
4. Florida State Museum Collection
5. Florida State Museum Collection
6. Florida State Museum Collection
7. Ford and Webb, 1956, fig. 40–1
8. Ford and Webb, 1956, fig. 41–a
9. Drucker, 1943a, pl. 17d
10. Weiant, 1943, fig. 19f
11. Weiant, 1943, fig. 17e
12. Weiant, 1943, pl. 66–12
13. Florida State Museum Collection
14. Florida State Museum Collection
15. Florida State Museum Collection
16. M.D. Coe, 1966, (unnumbered pages)
17. Piña Chán, 1958, vol. 1, fig. 45n
18. Vaillant, 1931, pl. 74n
19. Piña Chán, 1958, vol. 1, fig. 37e
20. Vaillant, 1930, pl. 6h
21. Piña Chán, 1958, vol. 1, fig. 34c
22. MacNeish, chart, personal communication
23. MacNeish, chart, personal communication
24. MacNeish, chart, personal communication
25. MacNeish, 1964, p. 536
26. Dixon, 1959, fig. 22f
27. Sanders, 1961, fig. 22
28. Lowe, 1962, pl. 25c–3
29. Dixon, 1959, fig. 1–c
30. Dixon, 1959, fig. 1–d
31. M.D. Coe, 1961, fig. 35i
32. M.D. Coe, 1961, fig. 35i
33. M.D. Coe, 1961, fig. 27 1
34. M.D. Coe, 1961, fig. 32
35. M.D. Coe, 1961, figs. 41a–b, 51q–r
36. M.D. Coe, 1961, figs. 20, 22p
37. Reichel-Dolmatoff, Gerardo and Alicia, 1956, fig. 9–5, 16
38. Reichel-Dolmatoff, Gerardo and Alicia, 1956, fig. 6–8
39. Reichel-Dolmatoff, Gerardo and Alicia 1956, fig. 6–4
40. Reichel-Dolmatoff, Gerardo and Alicia, 1956, fig. 7–o
41. Estrada, 1958, fig. 41–1
42. Meggers, Evans, and Estrada, 1965, fig. 80–2
43. Meggers, Evans, and Estrada, 1965, fig. 84–7
44. Meggers, Evans, and Estrada, 1965, pl. 16b
45. Tello, 1960, fig. 132
46. Izumi and Sono, 1963, pl. 111c–4
47. Izumi and Sono, 1963, pl. 131–2
48. Izumi and Sono, 1963, pl. 131–1
49. Izumi and Sono, 1963, fig. 46–9
50. Izumi and Sono, 1963, pl. 133–3
51. Izumi and Sono, 1963, pl. 145–43
52. Izumi and Sono, 1963, pl. 43b
53. Strong and Evans, 1952, figs. 35–4, 36–3
54. Tello, 1943, fig. 17b
55. Strong and Evans, 1952, p. 41
56. F. Engel, 1963, fig. 145
57. Suhm and Krieger, 1954, pl. 25j
58. Suhm and Krieger, 1954, pl. 57i
59. Ford, 1951, fig. 24j

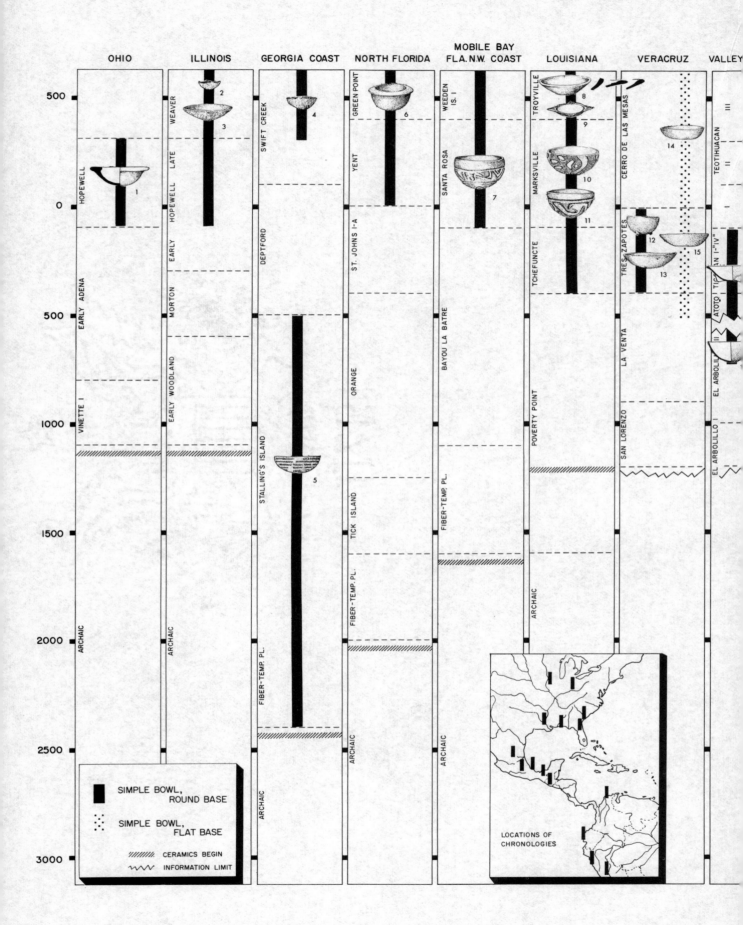

MOBILE BAY

OHIO	ILLINOIS	GEORGIA COAST	NORTH FLORIDA	FLA.N.W. COAST	LOUISIANA	VERACRUZ	VALLEY

500

0

500

1000

1500

2000

2500

3000

OHIO: HOPEWELL / EARLY ADENA / VINETTE I / ARCHAIC

ILLINOIS: WEAVER / LATE HOPEWELL / EARLY HOPEWELL / MORTON / EARLY WOODLAND / ARCHAIC

2 3

GEORGIA COAST: SWIFT CREEK / DEPTFORD / STALLING'S ISLAND / FIBER-TEMP. PL. / ARCHAIC

4

NORTH FLORIDA: GREEN POINT / YENT / ST. JOHNS I-A / ORANGE / TICK ISLAND / FIBER-TEMP. PL. / FIBER-TEMP. PL. / ARCHAIC

6

5

FLA.N.W. COAST: WEEDEN IS. I / SANTA ROSA / BAYOU LA BATRE / FIBER-TEMP. PL. / ARCHAIC

7

LOUISIANA: TROYVILLE / MARKSVILLE / TCHEFUNCTE / POVERTY POINT / ARCHAIC

8
9
10
11

VERACRUZ: CERRO DE LAS MESAS / TRES ZAPOTES / LA VENTA / SAN LORENZO

14
12
13

VALLEY: TEOTIHUACAN / ATOTO I TIC... I-"IV" / EL ARBOLILLO II / EL ARBOLILLO I

III
II
I
15

LOCATIONS OF CHRONOLOGIES

■ SIMPLE BOWL, ROUND BASE

⋮ SIMPLE BOWL, FLAT BASE

▨ CERAMICS BEGIN

〜 INFORMATION LIMIT

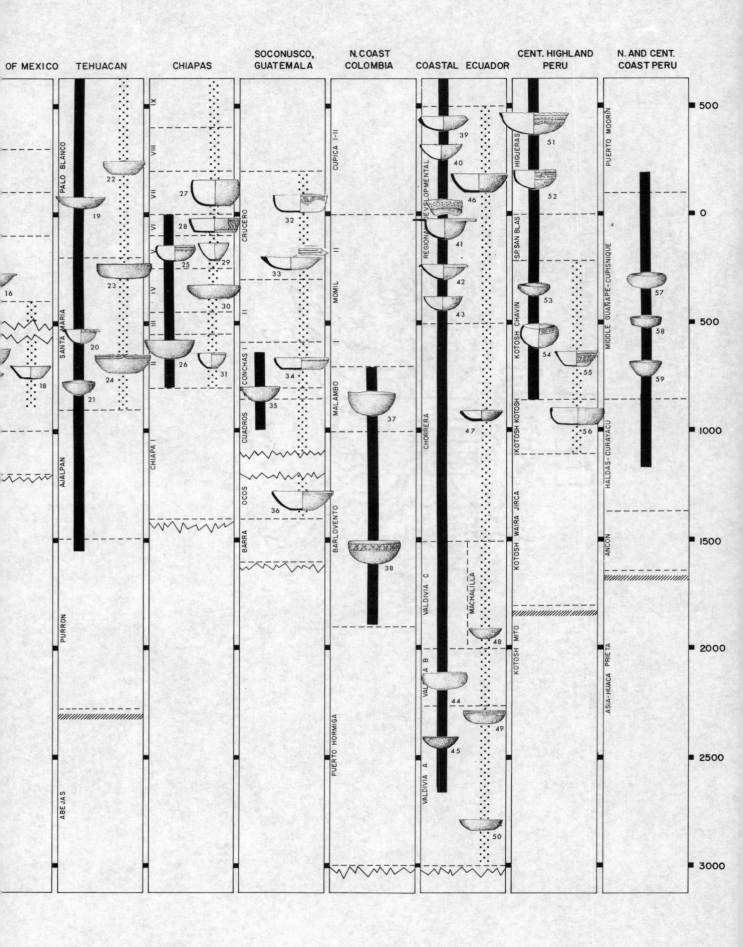

OF MEXICO TEHUACAN CHIAPAS SOCONUSCO, GUATEMALA N. COAST COLOMBIA COASTAL ECUADOR CENT. HIGHLAND PERU N. AND CENT. COAST PERU

ROUND-BASE AND FLAT-BASE SIMPLE BOWL

CHART 14

1. Shetrone, 1926, fig. 53
2. Griffin, 1952b, fig. 101
3. McGregor, 1959, fig. 6
4. Wauchope, 1966, fig. 13d
5. Claflin, 1931, pl. 18
6. Moore, 1903, fig. 25
7. Wimberly, 1960, fig. 46
8. Ford, 1951, fig. 20a, d, h
9. Ford, 1936, fig. 37
10. Ford and Willey, 1940, fig. 29b
11. Ford and Willey, 1940, fig. 40
12. Drucker, 1943a, pl. 15d
13. Drucker, 1943a, pl. 15f
14. Drucker, 1943a, pl. 15h
15. García Payón, 1966, pl. 46–23
16. Vaillant, 1931, pl. 76–f
17. Piña Chán, 1958, vol. 1, fig. 40a
18. Piña Chán, 1958, vol. 1, fig. 37a
19. MacNeish chart, personal communication
20. MacNeish chart, personal communication
21. MacNeish chart, personal communication
22. MacNeish chart, personal communication
23. MacNeish chart, personal communication
24. MacNeish chart, personal communication
25. Sanders, 1961, fig. 23
26. Sanders, 1961, fig. 18, p. 19
27. Sanders, 1961, fig. 21b
28. Sanders, 1961, fig. 33
29. Sanders, 1961, fig. 43
30. Sanders, 1961, fig. 23

31. Sanders, 1961, fig. 18
32. M. D. Coe, 1961, fig. 37f
33. M. D. Coe, 1961, fig. 29a
34. M. D. Coe, 1961, fig. 29f
35. M. D. Coe, 1961, fig. 23f
36. M. D. Coe, 1961, fig. 22n
37. Angulo Valdés, 1962b, pl. 1a
38. Reichel-Dolmatoff, 1955, p. 257
39. Estrada, Meggers, and Evans, 1964, fig. 39–4
40. Estrada, Meggers, and Evans, 1964, fig. 39–7
41. Estrada, 1962, fig. 45b
42. Estrada, Meggers, and Evans, 1964, fig. 39–5
43. Estrada, Meggers, and Evans, 1964, fig. 39–1
44. Meggers, Evans, and Estrada, 1965, fig. 54–3
45. Meggers, Evans, and Estrada, 1965, fig. 54–6
46. Meggers and Evans, personal communication
47. Meggers and Evans, personal communication
48. Meggers, Evans, and Estrada, 1965, fig. 22–6
49. Meggers, Evans, and Estrada, 1965, fig. 24–1
50. Meggers, Evans, and Estrada, 1965, fig. 24–2
51. Izumi and Sono, 1963, pl. 119–19
52. Izumi and Sono, 1963, pl. 123–12
53. Izumi and Sono, 1963, pl. 128–4
54. Izumi and Sono, 1963, fig. 46 VA
55. Izumi and Sono, 1963, pl. 132–11
56. Izumi and Sono, 1963, pl. 128–1
57. Ford, 1949, fig. 9
58. Ford, 1949, fig. 9
59. Ford, 1949, fig. 9

ROUND-BASE AND FLAT-BASE SIMPLE BOWL

CHART 11

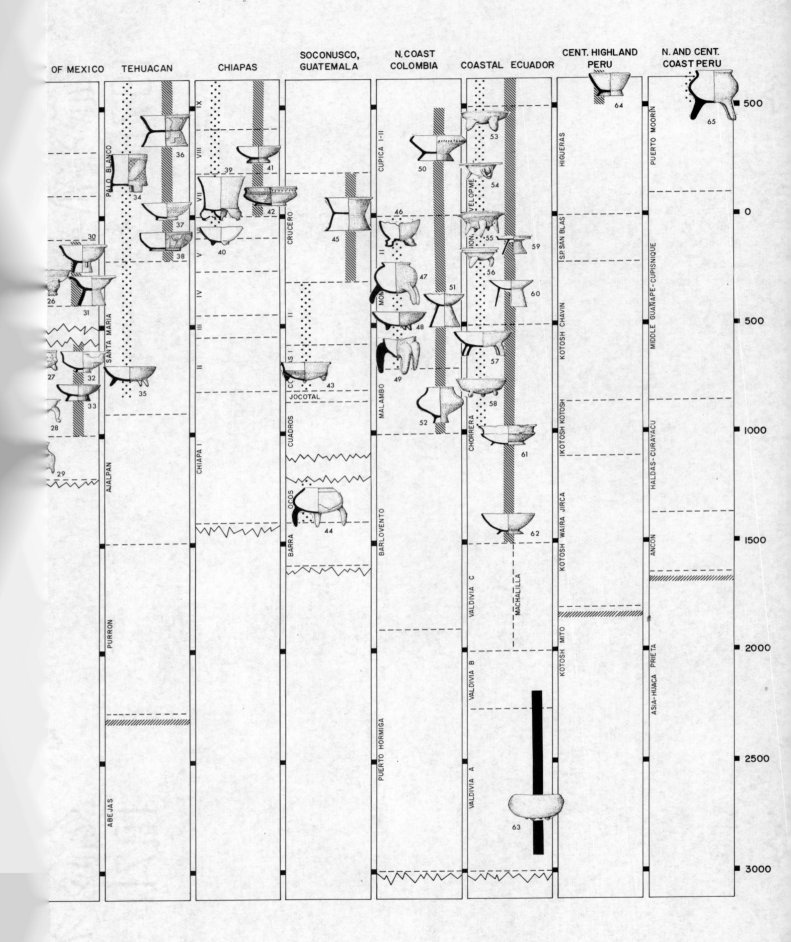

OF MEXICO   TEHUACAN   CHIAPAS   SOCONUSCO, GUATEMALA   N. COAST COLOMBIA   COASTAL ECUADOR   CENT. HIGHLAND PERU   N. AND CENT. COAST PERU

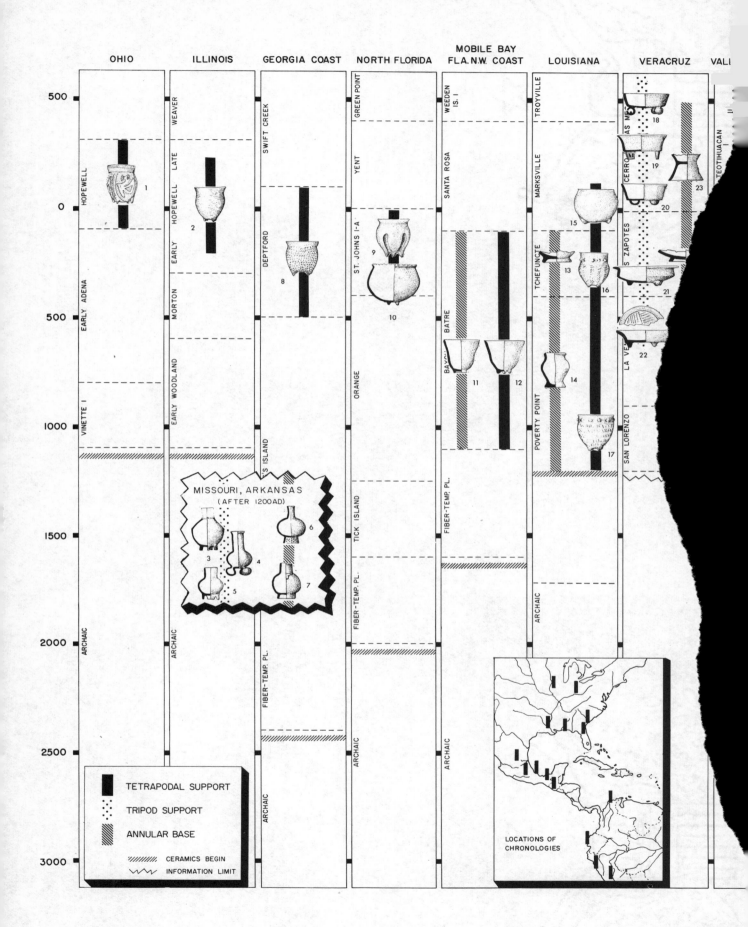

OHIO · ILLINOIS · GEORGIA COAST · NORTH FLORIDA · MOBILE BAY FLA. N.W. COAST · LOUISIANA · VERACRUZ · VALL

MISSOURI, ARKANSAS
(AFTER 1200 AD)

LOCATIONS OF CHRONOLOGIES

■ TETRAPODAL SUPPORT
⋮ TRIPOD SUPPORT
▨ ANNULAR BASE

////// CERAMICS BEGIN
〜〜 INFORMATION LIMIT

VESSEL FEET AND ANNULAR BASE

CHART 15

1. Griffin, 1952b, fig. 32s
2. Fowler, 1957, pl. 11
3. Phillips, Ford, and Griffin, 1951, fig. 105r
4. Phillips, Ford, and Griffin, 1951, fig. 105f
5. Phillips, Ford, and Griffin, 1951, fig. 105p
6. Phillips, Ford, and Griffin, 1951, fig. 103i
7. Phillips, Ford, and Griffin, 1951, fig. 103k
8. Wauchope, 1966, fig. 6b
9. Goggin, 1952, pl. 3A
10. Florida State Museum Collection
11. Wimberly, 1960, fig. 40
12. Wimberly, 1960, fig. 40
13. Ford and Quimby, 1945, fig. 18c, p. 52
14. Alexander Collection
15. Ford and Willey, 1940, fig. 22b
16. Louisiana State University Collection
17. Alexander Collection
18. Ekholm, 1944, fig. 6x
19. Drucker, 1943b, fig. 12k
20. Drucker, 1943b, fig. 12k′
21. Drucker, 1943a, pl. 15k
22. Florida State Museum Collection
23. Drucker, 1943b, fig. 81
24. Drucker, 1943a, fig. 30a
25. Drucker, 1952, fig. 41d
26. Vaillant, 1931, pl. 71g
27. Piña Chán, 1958, vol. 1, fig. 36t
28. Piña Chán, 1958, vol. 1, fig 34a
29. Piña Chán, 1958, vol. 1, fig. 36j
30. Vaillant, 1931, pl. 76m
31. Porter, 1953, fig. 3
32. Vaillant, 1930, pl. 4a
33. Vaillant, 1935b, p. 227
34. MacNeish chart, personal communication
35. MacNeish chart, personal communication
36. MacNeish chart, personal communication
37. MacNeish chart, personal communication
38. MacNeish chart, personal communication
39. Lowe, 1962, fig. 14c
40. Lowe, 1962, fig. 8d
41. Agrinier, 1964, fig. 80–3
42. Lowe, 1962, fig. 11b
43. M. D. Coe, 1961, fig. 26k
44. M. D. Coe, 1961, fig. 14
45. Coe and Flannery, 1967, fig. 35a, c
46. Reichel-Dolmatoff, Gerardo and Alicia, 1956, fig. 10–32
47. Duque, 1964, fig. 79, p. 329
48. Reichel-Dolmatoff, Gerardo and Alicia, 1956, fig. 10, 17–18
49. Reichel-Dolmatoff, Gerardo and Alicia, 1956, fig. 11–14
50. Reichel Dolmatoff, Gerardo and Alicia, 1962, pl. 3–2
51. Reichel-Dolmatoff, Gerardo and Alicia, 1956, fig. 10–4
52. Angulo Valdés, 1962b, pl. 1d
53. Estrada, 1957, fig. 51
54. Estrada, 1962, fig. 57
55. Estrada, 1962, fig. 56
56. Estrada, Meggers, and Evans, 1964, fig. 20–8
57. Estrada, 1958, fig. 55
58. Estrada, 1957, fig. 19a
59. Estrada, Meggers, and Evans, 1964, fig. 21–12
60. Estrada, Meggers, and Evans, 1964, fig. 21–13
61. Estrada, 1958, fig. 41–1
62. Estrada, 1958, fig. 43–5
63. Meggers, Evans, and Estrada, 1965, fig. 44–5
64. Strong and Evans, 1952, fig. 68–1
65. Bennett, 1944a, fig. 32D–2

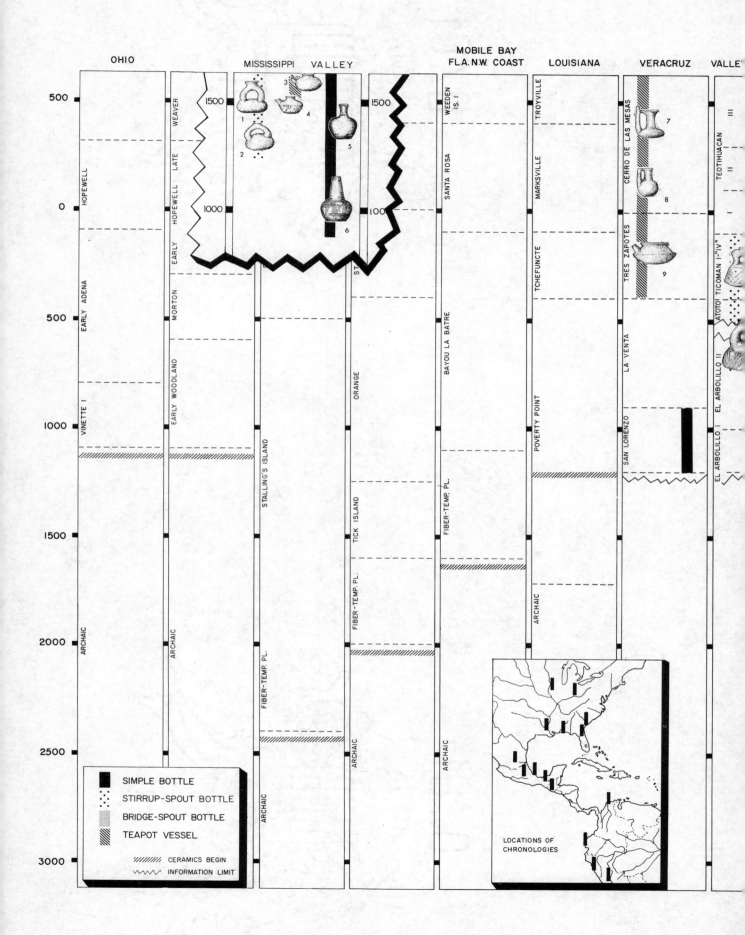

OHIO   MISSISSIPPI VALLEY   MOBILE BAY FLA.N.W. COAST   LOUISIANA   VERACRUZ   VALLE

500
0
500
1000
1500
2000
2500
3000

OHIO: HOPEWELL / EARLY ADENA / VINETTE I / ARCHAIC

WEAVER / LATE HOPEWELL / EARLY HOPEWELL / MORTON / EARLY WOODLAND / ARCHAIC

1500 / 1000

STALLING'S ISLAND / FIBER-TEMP. PL. / ARCHAIC

ORANGE / TICK ISLAND / FIBER-TEMP. PL. / ARCHAIC

1500 / 100

WEEDEN IS. I / SANTA ROSA / BAYOU LA BATRE / FIBER-TEMP. PL. / ARCHAIC

TROYVILLE / MARKSVILLE / TCHEFUNCTE / POVERTY POINT / ARCHAIC

CERRO DE LAS MESAS / TRES ZAPOTES / LA VENTA / SAN LORENZO

TEOTIHUACAN / ATOTOI TICOMAN I—"IV" / EL ARBOLILLO II / EL ARBOLILLO I

LOCATIONS OF CHRONOLOGIES

SIMPLE BOTTLE
STIRRUP-SPOUT BOTTLE
BRIDGE-SPOUT BOTTLE
TEAPOT VESSEL

///// CERAMICS BEGIN
\\\\\ INFORMATION LIMIT

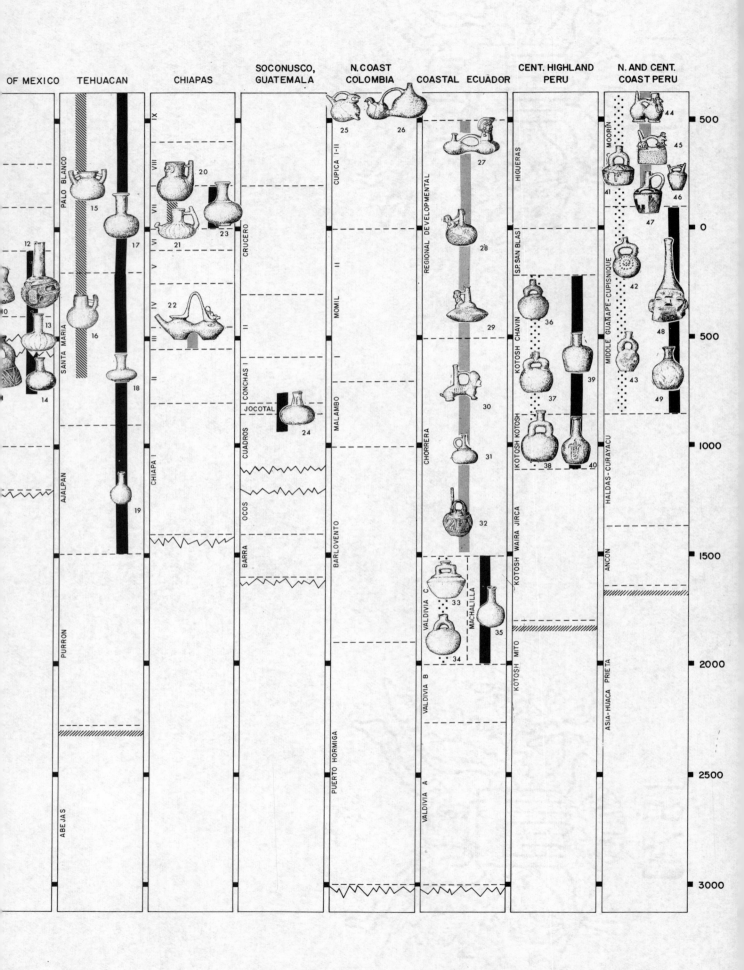

OF MEXICO   TEHUACAN   CHIAPAS   SOCONUSCO, GUATEMALA   N. COAST COLOMBIA   COASTAL ECUADOR   CENT. HIGHLAND PERU   N. AND CENT. COAST PERU

STIRRUP-SPOUT, SIMPLE, AND BRIDGE-SPOUT BOTTLES, AND TEAPOT VESSEL

Chart 16

1. Phillips, Ford, and Griffin, 1951, fig. 106a
2. Phillips, Ford, and Griffin, 1951, fig. 106b
3. Phillips, Ford, and Griffin, 1951, fig. 113b
4. Phillips, Ford, and Griffin, 1951, fig. 113i
5. Holmes, 1903, pl. 46
6. Newell and Krieger, 1949, fig. 31a
7. Drucker, 1943b, fig. 12x
8. Weiant, 1943, fig. 11d
9. Drucker, 1943a, fig. 24d
10. Porter, 1953, fig. 12
11. Porter, 1953, pl. 10ᴇ
12. Porter, 1953, pl. 6ʜ
13. Porter, 1953, pl. 7ʙ
14. Piña Chán, 1958, vol. 1, p.76
15. MacNeish chart, personal communication
16. MacNeish chart, personal communication
17. MacNeish, personal communication
18. MacNeish chart, personal communication
19. MacNeish chart, personal communication
20. Lowe, 1962, fig. 7a
21. Lowe, 1962, pl. 14i
22. Lowe, 1962, fig. 28, pl. 25a-l
23. Lowe, 1962, fig. 10b
24. Coe and Flannery, 1967, fig. 8
25. Bennett, 1944b, fig. 13d
26. Bennett, 1944b, fig. 13e
27. Estrada, 1962, fig. 50a-b
28. Estrada, 1957, fig. 52
29. Estrada, 1957, fig. 25A
30. Estrada, 1962, fig. 115
31. Estrada, 1958, fig. 55
32. Estrada, 1958, fig. 39
33. Meggers, Evans, and Estrada, 1965, fig. 78–8
34. Meggers, Evans, and Estrada, 1965, fig. 88–12
35. Meggers, Evans, and Estrada, 1965, fig. 88–11
36. Izumi and Sono, 1963, fig. 46
37. Tello, 1960, pl. 48
38. Izumi and Sono, 1963, pl. 128–6
39. Izumi and Sono, 1963, pl. 129–9
40. Izumi and Sono, 1963, pl. 135–2
41. Larco, 1945a, p. 14
42. Ford, 1949, fig. 9
43. Larco, 1945a, p. 12
44. Strong and Evans, 1952, fig. 57–9
45. Strong and Evans, 1952, fig. 58e
46. Strong and Evans, 1952, fig. 55–11
47. Ford, 1949, fig. 9
48. Larco Hoyle, 1945a, p. 10
49. Larco Hoyle, 1945a, p. 15

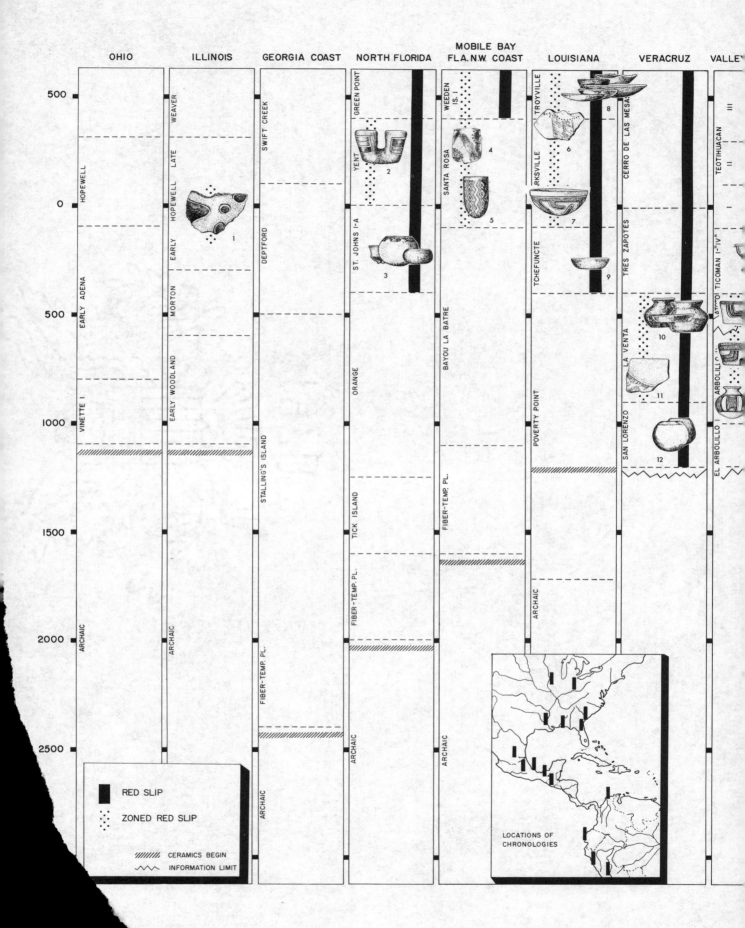

MOBILE BAY

OHIO	ILLINOIS	GEORGIA COAST	NORTH FLORIDA	FLA. N.W. COAST	LOUISIANA	VERACRUZ	VALLEY

500

0

500

1000

1500

2000

2500

OHIO: HOPEWELL · EARLY ADENA · VINETTE I · ARCHAIC

ILLINOIS: WEAVER · LATE HOPEWELL · EARLY HOPEWELL · MORTON · EARLY WOODLAND · ARCHAIC

GEORGIA COAST: SWIFT CREEK · DEPTFORD · STALLING'S ISLAND · FIBER-TEMP. PL. · ARCHAIC · ARCHAIC

NORTH FLORIDA: GREEN POINT · YENT · ST. JOHNS I-A · ORANGE · TICK ISLAND · FIBER-TEMP. PL. · ARCHAIC

FLA. N.W. COAST: WEEDEN IS. I · SANTA ROSA · BAYOU LA BATRE · FIBER-TEMP. PL. · ARCHAIC

LOUISIANA: TROYVILLE · ARKSVILLE · TCHEFUNCTE · POVERTY POINT · ARCHAIC

VERACRUZ: CERRO DE LAS MESAS · TRES ZAPOTES · LA VENTA · SAN LORENZO · EL ARBOLILLO I

VALLEY: III · TEOTIHUACAN · II · TICOMAN I-IV · ARBOLILLO

1 2 3 4 5 6 7 8 9 10 11 12

RED SLIP

ZONED RED SLIP

/////// CERAMICS BEGIN

∿∿∿ INFORMATION LIMIT

LOCATIONS OF
CHRONOLOGIES

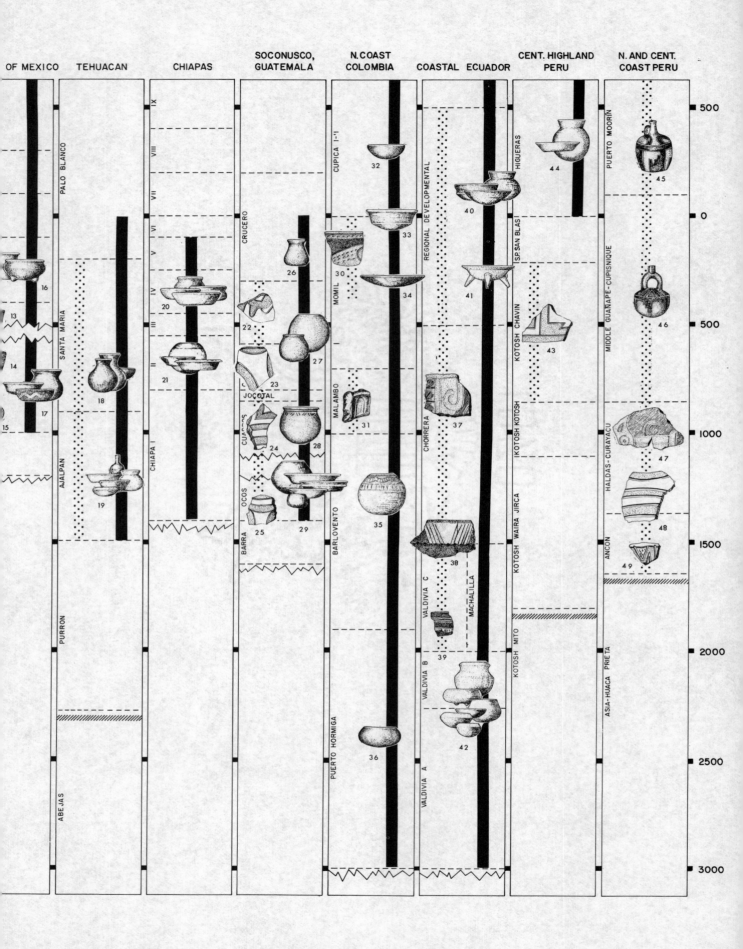

OF MEXICO · TEHUACAN · CHIAPAS · SOCONUSCO, GUATEMALA · N. COAST COLOMBIA · COASTAL ECUADOR · CENT. HIGHLAND PERU · N. AND CENT. COAST PERU

RED SLIP AND ZONED RED SLIP

Chart 17

1. Griffin, 1952a, pl. 35-R
2. Moore, 1902, fig. 155
3. Goggin, 1952, p. 102
4. Willey, 1949a, pl. 26h
5. Moore, 1902, fig. 270
6. Ford, 1951, pl. 11-6
7. Ford and Willey, 1940, fig. 40
8. Ford, 1951, fig. 19a–e
9. Ford and Quimby, 1945, pp. 54–56
10. Florida State Museum Collection
11. Florida State Museum Collection
12. M. D. Coe, 1966 (unnumbered pages)
13. Piña Chán, 1958, vol. 1, fig. 44h
14. Porter, 1953, fig. 8
15. Porter, 1953, pp. 35–36; Piña Chán, 1958, vol. 1, pp. 44–46
16. Vaillant, 1931, pl. 73f, 76k
17. Piña Chán, 1958, vol. 1, fig. 16d, f, i
18. MacNeish chart, personal communication
19. MacNeish chart, personal communication
20. Sanders, 1961, pp. 20–23
21. Dixon, 1959, fig. 1
22. M. D. Coe, 1961, fig. 33p
23. M. D. Coe, 1961, fig. 34b
24. M. D. Coe, 1961, fig. 17g
25. M. D. Coe, 1961, fig. 17k
26. Coe and Flannery, 1967, fig. 8
27. Coe and Flannery, 1967, fig. 8
28. Coe and Flannery, 1967, fig. 8
29. M. D. Coe, 1961, pp. 51–53
30. Reichel-Dolmatoff, Gerardo and Alicia, 1956, fig. 2–8
31. Angulo Valdés, 1962, p. 43, pl. 3n
32. Reichel-Dolmatoff, Gerardo and Alicia, 1961, pp. 269–271
33. Reichel-Dolmatoff, Gerardo and Alicia, 1956, fig. 7J
34. Reichel-Dolmatoff, Gerardo and Alicia, 1956, pp. 151–152, figs. 7–I, 8FF, 8GG
35. Reichel-Dolmatoff, 1955, pp. 257–258
36. Reichel-Dolmatoff, 1965, pp. 25–26
37. Estrada, 1958, fig. 43–6
38. Meggers, Evans, and Estrada, 1965, pl. 145d
39. Meggers, Evans, and Estrada, 1965, pl. 145o
40. Estrada, Meggers, and Evans, 1964, p. 530
41. Estrada, 1962, fig. 56
42. Meggers, Evans, and Estrada, 1965, pp. 76–80, pls. 97–99
43. Tello, 1960, fig. 169
44. Izumi and Sono, 1963, pls. 36f, 116–6
45. Larco Hoyle, 1948, p. 21
46. Larco Hoyle, 1945a, p. 14
47. F. Engel, 1956, fig. 11D
48. Willey and Corbett, 1954, fig. 8e
49. Willey and Corbett, 1954, fig. 8h

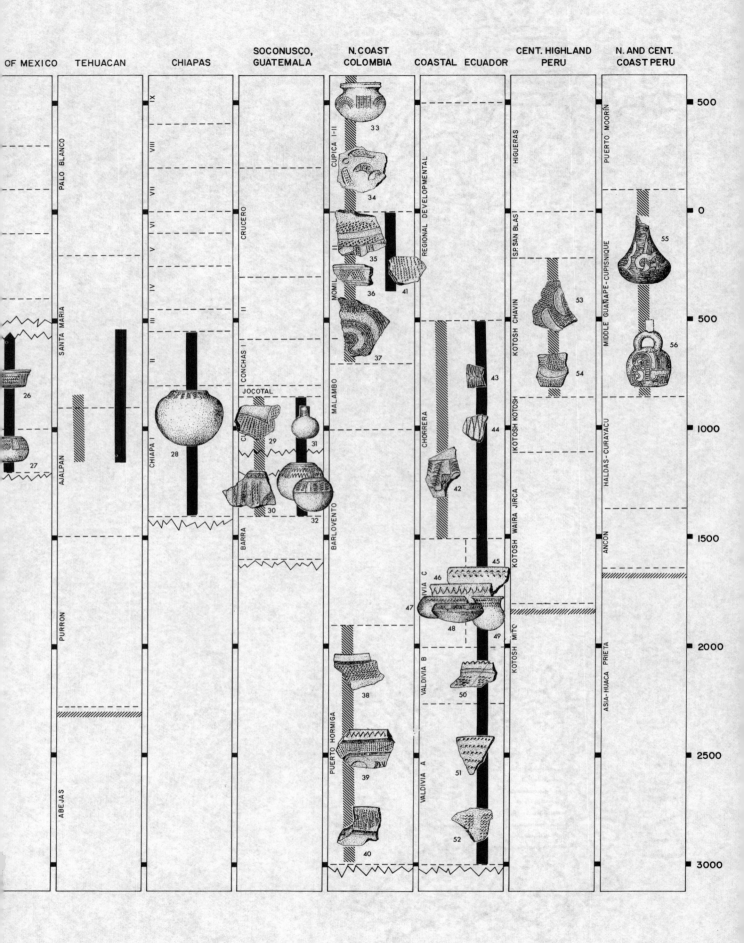

OF MEXICO | TEHUACAN | CHIAPAS | SOCONUSCO, GUATEMALA | N. COAST COLOMBIA | COASTAL ECUADOR | CENT. HIGHLAND PERU | N. AND CENT. COAST PERU

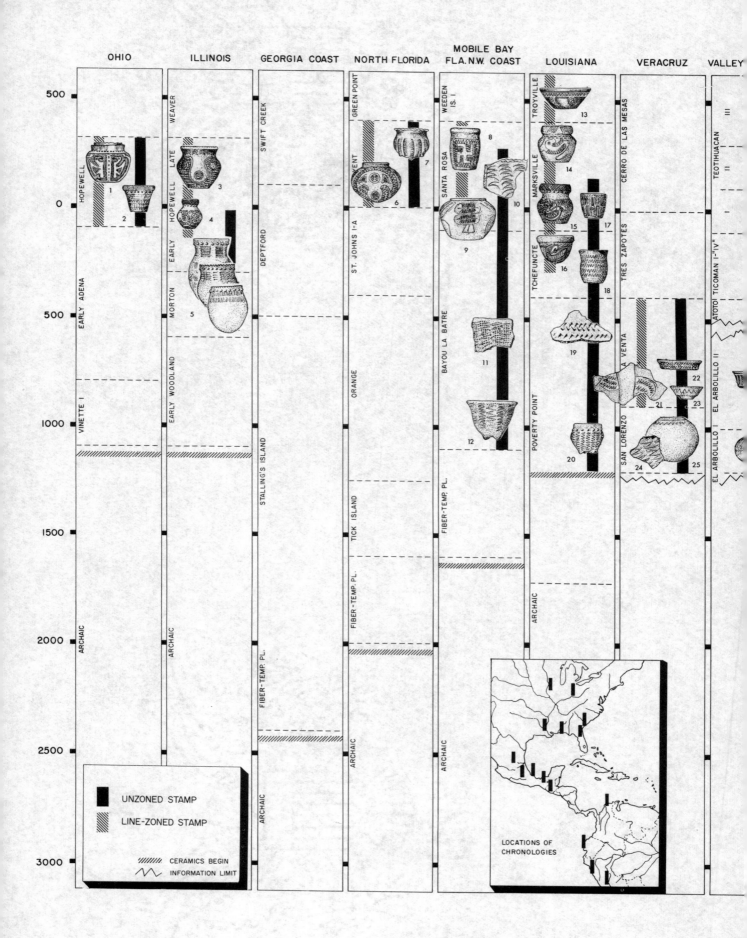

OHIO | ILLINOIS | GEORGIA COAST | NORTH FLORIDA | MOBILE BAY / FLA. N.W. COAST | LOUISIANA | VERACRUZ | VALLEY

500
0
500
1000
1500
2000
2500
3000

LEGEND:

■ UNZONED STAMP

▨ LINE-ZONED STAMP

▨▨ CERAMICS BEGIN

〰 INFORMATION LIMIT

LOCATIONS OF CHRONOLOGIES

UNZONED AND LINE-ZONED STAMPING

CHART 18

1. Florida State Museum Collection
2. Moorehead, 1922, fig. 70
3. McGregor, 1952, pl. 24a
4. McGregor, 1959, fig. 5
5. McGregor, 1952, pl. 21a-b
6. Griffin, 1952b, fig. 179e
7. Sears, 1962, fig. 3j
8. Florida State Museum Collection
9. Willey, 1949a, fig. 22d
10. Willey, 1949a, fig. 24
11. Wimberly, 1960, fig. 42
12. Wimberly, 1960, fig. 40–41
13. Ford, 1951, fig. 13c
14. Ford and Willey, 1940, fig. 31d
15. Ford and Willey, 1940, fig. 28f
16. Ford and Willey; 1940, fig. 39a
17. Ford and Willey, 1940, fig. 29c
18. Ford and Quimby, 1945, fig. 17a
19. Alexander Collection
20. Alexander Collection
21. Florida State Museum Collection
22. Florida State Museum Collection
23. Florida State Museum Collection
24. Florida State Museum Collection
25. Florida State Museum Collection
26. Piña Chán, 1958, vol. 1, fig. 37d
27. Porter, 1953, pl. 11F
28. Sanders, 1961, pl. 7A, fig. 19

29. Coe, 1961, fig. 48b
30. Coe, 1961, fig. 47f
31. Coe and Flannery, 1967, fig. 8
32. Coe and Flannery, 1967, fig. 8
33. Reichel-Dolmatoff, Gerardo and Alicia, 1961, pl. 3–5
34. Reichel-Dolmatoff, Gerardo and Alicia, 1961, pl. 5–3
35. Reichel-Dolmatoff, Gerardo and Alicia, 1956, pl. 9–6
36. Reichel-Dolmatoff, Gerardo and Alicia, 1956, pl. 11–2
37. Reichel-Dolmatoff, Gerardo and Alicia, 1956, pl. 9–5
38. Reichel-Dolmatoff, 1965, pl. 3–4
39. Reichel-Dolmatoff, 1965, pl. 3–10
40. Reichel-Dolmatoff, 1965, pl. 3–3
41. Reichel-Dolmatoff, Gerardo and Alicia, 1956, pl. 8–9
42. Estrada, 1962, fig. 41a
43. Estrada, 1962, fig. 41b
44. Estrada, 1962, fig. 41c
45. Meggers, Evans, and Estrada, 1965, pl. 109d
46. Meggers, Evans, and Estrada, 1965, pl. 108b
47. Meggers, Evans, and Estrada, 1965, pp. 82–84
48. Meggers, Evans, and Estrada, 1965, pp. 82–84
49. Meggers, Evans, and Estrada, 1965, pp. 82–84
50. Meggers, Evans, and Estrada, 1965, pl. 113b
51. Meggers, Evans, and Estrada, 1965, pl. 113k
52. Meggers, Evans, and Estrada, 1965, pl. 113c
53. Izumi and Sono, 1963, pl. 69a–3
54. Izumi and Sono, 1963, pl. 69a–4
55. Larco Hoyle, 1941, fig. 113
56. Larco Hoyle, 1945a, p. 9

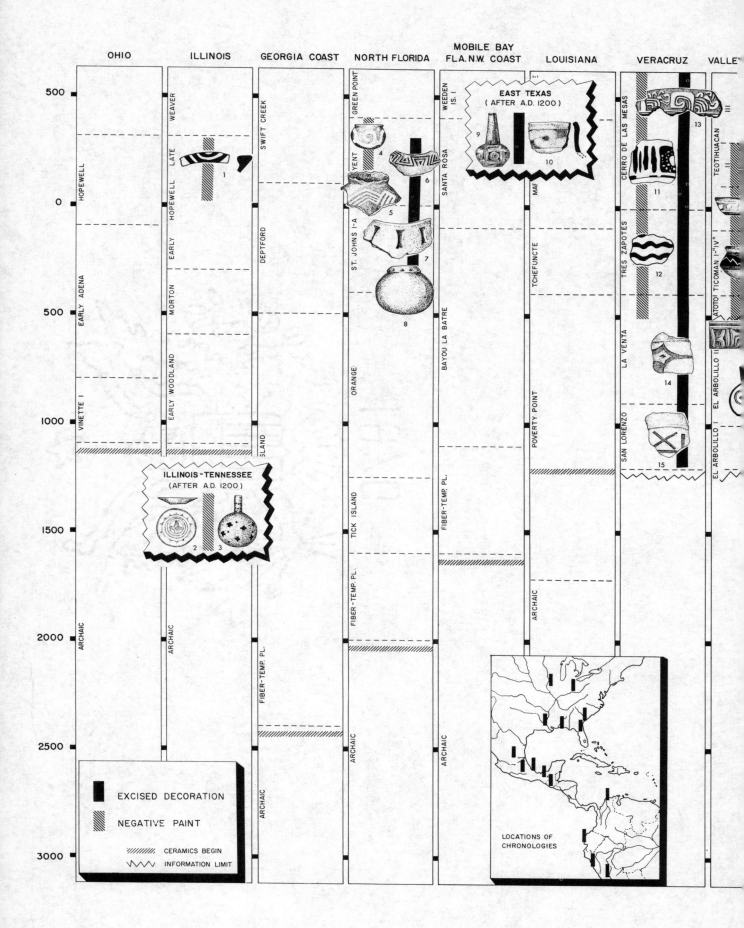

OHIO   ILLINOIS   GEORGIA COAST   NORTH FLORIDA   MOBILE BAY FLA. N.W. COAST   LOUISIANA   VERACRUZ   VALLEY

500

0

500

1000

1500

2000

2500

3000

OHIO
HOPEWELL
EARLY ADENA
VINETTE I
ARCHAIC

ILLINOIS
WEAVER
LATE HOPEWELL
EARLY HOPEWELL
MORTON
EARLY WOODLAND
ARCHAIC

ILLINOIS-TENNESSEE
(AFTER A.D. 1200)
2   3

GEORGIA COAST
SWIFT CREEK
DEPTFORD
ISLAND
FIBER-TEMP. PL.
ARCHAIC
ARCHAIC

NORTH FLORIDA
GREEN POINT
YENT
ST. JOHNS I-A
ORANGE
TICK ISLAND
FIBER-TEMP. PL.
ARCHAIC
4   6   5   7   8

MOBILE BAY FLA. N.W. COAST
WEEDEN IS. I
SANTA ROSA
BAYOU LA BATRE
FIBER-TEMP. PL.
ARCHAIC

EAST TEXAS
(AFTER A.D. 1200)
9   10

LOUISIANA
MAF
TCHEFUNCTE
POVERTY POINT
ARCHAIC

VERACRUZ
CERRO DE LAS MESAS
TRES ZAPOTES
LA VENTA
SAN LORENZO
11   12   14   15

VALLEY
III
TEOTIHUACAN
ATOTOTL TICOMAN I-"IV"
EL ARBOLILLO II
EL ARBOLILLO I
13

EXCISED DECORATION

NEGATIVE PAINT

CERAMICS BEGIN

INFORMATION LIMIT

LOCATIONS OF CHRONOLOGIES

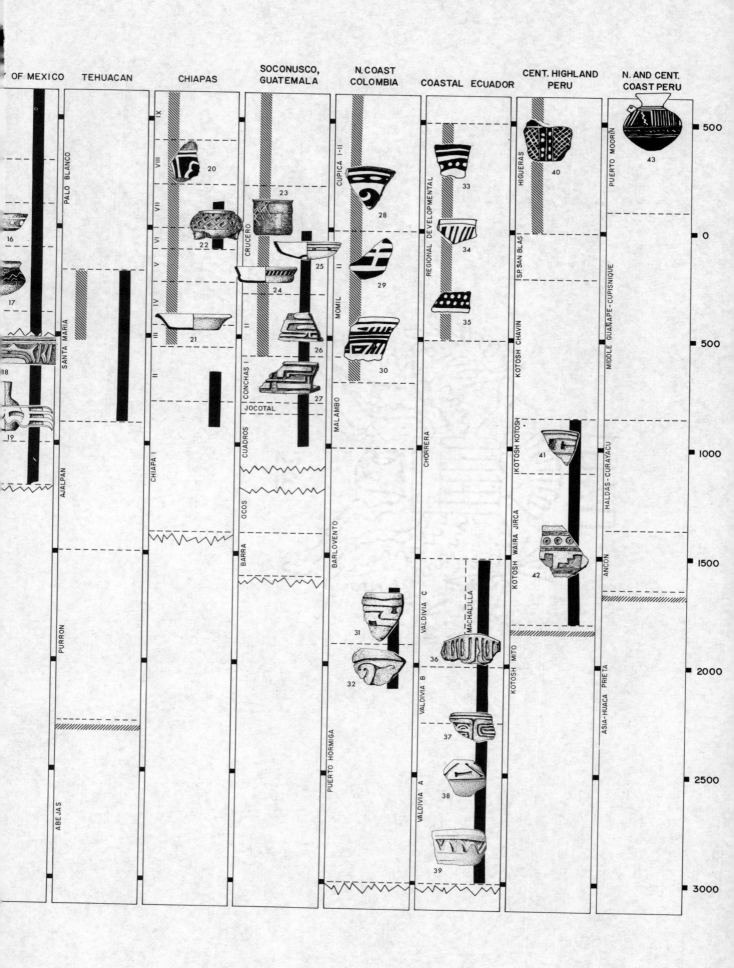

OF MEXICO · TEHUACAN · CHIAPAS · SOCONUSCO, GUATEMALA · N.COAST COLOMBIA · COASTAL ECUADOR · CENT. HIGHLAND PERU · N. AND CENT. COAST PERU

EXCISED DECORATION AND NEGATIVE PAINTING

CHART 19

1. Perino, personal communication (Snyders Site); Griffin, 1952c
2. Griffin, 1952b, fig. 108M
3. Griffin, 1952b, fig. 81b
4. Sears, 1962, fig. 3–d
5. Sears, 1962, fig. 3–E
6. Goggin, 1952, p. 103
7. Florida State Museum Collection
8. Florida State Museum Collection
9. Newell and Krieger, 1949, fig. 31A
10. Newell and Krieger, 1949, fig. 32T
11. Drucker, 1943b, fig. 139
12. Florida State Museum Collection
13. Drucker, 1943b, fig. 115
14. García Payón, 1966, pl. 25–14
15. García Payón, 1966, pl. 25–12
16. Millon, Drewitt, and Bennyhoff, 1965, fig. 114A
17. Vaillant, 1931, pl. 70–r
18. Piña Chán, 1958, vol. 1, fig. 49
19. Piña Chán, 1958, Vol. 1, fig. 49
20. Sanders, 1961, fig. 36–I
21. Peterson, 1963, fig. 11a
22. Lowe, 1962, pl. 15v
23. Coe and Flannery, 1967, fig. 25c
24. M. D. Coe, 1961, fig. 34i
25. Coe and Flannery, 1967, fig. 32e
26. M. D. Coe, 1961, fig. 28e
27. M. D. Coe, 1961, fig. 28e
28. Duque, 1964, drawing 11
29. Reichel-Dolmatoff, Gerardo and Alicia, 1956, fig. 4–10
30. Reichel-Dolmatoff, Gerardo and Alicia, 1956, fig. 4–4
31. Willey and McGimsey, 1954, fig. 12c
32. Willey and McGimsey, 1954, fig. 46g
33. Estrada, 1962, p. 39, fig. 54e
34. Estrada, Meggers, and Evans, 1964, fig. 30e
35. Estrada, Meggers, and Evans, 1964, fig. 30c
36. Estrada, 1958, fig. 11
37. Meggers, Evans, and Estrada, 1965, pl. 58E
38. Meggers, Evans, and Estrada, 1965, pl. 59K
39. Meggers, Evans, and Estrada, 1965, pl. 59E
40. Izumi and Sono, 1963, p. 158, pl. 117–4
41. Izumi and Sono, 1963, pl. 76–4
42. Izumi and Sono, 1963, pl. 84–2
43. Larco Hoyle, 1945b, p. 8

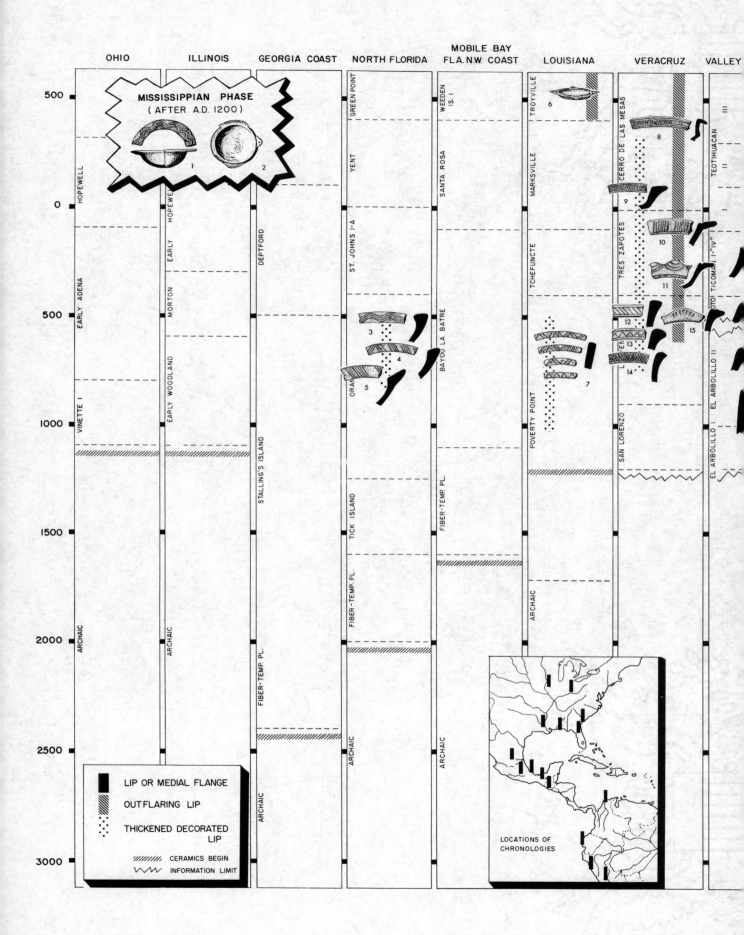

MOBILE BAY

| OHIO | ILLINOIS | GEORGIA COAST | NORTH FLORIDA | FLA. N.W. COAST | LOUISIANA | VERACRUZ | VALLEY |

MISSISSIPPIAN PHASE
(AFTER A.D. 1200)

LIP OR MEDIAL FLANGE

OUTFLARING LIP

THICKENED DECORATED LIP

CERAMICS BEGIN

INFORMATION LIMIT

LOCATIONS OF CHRONOLOGIES

OF MEXICO   TEHUACAN   CHIAPAS   SOCONUSCO, GUATEMALA   N. COAST COLOMBIA   COASTAL ECUADOR   CENT. HIGHLAND PERU   N. AND CENT. COAST PERU

LABIAL OR MEDIAL FLANGE, OUTFLARING LIP, AND THICKENED DECORATED LIP

CHART 20

1. Griffin, 1952b, fig. 110p
2. Griffin, 1952b, fig. 125e
3. Florida State Museum Collection
4. Florida State Museum Collection
5. Florida State Museum Collection
6. Ford, 1936, fig. 37
7. Ford and Webb, 1956, fig. 42
8. Drucker, 1943b, fig. 93
9. Drucker, 1943b, fig. 92
10. Weiant, 1943, fig 41c
11. Weiant, 1943, fig. 42d
12. García Payón, 1966, pl. 14–2
13. Florida State Museum Collection
14. Florida State Museum Collection
15. García Payón, 1966, pl. 19–22
16. Piña Chán, 1958, vol. 1, fig. 8o
17. Piña Chán, 1958, vol. 1, fig. 18q
18. Piña Chán, 1958, vol 1, fig. 18p
19. Piña Chán, 1958, vol. 1, fig. 15o
20. MacNeish chart, personal communication
21. MacNeish chart, personal communication
22. Lowe, 1962, fig. 17f
23. Peterson, 1963, fig. 46
24. Sanders, 1961, fig. 23
25. Dixon, 1959, fig. 27c
26. Dixon, 1959, fig. 40a
27. Dixon, 1959, fig. 49b
28. Dixon, 1959, fig. 27a
29. Sanders, 1961, fig. 21a
30. Coe and Flannery, 1967, fig. 31f
31. Coe and Flannery, 1967, fig. 31h
32. M. D. Coe, 1961, fig. 32e
33. M. D. Coe, 1961, fig. 32k
34. M. D. Coe, 1961, fig. 23r
35. Coe and Flannery, 1967, fig. 31d
36. M. D. Coe, 1961, fig. 23s
37. Reichel-Dolmatoff, Gerardo and Alicia, 1956, fig. 9–10
38. Reichel-Dolmatoff, Gerardo and Alicia, 1956, fig. 9–16
39. Reichel-Dolmatoff, Gerardo and Alicia, 1956, fig. 9–5
40. Reichel-Dolmatoff, Gerardo and Alicia, 1956, fig. 9–8
41. Angulo Valdés, 1962b, pl. 2a
42. Reichel-Dolmatoff, Gerardo and Alicia, 1956, fig. 6–1
43. Estrada, 1962, fig. 46b
44. Estrada, 1958, fig. 46–3
45. Meggers and Evans, notes
46. Estrada, 1958, fig. 27–1
47. Estrada, 1958, fig. 46–5
48. Estrada, 1958, fig. 27–3
49. Meggers, Evans, and Estrada, 1965, pl. 40c
50. Meggers, Evans, and Estrada, 1965, pl. 40a
51. Meggers and Evans, notes
52. Estrada, Meggers, and Evans, 1964, fig. 23b
53. Tello, 1960, fig. 155
54. Izumi and Sono, 1963, pl. 133–6
55. Izumi and Sono, 1963, pl. 133–5

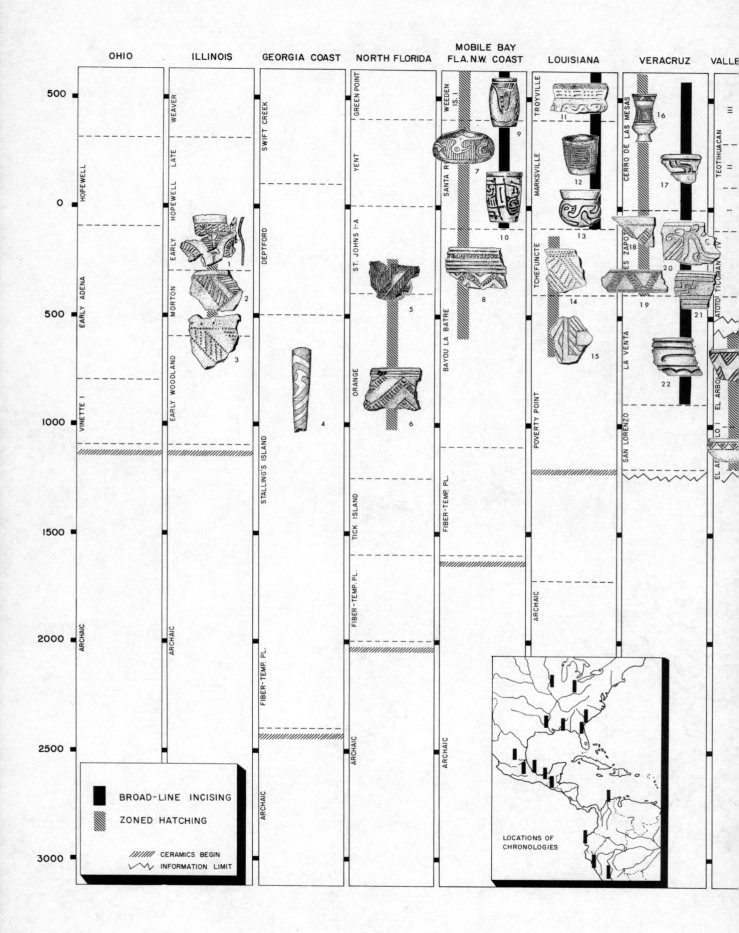

OHIO   ILLINOIS   GEORGIA COAST   NORTH FLORIDA   MOBILE BAY FLA. N.W. COAST   LOUISIANA   VERACRUZ   VALLE

BROAD-LINE INCISING
ZONED HATCHING
CERAMICS BEGIN
INFORMATION LIMIT

LOCATIONS OF CHRONOLOGIES

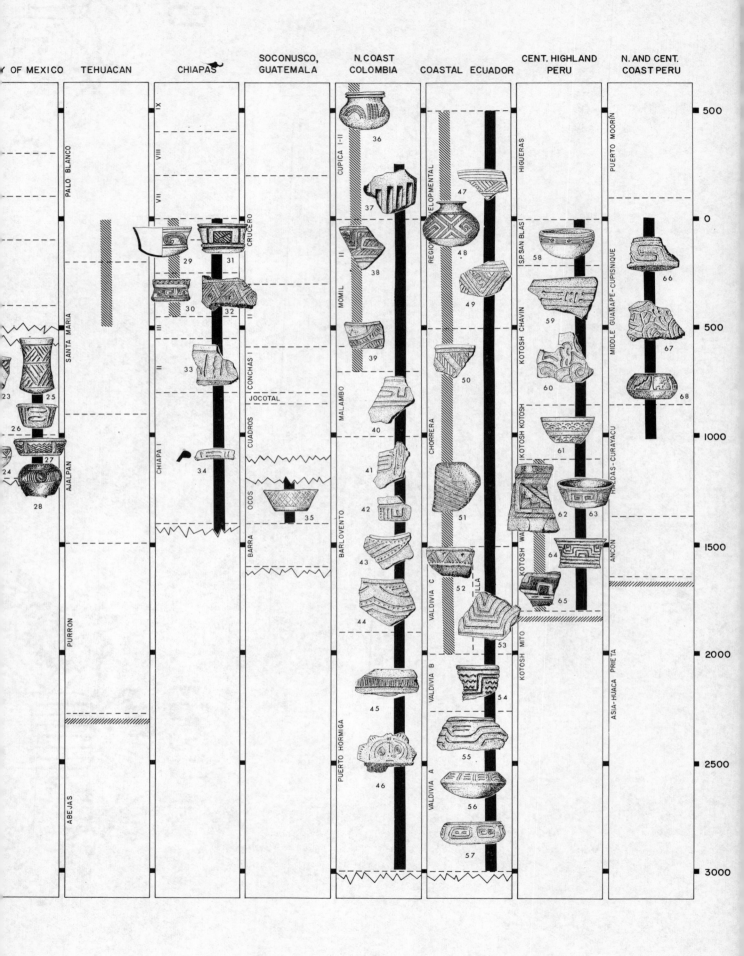

OF MEXICO TEHUACAN CHIAPAS SOCONUSCO, GUATEMALA N. COAST COLOMBIA COASTAL ECUADOR CENT. HIGHLAND PERU N. AND CENT. COAST PERU

BROAD-LINE INCISING AND ZONED HATCHING

CHART 21

1. Perino, personal communication (Snyder's site); Griffin, 1952c
2. Cole, et al., 1951, fig. 61
3. Cole, et al., 1951, fig. 60–8
4. Williams, ed., 1968, fig. 63d
5. Sears and Griffin, 1950 (unnumbered pages)
6. Florida State Museum Collection
7. Willey, 1949a, fig. 35a
8. Webb and DeJarnette, 1942, pl. 167 1–c
9. Willey, 1949a, fig. 22f
10. Moore, 1902, fig. 228
11. Moore, 1912, fig. 6
12. Ford and Willey, 1940, fig. 35e
13. Ford and Willey, 1940, fig. 36e
14. Ford and Quimby, 1945, pl. 4f
15. Haag, 1939 (unnumbered pages)
16. Drucker, 1943b, fig. 100, pl. 20a–b
17. Drucker, 1943b, fig. 99
18. Florida State Museum Collection
19. Weiant, 1943, fig. 4a
20. Weiant, 1943, fig. 48e
21. Weiant, 1943, fig. 45e
22. Drucker, 1952, fig. 25d
23. Piña Chán, 1958, vol. 1, fig. 16f
24. Piña Chán, 1958, vol. 1, fig. 33m
25. Piña Chán, 1958, vol. 1, fig. 39w
26. Piña Chán, 1958, vol. 1, fig. 39u
27. Porter, 1953, fig. 7
28. Vaillant, 1935b, fig. 19
29. Peterson, 1963, fig. 55c
30. Peterson, 1963, fig. 56a
31. Peterson, 1963, fig. 84d
32. Sanders, 1961, pl. 11B–e
33. Dixon, 1959, fig. 16b
34. Dixon, 1959, fig. 5e
35. M.D. Coe, 1961, fig. 50k
36. Reichel-Dolmatoff, Gerardo and Alicia, 1962, pl. 3–5
37. Reichel-Dolmatoff, Gerardo and Alicia, 1962, pl. 6–11
38. Reichel-Dolmatoff, Gerardo and Alicia, 1956, pl. 18–13
39. Reichel-Dolmatoff, Gerardo and Alicia, 1956, pl. 18–5
40. Angulo Valdés, 1962b, pl. 7d
41. Angulo Valdés, 1962b, pl. 3m
42. Reichel-Dolmatoff, 1955, pl. 5–2
43. Reichel-Dolmatoff, 1955, pl. 3–5
44. Reichel-Dolmatoff, 1955, pl. 3–7
45. Meggers, Evans, and Estrada, 1965, pl. 188 L
46. Reichel-Dolmatoff, 1965, pl. 4–1
47. Estrada, 1962, fig. 54b
48. Estrada, 1962, fig. 60
49. Estrada, 1962, fig. 54c
50. Estrada, 1962, fig. 41d
51. Meggers, Evans, and Estrada, 1965, pl. 135 L
52. Meggers, Evans, and Estrada, 1965, pl. 132g
53. Meggers, Evans, and Estrada, 1965, pl. 36c
54. Meggers, Evans, and Estrada, 1965, pl. 38b
55. Meggers, Evans, and Estrada, 1965, pl. 38j
56. Meggers, Evans, and Estrada, 1965, pl. 32a
57. Meggers, Evans, and Estrada, 1965, pl. 42a
58. Izumi and Sono, 1963, fig. 46
59. Izumi and Sono, 1963, fig. 63b–12
60. Izumi and Sono, 1963, pl. 43f
61. Izumi and Sono, 1963, pl. 47f
62. Izumi and Sono, 1963, pl. 82b–4
63. Izumi and Sono, 1963, fig. 46
64. Izumi and Sono, 1963, fig. 46
65. Izumi and Sono, 1963, pl. 83b–12
66. Willey and Corbett, 1954, fig. 1j
67. Willey and Corbett, 1954, fig. 8b
68. Larco Hoyle, 1941, fig. 79

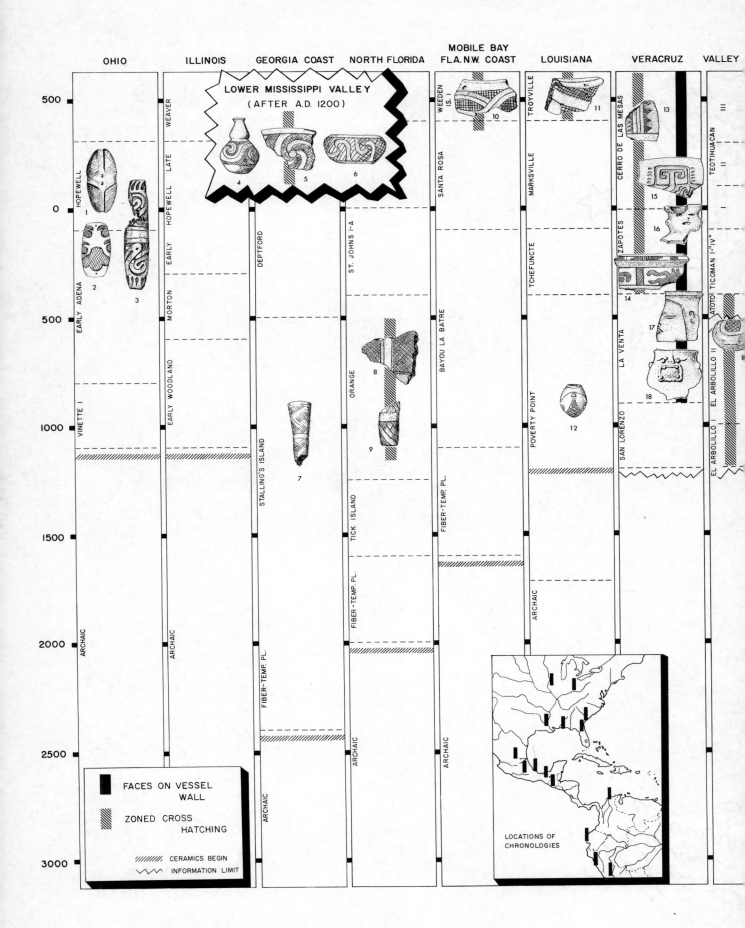

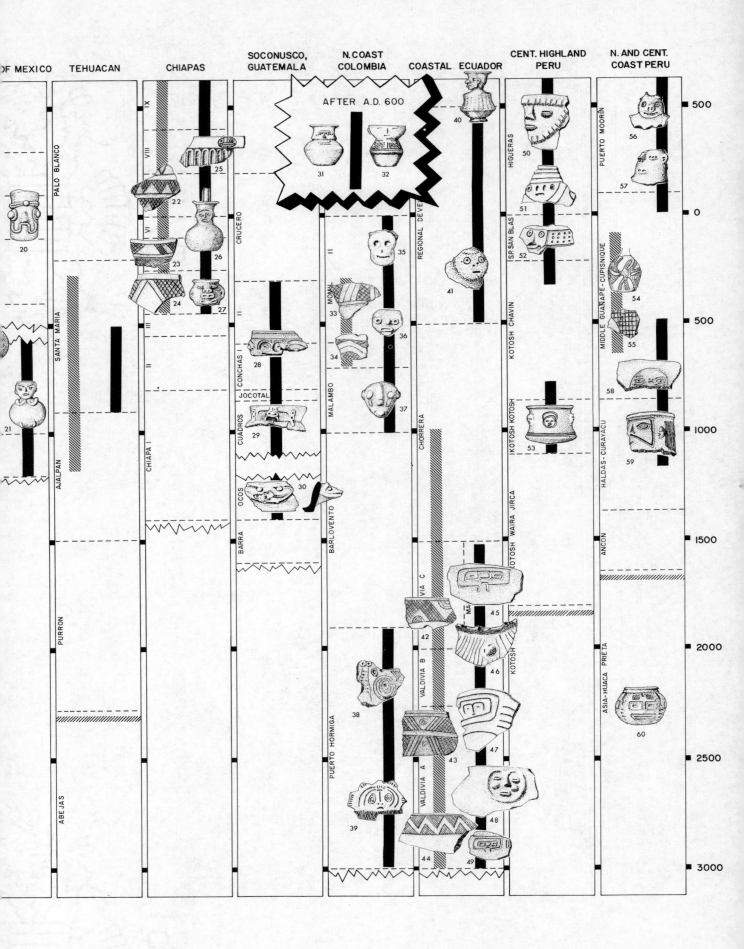

OF MEXICO TEHUACAN CHIAPAS SOCONUSCO, GUATEMALA N. COAST COLOMBIA COASTAL ECUADOR CENT. HIGHLAND PERU N. AND CENT. COAST PERU

AFTER A.D. 600

500

0

500

1000

1500

2000

2500

3000

PALO BLANCO

SANTA MARIA

AJALPAN

PURRON

ABEJAS

IX
VIII
VI
CRUCERO
CHIAPA I
II
III

20

21

22
23
24
25
26
27

CONCHAS I
CUADROS
JOCOTAL
OCOS
BARRA

28
29
30

II
I
MOMIL
MALAMBO
BARLOVENTO
PUERTO HORMIGA

31 32

33
34
35
36
37
38
39

REGIONAL DEVE
CHORRERA
VIA C
VALDIVIA B
VALDIVIA A

40
41
42
43
44
45
46
47
48
49

HIGUERAS
I.SP.SAN BLAS
KOTOSH CHAVIN
IKOTOSH KOTOSH
KOTOSH WAIRA JIRCA
KOTOSH

50
51
52
53

PUERTO MOORÍN
MIDDLE GUAÑAPE-CUPISNIQUE
HALDAS-CURAYACU
ANCON
ASIA-HUACA PRIETA

54
55
56
57
58
59
60

FACES ON VESSEL WALLS AND ZONED CROSSHATCHING

Chart 22

1. Mills, 1916, fig. 92
2. Mills, 1916, fig. 113
3. Moorehead, 1922, fig. 59
4. Webb, 1959, fig. 108h
5. Ford, 1936, fig. 20r
6. Ford, 1936, fig. 9j
7. Williams, ed., 1968, fig. 63b
8. Florida State Museum Collection
9. Rouse, 1951, fig. 14D
10. Willey, 1949a, pl. 26c
11. Ford, 1936, fig. 35a
12. Ford, Phillips, and Haag, 1955, fig. 50
13. Drucker, 1943b, fig. 84
14. Weiant, 1943, fig. 13b
15. Weiant, 1943, fig. 50d
16. Weiant, 1943, pl. 56–5
17. Drucker, 1952, fig. 64
18. Drucker, 1952, fig. 29, pl. 18b
19. Porter, 1953, pl. 6a
20. Millon, Drewitt, and Bennyhoff, 1965, fig. 95
21. Piña Chán, 1958, vol. 1, fig. 35y
22. Sanders, 1961, fig. 33
23. Sanders, 1961, fig. 23
24. Sanders, 1961, fig. 23
25. Sanders, 1961, fig. 34
26. Lowe, 1962, fig. 7b
27. Peterson, 1963, fig. 173c
28. M. D. Coe, 1961, fig. 33c
29. Coe and Flannery, 1967, pl. 27L
30. M. D. Coe, 1961, fig. 40g
31. W. C. Bennett, 1944b, fig. 25b
32. W. C. Bennett, 1944b, fig. 14d
33. Reichel-Dolmatoff, Gerardo and Alicia, 1956, pl. 7–9
34. Reichel-Dolmatoff, Gerardo and Alicia, 1956, pl. 2–7
35. Reichel-Dolmatoff, Gerardo and Alicia, 1956, fig.13–19
36. Reichel-Dolmatoff, Gerardo and Alicia, 1956, fig.13–12
37. Angulo Valdés, 1962b, pl. 6i
38. Reichel-Dolmatoff, 1965, pl. 5–9
39. Reichel-Dolmatoff, 1965, pl. 4–1
40. Estrada, 1957, fig. 9
41. Estrada, Meggers, and Evans, 1964, fig. 29c
42. Meggers, Evans, and Estrada, 1965, pl. 133v
43. Meggers, Evans, and Estrada, 1965, pl. 62b
44. Meggers, Evans, and Estrada, 1965, pl. 63n
45. Meggers, Evans, and Estrada, 1965, pl. 41a
46. Meggers, Evans, and Estrada, 1965, pl. 89d
47. Meggers, Evans, and Estrada, 1965, pl. 41h
48. Meggers, Evans, and Estrada, 1965, pl. 57d
49. Estrada, 1958, fig. 15–4
50. Izumi and Sono, 1963, pl. 92–19
51. Izumi and Sono, 1963, pl. 94a–1
52. Izumi and Sono, 1963, pl. 94a–7
53. Izumi and Sono, 1963, pl. 130–3
54. Larco Hoyle, 1941, fig. 99
55. Strong and Evans, 1952, fig. 51e
56. Strong and Evans, 1952, fig. 63j
57. Strong and Evans, 1952, fig. 64c
58. Willey and Corbett, 1954, fig. 8d
59. Willey and Corbett, 1954, fig. 2f
60. Bird, 1962, fig. 7